THE CRICKETERS' WHO'S WHO 1993

THE CRICKETERS' WHO'S WHO 1993

compiled and edited by
IAIN SPROAT

Introduction by
TIM CURTIS

Statistics by
RICHARD LOCKWOOD

Portraits photographed or researched by
BILL SMITH

Queen Anne Press

QUEEN ANNE PRESS
a division of Lennard Associates Limited
Mackerye End
Harpenden
Herts AL5 5DR

First published in Great Britain 1993

British Library Cataloguing in Publication
is available

ISBN 1 85291 526 9

Typeset in Times and Univers Condensed
Design by Forest Publication Services
Cover design by Cooper Wilson

Cover photographs
(*front, clockwise from top left*)
David Capel
Devon Malcolm
John Emburey
Neil Fairbrother and Richard Blakey
Neil Radford
Tim Munton
(*back*)
Representatives of all 18 counties
in their new Sunday League colours
(*all photographs by Colin Elsey of Colorsport*)

Reproduced, printed and bound by
Butler and Tanner Limited, Frome and London

PREFACE

The cricketers listed in this volume include all those who played for a first-class county at least once last season in any form of cricket and, for the first time, all those registered (at the time of going to press) to play for the 18 first-class counties in 1993, even those who have yet to make a first team appearance. All statistics are complete to the end of the last English season. Figures about 1000 runs and 50 wickets in a season refer to matches in England only. All first-class figures this year include figures for Test matches which are also extracted and listed separately. One-day 100s and 50s are for the English domestic competitions and all One-Day Internationals, home and abroad.

The following abbreviations apply: *means not out; All First – all first-class matches; 1-day Int – One-Day Internationals; Sunday – Sunday League; NatWest – NatWest Trophy; B&H – Benson & Hedges Cup. The figures for batting and bowling averages refer to the full first-class English list for 1992, followed in brackets by the 1991 figures. Inclusion in the batting averages depends on a minimum of six completed innings, and an average of at least 10 runs; a bowler has to have taken at least 10 wickets. The same qualification has been used for compiling the bowlers' strike rate.

Readers will notice occasional differences in the way the same kind of information is presented. This is because I have usually tried to follow the way in which the cricketers themselves have provided the relevant information.

Each year in *The Cricketers' Who's Who,* in addition to those cricketers who are playing during the current season, I also include the biographical and career details of those who played in the previous season but retired at the end of it. The purpose of this is to have, on the record, the full and final cricketing achievements of every player when his career has ended.

A book of this complexity and detail has to be prepared several months in advance of the cricket season, and occasionally there are recent changes in a player's circumstances which cannot be included in time. Many examples of facts and statistics which can quickly become outdated in the period between the actual compilation of the book and its publication, months later, will spring to the reader's mind, and I ask him or her to make the necessary commonsense allowance and adjustments.

Iain Sproat, March 1993

INTRODUCTION

1882 – the Ashes; 1933 – Bodyline; 1993 – the Murray Report. The present stir does not yet match that created by the first two pieces of cricket history. However, like it or not, 1993 will be remembered as the year when the Murray Report reshaped the English county game, particularly if we beat the Aussies. After all, isn't the idea to create a structure which will produce the best England Test side?

It is in our nature to become dissatisfied, to tinker and redesign, but our domestic programme has long cried out for attention: for a fixture list in which there is room to breathe and which strikes a better balance between one-day and Championship cricket. This year's programme of four-day and one-day matches goes a long way towards creating such a fixture list. So the 1993 diary will contain four less days of Championship cricket, fewer first-class venues, cricketless Wednesdays, a cut-throat start to the Benson & Hedges Cup and an 'ungodly' hour to start the new Sunday League. Progress? I think so, overall.

Four-day cricket has been coming for a long time. For the first time since the Championship contained 32 matches, the anomaly of some sides playing each other twice and others only once has been done away with. This is a good practical start, but more particularly each game should now be played to a natural conclusion. Each wicket taken and each run scored will be worth more because they cannot be traded in as they were in the bartering that had increasingly become a part of three-day matches. In the same way that a Test match is often decided by one poor session, so it is with four-day cricket (after all the difference is only 18 overs). The knowledge of this produces pressure and the players who prosper in such circumstances should be well-equipped for Test cricket. It's not just about Test cricket, though. The County Championship must be more than just a service industry for profit-making Test matches.

With an even fixture list, time to travel and prepare for each game, and real games played on true pitches the County Championship now has an integrity which it has lacked for some years.

So why, do I hear you ask, is there a technicolour jamboree taking place in the middle of each four-day game? Will the new Axa Equity and Law Sunday League create an American football-fashion offensive line-up very different from that which left the field clad in white on Saturday evening? Add a couple of shoulder-pads and those counties which have opted for the V-pattern shirt (viz John Emburey in Middlesex colours on the front cover) would certainly bear a passable likeness to rugby league players if not American footballers. Helmets and pads are currently being rounded up for respraying in appropriate colours to complete our colour-coordinated outfits. While helmets have brought anonymity to the game, the new kits will feature names on shirts and sweaters to be attached by velcro strips - a good thing for the spectators but pity the player who is dropped and who has his velcro name bands noisily removed, like a sergeant losing his stripes, to be replaced by someone else's.

Each April we receive from Lord's the admonition that whites only are to be worn on the ground. What will the men with the colourful ties make therefore of the rainbow cavalcade which will process through the Long Room every other Sunday to set foot on the hallowed turf? Will they blanche at the prospect or might it remind them of the colourful array of clothing worn in the game's infancy.

I have always favoured the old-fashioned myself: billowing cotton shirts, baggy flannels, etc., yet I, like the majority of my fellow professionals, regard the Sunday colours as not just a necessary financial step forward, but a welcome contrast. The one-day game is different. Let's make Sunday a family day. Good cricket, yes, played over fifty overs per side, but with a broad appeal to the initiate and uninitiated alike. Barbecued brunches at 11 o'clock before the game? Well, the players' Sunday lunch has certainly been knocked on the head by a midday start, but I think we are being hypocritical to complain at the extra work-load on a Sunday. The new schedule guarantees at least one day a week off and I think that with this 'pressure release valve' we will soon adjust.

After all, the complaint for many years has been that 40-over cricket is too instant; now we have a full-blooded league which will better reward quality cricket without losing the thrills of one-day cricket and can become a great family day.

The new Sunday format brings its own rule changes with the recently successful World Cup as the role model. Most noticeable will be the two close fielders for the first 15 overs. Shrewdly stationed they are still run savers, and as catchers they turn the batsmen's thoughts to watchfulness and the bowler's minds to attack. A game of cricket rather than a 40-over damage limitation exercise is what is intended. To this end leg-side fielding restrictions have been vetoed and only one white ball is to be used thus enabling spinners to play their part. That part may well be to flight the ball high above the black-draped sightscreens into the walls of white which traditionally encompass our cricket grounds. A return to lob bowling? Perhaps not, but sighting difficulties could produce some good 'What happened next?' moments this year.

The World Cup's worst rule was the one governing rain interruptions. Our own version is none too clear, invariably leading to success for the side batting second. Major discrepancies occur when the side batting first has finished its innings, there is rain and the side batting second has all their wickets to chase a target which is calculated as the first team's overall run rate multiplied by the number of overs left. It seems to me that a degree of flexibility is required, so how does this sound? Let's say the number of overs left were 20. Let the target be calculated as the number of runs scored by the side batting first in their last 20 overs (normally the most productive) or their best consecutive 20 overs. This probably raises as many questions as it answers, but nevertheless food for thought.

The board has resisted the temptation to tinker too much with rules for the County Championship. Raising the batting bonus points thresholds by fifty runs and increasing the number of overs by twenty in which to achieve them paves the way for an intriguing game within a game. With the new ball available at 100 overs there remain 20 overs in which to battle for outstanding bonus points, thus enlivening the end of the first day and the start of the second. Remembering, perhaps, the criticism they received for changing the quality of both ball and pitches after the 1989 season (if there were an improvement in play which factor would be responsible?), the board have eschewed further fiddling, that is except for the no ball regulation.

No balls have been decreed a bad thing and indeed they are a largely unnecessary hiccup in the proceedings, a licence for the fastidious umpire and an irritation to fielders and spectators alike. In Australia they have reduced the 'plague' by awarding a penalty of two runs in addition to any runs accrued. We are to follow suit, although as yet we are not sure whether these 'runs' will be added to the batsman's score, to extras or have a separate column all to themselves. One of our regular transgressors returned from a winter's club cricket in Australia to tell us how, in his first representative game, he had found the edge off a no ball, seen the catch dropped, the ball run to the boundary and then turned round to find the umpire signalling six. There is something particularly mortifying about that upraised-arm signal, and what if the irate fast bowler then delivers a no-ball bouncer which is hooked for six? What signal will this produce? By the time this is read, perhaps such signals will have already had a practical demonstration.

Bowlers will curse this new law; captains too until it takes effect, but the Aussies will be at home with it when they arrive in April to defend the Ashes. By then they will have completed their home series with the West Indies who will in turn have taken on Pakistan in the Caribbean. Something of a pecking order could well emerge from these closely grouped series. England will need no more motivation, however, than the memories of 1989 and the last West Indies series. That was the nadir of England's recent cricketing fortunes (this winter not included!). It spawned a rebel tour to South Africa and an England regime based on squad selection, dedication and fitness. That has brought some success and this summer's six Tests promise to deliver the third thrilling home series in a row.

Despite the rebel's availability and the events of the winter I would not rule out a recall for Lamb or Gower. The Australians, meanwhile, look likely to bring Langer and Martyn amongst their party, both products of the Australian Cricket Academy. Are we missing a trick here? Whittingdale's backing has facilitated a much more professional winter preparation for the England side. Would it not be possible to run an academy or its equivalent at Lilleshall, built around the 'A' tours, for a selected group of, say, U23 players? This would seem to be a more purposeful use for the money presently spent on guaranteeing year-round contracts for Test players.

With an Ashes tour and the Murray Report, 1993 will indeed be an auspicious year for cricket. Players will be coming to terms with a six-day week, travelling days and the logistical problems of cramming both Saturday and Sunday kit into the sponsored car; statisticians will, no doubt, be setting up new computer programmes for the new competitions and spectators will be counting the number of fourth days lost to early finishes and quietly wondering whether the extra two hours on a Sunday are worth it. No doubt there will be plenty more to debate and so, listening to David Mellor doing his stint on 606 through the winter months, the prospect presents itself of one of his friends taking over from Frances Edmonds for a while this summer - an alternative Prime Minister's question time?

Tim Curtis
March 1993

THE QUIZ

Throughout this book there are 200 quiz questions.

The answers can be found on page 650

ADAMS, C. J.   Derbyshire

Name: Christopher John Adams
Role: Right-hand bat, right-arm
medium pace bowler, slip fielder
Born: 6 May 1970, Whitwell, Derbyshire
Height: 6ft **Weight:** 13st 7lbs
Nickname: Grizzly
County debut: 1988
County cap: 1992
1000 runs in season: 1
1st-Class 50s scored: 11
1st-Class 100s scored: 8
1st-Class catches: 71
One-Day 50s: 7
One-Day 100s: 2
Place in batting averages: 61st av. 41.07
(1991 104th av. 31.40)
Strike rate: (career 59.80)
Parents: John and Eluned (Lyn)
Wife and date of marriage: Samantha,
26 September 1992
Family links with cricket: Brother David played 2nd XI cricket for Derbyshire and Gloucestershire. Father played for Yorkshire Schools and uncle played for Essex 2nd XI
Education: Tapton House School; Chesterfield Boys Grammar School; Repton School
Qualifications: 6 O-levels, NCA Coaching Awards
Off-season: 'Playing in the National Indoor League for Sheffield, getting as fit as possible, enjoying Christmas and the New Year and continuing to work on and improve my game.'
Overseas tours: Repton School to Barbados 1987; England NCA North to N. Ireland 1987
Overseas teams played for: Takapuna, New Zealand 1987-88; Te Puke, New Zealand 1989-90; Primrose, Cape Town, South Africa 1991-92
Cricketers particularly admired: Alan Hill for preparation, determination and whole approach to the game, Adrian Kuiper for his ability to win a game from any situation and Mohammad Azharuddin, a supreme architect in playing the cricket ball
Other sports followed: Football (Southend and Arsenal), golf, rallying and motor racing – any relatively interesting sport
Injuries: Muscle tear in neck in mid season, dislocated thumb in last game of the season
Relaxations: 'I like to ride my mountain bike. I like computer games, reading and the odd crossword.'
Extras: Beat Richard Hutton's 25-year-old record for most runs scored in a season at Repton. Represented ESCA at U15 and U19 levels, MCC Schools U19 and Young England in 1989. Took two catches fielding as 12th man for England v India at Old Trafford in 1990. Holds county records for the fastest hundred by a Derbyshire batsman (57 mins) and the highest score in the Sunday League (141*)

Opinions on cricket: 'I have mixed feelings about four-day cricket. I believe the idea of playing every county once a season is terrific, however, in retrospect I think the spectators may find the odd day's play a tad boring. I also think 50 overs on a Sunday is crazy. An enjoyable day's play has been made into another gruelling day's cricket. On the plus side the coloured clothing is tremendous.'
Best batting: 140* Derbyshire v Worcestershire, Worcester 1992
Best bowling: 4-29 Derbyshire v Lancashire, Derby 1991

1992 Season

	M	Inns	NO	Runs	HS	Avge	100s	50s	Ct	St	O	M	Runs	Wkts	Avge	Best	5wI	10wM
Test																		
All First	23	33	6	1109	140 *	41.07	4	4	20	-	66	5	260	2	130.00	1-47	-	-
1-day Int																		
NatWest	2	2	1	136	106 *	136.00	1	-	3	-	3	1	15	1	15.00	1-15	-	
B & H	5	4	0	29	18	7.25	-	-	2	-								
Sunday	16	15	3	519	141 *	43.25	1	4	10	-	5	0	41	0	-	-	-	-

Career Performances

	M	Inns	NO	Runs	HS	Avge	100s	50s	Ct	St	Balls	Runs	Wkts	Avge	Best	5wI	10wM
Test																	
All First	69	103	13	3014	140 *	33.48	8	11	71	-	598	375	10	37.50	4-29	-	-
1-day Int																	
NatWest	4	3	1	136	106 *	68.00	1	-	4	-	18	15	1	15.00	1-15	-	
B & H	13	11	2	127	44	14.11	-	-	5	-	6	3	0	-	-	-	-
Sunday	51	46	12	1171	141 *	34.44	1	7	22	-	30	41	0	-	-	-	-

AFFORD, J. A.   Nottinghamshire

Name: John Andrew Afford
Role: Slow left-arm bowler, right-hand bat and 'hopeless fielder'
Born: 12 May 1964, Crowland, Peterborough
Height: 6ft 1½in **Weight:** 13st
Nickname: Aff, Des
County debut: 1984
County cap: 1990
50 wickets in a season: 3
1st-Class 5 w. in innings: 9
1st-Class 10 w. in match: 2
1st-Class catches: 36
Place in bowling averages: 55th av. 31.35 (1991 63rd av. 31.87)
Strike rate: 59.90 (career 70.09)
Parents: Jill

Wife and date of marriage: Lynn,
1 October 1988
Children: Lily Meagan, 1 June 1991
Education: Spalding Grammar School;
Stamford College for Further Education
Qualifications: 5 O-levels,
NCA coaching certificate
Overseas tours: England A to
Kenya/Zimbabwe 1989-90
Overseas teams played for:
Upper Hutt, Taita and Petone,
all in Wellington, New Zealand
between 1984 and 1991.
Cricketers particularly admired:
Richard Hadlee, Clive Rice and Andy Pick
– 'he can't leave it alone'. Anyone who
bowls a lot
Other sports followed: Football –
Peterborough United FC
Relaxations: 'Now our house is finished I tend to lie on the sofa watching TV.'
Extras: Hat-trick against Leics 2nd XI in 1989, also took 100 wickets in that season, 47
in 2nd XI and 53 in 1st XI
Best batting: 22* Nottinghamshire v Leicestershire, Trent Bridge 1989
Best bowling: 6-68 Nottinghamshire v Sussex, Trent Bridge 1992

1992 Season

	M	Inns	NO	Runs	HS	Avge	100s	50s	Ct	St	O	M	Runs	Wkts	Avge	Best	5wI	10wM
Test																		
All First	18	17	6	42	12	3.81	-	-	4	-	509.1	128	1599	51	31.35	6-68	2	1
1-day Int																		
NatWest																		
B & H																		
Sunday	2	0	0	0	0	-	-	-	-	-	9	0	59	1	59.00	1-32	-	

Career Performances

	M	Inns	NO	Runs	HS	Avge	100s	50s	Ct	St	Balls	Runs	Wkts	Avge	Best	5wI	10wM
Test																	
All First	115	99	41	208	22 *	3.58	-	-	36	-	20748	9900	296	33.44	6-68	9	2
1-day Int																	
NatWest	5	2	2	2	2 *	-	-	-	-	-	348	164	5	32.80	3-32	-	
B & H	11	1	1	1	1 *	-	-	-	1	-	708	458	12	38.16	4-38	-	
Sunday	17	3	2	0	0 *	0.00	-	-	5	-	606	533	11	48.45	2-39	-	

AFTAB HABIB

Middlesex

Name: Aftab Habib
Role: Right-hand bat,
right-arm medium bowler
Born: 7 February 1972, Reading, Berks
Height: 5ft 11in
County debut: 1992
Marital status: Single
Family links with cricket: Cousin of
Zahid Sadiq (ex-Surrey and Derbyshire)
Education: Millfield School, Somerset
Overseas tours: England U19 to
New Zealand 1990-91
Best batting: 12 Middlesex v Surrey,
The Oval 1992

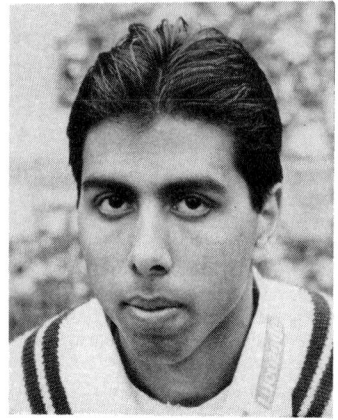

1992 Season

	M	Inns	NO	Runs	HS	Avge	100s	50s	Ct	St	O	M	Runs	Wkts	Avge	Best	5wl	10wM
Test																		
All First	1	2	1	19	12	19.00	-	-	-	-								
1-day Int																		
NatWest																		
B & H																		
Sunday																		

Career Performances

	M	Inns	NO	Runs	HS	Avge	100s	50s	Ct	St	Balls	Runs	Wkts	Avge	Best	5wl	10wM
Test																	
All First	1	2	1	19	12	19.00	-	-	-	-							
1-day Int																	
NatWest																	
B & H																	
Sunday																	

1. Which county won the Benson & Hedges Cup in 1992?

AGNEW, J. P.   Leicestershire

Name: Jonathan Philip Agnew
Role: Right-hand bat, right-arm fast bowler
Born: 4 April 1960, Macclesfield, Cheshire
Height: 6ft 4in **Weight:** 13st
Nickname: Spiro (after former US
Vice-President Spiro Agnew), Rambo
County debut: 1978
County cap: 1984
Test debut: 1984
No. of Tests: 3
50 wkts in a season: 7
100 wkts in a season: 1
1st-Class 5w. in innings: 37
1st-Class 10w. in match: 6
1st-Class catches: 39
1st-Class 50s: 2
Parents: Philip and Margaret
Wife and date of marriage: Beverley,
8 October 1983
Children: Jennifer, 31 October 1985; Rebecca, 18 September 1988
Family links with cricket: First cousin, Mary Duggan, was captain of England Women's team in the 1960s. Father was very keen cricketer
Education: Taverham Hall Prep School, Uppingham School
Qualifications: 9 O-levels, 2 A-levels
Career outside cricket: BBC Cricket Correspondent
Off-season: Commentating in India
Overseas tours: Young England to Australia 1978-79; Leicestershire to Zimbabwe 1981; England to India and Australia 1984-85; England B to Sri Lanka 1986
Overseas teams played for: Essendon, Melbourne 1978, 1980; Alexandra, Harare 1981-82; Central Cumberland District, Sydney 1982-83
Cricketers particularly admired: Imran Khan, Wayne Larkins
Other sports played: Hockey and golf
Relaxations: Music (all kinds). Plays piano and tuba.
Extras: Played for Surrey 2nd XI 1976-77. One of Wisden's Cricketers of the Year 1987. Leicestershire Player of the Year 1987. Author of *Eight Days A Week* (1988). BBC Radio cricket correspondent since 1991. Came out of retirement to play in NatWest Trophy semi-final win over Essex in 1992
Best batting: 90 Leicestershire v Yorkshire, Scarborough 1987
Best bowling: 9-70 Leicestershire v Kent, Leicester 1985

1992 Season

	M	Inns	NO	Runs	HS	Avge	100s	50s	Ct	St	O	M	Runs	Wkts	Avge	Best	5wI	10wM
Test																		
All First																		
1-day Int																		
NatWest	1	0	0	0	0	-	-	-	-	-	12	2	31	1	31.00	1-31	-	
B & H																		
Sunday																		

Career Performances

	M	Inns	NO	Runs	HS	Avge	100s	50s	Ct	St	Balls	Runs	Wkts	Avge	Best	5wI	10wM
Test	3	4	3	10	5	10.00	-	-	-	-	552	373	4	93.25	2-51	-	-
All First	218	232	49	2118	90	11.57	-	2	39	-	35388	19485	666	29.25	9-70	37	6
1-day Int	3	1	1	2	2 *	-	-	-	1	-	126	120	3	40.00	3-38	-	
NatWest	17	7	4	34	8 *	11.33	-	-	1	-	1080	635	20	31.75	3-31	-	
B & H	35	13	4	65	23 *	7.22	-	-	5	-	1820	1099	42	26.16	5-30	2	
Sunday	85	38	15	206	23 *	8.95	-	-	12	-	3401	2485	84	29.58	4-25	-	

ALIKHAN, R. I.   Surrey

Name: Rehan Iqbal Alikhan
Role: Right-hand opening bat
Born: 28 December 1962, London
Height: 6ft 1^1/$_2$in **Weight:** 13st
Nickname: Tiger, Prince
County debut: 1986 (Sussex), 1989 (Surrey)
1000 runs in a season: 1
1st-Class 50s scored: 31
1st-Class 100s scored: 2
1st-Class catches: 56
One-Day 50s: 2
Place in batting averages:
(1991 94th av. 32.96)
Parents: Akbar and Farida
Wife and date of marriage: Janine,
8 December 1991
Family links with cricket: Father played
college and club cricket
Education: King's College School,
Wimbledon
Qualifications: 8 O-levels, 2 A-levels
Career outside cricket: 'Have worked as a Lloyds re-insurance broker.'

Off-season: 3 months training, 3 months playing cricket in Perth

Overseas tours: CCC to Kenya 1986; Surrey to Dubai 1989, 1990

Overseas teams played for: Mossman Middle Harbour, Sydney 1982-84, Pakistan International Airlines 1986-87; Claremont Nedlands, Perth 1987-91; Melville, Perth 1991-93

Cricketers particularly admired: Imran Khan, Zaheer Abbas, Viv Richards, Sunil Gavaskar, Javed Miandad, Alec Stewart, Graham Thorpe

Other sports followed: Golf, rugby (union and league), Italian football, squash, tennis

Injuries: Out for two months with damaged nerve in left wrist

Relaxations: 'Spending time with Nenee, watching videos, eating out, seeing shows in the West End and trying to keep my body trim!'

Extras: Released by Sussex at end of 1988 season. Surrey 2nd XI Player of the Year 1989. Scored first first-class 100 in 1990. Had only 18 innings in all cricket in 1992 because of wrist injury, and only three first-class innings – 'the least amount of first-class cricket since my debut in 1986'.

Opinions on cricket: 'Four-day cricket is very good news because it will allow people to have a rest between games, thus allowing players to recharge batteries and therefore be able to provide a more motivated performance. A more balanced team should now be selected, allowing specialist batsmen to be selected for certain positions in the order and also allowing for the selection of specialist wicket-keepers.'

Best batting: 138 Surrey v Essex, The Oval 1990

Best bowling: 2-19 Sussex v West Indians, Hove 1988

1992 Season

	M	Inns	NO	Runs	HS	Avge	100s	50s	Ct	St	O	M	Runs	Wkts	Avge	Best	5wI	10wM
Test																		
All First	2	3	0	65	54	21.66	-	1	2	-								
1-day Int																		
NatWest																		
B & H																		
Sunday																		

Career Performances

	M	Inns	NO	Runs	HS	Avge	100s	50s	Ct	St	Balls	Runs	Wkts	Avge	Best	5wI	10wM
Test																	
All First	101	173	14	4547	138	28.59	2	31	56	-	347	274	7	39.14	2-19	-	-
1-day Int																	
NatWest	8	8	1	125	41	17.85	-	-	2	-							
B & H	3	3	0	137	71	45.66	-	2	1	-							
Sunday	12	8	2	72	23	12.00	-	-	-	-	54	47	0	-		-	-

ALLEYNE, M. W.   Gloucestershire

Name: Mark Wayne Alleyne
Role: Right-hand bat, right-arm medium
bowler, cover fielder, occasional
wicket-keeper
Born: 23 May 1968, Tottenham
Height: 5ft 10½in **Weight:** 12st 10lbs
Nickname: Boo-Boo
County debut: 1986
County cap: 1990
1000 runs in a season: 2
1st-Class 50s scored: 28
1st-Class 100s scored: 5
1st-Class 200s scored: 1
1st-Class catches: 103
1st-Class stumpings: 2
One-day 50s: 6
One-day 100s: 1
Place in batting averages: 111th av. 32.27

(1991 101st av. 32.02)
Place in bowling averages: 89th 35.85 (1991 123rd av. 43.09)
Strike rate: 59.21 (career 66.17)
Parents: Euclid Clevis and Hyacinth Cordeilla
Marital status: Single
Family links with cricket: Brother played for Gloucestershire 2nd XI and Middlesex
YCs. Father played club cricket in Barbados and England
Education: Harrison College, Barbados and Cardinal Pole School, E. London
Qualifications: 6 O-levels, NCA senior coaching award, and volleyball coaching certificate
Overseas tours: England YC to Sri Lanka 1987 and Australia 1988
Cricketers particularly admired: Gordon Greenidge, Viv Richards
Other sports followed: Football, volleyball, athletics
Relaxations: Watching films and sport; listening to music
Extras: Youngest player to score a century for Gloucestershire. In 1990 also became the
youngest to score a double hundred for the county. Graduate of Haringey Cricket College
Best batting: 256 Gloucestershire v Northamptonshire, Northampton 1990
Best bowling: 4-48 Gloucestershire v Glamorgan, Bristol 1988

---

2. In which year did Don Bradman begin his Test career?

20

1992 Season

	M	Inns	NO	Runs	HS	Avge	100s	50s	Ct	St	O	M	Runs	Wkts	Avge	Best	5wl	10wM
Test																		
All First	22	36	3	1065	93	32.27	-	7	23	-	138.1	32	502	14	35.85	3-25	-	-
1-day Int																		
NatWest	3	3	0	68	26	22.66	-	-	2	-	14	0	44	1	44.00	1-22	-	
B & H	5	4	0	49	24	12.25	-	-	1	-	42.1	4	149	1	149.00	1-25	-	
Sunday	17	16	3	589	134 *	45.30	1	4	5	-	93.5	2	447	14	31.92	4-35	-	

Career Performances

	M	Inns	NO	Runs	HS	Avge	100s	50s	Ct	St	Balls	Runs	Wkts	Avge	Best	5wl	10wM
Test																	
All First	124	194	25	5082	256	30.07	5	28	103	2	4103	2505	62	40.40	4-48	-	-
1-day Int																	
NatWest	17	13	4	136	45	15.11	-	-	7	-	462	302	9	33.55	5-30	1	
B & H	25	19	3	231	36	14.43	-	-	7	-	895	639	22	29.04	5-27	1	
Sunday	97	83	25	1805	134 *	31.12	1	6	28	-	2812	2368	81	29.23	4-35	-	

ALLOTT, P. J. W. Lancashire

Name: Paul John Walter Allott
Role: Right-hand bat, right-arm
fast-medium bowler
Born: 14 September 1956, Altrincham
Height: 6ft 4in **Weight:** 15st
Nickname: Walt
County debut: 1978
County cap: 1981
Benefit: 1990 (£109,617)
Test debut: 1981
Tests: 13
One-Day Internationals: 13
50 wickets in a season: 5
1st-Class 50s scored: 10
1st-Class 5 w. in innings: 30
1st-Class catches: 136
Place in batting averages:
(1991 254th av. 10.50)
Place in bowling averages:
(1991 100th av. 36.85)
Strike rate: (career 59.70)
Parents: John Norman and Lillian Patricia

Wife and date of marriage: Helen, 27 October 1979
Children: Ben and Susie
Family links with cricket: Father was dedicated club cricketer for twenty years with Ashley CC and is now a selector, administrator and junior organiser with Bowdon CC
Education: Altrincham Grammar School; Bede College, Durham
Qualifications: Qualified teacher and cricket coach
Overseas tours: With England to India 1981-82; India and Australia 1984-85
Cricketers particularly admired: Dennis Lillee
Injuries: Groin and back strains
Relaxations: Playing golf, watching all sports, listening to music, eating out, photography
Extras: Played football as goalkeeper for Cheshire schoolboys. Released by Lancashire at the end of the 1992 season. Will play for Staffordshire in 1993
Best batting: 88 Lancashire v Hampshire, Southampton 1987
Best bowling: 8-48 Lancashire v Northamptonshire, Northampton 1981

1992 Season

	M	Inns	NO	Runs	HS	Avge	100s	50s	Ct	St	O	M	Runs	Wkts	Avge	Best	5wI	10wM
Test																		
All First																		
1-day Int																		
NatWest																		
B & H	3	3	1	13	9	6.50	-	-	-	-	33	5	136	3	45.33	1-39	-	
Sunday	9	3	0	5	3	1.66	-	-	1	-	59.4	3	208	2	104.00	1-13	-	

Career Performances

	M	Inns	NO	Runs	HS	Avge	100s	50s	Ct	St	Balls	Runs	Wkts	Avge	Best	5wI	10wM
Test	13	18	3	213	52 *	14.20	-	1	4	-	2225	1084	26	41.69	6-61	1	-
All First	245	262	64	3360	88	16.97	-	10	136	-	38927	16665	652	25.56	8-48	30	-
1-day Int	13	6	1	15	8	3.00	-	-	2	-	819	552	15	36.80	3-41	-	
NatWest	26	13	5	67	19 *	8.37	-	-	4	-	1668	811	47	17.25	4-28	-	
B & H	62	27	8	176	23 *	9.26	-	-	18	-	3440	1786	74	24.13	4-23	-	
Sunday	164	65	30	527	43	15.05	-	-	27	-	6736	4401	151	29.14	4-28	-	

3. In which year did Derek Underwood begin his Test career?

4. In which year did John Hampshire begin his Test career?

AMBROSE, C. E. L.   Northamptonshire

Name: Curtly Elconn Lynwall Ambrose
Role: Left-hand bat, right-arm fast bowler;
'like the gully area'
Born: 21 September 1963, Antigua
Height: 6ft 7in **Weight:** 14st 4lbs
Nickname: Ambie
County debut: 1989
County cap: 1990
Test debut: 1987-88
Tests: 34
One-Day Internationals: 71
50 wickets in a season: 5
1st-Class 50s scored: 3
1st-Class 5 w. in innings: 19
1st-Class 10 w. in match: 3
1st-Class catches: 26
Place in batting averages: 189th av. 20.00
Place in bowling averages: 25th av. 26.14
(1991 2nd av. 17.03)
Strike rate: 65.24 (career 52.94)
Parents: Jasper (deceased) and Hillie
Wife and date of marriage: Bridgette, 6 September 1991
Children: Tanya
Family links with cricket: Brother used to play club cricket and got trials for Antigua.
Cousin Rolston Otto plays for Antigua and Leeward Islands
Education: Swetes Primary School; All Saints Secondary School
Qualifications: 3 O-levels, 3 A-levels, qualified carpenter
Off-season: Touring with the West Indies
Overseas tours: West Indies to England 1988, to Australia 1988-89, to India for Nehru
Cup 1989-90, to Pakistan 1990-91, to England 1991, to Pakistan 1991-92, to Australia for
Benson & Hedges World Series and World Cup 1991-92, to West Indies to Australia and
South Africa 1992-93
Overseas teams played for: Leeward Islands
Cricketers particularly admired: David Gower, Richard Hadlee, Robin Smith and all
West Indies Test cricketers
Other sports followed: NBA (American) basketball and tennis
Relaxations: Going to the movies, relaxing on the beach, listening to and playing music
(bass guitar)
Extras: A basketball player who only began playing cricket seriously at age 17. Took a
wicket with his first ball on Championship debut for Northamptonshire against Glamorgan
in 1989. Played in two NatWest finals in three years with Northants. Figures of 8 for 45
are the best in Tests for W Indies v England. One of *Wisden*'s Cricketers of the Year 1992

Opinions on cricket: 'Too much cricket played. It's almost impossible to play cricket every day for five months and still play international cricket. It could shorten your career. You get tired and when you are tired it affects your game.'
Best bowling: 8-45 West Indies v England, Bridgetown 1989-90

1992 Season

	M	Inns	NO	Runs	HS	Avge	100s	50s	Ct	St	O	M	Runs	Wkts	Avge	Best	5wI	10wM
Test																		
All First	18	20	10	200	49 *	20.00	-	-	5	-	543.4	151	1307	50	26.14	4-53	-	-
1-day Int																		
NatWest	5	2	1	12	8	12.00	-	-	-	-	50.5	15	82	8	10.25	4-7	-	
B & H	2	1	0	1	1	1.00	-	-	1	-	18	3	58	7	8.28	4-31	-	
Sunday	11	3	1	33	14 *	16.50	-	-	1	-	77.1	4	361	7	51.57	3-29	-	

Career Performances

	M	Inns	NO	Runs	HS	Avge	100s	50s	Ct	St	Balls	Runs	Wkts	Avge	Best	5wI	10wM
Test	34	51	9	513	53	12.21	-	1	7	-	8219	4021	148	27.16	8-45	6	1
All First	110	140	37	1603	59	15.56	-	3	26	-	22238	9993	420	23.79	8-45	19	3
1-day Int	71	41	19	294	26 *	13.36	-	-	17	-	3847	2263	111	20.38	5-17	3	
NatWest	13	5	1	82	48	20.50	-	-	4	-	833	309	18	17.16	4-7	-	
B & H	7	5	3	52	17 *	26.00	-	-	4	-	438	224	17	13.17	4-31	-	
Sunday	23	9	2	56	14 *	8.00	-	-	2	-	970	646	17	38.00	3-15	-	

ANDREW, S. J. W.   Essex

Name: Stephen Jon Walter Andrew
Role: Right-hand bat, right-arm medium bowler
Born: 27 January 1966, London
Height: 6ft 3in **Weight:** 14st
Nickname: Rip, Chinny, His Chinness, Le Grand Chien, G.O.S.
County debut: 1984 (Hants), 1990 (Essex)
1st-Class 5 w. in innings: 5
1st-Class catches: 21
Place in bowling averages: 85th av. 35.37 (1991 58th av. 31.44)
Strike rate: 66.25 (career 57.94)
Parents: Jon and Victoria
Marital status: Single
Education: Hordle House Prep School; Milton Abbey Public School
Qualifications: 3 O-levels
Overseas tours: Young England to West Indies 1985
Overseas teams played for: Pirates, Durban 1983-84; S.A.P., Durban 1984-86; Manly, Sydney 1987-88; Pinetown, Durban 1988-89; Taita, Wellington 1990-91

Cricketers particularly admired:
Dennis Lillee
Other sports followed:
Interested in most sports
Relaxations: Music, videos, films, books,
playing golf, sleeping, drinking
Best batting:
35 Essex v Northamptonshire,
Chelmsford 1990
Best bowling:
7-92 Hampshire v Gloucestershire,
Southampton 1987

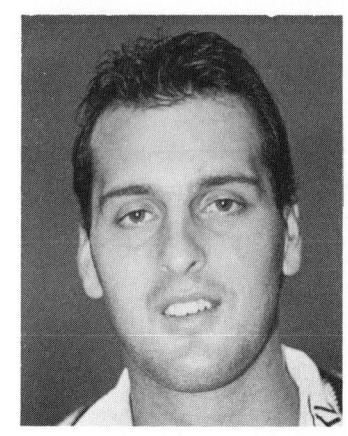

1992 Season

	M	Inns	NO	Runs	HS	Avge	100s	50s	Ct	St	O	M	Runs	Wkts	Avge	Best	5wI	10wM
Test																		
All First	10	12	4	38	14 *	4.75	-	-	-	-	265	45	849	24	35.37	4-54	-	-
1-day Int																		
NatWest																			
B & H																			
Sunday	1	0	0	0	0	-	-	-	-	-	8	0	41	1	41.00	1-41	-	

Career Performances

	M	Inns	NO	Runs	HS	Avge	100s	50s	Ct	St	Balls	Runs	Wkts	Avge	Best	5wI	10wM
Test																	
All First	100	69	31	292	35	7.68	-	-	21	-	15066	8349	260	32.11	7-92	5	-
1-day Int																	
NatWest	6	1	1	0	0 *	-	-	-	2	-	372	219	7	31.28	2-34	-	
B & H	11	3	3	5	4 *	-	-	-	1	-	654	363	20	18.15	5-24	1	
Sunday	31	5	2	20	8	6.66	-	-	2	-	1221	1050	23	45.65	4-50	-	

5. In which year did Fred Trueman begin his Test career?

6. In which year did Geoffrey Boycott begin his Test career?

ARCHER, G. F.   Nottinghamshire

Name: Graeme Francis Archer
Role: Right-hand bat
Born: 26 September 1970, Carlisle, Cumbria
Height: 6ft ³/₄in **Weight:** 12st 6lbs
Nickname: Archie Bunker and Astro Chimp
County debut: 1992
1st-Class 50s: 4
1st-Class 100s: 1
1st-Class catches: 6
Place in batting averages: 33rd av. 47.50
Parents: Christopher William and
Jean Elizabeth
Marital status: Single
Family links with cricket: Father played
for Carlisle in N Lancashire League; brother
Neil plays in the S Cheshire Alliance League
Education: King Edward VI High School;
Stafford College
Qualifications: 3 O-levels, City & Guilds
and BTEC National Diploma in Leisure Management
Career outside cricket: 'Not decided yet.'
Off-season: Getting physically fit for the 1993 season, taking NCA Coaching Award
Overseas teams played for: Hutt Districts, New Zealand 1991-92; also played for Hutt
Valley representative side
Cricketers particularly admired: Graeme Hick, Ian Botham, Derek Randall
Other sports followed: Watches football and rugby, plays badminton
Relaxations: Music and concerts, and 'the odd round of golf with friends'
Extras: Scored 200* in a 15 (8-ball) over match for Walsall U18s. Awarded the
A.A.Thompson Fielding Prize by The Cricket Society in 1990. Made 2nd XI debut for
Notts in 1987 aged 15. Played for Staffordshire in 1990-91
Opinions on cricket: 2nd XI pitches and grounds need to be improved
Best batting: 117 Nottinghamshire v Derbyshire, Trent Bridge 1992

1992 Season

	M	Inns	NO	Runs	HS	Avge	100s	50s	Ct	St	O	M	Runs	Wkts	Avge	Best	5wI	10wM
Test																		
All First	7	13	3	475	117	47.50	1	4	6	-								
1-day Int																		
NatWest																		
B & H																		
Sunday	4	1	0	9	9	9.00	-	-	-	-								

Career Performances

	M	Inns	NO	Runs	HS	Avge	100s	50s	Ct	St	Balls	Runs	Wkts	Avge	Best	5wl	10wM
Test																	
All First	7	13	3	475	117	47.50	1	4	6	-							
1-day Int																	
NatWest																	
B & H																	
Sunday	4	1	0	9	9	9.00	-	-	-	-							

ASIF DIN, M.   Warwickshire

Name: Mohamed Asif Din
Role: Right-hand bat, leg-spin bowler
Born: 21 September 1960, Kampala, Uganda
Height: 5ft 9in **Weight:** 10st 7lbs
Nickname: Gunga 'and many others'
County debut: 1981
County cap: 1987
1000 runs in a season: 2
1st-Class 50s scored: 39
1st-Class 100s scored: 8
1st-Class 5 w. in innings: 1
1st-Class catches: 108
One-Day 50s: 19
One-Day 100s: 5
Place in batting averages:
(1991 147th av. 26.34)
Strike rate: (career 85.93)
Parents: Jamiz and Mumtaz
Wife and date of marriage:

Ahmerin, 27 September 1987
Children: Zahra, 18 October 1990
Family links with cricket: Brothers Khalid and Abid play in Birmingham League
Education: Ladywood Comprehensive School, Birmingham
Qualifications: CSEs and O-levels
Cricketers particularly admired: Zaheer Abbas, Majid Khan
Injuries: Back trouble early in the season and a broken finger
Other sports followed: American football, basketball
Relaxations: Fishing and shooting
Best batting: 158* Warwickshire v Cambridge University, Fenner's 1988
Best bowling: 5-100 Warwickshire v Glamorgan, Edgbaston 1982

1992 Season

	M	Inns	NO	Runs	HS	Avge	100s	50s	Ct	St	O	M	Runs	Wkts	Avge	Best	5wI	10wM
Test																		
All First	2	3	0	103	40	34.33	-	-	-	-								
1-day Int																		
NatWest																		
B & H	4	4	1	128	71 *	42.66	-	1	1	-	10	0	40	0	-		-	-
Sunday	6	6	1	46	22	9.20	-	-	2	-	2	0	23	0	-		-	-

Career Performances

	M	Inns	NO	Runs	HS	Avge	100s	50s	Ct	St	Balls	Runs	Wkts	Avge	Best	5wI	10wM
Test																	
All First	199	326	44	8423	158 *	29.86	8	39	108	-	6273	4256	73	58.30	5-100	1	-
1-day Int																	
NatWest	26	23	7	645	94 *	40.31	-	3	6	-	139	88	7	12.57	5-40	1	
B & H	41	38	5	1177	137	35.66	2	5	5	-	126	102	1	102.00	1-26	-	
Sunday	145	131	23	3059	113	28.32	3	11	26	-	183	205	4	51.25	1-11	-	

ATHERTON, M. A. Lancashire

Name: Michael Andrew Atherton
Role: Right-hand bat, leg-spin bowler
Born: 23 March 1968, Manchester
Height: 6ft **Weight:** 12st 7lbs
Nickname: Athers, Dread
County debut: 1987
County cap: 1989
Test debut: 1989
Tests: 21
One-Day Internationals: 10
1000 runs in a season: 5
1st-Class 50s scored: 34
1st-Class 100s scored: 26
1st-Class 5 w. in innings: 3
1st-Class catches: 108
One-Day 50s: 18
One-Day 100s: 2
Place in batting averages: 21st av. 51.54
(1991 53rd av. 41.00)
Strike rate: (career 83.14)
Parents: Alan and Wendy
Marital status: Single

Family links with cricket: Father and brother both play league cricket
Education: Briscoe Lane Primary, Manchester GS; Downing College, Cambridge
Qualifications: 10 O-levels, 3 A-levels; BA (Hons) (Cantab)
Off-season: In India with England
Overseas tours: Young England to Sri Lanka 1987 and Australia 1988; England A to Zimbabwe 1989-90; England to Australia and New Zealand 1990-91, to India 1992-93
Cricketers particularly admired: Graham Gooch
Other sports followed: Golf, squash, football
Injuries: Back injury
Relaxations: 'Decent novels (Heller, Kundera, etc), good movies, food and wine, travelling, most sports, music'
Extras: In 1987 was first player to score 1000 runs in his debut season since Paul Parker in 1976. Youngest Lancastrian to score a Test century (151 v NZ at Trent Bridge in 1990); second Lancastrian to score a Test century at Old Trafford (138 v India in 1990). First captained England U19 aged 16. Selected for England tour to New Zealand and also England A tour to Bermuda and West Indies in 1991-92 but ruled out of both through injury
Opinions on cricket: 'In favour of four-day cricket if this means greater quality and less quantity. Not in favour of the idiotic 50 overs on a Sunday as it will exhaust bowlers who need the energy to bowl sides out on a Monday.'
Best batting: 199 Lancashire v Durham, Gateshead Fell 1992
Best bowling: 6-78 Lancashire v Nottinghamshire, Trent Bridge 1990

1992 Season

	M	Inns	NO	Runs	HS	Avge	100s	50s	Ct	St	O	M	Runs	Wkts	Avge	Best	5wI	10wM
Test	3	5	0	145	76	29.00	-	2	5	-								
All First	21	37	6	1598	199	51.54	5	7	24	-	74.1	9	343	4	85.75	2-109	-	-
1-day Int																		
NatWest	2	2	1	117	109 *	117.00	1	-	-	-	11.2	0	83	2	41.50	2-83	-	
B & H	3	3	0	41	24	13.66	-	-	-	-	9	0	60	0	-	-	-	
Sunday	14	14	0	450	76	32.14	-	2	2	-	7	0	58	2	29.00	1-28	-	

Career Performances

	M	Inns	NO	Runs	HS	Avge	100s	50s	Ct	St	Balls	Runs	Wkts	Avge	Best	5wI	10wM
Test	21	39	1	1311	151	34.50	3	9	20	-	366	282	1	282.00	1-60	-	-
All First	123	211	26	8424	199	45.53	26	34	108	-	8813	4666	106	44.01	6-78	3	-
1-day Int	10	10	1	335	74	37.22	-	3	3	-							
NatWest	9	9	2	346	109 *	49.42	1	1	4	-	188	154	6	25.66	2-15	-	
B & H	29	29	2	942	91	34.88	-	8	13	-	252	228	7	32.57	4-42	-	
Sunday	35	35	2	1075	111	32.57	1	6	11	-	216	248	7	35.42	3-33	-	

ATHEY, C. W. J. Sussex

Name: Charles William Jeffrey Athey
Role: Right-hand bat,
right-arm medium bowler
Born: 27 September 1957,
Middlesbrough
Height: 5ft 10in **Weight:** 12st
Nickname: Bumper, Wingnut, Ath
County debut: 1976 (Yorks),
1984 (Gloucs)
County cap: 1980 (Yorks),
1985 (Gloucs)
Benefit: 1990
Test debut: 1980
Tests: 23
One-Day Internationals: 31
1000 runs in a season: 10
1st-Class 50s scored: 99
1st-Class 100s scored: 42
1st-Class catches: 369
1st-Class stumpings: 2
One-Day 50s: 71
One-Day 100s: 9
Place in batting averages: 113th av. 31.93 (1991 40th av. 44.76)
Strike rate: (career 95.95)
Parents: Peter and Maree
Wife and date of marriage: Janet Linda, 9 October 1982
Family links with cricket: 'Father played league cricket in North Yorkshire and South Durham League for twenty-nine years, twenty-five of them with Middlesbrough. President of Middlesbrough CC since 1975. Brother-in-law Colin Cook played for Middlesex, other brother-in-law (Martin) plays in Thames Valley League. Father-in-law deeply involved in Middlesex Youth cricket.'
Education: Linthorpe Junior School; Stainsby Secondary School; Acklam Hall High School
Qualifications: 4 O-levels, some CSEs, NCA coaching certificate
Off-season: Looking for work, playing and watching football, keeping fit
Overseas tours: England U19 to West Indies 1976; England to West Indies 1980-81; Australia 1986-87; Pakistan, Australia and New Zealand 1987-88; England B to Sri Lanka 1985-86; unofficial English XI to South Africa 1989-90
Cricketers particularly admired: Gordon Greenidge, Malcolm Marshall, Chris Smith
Other sports followed: Most sports
Relaxations: Music, good films, good food
Extras: Played for Teesside County Schools U16 at age 12. Played for Yorkshire Colts

1974. Played football for Middlesbrough Schools U16 and Junior XI. Offered but declined apprenticeship terms with Middlesbrough FC. Captain of Gloucestershire in 1989. Suspension for playing in South Africa in 1990 was remitted in 1992. Allowed to move to Sussex for 1993 season

Opinions on cricket: 'The registration rule has got to be studied and changed. I believe the rule is meant to stop players moving regularly between counties for better financial deals, but when a player has been at a particular county for a long time and genuinely feels he needs to move on, providing he is out of contract, he should be able to go as a "free man".'

Best batting: 184 England B v Sri Lanka XI, Galle 1985-86

Best bowling: 3-3 Gloucestershire v Hampshire, Bristol 1985

1992 Season

	M	Inns	NO	Runs	HS	Avge	100s	50s	Ct	St	O	M	Runs	Wkts	Avge	Best	5wI	10wM
Test																		
All First	20	32	0	1022	181	31.93	2	4	19	-	58	7	184	2	92.00	1-16	-	-
1-day Int																		
NatWest	3	3	0	124	59	41.33	-	2	1	-	2	0	11	0	-		-	-
B & H	5	5	1	122	56 *	30.50	-	1	-	-	23	1	122	4	30.50	4-57	-	
Sunday	17	17	3	467	105	33.35	1	1	7	-	4.5	0	31	0	-		-	-

Career Performances

	M	Inns	NO	Runs	HS	Avge	100s	50s	Ct	St	Balls	Runs	Wkts	Avge	Best	5wI	10wM
Test	23	41	1	919	123	22.97	1	4	13	-							
All First	387	639	62	20129	184	34.88	42	99	369	2	4318	2339	45	51.97	3-3	-	-
1-day Int	31	30	3	848	142 *	31.40	2	4	16	-	6	10	0	-		-	-
NatWest	39	38	7	1338	115	43.16	1	11	21	-	145	131	1	131.00	1-18	-	-
B & H	68	64	10	1921	95	35.57	-	16	32	-	478	364	16	22.75	4-48	-	
Sunday	220	210	19	6420	121 *	33.61	6	40	85	-	735	691	24	28.79	5-35	1	

7. In which year did Richie Benaud begin his Test career?

8. In which year did Ian Botham begin his Test career?

ATKINS, P. D.

Name: Paul David Atkins
Role: Right-hand bat,
right-arm medium bowler
Born: 11 June 1966, Aylesbury, Bucks
Height: 6ft 1in **Weight:** 13st 11lbs
Nickname: Ripper
County debut: 1988
1st-Class 50s scored: 3
1st-Class 100s scored: 1
1st-Class catches: 5
One-Day 50s: 1
Place in batting averages: 135th av. 27.28
Parents: Brian and Thelma
Marital status: Single
Family links with cricket: 'Dad plays
for Dinton, Mum does the teas and
washes my gear.'
Education: Broughton First and
Middle Schools, Aylesbury G.S.
Qualifications: 7 O-levels, 3 A-levels
Off-season: 'In Durban, South Africa, playing cricket and golf, coaching and relaxing in
the sunshine far away from the Oval indoor nets. Trying to win a bet with D.Bicknell and
A.Brown.'
Overseas tours: NAYC to Bermuda 1985; Surrey to UAE 1988,1989,1990;
Buckinghamshire to Zimbabwe 1992
Overseas teams played for: Pietermaritzburg University 1985-86; Alexandrians 1986-
88; Perth 1988-90; New Era 1991-92
Cricketers particularly admired: Gordon Greenidge, Desmond Haynes, 'all my Surrey
team-mates past and present', all Aylesbury players especially Nigel Farrow
Other sports followed: Golf, rugby, football (Portsmouth FC)
Injuries: 'No major injury in 1992 for the first season in my career.'
Relaxations: Listening to music, sleeping, playing other sports and socialising with Tony
Murphy, Joey Benjamin and former team-mate Jon Robinson
Extras: Played for Buckinghamshire since 1985. Won Wilfred Rhodes Batting Trophy
1986. Seventh Surrey player to score century on his debut. Scored two first-class 99s
Best batting: 114* Surrey v Cambridge University, The Oval 1988

9. Who holds the record for the most sixes in one first-class innings?

	M	Inns	NO	Runs	HS	Avge	100s	50s	Ct	St	O	M	Runs	Wkts	Avge	Best	5wl	10wM
Test																		
All First	7	14	0	382	99	27.28	-	2	2	-								
1-day Int																		
NatWest																		
B & H																		
Sunday																		

Career Performances

	M	Inns	NO	Runs	HS	Avge	100s	50s	Ct	St	Balls	Runs	Wkts	Avge	Best	5wl	10wM
Test																	
All First	17	32	3	853	114 *	29.41	1	3	5	-							
1-day Int																	
NatWest	2	2	0	82	82	41.00	-	1	1	-							
B & H	3	3	1	15	9	7.50	-	-	-	-							
Sunday	1	1	0	2	2	2.00	-	-	-	-							

AUSTIN, I. D.   Lancashire

Name: Ian David Austin
Role: Left-hand bat,
right-arm medium bowler
Born: 30 May 1966, Haslingden, Lancs
Height: 5ft 10in **Weight:** 14st 7lbs
Nickname: Oscar, Bully
County debut: 1986
County cap: 1990
1st-Class 100s scored: 2
1st-Class 50s scored: 5
1st-Class 5 w. in innings: 1
1st-Class catches: 7
One-Day 50s: 2
Place in batting averages: 130th av. 28.75
(1991 149th av. 26.25)
Place in bowling averages: 121st av. 43.50
(1991 142nd av. 65.58)
Strike rate: 82.41 (career 78.76)
Parents: Jack and Ursula
Family links with cricket: Father opened batting for Haslingden CC
Education: Haslingden High School
Qualifications: 3 O-levels; NCA coaching certificate

Cricketers particularly admired: Ian Botham, Clive Lloyd
Overseas tours: England U19 to Bermuda 1985; Lancashire to Jamaica 1987 & 1988, Zimbabwe 1989, Tasmania and Western Australia 1990 & 1991
Other sports followed: Football, golf
Relaxations: Listening to music, playing golf
Extras: Holds amateur Lancashire League record for highest individual score (147*). Broke Lancashire CCC record for most wickets in the Sunday League in 1991.
Best batting: 115* Lancashire v Derbyshire, Blackpool 1992
Best bowling: 5-79 Lancashire v Surrey, The Oval 1988

1992 Season

	M	Inns	NO	Runs	HS	Avge	100s	50s	Ct	St	O	M	Runs	Wkts	Avge	Best	5wI	10wM
Test																		
All First	8	10	2	230	115 *	28.75	1	1	-	-	164.5	41	522	12	43.50	3-44	-	-
1-day Int																		
NatWest	2	2	2	36	33 *	-	-	-	-	-	21	3	85	2	42.50	2-27	-	
B & H	5	3	0	54	33	18.00	-	-	-	-	45.3	2	186	2	93.00	2-44	-	
Sunday	15	10	3	138	31	19.71	-	-	3	-	103.5	2	517	12	43.08	3-38	-	

Career Performances

	M	Inns	NO	Runs	HS	Avge	100s	50s	Ct	St	Balls	Runs	Wkts	Avge	Best	5wI	10wM
Test																	
All First	51	66	17	1249	115 *	25.49	2	5	7	-	6144	2919	78	37.42	5-79	1	-
1-day Int																	
NatWest	10	5	3	61	33 *	30.50	-	-	1	-	642	445	10	44.50	3-36	-	
B & H	24	14	4	282	80	28.20	-	2	3	-	1395	946	22	43.00	4-25	-	
Sunday	78	42	17	433	48	17.32	-	-	15	-	3110	2565	86	29.82	5-56	1	

AYLING, J. R.   Hampshire

Name: Jonathan Richard Ayling
Role: Right-hand bat, right-arm medium bowler
Born: 13 June 1967, Portsmouth
Height: 6ft 5in **Weight:** 14st 7lbs
Nickname: Victor, Kitty
County debut: 1988
County cap: 1991
1st-Class 50s scored: 11
1st-Class 100s scored: 1
1st-Class catches: 14
1st-Class 5 w. in innings: 1
One-Day 50s: 1

Place in batting averages: 168th av. 23.72
(1991 69th av. 46.00)
Place in bowling averages: 4th av. 20.60
(1991 15th av. 23.80)
Strike rate: 44.54 (career 54.09)
Parents: Christopher and Mary
Marital status: Single
Education: Portsmouth Grammar School
Qualifications: 8 O-levels, 1 A-level
Off-season: Training at Lilleshall,
working for BMW, touring in
California and South Africa
Overseas clubs played for: Pinelands,
Cape Town 1986-89
Cricketers particularly admired:
Graham Gooch, Mike Gatting,
John Emburey, Robin Smith, Allan Lamb
'and many of the senior Hants players'
Other sports followed: Athletics, soccer,
rugby union, snooker
Injuries: Knee problems, out for several weeks.
Relaxations: 'Getting away from cricket and spending time with family and friends.'
Extras: Wicket with first ball in first-class cricket; missed all of 1989 season with a serious
knee injury. One of only four players to play in two Lord's finals for Hampshire. Highest
English-qualified bowler in 1992 averages
Opinions on cricket: 'Too much cricket has been crammed into each season, reducing the
quality of performance from players. With any luck the new 1993 format will benefit
everyone.'
Best batting: 121 Hampshire v Oxford University, The Parks 1992
Best bowling: 5-12 Hampshire v Middlesex, Bournemouth 1992

1992 Season

	M	Inns	NO	Runs	HS	Avge	100s	50s	Ct	St	O	M	Runs	Wkts	Avge	Best	5wl	10wM
Test																		
All First	18	26	1	593	121	23.72	1	2	4	-	356.2	78	989	48	20.60	5-12	1	-
1-day Int																		
NatWest	1	0	0	0	0	-	-	-	-	-	12	0	70	0	-	-	-	-
B & H	6	5	3	41	18 *	20.50	-	-	1	-	58	4	236	6	39.33	2-25	-	
Sunday	15	14	5	273	45	30.33	-	-	4	-	85.3	1	389	8	48.62	2-24	-	

10.   Who holds the record for the most first-class sixes an English season?

Career Performances

	M	Inns	NO	Runs	HS	Avge	100s	50s	Ct	St	Balls	Runs	Wkts	Avge	Best	5wI	10wM
Test																	
All First	56	84	11	1993	121	27.30	1	11	14	-	7086	3254	131	24.84	5-12	1	-
1-day Int																	
NatWest	12	8	4	105	29	26.25	-	-	4	-	840	572	16	35.75	3-30	-	
B & H	15	10	5	66	18 *	13.20	-	-	3	-	846	584	16	36.50	2-22	-	
Sunday	57	46	15	791	56	25.51	-	1	10	-	2187	1780	52	34.23	4-37	-	

AYMES, A. N. Hampshire

Name: Adrian Nigel Aymes
Role: Right-hand bat, wicket-keeper
Born: 4 June 1964, Southampton
Height: 6ft **Weight:** 13st
Nickname: Aymser, Adi
County debut: 1987
County cap: 1991
1st-Class 50s scored: 8
1st-Class catches: 47 (career 121)
1st -Class stumpings: 4 (career 9)
Place in batting averages: 190th av. 19.94
(1991 135th av. 28.00)
Parents: Michael and Barbara
Wife and date of marriage: Marie,
12 November 1992
Education: Shirley Middle; Bellemoor
Secondary; Hill College
Qualifications: 4 O-levels, 1 A-level
Career outside cricket: Builder
Overseas tours: Hampshire XI to the Isle of Wight
Cricketers particularly admired: Bob Taylor, Alan Knott
Other sports followed: Football
Injuries: Split cartilage in left knee, out for four weeks
Relaxations: Watching videos
Extras: Half century on debut v Surrey; equalled club record of 6 catches in an innings and 10 in a match
Opinions on cricket: 'Good wickets and a bigger-seamed ball.'
Best batting: 75* Hampshire v Glamorgan, Pontypridd 1990
Best Bowling: 1-75 Hampshire v Sussex, Southampton 1992

1992 Season

	M	Inns	NO	Runs	HS	Avge	100s	50s	Ct	St	O	M	Runs	Wkts	Avge	Best	5wI	10wM
Test																		
All First	18	23	5	359	65	19.94	-	2	47	4	7	0	75	1	75.00	1-75	-	-
1-day Int																		
NatWest																		
B & H	6	1	0	11	11	11.00	-	-	4	2								
Sunday	13	6	3	73	23	24.33	-	-	8	1								

Career Performances

	M	Inns	NO	Runs	HS	Avge	100s	50s	Ct	St	Balls	Runs	Wkts	Avge	Best	5wI	10wM
Test																	
All First	50	63	17	1402	75 *	30.47	-	8	121	9	42	75	1	75.00	1-75	-	-
1-day Int																	
NatWest	5	1	0	2	2	2.00	-	-	6	1							
B & H	11	3	0	23	11	7.66	-	-	8	6							
Sunday	29	18	11	257	33 *	36.71	-	-	23	5							

BABINGTON, A. M.   Gloucestershire

Name: Andrew Mark Babington
Role: Left-hand bat, right-arm
fast-medium bowler
Born: 22 July 1963, London
Height: 6ft 2in **Weight:** 13st
Nickname: Gypsy, Vinny Jones, Oscar
County debut: 1986 (Sussex);
1991 (Gloucestershire)
1st-Class 50s scored: 1
1st-Class 5 w. in innings: 3
1st-Class catches: 31
Place in batting averages: 255th av. 10.71
Place in bowling averages: 124th av. 44.29
(1991 91st av. 35.40)
Strike rate: 66.35 (career 67.02)
Parents: Roy and Maureen
Marital status: Divorced
Family links with cricket: Father and
brother played club cricket.
Education: Reigate Grammar School; Borough Road PE College
Qualifications: 5 O-levels, 2 A-levels; NCA coaching certificate; Member of Institute of
Legal Executives; holds LAUTRO and consumer credit licence for the insurance industry

Career outside cricket: Working in insurance/broking
Off-season: In England training for the new season and working in the finance industry
Overseas tours: Surrey YCs to Australia 1980; Gloucestershire to Kenya 1991
Overseas teams played for: Gosnalls, Perth 1991-92
Cricketers particularly admired: Dennis Lillee, John Snow, David Smith, Martin Lee
Other sports followed: All motor sports, boxing, football
Injuries: Dislocated finger and damaged knee ligaments, out for three weeks
Relaxations: 'Driving, spending time with Charlotta, visiting Sweden. Eating and drinking at the Cherry Tree pub in Faygate, Reading. Listening to soul and Motown music.'
Extras: Took hat-trick (3rd, 4th & 5th Championship wickets) v Gloucestershire in 1986. Scored maiden 1st-class 50 off 30 balls (5 sixes) v Sussex at Cheltenham 1991
Opinions on cricket: 'Counties should do more for players over a 12-month period with regard to jobs etc. in the winter. 50-over cricket on Sundays will be hard work in the middle of a four-day game. Good to see coloured kit. Pitches should be harder and quicker if possible to provide more entertaining cricket'
Best batting: 58 Gloucestershire v Sussex, Cheltenham 1991
Best bowling: 8-107 Gloucestershire v Kent, Bristol 1992

1992 Season

	M	Inns	NO	Runs	HS	Avge	100s	50s	Ct	St	O	M	Runs	Wkts	Avge	Best	5wl	10wM
Test																		
All First	9	11	4	75	24	10.71	-	-	3	-	188	21	753	17	44.29	8-107	1	-
1-day Int																		
NatWest	3	1	1	1	1*	-	-	-	1	-	27	5	90	4	22.50	3-8	-	
B & H	5	2	1	35	27	35.00	-	-	1	-	49	7	160	6	26.66	2-27	-	
Sunday	15	5	3	10	6	5.00	-	-	3	-	98.1	7	410	16	25.62	4-21	-	

Career Performances

	M	Inns	NO	Runs	HS	Avge	100s	50s	Ct	St	Balls	Runs	Wkts	Avge	Best	5wl	10wM
Test																	
All First	87	92	37	475	58	8.63	-	1	31	-	13002	6911	194	35.62	8-107	3	-
1-day Int																	
NatWest	11	3	3	5	4*	-	-	-	4	-	582	387	15	25.80	3-8	-	
B & H	20	9	4	63	27	12.60	-	-	3	-	1166	694	28	24.78	4-29	-	
Sunday	72	18	7	39	11	3.54	-	-	17	-	2753	2111	64	32.98	4-21	-	

11.   Who is the only Test player to have been given out 'obstructing the field'?

BAILEY, R. J.   Northamptonshire

Name: Robert John Bailey
Role: Right-hand bat, off-spin bowler
Born: 28 October 1963, Biddulph,
Stoke-on-Trent
Height: 6ft 3in **Weight:** 14-15st
Nickname: Bailers, Nose Bag ('I eat a lot!')
County debut: 1982
County cap: 1985
Benefit: 1993
Test debut: 1988
Tests: 4
One-Day Internationals: 4
1000 runs in a season: 9
1st-Class 50s scored: 73
1st-Class 100s scored: 29
1st-Class 200s scored: 3
1st-Class catches: 166
One-Day 50s: 41
One-Day 100s: 7
Place in batting averages: 29th av. 49.12 (1991 58th av. 39.48)
Place in bowling averages: (1991 104th av. 38.09)
Strike rate: (career 76.92)
Parents: Marie, father deceased
Wife and date of marriage: Rachel, 11 April 1987
Children: Harry John, 7 March 1991
Family links with cricket: Father played in North Staffordshire League for thirty years for Knypersley and Minor Counties cricket for Staffordshire as wicket-keeper. Brother Simon now plays for Knypersley in the North Staffs/South Cheshire League
Education: Biddulph High School
Qualifications: 6 CSEs, 1 O-level, NCA Advanced Cricket Coach
Career outside cricket: Working in marketing for NCCC
Off-season: Organising benefit year
Overseas tours: England to Sharjah 1985 and 1987; West Indies 1989-90; Northants to Durban 1992, to Cape Town 1993
Cricketers particularly admired: Dennis Lillee, David Steele
Other sports followed: Football (Stoke City)
Relaxations: Walking and drinking at the local village pub
Extras: Played for Young England v Young Australia 1983. Selected for cancelled tour of India 1988-89. Youngest Northamptonshire player to score 10,000 runs
Opinions on cricket: 'I hope that 50-over Sunday League cricket doesn't take off. I think most players will find four-day cricket hard in 1993, i.e. longer spells in the field. I can't imagine players wanting to start at 12 noon on a Sunday. What time do we eat lunch – let's

get our priorities right!'
Best batting: 224* Northamptonshire v Glamorgan, Swansea 1986
Best bowling: 3-27 Northamptonshire v Glamorgan, Wellingborough 1988

1992 Season

	M	Inns	NO	Runs	HS	Avge	100s	50s	Ct	St	O	M	Runs	Wkts	Avge	Best	5wl	10wM
Test																		
All First	23	39	7	1572	167 *	49.12	2	8	22	-	120.1	31	291	9	32.33	1-0	-	-
1-day Int																		
NatWest	5	5	2	219	98 *	73.00	-	2	2	-	15	3	39	0	-	-	-	-
B & H	4	4	1	138	109 *	46.00	1	-	2	-								
Sunday	17	15	4	449	69	40.81	-	4	3	-	8	0	44	4	11.00	2-4	-	

Career Performances

	M	Inns	NO	Runs	HS	Avge	100s	50s	Ct	St	Balls	Runs	Wkts	Avge	Best	5wl	10wM
Test	4	8	0	119	43	14.87	-	-	-	-							
All First	233	390	60	13725	224 *	41.59	29	73	166	-	4231	2361	55	42.92	3-27	-	-
1-day Int	4	4	2	137	43 *	68.50	-	-	1	-	36	25	0	-	-	-	
NatWest	31	31	9	1025	145	46.59	1	6	6	-	198	113	6	18.83	3-47	-	
B & H	43	40	4	1546	134	42.94	2	11	9	-	60	29	1	29.00	1-22	-	
Sunday	135	128	18	3970	125 *	36.09	4	24	31	-	193	229	8	28.62	3-23	-	

BAINBRIDGE, M. R. Surrey

Name: Mark Robert Bainbridge
Role: Right-hand bat, left-arm bowler
Born: 11 May 1973, Isleworth, Middlesex
Height: 5ft 9½in **Weight:** 10st 7lbs
Nickname: Baino
Marital status: Single
Family links with cricket: 'Dad played ever since I can remember for his local side, Barnes.'
Education: Teddington School; Richmond upon Thames College
Qualifications: 8 GCSEs BTEC in Business Studies
Career outside cricket: 'Something in the leisure industry'
Off-season: Coaching in schools and working in the Ken Barrington Cricket Centre at the Oval

Overseas tours: England U18 to Canada 1991 (International Youth Tournament); England U19 to Barbados 1991, to Pakistan 1992

Cricketers particularly admired: Phil Tufnell, Graham Thorpe, David Gower and Mark Taylor (Australia)

Other sports followed: Rugby union, football

Injuries: Recurrence of groin injury, off for two weeks

Relaxations: Going out with friends, watching videos and watching Harlequins play rugby

Opinions on cricket: 'There is too much cricket played in short spaces of time. Some weeks you can play 14 days on the trot, have a break for a day or two and then a further 14 days solid cricket. It should be spread out so that players can have one or two days off each week when they can practice or rest.'

BAINBRIDGE, P.   Durham

Name: Philip Bainbridge
Role: Right-hand bat, right-arm medium bowler
Born: 16 April 1958, Stoke-on-Trent
Height: 5ft 9½in **Weight:** 12st 7lbs
Nickname: Bains, Robbo, Red
County debut: 1977 (Gloucestershire), 1992 (Durham)
County cap: 1981
Benefit: 1989
1000 runs in a season: 8
1st-Class 50s scored: 77
1st-Class 100s scored: 22
1st-Class 5 w. in innings: 8
1st-Class catches: 118
One-Day 50s: 22
One-Day 100s: 1
Place in batting averages: 46th av. 43.95
Place in bowling averages: 114th av. 40.64
Strike rate: 80.64 (career 73.24)
Parents: Leonard George and Lilian Rose
Wife and date of marriage: Barbara, 22 September 1979
Children: Neil, 11 January 1984; Laura, 15 January 1985
Family links with cricket: Cousin, Stephen Wilkinson, played for Somerset
Education: Hanley High School; Stoke-on-Trent Sixth Form College; Borough Road College of Education
Qualifications: 9 O-levels, 2 A-levels, BEd
Career outside cricket: Runs own corporate hospitality company and sports tour operators

– Rhodes Leisure, Bristol. In particular, runs sports tours to South Africa

Off-season: 'Working in the business.'

Overseas tours: British Colleges to W. Indies 1978; English Counties XI to Zimbabwe 1985; plus other tours to West Indies, Sri Lanka, Holland, South Africa, Pakistan and Zimbabwe

Cricketers particularly admired: Mike Procter, Wayne Larkins, Richard Hadlee

Other sports followed: All sports, particularly rugby union

Relaxations: Sport, music, travel. Coaching U10s mini rugby

Extras: Played for four 2nd XIs in 1976 – Gloucestershire, Derbyshire, Northamptonshire and Warwickshire. Played for Young England v Australia 1977. Scored first century for Stoke-on-Trent aged 14. One of *Wisden's* Cricketers of the Year, 1985. Joined Durham for their first season in first-class cricket after 14 seasons with Gloucestershire. Played for Leyland CC as professional in 1991 – they won the Northern League.

Opinions on cricket: 'Welcome the new formats due to take place in 1993, i.e. four-day cricket and coloured clothing. Although I thought the Sunday League should have stayed at 40 overs.'

Best batting: 169 Gloucestershire v Yorkshire, Cheltenham 1988

Best bowling: 8-53 Gloucestershire v Somerset, Bristol 1986

1992 Season

	M	Inns	NO	Runs	HS	Avge	100s	50s	Ct	St	O	M	Runs	Wkts	Avge	Best	5wI	10wM
Test																		
All First	17	30	9	923	92 *	43.95	-	8	8	-	188.1	39	569	14	40.64	5-100	1	-
1-day Int																		
NatWest	1	1	0	6	6	6.00	-	-	-	-	8	0	29	1	29.00	1-29	-	
B & H	4	4	0	70	27	17.50	-	-	1	-	36	1	160	5	32.00	4-38	-	
Sunday	8	7	0	148	57	21.14	-	1	2	-	45	2	276	5	55.20	2-41	-	

Career Performances

	M	Inns	NO	Runs	HS	Avge	100s	50s	Ct	St	Balls	Runs	Wkts	Avge	Best	5wI	10wM
Test																	
All First	274	454	69	13276	169	34.48	22	77	118	-	21022	10554	287	36.77	8-53	8	-
1-day Int																	
NatWest	27	23	3	643	89	32.15	-	6	4	-	1549	878	28	31.35	3-49	-	
B & H	50	46	9	1037	96	28.02	-	6	17	-	2349	1425	43	33.14	4-38	-	
Sunday	170	150	25	2675	106 *	21.40	1	10	35	-	5819	4997	164	30.47	5-22	1	

12.   Which bowler has taken the most wickets in one first-class match?

BAKKER, P.-J. Hampshire

Name: Paul-Jan Bakker
Role: Right-hand bat, right-arm
medium bowler,
fine-leg and mid-off/mid-on fielder
Born: 19 August 1957,
Vlaardingen, Holland
Height: 6ft 1in
Weight: 14st (very up and down)
Nickname: Nip, Peach, Dutchie
County debut: 1986
County cap: 1989
50 wickets in a season: 1
1st-Class 5 w. in innings: 7
1st-Class catches: 9
Place in batting averages: 248th av. 11.50
Place in bowling averages: 109th av. 40.09
(1991 69th av. 32.75)
Strike rate: 88.36 (career 59.71)

Parents: Hubertus Antonius Bakker and
Wilhelmina Hendrika Bakker-Goos
Marital status: Single
Family links with cricket: 'Father is scorer for Quick CC, my club in the Hague.'
Education: 1ᵉ VCL and Hugo de Groot College, The Hague, Holland
Qualifications: 'We have a different school system but finished my HAVO schooling.'
Ski-instructor
Career outside cricket: Ski holidays/ ski touring and ski lessons in Switzerland
Overseas tours: Several tours to England with Dutch clubs and with Holland national side,
including ICC Trophy 1986; MCC to USA 1989-90; Namibia 1990-91
Overseas teams played for: Quick, The Hague 1965-85; Green Point, Cape Town 1981-
86; Flamingo Touring Club 1986-91
Cricketers particularly admired: 'Malcolm Marshall – best bowler I've ever seen (but
he can't beat me at golf!) and Michael Holding – the most beautifully balanced run-up'
Other sports followed: Formula One motor racing, skiing, golf and most other sports
Relaxations: Golf – but is it relaxation when you double-bogey a par 3. Winter sports are
most relaxing, especially the end of a day's skiing
Extras: First ever Dutch player to play professional cricket. Played for Holland in 1986
and 1990 ICC Trophy competitions. 'To be invited for the Crickethon at Wembley was a
big thrill, especially being the only "European" in the side.' Released by Hampshire at the
end of 1992 season
Best batting: 22 Hampshire v Yorkshire, Southampton 1989
22 Hampshire v Glamorgan, Portsmouth 1992
Best bowling: 7-31 Hampshire v Kent, Bournemouth 1987

1992 Season

	M	Inns	NO	Runs	HS	Avge	100s	50s	Ct	St	O	M	Runs	Wkts	Avge	Best	5wI	10wM
Test																		
All First	6	7	1	69	22	11.50	-	-	-	-	162	48	441	11	40.09	4-38	-	-
1-day Int																		
NatWest																		
B & H																		
Sunday	4	2	1	14	14	14.00	-	-	-	-	24	0	122	1	122.00	1-41	-	

Career Performances

	M	Inns	NO	Runs	HS	Avge	100s	50s	Ct	St	Balls	Runs	Wkts	Avge	Best	5wI	10wM
Test																	
All First	69	54	19	333	22	9.51	-	-	9	-	11525	5406	193	28.01	7-31	7	-
1-day Int																	
NatWest	11	3	1	7	3 *	3.50	-	-	-	-	688	378	11	34.36	3-34	-	
B & H	10	2	0	11	7	5.50	-	-	1	-	648	332	10	33.20	2-19	-	
Sunday	41	12	9	40	14	13.33	-	-	3	-	1717	1281	55	23.29	5-17	2	

BALL, M. C. J. Gloucestershire

Name: Martyn Charles John Ball
Role: Right-hand bat, off-spin bowler,
slip fielder
Born: 26 April 1970, Bristol
Height: 5ft 9in **Weight:** 12st
Nickname: Benny
County debut: 1988
1st-Class 50s scored: 2
1st-Class 5 w. in innings: 2
1st-Class catches: 23
Place in batting averages: 233rd av. 13.40
(1991 249th av. 11.77)
Place in bowling averages: 103rd av. 38.28
(1991 53rd av. 30.63)
Strike rate: 69.00 (career 65.05)
Parents: Kenneth and Pamela
Wife and date of marriage: Mona,
28 September 1991
Children: Kristina, 9 May 1990
Education: King Edmund Secondary School, Yate; Bath College of Further Education
Qualifications: 6 O-levels, 2 AO-levels, 3 A-levels
Career outside cricket: Insurance and pensions

Off-season: Getting prepared for 1993 season, running around the fjords of Norway
Overseas tours: Gloucestershire to Namibia 1989, to Kenya 1990
Overseas teams played for: North Melbourne 1988-89;
Old Hararians (Zimbabwe) 1990-91
Cricketers most admired: Ian Botham, Vic Marks, John Emburey, David Graveney
Other sports followed: All sports except show-jumping and synchronised swimming
Injuries: Torn muscles of the lower back, out for four weeks
Relaxations: 'Listening to music, watching TV, spending time with my wife and daughter, and winding up my team-mate Tim Hancock.'
Extras: Played for Young England against New Zealand in 1989
Best batting: 54 Gloucestershire v Somerset, Taunton 1992
Best bowling: 5-101 Gloucestershire v Sussex, Cheltenham 1992

1992 Season

	M	Inns	NO	Runs	HS	Avge	100s	50s	Ct	St	O	M	Runs	Wkts	Avge	Best	5wI	10wM
Test																		
All First	12	21	6	201	54	13.40	-	2	6	-	322	61	1072	28	38.28	5-101	1	-
1-day Int																		
NatWest	2	1	1	16	16 *	-	-	-	1	-	8	2	33	1	33.00	1-24	-	
B & H	5	2	0	14	13	7.00	-	-	3	-	41	3	175	2	87.50	1-39	-	
Sunday	11	7	3	31	19	7.75	-	-	1	-	61.1	2	276	7	39.42	2-33	-	

Career Performances

	M	Inns	NO	Runs	HS	Avge	100s	50s	Ct	St	Balls	Runs	Wkts	Avge	Best	5wI	10wM
Test																	
All First	32	44	9	379	54	10.82	-	2	23	-	4554	2449	70	34.98	5-101	2	-
1-day Int																	
NatWest	3	1	1	16	16 *	-	-	-	1	-	120	75	4	18.75	3-42	-	
B & H	7	2	0	14	13	7.00	-	-	3	-	306	243	2	121.50	1-39	-	
Sunday	24	14	4	50	19	5.00	-	-	6	-	720	585	8	73.12	2-33	-	

13. Who won the NatWest Trophy in 1992?

BALLINGER, R. J. — Middlesex

Name: Richard John Ballinger
Role: Right-hand bat, right-arm
fast-medium bowler
Born: 18 September 1973
Height: 6ft 2in **Weight:** 13st 13lbs
Nickname: Bally
County debut: No first team appearance
Parents: John and Liz
Marital status: Single
Education: Newland House School,
Twickenham; Millfield School, Somerset
Qualifications: 3 A-levels
Career outside cricket: Student
Off-season: Studying at Durham University
Overseas tours: England U19 to
Pakistan 1992, to India 1993
Cricketers most admired: Dennis Lillee,
Richard Hadlee
Other sports followed: Soccer, rugby, golf
Relaxations: Music, cinema, socialising
Opinions on cricket: 'The one bouncer per over rule should be abolished. Players should not be branded as simply batsmen or bowlers which tends to happen at youth level.'

BARNETT, A. A. — Lancashire

Name: Alex Anthony Barnett
Role: Right-hand bat, slow left-arm bowler
Born: 11 September 1970, Malaga, Spain
Height: 5ft 11¾ **Weight:** 11st 7lbs
Nickname: Bung, AB, George
County debut: 1991 (Middlesex), 1992 (Lancashire)
1st-Class 5 w. in innings: 2
1st-Class catches: 7
Place in batting averages: 260th av. 10.00
Place in bowling averages: 129th av. 47.06 (1991 72nd av. 32.90)
Strike rate: 77.61 (career 78.17)
Parents: Michael and Patricia
Marital status: Single
Family links with cricket: Great uncle, Charlie J. Barnett was opening batsman for Gloucestershire and England. Father founded L.C.C.A. (London County Cricket

Association) and is chairman of the London Cricket College
Education: Primrose Hill Primary; William Ellis Secondary
Qualifications: 'Not many Os, no As, no degrees, but have got scuba diving novice certificate.'
Career outside cricket: 'Professional out-of-work cricketer'
Off-season: Playing cricket in Cape Town for 6 months
Overseas tours: England U19 to Australia 1989-90
Cricketers particularly admired: Don Wilson, Clive Radley, Mike Gatting, Simon Hughes
Other sports followed: Golf, boxing
Relaxations: Trying new restaurants with girlfriend Kate, playing golf, watching films

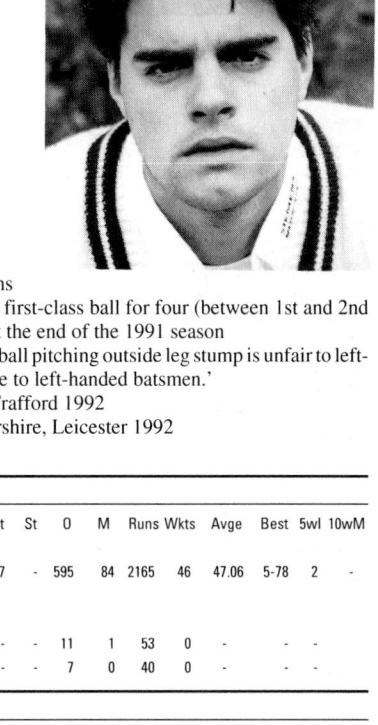

Extras: First-class debut aged 17. Hit first first-class ball for four (between 1st and 2nd slip). Joined Lancashire from Middlesex at the end of the 1991 season
Opinions on cricket: 'LBW law regarding ball pitching outside leg stump is unfair to left-arm spinners and seamers and an advantage to left-handed batsmen.'
Best batting: 17 Lancashire v Kent, Old Trafford 1992
Best bowling: 5-78 Lancashire v Leicestershire, Leicester 1992

1992 Season

	M	Inns	NO	Runs	HS	Avge	100s	50s	Ct	St	O	M	Runs	Wkts	Avge	Best	5wI	10wM
Test																		
All First	22	17	10	70	17	10.00	-	-	7	-	595	84	2165	46	47.06	5-78	2	-
1-day Int																		
NatWest																		
B & H	2	0	0	0	0	-	-	-	-	-	11	1	53	0	-	-	-	
Sunday	2	0	0	0	0	-	-	-	-	-	7	0	40	0	-	-	-	

Career Performances

	M	Inns	NO	Runs	HS	Avge	100s	50s	Ct	St	Balls	Runs	Wkts	Avge	Best	5wI	10wM
Test																		
All First	25	20	12	92	17	11.50	-	-	7	-	4378	2559	56	45.69	5-78	2	-
1-day Int																		
NatWest																		
B & H	2	0	0	0	0	-	-	-	-	-	66	53	0	-	-	-	
Sunday	2	0	0	0	0	-	-	-	-	-	42	40	0	-	-	-	

BARNETT, K. J.   Derbyshire

Name: Kim John Barnett
Role: Right-hand bat, leg-spin bowler, county captain
Born: 17 July 1960, Stoke-on-Trent
Height: 6ft **Weight:** 13st 7lbs
Nickname: Skippo, Barn
County debut: 1979
County cap: 1982
Benefit: 1993
Test debut: 1988
Tests: 4
One-Day Internationals: 1
1000 runs in a season: 10
1st-Class 50s scored: 98
1st-Class 100s scored: 38
1st-Class 200s scored: 2
1st-Class 5 w. in innings: 2
1st-Class catches: 216
One-Day 50s: 49
One-Day 100s: 9
Place in batting averages: 18th av. 52.91 (1991 67th av. 37.81)
Place in bowling averages: (1991 20th av. 24.80)
Strike rate: (career 78.48)
Parents: Derek and Doreen
Marital status: Engaged to Janet
Children: Michael Nicholas, 24 April 1990
Education: Leek High School, Staffs
Qualifications: 7 O-levels
Career outside cricket: Bank clerk
Off-season: Organising benefit
Overseas tours: With England Schools to India 1977-78; Young England to Australia 1978-79; England A to Sri Lanka 1986 (vice-captain); unofficial England XI to South Africa 1989-90
Overseas teams played for: Boland 1980-81, 1982-83
Cricketers particularly admired: Gordon Greenidge, Malcolm Marshall
Other sports followed: Horse racing – most sports
Injuries: Torn knee muscle, out for one month
Relaxations: Eating and sleeping
Extras: Played for Northamptonshire 2nd XI when aged 15, Staffordshire and Warwickshire 2nd XI. Became youngest captain of a first-class county when appointed in 1983. Banned from Test cricket after joining tour to South Africa, suspension remitted in 1992
Opinions on cricket: 'Forget all the trivia about pitches, how the game should be in length

of time, covering etc. Let's get on with playing attractive, entertaining cricket.'
Best batting: 239* Derbyshire v Leicestershire, Leicester 1988
Best bowling: 6-28 Derbyshire v Glamorgan, Chesterfield 1991

1992 Season

	M	Inns	NO	Runs	HS	Avge	100s	50s	Ct	St	O	M	Runs	Wkts	Avge	Best	5wl	10wM
Test																		
All First	19	29	5	1270	160	52.91	4	4	5	-	77.4	11	250	4	62.50	3-24	-	-
1-day Int																		
NatWest																		
B & H	5	5	1	252	84 *	63.00	-	2	4	-	12	0	59	1	59.00	1-26	-	
Sunday	14	14	1	389	55	29.92	-	3	7	-	4	0	23	2	11.50	2-23	-	

Career Performances

	M	Inns	NO	Runs	HS	Avge	100s	50s	Ct	St	Balls	Runs	Wkts	Avge	Best	5wl	10wM
Test	4	7	0	207	80	29.57	-	2	1	-	36	32	0	-	-	-	-
All First	333	533	47	18495	239 *	38.05	38	98	216	-	10752	5324	137	38.86	6-28	2	-
1-day Int	1	1	0	84	84	84.00	-	1	-	-							
NatWest	25	25	2	798	88	34.69	-	6	10	-	178	107	11	9.72	6-24	1	
B & H	64	55	3	1926	115	37.03	3	14	23	-	306	198	6	33.00	1-10	-	
Sunday	198	190	28	5481	131 *	33.83	6	28	69	-	683	608	18	33.77	3-39	-	

BARTLE, S. Yorkshire

Name: Steven Bartle
Role: Left-hand bat, right-arm
medium bowler
Born: 5 September 1971, Shipley
Height: 6ft 3in **Weight:** 14st 4lbs
Nickname: Squirrel, Barts
County debut: No first team appearance
Parents: John and Judith
Marital status: Single
Family links with cricket: Father played
for Windhill in the Bradford League
Education: Woodend Middle School;
Beckfoot GS; Windhill College of Education
Qualifications: 9 GCSEs, coaching
qualifications
Off-season: Coaching and taking part
in coaching courses. Keeping fit, running,
football, weight training

Overseas tours: England U19 to New Zealand 1990
Cricketers most admired: David Gower, Curtly Ambrose, Robin Smith
Other sports followed: Golf, snooker, American football, baseball
Relaxations: Playing various sports, watching TV, astronomy
Opinions on cricket: 'Enjoy Sunday League more than Championship, faster and more enjoyable for players and spectators.'

BARTLETT, R. J.   Somerset

Name: Richard James Bartlett
Role: Right-hand bat, off-spin bowler
Born: 8 October 1966, Ash Priors, Somerset
Height: 5ft 9in **Weight:** 12st 7lbs
Nickname: Pumpy
County debut: 1986
1st-Class 50s scored: 8
1st-Class 100s scored: 2
1st-Class catches: 35
One-Day 50s: 8
Place in batting averages: 139th av. 27.07
(1991 120th av. 29.50)
Parents: Richard and Barbara
Family links with cricket: 'Dad used to
play club cricket but now umpires in
the Somerset League.'
Education: Taunton School
Qualifications: 8 O-levels, 3 A-levels
Cricketers particularly admired:
Jimmy Cook, Steve Waugh, Adrian Jones, Trevor Gard, Viv Richards
Other sports followed: Golf, hockey (county U21 player) and most others
Relaxations: Music, socialising, playing golf
Extras: First Somerset player to score a century on first-class debut since Harold Gimblett.
Represented England Schools and England Young Cricketers. Rapid Cricketline 2nd XI
Player of the Season 1990. Released by Somerset at the end of 1992 season
Best batting: 117* Somerset v Oxford University, The Parks 1986
Best bowling: 1-9 Somerset v Glamorgan, Taunton 1988

---

14.   Who were the losing finalists in the 1992 NatWest Trophy final?

1992 Season

	M	Inns	NO	Runs	HS	Avge	100s	50s	Ct	St	O	M	Runs	Wkts	Avge	Best	5wI	10wM
Test																		
All First	8	13	0	352	72	27.07	-	2	5	-								
1-day Int																		
NatWest																		
B & H	4	4	0	32	22	8.00	-	-	1	-								
Sunday	6	6	0	79	37	13.16	-	-	-	-								

Career Performances

	M	Inns	NO	Runs	HS	Avge	100s	50s	Ct	St	Balls	Runs	Wkts	Avge	Best	5wI	10wM
Test																	
All First	51	82	6	1856	117 *	24.42	2	8	35	-	180	145	4	36.25	1-9	-	-
1-day Int																	
NatWest	3	3	1	147	85	73.50	-	2	1	-							
B & H	13	13	1	140	36	11.66	-	-	4	-							
Sunday	44	44	1	964	55	22.41	-	6	20	-							

BARWICK, S. R. Glamorgan

Name: Stephen Royston Barwick
Role: Right-hand bat, right-arm medium bowler
Born: 6 September 1960, Neath
Height: 6ft 2in **Weight:** 13st
Nickname: Bas
County debut: 1981
County cap: 1987
50 wickets in a season: 2
1st-Class 5 w. in innings: 9
1st-Class 10 w. in match: 1
1st-Class catches: 37
Place in bowling averages: 127th av. 45.19
(1991 34th av. 27.39)
Parents: Margaret and Roy
Wife and date of marriage: Margaret,
12 December 1987
Children: Michael Warren,
25 September 1990
Family links with cricket: 'My Uncle David played for Glamorgan 2nd XI.'
Education: Cwrt Sart Comprehensive; Dwr-y-Felin Comprehensive
Qualifications: 'Commerce, human biology, mathematics, English.'

Career outside cricket: Ex-steel worker
Overseas teams played for: Benoni, South Africa
Cricketers particularly admired: Ian Botham, Richard Hadlee
Other sports followed: Football and rugby
Relaxations: 'Spending time with my little boy, sea fishing and the odd pint or two.'
Best batting: 30 Glamorgan v Hampshire, Bournemouth 1988
Best bowling: 8-42 Glamorgan v Worcestershire, Worcester 1983

1992 Season

	M	Inns	NO	Runs	HS	Avge	100s	50s	Ct	St	O	M	Runs	Wkts	Avge	Best	5wI	10wM
Test																		
All First	18	15	4	31	9 *	2.81	-	-	6	-	602	155	1627	36	45.19	4-67	-	-
1-day Int																		
NatWest	3	1	1	0	0 *	-	-	-	-	-	36	9	110	9	12.22	5-26	1	
B & H	4	2	0	12	7	6.00	-	-	1	-	44	5	126	5	25.20	2-29	-	
Sunday	13	3	0	9	6	3.00	-	-	3	-	88	3	470	11	42.72	3-16	-	

Career Performances

	M	Inns	NO	Runs	HS	Avge	100s	50s	Ct	St	Balls	Runs	Wkts	Avge	Best	5wI	10wM
Test																	
All First	173	162	62	724	30	7.24	-	-	37	-	27850	12931	378	34.20	8-42	9	1
1-day Int																	
NatWest	19	8	4	21	6	5.25	-	-	2	-	1042	542	32	16.93	5-26	1	
B & H	40	23	12	87	18	7.90	-	-	9	-	2199	1368	49	27.91	4-11	-	
Sunday	120	40	23	188	48 *	11.05	-	-	16	-	4484	3534	110	32.12	4-23	-	

BASE, S. J.   Derbyshire

Name: Simon John Base
Role: Right-hand bat, right-arm fast-medium bowler
Born: 2 January 1960, Maidstone
Height: 6ft 3in **Weight:** 14st 7lbs
Nickname: Basey, Bok
County debut: 1986 (Glamorgan), 1988 (Derbys)
County cap: 1990
50 wickets in a season: 1
1st-Class 50s scored: 2
1st-Class 5 w. in innings: 12
1st-Class 10 w. in match: 1
1st-Class catches: 45
Place in batting averages: (1991 252nd av. 10.78)
Place in bowling averages: (1991 102nd av. 37.33)

Strike rate: (career 52.47)
Parents: Christine and Peter (deceased)
Wife and date of marriage: Louise Ann,
23 September 1989
Children: Christopher Peter Elliott,
15 December 1991
Family links with cricket: Grandfather
played, 'brother-in-law pretends he can!'
Education: Fish Hoek Primary School,
Fish Hoek High School, Cape Town,
South Africa
Qualifications: High School, School
Certificate Matriculation. Refrigeration
and air conditioning technician
Career outside cricket:
Hall-Thermotank in South Africa
as a technician, G.S.P.K. Electronics,
Rhodes Fabrics

Off-season: Rehabilitating after back
operation and holidaying in South Africa
Overseas tours: England XI to Holland 1989
Overseas teams played for: Western Province B 1982-83; Boland 1986-89;
Border 1989-92
Cricketers particularly admired: Graham Gooch, Graeme Pollock, Mike Procter,
Richard Hadlee, Malcolm Marshall
Other sports followed: Most other sports
Injuries: Trapped nerve in lower back, off for most of the season, spinal fusion in August
Relaxations: Spending time with family, swimming, windsurfing, braaing
Extras: Suspended from first-class cricket for ten weeks during 1988 season for a
supposed breach of contract, joining Derbyshire when he was still to be contracted to
Glamorgan. The TCCB fined Derbyshire £2000.
Opinions on cricket: 'Very pleased that four-day cricket has now been introduced and that
coloured clothing has been brought into Sunday League cricket – a long time overdue.'
Best batting: 58 Derbyshire v Yorkshire, Chesterfield 1990
Best bowling: 7-60 Derbyshire v Yorkshire, Chesterfield 1989

1992 Season

	M	Inns	NO	Runs	HS	Avge	100s	50s	Ct	St	O	M	Runs	Wkts	Avge	Best	5wI	10wM
Test																		
All First	2	2	1	3	3	3.00	-	-	2	-	35	8	100	7	14.28	5-35	1	-
1-day Int																		
NatWest																			
B & H																			
Sunday	4	2	1	19	13	19.00	-	-	3	-	32	0	176	3	58.66	1-31	-	

Career Performances

	M	Inns	NO	Runs	HS	Avge	100s	50s	Ct	St	Balls	Runs	Wkts	Avge	Best	5wl	10wM
Test																	
All First	103	130	33	1135	58	11.70	-	2	45	-	16948	8915	323	27.60	7-60	12	1
1-day Int																	
NatWest	2	2	0	6	4	3.00	-	-	1	-	90	61	2	30.50	2-49	-	
B & H	15	9	3	53	15*	8.83	-	-	-	-	870	629	15	41.93	3-33	-	
Sunday	62	25	4	93	19	4.42	-	-	19	-	2553	1927	76	25.35	4-14	-	

BASTIEN, S.   Glamorgan

Name: Steven Bastien
Role: Right-hand bat, right-arm
fast-medium bowler, outfielder
Born: 13 March 1963, Stepney
Height: 6ft 1in **Weight:** 13st
Nickname: Bassie
County debut: 1988
1st-Class 5 w. in innings: 5
1st-Class catches: 5
Place in bowling averages: 140th av. 50.21
(1991 128th av. 46.50)
Strike rate: 96.47 (career 73.52)
Parents: Anthony and Francisca
Marital status: Single
Children: Linden Kieron,
20 December 1990
Family links with cricket: Brother Roger
plays in the Essex League

Education: St Mary's Academy School,
Dominica; St Bonaventure School, London
Qualifications: 3 CSEs; NCA coaching certificate; carpentry and CCPR course
Cricketers particularly admired: Viv Richards, David Gower, Robin Smith, Michael
Holding, Malcolm Marshall
Other sports followed: Football, boxing, basketball, athletics
Injuries: Burst webbing on right hand
Relaxations: Listening to reggae, soul and calypso music
Extras: Took five wickets on first-class debut in 1988. Member of Haringey Cricket
College
Best batting: 36* Glamorgan v Warwickshire, Edgbaston 1988
Best bowling: 6-75 Glamorgan v Worcestershire, Worcester 1990

1992 Season

	M	Inns	NO	Runs	HS	Avge	100s	50s	Ct	St	O	M	Runs	Wkts	Avge	Best	5wI	10wM
Test																		
All First	10	10	3	21	9 *	3.00	-	-	2	-	305.3	73	954	19	50.21	5-95	1	-
1-day Int																		
NatWest	2	1	1	7	7 *	-	-	-	-	-	19	1	98	1	98.00	1-42	-	
B & H	2	1	1	3	3 *	-	-	-	-	-	22	4	73	1	73.00	1-29	-	
Sunday	4	1	1	0	0 *	-	-	-	-	-	26	0	100	3	33.33	1-24	-	

Career Performances

	M	Inns	NO	Runs	HS	Avge	100s	50s	Ct	St	Balls	Runs	Wkts	Avge	Best	5wI	10wM
Test																	
All First	44	33	13	152	36 *	7.60	-	-	5	-	7058	3715	96	38.69	6-75	5	-
1-day Int																	
NatWest	2	1	1	7	7 *	-	-	-	-	-	114	98	1	98.00	1-42	-	
B & H	4	2	1	10	7	10.00	-	-	-	-	198	137	1	137.00	1-29	-	
Sunday	11	2	1	1	1	1.00	-	-	1	-	354	265	6	44.16	2-42	-	

BATES, R. T. Nottinghamshire

Name: Richard Terry Bates
Role: Right-hand bat, off-spin bowler,
slip fielder
Born: 17 June 1972, Stamford, Lincs
Height: 6ft 1in **Weight:** 13st 5lbs
Nickname: Blast, Batesy
County debut: No first team appearance
Parents: Terry and Sue
Marital status: Single
Family links with cricket: Father is NCA
Development and Administration Manager
Education: Bourne G.S.;
Stamford College for Further Education
Qualifications: 8 GCSEs, BTEC in
Business and Finance,
NCA Coaching Award
Career outside cricket: Employed by
Notts CCC to coach during the winter
Off-season: Coaching, keeping fit, madisons
Overseas tours: Lincolnshire Colts (U19) to Australia 1990
Overseas teams played for: Redwood, New Zealand 1991-92
Cricketers particularly admired: Ian Botham, Derek Randall, Viv Richards

Other sports followed: Football, rugby
Injuries: Shin splints, missed the whole season after operations on both legs
Relaxations: Socialising, films, going out for a Chinese meal
Opinions on cricket: 'Improvement in the minimum wage for young cricketers! Better prospects for winter employment for all professional cricketers.'

BATTY, J. D. Yorkshire

Name: Jeremy David Batty
Role: Right-hand bat, off-spin bowler, cover fielder
Born: 15 May 1971, Bradford
Height: 6ft 1in **Weight:** 11st 10lbs
Nickname: Bullfrog, Sniper, Nora
County debut: 1989
1st-Class 50s scored: 1
1st-Class 5 w. in innings: 2
1st-Class catches: 16
Place in batting averages: 230th av. 14.09 (1991 203rd av. 18.36)
Place in bowling averages: 117th av. 42.66 (1991 88th av. 35.09)
Strike rate: 77.45 (career 71.51)
Parents: David and Rosemary
Marital status: Single
Family links with cricket: Father took over 1000 wickets in the Bradford League.
Education: Parkside Middle School; Bingley Grammar School; Horsforth College
Qualifications: 5 O-levels; BTEC: Diploma in Leisure Studies; coaching certificate
Overseas tours: England Young Cricketers to Australia 1989-90
Overseas teams played for: Sunrise 1989-90, Country Districts 1990-91 (both Zimbabwe)
Cricketers particularly admired: Phil Carrick, John Emburey, Ian Botham, Mike Gatting
Other sports followed: Rugby league, rugby union, football
Relaxations: Drink, food, music and movies
Extras: Took five wickets on first-class debut v Lancashire in 1989
Best batting: 51 Yorkshire v Sri Lanka, Headingley 1991
Best bowling: 6-48 Yorkshire v Nottinghamshire, Worksop 1991

---

15. Who was vice-captain of Pakistan on the England tour of 1992?

1992 Season

	M	Inns	NO	Runs	HS	Avge	100s	50s	Ct	St	O	M	Runs	Wkts	Avge	Best	5wI	10wM
Test																		
All First	18	15	4	155	49	14.09	-	-	4	-	426	85	1408	33	42.66	4-34	-	-
1-day Int																		
NatWest																		
B & H	1	1	1	2	2 *	-	-	-	1	-	7	0	34	0	-		-	-
Sunday	10	4	3	1	1 *	1.00	-	-	7	-	70	4	372	13	28.61	3-21	-	

Career Performances

	M	Inns	NO	Runs	HS	Avge	100s	50s	Ct	St	Balls	Runs	Wkts	Avge	Best	5wI	10wM
Test																	
All First	45	41	13	403	51	14.39	-	1	16	-	7080	3864	99	39.03	6-48	2	-
1-day Int																	
NatWest	1	1	0	4	4	4.00	-	-	-	-	36	17	1	17.00	1-17	-	
B & H	4	1	1	2	2 *	-	-	-	1	-	174	109	1	109.00	1-34	-	
Sunday	21	8	5	28	13 *	9.33	-	-	13	-	882	748	25	29.92	4-33	-	

BELL, M. A. V.   Warwickshire

Name: Michael Anthony Vincent Bell
Role: Right-hand bat, left-arm fast-medium
bowler
Born: 19 December 1967, Birmingham
Height: 6ft 2in **Weight:** 12st 8lbs
Nickname: Belly, Nelly, Breezer
County debut: 1992
Parents: Vincent and Adelheid
Marital status: Single
Family links with cricket: Father played
cricket mainly for Mitchell & Butler in
the Birmingham League. An uncle played
a few games for Jamaica
Education: Bishop Milner Comprehensive,
Dudley Technical College
Qualifications: 5 O-levels; City and Guilds
in Recreation and Leisure Parts 1 & 2
Career outside cricket: Casino croupier,
worked with the PE staff at Earls High School
and also worked in the corporate hospitality
department at EMP plc for two years
Off-season: Playing cricket in Perth, Australia

Overseas tours: BWIA to Barbados, Trinidad and Tobago 1989; John Morris's Madcap CC to Australia 1992
Overseas teams played for: Swanbourne, Perth 1986-87; Norwood, Melbourne 1989-90; Phoenix, Perth 1992-93
Cricketers particularly admired: Dennis Lillee, Viv Richards, Michael Holding, Imran Khan, Wasim Akram
Other sports followed: Any sport played by the best in that particular field
Relaxations: Listening to the Rebel MC, Bell Biv Devoe and holidaying in Montego Bay, Jamaica
Opinions on cricket: 'The rules and playing conditions should not be revised whenever bowlers discover new, consistently effective ways of dismissing opponents, so that the balance of power swings ever more in favour of the batsmen. Pitches with pace and bounce should be the rule not the exception. This would produce better cricketers, better cricket and a better spectacle for the paying public. Flat lifeless pitches are good for no one.'
Best batting: 5 Warwickshire v Nottinghamshire, Edgbaston 1992
Best bowling: 3-78 Warwickshire v Nottinghamshire, Edgbaston 1992

1992 Season

	M	Inns	NO	Runs	HS	Avge	100s	50s	Ct	St	O	M	Runs	Wkts	Avge	Best	5wI	10wM
Test																		
All First	3	5	2	10	5	3.33	-	-	-	-	79.2	17	247	8	30.87	3-78	-	-
1-day Int																		
NatWest																		
B & H																		
Sunday																		

Career Performances

	M	Inns	NO	Runs	HS	Avge	100s	50s	Ct	St	Balls	Runs	Wkts	Avge	Best	5wI	10wM
Test																	
All First	3	5	2	10	5	3.33	-	-	-	-	476	247	8	30.87	3-78	-	-
1-day Int																	
NatWest																	
B & H																	
Sunday																	

16. Who was vice-captain of England in the 1992 series v Pakistan?

17. For how many years was Micky Stewart manager of England?

BENJAMIN, J. E.   Surrey

Name: Joseph Emmanuel Benjamin
Role: Right-hand bat, right-arm
fast-medium bowler
Born: 2 February 1961, Christchurch,
St Kitts, West Indies
Height: 6ft 2in **Weight:** 12st
Nickname: Boggy, Moon Man
County debut: 1988 (Warwickshire),
1992 (Surrey)
1st-Class 5 w. in innings: 6
1st-Class catches: 12
Place in batting averages: 247th av. 11.60
Place in bowling averages: 107th av. 39.55
Strike rate: 77.64 (career 68.33)
Parents: Henry and Judith
Marital status: Single
Education: Cayon High School, St Kitts;
Mount Pleasant, Highgate, Birmingham
Qualifications: 4 O-levels
Career outside cricket: Landscape gardener, store manager
Off-season: Wintering and playing in Australia
Cricketers particularly admired: Desmond Haynes, Imran Khan, Salim Malik,
Malcolm Marshall
Other sports followed: Rugby, squash, soccer
Injuries: Groin strain, off for two weeks
Relaxations: Music, swimming, going to the cinema, reading
Extras: Released by Warwickshire at the end of the 1991 season and signed up by Surrey
for 1992. Enjoyed his best batting and bowling performances on the same day at Guildford
Opinions on cricket: 'Having four-day cricket will improve a lot of individual talent, and
the all-round team game. There will be more opportunity to win games with ample time.'
Best batting: 42 Surrey v Kent, Guildford 1992
Best bowling: 6-30 Surrey v Durham, Durham University 1992

1992 Season

	M	Inns	NO	Runs	HS	Avge	100s	50s	Ct	St	O	M	Runs	Wkts	Avge	Best	5wI	10wM
Test																		
All First	18	18	8	116	42	11.60	-	-	5	-	582.2	94	1780	45	39.55	6-30	2	-
1-day Int																		
NatWest	1	0	0	0	0	-	-	-	1	-	12	2	39	0	-		-	-
B & H	7	1	1	0	0 *	-	-	-	4	-	68	6	268	8	33.50	2-46	-	
Sunday	14	3	1	24	11	12.00	-	-	2	-	96.4	3	481	13	37.00	4-44	-	

Career Performances

	M	Inns	NO	Runs	HS	Avge	100s	50s	Ct	St	Balls	Runs	Wkts	Avge	Best	5wI	10wM
Test																	
All First	43	40	16	341	42	14.20	-	-	12	-	7449	3800	109	34.86	6-30	6	-
1-day Int																	
NatWest	5	4	2	27	19	13.50	-	-	2	-	294	190	3	63.33	2-37	-	
B & H	9	2	1	20	20	20.00	-	-	5	-	540	340	11	30.90	2-32	-	
Sunday	36	14	7	112	24	16.00	-	-	9	-	1498	1134	33	34.36	4-44	-	

BENJAMIN, K. C. G. Worcestershire

Name: Kenneth Charlie Griffith Benjamin
Role: Right-hand bat, right-arm
fast-medium bowler
Born: 8 April 1967
County debut: No first team appearance
Test debut: 1991-92
Tests: 1
1st-Class 5 w. in innings: 2
1st-Class catches: 2
Strike rate: (career 53.41)
Off-season: Touring with West Indies
Overseas tours: West Indies to
Australia and South Africa 1992-93
Overseas teams played for:
Leeward Islands 1988-93
Extras: Made Test debut for West Indies
v South Africa at Bridgetown 1991-92.
Played for World XI v Pakistan at
Scarborough 1992. Signed by Worcestershire
for 1993 season to replace Tom Moody
Best batting: 52* Leeward Isles v Trinidad & Tobago, Basseterre 1991-92
Best bowling: 7-51 Leeward Isles v Jamaica, Basseterre 1990-91

---

18.   What was remarkable about England's one-day victory over Pakistan
at Trent Bridge last season?

1992 Season

	M	Inns	NO	Runs	HS	Avge	100s	50s	Ct	St	O	M	Runs	Wkts	Avge	Best	5wI	10wM
Test																		
All First	1	1	1	0	0*	-	-	-	-	-	12	0	55	3	18.33	3-55	-	-
1-day Int																		
NatWest																		
B & H																		
Sunday																		

Career Performances

	M	Inns	NO	Runs	HS	Avge	100s	50s	Ct	St	Balls	Runs	Wkts	Avge	Best	5wI	10wM
Test	1	2	0	8	7	4.00	-	-	-	-	204	108	2	54.00	2-87	-	-
All First	25	33	10	321	52*	13.95	-	1	2	-	4326	1943	81	23.98	7-51	2	-
1-day Int																	
NatWest																	
B & H																	
Sunday																	

BENJAMIN, W. K. M.   Leicestershire

Name: Winston Keithroy Matthew Benjamin
Role: Right-hand bat,
right-arm fast bowler
Born: 31 December 1964,
St. John's, Antigua
Height: 6ft 3in
County debut: 1986
County Cap: 1989
Test debut: 1987-88
Tests: 8
One-Day Internationals: 60
1st-Class 50s scored: 14
1st-Class 100s scored: 1
1st-Class catches: 60
1st-Class 5 w. in innings: 17
1st-Class 10 w. in match: 2
One-Day 5 w. in innings: 3
50 wickets in a season: 1
Place in batting averages: 182nd av. 20.59
Place in bowling averages: 59th av. 31.87
Strike rate: 62.42 (career 54.56)
Education: All Saints School, Antigua

Off-season: Playing in South Africa
Overseas teams played for: Leeward Islands 1985-93
Overseas tours: West Indies to Australia 1986-87, 1988-89, to Pakistan 1986-87, to India 1987-88, to England 1988
Best batting: 101* Leicestershire v Derbyshire, Leicester 1992
Best bowling: 7-54 Leicestershire v Australia, Leicester 1992

1992 Season

	M	Inns	NO	Runs	HS	Avge	100s	50s	Ct	St	O	M	Runs	Wkts	Avge	Best	5wI	10wM
Test																		
All First	20	25	3	453	72	20.59	-	4	15	-	489	102	1498	47	31.87	4-34	-	-
1-day Int																		
NatWest	5	5	1	28	24 *	7.00	-	-	1	-	51.3	5	174	9	19.33	5-32	1	
B & H	2	2	0	84	45	42.00	-	-	-	-	21.3	5	85	2	42.50	1-37	-	
Sunday	9	8	0	30	8	3.75	-	-	2	-	67.2	6	269	10	26.90	2-20	-	

Career Performances

	M	Inns	NO	Runs	HS	Avge	100s	50s	Ct	St	Balls	Runs	Wkts	Avge	Best	5wI	10wM
Test	8	10	1	125	41 *	13.88	-	-	3	-	1248	564	26	21.69	4-52	-	-
All First	124	148	34	2630	101 *	23.07	1	14	60	-	18715	8946	343	26.08	7-54	17	2
1-day Int	60	36	7	190	31	6.55	-	-	11	-	3237	2235	69	32.39	3-21	-	
NatWest	12	9	2	59	24 *	8.42	-	-	1	-	795	417	19	21.94	5-32	1	
B & H	13	9	2	146	45	20.85	-	-	1	-	775	442	26	17.00	5-17	2	
Sunday	45	34	7	262	41 *	9.70	-	-	6	-	1924	1335	46	29.02	4-19	-	

BENSON, J. D. R.   Leicestershire

Name: Justin David Ramsay Benson
Role: Right-hand bat, right-arm medium bowler
Born: 1 March 1967, Dublin
Height: 6ft 3in **Weight:** 14st 7lbs
Nickname: Rambo, Archie
County debut: 1988
1st-Class 50s scored: 5
1st-Class 100s scored: 3
1st-Class catches: 52
One-Day 50s: 3
Place in batting averages: 164th av. 23.07 (1991 79th av. 35.72)
Parents: Malcolm and Liz
Marital status: Single
Family links with cricket: Father is a qualified first-class umpire and was a 'mean left-arm spinner'

Education: St Faith's; The Leys School, Cambridge; Cambridge College of Further Education
Qualifications: 10 O-levels
Career outside cricket: 'Yuppie and financial adviser (when required)'
Off-season: Keeping fit and working out
Overseas teams played for: Durbanville and Municiples, South Africa; Cotton Gound, West Indies
Cricketers particularly admired: Darren Maddy, Neil Smith
Other sports followed: Rugby and most TV sports
Injuries: 'Lack of form'
Relaxations: 'Being a socialite or playing Game Boy!'
Extras: Scored 85 and won the Man of the Match award for Cambridgeshire in his first NatWest Trophy match in 1986
Opinions on cricket: 'Should be paid all year round or clubs should find winter employment.'
Best batting: 133* Leicestershire v Hampshire, Bournemouth 1991
Best bowling: 2-24 Leicestershire v Yorkshire, Sheffield 1992

1992 Season

	M	Inns	NO	Runs	HS	Avge	100s	50s	Ct	St	O	M	Runs	Wkts	Avge	Best	5wI	10wM
Test																		
All First	18	28	1	623	122	23.07	1	1	30	-	43.4	6	142	5	28.40	2-24	-	-
1-day Int																		
NatWest	4	4	1	78	42	26.00	-	-	4	-	23.5	2	111	4	27.75	2-18	-	
B & H	5	4	1	48	23 *	16.00	-	-	2	-	21	0	92	4	23.00	2-27	-	
Sunday	15	15	0	301	51	20.06	-	1	6	-	47.3	0	304	5	60.80	2-35	-	

Career Performances

	M	Inns	NO	Runs	HS	Avge	100s	50s	Ct	St	Balls	Runs	Wkts	Avge	Best	5wI	10wM
Test																	
All First	50	76	8	1854	133 *	27.26	3	5	52	-	769	488	8	61.00	2-24	-	-
1-day Int																	
NatWest	6	6	1	174	85	34.80	-	1	4	-	156	124	4	31.00	2-18	-	
B & H	11	10	3	165	43	23.57	-	-	3	-	168	131	5	26.20	2-27	-	
Sunday	55	49	9	876	67	21.90	-	2	19	-	831	816	25	32.64	3-37	-	

BENSON, M. R.   Kent

Name: Mark Richard Benson
Role: Left-hand bat, off-spin bowler, county captain
Born: 6 July 1958, Shoreham, Sussex
Height: 5ft 10in **Weight:** 12st 7lbs
Nickname: Benny
County debut: 1980
County cap: 1981
Benefit: 1991 (£174,619)
Test debut: 1986
Tests: 1
One-Day Internationals: 1
1000 runs in a season: 11
1st-Class 50s scored: 88
1st-Class 100s scored: 42
1st-Class 200s scored: 1
1st-Class catches: 120
One-Day 50s: 46
One-Day 100s: 4
Place in batting averages: 44th av. 44.90 (1991 29th av. 47.46)
Parents: Frank and Judy
Wife and date of marriage: Sarah, 20 September 1986
Children: Laurence Mark Edward, 16 October 1987; Edward 23 June 1990
Family links with cricket: Father played for Ghana, sister Tina is Marketing Manager for Kent CCC
Education: Sutton Valence School
Qualifications: O and A-levels and 1 S-level. Qualified tennis coach
Career outside cricket: Marketing assistant with Shell UK Oil; financial adviser
Cricketers particularly admired: Malcolm Marshall, Jimmy Cook, Chris Tavare
Other sports followed: Baseball, golf, horse racing, athletics
Relaxations: Horse racing, cards, 'playing with my children'
Extras: Scored 1000 runs in first full season. Record for most runs in career and season at Sutton Valence School. Appointed Kent captain at end of 1990 season
Best batting: 257 Kent v Hampshire, Southampton 1991
Best bowling: 2-55 Kent v Surrey, Dartford 1986

---

19. Who replaced Graham Gooch in the fourth Texaco Trophy match at Lord's last season, when he withdrew through injury?

1992 Season

	M	Inns	NO	Runs	HS	Avge	100s	50s	Ct	St	O	M	Runs	Wkts	Avge	Best	5wl	10wM
Test																		
All First	21	35	2	1482	139	44.90	4	6	15	-	3	0	25	1	25.00	1-18	-	-
1-day Int																		
NatWest	3	3	0	126	58	42.00	-	2	2	-								
B & H	7	7	0	254	66	36.28	-	3	2	-								
Sunday	15	14	0	371	68	26.50	-	3	4	-								

Career Performances

	M	Inns	NO	Runs	HS	Avge	100s	50s	Ct	St	Balls	Runs	Wkts	Avge	Best	5wl	10wM
Test	1	2	0	51	30	25.50	-	-	-	-							
All First	248	419	31	16035	257	41.32	42	88	120	-	467	493	5	98.60	2-55	-	-
1-day Int	1	1	0	24	24	24.00	-	-	-	-							
NatWest	29	29	1	1000	113 *	35.71	1	7	9	-							
B & H	57	56	6	1989	118	39.78	3	14	7	-							
Sunday	134	127	1	3516	97	27.90	-	25	38	-							

BERRY, P. J.   Durham

Name: Philip John Berry
Role: Right-hand bat, off-spin bowler
Born: 28 December 1966, Saltburn
Height: 6ft **Weight:** 12st
Nickname: Chuck
County debut: 1986 (Yorkshire),
1992 (Durham)
1st-Class 50s scored: 1
1st-Class 5 w. in innings: 1
1st-Class 10 w. in innings: 1
1st-Class catches: 6
Place in batting averages: 211th av. 17.08
Place in bowling averages: 102nd av. 38.17
Strike rate: 63.00 (career 78.58)
Parents: John and Beryl
Wife: Judith
Family links with cricket: Brother used
to play league cricket for Saltburn
Education: Saltscar Comprehensive School;
Longlands College of FE
Qualifications: 1 O-level, City & Guilds passes in Public and Recreational Services
Off-season: Looking for a job. Working as clerk for Social Security

Overseas tours: NCA to Bermuda for U19 (International Youth Tournament) 1985
Cricketers particularly admired: John Emburey, David Gower
Other sports followed: Horse racing, rugby union, Middlesbrough FC, anything except motor racing
Injuries: Patella tendonitis, off for two weeks
Relaxations: Reading, crosswords, horse racing, eating and drinking
Extras: Enjoyed best batting and bowling performances in the same game against Middlesex at Lord's
Opinions on cricket: 'Not enough done for players once the season ends. No effort to find winter employment'
Best batting: 76 Durham v Middlesex, Lord's 1992
Best bowling: 7-113 Durham v Middlesex, Lord's 1992

1992 Season

	M	Inns	NO	Runs	HS	Avge	100s	50s	Ct	St	O	M	Runs	Wkts	Avge	Best	5wI	10wM
Test																		
All First	9	15	3	205	76	17.08	-	1	-	-	178.3	27	649	17	38.17	7-113	1	1
1-day Int																		
NatWest	1	1	0	9	9	9.00	-	-	-	-	11	0	48	0	-		-	-
B & H	1	0	0	0	0	-	-	-	-	-	11	0	49	0	-		-	-
Sunday	1	1	0	6	6	6.00	-	-	-	-	8	0	35	1	35.00	1-35	-	

Career Performances

	M	Inns	NO	Runs	HS	Avge	100s	50s	Ct	St	Balls	Runs	Wkts	Avge	Best	5wI	10wM
Test																	
All First	16	22	9	281	76	21.61	-	1	6	-	1886	1050	24	43.75	7-113	1	1
1-day Int																	
NatWest	1	1	0	9	9	9.00	-	-	-	-	66	48	0	-		-	-
B & H	2	0	0	0	0	-	-	-	-	-	96	77	0	-		-	-
Sunday	1	1	0	6	6	6.00	-	-	-	-	48	35	1	35.00	1-35	-	

20. Who was captain of Leicestershire in 1992?

21. Who was captain of Sussex in 1992?

BICKNELL, D. J. Surrey

Name: Darren John Bicknell
Role: Left-hand opening bat,
left-arm bowler, gully fielder
Born: 24 June 1967, Guildford
Height: 6ft 4^1/2in **Weight:** 13st 7lbs
Nickname: Denzil
County debut: 1987
County cap: 1990
1000 runs in a season: 4
1st-Class 50s scored: 36
1st-Class 100s scored: 17
1st-Class catches: 45
One-Day 50s: 12
One-Day 100s: 5
Place in batting averages: 91st av. 36.21
(1991 30th av. 47.20)
Parents: Vic and Valerie
Wife and date of marriage: Rebecca,
26 September 1992

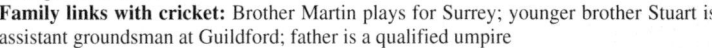

Family links with cricket: Brother Martin plays for Surrey; younger brother Stuart is assistant groundsman at Guildford; father is a qualified umpire
Education: Robert Haining County Secondary; Guildford County College of Technology
Qualifications: 2 O-levels, 7 CSEs, City and Guilds qualification in Recreation Administration and Sports Studies
Off-season: 'Hopefully working, playing football and practising my game'
Overseas tours: Surrey to Sharjah 1988 & 1989, to Dubai 1990; England A to Zimbabwe and Kenya 1989-90, to Pakistan 1990-91, to Bermuda and West Indies 1991-92
Overseas teams played for: Coburg, Melbourne 1987
Cricketers particularly admired: Waqar Younis, Robin Smith and Graham Gooch
Other sports followed: Football. 'Follow the fortunes of West Ham, used to follow Aldershot.'
Injuries: Achilles tendon injury – affected all season but only missed two Sunday League matches
Relaxations: Eating out and participating in many sports including golf and snooker
Extras: Shares county record third wicket stand of 413 with David Ward v Kent at Canterbury in 1990 – both made career bests
Opinions on cricket: 'Counties should endeavour to look after players better, possibly with 12-month contracts. The present economic climate means that it is very difficult for players to get work in the winter.'
Best batting: 186 Surrey v Kent, Canterbury 1990
Best bowling: 2-62 Surrey v Northamptonshire, Northampton 1991

1992 Season

	M	Inns	NO	Runs	HS	Avge	100s	50s	Ct	St	O	M	Runs	Wkts	Avge	Best	5wl	10wM
Test																		
All First	24	42	5	1340	120 *	36.21	2	7	6	-	9.2	0	90	0	-	-	-	-
1-day Int																		
NatWest	1	1	0	21	21	21.00	-	-	-	-								
B & H	7	7	1	410	86	68.33	-	5	3	-								
Sunday	15	15	2	651	125	50.07	3	1	4	-								

Career Performances

	M	Inns	NO	Runs	HS	Avge	100s	50s	Ct	St	Balls	Runs	Wkts	Avge	Best	5wl	10wM
Test																	
All First	122	213	22	7364	186	38.55	17	36	45	-	255	265	3	88.33	2-62	-	-
1-day Int																	
NatWest	9	9	1	305	135 *	38.12	1	-	-	-							
B & H	19	19	1	782	119	43.44	1	7	6	-							
Sunday	38	37	3	1221	125	35.91	3	5	9	-							

BICKNELL, M. P.   Surrey

Name: Martin Paul Bicknell
Role: Right-hand bat, right-arm fast-medium bowler
Born: 14 January 1969, Guildford
Height: 6ft 4in **Weight:** 14st 7lbs
Nickname: Bickers, Spandau
County debut: 1986
County cap: 1989
50 wickets in a season: 4
1st-Class 50s scored: 4
1st-Class 5 w. in innings: 13
1st-Class catches: 38
Place in batting averages: 162nd av. 24.83 (1991 207th av. 17.33)
Place in bowling averages: 22nd av. 25.67 (1991 14th av. 27.26)
Strike rate: 53.14 (career 57.44)
Parents: Vic and Valerie
Marital status: Single
Family links with cricket: All play to varying standards, brother Darren plays for Surrey
Education: Robert Haining County Secondary
Qualifications: 2 O-levels, 5 CSEs

Off-season: Playing cricket in Perth

Overseas tours: England YC to Sri Lanka 1986-87 and Australia 1987-88; England A to Zimbabwe and Kenya 1989-90, to Bermuda and West Indies 1991-92; England to Australia 1990-91

Cricketers particularly admired: Richard Hadlee, Dennis Lillee, Ian Botham, Alistair Brown

Other sports followed: 'Leeds United, and generally most sports.'

Injuries: Hamstring problems, missed a couple of games

Relaxations: 'Spending time with my fiancee Rebecca. Playing golf, following Leeds United.'

Extras: Youngest player to play for Surrey since David Smith. His figures of 9 for 45 were the best for the county for thirty years. One of four players on stand-by as reserves for England's World Cup squad 1992

Opinions on cricket: 'Four-day cricket is a good idea.'

Best batting: 88 Surrey v Hampshire, Southampton 1992

Best bowling: 9-45 Surrey v Cambridge University, Fenner's 1988

1992 Season

	M	Inns	NO	Runs	HS	Avge	100s	50s	Ct	St	O	M	Runs	Wkts	Avge	Best	5wI	10wM
Test																		
All First	19	26	8	447	88	24.83	-	2	7	-	628.5	116	1823	71	25.67	6-107	4	-
1-day Int																		
NatWest																		
B & H	7	4	0	31	19	7.75	-	-	1	-	68.5	6	263	8	32.87	3-43	-	
Sunday	15	7	5	60	18 *	30.00	-	-	2	-	118	8	544	26	20.92	4-48	-	

Career Performances

	M	Inns	NO	Runs	HS	Avge	100s	50s	Ct	St	Balls	Runs	Wkts	Avge	Best	5wI	10wM
Test																	
All First	119	133	40	1563	88	16.80	-	4	38	-	22000	10298	383	26.88	9-45	13	-
1-day Int	7	6	2	96	31 *	24.00	-	-	2	-	413	347	13	26.69	3-55	-	
NatWest	18	9	5	81	66 *	20.25	-	1	8	-	1131	619	22	28.13	4-49	-	
B & H	24	15	2	112	27 *	8.61	-	-	8	-	1432	931	36	25.86	3-28	-	
Sunday	77	28	16	183	20 *	15.25	-	-	21	-	3254	2289	86	26.61	4-14	-	

22. Who was captain of Gloucestershire in 1992?

BISHOP, I. R.   Derbyshire

Name: Ian Raphael Bishop
Role: Right-hand bat, right-arm fast bowler
Born: 24 October 1967, Port of Spain,
Trinidad,
West Indies
Height: 6ft 5$^{1}/_{2}$in **Weight:** 15st 10lbs
Nickname: Bish
County debut: 1989
County cap: 1990
Test debut: 1988-89
Tests: 11
One-Day Internationals: 35
50 wickets in a season: 2
1st-Class 100s scored: 1
1st-Class 50s scored: 1
1st-Class 5 w. in innings: 18
1st-Class 10 w. in match: 1
1st-Class catches: 19
Place in batting averages: 184th av. 20.42
Place in bowling averages: 3rd av. 17.46
Strike rate: 45.28 (career 44.52)
Parents: Randolph and Recalda
Marital status: Single

Family links with cricket: Uncle played for Young West Indies against England U20 in the Caribbean 1984-85
Education: Belmont Primary and Belmont Secondary Schools
Qualifications: 2 O-levels
Overseas tours: West Indies to England 1988, to Australia 1988-89, to India for Nehru Cup 1989-90, to Pakistan 1990-91, to Pakistan and Australia 1991-92, to Australia and South Africa 1992-93
Overseas teams played for: Trinidad & Tobago
Cricketers particularly admired: Malcolm Marshall, Michael Holding, Gordon Greenidge
Other sports followed: Athletics, soccer, basketball
Relaxations: Watching television, reading sports magazines and theological books
Extras: Played for Northumberland club Tynedale in 1987. Top of 1990 bowling averages. 'I am a born-again Christian.' Missed 1991 tour to England and 1991-92 World Cup through injury
Best batting: 103* Derbyshire v Yorkshire, Scarborough 1990
Best bowling: 7-34 Derbyshire v Hampshire, Portsmouth 1992

1992 Season

	M	Inns	NO	Runs	HS	Avge	100s	50s	Ct	St	O	M	Runs	Wkts	Avge	Best	5wI	10wM
Test																		
All First	20	21	2	388	90	20.42	-	1	6	-	483	116	1118	64	17.46	7-34	4	-
1-day Int																		
NatWest	2	2	0	6	6	3.00	-	-	-	-	22	3	61	0	-			
B & H	5	4	0	68	42	17.00	-	-	-	-	53	7	147	8	18.37	4-30	-	
Sunday	14	8	3	103	36 *	20.60	-	-	-	-	102.2	5	429	19	22.57	3-18	-	

Career Performances

	M	Inns	NO	Runs	HS	Avge	100s	50s	Ct	St	Balls	Runs	Wkts	Avge	Best	5wI	10wM
Test	11	17	7	156	30 *	15.60	-	-	1	-	2425	1091	53	20.58	6-87	3	-
All First	88	115	32	1342	103 *	16.16	1	1	19	-	14472	6659	325	20.48	7-34	18	1
1-day Int	35	16	8	148	33 *	18.50	-	-	8	-	1780	1199	59	20.32	5-27	1	
NatWest	2	2	0	6	6	3.00	-	-	-	-	132	61	0	-			
B & H	5	4	0	68	42	17.00	-	-	-	-	318	147	8	18.37	4-30	-	
Sunday	15	9	4	119	36 *	23.80	-	-	-	-	662	480	20	24.00	3-18	-	

BISHOP, J.   Glamorgan

Name: Jamie Bishop
Role: Left-hand bat, occasional wicket-keeper
Born: 14 January 1971, Swansea
Height: 5ft 11in **Weight:** 14st
Nickname: Bish, Bilge, Tuck Box
County debut: 1992
1st-Class 50s scored: 1
1st-Class catches: 4
Parents: Meirion and Patricia
Marital status: Single
Family links with cricket: 'Father played
local club cricket, mother makes the teas.'
Education: Pontardulais Comprehensive;
Gorseinon Tertiary College;
Cardiff Institute of Higher Education
Qualifications: BTEC National Diploma
in Leisure and Sports Studies
Off-season: Studying – final year
of degree course for BA in Human
Movement Studies (Science), playing rugby league
Overseas tours: Welsh Schools Cricket Association to Australia 1986, to Barbados 1988
(captain); South Wales Cricket Association to New Zealand/Australia 1992

Cricketers particularly admired: David Gower, Neil Fairbrother
Other sports followed: Rugby (league and union)
Injuries: Dislocated finger, missed four days
Relaxations: Swimming, squash, tennis, playing Game Boy
Extras: Scored 50 for Wales against West Indies in 1991
Best batting: 51* Glamorgan v Oxford University, The Parks 1992

1992 Season

	M	Inns	NO	Runs	HS	Avge	100s	50s	Ct	St	O	M	Runs	Wkts	Avge	Best	5wI	10wM
Test																		
All First	1	1	1	51	51 *	-		-	1	4	-							
1-day Int																		
NatWest																		
B & H																		
Sunday																		

Career Performances

	M	Inns	NO	Runs	HS	Avge	100s	50s	Ct	St	Balls	Runs	Wkts	Avge	Best	5wI	10wM
Test																	
All First	1	1	1	51	51 *	-		-	1	4	-						
1-day Int																	
NatWest																	
B & H																	
Sunday																	

BLAKEY, R. J.   Yorkshire

Name: Richard John Blakey
Role: Right-hand bat, wicket-keeper
Born: 15 January 1967, Huddersfield
Height: 5ft 10in **Weight:** 11st 4lbs
Nickname: Dick
County debut: 1985
County cap: 1987
One-day internationals: 1
1000 runs in a season: 4
1st-Class 50s scored: 38
1st-Class 100s scored: 9
1st-Class 200s scored: 2
1st-Class catches: 252
1st-Class stumpings: 25
One-Day 50s: 21

One-Day 100s: 3
Place in batting averages: 40th av. 46.30
(1991 151st av. 26.13)
Parents: Brian and Pauline
Wife and date of marriage: Michelle,
28 September 1991
Family links with cricket: Father played
local cricket
Education: Woodhouse Primary;
Rastrick Grammar School
Qualifications: 4 O-levels, Senior NCA
coaching certificate
Overseas tours: Young England to
West Indies 1985; Yorkshire to Barbados
1987, to Cape Town 1991; England A to
Zimbabwe and Kenya 1989-90, to
Pakistan 1990-91; England to India and
Sri Lanka 1992-93

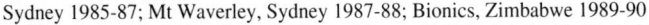

Overseas teams played for: Waverley,
Sydney 1985-87; Mt Waverley, Sydney 1987-88; Bionics, Zimbabwe 1989-90
Cricketers particularly admired: Martyn Moxon, Phil Carrick, Ian Botham, Alan Knott
Other sports followed: Any
Relaxations: Any sports, particularly golf and squash, eating out, drawing, photography
Extras: Established himself in Huddersfield League. Made record 2nd XI score – 273* v
Northamptonshire 1986. Yorkshire's Young Player of the Year 1989. Made Test debut in
Second Test at Madras, February 1993
Opinions on cricket: 'Hopefully four-day cricket will put an end to the ridiculous amount
of contrived finishes, providing that the pitches produce a good balance between bat and
ball. Coloured gear for all one-day cricket please. People should accept umpires decisions
without showing dissent.'
Best batting: 221 England A v Zimbabwe, Bulawayo 1989-90
Best bowling: 1-68 Yorkshire v Nottinghamshire, Sheffield 1986

1992 Season

	M	Inns	NO	Runs	HS	Avge	100s	50s	Ct	St	O	M	Runs	Wkts	Avge	Best	5wI	10wM
Test																		
All First	21	32	9	1065	125 *	46.30	2	5	44	5								
1-day Int	1	1	0	25	25	25.00	-	-	1	1								
NatWest	2	1	0	64	64	64.00	-	1	4	-								
B & H	4	4	0	85	39	21.25	-	-	7	-								
Sunday	14	14	1	486	105 *	37.38	1	2	9	4								

Career Performances

	M	Inns	NO	Runs	HS	Avge	100s	50s	Ct	St	Balls	Runs	Wkts	Avge	Best	5wl	10wM
Test																	
All First	157	254	35	7242	221	33.06	9	38	252	25	63	68	1	68.00	1-68	-	-
1-day Int	1	1	0	25	25	25.00	-	-	1	1							
NatWest	12	8	1	142	64	20.28	-	1	17	1							
B & H	28	25	3	655	79	29.77	-	5	23	-							
Sunday	67	66	11	2335	130 *	42.45	3	15	48	7							

BODEN, D. J. P. Essex

Name: David Jonathan Peter Boden
Role: Right-hand bat, right-arm
medium-fast bowler
Born: 26 November 1970,
Eccleshall, Staffs
Height: 6ft 3in **Weight:** 14st 7lbs
Nickname: Horse
County debut: 1989 (Middlesex),
1992 (Sussex)
1st-Class catches: 1
Parents: Peter and Mary
Marital status: Single
Family links with cricket: 'Dad is an
avid follower of the game and ferried
me everywhere when I was younger.'
Education: Stone Alleynes High School;
Stafford College of Further Education
Qualifications: 3 CSEs, 6 O-levels,
BTEC National Diploma in Business
Studies, NCA Coaching Certificate
Off-season: Playing cricket in Australia and relaxing on Bondi Beach
Overseas teams played for: Waverley, Sydney 1990-93
Cricketers particularly admired: Keith Fletcher, Ian Botham, Alex Richards,
Neil Foster
Other sports followed: Most ball games especially rugby union
Injuries: Ruptured ligaments in right ankle at the end of June, out for the rest of the season
Relaxations: Listening to music and playing Atari Lynx computer games, playing golf
Best batting: 5 Essex v Cambridge University, Fenner's 1992
Best bowling: 4-11 Middlesex v Oxford University, The Parks 1989

1992 Season

	M	Inns	NO	Runs	HS	Avge	100s	50s	Ct	St	O	M	Runs	Wkts	Avge	Best	5wI	10wM
Test																		
All First	1	1	0	5	5	5.00	-	-	1	-	16	6	42	0	-		-	-	-
1-day Int																		
NatWest																		
B & H																		
Sunday																		

Career Performances

	M	Inns	NO	Runs	HS	Avge	100s	50s	Ct	St	Balls	Runs	Wkts	Avge	Best	5wI	10wM
Test																	
All First	2	1	0	5	5	5.00	-	-	2	-	185	68	4	17.00	4-11	-	-
1-day Int																	
NatWest																	
B & H																	
Sunday																	

BOILING, J.   Surrey

Name: James Boiling
Role: Right-hand bat, right-arm off-spin bowler, gully fielder
Born: 8 April 1968, New Delhi
Height: 6ft 3in **Weight:** 13st 2lbs
Nickname: Steaming, Simmering, Kettlehead, Bubbling, Hot Man
County debut: 1988
1st-Class 5 w. in innings: 1
1st-Class 10 w. in innings: 1
1st-Class catches: 19
Place in batting averages: 200th av. 19.00
Place in bowling averages: 82nd av. 35.08 (1991 119th av. 42.08)
Strike rate: 78.82 (career 82.67)
Parents: Graham and Geraldine
Marital status: Single
Family links with cricket: 'Father umpired a school match once. Mother would like to see the front foot no ball law changed.'
Education: Rutlish School, Merton; Durham University and 'the Surrey dressing room!'

Qualifications: 10 O-levels, 3 A-levels, BA (Hons) in History, NCA Senior Coaching Award
Career outside cricket: Learning to play guitar in a band with Nick Peters (ex-Surrey) and Andrew Golding (ex-Essex)
Off-season: Touring Australia with England A
Overseas tours: Surrey Schools to Australia 1985-86; England YCs to Youth World Cup in Australia, 1988; England A to Australia 1992-93
Overseas teams plated for: Bionics, Harare, Zimbabwe 1991-92
Cricketers particularly admired: Jim Laker, David Gower, Andrew Golding
Other sports followed: Televised sport
Injuries: Bruised hand, out for a week
Relaxations: Music, good food and wine, the company of friends
Extras: Believed to be the only player to win a Gold Award against his own county, 8-3-9-3 analysis for Combined Universities against Surrey in 1989. Late call up for England A tour to Australia when Ian Salisbury stayed in India
Opinions on cricket: 'The English season is the most physically and mentally demanding in the world - such an arrangement can only be tolerated in the light of recent and welcome developments in the professional game as a result of strenuous efforts on the part of those concerned.'
Best batting: 29 Surrey v Glamorgan, Neath 1992
Best bowling: 6-84 Surrey v Gloucestershire, Bristol 1992

1992 Season

	M	Inns	NO	Runs	HS	Avge	100s	50s	Ct	St	O	M	Runs	Wkts	Avge	Best	5wI	10wM
Test																		
All First	19	21	11	190	29	19.00	-	-	19	-	591.1	156	1579	45	35.08	6-84	1	1
1-day Int																		
NatWest	1	0	0	0	0	-	-	-	1	-	12	2	37	2	18.50	2-37	-	
B & H	7	3	2	16	8 *	16.00	-	-	4	-	66	2	236	7	33.71	2-20	-	
Sunday	17	5	2	13	5	4.33	-	-	6	-	107	1	495	18	27.50	5-24	1	

Career Performances

	M	Inns	NO	Runs	HS	Avge	100s	50s	Ct	St	Balls	Runs	Wkts	Avge	Best	5wI	10wM
Test																	
All First	28	34	15	250	29	13.15	-	-	27	-	5126	2286	62	36.87	6-84	1	1
1-day Int																	
NatWest	5	2	0	29	22	14.50	-	-	4	-	360	202	5	40.40	2-22	-	
B & H	22	13	9	48	9 *	12.00	-	-	11	-	1246	828	20	41.40	3-9	-	
Sunday	26	9	4	33	12 *	6.60	-	-	6	-	1002	807	26	31.03	5-24	1	

23. Who is the new Director of Cricket at Northamptonshire?

BOON, T. J.   Leicestershire

Name: Timothy James Boon
Role: Right-hand bat, right-arm
medium bowler
Born: 1 November 1961,
Doncaster, South Yorkshire
Height: 6ft **Weight:** 12st 7lbs
Nickname: Boony, Ted
County debut: 1980
County cap: 1986
1000 runs in a season: 7
1st-Class 50s scored: 59
1st-Class 100s scored: 12
1st-Class catches: 106
One-Day 50s: 14
One-Day 100s: 1
Place in batting averages: 74th av. 38.10
(1991 106th av. 31.18)

Parents: Jeffrey and Elizabeth
Marital status: Single
Family links with cricket: Father played club cricket
Education: Mill Lane Primary; Edlington Comprehensive; three months at Doncaster Art School; Peter Van School of Business
Qualifications: 1 A-level, 6 O-levels. Advanced coach
Career outside cricket: Selling, owning a fitness studio, renovating property
Off-season: 'Making ends meet! Looking for other avenues to go down, maybe go abroad for a short while.'
Overseas tours: England YC to West Indies 1980; Leicestershire to Zimbabwe 1980-81
Overseas teams played for: Old Hararians, Zimbabwe 1980; Pirates, Pinetown, Natal 1990-91
Cricketers particularly admired: 'All those who have made it into international cricket, all those who have given me assistance (such as Chris Balderstone, Ken Higgs, Bob Simpson, Jackie Birkenshaw and many more).'
Other sports followed: Leicester Tigers (rugby union) and Leicester City FC
Relaxations: Keeping fit at the University, following local sport, 'producing zany ideas'
Extras: Captain England YC v West Indies 1980 and v India 1981; missed 1985 season due to broken leg sustained in a car crash in South Africa the previous winter. 'Would dearly love to play in a Leicestershire Championship-winning side in 1993'
Opinions on cricket: '50-over cricket will be too much on Sundays – particularly in the middle of four-day games. On a national scale more direction should be given to young cricketers off season by providing assistance with winter/future employment.'
Best batting: 144 Leicestershire v Gloucestershire, Leicester 1984
Best bowling: 3-40 Leicestershire v Yorkshire, Leicester 1986

1992 Season

	M	Inns	NO	Runs	HS	Avge	100s	50s	Ct	St	O	M	Runs	Wkts	Avge	Best	5wI	10wM
Test																		
All First	24	41	3	1448	139	38.10	2	10	15	-	29	4	175	4	43.75	2-0	-	-
1-day Int																		
NatWest	4	4	0	76	31	19.00	-	-	2	-								
B & H	5	5	1	164	59	41.00	-	2	2	-								
Sunday	8	8	0	159	49	19.87	-	-	2	-	5	0	41	1	41.00	1-23	-	

Career Performances

	M	Inns	NO	Runs	HS	Avge	100s	50s	Ct	St	Balls	Runs	Wkts	Avge	Best	5wI	10wM
Test																	
All First	208	350	39	10117	144	32.53	12	59	106	-	619	525	11	47.72	3-40	-	-
1-day Int																	
NatWest	16	14	4	281	76 *	28.10	-	1	6	-	6	2	0	-		-	-
B & H	29	26	6	752	103	37.60	1	5	6	-							
Sunday	100	88	10	1802	97	23.10	-	8	21	-	42	55	1	55.00	1-23	-	

BOOTH, P. A.   Warwickshire

Name: Paul Anthony Booth
Role: Left-hand bat, slow left-arm bowler
Born: 5 September 1965, Huddersfield
Height: 6ft **Weight:** 12st
Nickname: Boot, Linford
County debut: 1982 (Yorks),
1990 (Warwicks)
1st-Class 50s scored: 3
1st-Class 5 w. in innings: 1
1st-Class catches: 15
Place in batting averages: 253rd av. 12.70
(1991 237th av. 13.46)
Place in bowling averages: 118th av. 42.84
(1991 107th av. 38.33)
Strike rate: 88.31 (career 94.91)
Parents: Colin and Margaret
Wife and date of marriage: Beverley,
13 October 1990
Family links with cricket: Father played
local cricket for over 30 years
Education: Meltham C of E; Honley High School
Qualifications: 2 O-levels (maths and woodwork), coaching certificate

Career outside cricket: Postman, labourer
Off-season: Working for local builder
Overseas tours: England U19 to the West Indies 1984-85; Warwickshire to Trinidad 1991, to South Africa 1992
Cricketers particularly admired: Ray Illingworth, Derek Underwood, Bob Woolmer
Other sports followed: Football (Leeds United), golf
Relaxations: Playing golf and watching Leeds when possible
Extras: Yorkshire debut aged 17 years 3 days. Released by Yorkshire at end of 1989 season
Opinions on cricket: 'I am glad four-day cricket has come, but they should scrap the Sunday League.'
Best batting: 62 Warwickshire v Somerset, Taunton 1991
Best bowling: 5-98 Yorkshire v Lancashire, Old Trafford 1988

1992 Season

	M	Inns	NO	Runs	HS	Avge	100s	50s	Ct	St	O	M	Runs	Wkts	Avge	Best	5wI	10wM
Test																		
All First	8	11	4	78	22 *	11.14	-	-	-	-	279.4	74	814	19	42.84	4-29	-	-
1-day Int																		
NatWest																		
B & H																		
Sunday																		

Career Performances

	M	Inns	NO	Runs	HS	Avge	100s	50s	Ct	St	Balls	Runs	Wkts	Avge	Best	5wI	10wM
Test																	
All First	52	69	15	686	62	12.70	-	3	15	-	8637	3804	91	41.80	5-98	1	-
1-day Int																	
NatWest	2	1	1	6	6 *	-	-	-	-	-	66	33	0	-	-	-	-
B & H	7	5	2	34	13 *	11.33	-	-	4	-	240	200	5	40.00	2-28	-	
Sunday	4	0	0	0	0	-	-	-	1	-	144	146	3	48.66	1-33	-	

24   What do Derek Randall, Graeme Hick and Neil Taylor have in common?

25.   Who is the only current umpire to have scored a century on his first-class debut?

BOTHAM, I. T. Durham

Name: Ian Terence Botham
Role: Right-hand bat, right-arm
fast-medium bowler, slip fielder
Born: 24 November 1955, Heswall, Cheshire
Height: 6ft 2in **Weight:** 15st 5lbs
Nickname: Guy, Both, Beefy
County debut: 1974 (Som), 1987 (Worcs),
Durham (1992)
County cap: 1976 (Som), 1987 (Worcs)
Benefit: 1984 (£90,822)
Test debut: 1977
Tests: 102
One-Day Internationals: 116
1000 runs in a season: 4
50 wickets in a season: 7
1st-Class 50s scored: 94
1st-Class 100s scored: 37
1st-Class 200s scored: 2
1st-Class 5 w. in innings: 59
1st-Class 10 w. in match: 8
1st-Class catches: 346
One-Day 50s: 43
One-Day 100s: 7

Place in batting averages: 118th av. 31.00 (1991 45th av. 43.61)
Place in bowling averages: 112th av. 44.00 (1991 19th av. 24.47)
Strike rate: 79.84 (career 53.86)
Parents: Les and Marie
Wife and date of marriage: Kathryn, 31 January 1976
Children: Liam James, 26 August 1977; Sarah Lianne, 3 February 1979; Rebecca Kate,
13 November 1985
Family links with cricket: Father played for Navy and Fleet Air Arm; mother played for
VAD nursing staff; son Liam already a very promising all-rounder
Education: Millford Junior School; Buckler's Mead Secondary School, Yeovil
Off-season: Appearing in pantomime. Captain of celebrity team in the BBC quiz show 'A
Question of Sport.'
Overseas tours: England to Pakistan and New Zealand 1977-78, to Australia 1978-79, to
Australia and India 1979-80, to West Indies 1980-81, to India 1981-82, to Australia and
New Zealand 1982-83, to West Indies 1985-86, to Australia 1986-87, to New Zealand
1991-92, to Australia (World Cup) 1992
Cricketers particularly admired: Viv Richards, David Gower, Allan Border, Andy
Roberts ('the fastest bowler I ever faced')
Other sports followed: Rugby, football, American sports, 'virtually anything'

Relaxations: Golf, shooting, fishing (salmon and trout), flying

Extras: England captain for twelve Tests between 1980 and 1981. Played for Somerset 2nd XI 1971. On MCC staff 1972-73. Took five Australian wickets on his first day in Test cricket aged 21. One of *Wisden's* Five Cricketers of the Year, 1977. Best man at Viv Richards's wedding in Antigua in March 1981. Subject of 'This is Your Life' television programme in November 1981 and voted BBC TV Sports Review Sporting Personality of 1981 following his exploits against Australia. Scored 200 in 272 minutes for England v India at The Oval in 1982, third fastest Test double century by an Englishman, after Walter Hammond and Denis Compton. His published books include *High, Wide and Handsome,* an account of his record-breaking 1985 season; *It Sort of Clicks*, in collaboration with Peter Roebuck, and *Cricket My Way* with Jack Bannister. First cricketer since W.G. Grace to have painting commissioned by National Portrait Gallery. Captain of Somerset 1984-85. Holds record for having scored 1000 runs and taken 100 wickets in fewest Test matches. First player to score a century and take eight wickets in an innings in a Test match, v Pakistan at Lord's in 1978. Most sixes in a first-class season in 1985. Left Somerset at the beginning of 1987 to join Worcestershire after Somerset had decided not to renew the contracts of Richards and Garner. Missed nearly all 1988 season with back injury. Appeared on 'Desert Island Discs' in November 1989, when his choice of music ranged from The Beatles to Beethoven. The one book he wanted was an encyclopedia of fish, and his luxury was a fishing rod. Raised over £1,000,000 for Leukaemia Research with a series of fund-raising walks. Left Worcestershire at the end of 1991 season to join Durham. When he scored 105 for Durham against Leicestershire he became one of only eight players to score first-class centuries for three different counties. Awarded the OBE in 1992.

Opinions on cricket: 'The Comprehensive (school) system is a disgrace. How can we bring our youngsters on when there are 3000 kids in one school, and no facilities for cricket. When I was a lad we would stay on after school, being taught how to play by an experienced cricket master. Now the kids are just not being given the chance.'

Best batting: 228 Somerset v Gloucestershire, Taunton 1980

Best bowling: 8-34 England v Pakistan, Lord's 1978

1992 Season

	M	Inns	NO	Runs	HS	Avge	100s	50s	Ct	St	O	M	Runs	Wkts	Avge	Best	5wI	10wM
Test	2	2	0	8	6	4.00	-	-	2	-	24	8	61	0	-	-	-	-
All First	17	25	2	713	105	31.00	1	4	9	-	346	70	1144	26	44.00	4-72	-	-
1-day Int	5	4	2	76	40	38.00	-	-	2	-	54	2	214	5	42.80	2-45	-	
NatWest	2	2	1	68	63 *	68.00	-	1	-	-	24	2	107	2	53.50	1-53	-	
B & H	4	4	0	166	86	41.50	-	2	2	-	39	7	114	4	28.50	2-21	-	
Sunday	13	12	0	368	67	30.66	-	3	6	-	81.5	1	401	14	28.64	3-37	-	

26. What is the middle name of David Lawrence?

Career Performances

	M	Inns	NO	Runs	HS	Avge	100s	50s	Ct	St	Balls	Runs	Wkts	Avge	Best	5wl	10wM
Test	102	161	6	5200	208	33.54	14	22	120	-	21815	10878	383	28.40	8-34	27	4
All First	392	600	45	18983	228	34.20	37	94	346	-	62432	31386	1159	27.08	8-34	59	8
1-day Int	116	106	15	2113	79	23.22	-	9	36	-	6271	4139	145	28.54	4-31	-	
NatWest	44	36	9	1160	101	42.96	1	8	20	-	2722	1645	61	26.96	5-51	1	
B & H	86	72	11	1688	138 *	27.67	2	4	52	-	4882	2762	131	21.08	5-41	1	
Sunday	196	179	25	4903	175 *	31.83	4	22	79	-	7660	5885	247	23.82	5-27	1	

BOWEN, M. N.

Name: Mark Nicholas Bowen
Role: Right-hand bat, right-arm medium bowler
Born: 6 December 1967, Redcar
Height: 6ft 2in **Weight:** 13st 8lbs
Nickname: Jim ('or anything relating to Jim Bowen's Bullseye')
County debut: 1992
Parents: Keith and Teresa
Marital status: Single
Family links with cricket: Father has always played club cricket
Education: Sacred Heart Secondary School, Redcar; St Mary's Sixth Form College, Middlesbrough; Teesside Polytechnic
Qualifications: 8 O-levels, 3 A-levels, 2.1 Hons degree in Chemical Engineering
Career outside cricket: Chemical engineering, mainly in the nuclear industry
Off-season: Working as a commissioning engineer with British Nuclear Fuels at Sellafield
Overseas tours: Northamptonshire to South Africa 1991-92
Other sports followed: Hockey, rugby union and football (Middlesbrough FC)
Relaxations: Playing hockey, keeping fit, pub quizzes
Extras: Made debut for Northants first team in Natal on 1991-92 tour to South Africa before playing in the 2nd XI
Opinions on cricket: 'I believe that all cricket should be played on uncovered pitches. This, I hope, would remove the most frustrating element of the game, contrived cricket. If this is not possible then I think good cricket wickets should be prepared allowing an even contest. All too often wickets are made just to suit batsmen.'
Best batting: 13* Northamptonshire v Natal, Durban 1991-92
Best bowling: 1-23 Northamptonshire v Natal, Durban 1991-92

1992 Season

	M	Inns	NO	Runs	HS	Avge	100s	50s	Ct	St	O	M	Runs	Wkts	Avge	Best	5wI	10wM
Test																		
All First	2	1	0	5	5	5.00	-	-	-	-	43	6	159	1	159.00	1-35	-	-
1-day Int																		
NatWest																		
B & H																		
Sunday	3	1	0	9	9	9.00	-	-	-	-	18	0	98	1	98.00	1-33	-	

Career Performances

	M	Inns	NO	Runs	HS	Avge	100s	50s	Ct	St	Balls	Runs	Wkts	Avge	Best	5wI	10wM
Test																	
All First	3	3	2	26	13 *	26.00	-	-	-	-	408	247	2	123.50	1-23	-	-
1-day Int																	
NatWest																	
B & H																	
Sunday	3	1	0	9	9	9.00	-	-	-	-	108	98	1	98.00	1-33	-	

BOWLER, P. D. Derbyshire

Name: Peter Duncan Bowler
Role: Right-hand opening bat,
occasional off-spin bowler, wicket-keeper
Born: 30 July 1963, Plymouth
Height: 6ft 1in **Weight:** 13st 7lbs
Nickname: Croc
County debut: 1986 (Leics), 1988 (Derbys)
County cap: 1989
1000 runs in a season: 5
1st-Class 50s scored: 49
1st-Class 100s scored: 18
1st-Class 200s scored: 2
1st-Class catches: 82
1st-Class stumpings: 1
One-Day 50s: 25
One-Day 100s: 3
Place in batting averages: 6th av. 65.93
(1991 80th av. 35.56)
Parents: Peter and Etta
Wife and date of marriage: Joanne, 10 October 1992
Education: Daramalan College, Canberra, Australia
Qualifications: Australian Year 12 certificate

Career outside cricket: Has worked for BBC Radio as a sports journalist on occasions
Off-season: 'Spending more time enjoying my great hobbies, gardening and interior decorating, in and about my new home!'
Cricketers particularly admired: Rick McCosker, Chris Balderstone, Gus Valence
Other sports followed: Rugby union, football
Relaxations: Spending time with the family, reading, gardening, decorating
Extras: First Leicestershire player to score a first-class hundred on debut (100 not out v Hampshire 1986). Moved to Derbyshire at end of 1987 season and scored a hundred on his debut v Cambridge University in 1988. First batsman to 2000 runs in 1992. Finished equal leading runscorer (2044) with Mike Roseberry of Middlesex. Derbyshire Player of the Year 1992
Opinions on cricket: 'Traditional attire for all competitions please!'
Best batting: 241* Derbyshire v Hampshire, Portsmouth 1992
Best bowling: 3-41 Derbyshire v Leicestershire, Leicester 1991

1992 Season

	M	Inns	NO	Runs	HS	Avge	100s	50s	Ct	St	O	M	Runs	Wkts	Avge	Best	5wI	10wM
Test																		
All First	24	38	7	2044	241 *	65.93	6	11	13	-	23	3	92	0	-	-	-	-
1-day Int																		
NatWest	2	2	0	115	111	57.50	1	-	2	-	3	0	12	0	-		-	-
B & H	5	5	1	139	66 *	34.75	-	2	3	-								
Sunday	17	17	5	583	91 *	48.58	-	6	4	-	3	0	21	0	-		-	-

Career Performances

	M	Inns	NO	Runs	HS	Avge	100s	50s	Ct	St	Balls	Runs	Wkts	Avge	Best	5wI	10wM
Test																	
All First	128	223	22	8256	241 *	41.07	18	49	82	1	2283	1449	20	72.45	3-41	-	-
1-day Int																	
NatWest	9	9	0	213	111	23.66	1	-	5	-	36	26	0	-		-	-
B & H	24	23	1	776	109	35.27	2	6	16	1	246	125	4	31.25	1-15	-	
Sunday	87	84	10	2379	91 *	32.14	-	19	40	1	242	237	7	33.85	3-31	-	

27. What is the middle name of Graham Gooch?

28. What is the middle name of Mark Ramprakash?

BRAMHALL, S.   Nottinghamshire

Name: Stephen Bramhall
Role: Right-hand bat, wicket-keeper
Born: 27 November 1967, Warrington
Height: 6ft **Weight:** 13st
Nickname: Bram, Ginge, Bean
('plus many others, all unprintable')
County debut: 1990 (Lancashire),
1992 (Nottinghamshire)
1st-Class catches: 16
1st-Class stumpings: 6
Place in batting averages:
217th av. 16.28
Parents: Harry and Dorothy
Marital status: Single
Family links with cricket: 'Father
drove me everywhere.'
Education: Stockton Heath High School;
Newcastle University
Qualifications: 8 O-levels, 3 A-levels
Career outside cricket: Materials buyer in industry
Off-season: Resting
Overseas teams played for: South Canberra 1990-92
Cricketers particularly admired: Jack Russell, Alan Knott, John Wileman and Tim
Hindson
Other sports followed: Soccer, snooker, rugby league
Relaxations: 'Sleep – the odd lager'
Opinions on cricket: 'Lunch should be one hour and tea half-an-hour. 2nd XI wickets
could be better. Bring in floodlit cricket to attract bigger crowds.'
Best batting: 37* Nottinghamshire v Surrey, Trent Bridge 1992

1992 Season

	M	Inns	NO	Runs	HS	Avge	100s	50s	Ct	St	O	M	Runs	Wkts	Avge	Best	5wI	10wM
Test																		
All First	8	10	3	114	37 *	16.28	-	-	14	5								
1-day Int																		
NatWest																		
B & H																		
Sunday	6	1	0	1	1	1.00	-	-	4	3								

Career Performances

	M	Inns	NO	Runs	HS	Avge	100s	50s	Ct	St	Balls	Runs	Wkts	Avge	Best	5wl	10wM
Test																	
All First	10	13	5	115	37 *	14.37	-	-	16	6							
1-day Int																	
NatWest																	
B & H																	
Sunday	6	1	0	1	1	1.00	-	-	4	3							

BRIERS, M. P. Durham

Name: Mark Paul Briers
Role: Right-hand bat, leg-spin bowler
Born: 21 April 1968, Kegworth
Height: 5ft 11in **Weight:** 11st 5lbs
Nickname: The Duke, Wong
County debut: 1992
1st-Class 50s scored: 4
1st-Class catches: 7
One-Day 50s: 2
Place in batting averages: 198th av. 19.16
Place in bowling averages: 141st av. 51.75
Strike rate: 72.25 (career 72.25)
Parents: Graham and Mary
Marital Status: Single - 'but looking!'
Education: Shepshed Hindleys
Qualifications: Plumbing and Heating
Certificates
Overseas teams played for: South African
Police, Pretoria; Manaia, New Zealand and
Taranaki Province

Cricketers particularly admired: Ian Botham, Richard Stemp
Other sports followed: 'Golf, soccer, rugby – most sports.'
Extras: On Worcestershire staff in 1988
Best batting: 62* Durham v Sussex, Horsham 1992
Best bowling: 3-109 Durham v Gloucestershire, Stockton 1992

29. Which Test cricketer's middle name is Logo?

1992 Season

	M	Inns	NO	Runs	HS	Avge	100s	50s	Ct	St	O	M	Runs	Wkts	Avge	Best	5wl	10wM
Test																		
All First	16	28	4	460	62 *	19.16	-	4	7	-	144.3	22	621	12	51.75	3-109	-	-
1-day Int																		
NatWest	1	1	1	54	54 *	-	-	-	1	-	-	0.2	0	0	1	0.00	1-0	-
B & H																		
Sunday	7	6	0	147	69	24.50	-	1	1	-	13	0	95	1	95.00	1-47	-	

Career Performances

	M	Inns	NO	Runs	HS	Avge	100s	50s	Ct	St	Balls	Runs	Wkts	Avge	Best	5wl	10wM
Test																	
All First	16	28	4	460	62 *	19.16	-	4	7	-	867	621	12	51.75	3-109	-	-
1-day Int																	
NatWest	1	1	1	54	54 *	-	-	-	1	-	2	0	1	0.00	1-0	-	
B & H																	
Sunday	7	6	0	147	69	24.50	-	1	1	-	78	95	1	95.00	1-47	-	

BRIERS, N. E.   Leicestershire

Name: Nigel Edwin Briers
Role: Right-hand opening bat, right-arm medium bowler, county captain
Born: 15 January 1955, Leicester
Height: 6ft **Weight:** 12st 8lbs
Nickname: Kudu
County debut: 1971
County cap: 1981
Benefit: 1990
1000 runs in a season: 9
1st-Class 50s scored: 84
1st-Class 100s scored: 26
1st-Class 200s scored: 1
1st-Class catches: 144
One-Day 50s: 35
One-Day 100s: 4
Place in batting averages: 73rd av. 38.11
(1991 60th av. 39.07)
Parents: Leonard Arthur Roger and Eveline
Wife and date of marriage: Suzanne Mary Tudor, 3 September 1977
Children: Michael Edward Tudor, 25 March 1983; Andrew James Tudor, 30 June 1986
Family links with cricket: Father was captain and wicket-keeper of Narborough and

Littlethorpe CC in the South Leicestershire League for fifteen years and mother was scorer. Father was also captain of South Leicestershire Representative XI and played for the Royal Marines in the same team as Trevor Bailey. Cousin, Norman Briers, played once for Leicestershire in 1967
Education: Lutterworth Grammar School; Borough Road College
Qualifications: Qualified teacher (Cert Ed), BEd (Hons), MCC Advanced Cricket Coach
Career outside cricket: Teaching at Ludgrove School
Off-season: Teaching PE and History at Ludgrove School
Overseas tours: Derrick Robins tour to South America 1979; MCC to the Far East 1981; Leicestershire to Zimbabwe, Holland, Jersey and Guernsey; MCC to the Virgin and Leeward Islands 1991-92
Cricketers particularly admired: Ray Illingworth, Richard Hadlee, Geoff Boycott, Barry Richards
Other sports followed: Rugby (Leicester Tigers) and football (Leicester City)
Extras: Youngest player ever to appear for Leicestershire (aged 16 years 104 days). Shares record with Roger Tolchard for highest fifth wicket stand of 233 v Somerset, 1979. Appointed county captain in 1990. Captained MCC on 1991-92 tour of the Virgin and Leeward Islands. Wombwell Cricket Lovers' Society Captain of the Year
Best batting: 201* Leicestershire v Warwickshire, Edgbaston 1983
Best bowling: 4-29 Leicestershire v Derbyshire, Leicester 1985

992 Season

	M	Inns	NO	Runs	HS	Avge	100s	50s	Ct	St	O	M	Runs	Wkts	Avge	Best	5wI	10wM
Test																		
All First	24	42	6	1372	123	38.11	3	9	12	-								
1-day Int																		
NatWest	5	5	0	169	88	33.80	-	1	-	-								
B & H	5	5	1	300	102	75.00	1	2	4	-								
Sunday	16	16	0	330	43	20.62	-	-	7	-								

Career Performances

	M	Inns	NO	Runs	HS	Avge	100s	50s	Ct	St	Balls	Runs	Wkts	Avge	Best	5wI	10wM
Test																	
All First	335	547	55	15977	201 *	32.47	26	84	144	-	2047	988	32	30.87	4-29	-	-
1-day Int																	
NatWest	33	33	2	648	88	20.90	-	2	6	-	84	75	6	12.50	2-6	-	
B & H	54	49	4	1094	102	24.31	1	5	19	-	330	266	3	88.66	1-26	-	
Sunday	201	198	23	5319	119 *	30.39	3	28	51	-	482	384	10	38.40	3-29	-	

BRINKLEY, J. E. — Worcestershire

Name: James Edward Brinkley
Role: Right-hand bat, right-arm
fast-medium bowler
Born: 13 March 1974,
Helensburgh, Scotland
Height: 6ft 3in **Weight:** 14st
Nickname: JB
County debut: No first team appearance
Parents: Tom and Sharon
Marital status: Single
Family links with cricket: Father played
service cricket in the Royal Navy, mother
coaches junior teams in Western Australia
Education: Marist College, Canberra;
Trinity College, Perth
Qualifications: West Australian Tertiary
Entrance Examinations
Career outside cricket: Advertising
Off-season: Playing A Grade cricket in
Perth, Australia
Overseas teams played for: Scarborough, Perth 1990-93
Cricketers particularly admired: Michael Holding, Viv Richards, Ian Botham, David
Gower
Other sports followed: Rugby union and golf
Injuries: Groin strain, out for three weeks
Relaxations: Golf, fitness training, music, reading, cricket
Opinions on cricket: 'The transition to a more balanced programme of four-day and one-
day cricket will aid the progression of young cricketers through to the higher levels both
mentally and physically. I believe that the Bull Junior Development Programme gives
young county cricketers an immediate focus for their motivation in terms of representative
selection.'

---

30. What is the middle name of Graeme Hick?

31. What is the middle name of Cardigan Connor?

BROAD, B. C.   Gloucestershire

Name: Brian Christopher Broad
Role: Left-hand bat, right-arm
medium bowler
Born: 29 September 1957, Bristol
Height: 6ft 4in **Weight:** 14st 7lbs
Nickname: Walter, Broadie
County debut: 1979 (Gloucs),
1984 (Notts)
County cap: 1981 (Gloucs),
1984 (Notts)
Test debut: 1984
Tests: 25
One-Day Internationals: 34
1000 runs in a season: 10
1st-Class 50s scored: 95
1st-Class 100s scored: 47
1st-Class 200s scored: 1
1st-Class catches: 174
One-Day 50s: 64
One-Day 100s: 10
Place in batting averages: 50th av. 43.33
(1991 24th av. 49.68)
Parents: Nancy and Kenneth
Marital status: Divorced
Children: Gemma Joanne, 14 January 1984; Stuart Christopher John, 24 June 1986
Family links with cricket: Father and grandfather both played local cricket. Father member of Gloucestershire Committee until retired
Education: Colston's School, Bristol; St Paul's College, Cheltenham
Qualifications: 5 O-levels, NCA advanced coach
Career outside cricket: Runs his own furniture import business
Off-season: At home pursuing interests outside the game
Overseas tours: English Counties to Zimbabwe 1985; England to Australia 1986-87, to Pakistan, Australia and New Zealand 1987-88; unofficial English team to South Africa 1989-90
Overseas teams played for: Orange Free State 1985-86 (captain)
Cricketers particularly admired: Graham Gooch, Richard Hadlee, Clive Rice
Other sports followed: Rugby
Relaxations: 'Playing any sport, spending time with my family.'
Extras: Struck down by osteomyelitis at age 15. First played adult cricket for Downend CC, where W. G. Grace learnt to play; played with Allan Border in Gloucestershire 2nd XI. Published autobiography *Home Thoughts from Abroad* in 1987 after he had hit three centuries in a row in Test series v Australia, 1986-87. Banned from Test cricket for five

years for joining tour to South Africa. Passed 2000 runs in a season for the first time and made his first double hundred in 1990. Released by Notts before the end of the 1992 season and decided to return to Gloucestershire

Opinions on cricket: 'Cricket is a game played by professionals but run by amateurs. This needs to be changed for the game to go forward into the 21st century.'

Best batting: 227* Nottinghamshire v Kent, Tunbridge Wells 1990

Best bowling: 2-14 Gloucestershire v West Indians, Bristol 1980

1992 Season

	M	Inns	NO	Runs	HS	Avge	100s	50s	Ct	St	O	M	Runs	Wkts	Avge	Best	5wI	10wM
Test																		
All First	14	27	3	1040	159 *	43.33	5	-	7	-								
1-day Int																		
NatWest	2	2	0	80	72	40.00	-	1	-	-								
B & H	4	4	0	192	83	48.00	-	2	-	-								
Sunday	10	9	0	263	63	29.22	-	2	3	-								

Career Performances

	M	Inns	NO	Runs	HS	Avge	100s	50s	Ct	St	Balls	Runs	Wkts	Avge	Best	5wI	10wM
Test	25	44	2	1661	162	39.54	6	6	10	-	6	4	0	-	-	-	-
All First	311	557	38	20147	227 *	38.81	47	95	174	-	1625	1036	16	64.75	2-14	-	-
1-day Int	34	34	0	1361	106	40.02	1	11	10	-	6	6	0	-	-	-	-
NatWest	32	32	0	1178	115	36.81	1	11	8	-							
B & H	61	60	3	1874	122	32.87	3	10	14	-	348	308	6	51.33	2-73	-	
Sunday	161	158	10	5086	108	34.36	5	32	44	-	669	602	19	31.68	3-46	-	

32. What is the middle name of Sir Jack Hobbs?

33. What is the middle name of Chris Lewis?

BROADHURST, M.   Yorkshire

Name: Mark Broadhurst
Role: Right-hand (lower order) bat,
right-arm fast-medium bowler
Born: 20 June 1974, Barnsley
Height: 6ft **Weight:** 11st 5lbs
Nickname: Broady, Stanley, Ditherer, Gibby
County debut: 1991
Parents: Robert and Pamela
Marital status: Single
Family links with cricket: Father played
local league cricket for Ward Green
Education: Worsborough Common Junior
School; Kingstone Comprehensive
Qualifications: 8 GCSEs, City and Guilds
qualification in Leisure and Recreation
Overseas tours: England U19 to
New Zealand 1990-91; NCA YC to
Canada 1991
Cricketers particularly admired:
Dennis Lillee, Richard Hadlee, Michael Holding, Malcolm Marshall, Arnie Sidebottom,
Steve Oldham
Other sports followed: Football, golf, athletics
Relaxations: 'I enjoy watching cricket videos, listening to music and reading.'
Extras: Selected for England U19 squad aged 16. Made first class debut for Yorkshire at
age 16 becoming the third youngest in Yorkshire history. Contributor to Wombwell
Cricket Society's 12th Man magazine. Played for England U19 v Australia 1991. Selected
for England U19 tour to Pakistan 1991-92 but forced to drop out through back injury
Opinions on cricket: 'Not enough cricket played in Comprehensive schools. I think the
Bull Development of Excellence scheme offers great opportunities for young players,
giving such as myself a chance to compete in international matches at home and abroad.'
Best batting: 1 Yorkshire v Sri Lanka, Headingley 1991
Best bowling: 3-61 Yorkshire v Oxford University, The Parks 1991

1992 Season (did not make any first-class or one-day appearance)

---

34.   What is the middle name of Devon Malcolm?

Career Performances

	M	Inns	NO	Runs	HS	Avge	100s	50s	Ct	St	Balls	Runs	Wkts	Avge	Best	5wI	10wM
Test																	
All First	2	1	0	1	1	1.00	-	-	-	-	228	130	6	21.66	3-61	-	-
1-day Int																	
NatWest																		
B&H																		
Refuge	1	0	0	0	0	-	-	-	-	-	48	27	0	-		-	-

BROWN, A. D. Essex

Name: Adrian Desmond Brown
Role: Right-hand bat, wicket-keeper
Born: 18 May 1962, Clacton-on-Sea, Essex
Height: 5ft 11in **Weight:** 12st 5lbs
Nickname: Brownie, Hovis
County debut: 1988
1st-Class catches: 28
1st-Class stumpings: 5
One-Day 50s: 1
Parents: Desmond and Kathleen
Wife and date of marriage: Karen Ann,
10 October 1992
Family links with cricket: Father played
for Clacton
Education: Clacton County High School;
Magdalene College, Cambridge
Qualifications: 8 O-levels, 3 A-levels,
MA (Modern Languages), PGCE
Career outside cricket: Teacher

Off-season: Teaching at Ipswich School
Cricketers particularly admired: Alan Knott, Jack Russell
Other sports followed: Rugby union, football
Relaxations: Playing most sports, theatre, cinema, 'listening to Ray East talking about cricket'
Extras: Plays for Suffolk in the Minor Counties, former Cambridge Blue in 1986 and emergency wicket-keeper for Essex
Opinions on cricket: 'Four-day cricket will surely produce better batsmen and bowlers if good wickets are available. Perhaps Minor Counties cricket needs restructuring as many games are still very artificial when played over two days with four innings. Sponsorship would be a problem.'
Best batting: 30 Cambridge University v Surrey, Cambridge 1986

1992 Season

	M	Inns	NO	Runs	HS	Avge	100s	50s	Ct	St	O	M	Runs	Wkts	Avge	Best	5wl	10wM
Test																		
All First	1	0	0	0	0	-	-	-	4	1								
1-day Int																		
NatWest																		
B & H																		
Sunday	1	0	0	0	0	-	-	-	1	-								

Career Performances

	M	Inns	NO	Runs	HS	Avge	100s	50s	Ct	St	Balls	Runs	Wkts	Avge	Best	5wl	10wM
Test																	
All First	14	16	4	99	30	8.25	-	-	28	5							
1-day Int																	
NatWest	5	4	0	65	51	16.25	-	1	5	2							
B & H	4	4	2	24	10 *	12.00	-	-	1	1							
Sunday	1	0	0	0	0	-	-	-	1	-							

BROWN, A. D.   Surrey

Name: Alistair Duncan Brown
Role: Right-hand bat, occasional
leg-spin bowler, occasional wicket-keeper
Born: 11 February 1970, Beckenham
Height: 5ft 10in **Weight:** 12st
Nickname: Lordy
County debut: 1992
1st-Class 50s scored: 3
1st-Class 100s scored: 3
1st-Class catches: 6
One-Day 50s: 3
One-Day 100s: 2
Place in batting averages: 28th av. 49.33
Parents: Robert and Ann
Marital status: Single
Family links with cricket: Father played
for Surrey Young Amateurs
Education: Cumnor House School;
Caterham School
Qualifications: 5 O-levels, NCA senior coach
Career outside cricket: Cricket coach, insurance administrator, amateur golfer
Off-season: Coaching cricket in schools around Surrey and in Inner London

Overseas teams played for: North Perth, Australia 1990-91
Cricketers particularly admired: Ian Botham, Viv Richards, David Gower
Other sports followed: Horse racing, tennis, football, golf
Relaxations: Tennis and golf
Extras: Scored three of the eight fastest centuries of the 1992 season (71, 78 & 79 balls)
Opinions on cricket: 'Not sure that a short leg is required on a flat, non-turning wicket, except for target practice.'
Best batting: 175 Surrey v Durham, Durham University 1992

1992 Season

	M	Inns	NO	Runs	HS	Avge	100s	50s	Ct	St	O	M	Runs	Wkts	Avge	Best	5wI	10wM
Test																		
All First	11	16	1	740	175	49.33	3	3	6	-	16	1	78	0	-		-	-	-
1-day Int																		
NatWest																		
B & H	7	7	2	170	41	34.00	-	-	1	-								
Sunday	17	17	1	585	113	36.56	2	2	3	-								

Career Performances

	M	Inns	NO	Runs	HS	Avge	100s	50s	Ct	St	Balls	Runs	Wkts	Avge	Best	5wI	10wM
Test																	
All First	11	16	1	740	175	49.33	3	3	6	-	96	78	0	-		-	-	-
1-day Int																	
NatWest																	
B & H	8	8	2	207	41	34.50	-	-	1	-							
Sunday	28	27	1	832	113	32.00	2	3	7	-							

35. What is the middle name of Don Topley?

36. Who was the English umpire in the last World Cup?

BROWN, A. M.   Derbyshire

Name: Andrew Mark Brown
Role: Left-hand opening bat, right-arm medium bowler, occasional wicket-keeper
Born: 6 November 1964, Heanor, Derbys
Height: 5ft 9in **Weight:** 10st 7lbs
Nickname: Brownie
County debut: 1985
1st-Class 50s scored: 3
1st-Class 100s scored: 1
1st-Class catches: 19
Place in batting averages: 206th av. 18.00
Parents: John and Marion
Marital status: Single
Family links with cricket: 'Father is Youth Coaching Organiser for Derbyshire; brother Stephen played for Derbyshire youth teams; sister Helen also plays.'
Education: Langley Mill Junior School; Aldercar Comprehensive School; South-East Derbyshire College of PE
Qualifications: 8 O-levels, 1 A-level; coaching certificate
Off-season: Coaching in South Africa
Overseas teams played for: Metro and Counties, New Zealand 1983-84; Old Boys, Hastings and Hawkes Bay 1984-86; Kia Toa University and Manawatu 1987-90
Cricketers particularly admired: John Wright, Bob Taylor
Other sports followed: Football (Nottingham Forest)
Injuries: Dislocated shoulder and ligament damage, torn cruciate ligament in right knee, out for 12 weeks
Relaxations: 'Lying on beaches and attempting to surf.'
Extras: 'Born 100 yards away from where I made my first senior appearance for Derbyshire. Hold world record for opening partnership without either batsman scoring a hundred (246) with Neil Weighman (ex-Notts), 94* and 96* respectively.' Released by Derbyshire at the end of the 1992 season
Opinions on cricket: '2nd XI pitches should be of a similar standard to those used for first-class matches. Bowlers get too much help from over responsive pitches and batsman looking for form, or trying to make their way in the game, are at a disadvantage.'
Best batting: 139* Derbyshire v Northamptonshire, Chesterfield 1990

> 37.   Who has the best-ever bowling figures in a Test at Lord's, and what were they?

1992 Season

	M	Inns	NO	Runs	HS	Avge	100s	50s	Ct	St	O	M	Runs	Wkts	Avge	Best	5wI	10wM
Test																		
All First	7	8	0	144	43	18.00	-	-	7	-	3	0	9	0	-	-	-	-
1-day Int																		
NatWest																		
B & H																		
Sunday	4	0	0	0	0	-	-	-	1	-								

Career Performances

	M	Inns	NO	Runs	HS	Avge	100s	50s	Ct	St	Balls	Runs	Wkts	Avge	Best	5wI	10wM
Test																	
All First	22	31	3	815	139 *	29.10	1	3	19	-	18	9	0	-	-	-	-
1-day Int																	
NatWest																	
B & H																	
Sunday	7	1	1	2	2 *	-	-	-	2	-							

BROWN, D. R.   Warwickshire

Name: Douglas Robert Brown
Role: Right-hand bat, right-arm
fast-medium bowler
Born: 29 October 1969, Stirling
Height: 6ft 2¹/₂in **Weight:** 13st 2lbs
Nickname: 'Anything which sounds
remotely Scottish'
County debut: 1992
Parents: Alastair and Janette
Marital status: Engaged to Brenda
Family links with cricket: Both
grandfathers played club cricket
Education: Alloa Academy;
West London Institute of Higher
Education (Borough Road College)
Qualifications: 9 O-grades, 5 Higher
Grades; BEd (Hons) Physical Education;
qualified coach football, cricket,
basketball, trampolining and rugby league
Career outside cricket: PE teacher
Off-season: Coaching for Western Province Cricket Board
Overseas tours: Scotland XI to Pakistan 1989

Overseas teams played for: Primrose, Cape Town 1992-93
Cricketers particularly admired: Omar Henry, Tim Munton, Richard Hadlee, Dermot Reeve
Other sports followed: All sports especially rugby, football and golf
Injuries: Damaged tibia, tendon and ligaments in left foot, out for 12 weeks
Relaxations: 'Spending time with my girlfriend, eating out, listening to music, playing golf and watching sport.'
Extras: Played football at Hampden Park for Scotland U18. Played first-class and B & H cricket for Scotland in 1989, and played again for Scotland against Ireland in 1992
Opinions on cricket: 'What a great game!.'
Best batting: 44* Scotland v Ireland, Dublin 1992
Best bowling: 3-27 Warwickshire v Cambridge University, Fenner's 1992

1992 Season

	M	Inns	NO	Runs	HS	Avge	100s	50s	Ct	St	O	M	Runs	Wkts	Avge	Best	5wI	10wM
Test																		
All First	2	3	2	54	44 *	54.00	-	-	2	-	34	14	70	5	14.00	3-27	-	-
1-day Int																		
NatWest																		
B & H																		
Sunday	2	1	0	14	14	14.00	-	-	-	-	14	2	47	3	15.66	3-21	-	

Career Performances

	M	Inns	NO	Runs	HS	Avge	100s	50s	Ct	St	Balls	Runs	Wkts	Avge	Best	5wI	10wM
Test																	
All First	3	3	2	54	44 *	54.00	-	-	2	-	445	204	8	25.50	3-27	-	-
1-day Int																	
NatWest																	
B & H	3	3	0	57	24	19.00	-	-	1	-	183	140	3	46.66	3-50		
Sunday	3	1	0	14	14	14.00	-	-	-	-	120	82	4	20.50	3-21	-	

38. Which England Test captain won an Olympic gold medal at boxing?

39. Who is England's most capped Test player?

BROWN, G. K.   Durham

Name: Gary Kevin Brown
Role: Right-hand opening bat,
off-spin bowler
Born: 16 June 1965, Welling, Kent
Height: 5ft 10in **Weight:** 13st 7lbs
Nickname: Browny, Barry
County debut: 1986 (Middlesex),
1992 (Durham)
1st-Class 50s scored: 1
1st-Class 100s scored: 1
One-Day 50s: 1
1st-Class catches: 5
Parents: Kenneth William and
Margaret Sonia
Marital status: Single
Family links with cricket: Brother Keith
plays for Middlesex; father played club
cricket and is a qualified umpire
Education: Chace Comprehensive, Enfield
Qualifications: 3 O-levels, qualified cricket coach
Career outside cricket: Cricket coach at McEwan's Cricket Centre, Houghton-le-Spring
Overseas teams played for: Marist CC, New Zealand 1985-89
Cricketers particularly admired: All players who have reached Test level
Other sports followed: Most sports
Relaxations: 'Spending time with family, playing golf occasionally, pint down the local.'
Extras: Was on the Middlesex staff before moving to Durham. Plays first-class rugby for
Durham City RFC. Released by Durham at the end of the 1992 season
Best batting: 103 Minor Counties v India, Trowbridge 1990
Best bowling: 1-39 Minor Counties v India, Trowbridge 1990

1992 Season

	M	Inns	NO	Runs	HS	Avge	100s	50s	Ct	St	O	M	Runs	Wkts	Avge	Best	5wI	10wM
Test																		
All First	4	6	0	136	48	22.66	-	-	3	-	9	1	64	0	-	-	-	-
1-day Int																		
NatWest																		
B & H																		
Sunday																		

Career Performances

	M	Inns	NO	Runs	HS	Avge	100s	50s	Ct	St	Balls	Runs	Wkts	Avge	Best	5wI	10wM
Test																	
All First	6	10	1	345	103	38.33	1	1	5	-		108	103	1	103.00	1-39	-	-
1-day Int																	
NatWest	2	2	0	66	42	33.00	-	-	-	-							
B & H	12	12	0	298	82	24.83	-	1	4	-		6	8	0	-		-	-
Sunday																	

BROWN, K. R. Middlesex

Name: Keith Robert Brown
Role: Right-hand bat, wicket-keeper
Born: 18 March 1963, Edmonton
Height: 5ft 11in **Weight:** 13st 7lbs
Nickname: Browny, Scarface, Stally
County debut: 1984
County cap: 1990
1000 runs in a season: 2
1st-Class 50s scored: 31
1st-Class 100s scored: 10
1st-Class 200s scored: 1
1st-Class catches: 180
1st-Class stumpings: 11
One-Day 50s: 8
One-Day 100s: 2
Place in batting averages:
152nd av. 25.86 (1990 87th av. 33.82)
Parents: Kenneth William and
Margaret Sonia
Wife and date of marriage: Marie, 3 November 1984
Children: Zachary, 24 February 1987; Rosanna, 18 December 1989
Family links with cricket: Brother Gary was on Middlesex staff for three years and moved
to Durham. Father is a qualified umpire
Education: Chace Comprehensive School, Enfield
Qualifications: French O-level; NCA Senior Coaching Award
Jobs outside cricket: Plasterer, PE instructor, Coach
Off-season: Coaching and keeping fit
Overseas tours: NCA Youth tour to Denmark; Middlesex pre-season tours to La Manga
and Portugal

Overseas teams played for: Sydney University, Australia 1988-89; Motueka Cricket Association, New Zealand 1991-92

Cricketers particularly admired: Clive Radley and Derek Randall

Other sports followed: Rugby, boxing, most other sports apart from motor racing

Relaxations: 'Walking pet dog, couple of pints in local, DIY at home, spending time with family'

Extras: Had promising boxing career but gave it up in order to concentrate on cricket. Picked to play rugby for Essex

Opinions on cricket: '40-over game should have been left as it was.'

Best batting: 200* Middlesex v Nottinghamshire, Lord's 1990

Best bowling: 2-7 Middlesex v Gloucestershire, Bristol 1987

1992 Season

	M	Inns	NO	Runs	HS	Avge	100s	50s	Ct	St	O	M	Runs	Wkts	Avge	Best	5wl	10wM
Test																		
All First	25	37	7	776	106	25.86	1	3	39	11								
1-day Int																		
NatWest	2	2	1	46	44 *	46.00	-	-	2	-								
B & H	6	5	1	84	33	21.00	-	-	6	5								
Sunday	17	13	7	308	73 *	51.33	-	1	10	7								

Career Performances

	M	Inns	NO	Runs	HS	Avge	100s	50s	Ct	St	Balls	Runs	Wkts	Avge	Best	5wl	10wM
Test																	
All First	136	212	36	6059	200 *	34.42	10	31	180	11	231	162	5	32.40	2-7	-	-
1-day Int																	
NatWest	13	11	3	315	103 *	39.37	1	-	5	-	6	8	0	-	-	-	
B & H	21	19	3	367	56	22.93	-	1	10	5	6	0	0	-	-	-	
Sunday	84	71	20	1535	102	30.09	1	7	33	8	28	29	0	-	-	-	

40.   What was unusual about the Lancashire v Somerset match in the County Championship in August 1892?

BROWN, S. J. E.   Durham

Name: Simon John Emmerson Brown
Role: Right-hand bat, left-arm
medium pace bowler, gully fielder
Born: 29 June 1969,
Cleadon Village, Sunderland
Height: 6ft 3in **Weight:** 13st
Nickname: Chubby
County debut: 1987 (Northamptonshire),
1992 (Durham)
50 wickets in a season: 1
1st-Class 5 w. in innings: 3
1st-Class catches: 9
Place in batting averages: 207th av. 17.90
Place in bowling averages: 74th av. 34.01
Strike rate: 52.67 (57.62)
Parents: Ernest and Doreen
Marital status: Single
Education: Boldon Comprehensive,
Tyne & Wear; South Tyneside College
Qualifications: 5 O-levels, qualified electrician
Career outside cricket: Electrician
Overseas tours: England YC to Sri Lanka 1987, to Australia for Youth World Cup 1988
Overseas teams played for: Marist, Christchurch, New Zealand
Cricketers particularly admired: John Lever, Dennis Lillee, Richard Hadlee, Ian Botham
Other sports followed: Basketball and football
Relaxations: Playing basketball, football and most sports
Extras: Offered basketball scholarship in America. Durham supporters' Player of the Year
1992
Best batting: 47* Durham v Surrey, Durham University 1992
Best bowling: 7-150 Durham v Kent, Canterbury 1992

1992 Season

	M	Inns	NO	Runs	HS	Avge	100s	50s	Ct	St	O	M	Runs	Wkts	Avge	Best	5wI	10wM
Test																		
All First	20	24	13	197	47*	17.90	-	-	4	-	509.1	75	1973	58	34.01	7-105	3	-
1-day Int																		
NatWest	2	1	1	3	3*	-	-	-	-	-	23.3	3	96	2	48.00	1-43	-	
B & H	4	2	2	6	4*	-	-	-	-	-	37	4	129	4	32.25	2-36	-	
Sunday	11	1	0	1	1	1.00	-	-	2	-	73	0	393	11	35.72	3-32	-	

Career Performances

	M	Inns	NO	Runs	HS	Avge	100s	50s	Ct	St	Balls	Runs	Wkts	Avge	Best	5wI	10wM
Test																	
All First	35	38	19	267	47 *	14.05	-	-	9	-	4783	2787	83	33.57	7-105	3	-
1-day Int																	
NatWest	3	2	2	10	7 *	-	-	-	-	-	213	169	3	56.33	1-43	-	
B & H	5	2	2	6	4 *	-	-	-	-	-	264	162	4	40.50	2-36	-	
Sunday	24	4	1	5	3 *	1.66	-	-	2	-	939	860	24	35.83	3-26	-	

BRYSON, R. E. Surrey

Name: Rudi Edwin Bryson
Role: Right-hand bat, right-arm fast bowler
Born: 25 July 1968, Springs, South Africa
Height: 6ft 1in **Weight:** 13st 5lbs
Nickname: Bok
County debut: 1992
1st-Class 50s scored: 2
1st-Class 100s scored: 1
1st-Class catches: 9
1st-Class 5 w. in innings: 10
1st-Class 10 w. in match: 2
Place in batting averages: 172nd av. 23.36
Place in bowling averages: 146th av. 54.60
Strike rate: 87.04 (career 51.65)
Parents: Robert and Pam
Marital status: Engaged to Shelley
Education: Strubenvale Primary;
Springs Boys High School
Qualifications: Matriculation
Off-season: Playing in South Africa
Overseas tours: South Africa to Australia (World Cup) 1992
Overseas teams played for: Northern Transvaal and Eastern Province
Cricketers particularly admired: Malcolm Marshall, Patrick Patterson
Injuries: Shin problems
Relaxations: listening to music, shopping
Extras: Represented South African Schools at hockey. Released by Surrey at end of 1992 season
Opinions on cricket: 'Wickets too flat. One bouncer per over should be ruled out.'
Best batting: 100 Eastern Province v Boland, Worcester 1991-92
Best bowling: 7-68 Eastern Province B v Griqualand West, Kimberley 1988-89

1992 Season

	M	Inns	NO	Runs	HS	Avge	100s	50s	Ct	St	O	M	Runs	Wkts	Avge	Best	5wI	10wM
Test																		
All First	11	13	2	257	76	23.36	-	1	-	-	333.4	41	1256	23	54.60	5-48	2	-
1-day Int																		
NatWest																		
B & H	5	2	1	18	18 *	18.00	-	-	-	-	52	3	232	10	23.20	4-31	-	
Sunday	7	3	1	42	20	21.00	-	-	-	-	45.1	1	267	8	33.37	2-30	-	

Career Performances

	M	Inns	NO	Runs	HS	Avge	100s	50s	Ct	St	Balls	Runs	Wkts	Avge	Best	5wI	10wM
Test																	
All First	39	43	11	745	100	23.28	1	2	9	-	7025	3735	136	27.46	7-68	10	2
1-day Int																	
NatWest																	
B & H	5	2	1	18	18 *	18.00	-	-	-	-	312	232	10	23.20	4-31	-	
Sunday	7	3	1	42	20	21.00	-	-	-	-	271	267	8	33.37	2-30	-	

BURNS, M. Warwickshire

Name: Michael Burns
Role: Right-hand bat, right-arm medium bowler, wicket-keeper
Born: 6 February 1969, Barrow-in-Furness
Height: 6ft **Weight:** 13st 7lbs
Nickname: George, Red Hot
County debut: 1991
1st-Class 50s scored: 1
1st-Class catches: 7
1st-Class stumpings: 1
Parents: Robert and Linda, stepfather Stan
Marital status: Single
Family links with cricket: Grandfather was a great back-garden bowler
Education: Walney Comprehensive; Barrow College of Further Education
Qualifications: 'Few CSEs, couple of GCEs', qualified fitter at VSEL in Barrow, coaching award
Career outside cricket: Was a fitter, then a greengrocer
Off-season: Playing and coaching in New Zealand
Overseas teams played for: Gill College, South Africa 1991-92; Motueka, Nelson, New

Zealand 1992-93

Cricketers particularly admired: Dermot Reeve, Dominic Ostler, Keith Piper, Graeme Welch, Roger Twose, Viv Richards, Carlisle Best, Richie Richardson and Andy Moles ('winter agent')

Other sports followed: Rugby league and golf

Relaxations: 'Golf, couple of pints with Graeme Welch, going to the pictures with girlfriend Carolyn.'

Extras: Played for Cumberland 1989-90. Had a trial with Glamorgan, went to La Manga with Lancashire junior side 1984

Opinions on cricket: '2nd XI pitches should be of a similar standard to first-class pitches to prepare youngsters for the first-class game.'

Best batting: 78 Warwickshire v Cambridge University, Fenner's 1992

1992 Season

	M	Inns	NO	Runs	HS	Avge	100s	50s	Ct	St	O	M	Runs	Wkts	Avge	Best	5wI	10wM
Test																		
All First	2	3	0	85	78	28.33	-	1	7	1								
1-day Int																		
NatWest																		
B & H																		
Sunday	1	1	0	1	1	1.00	-	-	-	-								

Career Performances

	M	Inns	NO	Runs	HS	Avge	100s	50s	Ct	St	Balls	Runs	Wkts	Avge	Best	5wI	10wM
Test																	
All First	2	3	0	85	78	28.33	-	1	7	1							
1-day Int																	
NatWest																	
B & H	1	1	0	3	3	3.00	-	-	-	-							
Sunday	1	1	0	1	1	1.00	-	-	-	-							

41.   What England Test cricketer fought and won a duel with swords and refereed international bridge games?

42.   Which county were the last to achieve first-class status before Durham, and in which year?

BURNS, N. D. Somerset

Name: Neil David Burns
Role: Left-hand bat, wicket-keeper
Born: 19 September 1965, Chelmsford
Height: 5ft 10in **Weight:** 12st
Nickname: Burnsie, Ern, George
County debut: 1986 (Essex), 1987 (Som)
County cap: 1987 (Somerset)
1st-Class 50s scored: 24
1st-Class 100s scored: 4
1st-Class catches: 278
1st-Class stumpings: 28
One-Day 50s: 4
Place in batting averages: 86th av. 36.76
(1991 109th av. 31.07)
Parents: Roy and Marie
Wife and date of marriage: Susan,
26 September 1987
Family links with cricket: Father Roy

played club cricket for Finchley CC;
brother Ian captained Essex U19 and plays for Chelmsford, MCC and Stock Exchange
Education: Mildmay Junior; Moulsham High School
Qualifications: 6 O-levels, advanced cricket coach
Career outside cricket: 'Involved with my wife in running Neil Burns Company Ltd
(NBC), specialising in sports marketing and PR, plus cricket coaching'
Off-season: 'Coaching, after-dinner speaking and working at my business until New Year
when I will be playing and coaching in South Africa in preparation for the 1993 season.'
Overseas tours: England YC to West Indies 1985; Essex to Barbados 1986; Christians in
Sport to India 1990
Overseas teams played for: Northerns/Goodwood, Cape Town 1984-87 and 1992; Western
Province B 1985-86
Cricketers particularly admired: Alan Knott, Bob Taylor, Rod Marsh, Graham Gooch,
Allan Border, Graeme Pollock, David Gower
Other sports followed: Most sports but particularly soccer,(West Ham)
Relaxations: Watching/playing sport, reading newspapers,relaxing at home
Extras: Former schoolboy footballer with Tottenham Hotspur FC and Orient FC. Joined
Somerset in 1987 after spending four years at Essex. Took eight stumpings in match v Kent
2nd XI at Dartford in 1984. Once took a hat-trick of stumpings off Nasser Hussain's leg-
breaks for Essex U11 v Berkshire U11 Scored maiden first-class 100 against old county
at Chelmsford in 1988. Writes column for *Sunday Independent* during the cricket season
and contributes to *Cricket World* magazine. Holds one-day record of four stumpings in an
innings (v Kent 1991 in Sunday League). Stumped batsman (Mike Roseberry) off a wide
bowled by Ken Macleay at Lord's in 1992

Opinions on cricket: 'Delighted by go-ahead on four-day structure and coloured clothing. In favour of 50 overs on Sunday, but not in the middle of a four-day match.'
Best batting: 166 Somerset v Gloucestershire, Taunton 1990

1992 Season

	M	Inns	NO	Runs	HS	Avge	100s	50s	Ct	St	O	M	Runs	Wkts	Avge	Best	5wI	10wM
Test																		
All First	22	33	12	772	73 *	36.76	-	4	41	3								
1-day Int																		
NatWest	2	1	0	24	24	24.00	-	-	2	-								
B & H	6	6	3	98	39 *	32.66	-	-	5	1								
Sunday	16	11	5	148	30	24.66	-	-	17	1								

Career Performances

	M	Inns	NO	Runs	HS	Avge	100s	50s	Ct	St	Balls	Runs	Wkts	Avge	Best	5wI	10wM
Test																	
All First	143	211	50	4870	166	30.24	4	24	278	28	3	8	0	-	-	-	-
1-day Int																	
NatWest	12	9	3	99	25 *	16.50	-	-	10	3							
B & H	31	24	9	439	51	29.26	-	1	28	6							
Sunday	93	72	20	992	58	19.07	-	3	90	17							

BUTCHER, A. R.   Essex

Name: Alan Raymond Butcher
Role: Left-hand bat, slow left-arm or medium pace
bowler, county captain
Born: 7 January 1954, Croydon
Height: 5ft 8¹/₂in **Weight:** 12st 7lbs
Nickname: Butch, Bouché ('in a flamboyantly French
moment from Phil Tufnell')
County debut: 1972 (Surrey),
1987 (Glamorgan)
County cap: 1975 (Surrey),
1987 (Glamorgan)
Benefit: 1985
Test debut: 1979
Tests: 1
One-Day Internationals: 1
1000 runs in a season: 12

1st-Class 50s scored: 123
1st-Class 100s scored: 46
1st-Class 200s scored: 1
1st-Class 5 w. in innings: 1
1st-Class catches: 185
One-Day 50s: 55
One-Day 100s: 6
Place in batting averages: (1991 39th av. 45.32)
Strike rate: (career 71.48)
Parents: Raymond and Jackie
Wife and date of marriage: Madeleine, 29 February 1992
Children: Mark, 23 February 1972; Gary, 11 March 1975; Lisa, 29 July 1979
Family links with cricket: Brother Martin played for MCC Young Professionals. Brother Ian played for Leicestershire and Gloucestershire. Son Mark made his Surrey debut in 1991, son Gary on the Glamorgan staff, daughter Lisa plays for her school team
Education: Heath Clark GS
Qualifications: 5 O-levels, 1 A-level
Off-season: Getting fit after missing virtually all of 1992 season
Overseas tours: England Schools to India 1971; Rest of the World (nominally) to Jamaica; England XI (nominally) to Calcutta
Other sports followed: Football
Injuries: Right calf, right patella tendon, cartilege in right knee, left calf
Relaxations: Reading, writing ('no not 'rithmetic'), music, food, wine, real ale – 'the last three may explain last season's problems'
Extras: Released by Surrey at end of 1986 season. Joined Glamorgan in 1987. First Englishman to score 1000 runs in both 1989 and 1990. Appointed captain of Glamorgan during 1989 after Hugh Morris resigned in mid-season. Believed to be the first father to play against his son (Mark) in English county cricket – at least this century (Glamorgan v Surrey, The Oval August 1991). Joined Essex for the 1993 season as 2nd XI captain/ coach
Opinions on cricket: 'With four-day cricket I believe the game is moving in the right direction. It is now up to the players to provide a County Championship of the highest quality. This must take into account entertainment as well as technical excellence and stand in its own right, not just as a breeding ground for Test cricketers.'
Best batting: 216* Surrey v Cambridge University, Fenner's 1980
Best bowling: 6-48 Surrey v Hampshire, Guildford 1972

1992 Season

	M	Inns	NO	Runs	HS	Avge	100s	50s	Ct	St	O	M	Runs	Wkts	Avge	Best	5wI	10wM
Test																		
All First	3	3	1	90	59 *	45.00	-	1	2	-								
1-day Int																		
NatWest																		
B & H																		
Sunday																		

Career Performances

	M	Inns	NO	Runs	HS	Avge	100s	50s	Ct	St	Balls	Runs	Wkts	Avge	Best	5wI	10wM
Test	1	2	0	34	20	17.00	-	-	-	-	12	9	0	-	-	-	-
All First	401	682	60	22633	216 *	36.38	46	123	185	-	10008	5433	141	38.53	6-48	1	-
1-day Int	1	1	0	14	14	14.00	-	-	-	-							
NatWest	38	36	4	1083	104 *	33.84	1	5	12	-	404	249	5	49.80	1-27	-	
B & H	79	74	4	1982	127	28.31	1	15	22	-	1125	603	27	22.33	4-36	-	
Sunday	234	223	26	5478	113 *	27.80	4	35	51	-	2073	1556	38	40.94	5-19	1	

BUTCHER, G. P. Glamorgan

Name: Gary Paul Butcher
Role: Right-hand opening bat,
right-arm medium bowler
Born: 11 March 1975, Clapham,
South London
Height: 5ft 9in **Weight:** 10st 9lbs
County debut: No first team appearance
Parents: Alan and Elaine
Marital status: Single
Family links with cricket: Father Alan
played for Glamorgan and is now with
Essex, brother Mark plays for Surrey
and uncle Ian played for Gloucs and Leics
Education: Riddlesdown Comprehensive;
Heath Clark College
Qualifications: 4 GCSEs, BTEC
1st Diploma in leisure studies
Career outside cricket: Salesman
Off-season: 'Taking driving test, working
and keeping fit.'
Cricketers particularly admired: David Gower, Malcolm Marshall, Viv Richards
Other sports followed: Football, boxing, rugby
Injuries: Back injury; off cricket for just over a week
Relaxations: 'Music, the wife and playing in the band.'
Opinions on cricket: 'All 2nd XI games should be played at county grounds, with two
qualified umpires.'

BUTCHER, M. A. Surrey

Name: Mark Alan Butcher
Role: Left-hand bat, right-arm
medium bowler
Born: 23 August 1972, Croydon
Height: 5ft 11in **Weight:** 11st 7lbs
Nickname: Butch, Basil
County debut: 1991
Parents: Alan and Elaine
Marital status: Single
Family links with cricket: Father Alan
played for Glamorgan, Surrey and
England and is now with Essex.
Brother Gary plays for Glamorgan
Education: Cumnor House School,
Trinity School and Archbishop Tenison's,
Croydon
Qualifications: 5 O-levels, senior
coaching award
Off-season: 'Training three times a week
and coaching in the London area.'
Overseas tours: England U19 to New Zealand 1990-91
Cricketers particularly admired: David Gower, Michael Holding, Ian Botham, Richie
Richardson
Other sports followed: Football, gymnastics, athletics
Injuries: Torn groin; out for one month
Relaxations: Music, reading, clothes
Extras: Played his first game for Surrey against his father's Glamorgan in the Refuge
League at The Oval, the first ever match of any sort between first-class counties in which
a father and son have been in opposition
Opinions on cricket: 'As much as possible should be done to create interest for young
people trying to take up the game. More money for equipment should be made available
to schools.'
Best batting: 47 Surrey v Middlesex, The Oval 1992
Best bowling: 1-95 Surrey v Middlesex, The Oval 1992

---

43.   Who won the Oxford v Cambridge match at Lord's in 1992?

1992 Season

	M	Inns	NO	Runs	HS	Avge	100s	50s	Ct	St	O	M	Runs	Wkts	Avge	Best	5wI	10wM
Test																		
All First	2	2	1	52	47	52.00	-	-	-	-	44	10	115	1	115.00	1-95	-	-
1-day Int																		
NatWest	1	1	1	4	4 *	-	-	-	-	-	12	3	36	0	-		-	-
B & H																		
Sunday	2	2	1	7	6	7.00	-	-	-	-	13	0	78	3	26.00	3-23	-	

Career Performances

	M	Inns	NO	Runs	HS	Avge	100s	50s	Ct	St	Balls		Runs	Wkts	Avge	Best	5wI	10wM
Test																		
All First	2	2	1	52	47	52.00	-	-	-	-	264		115	1	115.00	1-95	-	-
1-day Int																		
NatWest	1	1	1	4	4 *	-	-	-	-	-	72		36	0	-		-	-
B & H																		
Sunday	3	3	2	55	48 *	55.00	-	-	-	-	96		94	3	31.33	3-23	-	

BUTLER, K. A. Essex

Name: Keith Andrew Butler
Role: Right-hand bat
Born: 20 January 1971, Camden Town
Height: 5ft 8in **Weight:** 11st 7lbs
Nickname: Billy
County debut: 1991
Parents: John and Kath
Marital status: Single
Education: Dagenham Priory CS
Qualifications: 2 O-levels,
coaching certificate
Career outside cricket: 'Looking for
something more interesting.'
Off-season: 'In the pub smoking fags.'
Overseas tours: Young England to
Australia 1989-90
Overseas teams played for: East Torrens,
Adelaide 1989-90
Cricketers particularly admired:
Chris Gladwin, Darren Cousins, Steve Andrew – 'He's my drinking partner'
Other sports followed: Football, golf, snooker
Injuries: Stress fracture of lower back; out for two months

Relaxations: 'Going to the pub and my girlfriend and playing Gameboy.'
Extras: Released by Essex at the end of the 1992 season
Best batting: 10* Essex v Cambridge University, Fenner's 1989

1992 Season

	M	Inns	NO	Runs	HS	Avge	100s	50s	Ct	St	O	M	Runs	Wkts	Avge	Best	5wI	10wM
Test																		
All First																		
1-day Int																		
NatWest																		
B & H																		
Sunday	1	1	1	5	5*	-	-	-	-	-	-							

Career Performances

	M	Inns	NO	Runs	HS	Avge	100s	50s	Ct	St	Balls	Runs	Wkts	Avge	Best	5wI	10wM
Test																	
All First	1	1	1	10	10*	-	-	-	-	-							
1-day Int																	
NatWest																	
B & H																	
Sunday	4	2	1	6	5*	6.00	-	-	1	-	6	5	0	-		-	-

BYAS, D.   Yorkshire

Name: David Byas
Role: Left-hand bat (No 3), right-arm
medium bowler
Born: 26 August 1963,
Middledale, Kilham
Height: 6ft 4in **Weight:** 15st
Nickname: Bingo, Gadgett
County debut: 1986
County cap: 1991
1000 runs in a season: 1
1st-Class 50s scored: 22
1st-Class 100s scored: 8
1st-Class catches: 99
One-Day 50s: 7
Place in batting averages: 124th av. 30.15
(1991 43rd av. 44.48)
Strike rate: (career 94.80)
Parents: Richard and Anne

Wife and date of marriage: Rachael Elizabeth, 27 October 1990
Children: Olivia Rachael Byas, 27th October 1990
Family links with cricket: Father played in local league
Education: Scarborough College
Qualifications: 1 O-level (Engineering)
Career outside cricket: Partner in family farm
Off-season: 'Working with father and brother on the farm.'
Overseas teams played for: Papetoetoe, Auckland 1989
Cricketers particularly admired: David Gower, Viv Richards, Ian Botham
Other sports followed: Hockey, motor racing, rallying
Relaxations: 'Gardening, shooting and eating out with my wife Rachael.'
Extras: Became youngest captain (aged 21) of Scarborough CC in 1985
Best batting: 153 Yorkshire v Nottinghamshire, Worksop 1991
Best bowling: 3-55 Yorkshire v Derbyshire, Chesterfield 1990

1992 Season

	M	Inns	NO	Runs	HS	Avge	100s	50s	Ct	St	O	M	Runs	Wkts	Avge	Best	5wI	10wM
Test																		
All First	20	30	4	784	100	30.15	1	6	30	-								
1-day Int																		
NatWest	2	2	1	56	32	56.00	-	-	2	-								
B & H	4	4	0	92	31	23.00	-	-	1	-								
Sunday	14	13	0	289	80	22.23	-	1	2	-								

Career Performances

	M	Inns	NO	Runs	HS	Avge	100s	50s	Ct	St	Balls	Runs	Wkts	Avge	Best	5wI	10wM
Test																	
All First	99	161	17	4488	153	31.16	8	22	99	-	948	612	10	61.20	3-55	-	-
1-day Int																	
NatWest	8	6	1	133	54	26.60	-	1	6	-	18	23	1	23.00	1-23	-	
B & H	18	16	1	391	92	26.06	-	2	3	-	283	155	5	31.00	2-38	-	
Sunday	73	70	13	1421	80	24.93	-	4	12	-	523	445	19	23.42	3-19	-	

44. Who was the first county cricketer to be capped by three counties?

BYRNE, J. R.   Hampshire

Name: Jamie Robert Byrne
Role: Right-hand bat, right-arm fast bowler
Born: 1 April 1973, Manchester
Height: 5ft 10in **Weight:** 11st 11lbs
County debut: No first team appearance
Parents: Christopher and Patricia
Marital status: Single
Education: St. Pauls, Davyhulme;
Salford College of Technology
Qualifications: BTEC in art & design
Off-season: 'Probably abroad again
(most likely South Africa).'
Overseas teams played for:
Rovers, Cairns, Queensland 1991-92;
Glenwood Old Boys, Durban,
South Africa 1992-93
Cricketers particularly admired:
Malcolm Marshall
Other sports followed: 'Most.'
Relaxations: 'Listening to music, especially Bob Marley.'

CADDICK, A. R.   Somerset

Name: Andrew Richard Caddick
Role: Right-hand bat, right-arm fast-medium bowler
Born: 21 November 1968, Christchurch, New Zealand
Height: 6ft 5in **Weight:** 14st
Nickname: Kiwi, Vic, Doo, Bean ('Quite a few')
County debut: 1991
1st-Class 50s scored: 1
1st-Class 5 w. in innings: 3
1st-Class 10 w. in match: 1
1st-Class catches: 6
Place in batting averages: 188th av. 20.07
Place in bowling averages: 30th av. 27.01
Strike rate: 49.66 (51.51)
Parents: Christopher and Audrey
Marital status: Single
Education: Papanui High School, Christchurch
Qualifications: Qualified plasterer and tiler

Career outside cricket: Plasterer and tiler
Off-season: 'Returning to my family and touring Australia with England A.'
Overseas tours: New Zealand U19 to Australia 1987-88 (Youth World Cup), to England 1988; England A to Australia 1992-93
Cricketers particularly admired: Dennis Lillee, Richard Hadlee, Jimmy Cook
Other sports followed: 'Mostly all'
Injuries: 'Slight left ankle injury; off for a couple of games'
Relaxations: Music, videos, most sports
Extras: Rapid Cricketline Player of the Year 1991
Opinions on cricket: 'For a bowler it's a very hard game.'
Best batting:
54* Somerset v Worcs, Weston 1992
Best bowling: 6-52 Somerset v Kent, Canterbury 1992

1992 Season

	M	Inns	NO	Runs	HS	Avge	100s	50s	Ct	St	O	M	Runs	Wkts	Avge	Best	5wI	10wM
Test																		
All First	20	19	6	261	54 *	20.07	-	1	6	-	587.4	99	1918	71	27.01	6-52	3	1
1-day Int																		
NatWest	2	1	0	0	0	0.00	-	-	1	-	24	4	88	7	12.57	6-30	1	
B & H	5	4	3	14	6 *	14.00	-	-	2	-	52	7	164	5	32.80	2-20	-	
Sunday	13	1	1	4	4 *	-	-	-	1	-	86.3	2	384	16	24.00	4-18	-	

Career Performances

	M	Inns	NO	Runs	HS	Avge	100s	50s	Ct	St	Balls	Runs	Wkts	Avge	Best	5wI	10wM
Test																	
All First	22	20	6	261	54 *	18.64	-	1	7	-	3915	2169	76	28.53	6-52	3	1
1-day Int																	
NatWest	2	1	0	0	0	0.00	-	-	1	-	144	88	7	12.57	6-30	1	
B & H	5	4	3	14	6 *	14.00	-	-	2	-	312	164	5	32.80	2-20	-	
Sunday	13	1	1	4	4 *	-	-	-	1	-	519	384	16	24.00	4-18	-	

CAIRNS, C. L.   Nottinghamshire

Name: Christopher Lance Cairns
Role: Right-hand bat, right-arm
fast-medium bowler
Born: 13 June 1970, Picton, New Zealand
Height: 6ft 2in **Weight:** 14st
Nickname: Sheep
County debut: 1988
Test debut: 1990-91
Tests: 5
One-Day Internationals: 10
50 wickets in a season: 1
1st-Class 50s scored: 11
1st-Class 100s scored: 3
1st-Class 5 w. in innings: 6
1st-Class 10 w. in match: 2
1st-Class catches: 24
Place in batting averages: 62nd av. 41.00
Place in bowling averages: 83rd av. 35.25
Parents: Lance and Sue
Family links with cricket: Father played for New Zealand, uncle played first-class cricket
in New Zealand
Education: Christchurch Boys' High School, New Zealand
Qualifications: 5th and 6th form certificates
Marital status: Single
Off-season: Playing for New Zealand
Overseas tours: New Zealand Youth XI to Australia for Youth World Cup 1988; New
Zealand to Australia 1989-90
Cricketers particularly admired: Mick Newell, Richard Hadlee, Dennis Lillee
Other sports followed: Most sports
Opinions on cricket: 'Great game.'
Best batting: 110 Northern Districts v Auckland, Hamilton 1988-89
Best bowling: 7-34 Canterbury v Central Districts, New Plymouth 1991-92

1992 Season

	M	Inns	NO	Runs	HS	Avge	100s	50s	Ct	St	O	M	Runs	Wkts	Avge	Best	5wI	10wM
Test																		
All First	21	30	6	984	107 *	41.00	2	6	8	-	592.3	110	1974	56	35.25	6-70	2	-
1-day Int																		
NatWest	2	2	0	91	77	45.50	-	1	1	-	24	2	66	3	22.00	2-38	-	
B & H	4	2	0	17	16	8.50	-	-	1	-	35	2	155	3	51.66	1-34	-	
Sunday	14	10	2	206	55 *	25.75	-	1	6	-	102	5	459	18	25.50	4-26	-	

Career Performances

	M	Inns	NO	Runs	HS	Avge	100s	50s	Ct	St	Balls	Runs	Wkts	Avge	Best	5wI	10wM
Test	5	8	0	165	61	20.62	-	1	4	-	1128	700	20	35.00	6-52	2	-
All First	59	77	14	1955	110	31.03	3	11	24	-	10062	5619	187	30.04	7-34	6	2
1-day Int	10	8	3	83	42	16.60	-	-	7	-	367	362	11	32.90	4-55	-	
NatWest	2	2	0	91	77	45.50	-	1	1	-	144	66	3	22.00	2-38	-	
B & H	4	2	0	17	16	8.50	-	-	1	-	210	155	3	51.66	1-34	-	
Sunday	16	12	2	214	55 *	21.40	-	1	7	-	690	527	20	26.35	4-26	-	

CAPEL, D. J. Northamptonshire

Name: David John Capel
Role: Right-hand bat, right-arm
fast-medium bowler, all-rounder,
slip fielder
Born: 6 July 1963, Northampton
Height: 5ft 11in **Weight:** 12st 4lbs
Nickname: Capes, Fiery
County debut: 1981
County cap: 1986
Test debut: 1987
Tests: 15
One-Day Internationals: 23
1000 runs in a season: 3
50 wickets in a season: 3
1st-Class 50s scored: 62
1st-Class 100s scored: 12
1st-Class 5 w. in innings: 12
1st-Class catches: 126
One-Day 50s: 19
One-Day 100s: 3
Place in batting averages: 126th av. 29.73 (1991 153rd av. 25.54)
Place in bowling averages: 18th av. 25.29 (1991 111th av. 40.25)
Strike rate: 55.75 (career 61.71)
Parents: John and Janet
Wife and date of marriage: Debbie, 21 September 1985
Children: Jenny, 21 October 1987
Family links with cricket: Father and brother Andrew both captained their local league
sides
Education: Roade Primary and Roade Comprehensive School
Qualifications: 3 O-levels, 4 CSEs, NCA advanced coaching certificate
Off-season: 'Coaching in schools and working with young pro's in 2nd team at the club.

Also touring Australia with England A team.'
Overseas tours: England to Sharjah 1986, to Pakistan, New Zealand and Australia 1987-88, to India (Nehru Cup) and West Indies 1989-90; England A to Australia 1992-93
Overseas teams played for: Eastern Province, South Africa 1985-87; Petersham-Marrickville, Sydney 1991-92
Other sports followed: 'Golf, local rugby and soccer teams.'
Relaxations: 'Walking with daughter'.
Extras: Only second Northampton-born man to play for England
Best batting: 134 Eastern Province v Western Province, Port Elizabeth 1986-87
Best bowling: 7-46 Northamptonshire v Yorkshire, Northampton 1987

1992 Season

	M	Inns	NO	Runs	HS	Avge	100s	50s	Ct	St	O	M	Runs	Wkts	Avge	Best	5wI	10wM
Test																		
All First	23	34	4	892	103	29.73	1	5	16	-	446	92	1214	48	25.29	5-61	1	-
1-day Int																		
NatWest	5	4	1	135	72 *	45.00	-	1	2	-	47	6	148	6	24.66	3-21	-	
B & H	4	4	0	90	44	22.50	-	-	1	-	33	2	182	2	91.00	1-33	-	
Sunday	17	16	3	373	97 *	28.69	-	1	7	-	92.5	3	460	13	35.38	4-41	-	

Career Performances

	M	Inns	NO	Runs	HS	Avge	100s	50s	Ct	St	Balls	Runs	Wkts	Avge	Best	5wI	10wM
Test	15	25	1	374	98	15.58	-	2	6	-	2000	1064	21	50.66	3-88	-	-
All First	261	394	58	10068	134	29.96	12	62	126	-	27091	14350	439	32.68	7-46	12	-
1-day Int	23	19	2	327	50 *	19.23	-	1	6	-	1038	805	17	47.35	3-38	-	
NatWest	32	28	8	845	101	42.25	1	4	8	-	1345	860	27	31.85	3-21	-	
B & H	44	38	5	701	97	21.24	-	1	9	-	2020	1258	47	26.76	4-29	-	
Sunday	141	129	27	3048	121	29.88	2	13	32	-	4136	3283	103	31.87	4-30	-	

CARR, J. D.   Middlesex

Name: John Donald Carr
Role: Right-hand bat, right-arm medium bowler
Born: 15 June 1963, St.Johns Wood
Height: 6ft **Weight:** 12st
Nickname: Carsy, Batesie, Gold
County debut: 1983
County cap: 1987
1000 runs in a season: 2
1st-Class 50s scored: 33
1st-Class 100s scored: 12
1st-Class 5 w. in innings: 3

1st-Class catches: 123
One-day 50s: 13
One-day 100s: 1
Place in batting averages: 72nd av. 38.37
Strike rate: (103.46)
Parents: Donald and Stella
Wife and date of marriage: Vicky,
5 May 1990
Family links with cricket: Father played
for Derbyshire and England and is
now the secretary of the TCCB.
Uncle, Major Douglas Carr was
secretary of Derbyshire CCC
Education: The Hall, Hampstead;
Repton School; Worcester College, Oxford
Qualifications: Degree in philosophy,
politics and economics.
Senior coaching certificate
Career outside cricket: One year
with Barclays Bank
Overseas tours: Oxbridge tour to Australia and Hong Kong 1985-86; Troubadours tour
to Argentina and Brazil 1990
Overseas teams played for: Sydney University 1986; Weston Creek, Canberra 1988;
Argentina Colts XI 1989-90
Cricketers particularly admired: Richard Hadlee, Imran Khan, Malcolm Marshall
Relaxations: Watching and playing a variety of sports – Eton fives, real tennis, golf,
squash, football – good food and the cinema
Opinions on cricket: 'The Sunday League should be 25 overs per side. The all-action
game would appeal to a wider audience and attract more youngsters to play the game. One
day cricket is in danger of becoming stale with little variety provided by the current 60, 55
and 50-over competitions.'
Extras: Oxford University blue in three sports. Retired from first-class cricket at the end
of 1990 season and played for Hertfordshire in 1991. Returned to full time cricket in 1992
Best batting: 156 Middlesex v Essex, Lord's 1987
Best bowling: 6-61 Middlesex v Gloucestershire, Lord's 1985

1992 Season

	M	Inns	NO	Runs	HS	Avge	100s	50s	Ct	St	O	M	Runs	Wkts	Avge	Best	5wI	10wM
Test																		
All First	25	39	7	1228	114	38.37	2	8	41	-	53	18	124	5	24.80	1-9	-	-
1-day Int																		
NatWest	2	2	0	60	45	30.00	-	-	1	-	7	2	13	0	-		-	-
B & H	6	5	0	174	70	34.80	-	1	5	-	30	3	103	4	25.75	3-25	-	
Sunday	17	13	5	497	104 *	62.12	1	4	9	-	58	1	295	11	26.81	3-42	-	

Career Performances

	M	Inns	NO	Runs	HS	Avge	100s	50s	Ct	St	Balls	Runs	Wkts	Avge	Best	5wI	10wM
Test																	
All First	138	223	28	6623	156	33.96	12	33	123	-	6622	2866	64	44.78	6-61	3	-
1-day Int																	
NatWest	14	14	0	322	83	23.00	-	1	4	-	204	93	4	23.25	2-19	-	
B & H	25	24	1	688	70	29.91	-	5	11	-	752	466	12	38.83	3-22	-	
Sunday	71	62	11	1518	104 *	29.76	1	7	30	-	1002	785	28	28.03	4-21	-	

CARRICK, P. Yorkshire

Name: Phillip Carrick
Role: Right-hand bat, slow left-arm bowler
Born: 16 July 1952, Leeds
Height: 6ft **Weight:** 14st
Nickname: Fergus
County debut: 1970
County cap: 1976
Benefit: 1985
50 wickets in a season: 11
1st-Class 50s scored: 41
1st-Class 100s scored: 3
1st-Class 5 w. in innings: 47
1st-Class 10 w. in match: 5
1st-Class catches: 196
One-Day 50s: 2
Place in batting averages:
235th av 13.05 (1991 126th av 28.78)
Place in bowling averages:
43rd av. 29.25 (1991 40th av. 28.65)
Strike rate: 80.44 (career 72.20)
Parents: Arthur and Ivy (deceased)

Wife and date of marriage: Elspeth, 2 April 1977
Children: Emma Elizabeth, 6 May 1980; Philippa Louise, 11 January 1982
Family links with cricket: Father and brother played league cricket
Education: Bramley CS; Intake CS; Park Lane College of Further Education
Qualifications: 2 O-levels, 8 CSEs, senior cricket coach
Career outside cricket: Runs Phil Carrick Sports and Promotions
Off-season: Working and playing golf
Overseas tours: Derrick Robins XI to South Africa 1976, to Far East 1977; MCC to Namibia 1991
Overseas teams played for: Eastern Province 1976-77; Northern Transvaal 1982-83

Cricketers particularly admired: Graeme Pollock, Gary Sobers, Malcolm Marshall
Other sports followed: Rugby League and golf
Injuries: 'Old age!'
Relaxations: Golf, rugby league. 'Watching my daughters with their ponies.'
Extras: Yorkshire captain 1987-1989. Won B & H Cup in first season. During 1992, was playing in a Yorks team where, often, over half were not even born when he first played for Yorks
Opinions on cricket: 'Lets hope the four-day system gets rid of contrived cricket.'
Best batting: 131* Yorkshire v Northamptonshire, Northampton 1980
Best bowling: 8-33 Yorkshire v Cambridge University, Fenner's 1973

1992 Season

	M	Inns	NO	Runs	HS	Avge	100s	50s	Ct	St	O	M	Runs	Wkts	Avge	Best	5wI	10wM
Test																		
All First	19	25	5	261	46	13.05	-	-	6	-	630.1	202	1375	47	29.25	6-58	1	-
1-day Int																		
NatWest	2	1	0	0	0	0.00	-	-	-	-	24	5	65	1	65.00	1-20	-	
B & H	4	4	2	34	18	17.00	-	-	1	-	44	3	112	2	56.00	1-28	-	
Sunday	11	6	2	26	11	6.50	-	-	5	-	85	2	408	11	37.09	2-17	-	

Career Performances

	M	Inns	NO	Runs	HS	Avge	100s	50s	Ct	St	Balls	Runs	Wkts	Avge	Best	5wI	10wM
Test																	
All First	441	568	102	10255	131 *	22.00	3	41	196	-	77839	32115	1078	29.79	8-33	47	5
1-day Int																	
NatWest	32	23	3	320	54	16.00	-	1	6	-	1662	741	24	30.87	3-8	-	
B & H	60	38	7	340	53	10.96	-	1	9	-	2979	1590	42	37.85	3-22	-	
Sunday	210	143	42	1481	48 *	14.66	-	-	54	-	6702	5030	170	29.58	5-22	2	

45. Who was Geoff Boycott's opening partner in his first Test?

46. Who was John Edrich's opening partner in his first Test?

CHAPMAN, C. A.   Yorkshire

Name: Colin Anthony Chapman
Role: Right-hand bat, wicket-keeper
Born: 8 June 1971, Bradford
Height: 5ft 8in **Weight:** 11st 7lbs
Nickname: Humpy, Turtle, Chappy
County debut: 1990
1st-Class catches: 3
Parents: Mick and Joyce
Marital status: Single
Education: Nabwood Middle;
Beckfoot Grammar; Bradford & Ilkley
Community College
Qualifications: 5 O-levels, BTEC
Diploma in Graphic Design,
coaching certificate
Career outside cricket: Working in
graphics
Overseas teams played for: Waitamata,
Auckland 1989-91
Cricketers particularly admired: Phil Carrick, Alan Knott
Other sports followed: 'Anything slightly interesting.'
Relaxations: 'Spending a few hours at the pub.'
Best batting: 20 Yorkshire v Middlesex, Uxbridge 1990

1992 Season

	M	Inns	NO	Runs	HS	Avge	100s	50s	Ct	St	O	M	Runs	Wkts	Avge	Best	5wI	10wM
Test																		
All First	1	1	1	8	8 *	-	-	-	1	-								
1-day Int																		
NatWest																		
B & H																		
Sunday	1	1	0	13	13	13.00	-	-	-	-								

Career Performances

	M	Inns	NO	Runs	HS	Avge	100s	50s	Ct	St	Balls	Runs	Wkts	Avge	Best	5wI	10wM
Test																	
All First	3	5	1	55	20	13.75	-	-	3	-							
1-day Int																	
NatWest																	
B & H																	
Sunday	5	4	1	52	36 *	17.33	-	-	1	-							

CHAPMAN, R. J.   Nottinghamshire

Name: Robert James Chapman
Role: Right-hand bat, right-arm
fast-medium bowler
Born: 28 July 1972, Nottingham
Height: 6ft 1in **Weight:** 13st 5lbs
Nickname: Bob, Bobby, Chappers
County debut: 1992
Parents: Robert Dennis and Hazel Janice
Marital status: Single
Education: Farnborough School, Clifton,
Nottingham; South Notts College of
Further Education, West Bridgeford
Qualifications: 7 O-Levels
Career outside cricket: 'Hopefully
civil engineering'
Off season: Coaching at Trent Bridge
with David Pennett and Richard Bates
Cricketers particularly admired:
Ian Botham, Dermot Reeve, Allan Donald,
Andy Walters (Notts CA)
Other sports followed: Football, golf
Injuries: Sore shins; off cricket for ten days
Relaxations: Reading and listening to music, particularly The Cure and U2
Opinions on cricket: 'Better venues for 2nd XI Cricket.'
Best bowling: 1-38 Nottinghamshire v Warwickshire, Edgbaston 1992

1992 Season

	M	Inns	NO	Runs	HS	Avge	100s	50s	Ct	St	O	M	Runs	Wkts	Avge	Best	5wI	10wM
Test																		
All First	1	0	0	0	0	-	-	-	-	-	13	1	77	2	38.50	1-38	-	-
1-day Int																		
NatWest																			
B & H																			
Sunday																			

47.   Who was Len Hutton's opening partner in his first Test?

Career Performances

	M	Inns	NO	Runs	HS	Avge	100s	50s	Ct	St	Balls	Runs	Wkts	Avge	Best	5wI	10wM
Test																	
All First	1	0	0	0	0	-	-	-	-	-	78	77	2	38.50	1-38	-	-
1-day Int																	
NatWest																	
B & H																	
Sunday																	

CHAPPLE, G. Lancashire

Name: Glen Chapple
Role: Right-hand bat, right-arm
medium bowler
Born: 23 January 1974, Skipton, Yorkshire
Height: 6ft 2in **Weight:** 12st 7lbs
Nickname: Chappy, Boris, Greg
County debut: 1992
Strike rate: 58.00 (career 58.00)
Parents: Eileen and Michael
Marital Status: Single
Family links with cricket: Father
played in Lancs League for Nelson and
was a professional for Darwen and Earby
Education: West Craven High
School; Nelson and Colne College
Qualifications: 8 GCSEs, 2 A-Levels in
Geography and Economics
Off-season: Touring India with
Young England

Overseas tours: England U18 to Canada 1991; England U19 to New Zealand 1991, to
Pakistan 1992
Cricketers particularly admired: Dennis Lillee, Robin Smith
Other sports followed: Football (Liverpool), golf
Relaxations: 'Watching films, cinema, music, socialising.'
Best batting: 18 Lancashire v Sussex, Hove 1992
Best bowling: 3-40 Lancashire v Warwickshire, Edgbaston 1992

---

48.   Who was Jack Hobbs's opening partner in his first Test?

1992 Season

	M	Inns	NO	Runs	HS	Avge	100s	50s	Ct	St	O	M	Runs	Wkts	Avge	Best	5wI	10wM
Test																		
All First	2	2	1	19	18	19.00	-	-	-	-	48	17	128	5	25.60	3-40	-	-
1-day Int																		
NatWest																		
B & H																		
Sunday																		

Career Performances

	M	Inns	NO	Runs	HS	Avge	100s	50s	Ct	St	Balls	Runs	Wkts	Avge	Best	5wI	10wM
Test																	
All First	2	2	1	19	18	19.00	-	-	-	-	288	128	5	25.60	3-40	-	-
1-day Int																	
NatWest																	
B & H																	
Sunday																	

CHILDS, J. H. — Essex

Name: John Henry Childs
Role: Left-hand bat, slow left-arm bowler
Born: 15 August 1951, Plymouth
Height: 6ft **Weight:** 12st 6lbs
Nickname: Charlie
County debut: 1975 (Gloucs), 1985 (Essex)
County cap: 1977 (Gloucs), 1986 (Essex)
Testimonial: 1985
Test debut: 1988
Tests: 2
50 wickets in a season: 7
1st-Class 5 w. in innings: 45
1st-Class 10 w. in match: 8
1st-Class catches: 103
Place in batting averages: 240th av. 12.22
(1991 225th av. 15.00)
Place in bowling averages: 31st av. 27.19
(1991 45th av. 29.33)
Strike rate: 61.28 (career 69.35)
Parents: Sydney and Barbara (both deceased)
Wife and date of marriage: Jane Anne, 11 November 1978
Children: Lee Robert, 28 November 1980; Scott Alexander, 21 August 1984

Education: Audley Park Secondary Modern, Torquay
Qualifications: Advanced cricket coach
Off-season: Working for Essex CCC marketing department
Cricketers particularly admired: Gary Sobers, Mike Procter
Relaxations: 'Watching rugby, decorating at home, walking on moors and beaches, enjoying my family.'
Extras: Played for Devon 1973-74. Released by Gloucestershire at end of 1984 and joined Essex. One of *Wisden's* Five Cricketers of the Year, 1986. Selected for England's cancelled tour to India 1988-89. Essex Player of the Year 1992
Best batting: 43 Essex v Hampshire, Chelmsford 1992
Best bowling: 9-56 Gloucestershire v Somerset, Bristol 1981

1992 Season

	M	Inns	NO	Runs	HS	Avge	100s	50s	Ct	St	O	M	Runs	Wkts	Avge	Best	5wI	10wM
Test																		
All First	22	17	8	110	43	12.22	-	-	5	-	684.2	205	1822	67	27.19	6-82	3	-
1-day Int																		
NatWest	1	1	1	13	13 *	-	-	-	-	-	12	1	51	0	-			
B & H																		
Sunday	4	1	0	1	1	1.00	-	-	2	-	23	1	132	2	66.00	2-30	-	

Career Performances

	M	Inns	NO	Runs	HS	Avge	100s	50s	Ct	St	Balls	Runs	Wkts	Avge	Best	5wI	10wM
Test	2	4	4	2	2 *	-	-	-	1	-	516	183	3	61.00	1-13	-	-
All First	326	290	136	1391	43	9.03	-	-	103	-	58256	25095	840	29.87	9-56	45	8
1-day Int																	
NatWest	10	5	4	35	14 *	35.00	-	-	-	-	646	378	10	37.80	2-15	-	
B & H	23	7	5	25	10	12.50	-	-	6	-	1272	688	21	32.76	3-36	-	
Sunday	78	28	16	104	16 *	8.66	-	-	13	-	2941	2243	56	40.05	4-15	-	

49.   Who was Chris Smith's opening partner in his first Test?

COBB, R. A.

Leicestershire

Name: Russell Alan Cobb
Role: Right-hand bat, slow left-arm bowler
Born: 18 May 1961, Leicester
Height: 5ft 11in **Weight:** 12st
Nickname: Cobby
County debut: 1980
County cap: 1986
Test debut: 1988
Tests: 2
1000 runs in a season: 1
1st-Class 50s scored: 22
One-Day 50s: 1
1st-Class catches: 65
Parents: Alan and Betty
Wife and date of marriage: Sharon,
30 March 1985
Family links with cricket: Father was a
club cricketer, godfather, Maurice Hallam,
was captain of Leicestershire
Education: Woodbank School, Leicester; Trent College, Nottingham
Qualifications: 7 O-levels, NCA Advanced Coaching Certificate
Overseas tours: Young England to Australia 1979, to West Indies 1980; Leicestershire
to Zimbabwe 1981, to Holland 1988
Overseas teams played for: Glenelg, Adelaide 1980-81; Teachers Training College,
Pretoria 1983-85; Natal B 1988-89
Cricketers particularly admired: 'All who have played top-class cricket for a number
of years.'
Other sports followed: Most sports, especially rugby
Relaxations: Gardening, walking, eating out and flying (has private pilot's licence)
Best batting: 91 Leicestershire v Northamptonshire, Leicester 1986

1992 Season (did not make any first-class or one-day appearance)

Career Performances

	M	Inns	NO	Runs	HS	Avge	100s	50s	Ct	St	Balls	Runs	Wkts	Avge	Best	5wI	10wM
Test																	
All First	122	195	15	4388	91	24.37	-	23	72	-	90	49	0	-	-	-	-
1-day Int																	
NatWest	8	8	1	182	66 *	26.00	-	1	4	-							
B & H	2	2	-	26	22	13.00	-	-	-	-							
Sunday	16	6	4	60	24	30.00	-	-	2	-							

CONNOR, C. A. Hampshire

Name: Cardigan Adolphus Connor
Role: Right-hand bat, right-arm
fast-medium bowler
Born: 24 March 1961, Anguilla
Height: 5ft 10in **Weight:** 11st 4lbs
Nickname: Cardi, CC
County debut: 1984
County cap: 1988
50 wickets in a season: 3
1st-Class 50s scored: 1
1st-Class 5 w. in innings: 10
1st-Class 10 w. in match: 1
1st-Class catches: 47
Place in batting averages: 222nd av. 15.87
Place in bowling averages: 120th av. 43.31
(1991 108th av. 38.41)
Strike rate: 78.25 (career 63.78)
Parents: Ethleen Snagg
Marital status: Single
Education: The Valley Secondary School, Anguilla; Langley College
Qualifications: Engineer
Cricketers particularly admired: Viv Richards, Richard Hadlee
Other sports followed: American football, athletics and most others
Relaxations: Keeping fit and playing golf
Extras: Played for Buckinghamshire in Minor Counties before joining Hampshire. First
Anguillan-born player to appear in the County Championship
Best batting: 51 Hampshire v Yorkshire, Headingley 1992
Best bowling: 7-31 Hampshire v Gloucestershire, Portsmouth 1989

1992 Season

	M	Inns	NO	Runs	HS	Avge	100s	50s	Ct	St	O	M	Runs	Wkts	Avge	Best	5wI	10wM
Test																		
All First	16	13	5	127	51	15.87	-	1	5	-	417.2	69	1386	32	43.31	5-58	1	-
1-day Int																		
NatWest	2	0	0	0	0	-	-	-	1	-	23.1	5	66	6	11.00	3-29	-	
B & H	7	1	0	0	0	0.00	-	-	1	-	67.4	13	215	12	17.91	4-32	-	
Sunday	16	6	0	16	7	2.66	-	-	5	-	119.1	6	514	14	36.71	3-30	-	

Career Performances

	M	Inns	NO	Runs	HS	Avge	100s	50s	Ct	St	Balls	Runs	Wkts	Avge	Best	5wI	10wM
Test																	
All First	160	129	38	889	51	9.76	-	1	47	-	25834	13326	405	32.90	7-31	10	1
1-day Int																	
NatWest	24	4	2	28	13	14.00	-	-	8	-	1547	948	47	20.17	4-29	-	
B & H	39	9	4	19	5 *	3.80	-	-	8	-	2246	1467	64	22.92	4-19	-	
Sunday	127	31	12	136	19	7.15	-	-	24	-	5489	4031	154	26.17	4-11	-	

COOK, G. Durham

Name: Geoffrey Cook
Role: Right-hand bat, slow left-arm bowler
Born: 9 October 1951, Middlesbrough
Height: 6ft **Weight:** 12st 10lbs
Nickname: Geoff
County debut: 1971 (Northamptonshire), 1992 (Durham – one-day)
County cap: 1975 (Northamptonshire)
Benefit: 1985
Test debut: 1981-82
Tests: 7
One-Day Internationals: 6
1000 runs in a season: 12
1st-Class 50s scored: 112
1st-Class 100s scored: 37
1st-Class 200s scored: 1
1st-Class catches: 419
1st-Class stumpings: 3
One-Day 50s: 51
One-Day 100s: 4
Parents: Harry and Helen
Wife and date of marriage: Judith, 22 November 1975
Children: Anna, 21 May 1980
Family links with cricket: Father and brother David very keen club cricketers. Father very involved in running cricket in Middlesbrough
Education: Middlesbrough High School
Qualifications: 6 O-levels, 1 A-level
Off-season: Continuing to work on the development of Durham CCC
Overseas tours: England to India and Sri Lanka 1981-82, to Australia 1982-83
Overseas teams played for: Eastern Province 1978-81
Cricketers particularly admired: Clive Rice

Relaxations: Walking, reading, crosswords
Extras: 'Great believer in organised recreation for young people. Would enjoy time and scope to carry my beliefs through.' Northants captain from 1981 to 1988. Secretary of Cricketers' Association. Retired at end of 1990 season and worked on the promotion of Durham's claim to first-class status. Subsequently appointed the county's Director of Cricket.
Best batting: 203 Northamptonshire v Yorkshire, Scarborough 1988
Best bowling: 3-47 England XI v South Australia, Adelaide 1982-83

1992 Season

	M	Inns	NO	Runs	HS	Avge	100s	50s	Ct	St	O	M	Runs	Wkts	Avge	Best	5wl	10wM
Test																		
All First																		
1-day Int																		
NatWest	1	1	0	16	16	16.00	-	-	1	-								
B & H																		
Sunday	2	2	0	63	49	31.50	-	-	-	-								

Career Performances

	M	Inns	NO	Runs	HS	Avge	100s	50s	Ct	St	Balls	Runs	Wkts	Avge	Best	5wl	10wM
Test	7	13	0	203	66	15.61	-	2	9	-	42	27	0	-		-	-
All First	460	793	65	23277	203	31.97	37	112	419	3	1238	806	15	53.73	3-47	-	-
1-day Int	6	6	0	106	32	17.66	-	-	2	-							
NatWest	44	44	2	1549	130	36.88	3	11	25	-							
B & H	78	71	6	1915	108	29.46	1	11	30	-							
Sunday	240	223	20	4846	98	23.87	-	29	94	-	12	10	0	-		-	-

COOK, N. G. B.   Northamptonshire

Name: Nicholas Grant Billson Cook
Role: Right-hand bat, slow left-arm bowler
Born: 17 June 1956, Leicester
Height: 6ft **Weight:** 12st 8lbs
Nickname: Beast, Strop
County debut: 1978 (Leics), 1986 (Northants)
County cap: 1982 (Leics), 1987 (Northants)
Test debut: 1983
Tests: 15
One-Day Internationals: 3
50 wickets in a season: 8
1st-Class 50s scored: 4
1st-Class 5 w. in innings: 31

1st-Class 10 w. in match: 4
1st-Class catches: 191
Place in batting averages:
(1991 250th av. 11.40)
Place in bowling averages:
15th av. 24.71 (1991 93rd av. 35.50)
Strike rate: 51.34 (career 72.09)
Parents: Peter and Cynthia
Wife and date of marriage: Shân,
20th September 1991
Family links with cricket:
Father played club cricket
Education: Stokes Croft Junior;
Lutterworth High; Lutterworth Upper
Qualifications: 7 O-levels, 1 A-level,
advanced cricket coach
Off-season: 'Looking for work yet again.'
Overseas tours: England to New Zealand
and Pakistan 1983-84, to Pakistan 1987-88,

to India (Nehru Trophy) 1989-90; English Counties XI to Zimbabwe 1984-85; England B
to Sri Lanka 1985-86
Cricketers particularly admired: John Emburey, Phil Carrick
Other sports followed: Soccer (especially Leicester City), rugby, horse racing
Injuries: Calf injury in April; pulled hamstring in May – 'or as my wife says "total body
failure"'
Relaxations: Crosswords, reading (especially Wilbur Smith), good comedy programmes,
good food
Extras: Played for ESCA 1975. Played for Young England v Young West Indies 1975.
Left Leicestershire to join Northamptonshire in 1986
Opinions on cricket: '17 x 50-over Sunday games, starting at 12.00 are a joke – nobody
will turn up at the start and players will be knackered!! Does nobody in authority listen to
what the players think? The whole Sunday League could be de-valued with sides playing
2nd XIs to save players for important Championship matches.'
Best batting: 75 Leicestershire v Somerset, Taunton 1980
Best bowling: 7-34 Leicestershire v Essex, Chelmsford 1992

1992 Season

	M	Inns	NO	Runs	HS	Avge	100s	50s	Ct	St	O	M	Runs	Wkts	Avge	Best	5wI	10wM
Test																		
All First	17	11	6	118	37	23.60	-	-	3	-	325.1	90	939	38	24.71	7-34	1	1
1-day Int																		
NatWest	3	0	0	0	0	-	-	-	1	-	28	0	98	1	98.00	1-45	-	
B & H	1	0	0	0	0	-	-	-	-	-	11	0	49	0	-	-	-	
Sunday	9	5	2	16	11	5.33	-	-	4	-	60	2	284	13	21.84	2-20	-	

Career Performances

	M	Inns	NO	Runs	HS	Avge	100s	50s	Ct	St	Balls	Runs	Wkts	Avge	Best	5wl	10wM
Test	15	25	4	179	31	8.52	-	-	5	-	4172	1689	52	32.48	6-65	4	1
All First	337	344	94	2989	75	11.95	-	4	191	-	61569	24380	854	28.54	7-34	31	4
1-day Int	3	0	0	0	0	-	-	-	2	-	144	95	5	19.00	2-18	-	
NatWest	22	7	2	42	13	8.40	-	-	8	-	1480	824	23	35.82	4-24	-	
B & H	34	15	5	128	23	12.80	-	-	10	-	1771	1061	21	50.52	3-35	-	
Sunday	109	45	21	224	17 *	9.33	-	-	36	-	4145	3110	102	30.49	3-20	-	

COOPER, K. E.   Nottinghamshire

Name: Kevin Edwin Cooper
Role: Left-hand bat, right-arm
fast-medium bowler
Born: 27 December 1957,
Sutton-in-Ashfield
Height: 6ft **Weight:** 12st 4lbs
Nickname: Henry
County debut: 1976
County cap: 1980
Benefit: 1990
50 wickets in a season: 8
1st-Class 5 w. in innings: 25
1st-Class 10 w. in match: 1
1st-Class catches: 85
Place in batting averages:
(1991 266th av. 11.35)
Strike rate: (career 60.46)
Parents: Gerald Edwin and Margaret
Wife and date of marriage: Linda Carol,
14 February 1981

Children: Kelly Louise, 8 April 1982; Tara Amy, 22 November 1984
Family links with cricket: Father played local cricket
Cricketers particularly admired: John Snow
Injuries: Missed most of 1991 season with double stress fracture of 4th vertebra, had bone graft and operation to insert two screws into fractures
Relaxations: Golf, clay pigeon shooting
Extras: In 1974 took 10-6 in one innings for Hucknall Ramblers against Sutton College in the Mansfield and District League. First bowler to 50 first-class wickets in 1988 season. Released by Notts at end of 1992 season
Best batting: 46 Nottinghamshire v Middlesex, Trent Bridge 1985
Best bowling: 8-44 Nottinghamshire v Middlesex, Lord's 1984

1992 Season

	M	Inns	NO	Runs	HS	Avge	100s	50s	Ct	St	O	M	Runs	Wkts	Avge	Best	5wI	10wM
Test																		
All First	2	2	0	2	2	1.00	-	-	-	-	38	15	63	6	10.50	4-41	-	-
1-day Int																		
NatWest																		
B & H																		
Sunday	2	2	1	2	1*	2.00	-	-	1	-	14	0	74	0	-		-	-

Career Performances

	M	Inns	NO	Runs	HS	Avge	100s	50s	Ct	St	Balls	Runs	Wkts	Avge	Best	5wI	10wM
Test																	
All First	273	281	67	2141	46	10.00	-	-	85	-	42994	19332	711	27.19	8-44	25	1
1-day Int																	
NatWest	23	8	1	45	11	6.42	-	-	6	-	1568	717	34	21.08	4-49	-	
B & H	63	22	13	118	25*	13.11	-	-	12	-	3667	2035	71	28.66	4-9	-	
Sunday	159	56	19	242	31	6.54	-	-	27	-	6706	4887	136	35.93	4-25	-	

CORDINGLEY, G. J.　　　　　Lancashire

Name: Gareth John Cordingley
Role: Right-hand bat, right-arm medium bowler
Born: 23 January 1973, Blackburn
Height: 5ft 10in **Weight:** 12st 12lbs
Nickname: Corders, GC
County debut: No first team appearance
Parents: Ian and Marjorie
Marital status: Single
Education: Queen Elizabeth's GS, Blackburn; Trinity and All Saints College, Leeds (affiliated to Leeds University)
Qualifications: 9 GCSEs, 4 A-Levels
career outside cricket: Student
Off-season: Studying for a degree at Trinity and All Saints College, Leeds in Geography and Business management and administration
Cricketers particularly admired:
Ian Botham, Viv Richards, Richie Richardson
Other sports followed: Football (Blackburn Rovers) and rugby league
Relaxations: Playing squash, listening to music, watching sports

CORK, D. G.   Derbyshire

Name: Dominic Gerald Cork
Role: Right-hand bat, right-arm
fast-medium bowler,
cover fielder
Born: 7 August 1971,
Newcastle-under-Lyme, Staffordshire
Height: 6ft 3in **Weight:** 13st
Nickname: Corky, Snafflers,
Son of Base, Spasm, Golden, AYM
County debut: 1990
One-Day Internationals: 1
50 wickets in a season: 1
1st-Class 50s scored: 3
1st-Class 5 w. in innings: 3
1st-Class 10 w. in match: 1
1st-Class catches: 23
Place in batting averages:
123rd av. 30.42 (1991 188th av. 21.15)
Place in bowling averages:
39th av. 28.45 (1991 27th av. 25.61)

Strike rate: 56.33 (career 54.84)
Parents: Gerald ('line and width') and Mary
Marital status: Engaged
Family links with cricket: Father and two brothers, Simon and Jonathan, all play in North Staffs and South Cheshire League. All four played for Betley at same time and mother made the teas
Education: St Joseph's College, Stoke-on-Trent; Newcastle College
Qualifications: History O-Level, leisure and recreation qualified coach
Career outside cricket: 'None at the moment but would like to become a sports physiotherapist. However, receiving treatment is as far as I've got yet.'
Off-season: 'Resting after a long and hard season and then training for the England A team tour to Australia.'
Overseas tours: England YCs to Australia 1989-90; England A to Bermuda and West Indies 1991-92, to Australia 1992-93
Overseas teams played for: East Shirley CC 1990-91, Christchurch, New Zealand
Cricketers particularly admired: Richard Hadlee, Ian Botham, Kim Barnett, Phil Russell, Alan Warner ('keeps going'), Simon Base ('mental attitude')
Other sports followed: Football, horse racing and greyhounds
Injuries: Groin tear, out for two and a half weeks; concussion, out for one and a half weeks
Relaxations: Listening to music, especially Simply Red, driving 'and, most of all, eating steaks'.
Extras: Scored a century as nightwatchman for England U19 in the third match v Pakistan

at Taunton. Took a wicket in first over in first-class cricket v New Zealand at Derby. First played cricket for Betley CC in the North Staffordshire and South Cheshire League. Played Minor Counties cricket for Staffordshire in 1989 and 1990. Played for England A in 1991–his first season of first-class cricket. The Cricket Association Young Player of 1991. 'Of all the players I've seen in my career, he has the opportunity to go furthest' – Kim Barnett
Opinions on cricket: 'The new format of 17 four-day games will be very taxing on all players involved, and with the Sunday League being increased too I feel that more injuries will start appearing. Apart from that I'm glad the TCCB have started putting more relevance on four-day cricket which will hopefully help future England players.'
Best batting: 72* Derbyshire v Warwickshire, Edgbaston 1992
Best bowling: 8-53 Derbyshire v Essex, Derby 1991

1992 Season

	M	Inns	NO	Runs	HS	Avge	100s	50s	Ct	St	O	M	Runs	Wkts	Avge	Best	5wI	10wM
Test																		
All First	19	21	2	578	72 *	30.42	-	3	12	-	450.4	74	1366	48	28.45	5-36	2	-
1-day Int	1	0	0	0	0	-	-	-	-	-	11	1	37	1	37.00	1-37	-	
NatWest	2	2	0	15	11	7.50	-	-	-	-	21.5	5	54	8	6.75	5-18	1	
B & H	5	4	2	13	8 *	6.50	-	-	3	-	53.2	1	170	4	42.50	4-26	-	
Sunday	13	10	2	56	20	7.00	-	-	2	-	93.5	0	518	14	37.00	3-26	-	

Career Performances

	M	Inns	NO	Runs	HS	Avge	100s	50s	Ct	St	Balls	Runs	Wkts	Avge	Best	5wI	10wM
Test																	
All First	42	56	12	1022	72 *	23.22	-	3	23	-	6307	3135	115	27.26	8-53	3	1
1-day Int	1	0	0	0	0	-	-	-	-	-	66	37	1	37.00	1-37	-	
NatWest	2	2	0	15	11	7.50	-	-	-	-	131	54	8	6.75	5-18	1	
B & H	5	4	2	13	8 *	6.50	-	-	3	-	320	170	4	42.50	4-26	-	
Sunday	22	15	2	139	30	10.69	-	-	6	-	935	809	25	32.36	3-26	-	

50. Who is currently the most capped player in Test history?

51. Which current county player is a regular Sunday morning soccer referee?

COTTAM, A. C.

Name: Andrew Colin Cottam
Role: Right-hand bat, slow left-arm bowler
Born: 14 July 1973, Northampton
Height: 6ft 1in **Weight:** 11st
Nickname: Worm, Cotts, Dogers
County debut: 1992
Parents: Bob and Jackie
Marital status: single
Family links with cricket: Father played
for Hampshire, Northants and England.
Brothers, Michael and David, played
for Devon
Education: Seaton Primary School;
Axminster Secondary School
Qualifications: Qualified cricket coach
Career outside cricket: Builder's labourer
Off-season: Coaching and playing in
Australia
Overseas tours: England U18 to Canada;
England U19 to Pakistan
Other sports followed: Football (Tottenham Hotspur)
Injuries: Split webbing in little finger; knee operation in September
Relaxations: Listening to music, especially Bob Marley, or watching TV
Extras: Somerset Young Player of the Year 1992
Opinions on cricket: 'Play on uncovered wickets.'
Best batting: 31 Somerset v Gloucestershire, Gloucester 1992
Best bowling: 1-1 Somerset v Gloucestershire, Gloucester 1992

1992 Season

	M	Inns	NO	Runs	HS	Avge	100s	50s	Ct	St	O	M	Runs	Wkts	Avge	Best	5wI	10wM
Test																		
All First	6	8	1	43	31	6.14	-	-	1	-	116.1	25	280	6	46.66	1-1	-	-
1-day Int																		
NatWest																		
B & H	1	0	0	0	0	-	-	-	-	-	7	0	34	0	-		-	-
Sunday																		

---

52. What do Allan Border, Viv Richards, Javed Miandad and Richard Hadlee
have in common?

Career Performances

	M	Inns	NO	Runs	HS	Avge	100s	50s	Ct	St	Balls	Runs	Wkts	Avge	Best	5wI	10wM
Test																	
All First	6	8	1	43	31	6.14	-	-	1	-	697	280	6	46.66	1-1	-	-
1-day Int																	
NatWest																	
B & H	1	0	0	0	0	-	-	-	-	-	42	34	0	-		-	-
Sunday																	

COTTEY, P. A.   Glamorgan

Name: Phillip Anthony Cottey
Role: Right-hand bat
Born: 2 June 1966, Swansea
Height: 5ft 5in **Weight:** 10st 7lbs
Nickname: Cotts, Lofty
County debut: 1986
County cap: 1992
1000 runs in season: 2
1st-Class 50s scored: 21
1st-Class 100s scored: 5
1st-Class catches: 46
One-Day 50s: 4
Place in batting averages: 37th av. 46.78
(1991 173rd av. 23.00)
Parents: Bernard and Ruth
Marital status: 'Getting married to Gail in
October in Antigua'
Family links with cricket: Father played
for Swansea CC
Education: Bishopston Comprehensive School, Swansea
Qualifications: 9 O-levels
Career outside cricket: Works for father in haulage business
Off-season: Working for Porteynon Transport and playing semi-pro soccer
Overseas tours: Glamorgan to La Manga, Barbados, Trinidad, Zimbabwe and Cape Town
1987-92
Overseas teams played for: Penrith, Sydney 1986-88; Benoni, Johannesburg 1989-90;
Eastern Transvaal 1991-92
Cricketers particularly admired: John Steele, Alan Jones
Other sports followed: All sports especially soccer
Injuries: Broke right thumb at Durham and snapped ligament on left-hand; no time off
Relaxations: 'Watching films, training, lager tasting.'

Extras: Left school at 16 to play for Swansea City FC for three years as a professional. Three Welsh Youth caps (one as captain)
Best batting: 156 Glamorgan v Oxford University, The Parks 1990
Best bowling: 2-42 East Transvaal v West Transvaal, Potchefstroom 1991-92

1992 Season

	M	Inns	NO	Runs	HS	Avge	100s	50s	Ct	St	O	M	Runs	Wkts	Avge	Best	5wI	10wM
Test																		
All First	20	28	5	1076	141	46.78	2	6	10	-	7	2	26	0	-		-	-	-
1-day Int																		
NatWest	3	3	0	50	24	16.66	-	-	-	-								
B & H	4	4	1	56	38	18.66	-	-	1	-	1	0	1	0	-		-	-	-
Sunday	14	9	3	104	51 *	17.33	-	1	3	-	12	0	52	2	26.00	2-30	-

Career Performances

	M	Inns	NO	Runs	HS	Avge	100s	50s	Ct	St	Balls		Runs	Wkts	Avge	Best	5wI	10wM
Test																		
All First	88	126	22	3582	156	34.44	5	21	46	-	492		303	6	50.50	2-42	-	-
1-day Int																		
NatWest	7	7	2	92	27	18.40	-	-	1	-								
B & H	11	11	1	163	68	16.30	-	1	2	-	6		1	0	-		-	-
Sunday	41	31	8	573	92 *	24.91	-	3	10	-	72		52	2	26.00	2-30	-

COUSINS, D. M.   Essex

Name: Darren Mark Cousins
Role: Right-hand bat, right-arm
fast-medium bowler, outfielder
Born: 24 September 1971
Height: 6ft 2in **Weight:** 12st 7lbs
Nickname: Mad Dog
County debut: No first team appearance
Parents: Dennis
Marital status: Single
Family links with cricket: Father played for
Cambridgeshire
Education: Netherhall Comprehensive;
Impington Village College
Qualifications: 7 GCSEs
Off-season: Having to rest and recover
after back operation
Cricketers particularly admired:
'Even though I am a bowler I admire

Robin Smith for his sheer brute force and David Gower for his elegance. I also admire all the great fast bowlers (e.g. Dennis Lillee) and at present Allan Donald and Waqar Younis.'

Other sports followed: Sports fanatic, especially football

Injuries: Stress fracture of the back, injured during the first week of the season and did not play a single game

Relaxations: Going out to pubs and clubs with friends and girlfriend. Watching TV and listening to music

Extras: Represented Cambridgeshire at football and swimming. Played for a Young England side against Australia, taking four wickets in each innings. Played 2nd XI cricket for Northants and Worcs.

Opinions on cricket: 'I haven't been in professional cricket long enough to have any particular opinions. Because I haven't played a game yet I don't really understand the structure of the system etc. but maybe after a full season (hopefully), I will have some relevant opinions.'

COWANS, N. G.   Middlesex

Name: Norman George Cowans
Role: Right-hand bat, right-arm fast bowler
Born: 17 April 1961,
Enfield St Mary, Jamaica
Height: 6ft 3in **Weight:** 14st 7lbs
Nickname: Flash, George, Seed
County debut: 1980
County cap: 1984
Benefit: 1993
Test debut: 1982-83
Tests: 19
One-Day Internationals: 23
50 wickets in a season: 6
1st-Class 50s scored: 1
1st-Class 5 w. in innings: 23
1st-Class 10 w. in match: 1
1st-Class catches: 59
Place in batting averages:
(1991 255th av. 10.33)

Place in bowling averages: (1991 80th av. 34.09)
Strike rate: (career 49.09)
Parents: Gloria and Ivan
Children: Kimberley, 27 December 1983
Education: Park High Secondary, Stanmore, Middlesex
Qualifications: Qualified coach
Overseas tours: England YCs to Australia 1979; England to Australia and New Zealand

1982-83, to New Zealand and Pakistan 1983-84, to India and Australia 1984-85; England B to Sri Lanka 1985-86
Cricketers particularly admired: Viv Richards, Malcolm Marshall
Other sports followed: Football (Arsenal FC), athletics, boxing
Injuries: Groin operation
Relaxations: Fishing, photography, travelling, being with friends, listening to reggae and soul music
Extras: Played for England YC. Won athletics championships in sprinting and javelin throwing and was a squash and real tennis professional. Played thirteen Tests for England before being awarded his Middlesex cap
Best batting: 66 Middlesex v Surrey, Lord's 1984
Best bowling: 6-31 Middlesex v Leicestershire, Leicester 1985

1992 Season

	M	Inns	NO	Runs	HS	Avge	100s	50s	Ct	St	O	M	Runs	Wkts	Avge	Best	5wl	10wM
Test																		
All First	1	0	0	0	0	-	-	-	-	-	7	3	9	0	-	-	-	-
1-day Int																		
NatWest																		
B & H																		
Sunday	1	0	0	0	0	-	-	-	1	-	7	1	44	2	22.00	2-44	-	

Career Performances

	M	Inns	NO	Runs	HS	Avge	100s	50s	Ct	St	Balls	Runs	Wkts	Avge	Best	5wl	10wM
Test	19	29	7	175	36	7.95	-	-	9	-	3452	2003	51	39.27	6-77	2	-
All First	221	228	61	1531	66	9.16	-	1	59	-	30440	15241	620	24.58	6-31	23	1
1-day Int	23	8	3	13	4 *	2.60	-	-	5	-	1282	913	23	39.69	3-44	-	
NatWest	32	12	2	43	12 *	4.30	-	-	9	-	1864	1018	47	21.66	4-24	-	
B & H	32	15	6	50	12	5.55	-	-	6	-	1861	1027	47	21.85	4-33	-	
Sunday	93	31	11	137	27	6.85	-	-	14	-	3943	2686	103	26.07	6-9	1	

COWDREY, C. S.   Glamorgan

Name: Christopher Stuart Cowdrey
Role: Right-hand bat, right-arm medium bowler
Born: 20 October 1957, Farnborough, Kent
Height: 6ft **Weight:** 14st
Nickname: Cow, Woody
County debut: 1977 (Kent), 1992 (Glamorgan)
County cap: 1979 (Kent)
Benefit: 1989 (£146,287)
Test debut: 1984-85

Tests: 6
One-Day Internationals: 3
1000 runs in a season: 4
1st-Class 50s scored: 58
1st-Class 100s scored: 21
1st-Class 5 w. in innings: 2
1st-Class catches: 295
One-Day 50s: 42
One-Day 100s: 2
Strike rate: 72.62
Parents: Michael Colin and Penelope Susan
Wife and date of marriage: Christel,
1 January 1989
Family links with cricket: Grandfather,
Stuart Chiesman, on Kent Committee,
twelve years as Chairman. Pavilion on
Kent's ground at Canterbury named after
him. Father played for Kent and England,
brother Graham made Kent debut 1984

Education: Wellesley House, Broadstairs; Tonbridge School
Career outside cricket: Director of Ten Tenths Travel. Consultant to Stuart Canvas Products
Overseas tours: Captained England YC to West Indies 1976; England to India and Australia 1984-85; unofficial England XI to South Africa 1989-90
Cricketers particularly admired: David Gower
Other sports followed: All sports
Extras: Played for Kent 2nd XI at age 15. County vice-captain 1984 and appointed captain in 1985. Captained England for one Test v West Indies in 1988; injury kept him out of next Test and was not selected again. Banned from Test cricket for joining tour to South Africa in 1989-90, suspension remitted in 1992. Resigned from Kent captaincy at end of 1990 season. David Gower was best man at his wedding. Published autobiography, *Good Enough?*, 1986. Released by Kent at end of 1991 season, joined Glamorgan for 1992 season. Accomplished after-dinner speaker. Released by Glamorgan at end of 1992 season
Best batting: 159 Kent v Surrey, Canterbury 1985
Best bowling: 5-46 Kent v Hampshire, Canterbury 1986

1992 Season

	M	Inns	NO	Runs	HS	Avge	100s	50s	Ct	St	O	M	Runs	Wkts	Avge	Best	5wI	10wM
Test																		
All First	2	1	0	50	50	50.00	-	1	5	-								
1-day Int																		
NatWest	1	1	0	6	6	6.00	-	-	-	-								
B & H	4	4	0	139	78	34.75	-	1	3	-	13	0	74	1	74.00	1-35	-	
Sunday	8	8	1	72	27 *	10.28	-	-	2	-	40.2	1	208	7	29.71	2-20	-	

141

Career Performances

	M	Inns	NO	Runs	HS	Avge	100s	50s	Ct	St	Balls	Runs	Wkts	Avge	Best	5wI	10wM
Test	6	8	1	101	38	14.42	-	-	5	-	399	309	4	77.25	2-65	-	-
All First	299	452	68	12252	159	31.90	21	58	295	-	14524	7962	200	39.81	5-46	2	-
1-day Int	3	3	1	51	46 *	25.50	-	-	-	-	52	55	2	27.50	1-3	-	
NatWest	35	32	6	847	122 *	32.57	1	8	14	-	1026	628	22	28.54	4-36	-	
B & H	74	67	10	1713	114	30.05	1	11	30	-	2164	1564	48	32.58	4-14	-	
Sunday	213	193	30	4175	95	25.61	-	23	61	-	4282	3562	124	28.72	5-28	1	

COWDREY, G. R.   Kent

Name: Graham Robert Cowdrey
Role: Right-hand bat, right-arm
medium bowler,
cover fielder
Born: 27 June 1964, Farnborough, Kent
Height: 5ft 11in **Weight:** 13st 9lbs
Nickname: Van, Mervyn
County debut: 1984
County cap: 1988
1000 runs in season: 3
1st-Class 50s scored: 33
1st-Class 100s scored: 11
1st-Class catches: 66
One-Day 50s: 12
One-Day 100s: 1
Place in batting averages: 20th av. 51.64
(1991 59th av. 39.16)
Parents: Michael Colin and Penelope Susan
Wife and date of marriage: Maxine,
20 February 1993
Family links with cricket: Father (M.C.) and brother (C.S.) played for, and captained,
Kent and England
Education: Wellesley House, Broadstairs; Tonbridge School; Durham University
Qualifications: 8 O-levels, 3 A-levels, qualified electrician, currently completing plumbing
exams
Off-season: Working for London Road of Romford (Mercedes Benz)
Overseas tours: Christians in Sport to India 1986 and 1990; MCC to West Indies 1992
Overseas teams played for: Avendale, Cape Town 1983-84; Mossman, Sydney 1985-86;
Randwick, Sydney 1986-87
Cricketers particularly admired: David Ward, Alan Fordham, Julian Wilson, Jeremy
Cornwallis

Other sports followed: Horse racing, wife Maxine (Juster) is a jockey
Injuries: Bout of conjunctivitis
Relaxations: Reading, theatre, and live music. Has seen Van Morrison 107 times in concert. Voracious reader (favourite authors Brian Moore and Jonathan Smith) and concert goer. Hates pubs
Extras: Played for England YC. Made 1000 runs for Kent 2nd XI first season on staff, and broke 2nd XI record with 1300 runs in 26 innings in 1985. Plays in contact lenses
Opinions on cricket: 'I am amazed the TCCB have changed the structure of the cricket season. The B&H and the Sunday League have been destroyed. Maybe the players themselves should have been more closely involved with the changes.'
Best batting: 147 Kent v Gloucestershire, Bristol 1992
Best bowling: 1-5 Kent v Warwickshire, Edgbaston 1988

1992 Season

	M	Inns	NO	Runs	HS	Avge	100s	50s	Ct	St	O	M	Runs	Wkts	Avge	Best	5wI	10wM
Test																		
All First	21	31	6	1291	147	51.64	3	7	6	-	48	9	213	2	106.50	1-15	-	-
1-day Int																		
NatWest	3	3	0	42	33	14.00	-	-	1	-	3	1	4	2	2.00	2-4	-	
B & H	7	7	0	75	27	10.71	-	-	1	-	3	0	14	0	-	-	-	
Sunday	15	13	1	245	56	20.41	-	2	5	-	4	0	17	0	-	-	-	

Career Performances

	M	Inns	NO	Runs	HS	Avge	100s	50s	Ct	St	Balls	Runs	Wkts	Avge	Best	5wI	10wM
Test																	
All First	124	193	27	6009	147	36.19	11	33	66	-	1087	749	11	68.09	1-5	-	-
1-day Int																	
NatWest	15	12	3	215	37	23.88	-	-	2	-	285	130	8	16.25	2-4	-	
B & H	33	30	3	660	70 *	24.44	-	5	11	-	130	76	2	38.00	1-8	-	
Sunday	94	86	13	1776	102 *	24.32	1	7	33	-	600	458	21	21.81	4-15	-	

---

53. Who holds the record for the most wickets taken in a career in Sheffield Shield cricket?

54. Which Test captain of South Africa was born in Yorkshire?

COX, D. M.   Durham

Name: David Matthew Cox
Role: Left-hand bat, slow left-arm bowler
Born: 2 March 1972, Southall
Height: 5ft 11in **Weight:** 12st 7lbs
Nickname: Coxy, Zico
County debut: No first team appearance
Parents: Charles and Georgina
Marital status: Single
Family links with cricket: Father played
for Guinness Brewery and Old Actonians
Education: Greenford High School
Qualifications: 5 GCSEs
Career outside cricket:
Apprentice plasterer
Off-season: Coaching, plastering and
trying to keep fit
Cricketers particularly admired:
Don Wilson, Clive Radley and
Phil Edmonds
Other sports followed: Football (QPR), snooker and horse racing
Relaxations: 'Going out with my two mates Pete and Paul', playing snooker, golf and
watching TV
Extras: Missed most of the 1991 season with a broken hand. Was on the Lord's staff for
3 years

COX, R. M. F.   Hampshire

Name: Rupert Michael Fiennes Cox
Role: Left-hand bat, off-spin bowler
Born: 20 August 1967, Guildford
Height: 5ft 9in **Weight:** 11st
Nickname: Coxy, Ucca, MC and Nautilus
County debut: 1990
1st-Class 100s scored: 1
1st-Class catches: 5
Parents: Mike and Jo
Marital status: Single
Family links with cricket: Father played for MCC and Hampshire Hogs
Education: Cheam Prep School and Bradfield College
Qualifications: 8 O-levels, 2 A-levels

144

Career outside cricket:
'Anything that transpires'
Off-season: Resting, writing, holidaying, getting fit and playing a little in Cape Town
Overseas teams played for:
Techs-Mutual, Cape Town 1986-92
Cricketers particularly admired:
Geoffrey Boycott, Robin Smith and Malcolm Marshall
Other sports followed: Golf and football
Injuries: Glandular virus – back strain, 'missed three or four games while trying to throw off the virus'
Relaxations: 'Having a laugh, eating out and watching Darren Flint play cricket.'
Extras: Scored century in second first-class match. Wears one contact lens
Opinions on cricket: 'The format for the 1993 season will,

I'm sure be beneficial to the players, in particular the travel should be eased. However, its financial viability is very significant – in this respect I hope four-day cricket succeeds. The new Sunday venture I feel sure will bring a renewed surge of interest, especially with kids, now they can wear their team's strip. '

Best batting: 104* Hampshire v Worcestershire, Worcester 1990

1992 Season

	M	Inns	NO	Runs	HS	Avge	100s	50s	Ct	St	O	M	Runs	Wkts	Avge	Best	5wI	10wM
Test																		
All First	3	3	0	26	13	8.66	-	-	1	-								
1-day Int																		
NatWest																		
B & H																		
Sunday	1	1	0	5	5	5.00	-	-	-	-								

Career Performances

	M	Inns	NO	Runs	HS	Avge	100s	50s	Ct	St	Balls	Runs	Wkts	Avge	Best	5wI	10wM
Test																	
All First	9	12	2	287	104 *	28.70	1	-	5	-	6	1	0	-	-	-	-
1-day Int																	
NatWest																	
B & H																	
Sunday	4	4	1	22	13	7.33	-	-	1	-							

CRAWLEY, J. P.   Lancashire

Name: John Paul Crawley
Role: Right-hand bat,
occasional wicket-keeper
Born: 21 September 1971, Malden, Essex
Height: 6ft 2in **Weight:** 13st 12lbs
Nickname: Creeps, Jonty, JC
County debut: 1990
1000 runs in a season: 1
1st-Class 50s scored: 16
1st-Class 100s scored: 3
1st-Class catches: 14
Place in batting averages: 43rd av. 45.19
(1991 33rd av. 47.16)
Parents: Frank and Jean
Marital status: Single
Family links with cricket: Father played
in Manchester Association; brother Mark
played for Lancashire before moving to
Notts; other brother Peter plays for

Warrington CC and has played for Scottish Universities and Cambridge University; uncle
was excellent fast bowler; godfather umpires in Manchester Association
Education: Manchester Grammar School and Trinity College, Cambridge
Qualifications: 10 O-levels, 3 A-levels, 2 S-levels, qualified cricket coach
Off-season: At Cambridge University
Overseas tours: England U19 to Australia 1989-90, to New Zealand 1990-91
Overseas teams played for: Midland Guildford, Perth 1991
Cricketers particularly admired: Michael Atherton, Neil Fairbrother, Graham Gooch,
Alec Stewart, David Gower, Allan Donald, Ian Salisbury
Other sports followed: Soccer (Man Utd), golf
Injuries: Wisdom teeth operation, missed one game
Relaxations: Golf, soccer, squash, listening to music, dining out
Extras: Captained England U19 to New Zealand 1990-91 and played for England U19 in
three home series v New Zealand 1989, Pakistan 1990 and Australia (as captain) 1991.
Made his maiden first-class century for Cambridge University on the same day that brother
Mark made his for Notts. First to score 1000 runs in U19 Tests
Opinions on cricket: 'I think it's good that the four-day schedule has been introduced, and
that the Sunday League has been commercialised. Hopefully the four-day schedule will cut
down the major problem of county cricket – too much travelling.'
Best batting: 172 Lancashire v Surrey, Lytham 1992
Best bowling: 1-90 Lancashire v Sussex, Hove 1992

1992 Season

	M	Inns	NO	Runs	HS	Avge	100s	50s	Ct	St	O	M	Runs	Wkts	Avge	Best	5wl	10wM
Test																		
All First	17	29	3	1175	172	45.19	2	7	11	-	10	0	90	1	90.00	1-90	-	-
1-day Int																		
NatWest																			
B & H	4	4	0	80	42	20.00	-	-	2	-								
Sunday	2	2	0	14	8	7.00	-	-	-	-								

Career Performances

	M	Inns	NO	Runs	HS	Avge	100s	50s	Ct	St	Balls	Runs	Wkts	Avge	Best	5wl	10wM
Test																	
All First	32	52	6	2127	172	46.23	3	16	25	-	72	104	1	104.00	1-90	-	-
1-day Int																	
NatWest																		
B & H	8	8	0	138	42	17.25	-	-	3	-							
Sunday	2	2	0	14	8	7.00	-	-	-	-							

CRAWLEY, M. A.   Nottinghamshire

Name: Mark Andrew Crawley
Role: Right-hand bat, right-arm medium bowler, slip fielder
Born: 16 December 1967, Newton-le-Willows
Height: 6ft 3½in **Weight:** 13st 8lbs
Nickname: Creeps, Flat-cap-whippet, Perch
County debut: 1990 (Lancashire), 1991 (Nottinghamshire)
1000 runs in a season: 1
1st-Class 50s scored: 13
1st-Class 50s scored: 8
1st-Class catches: 51
One-day 50s: 5
Place in batting averages: 85th av. 37.05 (1991 115th av. 30.22)
Place in bowling averages: 75th av. 34.05 (1991 120th av. 42.09)
Strike rate: 70.00 (career 93.21)
Parents: Frank and Jean
Wife and date of marriage: Natasha, 27 December 1991
Family links with cricket: Father and uncle both excellent league players; brother John

plays for Lancashire; other brother Peter plays for Warrington CC and has played for Scottish Universities and Cambridge University

Education: Manchester Grammar School; Oxford University

Qualifications: 10 O-levels, 3 A-levels, BA (Hons) in Chemistry, Special Diploma in Social Studies

Off-season: Working in Nottingham

Overseas tours: North of England U19 to Bermuda 1985; Young England to Sri Lanka 1987; Oxbridge to Holland 1987

Overseas teams played for: University of New South Wales, Sydney 1990-91

Cricketers particularly admired: Dennis Lillee, Jeff Thomson, David Gower, Jim Robson

Other sports followed: Soccer (Liverpool), golf, American football, rugby

Relaxations: Soccer, golf, squash and playing most sports. Reading, crosswords

Extras: Third Notts player to score a century on his first-class debut. Nottinghamshire Young Player of the Year 1992

Opinions on cricket: 'I welcome the changes for the 1993 season, though why the Sunday League should be 50 instead of 40 overs is hard to understand.'

Best batting: 160* Nottinghamshire v Derbyshire, Derby 1992

Best Bowling 6-92 Oxford University v Glamorgan, The Parks 1990

1992 Season

	M	Inns	NO	Runs	HS	Avge	100s	50s	Ct	St	O	M	Runs	Wkts	Avge	Best	5wl	10wM
Test																		
All First	25	44	9	1297	160*	37.05	4	5	20	-	221.4	56	647	19	34.05	3-18	-	-
1-day Int																		
NatWest	1	1	0	4	4	4.00	-	-	2	-								
B & H	4	4	0	105	57	26.25	-	1	-	-	15	0	52	0	-		-	-
Sunday	11	10	4	213	94*	35.50	-	1	3	-	47.5	0	263	6	43.83	3-41	-	

Career Performances

	M	Inns	NO	Runs	HS	Avge	100s	50s	Ct	St	Balls	Runs	Wkts	Avge	Best	5wl	10wM
Test																	
All First	62	94	19	2900	160*	38.66	8	13	51	-	5313	2682	57	47.05	6-92	1	-
1-day Int																	
NatWest	3	3	2	113	74*	113.00	-	1	2	-	78	29	4	7.25	4-26	-	
B & H	18	17	2	373	58	24.86	-	3	4	-	818	488	7	69.71	2-72	-	
Sunday	21	17	5	287	94*	23.91	-	1	6	-	539	459	14	32.78	3-41	-	

55.   In what year did Mike Gatting lead an unofficial England tour to South Africa?

CROFT, R. D. B.   Glamorgan

Name: Robert Damien Bale Croft
Role: Right-hand bat, off-spinner
Born: 25 May 1970, Swansea
Height: 5ft 11in **Weight:** 11st 5lbs
Nickname: Crofty
County debut: 1989
County cap: 1992
50 wickets in a season: 1
1st-Class 50s scored: 8
1st-Class 5 w. in innings: 5
1st-Class 10 w. in match: 1
1st-Class catches: 28
Place in batting averages: 138th av. 27.08
(1991 226th av. 15.00)
Place in bowling averages: 58th av. 31.64
(1991 136th av. 50.78)
Strike rate: 57.98 (career 81.88)
Parents: Malcolm and Susan
Family links with cricket: Father and
grandfather played local cricket
Education: St John Lloyd Catholic School; Neath Trinity College; West Glamorgan
Institute of Higher Education
Qualifications: 6 O-levels; OND Business Studies; HND Business Studies; NCA senior
coaching certificate
Career outside cricket: Personnel management ('not as yet!')
Overseas tours: England A to Bermuda and West Indies 1991-92
Cricketers particularly admired: Alan Jones, Tom Cartwright, Don Shepherd, John
Steele, John Emburey
Other sports followed: Rugby, soccer
Relaxations: Shooting, fishing, driving, music, golf
Extras: Captained England South to victory in International Youth Tournament 1989; also
voted Player of the Tournament. Glamorgan Young Player of the Year 1992
Opinions on cricket: 'Enjoyment is of the utmost importance.'
Best batting: 91* Glamorgan v Worcestershire, Abergavenny 1990
Best bowling: 8-66 Glamorgan v Warwickshire, Swansea 1992

56.   How many years suspension from playing for England was imposed on
those who toured South Africa unofficially under Mike Gatting?

1992 Season

	M	Inns	NO	Runs	HS	Avge	100s	50s	Ct	St	O	M	Runs	Wkts	Avge	Best	5wI	10wM
Test																		
All First	24	34	10	650	60 *	27.08	-	3	10	-	657.1	124	2152	68	31.64	8-66	5	1
1-day Int																		
NatWest	3	3	1	35	17 *	17.50	-	-	-	-	22	2	78	1	78.00	1-45	-	
B & H	4	4	3	58	30 *	58.00	-	-	5	-	37	7	110	4	27.50	3-28	-	
Sunday	15	9	5	100	31 *	25.00	-	-	2	-	70	4	366	4	91.50	1-26	-	

Career Performances

	M	Inns	NO	Runs	HS	Avge	100s	50s	Ct	St	Balls	Runs	Wkts	Avge	Best	5wI	10wM
Test																	
All First	73	100	27	1902	91 *	26.05	-	8	28	-	11710	6076	143	42.49	8-66	6	1
1-day Int																	
NatWest	6	5	1	74	26	18.50	-	-	-	-	294	168	3	56.00	2-28	-	
B & H	5	5	3	58	30 *	29.00	-	-	5	-	276	159	6	26.50	3-28	-	
Sunday	29	19	6	188	31 *	14.46	-	-	7	-	1008	858	15	57.20	2-30	-	

CUMMINS, A. C.   Durham

Name: Anderson Cleophas Cummins
Role: Right-hand bat, right-arm
fast-medium bowler
Born: 7 April 1966
County debut: No first team appearance
One-Day Internationals: 19
1st-Class catches: 3
Strike rate: (career 50.81)
Career outside cricket: Works in a
bank in Barbados,
and spent summer 1992 working for
Barclays in Solihull
Overseas tours: West Indies to Australia
and New Zealand (World Cup) 1991-92,
to Australia and South Africa 1992-93
Overseas teams played for: Barbados
Extras: Played for Blossomfield CC,
Birmingham, during Summer 1992.
Was centre of public boycott of
historic West Indies v South Africa Test match, when not selected. Signed for Durham in
place of Dean Jones, who was expected to be touring with Australia. Made his Test debut
against Australia on 1992-93 tour

Best batting: 45* Barbados v Leeward Islands, Bridgetown 1991-92
Best bowling: 4-26 Barbados v Leeward Islands, St John's 1990-91

1992 Season (did not make any first-class or one-day appearance)

Career Performances

	M	Inns	NO	Runs	HS	Avge	100s	50s	Ct	St	Balls	Runs	Wkts	Avge	Best	5wI	10wM
Test																	
All First	11	15	3	208	45*	17.33	-	-	3	-	1931	964	38	25.36	4-26	-	-
1-day Int	19	9	4	62	24	12.40	-	-	1	-	1011	690	29	23.79	5-31	1	-
NatWest																	
B & H																	
Sunday																	

CUNLIFFE, R. J.   Gloucestershire

Name: Robert John Cunliffe
Role: Right-hand bat, cover fielder, occasional wicket-keeper
Born: 8 November 1973, Oxford
Height: 5ft 10in **Weight:** 12st 10lbs
Nickname: Arsie, Bertie
County debut: No first team appearance
Parents: Barry and Janet
Marital status: Single
Family links with cricket: 'Dad played in his younger days for his wife's village team and was groundsman for nine years at Banbury Twenty CC.'
Education: Banbury School and Banbury Technical College
Qualifications: 'None (only GCSE in Physical Education)'
Off-season: Hoping to play abroad
Overseas tours: England U19 to India 1993
Cricketers particularly admired: Robin Smith, David Gower, Ian Salisbury, Graham Gooch
Other sports followed: Football, rugby
Relaxations: 'Mainly sports – and seeing girlfriend Fliss!'

151

CURRAN, K. M.   Northamptonshire

Name: Kevin Malcolm Curran
Role: Right-hand bat, right-arm
fast-medium bowler
Born: 7 September 1959, Rusape, Rhodesia
Height: 6ft 2in **Weight:** 14st
Nickname: KC
County debut: 1985 (Gloucs)
1991 (Northamptonshire)
County cap: 1985 (Gloucs),
1992 (Northamptonshire)
One-Day Internationals: 11
1000 runs in a season: 5
50 wickets in a season: 4
1st-Class 50s scored: 42
1st-Class 100s scored: 18
1st-Class 5 w. in innings: 12
1st-Class 10 w. in match: 4
1st-Class catches: 118
One-Day 50s: 23
Place in batting averages: 159th av. 25.17 (1991 85th av. 34.50)
Place in bowling averages: 34th av. 27.52 (1991 22nd av. 25.08)
Strike rate: 54.32 (career 49.83)
Parents: Kevin and Sylvia
Marital status: Single
Family links with cricket: Father played for Rhodesia 1947-54. Cousin Patrick Curran played for Rhodesia 1975
Education: Marandellas High School, Zimbabwe
Qualifications: 6 O-levels, 2 M-levels
Career outside cricket: Tobacco buyer/farmer
Overseas tours: Zimbabwe to Sri Lanka 1982 and 1984, to England 1982 and for World Cup 1983, to Pakistan and India for World Cup 1987
Overseas teams played for: Zimbabwe and Natal 1988-92
Other sports followed: Rugby union
Relaxations: 'Game fishing, especially along the North Natal coast, the Mozambique coast, and Magaruque Island.'
Extras: First player to take a Sunday League hat-trick, and score a 50 in the same match, Gloucestershire v Warwickshire, Edgbaston 1989. Released by Gloucestershire at end of 1990 after he had completed the season's double of 1000 runs and 50 wickets. Chose to join Northamptonshire for the 1991 season after he had been approached by several counties. Eligible to play for England in 1994
Best batting: 144* Gloucestershire v Sussex, Bristol 1990
Best bowling: 7-54 Natal v Transvaal, Johannesburg 1988-89

1992 Season

	M	Inns	NO	Runs	HS	Avge	100s	50s	Ct	St	O	M	Runs	Wkts	Avge	Best	5wI	10wM
Test																		
All First	21	30	1	730	82	25.17	-	5	10	-	452.4	96	1376	50	27.52	6-45	1	-
1-day Int																		
NatWest	5	4	1	139	78 *	46.33	-	1	2	-	48	3	153	12	12.75	3-33	-	
B & H	4	4	0	46	29	11.50	-	-	1	-	36	0	192	7	27.42	2-32	-	
Sunday	14	11	6	296	80 *	59.20	-	2	1	-	78	2	409	12	34.08	4-21	-	

Career Performances

	M	Inns	NO	Runs	HS	Avge	100s	50s	Ct	St	Balls	Runs	Wkts	Avge	Best	5wI	10wM
Test																	
All First	210	320	53	9441	144 *	35.36	18	42	118	-	20381	10589	409	25.89	7-47	12	4
1-day Int	11	11	0	287	73	26.09	-	2	1	-	506	398	9	44.22	3-65	-	
NatWest	26	23	5	587	78 *	32.61	-	3	5	-	1253	698	27	25.85	4-34	-	
B & H	32	28	6	613	57	27.86	-	3	6	-	1507	1005	42	23.92	4-41	-	
Sunday	112	106	25	2607	92	32.18	-	15	19	-	3301	2658	107	24.84	5-15	1	

CURTIS, T. S.   Worcestershire

Name: Timothy Stephen Curtis
Role: Right-hand bat, leg-spin bowler,
county captain
Born: 15 January 1960, Chislehurst, Kent
Height: 5ft 11in **Weight:** 12st 5lbs
Nickname: TC, Duracell, Professor
County debut: 1979
County cap: 1984
Test debut: 1988
Tests: 5
1000 runs in a season: 9
1st-Class 50s scored: 82
1st-Class 100s: 27
1st-Class 200s scored: 2
1st-Class catches: 131
One-Day 50s: 62
One-Day 100s: 4
Place in batting averages: 25th av. 50.80
(1991 41st av. 44.67)
Strike rate: (career 84.18)
Parents: Bruce and Betty
Wife and date of marriage: Philippa, 21 September 1985

Children: Jennifer May, 9 February 1991
Family links with cricket: Father played good club cricket in Bristol and Stafford
Education: The Royal Grammar School, Worcester; Durham University; Cambridge University
Qualifications: 12 O-levels, 4 A-levels, BA (Hons) in English, PCGE in English and Games
Off-season: Teaching
Overseas tours: NCA U19 tour of Canada 1979
Other sports followed: Rugby, tennis, squash, golf
Injuries: 'Innumerable bruises!'
Extras: Captained Durham University to UAU Championship. Chairman of the Cricketers' Association. Appointed county captain for 1992 season. Worcestershire supporters' Player of the Year 1992
Opinions on cricket: 'Looking forward to seeing how the new format works.'
Best batting: 248 Worcestershire v Somerset, Taunton 1991
Best bowling: 2-17 Worcestershire v Oxford University, The Parks 1991

1992 Season

	M	Inns	NO	Runs	HS	Avge	100s	50s	Ct	St	O	M	Runs	Wkts	Avge	Best	5wI	10wM
Test																		
All First	23	41	5	1829	228 *	50.80	4	7	15	-	24	2	116	2	58.00	2-72	-	-
1-day Int																		
NatWest	1	1	0	12	12	12.00	-	-	2	-								
B & H	5	5	0	274	78	54.80	-	3	2	-								
Sunday	15	14	1	488	77 *	37.53	-	5	5	-								

Career Performances

	M	Inns	NO	Runs	HS	Avge	100s	50s	Ct	St	Balls	Runs	Wkts	Avge	Best	5wI	10wM
Test	5	9	0	140	41	15.55	-	-	3	-	18	7	0	-	-	-	-
All First	249	423	54	15311	248	41.49	27	82	139	-	926	657	11	59.72	2-17	-	-
1-day Int																	
NatWest	28	27	3	1170	120	48.75	2	8	9	-	24	15	2	7.50	1-6	-	
B & H	46	46	3	1452	97	33.76	-	13	9	-	2	4	0	-	-	-	
Sunday	133	129	20	4796	124	44.00	2	41	38	-							

57. Who was the first batsman to hit 1000 first-class runs in 1992?

DALE, A. Glamorgan

Name: Adrian Dale
Role: Right-hand bat, right-arm
medium bowler
Born: 24 October 1968,
Germiston, South Africa
Height: 5ft 11in **Weight:** 11st 10lbs
Nickname: Arthur
County debut: 1989
County cap: 1992
1000 runs in a season: 1
1st-Class 50s scored: 13
1st-Class 100s scored: 4
1st-Class catches: 23
One-Day 50s: 6
Place in batting averages: 59th av. 41.39
(1991 51st av. 41.38)
Place in bowling averages: 61st av. 32.20
Strike rate: 70.20 (76.28)
Parents: John and Maureen
Marital status: Single

Family links with cricket: Father played for Glamorgan 2nd XI and Chepstow CC
Education: Pembroke Primary; Chepstow Comprehensive; Swansea University
Qualifications: 9 O-levels, 3 A-levels, BA (Hons) in Economics
Off-season: Playing and coaching in Auckland, New Zealand
Overseas tours: Welsh Schools U16 to Australia 1986-87; Combined Universities to Barbados 1989; Glamorgan to Trinidad 1990, to Zimbabwe 1991
Overseas teams played for: Bionics, Zimbabwe 1990-91; Cornwall, New Zealand 1991-93
Cricketers particularly admired: Ian Botham, Michael Holding
Other sports followed: Football (Arsenal), athletics, US basketball
Injuries: Back spasm for a couple of days and aggravated hamstring, missed one week
Relaxations: 'Eating out, crosswords, videos, most other sports, sleeping!'
Extras: Played in successful Combined Universities sides of 1989 and 1990. Only batsman to score two half-centuries against the West Indies tourists in the same match in 1991. Took a wicket with his first delivery at Lord's.
Opinions on cricket: 'The four-day programme is a positive step forward for county cricket.'
Best batting: 150* Glamorgan v Nottinghamshire, Trent Bridge 1992
Best bowling: 3-21 Glamorgan v Indians, Swansea 1990

1992 Season

	M	Inns	NO	Runs	HS	Avge	100s	50s	Ct	St	O	M	Runs	Wkts	Avge	Best	5wI	10wM
Test																		
All First	22	33	5	1159	150 *	41.39	2	7	8	-	234	62	644	20	32.20	3-30	-	-
1-day Int																		
NatWest	3	3	0	41	20	13.66	-	-	1	-	29	2	110	4	27.50	2-46	-	
B & H	2	2	0	83	53	41.50	-	1	-	-	15	2	64	3	21.33	2-40	-	
Sunday	14	11	2	255	55 *	28.33	-	2	1	-	82	2	378	12	31.50	4-27	-	

Career Performances

	M	Inns	NO	Runs	HS	Avge	100s	50s	Ct	St	Balls	Runs	Wkts	Avge	Best	5wI	10wM
Test																	
All First	53	83	12	2509	150 *	35.33	4	13	23	-	2899	1547	38	40.71	3-21	-	-
1-day Int																	
NatWest	10	8	1	159	86	22.71	-	1	3	-	526	337	9	37.44	2-32	-	
B & H	12	11	1	207	53	20.70	-	1	2	-	522	355	12	29.58	3-24	-	
Sunday	46	36	7	720	67 *	24.82	-	4	11	-	1476	1348	39	34.56	4-27	-	

DALEY, J. A.   Durham

Name: James Arthur Daley
Role: Right-hand bat
Born: 24 September 1973, Sunderland
Height: 5ft 10in **Weight:** 11st 10lbs
County Debut: 1992
1st-Class 50s scored: 2
1st-Class catches: 2
Parents: William and Christine
Marital status: Single
Education: Hetton Comprehensive
Qualifications: 4 GCSEs
Off-season: Overseas
Overseas tours: Durham to Zimbabwe, 1991-92
Cricketers particularly admired:
'Robin Smith and Mark Ramprakash for their cool temperament and remarkable ability.'
Other sports followed: Most sports
Relaxations: Watching TV
Extras: Scored three centuries in 1991 for MCC Young Cricketers at Lord's.
Opinions on cricket: 'Cricket is a great game for travelling and meeting people.'

Best batting: 88 Durham v Somerset, Taunton 1992

1992 Season

	M	Inns	NO	Runs	HS	Avge	100s	50s	Ct	St	O	M	Runs	Wkts	Avge	Best	5wI	10wM
Test																		
All First	2	4	1	190	88	63.33	-	2	2	-								
1-day Int																		
NatWest																		
B & H																		
Sunday																		

Career Performances

	M	Inns	NO	Runs	HS	Avge	100s	50s	Ct	St	Balls	Runs	Wkts	Avge	Best	5wI	10wM
Test																	
All First	2	4	1	190	88	63.33	-	2	2	-							
1-day Int																	
NatWest																	
B & H																	
Sunday																	

DALTON, A. J.   Glamorgan

Name: Alistair John Dalton
Born: 27 April 1973, Bridgend
Height: 5ft 9in **Weight:** 11st
Nickname: Ali
County debut: No first team appearance
Parents: John and Christine
Marital status: Single
Family links with cricket: Father
captained Bridgend Town 1st XI for
10 years, brother Simon now plays for
the same 1st XI
Education: Millfield School
Qualifications: 8 GCSEs, 3 A-levels
Off-season: Playing in Australia
Overseas tours: Millfield School to
Jamaica 1990; Glamorgan Schools to
Singapore/Malaysia 1992; Wales Schools
 to Scotland for Home International
Competition 1992
Overseas teams played for: Paramatta, Sydney 1992-93

157

Cricketers particularly admired: Richie Richardson, Dean Jones
Other sports followed: Rugby (played scrum half for Millfield 1st XV)
Relaxations: Music and golf
Extras: Offered a contract while still at school
Opinions on cricket: 'I cannot believe how lucky I am to play the game as a professional. It's been my lifelong ambition.'

DAVIES, M.   Gloucestershire

Name: Mark Davies
Role: Right-hand bat, slow left-arm bowler
Born: 18 April 1969, Neath
Height: 5ft 7in **Weight:** 11st 4lb
Nickname: Sparky, Josey, Rourksie
County debut: 1990 (Glamorgan)
1992 (Gloucestershire)
50 wickets in a season: 1
1st class catches: 11
Place in batting averages: 250th av. 11.76
Place in bowling averages: 44th av. 29.94
Strike rate: 60.08 (60.94)
Parents: Peter and Dorothy
Marital status: Engaged to Carol
Family links with cricket: Brother is
club opening bat and has represented
the South Wales Cricket Association
Education: Cwrt Sart Comprehensive;
Neath Tertiary College
Qualifications: 6 O-levels; BTEC OND in Science; NCA junior and senior coaching awards; qualified lifeguard
Career outside cricket: Production technician in pharmaceutical company
Off-season: Playing in Pretoria, South Africa
Overseas tours: Fred Rumsey's XI to Barbados
Overseas teams played for: Newcastle City, New South Wales 1990-91
Cricketers particularly admired: Courtney Walsh, Bishen Bedi, John Steele
Other sports followed: Rugby union and league, boxing
Relaxations: Going to the cinema, ten-pin bowling, singing ('budding Aled Jones')
Extras: Was on the MCC groundstaff in 1987. Glamorgan 2nd XI Player of the Year 1991. Released by Glamorgan at the end of 1991, signed to play for Gloucs on a two-year contract
Opinions on cricket: 'Greater emphasis on specialist coaching for players. Better standard of practice facilities now that there is more time between four-day games.'
Best batting: 32* Gloucestershire v Yorkshire, Cheltenham 1992
Best bowling: 4-73 Gloucestershire v Durham, Stockton 1992

	M	Inns	NO	Runs	HS	Avge	100s	50s	Ct	St	O	M	Runs	Wkts	Avge	Best	5wI	10wM
Test																		
All First	19	23	10	148	32 *	11.38	-	-	10	-	560.5	143	1661	56	29.66	4-73	-	-
1-day Int																		
NatWest																		
B & H																		
Sunday	2	0	0	0	0	-	-	-	-	-								

Career Performances

	M	Inns	NO	Runs	HS	Avge	100s	50s	Ct	St	Balls	Runs	Wkts	Avge	Best	5wI	10wM
Test																	
All First	20	24	11	153	32 *	11.76	-	-	11	-	3413	1677	56	29.94	4-73	-	-
1-day Int																	
NatWest																	
B & H																	
Sunday	2	0	0	0	0	-	-	-	-	-							

DAVIS, R. P.   Kent

Name: Richard Peter Davis
Role: Right-hand bat, slow left-arm bowler
Born: 18 March 1966, Westbook, Margate
Height: 6ft 4in **Weight:** 14st 4lbs
Nickname: Dicky, Scud (missile)
County debut: 1986
County cap: 1990
50 wickets in season: 2
1st-Class 50s scored: 4
1st-Class 5 w. in innings: 11
1st-Class 10 w. in match: 1
1st-Class catches: 94
Place in batting averages: 167th av. 24.00
(1991 206th av. 17.40)
Place in bowling averages: 6th av. 21.74
(1991 116th av. 41.37)
Strike rate: 47.18 (career 74.91)
Parents: Brian and Silvia
Wife and date of marriage:
Samantha Jane, 3 March 1990
Family links with cricket: Father played club cricket and is an NCA coach; father-in-law
Colin Tomlin helps with England's fitness training

Education: King Ethelbert's School, Birchington; Thanet Technical College, Broadstairs
Qualifications: 8 CSEs; NCA coaching certificate
Career outside cricket: 'All sorts – carpentry, roofing, general labouring'
Off-season: 'At home – coaching, keeping fit and working at my game.'
Overseas tours: Kent Schools U17 to Canada 1983
Overseas teams played for: Hutt Districts, New Zealand 1986-88
Cricketers particularly admired: Graham Gooch, Carl Hooper, Viv Richards, Courtney Walsh
Other sports followed: Football, rugby, squash, 'any'
Relaxations: 'Reading, sport, TV, meal with my wife.'
Opinions on cricket: 'Looking forward to 17 four-day games. I like the idea of coloured clothing, but not the idea of the 50-over game. I feel that it should have stayed at 40 overs per side.'
Best batting: 67 Kent v Hampshire, Southampton 1989
Best bowling: 7-64 Kent v Durham, Gateshead Fell 1992

1992 Season

	M	Inns	NO	Runs	HS	Avge	100s	50s	Ct	St	O	M	Runs	Wkts	Avge	Best	5wI	10wM
Test																		
All First	18	24	11	312	54 *	24.00	-	1	11	-	582	150	1609	74	21.74	7-64	5	-
1-day Int																		
NatWest	3	2	0	31	22	15.50	-	-	5	-	32	0	129	4	32.25	2-40	-	
B & H	6	4	1	26	12 *	8.66	-	-	5	-	60	10	173	4	43.25	2-40	-	
Sunday	13	9	3	46	26	7.66	-	-	2	-	83.4	0	407	11	37.00	3-35	-	

Career Performances

	M	Inns	NO	Runs	HS	Avge	100s	50s	Ct	St	Balls	Runs	Wkts	Avge	Best	5wI	10wM
Test																	
All First	110	136	37	1620	67	16.36	-	4	94	-	20976	10010	280	35.75	7-64	11	1
1-day Int																	
NatWest	12	6	1	46	22	9.20	-	-	10	-	693	372	14	26.57	3-19	-	
B & H	15	7	3	27	12 *	6.75	-	-	6	-	871	556	10	55.60	2-33	-	
Sunday	75	35	13	212	40 *	9.63	-	-	24	-	2832	2186	77	28.39	5-52	1	

58.   Who is the manager of Nottinghamshire CCC?

DAWSON, R. I. Gloucestershire

Name: Robert Ian Dawson
Role: Right-hand bat, right-arm
medium bowler
Born: 29 March 1970, Exmouth, Devon
Height: 5ft 11in **Weight:** 12st
Nickname: Daws
County debut: 1991 (one-day),
1992 (first-class)
1st-Class catches: 2
Place in batting averages: 254th av. 11.00
Parents: Barry and Shirley
Marital status: Single
Family links with cricket: Father and
brother both played club cricket
Education: Millfield School;
Newcastle Polytechnic
Qualifications: 8 O-levels, 3 A-levels
Cricketers particularly admired:
Ian Botham, David Gower,
Viv Richards

Other sports followed: Football and rugby
Relaxations: Watching most sports and 'a night out with my mates'
Extras: Played in NatWest for Devon (from 1988), before joining Gloucestershire
Best batting: 29 Gloucestershire v Middlesex, Lord's 1992

1992 Season

	M	Inns	NO	Runs	HS	Avge	100s	50s	Ct	St	O	M	Runs	Wkts	Avge	Best	5wl	10wM
Test																		
All First	6	8	0	88	29	11.00	-	-	2	-								
1-day Int																		
NatWest	1	0	0	0	0	-	-	-	-	-								
B & H																		
Sunday	13	9	1	124	35	15.50	-	-	5	-	8	0	36	0	-		-	-

Career Performances

	M	Inns	NO	Runs	HS	Avge	100s	50s	Ct	St	Balls	Runs	Wkts	Avge	Best	5wl	10wM
Test																	
All First	6	8	0	88	29	11.00	-	-	2	-							
1-day Int																	
NatWest	3	2	0	13	13	6.50	-	-	-	-	24	37	1	37.00	1-37	-	
B & H																	
Sunday	13	9	1	124	35	15.50	-	-	5	-	48	36	0	-		-	-

DEAN, J. W. Sussex

Name: Jacob Winston Dean
Role: Right-hand bat, slow left-arm bowler
Born: 23 August 1970, Cuckfield, Sussex
Height: 5ft 10¹/₂in **Weight:** 11st 5lbs
Nickname: Marley
County debut: No first team appearance
Parents: Dudley John and Querida Anne
Marital status: Single
Family links with cricket: Brother plays
club cricket
Education: Chailey Comprehensive;
Haywards Heath Sixth Form College;
Crawley College
Qualifications: 5 O-levels, 2 A-levels,
HND in Business and Finance,
Senior Coaching Award
Off-season: Playing and coaching overseas
Cricketers particularly admired:
Richard Seager, Norman Gifford,
Phil Edmonds, Peter Moores

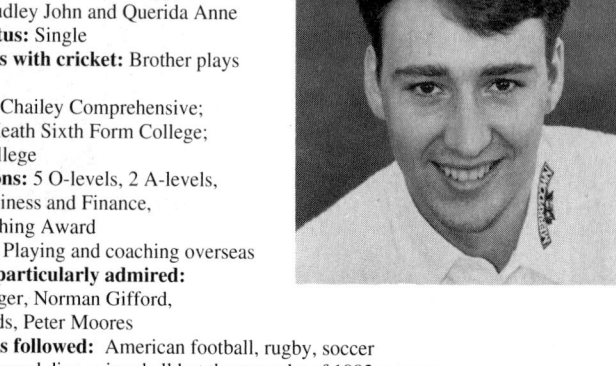

Other sports followed: American football, rugby, soccer
Injuries: Slipped disc, missed all but three weeks of 1992 season
Relaxations: Playing hockey and other sports, music and eating

DEFREITAS, P. A. J. Lancashire

Name: Phillip Anthony Jason DeFreitas
Role: Right-hand bat, right-arm fast bowler
Born: 18 February 1966,
Scotts Head, Dominica
Height: 6ft **Weight:** 13st 7lbs
Nickname: Daffy, Lunchy
County debut: 1985 (Leics), 1989 (Lancs)
County cap: 1986 (Leics), 1989 (Lancs)
Test debut: 1986-87
Tests: 31
One-Day Internationals: 78
50 wickets in a season: 5
1st-Class 50s scored: 22
1st-Class 100s scored: 4

1st-Class 5 w. in innings: 27
1st-Class 10 w. in match: 2
1st-Class catches: 43
One-Day 50s: 3
Place in batting averages: 160th av. 25.00
(1991 190th av. 20.79)
Place in bowling averages: 60th av. 32.08
(1991 18th av. 24.38)
Strike rate: 61.73 (career 56.55)
Parents: Sybil and Martin
Wife and date of marriage:
Nicola, 10 December 1990
Children: Alexandra Elizabeth Jane,
5 August 1991
Family links with cricket: Father played
in Windward Islands. All six brothers play
Education: Willesden High School
Qualifications: 2 O-levels
Career outside cricket: 'Full-time dad!'
Off-season: Touring with England
Overseas tours: Young England to West Indies 1985; England to Australia 1986-87, to Pakistan, Australia and New Zealand 1987-88, to India and West Indies 1989-90, to Australia 1990-91, to New Zealand 1991-92, to India and Sri Lanka 1992-93
Overseas teams played for: Port Adelaide, S Australia 1985; Mossman, Sydney 1988
Cricketers particularly admired: Ian Botham, Graham Gooch, Geoff Boycott, Mike Gatting
Other sports followed: Football (Manchester City) and rugby league (Warrington)
Relaxations: 'Golf, gardening, visiting stately homes, spending spare time with wife and daughter Alexandra.'
Extras: Left Leicestershire and joined Lancashire at end of 1988 season. Originally agreed to join unofficial English tour of South Africa 1989-90, but withdrew under pressure. Man of the match in 1990 NatWest Trophy final. One of *Wisden's* Cricketers of the Year 1992
Opinions on cricket: 'Pyjama cricket more interesting for children on a Sunday. New rule allowing only one bouncer per over not a good idea.'
Best batting: 113 Leicestershire v Nottinghamshire, Worksop 1988
Best bowling: 7-21 Lancashire v Middlesex, Lord's 1989

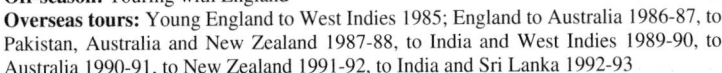

1992 Season

	M	Inns	NO	Runs	HS	Avge	100s	50s	Ct	St	O	M	Runs	Wkts	Avge	Best	5wI	10wM
Test	2	2	0	3	3	1.50	-	-	-	-	59	14	179	7	25.57	4-121	-	-
All First	13	14	1	325	72	25.00	-	3	1	-	349.5	65	1091	34	32.08	6-94	1	-
1-day Int	5	2	1	5	5 *	5.00	-	-	-	-	51.5	6	200	8	25.00	3-33	-	
NatWest	1	1	0	0	0	0.00	-	-	1	-	0.3	0	5	0	-	-	-	
B & H	5	3	1	35	24	17.50	-	-	1	-	52	7	176	12	14.66	5-16	1	
Sunday	10	8	2	193	49 *	32.16	-	-	-	-	79	1	440	12	36.66	3-53	-	

Career Performances

	M	Inns	NO	Runs	HS	Avge	100s	50s	Ct	St	Balls	Runs	Wkts	Avge	Best	5wI	10wM
Test	31	46	4	527	55 *	12.54	-	1	6	-	6628	3017	93	32.44	7-70	3	-
All First	167	224	24	4297	113	21.48	4	22	43	-	30652	14847	542	27.39	7-21	27	2
1-day Int	78	51	19	494	49 *	15.43	-	-	21	-	4417	2856	90	31.73	4-35	-	
NatWest	19	13	3	186	69	18.60	-	1	2	-	1121	556	29	19.17	5-13	3	
B & H	36	22	5	381	75 *	22.41	-	2	9	-	2160	1192	61	19.54	5-16	1	
Sunday	89	64	13	799	49 *	15.66	-	-	11	-	3563	2805	107	26.21	4-20	-	

DESSAUR, W. A. Nottinghamshire

Name: Wayne Anthony Dessaur
Role: Right-hand bat, off-spin bowler
Born: 4 February 1971, Nottingham
Height: 6ft **Weight:** 12st
Nickname: Bed
County debut: 1992
1st-Class 100s scored: 1
1st-Class catches: 1
Parents: Pat and Tony
Marital status: Single
Family links with cricket: Father and
brother play local league cricket, father is
coach of county U15 side
Education: Loughborough Grammar School
Qualifications: 6 O-levels, 2 A-levels,
qualified coach
Off-season: Playing in Australia
Overseas teams played for: Grange,
Adelaide 1991-93
Cricketers particularly admired: Tim Robinson, Derek Randall. Martin Crowe
Other sports followed: Football
Injuries: Ankle ligament injury
Relaxations: Sleeping, reading, listening to music, 'receiving mail from Mick Newell'
Extras: Scored century in second first-class match
Opinions on cricket: 'Four-day cricket is a good thing as it will help stop contrived
finishes. The introduction of coloured clothing and white balls will also help to market the
game and bring in more spectators on Sundays. But after a certain number of seasons the
attraction may fade out and so new ideas may be needed, i.e. floodlit games etc. It is good
to see that more counties are interested in employment for their players in the winter. 12-
month contracts would be ideal for the players and hopefully we will see this shortly.'
Best batting: 148 Nottinghamshire v Cambridge University, Trent Bridge 1992

1992 Season

	M	Inns	NO	Runs	HS	Avge	100s	50s	Ct	St	O	M	Runs	Wkts	Avge	Best	5wI	10wM
Test																		
All First	2	3	0	164	148	54.66	1	-	1	-								
1-day Int																		
NatWest																		
B & H																		
Sunday	2	2	1	16	13 *	16.00	-	-	-	-								

Career Performances

	M	Inns	NO	Runs	HS	Avge	100s	50s	Ct	St	Balls	Runs	Wkts	Avge	Best	5wI	10wM
Test																	
All First	2	3	0	164	148	54.66	1	-	1	-							
1-day Int																	
NatWest																	
B & H																	
Sunday	2	2	1	16	13 *	16.00	-	-	-	-							

DILLEY, G. R. — Worcestershire

Name: Graham Roy Dilley
Role: Left-hand bat, right-arm fast bowler
Born: 18 May 1959, Dartford
Height: 6ft 4in **Weight:** 15st
Nickname: Picca
County debut: 1977 (Kent), 1987 (Worcs)
County cap: 1980 (Kent), 1987 (Worcs)
Test debut: 1979-80
Tests: 41
One-Day Internationals: 36
50 wickets in a season: 3
1st-Class 50s scored: 4
1st-Class 5 w. in innings: 34
1st-Class 10 w. in match: 3
1st-Class catches: 75
Place in bowling averages:
(1991 9th av. 22.24)
Strike rate: (career 53.11)
Parents: Geoff and Jean
Wife and date of marriage: Helen, 6 November 1980
Children: Paul and Christopher
Family links with cricket: Father and grandfather both played local cricket. Wife is sister

of former Kent colleague Graham Johnson
Education: Dartford West Secondary School
Qualifications: 3 O-levels
Overseas tours: England to Australia and India 1979-80, to West Indies 1980-81, to India and Sri Lanka 1981-82, to New Zealand and Pakistan 1983-84, to Australia 1986-87, to Pakistan, New Zealand and Australia 1987-88; unofficial England XI to S Africa 1989-90
Overseas teams played for: Natal 1985-86
Injuries: Knee, ankle and neck injuries, played only one first-class game in 1992
Relaxations: Music, playing golf
Extras: Cricket Writers' Club Young Cricketer of the Year 1980. Missed 1984 season after suffering back injury on 1983-84 tour. Joined Worcestershire in 1987. Banned from Test cricket for joining tour to South Africa in 1989-90, suspension remitted in 1992. Autobiography *Swings and Roundabouts*, 1988. Retired at the end of the 1992 season
Best batting: 81 Kent v Northamptonshire, Northampton 1979
Best bowling: 7-63 Natal v Transvaal, Johannesburg 1985-86

1992 Season

	M	Inns	NO	Runs	HS	Avge	100s	50s	Ct	St	O	M	Runs	Wkts	Avge	Best	5wl	10wM
Test																		
All First	2	3	1	61	39	30.50	-	-	-	-	25	7	57	0	-	-	-	-
1-day Int																		
NatWest																		
B & H	1	0	0	0	0	-	-	-	-	-	7	0	33	0	-	-	-	
Sunday																		

Career Performances

	M	Inns	NO	Runs	HS	Avge	100s	50s	Ct	St	Balls	Runs	Wkts	Avge	Best	5wl	10wM
Test	41	58	19	521	56	13.35	-	2	10	-	8192	4107	138	29.76	6-38	6	-
All First	234	252	93	2339	81	14.71	-	4	75	-	34418	17395	648	26.84	7-63	34	3
1-day Int	36	18	8	114	31*	11.40	-	-	4	-	2043	1291	48	26.89	4-23	-	
NatWest	23	14	5	112	25	12.44	-	-	6	-	1396	716	37	19.35	5-29	1	
B & H	56	27	9	159	37*	8.83	-	-	8	-	3063	1766	88	20.06	4-14	-	
Sunday	73	27	8	252	33	13.26	-	-	21	-	2900	2060	79	26.07	4-20	-	

DIWAN, M. Essex

Name: Muneeb Diwan
Born: 20 March 1972, St Stephens, New Brunswick, Canada
Height: 5ft 10in **Weight:** 11st 6lbs
Nickname: Sammy
County debut: No first team appearance
Parents: Azeem and Kishwar

Marital status: Single
Family links with cricket: Father and uncles played club cricket
Education: Penge Primary School; Haringey Cricket College
Qualifications: Qualified as player, coach and umpire from Haringey Cricket College
Off-season: Playing in Kenya
Overseas tours: Haringey Cricket College to West Indies 1989 and 1990; Walthamstow Asian Cricket Club to Pakistan 1990
Overseas teams played for: Nairobi Gymkhana, Kenya 1992-93
Cricketers particularly admired: Graeme Hick, Viv Richards, Dean Jones
Other sports followed: Tennis and football
Relaxations: Movies
Extras: 'My ambition is to play for England.' Scored 120 and 74* in his first game for Essex 2nd XI. Has also played for Derbyshire 2nd XI
Opinions on cricket: 'A truly great and noble game! I believe in this game so much that I intend to promote, dignify and popularise it wherever I can.'

DOBSON, M. C. Glamorgan

Name: Mark Christopher Dobson
Role: Right-hand opening bat, slow left-arm bowler
Born: 24 October 1967, Canterbury
Height: 5ft 10in **Weight:** 12st 10lbs
Nickname: Dobbo
County debut: 1989 (Kent), 1992 (Glamorgan)
1st-Class 50s scored: 2
1st-Class catches: 2
Parents: Bryan and Yvonne
Wife and date of marriage: Michele
Children: Benjamin; Hollie
Family links with cricket: Father was top club cricketer
Education: Simon Langton Grammar School for Boys, Canterbury
Qualifications: 8 O-levels, 2 A-levels;

qualified coach
Career outside cricket: Builder
Off-season: Working in Canterbury
Overseas tours: Kent Schools U17 to Canada 1983
Overseas teams played for: Glenwood OB, Durban 1988-89; Green Point, Cape Town 1989-90
Cricketers particularly admired: Hartley Alleyne, Roy Pienaar
Other sports followed: Football, 'my grandfather was a professional footballer with QPR'
Relaxations: Physical training, music and reading
Extras: Released by Kent in early August 1991 after scoring 750 runs in only 10 matches at an average of 50 in the 2nd XI Championship, and taking 17 wickets. Joined Glamorgan in 1992 and carried bat with 95* out of 175 for Glamorgan 2nd XI v Middlesex 2nd XI
Best batting: 52 Kent v Glamorgan, Canterbury 1989
Best bowling: 2-20 Kent v Glamorgan, Canterbury 1989

1992 Season

	M	Inns	NO	Runs	HS	Avge	100s	50s	Ct	St	O	M	Runs	Wkts	Avge	Best	5wI	10wM
Test																		
All First	1	1	1	5	5*	-	-	-	1	-	18	7	45	1	45.00	1-42	-	-
1-day Int																		
NatWest																		
B & H																		
Sunday																		

Career Performances

	M	Inns	NO	Runs	HS	Avge	100s	50s	Ct	St	Balls	Runs	Wkts	Avge	Best	5wI	10wM
Test																	
All First	10	15	3	211	52	17.58	-	2	2	-	886	486	9	54.00	2-20	-	-
1-day Int																	
NatWest																	
B & H																	
Sunday	1	1	0	21	21	21.00	-	-	1	-							

59. What is the title of Brian Johnston's latest autobiography?

D'OLIVEIRA, D. B.   Worcestershire

Name: Damian Basil D'Oliveira
Role: Right-hand bat, off-spin bowler, slip
or boundary fielder
Born: 19 October 1960, Cape Town, South
Africa
Height: 5ft 8in **Weight:** 11st 10lbs
Nickname: Dolly
County debut: 1982
County cap: 1985
Benefit: 1993 (joint benefit with Martin
Weston)
1000 runs in a season: 4
1st-Class 50s scored: 41
1st-Class 100s scored: 10
1st-Class 200s scored: 1
1st-Class catches: 188
One-Day 50s: 17
One-Day 100s: 1
Place in batting averages: 127th av. 29.72
(1991 145th av. 26.63)
Place in bowling averages: 143rd av. 53.60
Strike rate: 92.20 (career 78.21)
Parents: Basil and Naomi
Wife and date of marriage: Tracey Michele, 26 September 1983
Children: Marcus Damian, 27 April 1986; Dominic James, 29 April 1988; 3rd child
expected February 1992
Family links with cricket: Father played for Worcestershire and England
Education: St George's RC Primary School; Blessed Edward Oldcorne Secondary School
Qualifications: 3 O-levels, 5 CSEs
Overseas tours: English Counties XI to Zimbabwe 1985
Cricketers particularly admired: Greg Chappell, Viv Richards, Dennis Lillee, Malcolm
Marshall, Richard Hadlee
Other sports followed: 'Most others, but not horse racing.'
Relaxations: Watching films, TV, eating out, and playing with the kids.
Best batting: 237 Worcestershire v Oxford University, The Parks 1991
Best bowling: 2-17 Worcestershire v Gloucestershire, Cheltenham 1986

60.   Whose new biography is entitled *England Expects*?

1992 Season

	M	Inns	NO	Runs	HS	Avge	100s	50s	Ct	St	O	M	Runs	Wkts	Avge	Best	5wI	10wM
Test																		
All First	13	19	1	535	100	29.72	1	2	14	-	153.4	29	536	10	53.60	2-44	-	-
1-day Int																		
NatWest	1	1	0	37	37	37.00	-	-	-	-								
B & H	2	2	0	11	8	5.50	-	-	2	-	1	0	2	0	-		-	-
Sunday	15	13	3	283	58	28.30	-	1	5	-								

Career Performances

	M	Inns	NO	Runs	HS	Avge	100s	50s	Ct	St	Balls	Runs	Wkts	Avge	Best	5wI	10wM
Test																	
All First	212	331	22	8667	237	28.04	10	41	188	-	2894	1712	37	46.27	2-17	-	-
1-day Int																	
NatWest	23	22	4	505	99	28.05	-	3	3	-	258	151	8	18.87	2-17	-
B & H	46	42	4	787	66	20.71	-	4	19	-	234	150	5	30.00	3-12	-
Sunday	152	136	16	2859	103	23.82	1	10	35	-	234	232	7	33.14	3-23	-

DONALD, A. A.   Warwickshire

Name: Allan Anthony Donald
Role: Right-hand bat, right-arm fast bowler
Born: 20 October 1966, Bloemfontein, South Africa
Height: 6ft 3in **Weight:** 14st
County debut: 1987
County cap: 1989
Test debut: 1992
Tests: 1
One-Day Internationals: 14
50 wickets in a season: 3
1st-Class 5 w. in innings: 30
1st-Class 10 w. in match: 3
1st-Class catches: 53
Place in batting averages: 193rd av. 19.50
Place in bowling averages: 7th av. 22.25 (1991 4th av. 19.68)
Strike rate: 46.64 (career 47.41)
Parents: Stuart and Francine
Wife and date of marriage: Tina, 21 September 1991
Family links with cricket: Father and uncle played club cricket
Education: Grey College High School and Technical High School, Bloemfontein

Qualifications: Matriculation
Off-season: Playing cricket in South Africa
Overseas tours: South Africa to India 1991-92, to Australia and New Zealand (World Cup) 1991-92, to West Indies 1991-92
Overseas teams played for: Orange Free State, South Africa 1985-93
Cricketers particularly admired: Richard Hadlee, Malcolm Marshall, Gladstone Small, Andy Lloyd, Eddie Barlow
Other sports followed: Rugby, golf, tennis
Injuries: Missed one game with side strain
Relaxations: 'Listening to music, having a barbecue, playing golf and having a few beers with my friends.'
Extras: Played for South African XI v Australian XI in 1986-87 and v English XI in 1989-90. Retained by Warwickshire for 1991 season ahead of Tom Moody. Toured with South Africa on first-ever visit to India 1991.
Opinions on cricket: 'Think that the one bouncer an over rule is a load of crap.'
Best batting: 46* Orange Free State v Western Province, Cape Town 1990-91
Best bowling: 8-37 Orange Free State v Transvaal, Johannesburg 1986-87

1992 Season

	M	Inns	NO	Runs	HS	Avge	100s	50s	Ct	St	O	M	Runs	Wkts	Avge	Best	5wI	10wM
Test																		
All First	21	22	10	234	41	19.50	-	-	14	-	575.2	139	1647	74	22.25	7-37	6	-
1-day Int																		
NatWest	4	2	2	23	14 *	-					45.5	11	108	11	9.81	5-28	1	
B & H	3	1	0	10	10	10.00	-	-	-	-	33	4	102	4	25.50	2-33	-	
Sunday	9	2	1	1	1 *	1.00	-	-	1	-	51	1	185	9	20.55	4-23	-	

Career Performances

	M	Inns	NO	Runs	HS	Avge	100s	50s	Ct	St	Balls	Runs	Wkts	Avge	Best	5wI	10wM
Test	1	2	0	0	0	0.00	-	-	-	-	270	144	6	24.00	4-77	-	-
All First	151	178	69	1282	46 *	11.76	-	-	53	-	25891	12586	546	23.05	8-37	30	3
1-day Int	14	3	1	8	5 *	4.00	-	-	1	-	742	545	24	22.70	5-29	1	
NatWest	16	5	3	26	14 *	13.00	-	-	1	-	989	465	41	11.34	5-12	3	
B & H	16	8	5	48	23 *	16.00	-	-	2	-	955	659	25	26.36	4-28	-	
Sunday	37	17	7	119	18 *	11.90	-	-	9	-	1584	1087	43	25.27	4-23	-	

61. What was the prize money for the winners of the Britannic Assurance Championship last season?

DONELAN, B. T. P.   Sussex

Name: Bradleigh Thomas Peter Donelan
Role: Right-hand bat, off-spin bowler
Born: 3 January 1968, Park Royal,
Middlesex
Height: 6ft 1in **Weight:** 12st 7lbs
Nickname: Rooster, Freddie, Claw
County debut: 1989
1st-Class 50s: 5
1st-Class 5 w. in innings: 3
1st-Class 10 w. in match: 1
1st-Class catches: 13
Place in batting averages: 172nd av. 22.15
(1991 81st av. 35.30)
Place in bowling averages: 130th av. 47.25
(1991 81st av. 34.17)
Strike rate: 86.57 (career 83.01)
Parents: Terry and Patricia
Marital status: Single

Education: Our Lady of Grace Junior School,
Finchley Catholic High School
Qualifications: 8 CSEs, NCA coaching certificate
Off-season: Coaching at Lord's and working on my game
Overseas tours: Christians in Sport to India 1990; MCC to Leeward Islands 1992
Overseas teams played for: Northcote, Melbourne 1987-88; Southland Cricket Association,
New Zealand 1988-90; Otago B 1988-89; Wellington B 1990-91
Cricketers particularly admired: Martin Crowe, Dean Jones, John Emburey, Ian Botham
Other sports followed: Football, golf, tennis, snooker, darts
Injuries: Patella tendonitis, had an operation on right knee in September 1992
Relaxations: 'Eating out in restaurants and generally spending my spare time with my
fiancee Kim.'
Extras: Was a product of the MCC ground staff – there for 2^{1}/$_{2}$years before joining Sussex
in 1989
Opinions on cricket: 'It will be interesting to see how four-day cricket will go on these
present-day wickets, but Sunday will be a long day. Heading in the right direction for
producing better quality Test players.'
Best batting: 68* Sussex v Hampshire, Southampton 1992
Best bowling: 6-62 Sussex v Gloucestershire, Hove 1991

1992 Season

	M	Inns	NO	Runs	HS	Avge	100s	50s	Ct	St	O	M	Runs	Wkts	Avge	Best	5wl	10wM
Test																		
All First	16	25	6	421	68 *	22.15	-	2	2	-	404	85	1323	28	47.25	6-77	1	-
1-day Int																		
NatWest																		
B & H	2	2	2	17	9 *	-	-	-	1	-	18	1	73	1	73.00	1-41	-	
Sunday	3	1	0	1	1	1.00	-	-	-	-	15	0	95	2	47.50	2-39	-	

Career Performances

	M	Inns	NO	Runs	HS	Avge	100s	50s	Ct	St	Balls	Runs	Wkts	Avge	Best	5wl	10wM
Test																	
All First	49	62	20	1026	68 *	24.42	-	5	13	-	7969	4118	96	42.89	6-62	3	1
1-day Int																	
NatWest																	
B & H	3	3	3	25	9 *	-	-	-	1	-	174	127	1	127.00	1-41	-	
Sunday	9	3	0	24	19	8.00	-	-	1	-	318	270	5	54.00	2-39	-	

DOWMAN, M. P.   Nottinghamshire

Name: Mathew Peter Dowman
Role: Left-hand bat, right-arm medium bowler
Born: 10 May 1974, Grantham, Lincs
Height: 5ft 10in
County debut: 1992 (one-day)
Marital status: Single
Education: Grantham College
Career outside cricket: Student
Off-season: Touring with England U19
Overseas tours: England U19 to India
Extras: Made only first team appearance in Tilcon Trophy at Scarborough

DUTCH, K. P.   Middlesex

Name: Keith Peter Dutch
Role: Right-hand bat, off-spin bowler
Born: 21 March 1973, Harrow, Middlesex
Height: 5ft 7in **Weight:** 11st 2lbs
Nickname: Dutchy, Kitten
County debut: No first team appearance
Parents: Alan and Ann
Marital status: Single
Family links with cricket: Father is a
qualified cricket coach
Education: Nower Hill High School, Pinner;
Weald College, Harrow
Qualifications: 5 GCSEs and AS-level in
English
Off-season: Playing in South Africa
Overseas teams played for:
Worcester United, South Africa 1992-92
Cricketers particularly admired:
Mark Ramprakash, Philip Tufnell,
Clive Radley, Robin Smith, Matthew Church

Other sports followed: Most sports, especially football (Arsenal)
Injuries: Back injury, out for 3 weeks
Relaxations: Socialising, watching and playing soccer, listening to music (except heavy
metal)
Extras: On MCC groundstaff for one year before becoming a contracted player
Opinions on cricket: 'I favour more one-day cricket. It seems to attract a bigger audience
and the atmosphere and excitement is a lot better.'

---

62. What was the prize money for the winners of the NatWest Trophy
last seaon?

63. What was the prize money for the winners of the Benson & Hedges
Cup last season?

EALHAM, M. A. Kent

Name: Mark Alan Ealham
Role: Right-hand bat, right-arm medium
bowler
Born: 27 August 1969, Ashford
Height: 5ft 10in **Weight:** 13st
Nickname: Ealy
County debut: 1989
County cap: 1992
1st-Class 50s scored: 4
1st-Class 5 w. in innings: 2
1st-Class catches: 7
Place in batting averages: 183rd av. 20.54
(1991 178th av. 22.50)
Place in bowling averages: 72nd av. 33.59
(1991 5th av. 20.82)
Strike rate 86.57 (career 83.01)
Parents: Alan and Sue
Marital status: Single
Family links with cricket: Father played
county cricket for Kent
Education: Stour Valley Secondary School
Qualifications: 9 CSEs
Off-season: Coaching before Christmas, then going to Perth, Australia to play for three
months
Overseas teams played for: South Perth, Australia 1992-93
Cricketers particularly admired: Ian Botham, Viv Richards, Malcolm Marshall, Robin
Smith, Mike Gatting
Other sports followed: Golf, snooker and most other sports
Relaxations: Playing golf and snooker, watching films
Best batting: 67* Kent v Gloucestershire, Bristol 1992
Best bowling: 5-39 Kent v Sussex, Hove 1991

1992 Season

	M	Inns	NO	Runs	HS	Avge	100s	50s	Ct	St	O	M	Runs	Wkts	Avge	Best	5wI	10wM
Test																		
All First	17	27	5	452	67 *	20.54	-	4	4	-	406.1	70	1243	37	33.59	4-67	-	-
1-day Int																		
NatWest	3	3	1	58	33 *	29.00	-	-	-	-	31	1	95	2	47.50	2-33	-	
B & H	7	7	2	85	26	17.00	-	-	5	-	65	8	208	10	20.80	4-29	-	
Sunday	15	12	4	179	43 *	22.37	-	-	4	-	91	2	419	10	41.90	3-24	-	

Career Performances

	M	Inns	NO	Runs	HS	Avge	100s	50s	Ct	St	Balls	Runs	Wkts	Avge	Best	5wI	10wM
Test																	
All First	25	39	8	656	67 *	21.16	-	4	7	-	3526	1835	58	31.63	5-39	2	-
1-day Int																	
NatWest	3	3	1	58	33 *	29.00	-	-	-	-	186	95	2	47.50	2-33	-	
B & H	13	11	4	107	26	15.28	-	-	8	-	684	427	19	22.47	4-29	-	
Sunday	38	28	9	329	43 *	17.31	-	-	15	-	1392	1106	31	35.67	3-24	-	

EDMONDS, P. H.   Middlesex

Name: Phillippe Henri Edmonds
Role: Right-hand bat, slow left-arm bowler
Born: 8 March 1951, Lusaka, Zambia
Height: 6ft 2in
County debut: 1971
County cap: 1974
Benefit: 1983 (£80,000)
Test debut: 1975
Tests: 51
One-Day Internationals: 29
50 wickets in a season: 11
1st-Class 50s scored: 22
1st-Class 100s scored: 3
1st-Class 5 w. in innings: 47
1st-Class 10 w. in match: 9
One-Day 50s: 2
One-Day 5w. in innings: 2
1st-Class catches: 345
Strike rate: (career 69.11)
Wife and date of marriage: Frances
Education: Gilbert Rennie High School, Lusaka; Skinner's School, Tunbridge Wells; Cranbrook School; Cambridge University
Overseas tours: International Wanderers to South Africa 1975-76; England to Pakistan and New Zealand 1977-78, to Australia 1978-79, to India, Sri Lanka and Australia 1984-85, to West Indies 1985-86, to Australia 1986-87
Overseas teams played for: Eastern Province, South Africa 1975-76
Other sports followed: Played rugby for Cambridge but missed Blue, squash
Extras: Cambridge University 1971, 1972, 1973 (captain). Retired at the end of 1987 season, persuaded by Middlesex to play against Notts at Trent Bridge in June 1992
Best batting: 142 Middlesex v Glamorgan, Swansea 1984
Best bowling: 8-53 Middlesex v Hampshire, Bournemouth 1984

1992 Season

	M	Inns	NO	Runs	HS	Avge	100s	50s	Ct	St	O	M	Runs	Wkts	Avge	Best	5wI	10wM
Test																		
All First	1	0	0	0	0	-	-	-	-	-	28	10	48	4	12.00	4-48	-	-
1-day Int																		
NatWest																			
B & H																			
Sunday																			

Career Performances

	M	Inns	NO	Runs	HS	Avge	100s	50s	Ct	St	Balls	Runs	Wkts	Avge	Best	5wI	10wM
Test	51	65	15	875	64	17.50	-	2	42	-	12028	4273	125	34.18	7-66	2	-
All First	391	495	91	7651	142	18.93	3	22	345	-	86116	31981	1246	25.66	8-53	47	9
1-day Int	29	18	7	116	20	10.54	-	-	6	-	1534	965	26	37.11	3-39	-	
NatWest	38	28	9	368	63 *	19.36	-	1	15	-	2455	1245	45	27.66	5-12	1	
B & H	61	41	9	533	44 *	16.65	-	-	14	-	2852	1457	66	22.07	5-4	1	
Sunday	153	115	29	1283	52	14.91	-	1	48	-	5832	4064	175	23.22	3-19	-	

EDWARDS, T.   Worcestershire

Name: Tim Edwards
Role: Right-hand bat, wicket-keeper
Born: 24 June 1974, Penzance, Cornwall
Height: 5ft 3in
Nickname: Ted, Pasty
County debut: No first team appearance
Parents: Chris and Heather
Marital status: Single
Family links with cricket: Father played for Cornwall
Education: Mount's Bay School, Penzance
Off-season: Preparing for the new season
Overseas tours: West of England U14 to Trinidad 1988; West of England U15 to Holland 1989
Cricketers particularly admired: Alan Knott, Ian Botham
Other sports followed: Football
Relaxations: 'Going out and enjoying myself.'
Extras: Played for Somerset 2nd XI during two years with Somerset on YTS scheme.

Name: Richard Mark Ellison
Role: Left-hand bat, right-arm medium bowler
Born: 21 September 1959, Ashford, Kent
Height: 6ft 2¹/₂in **Weight:** 14st
Nickname: Elly
County debut: 1981
County cap: 1983
Benefit: 1993
Test debut: 1984
Tests: 11
One-Day Internationals: 14
50 wickets in a season: 4
1st-Class 50s scored: 20
1st-Class 100s scored: 1
1st-Class 5 w. in innings: 18
1st-Class 10 w. in match: 2
One-Day 50s: 4
1st-Class catches: 85

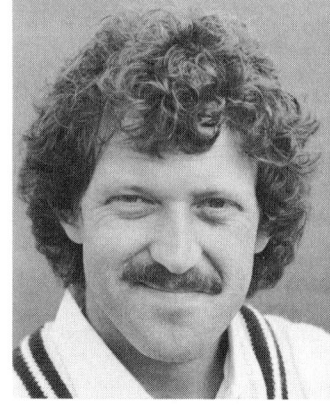

Place in batting averages: 165th av. 23.07
(1991 181st av. 21.841)
Place in bowling averages: 116th av. 41.51 (1991 59th av. 31.48)
Strike rate: 83.13 (career 63.01)
Parents: Peter Richard Maxwell (deceased) and Bridget Mary
Wife and date of marriage: Fiona, 28 September 1985
Children: Charles Peter, 26 January 1991
Family links with cricket: Brother Charles Christopher gained blue at Cambridge University 1981-86. Grandfather played with Grace brothers and was secretary of Derby CCC in about 1915
Education: Friars Preparatory School, Great Chart, Ashford; Tonbridge School; St Luke's College; Exeter University
Qualifications: 8 O-levels, 2 A-levels, Bed
Off-season: Working on benefit year
Overseas tours: With England to India and Australia 1984-85; Sharjah 1984-85; West Indies 1985-86; unofficial English tour to South Africa 1989-90
Cricketers particularly admired: Malcolm Marshall, Richard Hadlee, Chris Tavare, Terry Alderman
Other sports followed: Anything but horse racing and greyhounds
Relaxations: Social drinking, good food, music – Chris Rea, Dire Straits, New Order
Extras: Did not play at all in 1987 due to back injury. One of *Wisden's* Five Cricketers of the Year, 1985. Debut for Canterbury Amateur Operatic Society in April 1989, in 'Fiddler on the Roof'. Banned from Test cricket after touring South Africa in 1989-90, suspension

remitted in 1992
Best batting: 108 Kent v Oxford University, The Parks 1984
Best bowling: 7-33 Kent v Warwickshire, Tunbridge Wells 1991

1992 Season

	M	Inns	NO	Runs	HS	Avge	100s	50s	Ct	St	O	M	Runs	Wkts	Avge	Best	5wI	10wM
Test																		
All First	19	22	8	323	64	23.07	-	1	13	-	401.5	80	1204	29	41.51	6-95	2	-
1-day Int																		
NatWest	1	0	0	0	0	-	-	-	-	-	7	1	21	0	-	-	-	-
B & H	1	1	0	3	3	3.00	-	-	1	-	11	0	27	2	13.50	2-27	-	
Sunday	4	2	1	19	17 *	19.00	-	-	1	-	13.2	0	77	3	25.66	2-43	-	

Career Performances

	M	Inns	NO	Runs	HS	Avge	100s	50s	Ct	St	Balls	Runs	Wkts	Avge	Best	5wI	10wM
Test	11	16	1	202	41	13.46	-	-	2	-	2264	1048	35	29.94	6-77	3	1
All First	204	280	71	4954	108	23.70	1	20	85	-	29680	13604	471	28.88	7-33	18	2
1-day Int	14	12	4	86	24	10.75	-	-	2	-	696	510	12	42.50	3-42	-	
NatWest	21	16	7	302	49 *	33.55	-	-	1	-	1245	641	29	22.10	4-19	-	
B & H	36	29	7	447	72	20.31	-	1	9	-	2065	1156	47	24.59	4-28	-	
Sunday	97	75	34	1102	84	26.87	-	3	14	-	3608	2755	98	28.11	4-25	-	

EMBUREY, J. E.   Middlesex

Name: John Ernest Emburey
Role: Right-hand bat, off-spin bowler
Born: 20 August 1952, Peckham
Height: 6ft 2in **Weight:** 14st
Nickname: Embers, Ern
County debut: 1973
County cap: 1977
Benefit: 1986
Test debut: 1978
Tests: 60
One-Day Internationals: 58
50 wickets in a season: 14
1st-Class 50s scored: 45
1st-Class 100s scored: 5
1st-Class 5 w. in innings: 63
1st-Class 10 w. in match: 9
1st-Class catches: 403
One-Day 50s: 2

Place in batting averages: 146th av. 26.38 (1991 183rd av. 21.72)
Place in bowling averages: 20th av. 25.54 (1991 64th av. 31.91)
Strike rate: 63.22 (career 70.53)
Parents: John (deceased) and Rose
Wife and date of marriage: Susie, 20 September 1980
Children: Clare, 1 March 1983; Chloe, 31 October 1985
Education: Peckham Manor Secondary School
Qualifications: O-levels, advanced cricket coaching certificate
Off-season: Assisting Middlesex CCC
Overseas tours: With England to Australia 1978-79, to Australia and India 1979-80, to West Indies 1980-81, to India and Sri Lanka 1981-82, to West Indies 1985-86, to Australia 1986-87, to Pakistan, Australia and New Zealand 1987-88, to India 1992-93; unofficial English tours to South Africa 1981-82 and 1989-90
Overseas teams played for: Western Province 1982-84
Cricketers particularly admired: Ken Barrington, Derek Underwood
Other sports followed: Golf
Relaxations: Reading, gardening
Extras: Played for Surrey Young Cricketers 1969-70. Phil Edmonds of Middlesex and England was the best man at his wedding. Middlesex vice-captain since 1983. One of *Wisden's* Five Cricketers of the Year, 1983. Captain of England v West Indies for two Tests in 1988. Banned from Test cricket for three years for touring South Africa in 1981-82, and for five more for touring in 1989-90, suspension remitted in 1992. Published autobiography *Emburey* in 1988. Became only 9th player to take 1,000 wickets for Middlesex in the match against Somerset at Lord's, 1992
Best batting: 133 Middlesex v Essex, Chelmsford 1983
Best bowling: 7-27 Middlesex v Gloucestershire, Cheltenham 1989

1992 Season

	M	Inns	NO	Runs	HS	Avge	100s	50s	Ct	St	O	M	Runs	Wkts	Avge	Best	5wl	10wM
Test																		
All First	23	27	6	554	102	26.38	1	3	21	-	854.5	249	2069	81	25.54	5-23	3	-
1-day Int																		
NatWest	2	2	0	4	4	2.00	-	-	2	-	21.3	4	62	1	62.00	1-26	-	
B & H	6	3	0	35	19	11.66	-	-	3	-	57.5	8	198	9	22.00	3-14	-	
Sunday	16	4	4	54	30*	-	-	-	3	-	115.2	3	580	22	26.36	3-39	-	

Career Performances

	M	Inns	NO	Runs	HS	Avge	100s	50s	Ct	St	Balls	Runs	Wkts	Avge	Best	5wl	10wM
Test	60	89	18	1540	75	21.69	-	8	33	-	14227	5105	138	36.99	7-78	6	-
All First	446	562	112	10316	133	22.92	5	45	403	-	96355	35599	1366	26.06	7-27	63	9
1-day Int	58	43	10	471	34	14.27	-	-	19	-	3281	2226	75	29.68	4-37	-	
NatWest	51	33	11	456	36*	20.72	-	-	19	-	3420	1568	52	30.15	3-11	-	
B & H	72	51	14	609	50	16.45	-	1	38	-	3803	1978	75	26.37	5-37	1	
Sunday	223	149	52	1691	50	17.43	-	1	71	-	9446	6949	320	21.71	5-23	2	

EVANS, K. P.   Nottinghamshire

Name: Kevin Paul Evans
Role: Right-hand bat, right-arm medium bowler, slip fielder and occasional wicket-keeper
Born: 10 September 1963, Calverton, Nottingham
Height: 6ft 2in **Weight:** 13st
Nickname: Ghost
County debut: 1984
County cap: 1990
1st-Class 50s scored: 11
1st-Class 100s scored: 2
1st-Class 5 w. in innings: 3
1st-Class catches: 69
Place in batting averages: 174th av. 21.90 (1991 148th av. 26.27)
Place in bowling averages: 90th av. 35.89 (1991 67th av. 31.95)
Strike rate: 74.58 (career 67.71)
Parents: Eric and Eileen
Wife and date of marriage: Sandra, 19 March 1988
Family links with cricket: Brother Russell played for Notts. Father played local cricket
Education: William Lee Primary; Colonel Frank Seely Comprehensive, Calverton
Qualifications: 10 O-levels, 3 A-levels. Qualified coach
Off-season: Working for Pork Farms, Nottingham
Cricketers particularly admired: Richard Hadlee
Other sports followed: Football, tennis, squash
Injuries: Missed three weeks with pulled side muscle and one game after breaking thumb
Relaxations: Listening to music, reading, DIY, gardening
Extras: With brother Russell, first brothers to bat together for Nottinghamshire in first-class cricket for fifty years. Kept wicket for the first time in the Championship match against Essex at Colchester
Best batting: 104 Nottinghamshire v Surrey, Trent Bridge 1992
Best bowling: 5-27 Nottinghamshire v Northamptonshire, Northampton 1992

64. What was the prize money for the winners of the Sunday League last season?

1992 Season

	M	Inns	NO	Runs	HS	Avge	100s	50s	Ct	St	O	M	Runs	Wkts	Avge	Best	5wl	10wM
Test																		
All First	19	24	4	438	104	21.90	1	2	12	-	596.4	132	1723	48	35.89	5-27	1	-
1-day Int																		
NatWest	2	2	1	16	10	16.00	-	-	-	-	22.4	4	68	4	17.00	4-43	-	
B & H	4	2	0	8	6	4.00	-	-	-	-	41.4	4	176	3	58.66	2-38	-	
Sunday	11	6	2	71	30	17.75	-	-	1	-	78.2	1	409	10	40.90	3-31	-	

Career Performances

	M	Inns	NO	Runs	HS	Avge	100s	50s	Ct	St	Balls	Runs	Wkts	Avge	Best	5wl	10wM
Test																	
All First	89	123	30	2374	104	25.52	2	11	69	-	12325	6405	182	35.19	5-27	3	-
1-day Int																	
NatWest	14	10	2	65	20	8.12	-	-	4	-	844	461	15	30.73	4-30	-	
B & H	19	13	4	138	31 *	15.33	-	-	7	-	1074	726	24	30.25	4-43	-	
Sunday	81	45	17	431	30	15.39	-	-	12	-	3238	2840	82	34.63	4-28	-	

EYERS, C. J.   Worcestershire

Name: Christopher John Eyers
Role: Right-hand bat, right-arm medium bowler
Born: 28 March 1972, Aylesbury, Bucks
Height: 6ft 1in **Weight:** 13st 6lbs
Nickname: Pam
County debut: No first team appearance
Parents: Brian and Jean
Marital status: Single
Education: Royal Grammar School, Worcester; Staffordshire University
Qualifications: 2 O-levels, 6 GCSEs, 3 A-levels, NCA Coaching Award
Off-season: In final year of degree course in geography
Cricketers particularly admired: David Gower, Sir Richard Hadlee, Malcolm Marshall
Other sports followed: Football (Liverpool), rugby, golf, tennis
Injuries: Shin splints
Relaxations: Listening to music, cinema and films, playing golf

Extras: Best 2nd XI performance 9 wickets and 85 runs in the match against Somerset in 1992

Opinions on cricket: 'I'd like to see two one-day matches played at weekends, allowing a greater proportion of the public to see exciting limited-over matches which will give a result. Leave the four-day games to the weekdays for the purist to enjoy. Also glad to see the introduction of the new Sunday League format.'

FAIRBROTHER, N. H. Lancashire

Name: Neil Harvey Fairbrother
Role: Left-hand bat, left-arm medium bowler, county captain
Born: 9 September 1963, Warrington, Cheshire
Height: 5ft 8in **Weight:** 11st
Nickname: Harvey
County debut: 1982
County cap: 1985
Test debut: 1987
Tests: 7
One-Day Internationals: 29
1000 runs in a season: 8
1st-Class 50s scored: 70
1st-Class 100s scored: 26
1st-Class 200s scored: 1
1st-Class 300s scored: 1
1st-Class catches: 140
One-Day 50s: 42
One-Day 100s: 6
Place in batting averages: 7th av. 62.63 (1991 37th av. 46.26)
Parents: Les and Barbara
Wife and date of marriage: Audrey, 23 September 1988
Children: Rachael Elizabeth, 4 April 1991
Family links with cricket: Father and two uncles played local league cricket
Education: St Margaret's Church of England School, Oxford; Lymn Grammar School
Qualifications: 5 O-levels
Off-season: Touring with England
Overseas tours: England to Sharjah 1986-87, to India and Pakistan (World Cup), Australia and New Zealand 1987-88; England A to Pakistan 1990-91; England to New Zealand 1991-92, to India 1992-93
Cricketers particularly admired: Clive Lloyd, Allan Border, David Gower
Other sports followed: Football, rugby Union, rugby League
Relaxations: Music and playing sport

Extras: 'I was named after the Australian cricketer Neil Harvey, who was my mum's favourite cricketer.' England YC v Australia 1983. His innings of 366 in 1990 was the third highest score ever made in the County Championship, the second highest first-class score by a Lancashire batsman and the best at The Oval. Appointed Lancashire captain for 1992
Opinions on cricket: 'There is too much cricket. The game has to be made more entertaining. I'm all for coloured clothing.'
Best batting: 366 Lancashire v Surrey, The Oval 1990
Best bowling: 2-91 Lancashire v Nottinghamshire, Old Trafford 1987

1992 Season

	M	Inns	NO	Runs	HS	Avge	100s	50s	Ct	St	O	M	Runs	Wkts	Avge	Best	5wI	10wM
Test																		
All First	12	18	7	689	166 *	62.63	1	5	8	-								
1-day Int	5	5	0	198	63	39.60	-	2	-	-	1	0	9	0	-	-	-	-
NatWest	1	1	0	28	28	28.00	-	-	-	-								
B & H	4	4	1	155	79	51.66	-	1	1	-	6	0	50	0	-	-	-	-
Sunday	8	8	3	139	64 *	27.80	-	1	5	-								

Career Performances

	M	Inns	NO	Runs	HS	Avge	100s	50s	Ct	St	Balls	Runs	Wkts	Avge	Best	5wI	10wM
Test	7	9	1	64	33 *	8.00	-	-	4	-	12	9	0	-	-	-	-
All First	221	345	55	12177	366	41.99	26	70	140	-	656	423	5	84.60	2-91	-	-
1-day Int	29	27	6	860	113	40.95	1	7	13	-	6	9	0	-	-	-	-
NatWest	24	23	4	1021	93 *	53.73	-	9	9	-	18	16	0	-	-	-	-
B & H	43	42	12	1349	116 *	44.96	1	9	21	-	36	50	0	-	-	-	-
Sunday	128	118	28	3327	116 *	36.96	4	17	34	-	12	15	0	-	-	-	-

65. What was the prize money for the team that won each Test Match last season?

FARBRACE, P.   Middlesex

Name: Paul Farbrace
Role: Right-hand bat, wicket-keeper
Born: 7 July 1967, Ash, nr Canterbury
Height: 5ft 10in **Weight:** 12st 8lbs
Nickname: Farby
County debut: 1987 (Kent), 1990 (Middx)
1st-Class 50s scored: 4
1st-Class catches: 86
1st-Class stumpings: 12
Place in batting averages:
(1991 221st av. 15.45)
Parents: David and Betty
Wife and date of marriage: Elizabeth Jane,
27 July 1985
Children: Jemma Elizabeth, 30 March 1985;
Eleanor Kate, 3 September 1988
Family links with cricket: Father played
village cricket.

Two brothers, Ian and Colin play for the
same village, Ash
Education: Ash CE Primary School; Geoffrey Chaucer School, Canterbury
Qualifications: O-levels, NCA Senior/Advanced/Staff Coach
Career outside cricket: HM Customs and Excise; BBC Radio Kent sports reporter;
postman; cricket and football coach
Off-season: Working for BBC Radio Kent, and coaching cricket and football at Hampton
School
Overseas tours: Kent Schools to Canada 1983; Middlesex to Portugal 1991, 1992
Cricketers particularly admired: Alan Knott, Dean Headley, Robin Sims, Nigel
Mullarkey
Other sports followed: All sports except those with horses
Relaxations: 'Football, reading, my wife and children. Finding ways to get out of doing
DIY, mowing the grass and washing the cars.'
Extras: Played County Schools football, had England Schools U18 trial, attracted
attention from Notts County and Coventry City. Captained Kent v Essex in a five-a-side
cricket game in Dartford Tunnel in February 1989 to raise money for Children in Need. Has
only bowled once in first-class cricket and took the wicket of Graham Gooch at Lord's
Opinions on cricket: 'Disappointed with 50-over cricket on Sundays. It's too long a game
for Sundays, it should be only 40 overs with coloured clothing. Players don't do enough
to promote themselves through cricket, so encouraging children into the game. Sunday
lunchtimes could have been put to better use. Invite schools to midweek games when
crowds are low, surely this would benefit everybody.'
Best batting: 79 Middlesex v Cambridge University, Fenner's 1990

Best bowling: 1-64 Middlesex v Essex, Lord's 1991

1992 Season

	M	Inns	NO	Runs	HS	Avge	100s	50s	Ct	St	O	M	Runs	Wkts	Avge	Best	5wl	10wM
Test																		
All First	2	1	1	51	51 *	-		-	1	5	-							
1-day Int																		
NatWest																		
B & H																		
Sunday																		

Career Performances

	M	Inns	NO	Runs	HS	Avge	100s	50s	Ct	St	Balls	Runs	Wkts	Avge	Best	5wl	10wM
Test																	
All First	38	48	11	694	79	18.75	-	4	86	12	25	64	1	64.00	1-64	-	-
1-day Int																	
NatWest	6	4	1	41	17	13.66	-	-	8	1							
B & H																	
Sunday	18	12	4	73	26 *	9.12	-	-	11	10							

FELTHAM, M. A.   Middlesex

Name: Mark Andrew Feltham
Role: Right-hand bat, right-arm fast-medium
bowler
Born: 26 June 1963, London
Height: 6ft 2in **Weight:** 14st
Nickname: Felts, Felpsy, Boff or Douglas
County debut: 1983 (Surrey)
County cap: 1990 (Surrey)
50 wickets in a season: 1
1st-Class 50s scored: 7
1st-Class 100s scored: 1
1st-Class 5 w. in innings: 6
1st-Class catches: 48
One-Day 50s: 2
Place in batting averages: 107th av. 33.61
(1991 124th av. 28.84)
Place in bowling averages: 126th av. 45.00
(1991 54th av. 30.71)
Strike rate: 78.28 (career 60.69)
Parents: Leonard William and Patricia Louise

Wife and date of marriage: Debra Elizabeth, 22 September 1990
Children: Zoë Elizabeth, 23 June 1992
Family links with cricket: 'Mum responsible for fund-raising to build new development at Foster's Oval.'
Education: Roehampton Church School; Tiffin Boys' School
Qualifications: 7 O-levels; advanced cricket coach
Career outside cricket: Marketing and sales
Off-season: Working in London
Cricketers particularly admired: Ian Botham, Gordon Greenidge, Waqar Younis and Sylvester Clarke
Other sports followed: Football, American football and most others
Injuries: Shin splints, missed two games, and achilles injury, missed one game
Relaxations: Music, particularly Luther Vandross; Woody Allen films
Extras: 'I write a weekly column in *Wandsworth Borough News*. Dismissed both Clive Rice and Richard Hadlee in their last innings in county cricket.' Released by Surrey at the end of 1992 season and signed by Middlesex for 1993
Best batting: 101 Surrey v Middlesex, The Oval 1990
Best bowling: 6-53 Surrey v Leicestershire, The Oval 1990

1992 Season

	M	Inns	NO	Runs	HS	Avge	100s	50s	Ct	St	O	M	Runs	Wkts	Avge	Best	5wI	10wM
Test																		
All First	13	19	6	437	50	33.61	-	1	3	-	326.1	61	1125	25	45.00	4-75	-	-
1-day Int																		
NatWest	1	1	0	4	4	4.00	-	-	-	-	5.1	0	39	0	-	-	-	-
B & H	7	4	1	59	35	19.66	-	-	4	-	69.5	7	234	18	13.00	5-30	1	
Sunday	14	10	4	73	14 *	12.16	-	-	7	-	99	3	453	14	32.35	3-24	-	

Career Performances

	M	Inns	NO	Runs	HS	Avge	100s	50s	Ct	St	Balls	Runs	Wkts	Avge	Best	5wI	10wM
Test																	
All First	114	142	38	2526	101	24.28	1	7	48	-	17724	9266	292	31.73	6-53	6	-
1-day Int																	
NatWest	14	10	3	76	19 *	10.85	-	-	1	-	815	626	13	48.15	2-27	-	
B & H	31	20	4	202	35	12.62	-	-	10	-	1761	1154	51	22.62	5-28	2	
Sunday	99	69	21	850	61	17.70	-	2	25	-	3858	3260	92	35.43	4-35	-	

66.   What was the prize money for the team that won each Texaco Trophy match last season?

FELTON, N. A.   Northamptonshire

Name: Nigel Alfred Felton
Role: Left-hand bat
Born: 24 October 1960, Guildford
Height: 5ft 7in **Weight:** 10st 7lbs
Nickname: Gringo, Ninja
County debut: 1982 (Somerset),
1989 (Northants)
County cap: 1986 (Somerset),
1990 (Northants)
1000 runs in a season: 4
1st-Class 50s scored: 52
1st-Class 100s scored: 13
1st-Class catches: 101
One-Day 50s: 19
Place in batting averages: 115th av. 31.64
(1991 99th av. 41.56)
Parents: Ralph and Enid
Wife and date of marriage: Jill-Marie,
October 1989

Family links with cricket: Father played non-white cricket in Cape Town and club cricket in the UK
Education: Hawes Down Secondary School, Kent; Millfield School, Somerset; Loughborough University
Qualifications: 6 O-levels, 2 A-levels, BSc (Hons), Certificate of Education PE/Sports Sciences, qualified teacher
Career outside cricket: Sales and Marketing, Kerrypak, Bristol, manufacturers of netting and suppliers throughout the world
Overseas tours: England ESCA to India 1976-77; England YC to Australia 1979; Somerset to Barbados 1986; to Sierra Leone 1988
Overseas teams played for: Waneroo, Perth, Western Australia 1984-86; Cape Town CC 1988; Primrose, Cape Town 1991-92
Cricketers particularly admired: Richard Hadlee, Graham Gooch
Other sports followed: Most ball games
Injuries: Calf problems and back problems since car accident in 1988
Relaxations: 'Spending time with my wife.'
Extras: Played a season for Kent in 1980 after leaving Millfield and joined Somerset at end of first year at Loughborough. Released by Somerset at end of 1988 season
Best batting: 173* Somerset v Kent, Taunton 1983
Best bowling: 1-48 Northamptonshire v Derbyshire, Northampton 1990

1992 Season

	M	Inns	NO	Runs	HS	Avge	100s	50s	Ct	St	O	M	Runs	Wkts	Avge	Best	5wI	10wM
Test																		
All First	22	37	3	1076	103	31.64	1	9	18	-	14	2	93	0	-	-	-	-
1-day Int																		
NatWest	5	5	0	128	58	25.60	-	1	3	-	1	0	20	0	-	-	-	
B & H	4	4	0	121	82	30.25	-	1	2	-								
Sunday	17	15	1	513	77 *	36.64	-	3	2	-								

Career Performances

	M	Inns	NO	Runs	HS	Avge	100s	50s	Ct	St	Balls	Runs	Wkts	Avge	Best	5wI	10wM
Test																	
All First	183	312	18	8771	173 *	29.83	13	52	101	-	288	345	2	172.50	1-48	-	-
1-day Int																	
NatWest	23	23	2	715	87	34.04	-	6	10	-	6	20	0	-	-	-	
B & H	21	21	0	402	82	19.14	-	2	6	-	6						
Sunday	88	81	10	1908	96	26.87	-	11	25	-	6	7	0	-	-	-	

FIELD-BUSS, M. G.   Nottinghamshire

Name: Michael Gwyn Field-Buss
Role: Right-hand bat, off-spin bowler
Born: 23 September 1964, Malta
Height: 5ft 10in **Weight:** 11st
Nickname: Mouse
County debut: 1987 (Essex), 1989 (Notts)
1st-Class catches: 7
Place in bowling averages: 144th av. 53.63
Strike rate: 92.18 (career 86.95)
Parents: Gwyn and Monica
Marital status: Engaged to Paula
Family links with cricket: Father played local cricket with Ilford RAFA
Education: Wanstead High School
Qualifications: Qualified coach
Off-season: 'Finding work – hopefully'
Overseas teams played for: Werribee, Melbourne 1987-88
Cricketers particularly admired:
'Bill Morris (coach at Ilford Cricket School) during my early years, Ray East and David Acfield at Essex, Eddie Hemmings at Notts.'
Other sports followed: 'Watching Leyton Orient (although I support Arsenal). Keen on

most other sports except horse racing and showjumping.'
Injuries: Split spinning finger, out for two weeks
Relaxations: 'Spending as much time as possible with my fiancee, Paula, and my family, listening to music, playing football and sleeping.'
Opinions on cricket: 'More 2nd XI games should be played on first-class grounds.'
Best batting: 34* Essex v Middlesex, Lord's 1987
Best bowling: 4-33 Nottinghamshire v Somerset, Trent Bridge 1989

1992 Season

	M	Inns	NO	Runs	HS	Avge	100s	50s	Ct	St	O	M	Runs	Wkts	Avge	Best	5wl	10wM
Test																		
All First	8	7	2	27	13	5.40	-	-	5	-	169	29	590	11	53.63	4-71	-	-
1-day Int																		
NatWest	2	1	0	1	1	1.00	-	-	1	-	24	5	85	7	12.14	4-62	-	
B & H																		
Sunday	9	3	1	19	10 *	9.50	-	-	1	-	60	1	301	7	43.00	2-41	-	

Career Performances

	M	Inns	NO	Runs	HS	Avge	100s	50s	Ct	St	Balls	Runs	Wkts	Avge	Best	5wl	10wM
Test																	
All First	18	18	4	136	34 *	9.71	-	-	7	-	1913	1004	22	45.63	4-33	-	-
1-day Int																	
NatWest	2	1	0	1	1	1.00	-	-	1	-	144	85	7	12.14	4-62	-	
B & H																	
Sunday	13	6	2	24	10 *	6.00	-	-	1	-	510	420	11	38.18	2-22	-	

FIELDING, J. M.   Lancashire

Name: Jonathan Mark Fielding
Role: Right-hand bat, slow left-arm bowler
Born: 13 March 1973, Bury, Lancs
Height: 6ft **Weight:** 12st 7lbs
Nickname: Trigga, Fieldo
County debut: No first team appearance
Parents: Brian and Marjorie
Marital status: Single
Family links with cricket: Father was professional in Ribblesdale League and captained Ramsbottom in Lancashire League
Education: Woodey High School; Bury Technical College
Qualifications: 4 GCSEs, OND in Business and Finance
Career outside cricket: Dealing with electrical components at Rowe Hankins
Off-season: 'Was hoping to go to South Africa but this fell through due to lack of jobs

abroad. Forced to stay at home, working and training.'
Overseas tours: Lancashire to Barbados and St Lucia 1992
Cricketers particularly admired:
David Gower, Keith Arthurton, Clive Rice ('model sportsman')
Other sports followed: Football, rugby union, 'enjoy all sports, hate watching swimming'
Injuries: Torn ligaments in spinning finger, out for two weeks
Relaxations: Listening to music, watching TV, playing pool and darts
Extras: Won Lancashire League with Ramsbottom in 1992, with best performance of 9 for 53 against Burnley; top amateur wicket-taker in 1991 Lancashire League (73 wickets). Represented Lancashire

Federation at U15, U16 and U19. Played for England U19 in a friendly against Sri Lanka.
Opinions on cricket: 'Good idea to introduce coloured clothing – should bring more interest into the game. Don't agree on a third umpire and TV replays. Umpires decision on the field should be final.'

FITTON, J. D. Lancashire

Name: John Dexter Fitton
Role: Left-hand bat, off-spin bowler
Born: 24 August 1965, Rochdale
Height: 5ft 10in **Weight:** 12st 8lbs
Nickname: Orbury, Ted, Philbert
County debut: 1987
1st-Class 50s: 1
1st-Class 5 w. in innings: 3
1st-Class catches: 11
Place in batting averages: 195th av. 19.42 (1991 184th av. 21.70)
Place in bowling averages: 87th av. 35.76 (1991 143rd av. 69.08)
Strike rate: 79.00 (career 102.32)
Parents: Derek (deceased) and Jean
Marital status: Single
Family links with cricket: Father dedicated cricketer for 20 years with Littleboro in

Central Lancashire League and Robinsons in North Manchester League
Education: Redbrook High School; Oulder Hill Upper School; Rochdale College
Qualifications: 4 O-levels, Diploma in Business Studies
Career outside cricket: Export administration at Hanson Springs, Rochdale
Off-season: Looking for a job, playing soccer
Overseas tours: Lancashire to Jamaica, Zimbabwe and Western Australia
Overseas teams played for: Sydenham, Christchurch, New Zealand 1988-92
Cricketers particularly admired: 'David Gower, Mike Gatting and Ian Salisbury and most at Old Trafford.'
Other sports followed: Greyhound racing, Manchester City FC and Rochdale Hornets
Relaxations: Watching 'Only Fools and Horses' and 'Fawlty Towers', listening to Luther Vandross and Simply Red
Extras: Was the youngest player to take 50 wickets and score 500 runs for Rochdale in the Central Lancashire League. Captained Lancashire U19, North of England, and NAYC in 1984
Opinions on cricket: 'Clubs should do more for players in the off-season. Tea should be 30 minutes.'
Best batting: 60 Lancashire v Northamptonshire, Lytham 1991
Best bowling: 6-59 Lancashire v Yorkshire, Old Trafford 1988

1992 Season

	M	Inns	NO	Runs	HS	Avge	100s	50s	Ct	St	O	M	Runs	Wkts	Avge	Best	5wI	10wM
Test																		
All First	8	9	2	136	48 *	19.42	-	-	1	-	171.1	38	465	13	35.76	4-81	-	-
1-day Int																		
NatWest	2	1	1	17	17 *	-	-	-	-	-	13	1	49	1	49.00	1-49	-	
B & H	1	1	0	14	14	14.00	-	-	-	-	11	0	56	2	28.00	2-56	-	
Sunday	11	5	2	77	36	25.66	-	-	2	-	66	2	359	13	27.61	4-26	-	

Career Performances

	M	Inns	NO	Runs	HS	Avge	100s	50s	Ct	St	Balls	Runs	Wkts	Avge	Best	5wI	10wM
Test																	
All First	52	61	15	872	60	18.95	-	1	11	-	8391	4359	82	53.15	6-59	3	-
1-day Int																	
NatWest	2	1	1	17	17 *	-	-	-	-	-	78	49	1	49.00	1-49	-	
B & H	2	1	0	14	14	14.00	-	-	-	-	132	103	3	34.33	2-56	-	
Sunday	14	6	3	77	36	25.66	-	-	2	-	492	437	15	29.13	4-26	-	

67. Who was Durham's first captain, as a first-class county?

FLEMING, M. V.   Kent

Name: Matthew Valentine Fleming
Role: Right-hand bat, right-arm medium
bowler
Born: 12 December 1964, Macclesfield
(by mistake - one month early!)
Height: 6ft **Weight:** 12st 4lbs
Nickname: Jazzer, Swan Vestas
County debut: 1988
County cap: 1990
1st-Class 50s scored: 15
1st-Class 100s scored: 4
1st-Class catches: 34
One-Day 50s: 3
Place in batting averages: 144th av. 26.56
(1991 103rd av. 31.62)
Place in bowling averages: 41st av. 29.00
(1991 98th av. 35.81)
Strike rate: 61.25 (career 87.69)
Parents: Valentine and Elizabeth
Wife and date of marriage: Caroline, 23 September 1989
Family links with cricket: Great-grandfather C.F.Leslie played for England in 1880s
Education: St Aubyns School, Rottingdean; Eton College
Qualifications: 8 O-levels, 3 A-levels
Career outside cricket: House husband this winter
Off-season: Baby due also working for Andy Needham (ex-Surrey and Middlesex)
Overseas teams played for: Avendale, Cape Town 1984
Cricketers particularly admired: Robin Smith – 'he destroyed me in the B&H final',
Martin McCague – 'smallest, but most pertinent vocabulary', and 'anyone who is still
smiling on Monday mornings during 1993'
Other sports followed: Shooting, fishing, golf
Extras: Ex-army officer in the Royal Green Jackets. First two scoring shots in Championship
cricket were sixes
Opinions on cricket: 'Four-day cricket is a good idea, but why change the Sunday League
and cancel the B&H zonal rounds. We now have three very similar one-day competitions.
Sponsored estate cars necessary to carry all our kit now (coloured clothing etc).'
Best batting: 116 Kent v West Indies, Canterbury 1991
Best bowling: 4-63 Kent v Glamorgan, Canterbury 1992

---

68. Who is the current editor of *Wisden Cricketers' Almanack*?

1992 Season

	M	Inns	NO	Runs	HS	Avge	100s	50s	Ct	St	O	M	Runs	Wkts	Avge	Best	5wI	10wM
Test																		
All First	21	32	2	797	100 *	26.56	1	4	13	-	245	46	696	24	29.00	4-63	-	-
1-day Int																		
NatWest	3	3	0	65	53	21.66	-	1	-	-	18	3	58	5	11.60	3-34	-	
B & H	7	7	0	258	69	36.85	-	2	3	-	49	0	245	8	30.62	2-32	-	
Sunday	15	13	1	264	45 *	22.00	-	-	1	-	86	0	435	16	27.18	2-25	-	

Career Performances

	M	Inns	NO	Runs	HS	Avge	100s	50s	Ct	St	Balls	Runs	Wkts	Avge	Best	5wI	10wM
Test																	
All First	68	108	14	2898	116	30.83	4	15	34	-	5963	2786	68	40.97	4-63	-	-
1-day Int																	
NatWest	7	7	1	140	53	23.33	-	1	1	-	272	143	9	15.88	3-34	-	
B & H	19	18	0	433	69	24.05	-	3	4	-	888	599	18	33.27	2-32	-	
Sunday	56	52	8	951	77	21.61	-	2	13	-	2175	1869	62	30.14	4-45	-	

FLETCHER, I. Somerset

Name: Ian Fletcher
Role: Right-hand bat, right-arm medium bowler
Born: 31 August 1971, Sawbridgeworth, Herts
Height: 5ft 11in
County debut: 1991
1st-Class 50s: 1
1st-Class catches: 0
Education: Millfield School, Somerset
Extras: Played for Hertfordshire in NatWest Trophy 1990 and for Combined Universities in B&H Cup 1991
Best batting: 56 Somerset v Hampshire, Southampton 1991

1992 Season (did not make any first-class or one-day appearance)

Career Performances

	M	Inns	NO	Runs	HS	Avge	100s	50s	Ct	St	Balls	Runs	Wkts	Avge	Best	5wI	10wM
Test																	
All First	1	2	1	58	56	58.00	-	1	-	-							
1-day Int																	
NatWest	1	1	0	1	1	1.00	-	-	-	-							
B&H	1	1	0	9	9	9.00	-	-	1	-							
Sunday																	

FLETCHER, S. D.   Lancashire

Name: Stuart David Fletcher
Role: Right-hand bat, right-arm medium bowler
Born: 8 June 1964, Keighley
Height: 5ft 10in **Weight:** 12st 6lbs
Nickname: Fletch, Norm
County debut: 1983 (Yorkshire), 1992 (Lancashire)
County cap: 1988 (Yorkshire)
50 wickets in a season: 1
1st-Class 5 w. in innings: 5
1st-Class catches: 27
Place in bowling averages: (1991 105th av. 38.25)
Strike rate: (career 63.20)
Parents: Brough and Norma Hilda
Wife and date of marriage: Katharine, 4 October 1986
Children: Craig Stuart, 26 July 1989; Melissa Kate, 8 June 1992
Family links with cricket: Father played league cricket
Education: Woodhouse Primary; Reins Wood Secondary
Qualifications: O-level English and Woodwork, City and Guilds in coachbuilding
Off-season: Getting fit for the next season
Cricketers particularly admired: Ian Botham, Arnie Sidebottom
Other sports followed: Watches Leeds United FC
Injuries: Cartilage operation
Relaxations: Watching TV, snooker and golf
Extras: Released by Yorkshire at end of 1991 season and signed 3-year contract with Lancashire
Best batting: 28* Yorkshire v Kent, Tunbridge Wells 1984

Best bowling: 8-58 Yorkshire v Essex, Sheffield 1988

1992 Season

	M	Inns	NO	Runs	HS	Avge	100s	50s	Ct	St	O	M	Runs	Wkts	Avge	Best	5wI	10wM
Test																		
All First	6	5	1	62	23	15.50	-	-	2	-	101	23	409	6	68.16	2-53	-	-
1-day Int																		
NatWest																		
B & H																		
Sunday	2	1	1	6	6 *	-	-	-	-	-	11.1	0	77	2	38.50	2-45	-	

Career Performances

	M	Inns	NO	Runs	HS	Avge	100s	50s	Ct	St	Balls	Runs	Wkts	Avge	Best	5wI	10wM
Test																	
All First	113	96	32	476	28 *	7.43	-	-	27	-	15168	8375	240	34.89	8-58	5	-
1-day Int																	
NatWest	15	7	4	36	16 *	12.00	-	-	2	-	913	576	15	38.40	3-34	-	
B & H	27	6	3	20	15 *	6.66	-	-	6	-	1405	974	35	27.82	4-34	-	
Sunday	88	19	12	55	11 *	7.85	-	-	26	-	3699	3212	116	27.69	4-11	-	

FLINT, D. P. J.   Hampshire

Name: Darren Peter John Flint
Role: Right-hand bat, slow left-arm bowler
Born: 14 June 1970,
Height: 6ft **Weight:** 14st
County debut: No first team appearance
Parents: Peter and Linda
Marital status: Single
Education: Cranbourne Comprehensive;
Queen Mary's College, Basingstoke
Qualifications: 5 O-levels, NCA senior
coach
Off-season: Coaching and working for the
family business
Cricketers particularly admired:
Derek Underwood, John Emburey,
Malcolm Marshall, Gary Sobers
Other sports followed: Rugby, snooker
Relaxations: Enjoying good food and drink
Extras: Rapid Cricketline Player of the
Month August/September 1991

Opinions on cricket: 'Left-arm bowlers should be able to bowl over the wicket and get an lbw decision if the ball pitches outside the leg stump.'

FOLLAND, N. A. Somerset

Name: Nicholas Arthur Folland
Role: Left-hand bat, right-arm medium bowler
Born: 17 September 1963, Bristol
Height: 6ft ½in **Weight:** 13st
County debut: 1992
1st-Class 50s: 2
1st-Class catches: 1
One-Day 50s: 2
Parents: Geoffrey and Maureen
Wife and date of marriage:
Diane, 4 April 1992
Family links with cricket: Brother Neil played for Devon and now plays for Bedfordshire
Education: Exmouth School
Qualifications: Degree in Sports Science and Recreation Management
Career outside cricket: Teaching PE and geography at Blundells School, Tiverton
Off-season: Teaching
Cricketers particularly admired: David Gower, Viv Richards, Malcolm Marshall, Richard Hadlee
Other sports followed: All sports, especially rugby
Relaxations: Watching sport, reading, good food
Extras: Had trial for Gloucestershire in 1979. Played for Devon in the NatWest Trophy since 1984 and Minor Counties in the B&H Cup 1989-1992. Captained Minor Counties to victory over Pakistanis
Opinions on cricket: 'Very new to the professional game – I may have more opinions in a year or so.'
Best batting: 82* Somerset v Worcestershire, Weston-super-Mare 1992

---

69.   What do the following cricketers have in common - A.C. MacLaren, A.P.F. Chapman, M.D. Moxon and J.D. Glendenen?

1992 Season

	M	Inns	NO	Runs	HS	Avge	100s	50s	Ct	St	O	M	Runs	Wkts	Avge	Best	5wI	10wM
Test																		
All First	1	2	1	104	82 *	104.00	-	1	1	-								
1-day Int																		
NatWest	1	1	0	20	20	20.00	-	-	2	-								
B & H	5	5	0	155	63	31.00	-	2	5	-								
Sunday	1	1	0	3	3	3.00	-	-	2	-								

Career Performances

	M	Inns	NO	Runs	HS	Avge	100s	50s	Ct	St	Balls		Runs	Wkts	Avge	Best	5wI	10wM
Test																		
All First	2	4	1	212	82 *	70.66	-	2	1	-								
1-day Int																		
NatWest	7	7	0	130	55	18.57	-	1	4	-	20		55	1	55.00	1-52	-	
B & H	17	17	3	660	100 *	47.14	1	6	10	-								
Sunday	1	1	0	3	3	3.00	-	-	2	-								

FORDHAM, A.   Northamptonshire

Name: Alan Fordham
Role: Right-hand bat, occasional right-arm medium bowler
Born: 9 November 1964, Bedford
Height: 6ft 1in **Weight:** 13st
Nickname: Forders
County debut: 1986
County cap: 1990
1000 runs in a season: 3
1st-Class 50s scored: 33
1st-Class 100s scored: 14
1st-Class 200s scored: 1
1st-Class catches: 65
One-Day 50s: 22
One-Day 100s: 3
Place in batting averages: 47th av. 43.84 (1991 32nd av. 47.17)
Parents: Clifford and Ruth
Marital status: Single
Family links with cricket: Brother John played school and college cricket
Education: Bedford Modern School; Durham University
Qualifications: 9 O-levels, 3 A-levels, BSc (Hons) Chemistry, NCA senior coaching

award
Career outside cricket: 'Still no definite plans.'
Off-season: Playing and coaching in Cape Town
Overseas tours: Bedford Modern to Barbados 1983; Gentlemen of Leicestershire to Jersey and Guernsey 1987; International Ambassadors XI/Christians in Sport to India 1990; MCC to Leeward Islands 1992; Northants to Natal 1992
Overseas teams played for: Richmond, Melbourne 1983-84; Camberwell, Melbourne 1987-88; Curtin University, Perth, Western Australia 1988; Nirman Schools XI, Dhaka, Bangladesh 1989-90
Cricketers particularly admired: Allan Lamb, Bob Willis, Mike Brearley
Other sports followed: Rugby union
Relaxations: TV, music, travel
Extras: Has appeared for Bedfordshire in Minor Counties Championship. Played for Combined Universities in B & H Cup 1987. Shared county record stand of 393 with Allan Lamb v Yorkshire at Headingley in 1990. Only white man to have played league cricket in Bangladesh
Opinions on cricket: 'I'm sure I won't be the only one to say it's a shame to lose the B&H zonals. Disastrous format for Sundays, am I allowed a life in summer outside cricket? But I think most of us are looking forward to the four-day Championship programme.'
Best batting: 206* Northamptonshire v Yorkshire, Headingley 1990
Best bowling: 1-25 Northamptonshire v Yorkshire, Northampton 1990

1992 Season

	M	Inns	NO	Runs	HS	Avge	100s	50s	Ct	St	O	M	Runs	Wkts	Avge	Best	5wI	10wM
Test																		
All First	23	41	2	1710	192	43.84	4	7	14	-	12.2	0	72	0	-	-	-	-
1-day Int																		
NatWest	5	5	0	223	91	44.60	-	2	1	-								
B & H	4	4	0	182	103	45.50	1	1	-	-								
Sunday	16	15	0	520	89	34.66	-	5	5	-	1	0	10	0	-	-	-	

Career Performances

	M	Inns	NO	Runs	HS	Avge	100s	50s	Ct	St	Balls	Runs	Wkts	Avge	Best	5wI	10wM
Test																	
All First	103	182	16	6759	206 *	40.71	14	33	65	-	362	238	3	79.33	1-25	-	-
1-day Int																	
NatWest	14	14	1	766	132 *	58.92	2	5	3	-	21	6	1	6.00	1-3	-	
B & H	15	14	1	474	103	36.46	1	4	2	-							
Sunday	58	54	1	1615	89	30.47	-	13	14	-	6	10	0	-	-	-	

FOSTER, D. J.   Glamorgan

Name: Daren Joseph Foster
Role: Right-hand bat, right-arm fast-medium
bowler, specialist fine-leg
Born: 14 March 1966, London
Height: 5ft 9in **Weight:** 9st 4lbs
Nickname: Fozzie, Smiler, Stick Insect
County debut: 1986 (Somerset),
1991 (Glamorgan)
1st-Class 5 w. in innings: 2
1st-Class catches: 8
Place in bowling averages: 96th av. 37.27
(1991 68th av. 32.56)
Strike rate: 52.22 (career 63.16)
Parents: Vivian and Sadie
Marital status: Single
Children: Marcella and Daren Danny
Family links with cricket: Cousin Morris
Foster played for Jamaica
Education: Somerset School; Haringey
College; Southgate Technical College, 'Glamorgan dressing room'
Qualifications: 2 O-levels, 1 CSE, 'Provocational' Studies pass, Commercial Studies pass
and credit, qualifying as a physio 'so that I can treat myself'
Career outside cricket: Physio (as above), would like to run a gym eventually
Off-season: Working on career, relaxing after a hard season, 'maybe learn to drive
properly'
Overseas teams played for: West Geelong, Victoria 1988-89
Cricketers particularly admired: Clive Lloyd, Vivian Richards, Malcolm Marshall, Ian
Botham, Michael Holding, Matthew Maynard, Steve Bastien, R. Needham
Other sports followed: Rugby league, pool, 'any really'. Supports Tottenham
Injuries: Back, missed several games
Relaxations: Training, music (light classical and reggae), reading, 'talking politics with
Steve Bastien and Sam Kirnon'
Extras: Took career best 6-84 on his first Championship appearance for Glamorgan,
against his old county Somerset (1986-89). Appeared for both Surrey and Middlesex 2nd
XIs in 1985. Released by Glamorgan at the end of the 1992 season
Opinions on cricket: 'Good to see four-day cricket and coloured clothing on Sundays.
Cricketers should only go into the game if they really want to make a go of it. Too many
treat it as a game not a job. Steve Bastien for England!'
Best batting: 20 Somerset v Hampshire, Southampton 1988
Best bowling: 6-84 Glamorgan v Somerset, Taunton 1991

1992 Season

	M	Inns	NO	Runs	HS	Avge	100s	50s	Ct	St	O	M	Runs	Wkts	Avge	Best	5wI	10wM
Test																		
All First	8	4	1	40	17 *	13.33	-	-	1	-	191.3	27	820	22	37.27	5-87	1	-
1-day Int																		
NatWest	1	1	0	2	2	2.00	-	-	-	-	12	3	40	1	40.00	1-40	-	
B & H	1	0	0	0	0	-	-	-	-	-	11	0	42	2	21.00	2-42	-	
Sunday	10	4	3	21	10 *	21.00	-	-	1	-	68.3	3	400	9	44.44	3-32	-	

Career Performances

	M	Inns	NO	Runs	HS	Avge	100s	50s	Ct	St	Balls	Runs	Wkts	Avge	Best	5wI	10wM
Test																	
All First	45	39	15	201	20	8.37	-	-	8	-	6064	3844	96	40.04	6-84	2	-
1-day Int																	
NatWest	3	2	0	2	2	1.00	-	-	1	-	162	72	2	36.00	1-15	-	
B & H	8	1	0	0	0	0.00	-	-	-	-	486	305	8	38.12	2-26	-	
Sunday	32	13	10	36	10 *	12.00	-	-	4	-	1226	1035	27	38.33	4-26	-	

FOSTER, M.   Yorkshire

Name: Michael Foster
Born: 17 September 1972, Leeds
Height: 6ft 2in **Weight:** 14st 7lbs
Nickname: Foz
County debut: No first team appearance
Parents: Paul and Margaret
Marital status: Single
Family links with cricket: Grandfather and father play local cricket; sister played for Yorkshire
Education: Park High School, Pontefract; New College, Pontefract
Qualifications: 5 O-levels, 2 A-levels
Off-season: Playing in Australia
Overseas tours: England U19 to Pakistan 1991-92
Overseas teams played for: Freemantle, Western Australia 1991-92; Ringwood, Victoria 1992-93
Cricketers particularly admired: Robin Smith, Malcolm Marshall
Other sports followed: Rugby

Injuries: Broken finger, out for two weeks
Relaxations: Gym, running, socialising
Extras: Captained Yorkshire at all junior age levels

FOSTER, N. A. Essex

Name: Neil Alan Foster
Role: Right-hand bat, right-arm fast-medium
bowler, outfielder
Born: 6 May 1962, Colchester
Height: 6ft 3in **Weight:** 13st 7lbs
Nickname: Fozzie, Norbert, Norbie, Sniffer
County debut: 1980
County cap: 1983
Benefit: 1993
Test debut: 1983
Tests: 28
One-Day Internationals: 48
50 wickets in a season: 9
1st-Class 50s scored: 11
1st-Class 100s scored: 2
1st-Class 5 w. in innings: 49
1st-Class 10 w. in match: 8
1st-Class catches: 115

Place in batting averages: 173rd av. 23.28
(1991 131st av. 28.50)
Place in bowling averages: 46th av. 30.16 (1990 6th av. 20.96)
Strike rate: 64.00 (career 49.47)
Parents: Jean and Alan
Wife and date of marriage: Romany, 21 September 1985
Family links with cricket: Father played local cricket
Education: Broomgrove Infant & Junior Schools; Philip Morant Comprehensive, Colchester
Qualifications: 8 O-levels, 1 A-level, NCA coaching award. Has consumer credit licence
for Financial Consultancy
Career outside cricket: PE teacher at Holmwood House Prep School, Colchester
Off-season: Preparing for benefit and recovering from knee surgery
Overseas tours: England YC to West Indies 1980; England to New Zealand and Pakistan
1983-84; India and Australia 1984-85; West Indies 1985-86; Australia 1986-87; Pakistan,
Australia and New Zealand 1987-88; unofficial English team to South Africa 1989-90
Overseas teams played for: Transvaal, South Africa 1991-92
Cricketers particularly admired: Dennis Lillee, Graham Gooch, Viv Richards, Malcolm
Marshall, Imran Khan, John Lever, Sir Richard Hadlee, Keith Fletcher
Other sports followed: Most sports, particularly golf and football

Injuries: Operation on medial femoral condyle of left knee, out from August 1st to the end of the season

Relaxations: Music, golf

Extras: Was summoned from school at short notice to play for Essex v Kent at Ilford. First ball went for 4 wides, but he finished with figures of 3 for 51. Played for England YC v India 1981. Banned from Test cricket for touring South Africa in 1989-90, suspension remitted in 1992. Leading first-class wicket-taker in 1990 season. Britannic Assurance/*Sunday Express* Cricketer of the Year 1991

Opinions on cricket: 'Pleased to be playing four-day cricket, though disappointed to have 50 overs on a Sunday. Also pleased to be 'unbanned' and have been interested to see our fellow professionals attitude change from being opposed to the ban, as being against a cricketer's democratic rights to earn a living where he chooses, to being opposed to the lifting of the ban, as we knew what we were letting ourselves in for. We were always prepared to see the ban through but those who changed their minds are just completely two-faced!'

Best batting: 107* Essex v Sussex, Horsham 1991

Best bowling: 8-99 Essex v Lancashire, Old Trafford 1991

1992 Season

	M	Inns	NO	Runs	HS	Avge	100s	50s	Ct	St	O	M	Runs	Wkts	Avge	Best	5wI	10wM
Test																		
All First	11	14	0	326	54	23.28	-	2	12	-	256	63	724	24	30.16	4-47	-	-
1-day Int																		
NatWest	2	1	0	11	11	11.00	-	-	-	-	24	4	72	1	72.00	1-25	-	
B & H	3	3	0	64	62	21.33	-	1	1	-	22.2	2	61	2	30.50	1-25	-	
Sunday	5	3	0	29	18	9.66	-	-	3	-	29	0	153	2	76.50	1-16	-	

Career Performances

	M	Inns	NO	Runs	HS	Avge	100s	50s	Ct	St	Balls	Runs	Wkts	Avge	Best	5wI	10wM
Test	28	43	7	410	39	11.38	-	-	7	-	6081	2797	88	31.78	8-107	5	1
All First	222	257	56	4108	107 *	20.43	2	11	115	-	44330	21473	896	23.96	8-99	49	8
1-day Int	48	25	12	150	24	11.53	-	-	12	-	2627	1836	59	31.11	3-20	-	
NatWest	22	13	2	149	26	13.54	-	-	3	-	1465	751	39	19.25	4-9	-	
B & H	48	20	8	269	62	22.41	-	1	8	-	2850	1662	77	21.58	5-32	1	
Sunday	79	45	16	581	57	20.03	-	1	20	-	3236	2366	99	23.89	5-17	1	

70.   Who is current President of the MCC?

FOTHERGILL, A. R.   Durham

Name: Andrew Robert Fothergill
Role: Right-hand bat, wicket-keeper
Born: 10 February 1962,
Newcastle-upon-Tyne
Height: 6ft **Weight:** 13st
Nickname: Fothers
County debut: 1992
1st-Class catches: 10
1st-Class stumpings: 1
Place in batting averages: 259th av. 10.14
Parents names:
Bill and Dorothy (stepmother)
Marital status: Divorced
Education: Eastbourne Comprehensive,
Darlington
Career outside cricket:
Sales Executive – selling fixtures and
fittings to the retail industry
Off-season: as above
Cricketers particularly admired:
Alan Knott and Jack Russell

Other sports followed: Football (played for Bishop Auckland)
Relaxations: Going to restaurants and sleeping ('but not in the restaurant!')
Extras: First played for Durham in the NatWest Trophy in 1983. Played for Minor
Counties in the B&H Cup 1989-91
Best batting: 23 Durham v Kent, Canterbury 1992

1992 Season

	M	Inns	NO	Runs	HS	Avge	100s	50s	Ct	St	O	M	Runs	Wkts	Avge	Best	5wI	10wM
Test																		
All First	6	8	1	71	23	10.14	-	-	10	1								
1-day Int																		
NatWest	3	2	0	11	7	5.50	-	-	7	1								
B & H	3	3	1	32	17	16.00	-	-	2	1								
Sunday	15	11	4	160	42 *	22.85	-	-	12	5								

> 71. Who is the only player to have scored 1000 runs on a - to him -
> foreign Test ground?

Career Performances

	M	Inns	NO	Runs	HS	Avge	100s	50s	Ct	St	Balls	Runs	Wkts	Avge	Best	5wl	10wM
Test																	
All First	7	9	1	74	23	9.25	-	-	10	1							
1-day Int																	
NatWest	10	8	2	76	24	12.66	-	-	13	4							
B & H	12	11	3	121	45 *	15.12	-	-	11	1							
Sunday	15	11	4	160	42 *	22.85	-	-	12	5							

FOWLER, G.   Durham

Name: Graeme Fowler
Role: Left-hand opening bat, occasional wicket-keeper, 1st slip, 'slow right-hand declaration bowler'
Born: 20 April 1957, Accrington
Height: 5ft 9in **Weight:** 'Near 11st'
Nickname: Fow, Foxy
County debut: 1979
County cap: 1981
Benefit: 1991 (£152,000)
Test debut: 1982
Tests: 21
One-Day Internationals: 26
1000 runs in a season: 8
1st-Class 50s scored: 79
1st-Class 100s scored: 35
1st-Class 200s scored: 2
1st-Class catches: 143
1st-Class stumpings: 5
One-Day 50s: 49
One-Day 100s: 8
Place in batting averages: 101st av. 34.61 (1991 112th av. 30.74)
Marital status: Single
Education: Accrington Grammar School; Bede College, Durham University
Qualifications: Certificate of Education, advanced cricket coach
Career outside cricket: 'Some radio and TV work.'
Overseas tours: England to Australia and New Zealand 1982-83; New Zealand and Pakistan 1983-84; India and Australia 1984-85
Overseas teams played for: Tasmania 1981-82
Cricketers particularly admired: David Lloyd and Paul Allott
Other sports followed: 'Bits of everything.'

Injuries: 'Plastic surgery on my top lip. Ball came off wicket-keeper's elbow into my face at first slip. Couldn't laugh without pain for two weeks.'
Relaxations: Music, gardening, playing drums
Extras: Played for Accrington and Rawtenshall in Lancashire League: at 15 he was the youngest opener in the League. Played for England YC in 1976. Published *Fox on the Run*, a cricketing diary from 1984 to 1986, which won Channel 4's Sports Book of the Year Award. First Englishman to score a double century in India. Released by Lancashire at the end of the 1992 season and joined Durham
Opinions on cricket: 'Good game isn't it!'
Best batting: 226 Lancashire v Kent, Maidstone 1984
Best bowling: 2-34 Lancashire v Warwickshire, Old Trafford 1986

1992 Season

	M	Inns	NO	Runs	HS	Avge	100s	50s	Ct	St	O	M	Runs	Wkts	Avge	Best	5wI	10wM
Test																		
All First	11	20	2	623	106	34.61	1	4	7	-	5	0	60	1	60.00	1-60	-	-
1-day Int																		
NatWest	2	2	0	69	66	34.50	-	1	-	-								
B & H	2	2	0	58	36	29.00	-	-	-	-								
Sunday	10	10	1	263	57	29.22	-	2	1	-								

Career Performances

	M	Inns	NO	Runs	HS	Avge	100s	50s	Ct	St	Balls	Runs	Wkts	Avge	Best	5wI	10wM
Test	21	37	0	1307	201	35.32	3	8	10	-	18	11	0	-		-	-
All First	274	464	27	15803	226	36.16	35	79	143	5	407	366	10	36.60	2-34	-	-
1-day Int	26	26	2	744	81 *	31.00	-	4	4	2							
NatWest	30	30	0	880	122	29.33	2	4	9	2							
B & H	60	59	1	1689	136	29.12	1	12	17	1							
Sunday	167	162	11	4853	112	32.13	5	29	61	-	6		1	0	-	-	-

72. Which county entered the Minor Counties championship to replace Durham?

FRASER, A. G. J.   Essex

Name: Alastair Gregory James Fraser
Role: Right-hand bat, right-arm fast-medium
bowler
Born: 17 October 1967, Edgware
Height: 6ft 1in **Weight:** 13st
County debut: 1986 (Middx), 1991 (Essex)
1st-Class 50s scored: 1
1st-Class catches: 1
Strike rate: (career 62.08)
Parents: Don and Irene
Marital status: Single
Family links with cricket: Father played
club cricket,
brother Angus plays for Middlesex and
England
Education: Gayton High School, Harrow;
John Lyon
School, Harrow Weald Sixth Form College
Qualifications: 4 O-levels, qualified cricket
coach

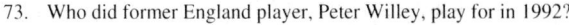

Off-season: Playing in Trinidad
Overseas tours: NCA U19 to Bermuda 1985; England YC to Sri Lanka 1987
Overseas teams played for: Plimmerton, Wellington 1986-88; Green Point, Cape Town
1988-89; Western Suburbs, Sydney 1989-90; Northerns-Goodwood, Cape Town 1991-
92; Queens Park, Trinidad 1992-93
Cricketers particularly admired: Graham Gooch, Malcolm Marshall
Other sports followed: Rugby union and league, football
Relaxations: Following Liverpool FC, having a pint with friends, playing football for Old
Lyonians (Southern Amateur League)
Extras: Joined Essex from Middlesex in 1990.
Opinions on cricket: 'Pleased to see four-day cricket in 1993 and looking forward to
Sunday cricket. Perhaps it should still be 40 overs.'
Best batting: 52* Essex v Sussex, Horsham 1991
Best bowling: 3-46 Middlesex v New Zealand, Lord's 1986

---

73.   Who did former England player, Peter Willey, play for in 1992?

1992 Season

	M	Inns	NO	Runs	HS	Avge	100s	50s	Ct	St	O	M	Runs	Wkts	Avge	Best	5wI	10wM
Test																		
All First	2	3	1	11	5	5.50	-	-	1	-	20.3	5	95	3	31.66	2-37	-	-
1-day Int																		
NatWest																		
B & H	1	1	0	6	6	6.00	-	-	-	-	5.1	0	31	1	31.00	1-31	-	
Sunday	6	4	1	25	12	8.33	-	-	-	-	36	0	177	6	29.50	2-39	-	

Career Performances

	M	Inns	NO	Runs	HS	Avge	100s	50s	Ct	St	Balls		Runs	Wkts	Avge	Best	5wI	10wM
Test																		
All First	10	10	5	137	52 *	27.40	-	1	1	-	745		386	12	32.16	3-46	-	-
1-day Int																		
NatWest																		
B & H	1	1	0	6	6	6.00	-	-	-	-	31		31	1	31.00	1-31	-	
Sunday	13	5	2	27	12	9.00	-	-	1	-	504		368	12	30.66	2-35	-	

FRASER, A. R. C. Middlesex

Name: Angus Robert Charles Fraser
Role: Right-hand bat, right-arm medium-fast bowler
Born: 8 August 1965, Billinge, Lancashire
Height: 6ft 5^{1}/2in **Weight:** 15st 7lbs
Nickname: Gus, Lard
County debut: 1984
County cap: 1988
Test debut: 1989
Tests: 11
One-Day Internationals: 24
50 wickets in a season: 3
1st-Class 50s scored: 1
1st-Class 5 w. in innings: 16
1st-Class 10 w. in match: 2
1st-Class catches: 16
Place in batting averages: 213th av. 16.76
Place in bowling averages: 147th av. 55.34
Strike rate: 111.30 (career 62.84)
Parents: Don and Irene
Marital status: Single
Family links with cricket: Brother Alastair plays for Essex. Parents are keen followers

Education: Gayton High School, Harrow; Orange Senior High School, Edgware
Qualifications: 7 O-levels, qualified cricket coach
Career outside cricket: Learning more about unit trust and gilts with Whittingdale
Off-season: Probably working for Whittingdale Unit Trust Ltd. Getting as fit as possible for summer
Overseas tours: Thames Valley Gentlemen to Barbados 1985; Middlesex to La Manga 1985 and 1986, to Portugal 1991; England to India (Nehru Cup) and West Indies 1989-90, to Australia 1990-91; Middlesex to Val de Lobo, Portugal 1991, 1992
Overseas teams played for: Plimmerton, Wellington 1985-86 and 1987-88; Western Suburbs, Sydney 1988-89
Cricketers particularly admired: Richard Hadlee, Allan Border, Graham Gooch and Dennis Lillee
Other sports followed: 'Watch Liverpool FC when I can, follow local rugby club, Harrow, watch rugby internationals when I can get tickets, golf'
Injuries: Hip, backside, leg pains throughout season, out for 2-3 weeks
Relaxations: 'Trying to work out which rule will be changed next – have they got any left? Sorting out the problems of the world over a pint with mates. '
Extras: Middlesex Player of the Year 1988 and 1989. Selected for England tour to New Zealand 1991-92 but ruled out by injury.
Opinions on cricket: 'The game is becoming a joke. I don't know what the people who make changes to the rules are trying to achieve but they do it without talking to the players. I haven't been spoken to yet about no ball changes, bouncers etc. and I don't know anyone other than captains (who happen to be batsmen) who have. We couldn't accuse captains of looking after themselves though could we? At least bowling machines wouldn't argue about field placings!'
Best batting: 92 Middlesex v Surrey, The Oval 1990
Best bowling: 7-77 Middlesex v Kent, Canterbury 1989

1992 Season

	M	Inns	NO	Runs	HS	Avge	100s	50s	Ct	St	O	M	Runs	Wkts	Avge	Best	5wI	10wM
Test																		
All First	18	20	7	218	33	16.76	-	-	3	-	426.4	90	1273	23	55.34	3-16	-	-
1-day Int																		
NatWest	2	1	1	1	1*	-	-	-	-	-	19	4	55	2	27.50	1-10	-	
B & H	6	2	1	2	2	2.00	-	-	2	-	61	11	227	8	28.37	3-30	-	
Sunday	17	2	0	9	9	4.50	-	-	2	-	114.2	9	479	14	34.21	3-40	-	

74.   Who is the only New Zealand player to have scored 1000 Test runs on one ground?

Career Performances

	M	Inns	NO	Runs	HS	Avge	100s	50s	Ct	St	Balls	Runs	Wkts	Avge	Best	5wI	10wM
Test	11	14	1	88	29	6.76	-	-	1	-	3106	1255	47	26.70	6-82	4	-
All First	119	134	34	1240	92	12.40	-	1	19	-	22309	9376	355	26.41	7-77	16	2
1-day Int	24	10	4	69	38 *	11.50	-	-	-	-	1336	797	23	34.65	3-22	-	
NatWest	17	4	3	28	19	28.00	-	-	-	-	1179	584	30	19.46	4-34	-	
B & H	21	10	4	38	13 *	6.33	-	-	5	-	1279	744	23	32.34	3-30	-	
Sunday	78	29	13	173	30 *	10.81	-	-	10	-	3317	2205	76	29.01	4-28	-	

FRENCH, B. N.   Nottinghamshire

Name: Bruce Nicholas French
Role: Right-hand bat, wicket-keeper
Born: 13 August 1959, Warsop, Notts
Height: 5ft 8in **Weight:** 10st
Nickname: Frog
County debut: 1976
County cap: 1980
Benefit: 1991
Test debut: 1986
Tests: 16
One-Day Internationals: 13
1st-Class 50s scored: 24
1st-Class 100s scored: 1
1st-Class catches: 772
1st-Class stumpings: 95
Place in batting averages: 218th av. 16.25
(1991 217th av. 15.75)
Parents: Maurice and Betty
Wife and date of marriage:
Ellen Rose, 9 March 1978
Children: Charles Daniel, 31 August 1978; Catherine Ellen, 28 December 1980
Family links with cricket: Brothers, Neil, David, Charlie, Joe, play for Welbeck CC and father is Treasurer. Neil also plays for Lincolnshire
Education: Meden School, Warsop
Qualifications: O-level and CSE
Overseas tours: England to India and Sri Lanka 1984-85, to West Indies 1985-86, to Australia 1986-87, to India and Pakistan (World Cup), Australia and New Zealand 1987-88; unofficial England XI to South Africa 1989-90
Cricketers particularly admired: Bob Taylor
Other sports followed: Rock climbing, fell walking and all aspects of mountaineering
Injuries: Missed most of 1988 season following operations in May on index finger of left

hand, and in 1989 broke the same finger again, missing end of season. Previously, French was bitten by a dog whilst jogging in the Caribbean in 1985-86; had to be carried off the field with a cut head and concussion after being struck by a short-pitched delivery from Richard Hadlee; contracted a chest infection after being hit in the chest by a ball in Australia in 1986-87; in Pakistan in 1987-88, he needed stitches in a cut eye and on the way to hospital a car struck his legs

Relaxations: Reading, pipe smoking and drinking Theakston's Ale

Extras: Youngest player to play for Nottinghamshire, aged 16 years 10 months. Equalled Nottinghamshire record for dismissals in match with 10 (7ct, 3st), and in innings with 6 catches; also set new county record for dismissals in a season with 87 (75ct, 12st). Banned from Test cricket for touring South Africa in 1989-90, suspension remitted in 1992. Made his maiden first-class 100 in 1990 in 15th season of county cricket

Best batting: 105* Nottinghamshire v Derbyshire, Derby 1990

Best bowling: 1-37 Nottinghamshire v Derbyshire, Derby 1991

1992 Season

	M	Inns	NO	Runs	HS	Avge	100s	50s	Ct	St	O	M	Runs	Wkts	Avge	Best	5wl	10wM
Test																		
All First	17	20	4	260	55	16.25	-	1	41	4								
1-day Int																		
NatWest	2	2	1	20	12	20.00	-	-	-	-								
B & H	4	2	0	15	10	7.50	-	-	4	-								
Sunday	8	6	4	52	22 *	26.00	-	-	2	-								

Career Performances

	M	Inns	NO	Runs	HS	Avge	100s	50s	Ct	St	Balls	Runs	Wkts	Avge	Best	5wl	10wM
Test	16	21	4	308	59	18.11	-	1	38	1							
All First	340	444	88	6721	105 *	18.87	1	24	772	95	90	70	1	70.00	1-37	-	-
1-day Int	13	8	3	34	9 *	6.80	-	-	13	3							
NatWest	30	25	6	366	49	19.26	-	-	45	4							
B & H	60	42	12	416	48 *	13.86	-	-	62	11							
Sunday	160	98	35	954	37	15.14	-	-	122	17							

75. Who is the only Australian player to have taken 50 Test wickets on one ground?

FROST, M.   Glamorgan

Name: Mark Frost
Role: Right-hand bat, right-arm medium-fast bowler
Born: 21 October 1962, Barking
Height: 6ft 2in **Weight:** 14st
Nickname: Harold, Frosty, Jack
County debut: 1988 (Surrey), 1990 (Glamorgan)
County cap: 1991
50 wickets in a season: 2
1st-Class 5 w. in innings: 4
1st-Class 10 w. in match: 2
1st-Class catches: 7
Place in bowling averages: 150th av. 64.07 (1991 41st av. 28.73)
Strike rate: 91.46 (career 59.06)
Parents: George and Joyce
Wife and date of marriage:
Janet, 28 September 1991
Family links with cricket:
All three brothers play
Education: Alexandra High School, Tipton; St Peter's, Wolverhampton; University of Durham
Qualifications: 10 O-levels, 4 A-levels, BA (Hons) Geography
Off-season: Working for South Glamorgan County Council, writing marketing publicity for the Economic Development Unit
Overseas tours: Christians in Sport to India 1985; Surrey to Sharjah 1988; Glamorgan to Zimbabwe 1991
Cricketers particularly admired: Jack Breakwell, Andy Webster, Ron Headley, Chris Derham, Nick Peters, Geoff Arnold, Pete Frost
Other sports followed: Soccer, rugby, tennis, athletics
Relaxations: Hill walking, climbing, listening to compact discs, theatre going. 'Climbing snowy mountains in Scotland with Janet. Converting Tony Cottey.'
Extras: Member of Christians in Sport. Played for Old Hill CC, winners of Cockspur Cup in 1987 and for Staffordshire before joining Surrey. Released by Surrey at end of 1989 season and joined Glamorgan
Opinions on cricket: 'The cricket ball should be standardised so that they all deteriorate, shine, or go soft in the same way. There should be no declarations so that batsmen have to give up their wickets to tired seamers!'
Best batting: 12 Glamorgan v Warwickshire, Edgbaston 1990
Best bowling: 7-99 Glamorgan v Gloucestershire, Cheltenham 1991

1992 Season

	M	Inns	NO	Runs	HS	Avge	100s	50s	Ct	St	O	M	Runs	Wkts	Avge	Best	5wl	10wM
Test																		
All First	8	5	2	4	4	1.33	-	-	2	-	198.1	29	833	13	64.07	3-100	-	-
1-day Int																		
NatWest																		
B & H	3	2	1	5	4	5.00	-	-	1	-	30	5	109	5	21.80	4-26	-	
Sunday	9	1	1	6	6 *	-	-	-	1	-	57.3	2	290	8	36.25	3-52	-	

Career Performances

	M	Inns	NO	Runs	HS	Avge	100s	50s	Ct	St	Balls	Runs	Wkts	Avge	Best	5wl	10wM
Test																	
All First	62	48	16	87	12	2.71	-	-	7	-	9569	5825	162	35.95	7-99	4	2
1-day Int																	
NatWest	6	1	0	3	3	3.00	-	-	3	-	372	260	5	52.00	3-50	-	
B & H	11	6	3	9	4	3.00	-	-	1	-	656	432	19	22.73	4-25	-	
Sunday	33	7	5	17	6 *	8.50	-	-	5	-	1321	1152	38	30.31	4-30	-	

FULTON, D. P.　　　　　　　　　　　Kent

Name: David Paul Fulton
Role: Right-hand bat, slow left-arm
Born: 15 November 1971, Lewisham
Height: 6ft 2in **Weight:** 11st 7lbs
Nickname: Rave, Fults, Don
County debut: 1992
1st-Class catches: 2
Parents: George and Joyce
Marital status: Single
Family links with cricket: Father plays for
Otford village side
Education: Otford County Primary;
The Judd School, Tonbridge;
Kent University
Qualifications: 10 GCSEs, 3 A-levels,
BA (Hons) ('provisionally') Politics and
International Relations; Senior NCA coach
Off-season: Studying, playing football,
boxing, weight-training

Overseas tours: Kent Schools U17 to Singapore and New Zealand 1986-87
Cricketers particularly admired: David Gower, Gordon Greenidge, Viv Richards and
all Kent players

Other sports followed: Rugby (Harlequins) and football (Nottingham Forest)

Relaxations: 'All other kinds of sport other than swimming. Socialising with team-mates. Watching and learning as Andy Tutt talks subtly and eloquently to women. Going on holidays with girlfriends.'

Extras: Played mainly Kent 2nd XI in 1992. Rapid Cricketline Player of the Month for July. Helped Kent University reach the final of UAU. '1992 was best season yet. Scored 1022 runs after returning from University in June (av. 64).'

Opinions on cricket: 'Concerned that as counties reduce the size of their staffs the gap between first-class and 2nd XI cricket will grow too large. Concerned that Kent's top five batsmen will still be playing first-class cricket in the year 2000 – they are good enough to do so. Concerned that the 50 over Sunday League is too long. The spectators might find it too drawn out.'

Best batting: 42 Kent v Cambridge University, Fenner's 1992

1992 Season

	M	Inns	NO	Runs	HS	Avge	100s	50s	Ct	St	O	M	Runs	Wkts	Avge	Best	5wI	10wM
Test																		
All First	1	2	0	58	42	29.00	-	-	2	-								
1-day Int																		
NatWest																		
B & H																		
Sunday																		

Career Performances

	M	Inns	NO	Runs	HS	Avge	100s	50s	Ct	St	Balls	Runs	Wkts	Avge	Best	5wI	10wM
Test																		
All First	1	2	0	58	42	29.00	-	-	2	-								
1-day Int																		
NatWest																		
B & H																		
Sunday																		

76. Which Durham bowler took two wickets in his first over in first-class cricket?

GALLIAN, J. E. R. Lancashire

Name: Jason Edward Riche Gallian
Role: Right-hand bat, right-arm medium
bowler
Born: 25 June 1971, Manly, NSW, Australia
Height: 6ft **Weight:** 13st
Nickname: Galliflap, Gallers, Winston
County debut: 1990
1st-Class 50s scored: 3
1st-Class 100s scored: 1
1st-Class catches: 7
One-Day 50s: 2
Place in batting averages: 117th av. 31.20
Place in bowling averages: 81st av. 34.88
Strike rate: 69.33 (career 72.31)
Parents: Ray and Marilyn
Marital status: Single
Education: The Pitwater House Schools,
Australia; Oxford University
Qualifications: Higher School Certificate
Off-season: Studying

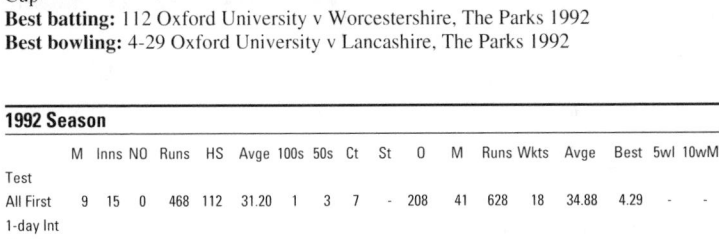

Overseas tours: Australia U20 to West Indies 1990
Overseas teams played for: NSW and Australia U19 1988-89; NSW Colts and NSW 2nd
XI 1990-91; Australia U20 and U21 1991-92
Cricketers particularly admired: Desmond Haynes, Michael Bevan
Other sports followed: Golf, tennis, rugby
Relaxations: Listening to music, watching television, playing golf
Extras: Played for Oxford University in 1992 and for Combined Universities in the B&H
Cup
Best batting: 112 Oxford University v Worcestershire, The Parks 1992
Best bowling: 4-29 Oxford University v Lancashire, The Parks 1992

1992 Season

	M	Inns	NO	Runs	HS	Avge	100s	50s	Ct	St	O	M	Runs	Wkts	Avge	Best	5wI	10wM
Test																		
All First	9	15	0	468	112	31.20	1	3	7	-	208	41	628	18	34.88	4.29	-	-
1-day Int																		
NatWest																		
B & H	4	4	0	114	50	28.50	-	2	-	-	23	0	102	2	51.00	1-26	-	
Sunday																		

Career Performances

	M	Inns	NO	Runs	HS	Avge	100s	50s	Ct	St	Balls	Runs	Wkts	Avge	Best	5wI	10wM
Test																	
All First	10	16	1	485	112	32.33	1	3	7	-	1374	693	19	36.47	4-29	-	-
1-day Int																	
NatWest																		
B & H	4	4	0	114	50	28.50	-	2	-	-	138	102	2	51.00	1-26	-	

GARAWAY, M. Hampshire

Name: Mark Garaway
Role: Right-hand bat, wicket-keeper
Born: 20 July 1973, Swindon, Wilts
Height: 5ft 7in **Weight:** 11st 7lbs
Nickname: Garas
County debut: No first team appearance
Parents: Sam and Valerie Anne
Marital status: Single
Family links with cricket: Grandfather kept
wicket for 40 years in club cricket. Father
still opens the batting for Ventnor 1st XI
Education: Carhampton Primary, Somerset;
Ventnor Middle and Sandown High School,
Isle of Wight
Qualifications: 10 GCSEs, 2 A-levels,
NCA cricket coach
Career outside cricket: 'Yet to find one!'
Off-season: 'Taking a break from playing
cricket after more than two years non-stop.
Coaching young cricketers on the Isle of
Wight and spending the winter at home.'
Overseas teams played for: Worcester, Boland, South Africa 1991-92
Cricketers particularly admired: Ian Botham, Gordon Greenidge, Robin Smith, David
Gower
Other sports followed: Squash, golf, soccer, rugby – 'basically any ball-playing sport'
Injuries: Torn ligaments in left index finger, out for a month
Relaxations: Music (any type), letter-writing, reading (particularly sports magazines and
novels)
Extras: Represented England at U15, U17 and U19 level. Played for Isle of Wight at U16,
U17, U21 and senior level in the same season. Spent two years (1991 and 1992) as MCC
Young Professional.
Opinions on cricket: 'Much more money should be designated for youth cricket, especially

Opinions on cricket: 'Much more money should be designated for youth cricket, especially within the Minor Counties and outskirts where there is a great deal of talent which has yet to be realised and/or developed.'

GARNHAM, M. A. — Essex

Name: Michael Anthony Garnham
Role: Right-hand bat, wicket-keeper
Born: 20 August 1960, Johannesburg
Height: 5ft 10³/₄in **Weight:** 12st
Nickname: Bones, Fred
County debut: 1979 (Gloucs), 1980 (Leics), 1989 (Essex)
County cap: 1989 (Essex)
1st-Class 50s scored: 26
1st-Class 100s scored: 4
1st-Class catches: 362
1st-Class stumpings: 31
One-Day 50s: 3
One-Day 100s: 1
Place in batting averages: 169th av. 23.70 (1991 34th av. 46.95)
Parents: Pauline Anne and Robert Arthur
Wife and date of marriage: Lorraine, 15 September 1984
Children: Laura Clare, 3 November 1988; Eleanor Louise, 22 October 1990
Family links with cricket: Father was a club cricketer in Essex. He lost the sight of an eye keeping wicket
Education: Camberwell Grammar, Melbourne, Australia; Scotch College, Perth, Australia; Park School, Barnstaple, North Devon; North Devon College; University of East Anglia (for one year)
Qualifications: 10 O-levels, 2 A-levels
Overseas tours: England Schools to India 1977-78; England YC to Australia 1979
Cricketers particularly admired: Bob Taylor
Other sports followed: Squash
Injuries: Cut around the eye requiring 16 stitches
Relaxations: Carpentry – furniture making, building and DIY
Extras: Moved to England in 1975 after living in Australia for ten years and in South Africa for four years. Played for Devon in 1976 and 1977 before joining Gloucestershire. Signed for Leicestershire in 1980 and was banned by the registration committee from competitive first-team cricket for a month for breach of registration regulations. Retired at end of 1985, but returned for one one-day and one three-day game in 1988 following

injury to Phil Whitticase. Signed for Essex in 1989, having been playing for Cambridgeshire. 'Having run a business making keeping gloves, I wear gloves I have made myself.'
Best batting: 123 Essex v Leicestershire, Leicester 1991

1992 Season

	M	Inns	NO	Runs	HS	Avge	100s	50s	Ct	St	O	M	Runs	Wkts	Avge	Best	5wI	10wM
Test																		
All First	24	28	4	569	82 *	23.70	-	4	42	3								
1-day Int																		
NatWest	4	3	1	66	53 *	33.00	-	1	3	1								
B & H	4	4	2	39	17 *	19.50	-	-	5	2								
Sunday	16	10	5	99	33 *	19.80	-	-	9	-								

Career Performances

	M	Inns	NO	Runs	HS	Avge	100s	50s	Ct	St	Balls	Runs	Wkts	Avge	Best	5wI	10wM
Test																	
All First	171	221	46	4956	123	28.32	4	26	362	31	24	39	0	-	-	-	-
1-day Int																	
NatWest	23	19	6	384	110	29.53	1	1	16	3							
B & H	53	38	14	506	55	21.08	-	1	50	7							
Sunday	140	101	26	1261	79 *	16.81	-	1	118	16							

GATTING, M. W. Middlesex

Name: Michael William Gatting
Role: Right-hand bat, right-arm medium bowler, slip fielder
Born: 6 June 1957, Kingsbury, Middlesex
Height: 5ft 10in **Weight:** 15st 7lbs
Nickname: Gatt, Jabba
County debut: 1975
County cap: 1977
Benefit: 1988 (£205,000)
Test debut: 1977-78
Tests: 68
One-Day Internationals: 85
1000 runs in a season: 14
1st-Class 50s scored: 144
1st-Class 100s scored: 72
1st-Class 200s scored: 5
1st-Class 5 w. in innings: 2
1st-Class catches: 376

One-Day 50s: 72
One-Day 100s: 11
Place in batting averages: 5th av. 66.66 (1991 3rd av. 73.46)
Parents: Bill and Vera
Wife and date of marriage: Elaine, September 1980
Children: Andrew, 21 January 1983; James, 11 July 1986
Family links with cricket: Father used to play club cricket. Brother Steve played for Middlesex 2nd XI
Education: Wykeham Primary School; John Kelly Boys' High School
Qualifications: 4 O-levels
Off-season: Touring India with England, playing golf and having a family holiday
Overseas tours: England to New Zealand and Pakistan 1977-78; West Indies 1980-81; India and Sri Lanka 1981-82; New Zealand and Pakistan 1983-84; India 1984-85; West Indies 1985-86; Australia 1986-87; India and Pakistan (World Cup), Australia and New Zealand 1987-88; unofficial English team to South Africa 1989-90; England to India and Sri Lanka 1992-93
Cricketers particularly admired: Sir Gary Sobers, Sir Leonard Hutton
Other sports followed: Football, golf
Injuries: 8 stitches in forehead wound
Relaxations: Golf, swimming, reading, music
Extras: Awarded OBE in Queen's Birthday Honours for services to cricket. Captain of Middlesex since 1983. Captain of England from 1986 to 1988. Published autobiography *Leading From the Front* in 1988. Won a bronze medal for ballroom dancing at the Neasden Ritz. Played football for Edgware Town as a teenager. Started as a goalkeeper, but also played centre-half for Middlesex Schools. Was recommended to West Ham, had a trial with QPR and offered an apprenticeship by Watford. His brother Steve has had a successful football career with Arsenal and Brighton. Mike started his cricket career as wicket-keeper for his school team. He toured West Indies with England Young Cricketers in 1976 and 'to my immense pleasure (and to most other people's total disbelief) I was given the job of opening the bowling in the 'Test' matches.' One of *Wisden's* Five Cricketers of the Year, 1983. His finest achievement was as captain of England on victorious tour of Australia, 1986-87, when they won the Ashes, the Perth Challenge Cup and World Series Cup. Was relieved of England captaincy after the First Test against West Indies in 1988. Captain of unofficial English team in South Africa in 1989-90 and was banned from Test cricket for five years; suspension remitted in 1992. Captained Middlesex to Championship title in 1990
Opinions on cricket: 'Best kept to myself.'
Best batting: 258 Middlesex v Somerset, Bath 1984
Best bowling: 5-34 Middlesex v Glamorgan, Swansea 1982

---

77.   Which countries will tour England in 1994?

1992 Season

	M	Inns	NO	Runs	HS	Avge	100s	50s	Ct	St	O	M	Runs	Wkts	Avge	Best	5wI	10wM
Test																		
All First	24	36	6	2000	170	66.66	6	10	16	-	9	3	38	0	-	-	-	-
1-day Int																		
NatWest	1	1	0	57	57	57.00	-	1	-	-								
B & H	6	5	0	106	38	21.20	-	-	2	-								
Sunday	16	16	2	540	96	38.57	-	4	9	-	3	0	32	0	-		-	-

Career Performances

	M	Inns	NO	Runs	HS	Avge	100s	50s	Ct	St	Balls	Runs	Wkts	Avge	Best	5wI	10wM
Test	68	117	14	3870	207	37.57	9	18	51	-	752	317	4	79.25	1-14	-	-
All First	432	676	107	28512	258	50.10	72	144	376	-	9731	4466	154	29.00	5-34	2	-
1-day Int	85	82	17	2049	115 *	31.52	1	9	22	-	386	334	10	33.40	3-32	-	
NatWest	54	53	13	1951	132 *	48.77	2	14	21	-	1004	643	19	33.84	2-14	-	
B & H	79	73	17	2550	143 *	45.53	3	17	24	-	1382	940	41	22.92	4-49	-	
Sunday	206	191	25	5418	124 *	32.63	5	32	69	-	3100	2619	85	30.81	4-30	-	

GERRARD, M. J.   Gloucestershire

Name: Martin James Gerrard
Role: Right-hand bat, left-arm medium-fast bowler
Born: 19 May 1967, Bristol
Height: 6ft 2in **Weight:** 13st 7lbs
Nickname: Noddy, Clunk
County debut: 1991
1st-Class 5 w. in innings: 1
1st-Class 10 w. in match: 1
1st-Class catches: 4
Strike rate: (career 75.88)
Parents: Donald and Jean
Marital status: Single
Education: Grittleton House School; St Brendan's Sixth Form College; Polytechnic of Wales
Qualifications: 8 O-levels, A-level Geography, HND in Mineral Surveying
Career outside cricket: Construction engineer
Off-season: Working for a financial services company, also working indoors with the county coach

Overseas teams played for: Vaal Reefs and Western Transvaal 1991-92
Cricketers particularly admired: Ian Botham, Sir Richard Hadlee, Jack Russell, Graham Gooch
Other sports followed: All sport, especially rugby, football and golf
Injuries: Glandular fever, out for 3-4 weeks
Relaxations: Playing golf, relaxing in front of Sky TV and going to the local with a few friends on days off
Extras: Recorded his first 10 wickets in a match on only his fifth first-class appearance
Opinions on cricket: 'General standard of 2nd XI umpiring should be better. The improvements made to the game for the start of the 1993 season should produce better cricket but Sunday League should remain 40 overs.'
Best batting: 42 Gloucestershire v Somerset, Bristol 1991
Best bowling: 6-40 Gloucestershire v Sri Lanka, Bristol 1991

1992 Season

	M	Inns	NO	Runs	HS	Avge	100s	50s	Ct	St	O	M	Runs	Wkts	Avge	Best	5wI	10wM
Test																		
All First	4	4	1	6	4	2.00	-	-	1	-	93	20	297	7	42.42	2-51	-	-
1-day Int																		
NatWest																		
B & H	2	1	1	1	1 *	-	-	-	1	-	13.5	2	53	0	-		-	-
Sunday	2	1	1	0	0 *	-	-	-	-	-	16	0	59	3	19.66	2-35	-	

Career Performances

	M	Inns	NO	Runs	HS	Avge	100s	50s	Ct	St	Balls	Runs	Wkts	Avge	Best	5wI	10wM
Test																	
All First	16	19	7	81	42	6.75	-	-	4	-	1973	1016	26	39.07	6-40	1	1
1-day Int																	
NatWest	1	0	0	0	0	-	-	-	-	-	12	10	0	-		-	-
B & H	2	1	1	1	1 *	-	-	-	1	-	83	53	0	-		-	-
Sunday	6	5	2	17	7	5.66	-	-	-	-	270	223	6	37.16	2-35	-	

78. Which national cricket team did Simon Hewitt captain in 1992?

GIDDINS, E. S. H.   Sussex

Name: Edward Simon Hunter Giddins
Role: Right-hand bat, right-arm medium-fast
bowler
Born: 20 July 1971, Eastbourne
Height: 6ft 4in **Weight:** 14st
Nickname: Hunter
County debut: 1991
1st-Class catches: 4
1st-Class 5 w. in innings: 2
Place in bowling averages: 36th av. 27.64
Strike rate: 47.96 (career 55.30)
Parents: Simon and Pauline
Marital status: Single
Family links with cricket:
Great-grandmother played cricket for
England Ladies
Education: St Bede's Prep School,
Eastbourne College
Qualifications: 'Various O and A-levels,
National Coaching Certificate, recorder (grade 2)'
Career outside cricket: 'Professional traveller'
Off-season: Travelling
Overseas tours: Eastbourne College cricket/drama/debating tour to New Zealand 1988
Overseas teams played for: Discovery Bay Hotel, Barbados 1991; Bondi Surf CC,
Sydney 1991-92; Bayswater Morley, Perth 1992;
Cricketers particularly admired: Simon Aldis, Rachel Heyhoe-Flint
Other sports followed: 'Most sports but not football.'
Injuries: 'Dodgy ankle – missed one game in June.'
Relaxations: Raving at garage parties. Videos (especially Coming to America, Pretty
Woman, Cocktail)
Extras: Took four wickets for no runs in 10 balls against Derbyshire at Eastbourne
Opinions on cricket: 'Wickets are like buses...they all come at the same time or not at all.
Professional cricket provides many things other than fun, competitive cricket. It provides
friends, acquaintances and a damn good social life.'
Best batting: 14* Sussex v Middlesex, Lord's 1991
Best bowling: 5-32 Sussex v Derbyshire, Eastbourne 1992

---

79.   What do Kepler Wessels, Gul Mahomed, and the Nawab of Pataudi
(senior) have in common?

1992 Season

	M	Inns	NO	Runs	HS	Avge	100s	50s	Ct	St	O	M	Runs	Wkts	Avge	Best	5wI	10wM
Test																		
All First	11	8	6	15	10 *	7.50	-	-	4	-	247.5	52	857	31	27.64	5-32	2	-
1-day Int																		
NatWest																		
B & H																		
Sunday	6	3	0	4	2	1.33	-	-	2	-	42	0	246	5	49.20	3-37	-	

Career Performances

	M	Inns	NO	Runs	HS	Avge	100s	50s	Ct	St	Balls	Runs	Wkts	Avge	Best	5wI	10wM
Test																	
All First	13	9	7	29	14 *	14.50	-	-	4	-	1825	1043	33	31.60	5-32	2	-
1-day Int																	
NatWest																	
B & H	1	1	0	0	0	0.00	-	-	-	-	48	46	1	46.00	1-46	-	
Sunday	8	3	0	4	2	1.33	-	-	2	-	294	284	5	56.80	3-37	-	

GIDLEY, M. I. Leicestershire

Name: Martyn Ian Gidley
Role: Left-hand bat, off-spin bowler
Born: 30 September 1968, Leicester
Height: 6ft 1in **Weight:** 11st 7lbs
Nickname: Gidders
County debut: 1989
1st-Class 50s scored: 3
1st-Class catches: 11
One-Day 50s: 1
Place in batting averages: 208th av. 17.87
(1991 222nd av. 15.28)
Parents: Barry and Susan
Marital status: Single
Family links with cricket: Father is former
chairman of Loughborough Town CC and
now compiling a book on the club's history
Education: Loughborough Grammar School
Qualifications: 7 O-levels, 3 A-levels,
NCA Coaching Certificate

Off-season: Playing and coaching in South Africa
Overseas teams played for: Harmony, OFS 1989-91; Orange Free State Colts 1989-92;
Orange Free State B 1990-91

Leicester City'
Relaxations: Reading, confessed Gameboy addict
Extras: Leicestershire U19 Player of the Year 1987, England Schools U19 1987
Opinions on cricket: 'Even though I was banned for playing in South Africa, I feel that
Mike Gatting's rebel side should not have had their 5-year ban lifted. They should not be
allowed to play for England. Players who refused to take the money must feel particularly
aggrieved.'
Best batting: 80 Leicestershire v Derbyshire, Leicester 1991
Best bowling: 3-51 Orange Free State B v Western Province B, Bloemfontein 1990-91

1992 Season

	M	Inns	NO	Runs	HS	Avge	100s	50s	Ct	St	O	M	Runs	Wkts	Avge	Best	5wI	10wM
Test																		
All First	5	10	2	143	39	17.87	-	-	2	-	80	20	248	2	124.00	1-51	-	-
1-day Int																		
NatWest																		
B & H																		
Sunday	6	5	1	104	55 *	26.00	-	1	2	-	27	0	149	3	49.66	1-25	-	

Career Performances

	M	Inns	NO	Runs	HS	Avge	100s	50s	Ct	St	Balls	Runs	Wkts	Avge	Best	5wI	10wM
Test																	
All First	21	32	7	559	80	22.36	-	3	11	-	2303	1116	16	69.75	3-51	-	-
1-day Int																	
NatWest																	
B & H	3	2	2	21	20 *	-	-	-	-	-	72	39	0	-		-	-
Sunday	14	12	6	155	55 *	25.83	-	1	2	-	373	370	8	46.25	3-45	-	

GILES, A. F. Warwickshire

Name: Ashley Fraser Giles
Role: Right-hand bat, slow left-arm bowler
Born: 19 March 1973, Chertsey, Surrey
Height: 6ft 3in **Weight:** 14st
Nickname: Splash, Skater, Shanks
County debut: No first team appearance
Parents: Michael and Paula
Marital status: Single
Family links with cricket: Brother and
other family members play local club cricket
Education: George Abbot County

Secondary, Guildford
Qualifications: 9 GCSEs, 1 A-levels
Off-season: Coaching and playing in South
Africa
Overseas tours:
Surrey U19 to Barbados 1991
Overseas teams played for:
Vredenburg/Saldanha, South Africa 1992-93
Cricketers particularly admired:
Ian Botham, David Gower, Ian Ward,
Steve Perryman
Other sports followed: Football, golf,
basketball
Relaxations: Music, eating, drinking,
relaxing with girlfriend, watching sport
Opinions on cricket: 'Introduction of
four-day cricket good for the game and
coloured clothing should be a big
spectator puller, which can only be
better for the game.'

GLENDENEN, J. D. Durham

Name: John David Glendenen
Role: Right-hand opening bat, right-arm
medium bowler
Born: 20 June 1965, Middlesbrough
Height: 6ft 1in **Weight:** 13st
Nickname: Glendo, Raymond
1st-Class 50s scored: 3
1st-Class 100s scored: 1
1st-Class catches: 5
One-Day 50s: 5
One-Day 100s: 1
Place in batting averages: 170th av. 22.48
Parents: David and Jackie
Marital status: 'Still looking'
Family links with cricket: Father played
cricket for Middlesbrough for 25 years in
the NYSD League, 'alongside my godfather
Peter Athey – Bill's dad'
Education: Ormesby Secondary School
Qualifications: 2 O-levels

Career outside cricket: Sales manager, 'ferret breeder'
Off-season: Playing in South Africa
Overseas teams played for: Manly, Sydney 1986-87 and 1990-92; Alberton, Johannesburg 1992-93
Cricketers particularly admired: Wayne Larkins and Matthew Maynard – 'for their immense talent', Geoff Cook – 'who says the right thing at the right time' and Mike Gatting
Other sports followed: Bungee jumping
Injuries: Eye injury and reaction to substance on the pitch
Relaxations: 'Shooting with Dad in the winter when I can, listening to soul music, walking the dogs with girlfriend, good pint in the Dun Cow.'
Extras: Had scored six centuries for Durham prior to first-class status including 109 against Glamorgan in the NatWest Trophy 1991. Has played 2nd XI cricket for Yorkshire (1983-86), Gloucestershire (1988) and Somerset (1989). Scored a century on his first-class debut against Oxford University.
Best batting: 117 Durham v Oxford University, The Parks 1992

1992 Season

	M	Inns	NO	Runs	HS	Avge	100s	50s	Ct	St	O	M	Runs	Wkts	Avge	Best	5wI	10wM
Test																		
All Firs	17	28	1	607	117	22.48	1	3	5	-								
1-day Int																		
NatWest	3	3	0	114	57	38.00	-	1	-	-								
B & H	4	4	0	132	60	33.00	-	1	2	-								
Sunday	15	13	2	424	78	38.54	-	3	3	-								

Career Performances

	M	Inns	NO	Runs	HS	Avge	100s	50s	Ct	St	Balls	Runs	Wkts	Avge	Best	5wI	10wM
Test																	
All First	17	28	1	607	117	22.48	1	3	5	-							
1-day Int																	
NatWest	6	6	0	243	109	40.50	1	1	-	-							
B & H	4	4	0	132	60	33.00	-	1	2	-							
Sunday	15	13	2	424	78	38.54	-	3	3	-							

80. What do Ian Botham, David Smith and Trevor Jesty all have in common?

81. Who was the first and only Australian this century to do the double of 50 wickets and 500 runs in the Australian season?

GOFTON, R. P.   Leicestershire

Name: Robert Paul Gofton
Role: Right-hand bat, right-arm medium-fast bowler
Born: 10 September 1968, Scarborough
Height: 5ft 11in **Weight:** 12st 5lbs
Nickname: Goffy
County debut: 1992
1st-Class 50s: 1
1st-Class catches: 2
Place in batting averages: 186th av. 20.28
Parents: Ken and Jean
Marital status: Single
Family links with cricket: 'Father played a good game in the back garden, and kept wicket for Scarborough Boys High School.'
Education: Wolfreton School, Kirkella, Hull; De Montfort University, Leicester
Qualifications: 7 O-levels, 1 A-levels, NCA Coaching Award
Career outside cricket: 'Open to offers'
Off-season: Studying at university
Overseas tours: NCA U19 tournament in Belfast 1987
Overseas teams played for: Randburg, Johannesburg 1988-89; University, Wellington, NZ 1989-90; Brothers, Bundaberg, Australia 1991-92
Cricketers particularly admired: Richard Stemp and Justin Benson – 'for making the game more enjoyable by their approach to it'
Other sports followed: Football and 'non-cricket'
Injuries: Dislocated collar bone, tear in left hamstring, out for three weeks on each occasion
Relaxations: 'Listening to Justin Benson and Paul Nixon's dressing-room stories.'
Extras: Was an MCC Young Professional at Lord's. Released by Leicestershire at the end of 1992 season
Opinions on cricket: 'Disappointed not to be receiving any coloured clothing next year. Training either in education or a career could be provided during the off-season, so that after the retainers meeting it might be easier to find alternative employment.'
Best batting: 75 Leicestershire v Surrey, The Oval 1992
Best bowling: 4-81 Leicestershire v Derbyshire, Ilkestone 1992

1992 Season

	M	Inns	NO	Runs	HS	Avge	100s	50s	Ct	St	O	M	Runs	Wkts	Avge	Best	5wI	10wM
Test																		
All First	5	8	1	142	75	20.28	-	1	2	-	81.4	15	348	6	58.00	4-81	-	-
1-day Int																		
NatWest																		
B & H																		
Sunday	7	3	1	4	2*	2.00	-	-	2	-	41.4	0	260	3	86.66	1-33	-	

Career Performances

	M	Inns	NO	Runs	HS	Avge	100s	50s	Ct	St	Balls	Runs	Wkts	Avge	Best	5wI	10wM
Test																	
All First	5	8	1	142	75	20.28	-	1	2	-	490	348	6	58.00	4-81	-	-
1-day Int																	
NatWest																	
B & H																	
Sunday	7	3	1	4	2*	2.00	-	-	2	-	250	260	3	86.66	1-33	-	

GOLDSMITH, S. C.   Derbyshire

Name: Steven Clive Goldsmith
Role: Right-hand bat, right-arm medium-slow 'nagger'
Born: 19 December 1964, Ashford, Kent
Height: 5ft 10$\frac{1}{2}$in **Weight:** 12st 10lbs
Nickname: Goldy, Nagger, Ox
County debut: 1987 (Kent), 1988 (Derbyshire)
1000 runs in a season: 1
1st-Class 50s: 12
1st-Class 100s: 2
1st-Class catches: 37
One-Day 50s: 3
Place in batting averages: 103rd av. 34.12 (1991 146th av. 26.52)
Place in bowling averages: (1991 76th av. 33.72)
Strike rate: (career 99.93)
Parents: Tony and Daphne
Wife and date of marriage: Joanne, 10 March 1990
Family links with cricket: Father played club cricket in Kent and Surrey leagues
Education: Simon Langton Grammar School, Canterbury

Qualifications: 8 O-levels, NCA coaching qualification
Career outside cricket: Sales executive for Smudge Products Ltd – 'my own business'
Off-season: Coaching, working at Clovelly Hotel, Smudge Products Ltd
Overseas teams played for: Essendon, Melbourne 1984-85; Pirates, Durban 1989-91
Cricketers particularly admired: David Gower, Peter Bowler, Mohammad Azharuddin, Ian Bishop, Dominic Cork and Mark Spencer
Other sports followed: Motor sport, golf, hockey 'and most others'
Injuries: Severe cut across right knee whilst fielding at The Oval on July 14th, out from then on
Relaxations: Classic cars, golf and watching Nick Owen on TV, Tony Hancock and comedy
Extras: Spent four years on Kent staff until released at end of the 1987 season. Released by Derbyshire at the end of 1992 season.
Opinions on cricket: 'Coloured clothing – about time!'
Best batting: 127 Derbyshire v Sri Lanka, Derby 1991
Best bowling: 3-42 Derbyshire v Yorkshire, Scarborough 1991

1992 Season

	M	Inns	NO	Runs	HS	Avge	100s	50s	Ct	St	O	M	Runs	Wkts	Avge	Best	5wI	10wM
Test																		
All First	10	11	3	273	100 *	34.12	1	1	3	-	119	22	419	3	139.66	1-9	-	-
1-day Int																		
NatWest	2	2	0	0	0	0.00	-	-	-	-	3	0	5	0	-		-	-
B & H	1	1	0	9	9	9.00	-	-	-	-	5.1	0	25	2	12.50	2-25	-	
Sunday	9	9	2	134	33	19.14	-	-	3	-	50.2	0	286	7	40.85	2-41	-	

Career Performances

	M	Inns	NO	Runs	HS	Avge	100s	50s	Ct	St	Balls	Runs	Wkts	Avge	Best	5wI	10wM
Test																	
All First	75	118	12	2646	127	24.96	2	12	37	-	2898	1571	29	54.17	3-42	-	-
1-day Int																	
NatWest	7	6	0	42	21	7.00	-	-	-	-	80	48	1	48.00	1-20	-	
B & H	15	11	3	168	45 *	21.00	-	-	9	-	91	63	5	12.60	3-38	-	
Sunday	54	47	11	866	67 *	24.05	-	3	16	-	764	751	14	53.64	3-48	-	

82. Who had the highest batting average in the last World Cup?

GOOCH, G. A. Essex

Name: Graham Alan Gooch
Role: Right-hand bat, right-arm medium
bowler
Born: 23 July 1953, Leytonstone
Height: 6ft **Weight:** 13st
Nickname: Zap, Goochie
County debut: 1973
County cap: 1975
Benefit: 1985 (£153,906)
Test debut: 1975
Tests: 99
One-Day Internationals: 111
1000 runs in a season: 16
1st-Class 50s scored: 178
1st-Class 100s scored: 99
1st-Class 200s scored: 9
1st-Class 5 w. in innings: 3
1st-Class catches: 478
One-Day 50s: 113
One-Day 100s: 36

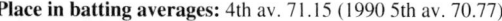

Place in batting averages: 4th av. 71.15 (1990 5th av. 70.77)
Strike rate: (career 77.36)
Parents: Alfred and Rose
Wife and date of marriage: Brenda, 23 October 1976
Children: Hannah; Megan and Sally (twins)
Family links with cricket: Father played local cricket for East Ham Corinthians. Second
cousin, Graham Saville, played for Essex CCC and is now England YC team manager
Education: Cannhall School and Norlington Junior High School, Leytonstone; Redbridge
Technical College
Qualifications: 6 CSEs; four-year apprenticeship in tool-making
Off-season: Captaining England in India
Overseas tours: England YC to West Indies 1972; England to Australia 1978-79, to
Australia and India 1979-80, to West Indies 1980-81, to India and Sri Lanka 1981-82, to
World Cup and Pakistan 1987-88, to India and West Indies 1989-90, to Australia 1990-91,
to New Zealand 1991-92, to Australia (World Cup) 1991-92, to India 1992-93; unofficial
England XI to South Africa 1981-82
Overseas teams played for: Western Province, South Africa 1982-84
Cricketers particularly admired: Bob Taylor, a model sportsman; Mike Procter for his
enthusiasm; Barry Richards for his ability
Other sports followed: Squash, soccer, golf. Has trained with West Ham United FC
Relaxations: 'Relaxing at home.'
Extras: One of *Wisden's* Five Cricketers of the Year, 1979. Captained English rebel team

in South Africa in 1982 and was banned from Test cricket for three years. Hit a hole in one at Tollygunge Golf Club during England's tour in India, 1981-82. Appointed Essex captain 1986, but resigned captaincy at end of 1987; reappointed in 1989 following retirement of Keith Fletcher. Captain of England for last two Tests of 1988 season against West Indies and Sri Lanka in 1988 and chosen to captain England on the cancelled tour of India in 1988-89. Reappointed captain for the tour to India and West Indies in 1989-90, and led England to their first Test victory over West Indies for sixteen years. His 333 in the Lord's Test against India was the third highest score ever by an English batsman in a Test match, and by also hitting 123 in the second innings he created a record Test aggregate of 456 runs and became the first man to hit a triple century and a century in the same first-class match. His aggregate for the season (2746 runs at 101.70) was the best since 1961 and he was only the fourth batsman to finish an English season with an average better than 100. When he first joined Essex, he was a wicket-keeper and batted at number 11 in his first match. He went on a Young England tour to the West Indies as second wicket-keeper to Andy Stovold of Gloucestershire. Autobiography *Out of the Wilderness* published in 1988; *Test of Fire,* an account of the West Indies tour, published in 1990; *Captaincy* published in 1992. Would have scored his 100th first-class hundred during the tour of India, had the ICC not declared the rebel tour matches not to be first-class

Best batting: 333 England v India, Lord's 1990
Best bowling: 7-14 Essex v Worcestershire, Ilford 1982

1992 Season

	M	Inns	NO	Runs	HS	Avge	100s	50s	Ct	St	O	M	Runs	Wkts	Avge	Best	5wI	10wM
Test	5	8	0	384	135	48.00	1	2	2	-	51	15	94	5	18.80	3-39	-	-
All First	18	29	3	1850	160	71.15	8	7	19	-	134	38	305	9	33.88	3-39	-	-
1-day Int	4	4	0	121	45	30.25	-	-	2	-								
NatWest	4	4	1	239	105 *	79.66	1	1	1	-	9	0	39	0	-		-	-
B & H	4	4	0	246	127	61.50	2	-	-	-	7	1	28	0	-		-	-
Sunday	11	11	1	483	79	48.30	-	4	7	-	14	1	55	2	27.50	2-24	-	

Career Performances

	M	Inns	NO	Runs	HS	Avge	100s	50s	Ct	St	Balls	Runs	Wkts	Avge	Best	5wI	10wM
Test	99	179	6	7573	333	43.77	17	41	96	-	2295	894	22	40.63	3-39	-	-
All First	484	816	66	36126	333	48.16	99	178	478	-	17872	8034	231	34.77	7-14	3	-
1-day Int	111	109	6	4071	142	39.52	8	23	38	-	1946	1423	36	39.52	3-19	-	
NatWest	46	45	3	2261	144	53.83	6	14	21	-	1639	847	28	30.25	3-31	-	
B & H	97	96	10	4402	198 *	51.18	11	29	61	-	3605	2107	67	31.44	3-24	-	
Sunday	228	224	21	7165	176	35.29	11	47	84	-	2456	4128	138	29.91	4-33	-	

GOUGH, D.   Yorkshire

Name: Darren Gough
Role: Right-hand bat, right-arm fast-medium
bowler
Born: 18 September 1970, Barnsley
Height: 5ft 11in **Weight:** 12st 9lbs
Nickname: Dazzler, Guzzler, Magnus,
Son of
County debut: 1989
1st-Class 50s: 2
1st-Class 5 w. in innings: 1
1st-Class catches: 6
One-Day 50s: 1
Place in batting averages:
(1991 137th av. 27.90)
Place in bowling averages: 93rd av. 36.40
(1991 137th av. 52.50)
Strike rate: 61.24 (career 67.43)
Parents: Trevor and Christine
Marital status: Single

Family links with cricket: Brother plays
for Barnsley in Yorkshire League
Education: St Helens Junior; Priory Comprehensive; Airedale and Wharfedale College
(part-time)
Qualifications: 2 O-levels, 5 CSEs, BTEC Leisure, Distinction Coaching Award 1
Career outside cricket: Motorway maintenance
Off-season: Coaching cricket around Yorkshire, relaxing and making every effort to be
fitter than in 1992
Overseas tours: England YC to Australia 1989-90; Yorkshire to Barbados 1990, to South
Africa 1992
Overseas teams played for: East Christchurch Shirley, New Zealand 1990-91
Cricketers particularly admired: 'Ian Botham and Richard Hadlee, for their all round
ability, and Peter Hartley for his approach to the game.'
Other sports followed: Football, golf
Injuries: Bruised ribs, missed one week, and twisted ankle, out for two weeks
Relaxations: Cinema
Extras: 'Had trials with Rotherham United FC but wasn't good enough.'
Opinions on cricket: 'It's a batter's game. I think four-day cricket will mean less
excitement for the spectators leading to smaller crowds.'
Best batting: 72 Yorkshire v Northamptonshire, Northampton 1991
Best bowling: 5-41 Yorkshire v Lancashire, Scarborough 1991

1992 Season

	M	Inns	NO	Runs	HS	Avge	100s	50s	Ct	St	O	M	Runs	Wkts	Avge	Best	5wI	10wM
Test																		
All First	11	12	4	72	22 *	9.00	-	-	2	-	255.1	53	910	25	36.40	4-43	-	-
1-day Int																		
NatWest	2	1	0	4	4	4.00	-	-	-	-	23	4	91	4	22.75	2-18	-	
B & H	4	3	1	18	7 *	9.00	-	-	-	-	35	6	124	6	20.66	2-29	-	
Sunday	13	7	2	10	5 *	2.00	-	-	2	-	90	6	399	15	26.60	3-30	-	

Career Performances

	M	Inns	NO	Runs	HS	Avge	100s	50s	Ct	St	Balls	Runs	Wkts	Avge	Best	5wI	10wM
Test																	
All First	41	47	14	532	72	16.12	-	2	6	-	5327	3105	79	39.30	5-41	1	-
1-day Int																	
NatWest	5	2	0	6	4	3.00	-	-	1	-	300	176	8	22.00	2-18	-	
B & H	6	4	1	19	7 *	6.33	-	-	-	-	294	192	8	24.00	2-29	-	
Sunday	28	16	4	136	72 *	11.33	-	1	8	-	1058	861	24	35.87	3-30	-	

GOWER, D. I.   Hampshire

Name: David Ivon Gower
Role: Left-hand bat, off-spin bowler
Born: 1 April 1957, Tunbridge Wells
Height: 6ft **Weight:** 11st 11lbs
Nickname: Lubo
County debut: 1975 (Leicestershire), 1990 (Hampshire)
County cap: 1977 (Leicestershire), 1990 (Hampshire)
Benefit: 1987 (£121,546)
Test debut: 1978
Tests: 117
One-Day Internationals: 114
1000 runs in a season: 12
1st-Class 50s scored: 131
1st-Class 100s scored: 49
1st-Class 200s scored: 2
1st-Class catches: 269
1st-Class stumpings: 1
One-Day 50s: 53
One-Day 100s: 19
Place in batting averages: 35th av. 47.11 (1991 84th av. 34.60)

Parents: Richard Hallam and Sylvia Mary
Wife and date of marriage: Thorunn, 18 September 1992
Family links with cricket: Father was club cricketer
Education: Marlborough House School; King's School, Canterbury; University College, London (did not complete law course)
Qualifications: 8 O-levels, 3 A-levels
Career outside cricket: Head PR Ltd
Off-season: Working for Channel Nine in Australia and Sky Sports in India
Overseas tours: English Schools XI to South Africa 1974-75; England YC to West Indies 1976; England to Australia 1978-79; Australia and India 1979-80; West Indies 1980-81; India and Sri Lanka 1981-82; Australia and New Zealand 1982-83; New Zealand and Pakistan 1983-84; India and Australia 1984-85; West Indies 1985-86; Australia 1986-87; Australia 1990-91
Cricketers particularly admired: Graeme Pollock, Gary Sobers, Allan Border
Other sports followed: Rugby, tennis, golf, soccer
Injuries: 'No excuses!'
Relaxations: Wildlife photography, wine, winter sports, flying, lawn mowing
Extras: Played for King's Canterbury 1st XI for three years. One of *Wisden's* Five Cricketers of the Year, 1978. Books include *Anyone for Cricket* (1979), *With Time to Spare* (1980), *Heroes and Contemporaries* (1983), *A Right Ambition* (1986), and he writes regular column for *Wisden Cricket Monthly*. England and Leicestershire captain 1984-86. Declared himself not available for England tour 1987-88. Reappointed Leicestershire captain for 1988 and reappointed captain of England v Australia in 1989. Sacked as captain and player after losing the Ashes to Allan Border's team. Resigned the Leicestershire captaincy at the end of the season and decided to join Hampshire. Surprisingly not selected for England's winter tours to either India or West Indies, but when in the Caribbean writing for *The Times*, he was called into the England side for their match v Barbados. Made sure of a fifth tour to Australia with 157* v India at The Oval. In the absence of Mark Nicholas through injury, captained Hampshire to victory in the NatWest Trophy final 1991. Awarded OBE in 1992. *Gower: The Autobiography* published 1992 – 'covers this section admirably!' Recalled to England team against Pakistan in 1992 and became England's leading run-maker by overtaking Geoff Boycott's aggregate of 8114 during the Old Trafford Test. Not selected to tour India which prompted an MCC meeting to discuss selectorial decisions
Best batting: 228 Leicestershire v Glamorgan, Leicester 1989
Best bowling: 3-47 Leicestershire v Essex, Leicester 1977

1992 Season

	M	Inns	NO	Runs	HS	Avge	100s	50s	Ct	St	O	M	Runs	Wkts	Avge	Best	5wl	10wM
Test	3	5	2	150	73	50.00	-	1	1	-								
All First	20	33	7	1225	155	47.11	1	8	14	-								
1-day Int																		
NatWest	2	1	0	6	6	6.00	-	-	-	-								
B & H	7	7	2	288	118 *	57.60	1	-	5	-								
Sunday	13	13	1	276	56	23.00	-	1	3	-								

Career Performances

	M	Inns	NO	Runs	HS	Avge	100s	50s	Ct	St	Balls	Runs	Wkts	Avge	Best	5wI	10wM
Test	117	204	18	8231	215	44.25	18	39	74	-	36	20	1	20.00	1-1	-	-
All First	432	699	69	25203	228	40.00	49	131	269	1	260	227	4	56.75	3-47	-	-
1-day Int	114	111	8	3170	158	30.77	7	12	44	-	5	14	0	-		-	-
NatWest	45	41	6	1763	156	50.37	5	8	15	-	15	16	0	-		-	-
B & H	68	67	9	1655	118 *	28.53	2	3	29	-							
Sunday	173	170	24	4976	135 *	34.08	5	30	67	-							

GRAVENEY, D. A.   Durham

Name: David Anthony Graveney
Role: Right-hand bat, slow left-arm bowler, county captain
Born: 2 January 1953, Bristol
Height: 6ft 4in **Weight:** 14st
Nickname: Gravity, Grav
County debut: 1972 (Gloucestershire), 1991 (Somerset), 1992 (Durham)
County cap: 1976 (Gloucestershire)
Benefit: 1986
50 wickets in a season: 7
1st-Class 50s scored: 15
1st-Class 100s scored: 2
1st-Class 5 w. in innings: 38
1st-Class 10 w. in match: 7
1st-Class catches: 224
One-Day 50s: 1
Place in batting averages: 214th av. 16.65
Place in bowling averages: 119th av. 42.89
(1991 110th av. 39.27)
Strike rate: 81.57 (career 69.39)
Parents: Ken and Jeanne (deceased)
Wife and date of marriage: Julie, 23 September 1978
Children: Adam, 13 October 1982
Family links with cricket: Son of J. K. Graveney, captain of Gloucestershire, who took 10 wickets for 66 runs v Derbyshire at Chesterfield in 1949, and nephew of Tom Graveney of Gloucestershire, Worcestershire and England. Brother, John, selected for English Public Schools v English Schools at Lord's
Education: Millfield School, Somerset
Career outside cricket: Company director. Accountant
Overseas tours: Unofficial England tour to South Africa 1989-90

Other sports followed: Golf, soccer, squash

Relaxations: 'Playing sport, TV and cinema. Relaxing at a good pub.'

Extras: Treasurer of Cricketers' Association. Captain of Gloucestershire, 1981 to 1988. Third member of the Graveney family to be dismissed by Gloucester CCC – Uncle Tom as captain in 1960 and father Ken as chairman in 1982 – when he was sacked as captain. Player-manager of unofficial tour to South Africa 1989-90, banned for 5 years but suspension remitted in 1992. Left Gloucestershire at end of 1990 season and joined Somerset. Left Somerset at the end of the 1991 season to captain Durham in their first season as a first-class county. Co-author with Jack Bannister of *Durham CCC: Past, Present and Future* published in 1993

Best batting: 119 Gloucestershire v Oxford University, The Parks 1980

Best bowling: 8-85 Gloucestershire v Nottinghamshire, Cheltenham 1974

1992 Season

	M	Inns	NO	Runs	HS	Avge	100s	50s	Ct	St	O	M	Runs	Wkts	Avge	Best	5wI	10wM
Test																		
All First	21	29	9	333	36	16.65	-	-	13	-	380.4	87	1201	28	42.89	3-22	-	-
1-day Int																		
NatWest	1	0	0	0	0	-												
B & H	2	2	0	34	21	17.00	-	-	1	-	12	1	54	0	-		-	-
Sunday	13	4	2	26	11 *	13.00	-	-	3	-	72.3	1	365	14	26.07	3-40	-	

Career Performances

	M	Inns	NO	Runs	HS	Avge	100s	50s	Ct	St	Balls	Runs	Wkts	Avge	Best	5wI	10wM
Test																	
All First	425	530	158	6501	119	17.47	2	15	224	-	63285	27314	912	29.95	8-85	38	7
1-day Int																	
NatWest	42	25	9	292	44	18.25	-	-	18	-	2296	1225	51	24.02	5-11	1	
B & H	70	45	16	459	49 *	15.82	-	-	17	-	2864	1759	51	34.49	3-13	-	
Sunday	233	137	53	1315	56 *	15.65	-	1	56	-	6478	5031	155	32.45	4-22	-	

83. Which English player came highest in the batting averages in the last World Cup?

GRAYSON, A. P. — Yorkshire

Name: Adrian Paul Grayson
Role: Right-hand bat, slow left-arm bowler
Born: 31 March 1971, Ripon
Height: 6ft 2in **Weight:** 12st
Nickname: PG, Larry, Ravi, BK
County debut: 1990
1st-Class 50s: 1
1st-Class catches: 7
Place in batting averages: 197th av. 19.33
Parents: Adrian and Carol
Marital status: Single
Family links with cricket: 'Dad played good league cricket and is also an NCA staff coach; brother also plays when free from football commitments.'
Education: Bedale Comprehensive School
Qualifications: 8 CSEs, BTEC in Leisure, NCA senior coaching award
Off-season: Cricket coaching, watching and playing football
Overseas tours: England YC to Australia 1989-90; Yorkshire to Barbados 1990, to Cape Town 1992
Overseas teams played for: Petone, Wellington 1991-92
Cricketers particularly admired: Graham Gooch, Martyn Moxon, Robin Smith
Other sports followed: Keen supporter of Leeds United and now follows Leicester City, where his elder brother Simon plays
Injuries: Asthma sufferer, had attack during season and spent three weeks in hospital
Relaxations: Playing golf, watching football, reading
Extras: Played for England YC v New Zealand 1989 and Pakistan 1990. Turned down an offer by Middlesex
Best batting: 57 Yorkshire v Surrey, The Oval 1992
Best bowling: 1-3 Yorkshire v Oxford University, The Parks 1991

1992 Season

	M	Inns	NO	Runs	HS	Avge	100s	50s	Ct	St	O	M	Runs	Wkts	Avge	Best	5wI	10wM
Test																		
All First	6	6	0	116	57	19.33	-	1	3	-	50	5	186	1	186.00	1-79	-	-
1-day Int																		
NatWest																			
B & H	3	3	0	43	22	14.33	-	-	-	-								
Sunday	2	1	0	8	8	8.00	-	-	-	-								

Career Performances

	M	Inns	NO	Runs	HS	Avge	100s	50s	Ct	St	Balls	Runs	Wkts	Avge	Best	5wI	10wM
Test																	
All First	14	18	5	291	57	22.38	-	1	7	-	960	523	3	174.33	1-3	-	-
1-day Int																	
NatWest																	
B & H	3	3	0	43	22	14.33	-	-	-	-							
Sunday	3	1	0	8	8	8.00	-	-	-	-	30	32	1	32.00	1-32	-	

GREENFIELD, K. Sussex

Name: Keith Greenfield
Role: Right-hand bat, right-arm off-spin or medium bowler
Born: 6 December 1968, Brighton
Height: 6ft **Weight:** 12st 6lbs
Nickname: Grubby
County debut: 1987
1st-Class 50s scored: 2
1st-Class 100s scored: 3
1st-Class catches: 27
One-Day 50s: 8
Place in batting averages: 156th av. 25.62 (1991 114th av. 30.30)
Parents: Leslie Ernest and Sheila
Wife and date of marriage: Caroline Susannah, 22 February 1992
Family links with cricket: Father keen spectator, father-in-law played club cricket for 20 years and now umpires
Education: Coldean First and Middle Schools, Falmer High School
Qualifications: 3 O-level, BTEC National Diploma in Leisure and Management, junior, senior and advanced coaching certificates
Off-season: Coaching at schools around Sussex and at the county ground, Hove
Overseas teams played for: Cornwall, Auckland 1988-90
Cricketers particularly admired: Derek Randall, Ian Botham, Peter Moores, Ian Gould
Other sports followed: 'All sports interest me.'
Injuries: Pulled quad in May, out for a week, and bruised hip bone, out from August to mid-September
Relaxations: 'Eating out, music, spending time at home, drinking at Long Man of Wilmington, concerts, and Caroline.'

Extras: First person taken on Youth Training Scheme to become a professional cricketer at Sussex. Only uncapped player to have captained Sussex at Hove (v Cambridge Univ), scored century in this game. Captained 2nd XI to Championship title in 1990
Opinions on cricket: 'Wrong to change Sunday League to 50 overs, should stay at 40. Coloured clothing good idea and four-day cricket a good thing.'
Best batting: 127* Sussex v Cambridge University, Hove 1991

1992 Season

	M	Inns	NO	Runs	HS	Avge	100s	50s	Ct	St	O	M	Runs	Wkts	Avge	Best	5wI	10wM
Test																		
All First	6	10	2	205	48	25.62	-	-	5	-	17	0	84	0	-		-	-	-
1-day Int																		
NatWest	2	2	0	19	19	9.50	-	-	1	-	12	5	33	1	33.00	1-33	-	
B & H	5	5	0	193	62	38.60	-	2	2	-	12	0	52	0	-		-	-
Sunday	13	13	0	347	79	26.69	-	3	4	-	28	0	201	4	50.25	2-36	-	

Career Performances

	M	Inns	NO	Runs	HS	Avge	100s	50s	Ct	St	Balls	Runs	Wkts	Avge	Best	5wI	10wM
Test																	
All First	25	42	5	995	127 *	26.89	3	2	27	-	159	133	0	-		-	-
1-day Int																	
NatWest	2	2	0	19	19	9.50	-	-	1	-	72	33	1	33.00	1-33	-	
B & H	8	8	1	226	62	32.28	-	2	5	-	180	141	1	141.00	1-35	-	
Sunday	34	32	4	736	79	26.28	-	6	6	-	321	355	4	88.75	2-36	-	

84. In what year was Durham CCC founded?

85. Who captained South Africa in the last World Cup?

GREIG, I. A. — Surrey

Name: Ian Alexander Greig
Role: Right-hand bat, right-arm medium
bowler, slip fielder
Born: 8 December 1955, Queenstown,
South Africa
Height: 5ft 11^1/$_2$in **Weight:** 12st
Nickname: Wash, Greigy
County debut: 1980 (Sussex), 1987 (Surrey)
County cap: 1981 (Sussex), 1987 (Surrey)
Benefit: 1992
Test debut: 1982
Tests: 2
1000 runs in a season: 2
50 wickets in a season: 3
1st-Class 50s scored: 40
1st-Class 100s scored: 8
1st-Class 200s scored: 1
1st-Class 5 w. in innings: 10
1st-Class 10 w. in match: 2
1st-Class catches: 152
One-Day 50s: 6

Place in batting averages: (1991 177th av. 22.59)
Place in bowling averages: (1991 121st av. 42.60)
Strike rate: (career 59.82)
Parents: Sandy (deceased) and Joyce
Wife and date of marriage: Cheryl, 8 January 1983
Children: Michelle, 17 December 1984; Andrew, 20 January 1987
Family links with cricket: Brother of Tony, former captain of Sussex and England;
brother-in-law Phillip Hodson played for Cambridge University and Yorkshire
Education: Queens College, Queenstown; Downing College, Cambridge
Qualifications: MA Law (Cantab)
Overseas teams played for: Border, South Africa 1974-75, 1979-80; Griqualand West,
South Africa 1975-76
Cricketers particularly admired: Garth le Roux, Richard Hadlee
Other sports followed: Rugby
Relaxations: Relaxing with family, barbecues, fly-fishing
Extras: Wombwell Cricket Lovers' Society County Captain of the Year 1991. Retired as
captain of Surrey at the end of the 1991 season, retired from first-class cricket after 1992
season
Best batting: 291 Surrey v Lancashire, The Oval 1990
Best bowling: 7-43 Sussex v Cambridge University, Fenner's 1981

1992 Season

	M	Inns	NO	Runs	HS	Avge	100s	50s	Ct	St	O	M	Runs	Wkts	Avge	Best	5wI	10wM
Test																		
All First																		
1-day Int																		
NatWest																		
B & H																		
Sunday	4	3	0	40	27	13.33	-	-	1	-	3	0	40	0	-		-	-

Career Performances

	M	Inns	NO	Runs	HS	Avge	100s	50s	Ct	St	Balls	Runs	Wkts	Avge	Best	5wI	10wM
Test	2	4	0	26	14	6.50	-	-	-	-	188	114	4	28.50	4-53	-	-
All First	253	339	50	8301	291	28.72	8	40	152	-	25065	13023	419	31.08	7-43	10	2
1-day Int																	
NatWest	24	20	3	390	82	22.94	-	2	6	-	970	579	22	26.31	4-31	-	
B & H	57	52	4	685	51	14.27	-	1	12	-	2602	1630	59	27.62	5-35	1	
Sunday	148	124	35	2036	68 *	22.87	-	3	35	-	4319	3682	126	29.22	5-30	2	

GRIFFITH, F. A. Derbyshire

Name: Frank Alexander Griffith
Role: Right-hand bat, right-arm medium bowler
Born: 15 August 1968, Leyton
Height: 6ft **Weight:** 12st
Nickname: Sir Learie
County debut: 1988
1st-Class 50s: 1
1st-Class catches: 12
Place in batting averages: 95th av. 35.42
Place in bowling averages: 16th av. 24.86
Strike rate: 45.20 (career 53.72)
Parents: Alex and Daisy
Marital status: Single
Education: William Morris High School, Walthamstow
Qualifications: Food and nutrition and art O-levels; NCA coaching certificate
Cricketers particularly admired:
Collis King, Franklyn Stephenson
Other sports followed: Table tennis, basketball, football
Relaxations: Listening to music

Extras: Attended Haringey Cricket College
Best batting: 81 Derbyshire v Glamorgan, Chesterfield 1992
Best bowling: 4-33 Derbyshire v Leicestershire, Ilkeston 1992

1992 Season

	M	Inns	NO	Runs	HS	Avge	100s	50s	Ct	St	O	M	Runs	Wkts	Avge	Best	5wI	10wM
Test																		
All First	7	10	3	248	81	35.42	-	1	6	-	113	31	373	15	24.86	4-33	-	-
1-day Int																		
NatWest																		
B & H																		
Sunday	3	2	1	5	4 *	5.00	-	-	2	-	11	0	82	4	20.50	2-20	-	

Career Performances

	M	Inns	NO	Runs	HS	Avge	100s	50s	Ct	St	Balls	Runs	Wkts	Avge	Best	5wI	10wM
Test																	
All First	20	31	4	467	81	17.29	-	1	12	-	1773	1017	33	30.81	4-33	-	-
1-day Int																	
NatWest																	
B & H	1	1	0	10	10	10.00	-	-	-	-							
Sunday	18	15	3	88	20	7.33	-	-	2	-	534	496	16	31.00	3-37	-	

HALL, J. W. Sussex

Name: James William Hall
Role: Right-hand opening batsman
Born: 30 March 1968, Chichester
Height: 6ft 3in **Weight:** 13st 7lbs
Nickname: Gus
County debut: 1990
County cap: 1992
1000 runs in a season: 2
1st-Class 50s scored: 17
1st-Class 100s scored: 4
1st-Class catches: 21
Place in batting averages: 68th av. 38.79
(1991 128th av. 28.58)
Parents: Maurice and Marlene (deceased)
Marital status: Single
Family links with cricket: Father played
club cricket for Chichester Priory Park
Education: Chichester Boys' High School

Qualifications: 9 O-levels

Off-season: At home resting

Overseas teams played for: Southern Districts, Perth, Western Australia 1986-87; Swanbourne, Perth 1988-89; University St Helliers, Auckland 1991-92

Cricketers particularly admired: Alan Wells, Allan Green, David Smith, Murray Lee-Smith, Franklyn Barrett

Other sports followed: Football (Brighton & Hove Albion and Carlisle United)

Injuries: Back spasms, inflamed disc and groin strain

Relaxations: Eating, drinking, sleeping

Extras: Scored 53 on first XI debut v Zimbabwe and scored maiden first-class 100 in same week (120* v New Zealand). Over 1000 runs in debut season of first-class cricket. Run out without facing a ball on NatWest debut v Glamorgan ('thanks Neil'). Whittingdale Young Cricketer of the Month for May 1991

Opinions on cricket: 'Four-day cricket is a step forward for producing good Test players. Sunday League should return to 40 overs – I don't know anyone who wants 50 overs and midday start.'

Best batting: 140* Sussex v Lancashire, Hove 1992

1992 Season

	M	Inns	NO	Runs	HS	Avge	100s	50s	Ct	St	O	M	Runs	Wkts	Avge	Best	5wl	10wM
Test																		
All First	20	34	5	1125	140 *	38.79	1	8	7	-	2	1	14	0	-		-	-	-
1-day Int																		
NatWest	2	2	0	47	47	23.50	-	-	-	-								
B & H	5	5	0	189	81	37.80	-	2	1	-								
Sunday	15	14	0	399	77	28.50	-	4	5	-								

Career Performances

	M	Inns	NO	Runs	HS	Avge	100s	50s	Ct	St	Balls	Runs	Wkts	Avge	Best	5wl	10wM
Test																		
All First	55	97	9	2951	140 *	33.53	4	17	21	-	12	14	0	-		-	-	-
1-day Int																		
NatWest	3	3	0	47	47	15.66	-	-	-	-								
B & H	9	9	0	339	81	37.66	-	3	1	-								
Sunday	18	17	0	495	77	29.11	-	5	5	-								

86.   Of whom did Brian Johnston say 'He did more than any other man to spread the gospel of cricket across the world'?

HALLETT, J. C. Somerset

Name: Jeremy Charles Hallett
Role: Right-hand bat, right-arm medium-fast bowler
Born: 18 October 1970, Yeovil
Height: 6ft 2in **Weight:** 12st
Nickname: Chicks, Pikey
County debut: 1990
1st-Class catches: 4
Place in bowling averages:
(1991 138th av. 53.08)
Strike rate: (career 81.44)
Parents: Glyn and Rosemarie
Marital status: Single
Family links with cricket: 'Father has played Somerset League cricket for years.'
Education: Wells Cathedral Junior School; Millfield School; Durham University
Qualifications: 10 O-levels, 3 A-levels
Overseas tours: England YC to Australia 1989-90
Cricketers particularly admired: Malcolm Marshall, Viv Richards, Terry Alderman, Richard Hadlee, Martin Crowe, Jimmy Cook
Other sports followed: Soccer (Yeovil Town), golf, 'all sports really'
Relaxations: 'Films, music, playing golf, a good pub, food!'
Extras: Cricketer of the Series, England YC v Australia 1989-90. Also played v New Zealand 1989 and Pakistan 1990. Somerset Young Player of the Year 1990. Played for Combined Universities in B&H Cup 1991 and 1992
Best batting: 15 Somerset v Gloucestershire, Bristol 1991
Best bowling: 3-154 Somerset v Worcestershire, Worcester 1991

1992 Season

	M	Inns	NO	Runs	HS	Avge	100s	50s	Ct	St	O	M	Runs	Wkts	Avge	Best	5wI	10wM
Test																		
All First																		
1-day Int																		
NatWest																		
B & H	3	2	1	6	5 *	6.00	-	-	-	-	19	3	67	0	-		-	-
Sunday																		

Career Performances

	M	Inns	NO	Runs	HS	Avge	100s	50s	Ct	St	Balls	Runs	Wkts	Avge	Best	5wI	10wM
Test																	
All First	11	6	1	35	15	7.00	-	-	4	-	1466	875	18	48.61	3-154	-	-
1-day Int																	
NatWest	1	0	0	0	0	-	-	-	-	-	72	31	0	-	-	-	
B & H	9	4	1	11	5 *	3.66	-	-	1	-	439	286	7	40.85	3-36	-	
Sunday	15	4	3	8	4 *	8.00	-	-	1	-	513	444	12	37.00	3-41	-	

HANCOCK, T. H. C.   Gloucestershire

Name: Timothy Harold Coulter Hancock
Role: Right-hand bat, occasional right-arm medium bowler, short-leg or cover fielder
Born: 20 April 1972
Height: 5ft 11in **Weight:** 14st (approx)
Nickname: Herbie, Dumper
County debut: 1991
1st-Class 50s: 3
1st-Class 100s: 1
1st-Class catches: 15
Place in batting averages: 136th av. 27.25
(1991 241st av. 13.28)
Parents: John and Jenifer
Marital status: Single
Family links with cricket: 'Dad plays and brother plays for Nottingham University plus league cricket.'
Education: St Edwards, Oxford; Henley College
Qualifications: 8 GCSEs
Off-season: In Brisbane
Overseas tours: Gloucestershire to Kenya 1991
Overseas teams played for: CBC Old Boys, Bloemfontein 1991-92
Cricketers particularly admired: Ian Botham, Robin Smith, Graham Gooch, Courtney Walsh 'and many others'
Other sports followed: Rugby union
Relaxations: 'Like having a good pint in a nice pub, and playing a bit of golf.'
Extras: Played hockey for Oxfordshire U19
Opinions on cricket: 'I think that four-day cricket is a good idea and is definitely worth a try. I can't really understand why the Sunday League has been extended to 50 overs, but I like the idea of coloured clothing which will make the game more attractive for the

spectator.'
Best batting: 102 Gloucestershire v Somerset, Taunton 1992
Best bowling: 2-48 Gloucestershire v Northamptonshire, Bristol 1992

1992 Season

	M	Inns	NO	Runs	HS	Avge	100s	50s	Ct	St	O	M	Runs	Wkts	Avge	Best	5wI	10wM
Test																		
All First	10	17	1	436	102	27.25	1	2	8	-	33.4	4	136	4	34.00	2-43	-	-
1-day Int																		
NatWest																		
B & H	5	3	0	25	12	8.33	-	-	2	-								
Sunday	4	4	0	21	8	5.25	-	-	1	-	2	0	9	0	-	-	-	

Career Performances

	M	Inns	NO	Runs	HS	Avge	100s	50s	Ct	St	Balls	Runs	Wkts	Avge	Best	5wI	10wM
Test		.															
All First	15	26	3	529	102	23.00	1	3	15	-	202	136	4	34.00	2-43	-	-
1-day Int																	
NatWest																	
B & H	5	3	0	25	12	8.33	-	-	2	-							
Sunday	9	7	0	41	20	5.85	-	-	2	-	12	9	0	-	-	-	

HANLEY, R.   Sussex

Name: Robin Hanley
Role: Right-hand bat
Born: 5 January 1968, Tonbridge, Kent
Height: 6ft 2in **Weight:** 14st
Nickname: Ninj, Ninja, Spook
County debut: 1990
Parents: Peter and Janet
Marital status: Single
Family links with cricket: Brother good
local player, grandfather founded Woodside
Green CC in Surrey
Education: Willingdon School; Eastbourne
Sixth Form College
Qualifications: 6 O-levels
Overseas teams played for: Bayswater
Morley, Perth, Western Australia, 1987-88;
Lake View, Kalgoorlie 1989-90;
Brighton, Tasmania 1990-91

Cricketers particularly admired: John Tompsett and Mike Turner (Eastbourne CC)
Other sports followed: Boxing
Relaxations: Fitness training, martial arts, archery
Extras: Played a season of Central Lancashire League cricket for Rochdale in 1989. Has also played for NCA YC, NAYC, English Schools U19. Released by Sussex at the end of the 1992 season
Best batting: 28 Sussex v Warwickshire, Eastbourne 1990

1992 Season

	M	Inns	NO	Runs	HS	Avge	100s	50s	Ct	St	O	M	Runs	Wkts	Avge	Best	5wl	10wM
Test																		
All First	1	1	0	1	1	1.00	-	-	-	-								
1-day Int																		
NatWest																		
B & H																		
Sunday	2	1	0	3	3	3.00	-	-	1	-								

Career Performances

	M	Inns	NO	Runs	HS	Avge	100s	50s	Ct	St	Balls	Runs	Wkts	Avge	Best	5wl	10wM
Test																	
All First	5	7	0	52	28	7.42	-	-	-	-							
1-day Int																	
NatWest																	
B & H																	
Sunday	5	3	0	16	11	5.33	-	-	3	-							

87. Which current Test cricketer has been described as 'White Lightening'?

88. Who was the last man to play for England at cricket and soccer?

HANSFORD, A. R.   Sussex

Name: Alan Roderick Hansford
Role: Right-hand bat, right-arm
medium-fast bowler
Born: 1 October 1968, Burgess Hill,
West Sussex
Height: 6ft **Weight:** 14st
Nickname: Skater
County debut: 1989
1st-Class 5 w. in innings: 1
1st-Class catches: 3
Parents: John and Muriel
Marital status: Single
Family links with cricket: Father played
club cricket primarily in Dorset. Four
brothers all play or played county youth and
club cricket, brother Robert played
ESCA (South) U15
Education: Oakmeeds Community School,
Burgess Hill; Haywards Heath Sixth Form
College; University of Surrey
Qualifications: 10 O-levels, 3 A-levels, BSc (Hons) Maths and Statistics
Cricketers particularly admired: Ian Botham, Viv Richards, Malcolm Marshall, Sylvester
Clarke, Phil Edmonds
Relaxations: Eating out, crosswords, brain-teasers
Extras: Took wicket with 4th ball in first-class cricket. Was member of 1989 and 1991
Combined Universities side. Rapid Cricketline Player of the Month for June 1992. Retired
from first-class cricket at the end of the 1992 season
Opinions on cricket: 'The lunch and tea intervals should be lengthened to one hour and
half-an-hour respectively in all games. Capped player system should be abolished.
Running on wicket line should be extended to five foot and strictly adhered to.'
Best batting: 29 Sussex v Hampshire, Southampton 1990
Best bowling: 5-79 Sussex v Hampshire, Hove 1989

1992 Season

	M	Inns	NO	Runs	HS	Avge	100s	50s	Ct	St	O	M	Runs	Wkts	Avge	Best	5wI	10wM
Test																		
All First	1	1	0	1	1	1.00	-	-	-	-	29	5	81	3	27.00	3-81	-	-
1-day Int																		
NatWest																		
B & H	3	1	1	4	4 *	-	-	-	1	-	30	1	122	2	61.00	1-30	-	
Sunday	3	2	1	5	5 *	5.00	-	-	-	-	16	0	126	1	126.00	1-30	-	

Career Performances

	M	Inns	NO	Runs	HS	Avge	100s	50s	Ct	St	Balls	Runs	Wkts	Avge	Best	5wI	10wM
Test																	
All First	10	11	3	109	29	13.62	-	-	3	-	1921	991	30	33.03	5-79	1	-
1-day Int																	
NatWest	1	1	1	5	5 *	-	-	-	-	-	72	48	2	24.00	2-48	-	
B & H	16	7	5	29	13 *	14.50	-	-	2	-	953	679	10	67.90	2-11	-	
Sunday	15	6	3	15	5 *	5.00	-	-	1	-	624	586	18	32.55	5-32	1	

HARDEN, R. J.   Somerset

Name: Richard John Harden
Role: Right-hand bat, left-arm medium
bowler
Born: 16 August 1965, Bridgwater
Height: 5ft 11½in **Weight:** 13st 7lbs
Nickname: Sumo, Curtis
County debut: 1985
County cap: 1989
1000 runs in a season: 3
1st-Class 50s scored: 42
1st-Class 100s scored: 15
One-Day 50s: 15
One-Day 100s: 1
1st-Class catches: 100
Place in batting averages: 26th av. 49.53
(1991 44th av. 43.71)
Parents: Chris and Ann
Wife and date of marriage:
Nicki Rae, 25 July 1992
Family links with cricket:
Grandfather played club cricket for Bridgwater
Education: Kings College, Taunton
Qualifications: 8 O-levels, 2 A-levels. Coaching award
Off-season: Working for Pennine Dataforms
Overseas teams: Central Districts, New Zealand
Cricketers particularly admired: Viv Richards,
Jimmy Cook
Other sports followed: Squash, golf, rugby
Injuries: Broken hand, off for a month
Relaxations: 'Love my domestic duties (dusting, hoovering, etc) rather than golf. Good
food and the odd drink.'

Opinions on cricket: 'The introduction of four-day cricket should be good provided we play on good cricket wickets.'
Best batting: 187 Somerset v Nottinghamshire, Taunton 1992
Best bowling: 2-7 Central Districts v Canterbury, Blenheim 1987-88

1992 Season

	M	Inns	NO	Runs	HS	Avge	100s	50s	Ct	St	O	M	Runs	Wkts	Avge	Best	5wI	10wM
Test																		
All First	20	33	5	1387	187	49.53	3	6	14	-	3	0	31	0	-		-	-
1-day Int																		
NatWest	2	2	1	147	108 *	147.00	1	-	-	-								
B & H	6	6	0	145	76	24.16	-	1	1	-								
Sunday	14	12	3	454	90 *	50.44	-	5	7	-								

Career Performances

	M	Inns	NO	Runs	HS	Avge	100s	50s	Ct	St	Balls	Runs	Wkts	Avge	Best	5wI	10wM
Test																	
All First	155	245	41	7902	187	38.73	15	42	100	-	1397	952	19	50.10	2-7	-	-
1-day Int																	
NatWest	11	9	1	259	108 *	32.37	1	-	5	-							
B & H	34	33	3	565	76	18.83	-	2	8	-							
Sunday	99	94	18	2310	90 *	30.39	-	13	26	-	1	0	0	-		-	-

HARRISON, J. C.   Middlesex

Name: Peter John Hartley
Role: Right-hand bat, off-spin bowler, short leg fielder
Born: 115 January 1972, Amersham, Bucks
Height: 6ft 3in **Weight:** 13st 10lbs
Nickname: Beadles, Fingers
County debut: No first team appearance
Parents: Paul and Carey
Marital status: Single
Education: Great Marlow, Bucks, College of Higher Education
Qualifications: 6 GCSEs, NCA Coaching Certificate, City & Guilds Apprenticeship in Sheet Metal Fabrication
Career outside cricket:
Sheet Metal Fabricator
Off-season: Training on general fitness in gym, working hard on game and coaching

Overseas tours: Middlesex to Portugal 1992
Cricketers particularly admired: Wilf Slack, Graeme Fowler, Norman Cowans, John Emburey, Malcolm Roberts
Other sports followed: Football (Wycombe Wanderers)
Relaxations: Listening to music
Extras: Played for Buckinghamshire 1991 and 1992. NCA U19 and NAYC in 1991. Offered contract by Leicestershire as well as Middlesex
Opinions on cricket: 'I personally think that four-day programme will produce better players and will help bridge the gap between Test and county cricket. I also think the one bouncer per over rule should be abolished.'

HARTLEY, P. J. Yorkshire

Name: Peter John Hartley
Role: Right-hand bat, right-arm fast-medium bowler
Born: 18 April 1960, Keighley
Height: 6ft **Weight:** 13st 2lbs
Nickname: Jack
County debut: 1982 (Warwicks), 1985 (Yorks)
County cap: 1987 (Yorks)
50 wickets in a season: 3
1st-Class 50s scored: 8
1st-Class 100s scored: 1
1st-Class 5 w. in innings: 12
1st-Class catches: 42
Place in batting averages: 209th av. 17.65 (1991 174th av. 23.00)
Place in bowling averages: 47th av. 30.17 (1991 87th av. 35.02)
Strike rate: 58.91 (career 58.86)
Parents: Thomas and Molly
Wife and date of marriage: Sharon, 12 March 1988
Children: Megan Grace, 25 April 1992
Family links with cricket: Father played local league cricket
Education: Greenhead Grammar School; Bradford College
Qualifications: City & Guilds in textile design and management
Career outside cricket: Textiles, Promotions Manager
Off-season: 'Looking after my daughter and playing golf.'
Overseas tours: Yorkshire pre-season tours to West Indies and South Africa
Overseas teams played for: Melville, New Zealand; Adelaide, Australia; Harmony and Orange Free State, South Africa

Cricketers particularly admired: Dennis Lillee, Malcolm Marshall
Other sports followed: Golf, football (Chelsea)
Injuries: Missed one match with a sore back
Relaxations: Golf (handicap of 4), spending time with daughter, drinking Budweiser
Opinions on cricket: 'Four-day cricket will, or should, be better for standards, but if wickets are over-prepared in favour of batsmen then games will still be decided by captains on the last day.'
Best batting: 127* Yorkshire v Lancashire, Old Trafford 1988
Best bowling: 8-111 Yorkshire v Sussex, Hove 1992

1991 Season

	M	Inns	NO	Runs	HS	Avge	100s	50s	Ct	St	O	M	Runs	Wkts	Avge	Best	5wI	10wM
Test																		
All First	20	23	3	353	69	17.65	-	2	6	-	549.5	101	1690	56	30.17	8-111	3	-
1-day Int																		
NatWest	2	1	0	0	0	0.00	-	-	-	-	22	2	104	1	104.00	1-33	-	
B&H	4	3	1	12	6 *	6.00	-	-	2	-	40.1	11	128	7	18.28	3-32	-	
Sunday	14	10	4	69	19	11.50	-	-	2	-	105.5	4	457	17	26.88	3-19	-	

Career Performances

	M	Inns	NO	Runs	HS	Avge	100s	50s	Ct	St	Balls	Runs	Wkts	Avge	Best	5wI	10wM
Test																	
All First	125	140	36	2279	127 *	21.91	1	8	42	-	18719	10863	318	34.16	8-111	12	-
1-day Int																	
NatWest	12	7	3	104	52	26.00	-	1	-	-	731	465	25	18.60	5-46	1	
B&H	26	15	5	78	29 *	7.80	-	-	8	-	1477	962	41	23.46	5-43	1	
Sunday	75	51	18	392	51	11.87	-	1	10	-	3154	2455	89	27.58	5-38	1	

HARVEY, M. E.   Lancashire

Name: Mark Edward Harvey
Role: Right-hand bat, occasional leg-spin bowler
Born: 26 June 1974, Burnley, Lancs
Height: 5ft 9in **Weight:** 11st 8lbs
Nickname: Harv, Vadge, Baz
County debut: No first team appearance
Parents: David and Wendy
Marital status: Single
Family links with cricket: Brother Jonathan was on MCC groundstaff 1989-92, father played local club cricket
Education: Worsthorne County Primary; Habergham High School, Burnley; Loughborough University
Qualifications: 8 GCSEs, 3 A-levels

Off-season: Studying physical education, sports science and recreation management at university

Cricketers particularly admired: David Gower – 'someone who makes it all look so easy', Dean Jones – 'exciting both batting and fielding', Mudassar Nazar – 'an admired professional for many years at Burnley'

Other sports followed: Football (Burnley and Oxford United), golf and 'anything else that keeps me interested'

Relaxations: Football, golf, most sports, listening to music (especially New Order) and watching comedies

Extras: Captained England U17, represented England at U17 and U18 levels, Represented Lancashire Youth cricket from U13 to U19

HAWKES, C. J. — Leicestershire

Name: Christopher James Hawkes
Role: Left-hand bat, slow left-arm bowler
Born: 14 July 1972, Loughborough
Height: 6ft 3½in **Weight:** 13st 8lbs
Nickname: Ches
County debut: 1991
1st-Class catches: 1
Parents: Richard and Mavis
Marital status: Single
Family links with cricket: Both father and brother played club cricket. Father is a qualified coach
Education: Loughborough Grammar School; Durham University
Qualifications: 10 GCSEs, 4 A-levels, in final year studying for BA (Hons) degree in English Literature
Off-season: At university and touring South Africa
Overseas tours: England U19 to New Zealand 1990-91; Durham University to South Africa 1992
Cricketers particularly admired: 'Those who have the ability to make the most of their talent.'

Other sports followed: Golf, rugby union, football and most sports
Injuries: Tendonitis in right knee
Relaxations: Most sports, pubs and travelling
Extras: Released by Leicestershire at the end of the 1992 season
Opinions on cricket: 'Commercialisation of the game seems to be becoming an increasingly more important factor in cricket's growth, and seems a necessary factor in encouraging youngsters to take up the game. However financial motivation should only be taken so far – and not at the expense of younger players, otherwise the game has no future.'
Best batting: 18 Leicestershire v Somerset, Leicester 1992
Best bowling: 4-18 Leicestershire v Lancashire, Southport 1992

1992 Season

	M	Inns	NO	Runs	HS	Avge	100s	50s	Ct	St	O	M	Runs	Wkts	Avge	Best	5wI	10wM
Test																		
All First	3	4	1	60	18	20.00	-	-	1	-	42	11	122	5	24.40	4-18	-	-
1-day Int																		
NatWest																		
B & H																		
Sunday																		

Career Performances

	M	Inns	NO	Runs	HS	Avge	100s	50s	Ct	St	Balls	Runs	Wkts	Avge	Best	5wI	10wM
Test																	
All First	4	6	2	65	18	16.25	-	-	2	-	336	162	5	32.40	4-18	-	-
1-day Int																	
NatWest																	
B & H																	
Sunday																	

89. Who was born in Australia, played for New South Wales, captained Lancashire and played in goal for Bolton Wanderers?

HAYE, A. F.   Leicestershire

Name: Andrew Fitzpatrick Haye
Role: Right-hand bat, right-arm fast-medium bowler
Born: 10 November 1972, St Anne, Jamaica
Height: 6ft 2in **Weight:** 13st 7lbs
Nickname: Ninja Man, Turtle
County debut: No first team appearance
Parents: Vera and Claude Duncan
Marital status: Single
Education: Copeland Community High School, Wembley
Qualifications: 1 O-level, 4 GCSEs, BTEC Business Studies
Off-season: Studying
Overseas tours: England U18 to Canada 1991
Cricketers particularly admired:
Graham Gooch, Malcolm Marshall, Justin Benson ('Rambo')
Other sports followed: Football (Aston Villa)
Relaxations: Watching TV, music, eating out
Extras: Was on MCC staff and has played for Middlesex 2nd XI

HAYHURST, A. N.   Somerset

Name: Andrew Neil Hayhurst
Role: Right-hand bat, right-arm medium bowler
Born: 23 November 1962, Davyhulme, Manchester
Height: 6ft **Weight:** 13st 7lbs
Nickname: Bull
County debut: 1985 (Lancs), 1990 (Somerset)
1000 runs in a season: 2
1st-Class 50s scored: 22
1st-Class 100s scored: 9
1st-Class catches: 31
One-Day 50s: 15
Place in batting averages: 108th av. 33.25 (1991 88th av. 33.70)

Place in bowling averages: (1991 144th av. 70.90)
Strike rate: (career 81.94)
Parents: William and Margaret
Wife and date of marriage: April, 17 February 1990
Children: Myles William David
Family links with cricket: Father played club cricket for Worsley in the Manchester and District Cricket Association
Education: St Mark's Primary School; Worsley Wardley High; Eccles Sixth Form College; Leeds Polytechnic (Carnegie College of PE)
Qualifications: 8 O-levels, 3 A-levels, BA (Hons) Human Movement, Advance Cricket Coach
Career outside cricket: Teaching PE or 'any other winter job I can get!'
Off-season: Legal and General Financial Consultant
Overseas tours: Lancashire to Jamaica 1987 and 1988; Zimbabwe 1989; Somerset to Bahamas 1990
Overseas teams played for: South Launceston, Tasmania 1987-89
Cricketers particularly admired: Viv Richards, Jimmy Cook, Clive Lloyd
Other sports followed: All sports, especially football (Manchester United) and rugby league (Salford)
Relaxations: Animals, gardening, good food
Extras: Played for Greater Manchester U19 at football. Scored a record 197 runs whilst playing for North of England v South, Southampton 1982. Holds record for number of runs in Manchester & District Cricket Association League, whilst playing for Worsley CC in 1984: 1193 runs (av. 70.17). Represented Greater Manchester U19s at football. Released by Lancashire at the end of 1989 season and joined Somerset on a three-year contract, 1990. Made 110* on his first-class debut for Somerset
Opinions on cricket: 'Glad to see four-day cricket. On good wickets like Taunton games can run their natural course instead of having contrived results. Hopefully coloured clothing will bring renewed interest and therefore revenue, although the 50-over format is too much, especially during a four-day game.'
Best batting: 172* Somerset v Gloucestershire, Bath 1991
Best bowling: 4-27 Lancashire v Middlesex, Old Trafford 1987

1992 Season

	M	Inns	NO	Runs	HS	Avge	100s	50s	Ct	St	O	M	Runs	Wkts	Avge	Best	5wI	10wM
Test																		
All First	23	38	2	1197	102	33.25	1	9	6	-	142	30	407	9	45.22	3-27	-	-
1-day Int																		
NatWest	2	2	0	68	47	34.00	-	-	-	-	6.4	0	37	2	18.50	2-22	-	
B & H	6	6	0	237	95	39.50	-	2	1	-	33	3	154	9	17.11	2-19	-	
Sunday	16	15	3	442	73	36.83	-	4	1	-	32.1	0	190	7	27.14	3-24	-	

Career Performances

	M	Inns	NO	Runs	HS	Avge	100s	50s	Ct	St	Balls	Runs	Wkts	Avge	Best	5wI	10wM
Test																	
All First	106	168	21	4851	172 *	33.00	9	22	31	-	7047	3918	86	45.55	4-27	-	-
1-day Int																	
NatWest	14	13	2	467	91 *	42.45	-	3	3	-	696	453	19	23.84	5-60	1	
B & H	22	20	1	494	95	26.00	-	4	2	-	762	525	22	23.86	4-50	-	
Sunday	83	67	14	1492	84	28.15	-	8	11	-	2221	1940	49	39.59	4-37	-	

HAYNES, D. L. Middlesex

Name: Desmond Leo Haynes
Role: Right-hand bat, right-arm bowler
Born: 15 February 1956, St James,
Barbados, West Indies
County debut: 1989
County cap: 1989
Test debut: 1977-78
Tests: 103
One-Day Internationals: 203
1000 runs in a season: 3
1st-Class 50s scored: 112
1st-Class 100s scored: 50
1st-Class 200s scored: 4
1st-Class catches: 162
1st-Class stumpings: 1
One-Day 50s: 75
One-Day 100s: 20
Place in batting averages: 42nd av. 45.84
(1991 48th av. 42.41)
Wife and date of marriage:
Dawn, 14 September 1991
Education: Federal HS, Barbados
Off-season: Touring with West Indies in Australia
Overseas teams played for: Barbados 1976-92
Overseas tours: World Series Cricket (Kerry Packer) 1978-79; West Indies to Australia 1979-80, 1981-82, 1984-85, 1988-89, 1991-92 (World Cup), 1992-93, to New Zealand 1979-80, 1986-87, to England 1980, 1984, 1988, 1991, to Pakistan 1980-81, 1986-87, 1990-91, 1991-92, to India 1983-84, 1987-88, 1989-90, to South Africa 1992-93; West Indies B to Zimbabwe 1981
Extras: Played for Scotland in the B&H Cup. Captained West Indies v England, Port of Spain in 1989-90 and on tour of Pakistan 1990-91. Vice-captain (to Viv Richards) on

England tour 1991 and promoted to vice-captain (to Richie Richardson) of tours to Pakistan and Australia 1991-92 when Gus Logie was ruled out after being injured in a car accident. Britannic Assurance Player of the Year 1990
Best batting: 255* Middlesex v Sussex, Lord's 1990
Best bowling: 1-2 West Indies v Pakistan, Lahore 1980-81

1992 Season

	M	Inns	NO	Runs	HS	Avge	100s	50s	Ct	St	O	M	Runs	Wkts	Avge	Best	5wI	10wM
Test																		
All First	20	35	2	1513	177	45.84	3	10	8	-	2.4	0	5	1	5.00	1-4	-	-
1-day Int																		
NatWest	2	2	0	121	101	60.50	1	-	-	-	2	0	7	0	-		-	-
B & H	4	4	1	250	89	83.33	-	3	1	-	2	0	21	1	21.00	1-21	-	-
Sunday	15	15	3	839	95 *	69.91	-	10	4	-								

Career Performances

	M	Inns	NO	Runs	HS	Avge	100s	50s	Ct	St	Balls	Runs	Wkts	Avge	Best	5wI	10wM
Test	103	179	21	6725	184	42.56	16	37	59	-	18	8	1	8.00	1-2	-	-
All First	298	509	58	21176	255 *	46.95	50	112	162	1	416	201	7	28.71	1-2	-	-
1-day Int	203	202	25	7514	152 *	42.45	16	46	49	-	30	24	0	-		-	-
NatWest	11	11	2	696	149 *	77.33	2	6	2	-	132	66	1	66.00	1-41	-	
B & H	13	13	1	707	131	58.91	1	6	7	-	192	110	3	36.66	1-9	-	
Sunday	41	40	5	1669	107 *	47.68	1	17	16	-	302	284	3	94.66	1-17	-	

HAYNES, G. R. Worcestershire

Name: Gavin Richard Haynes
Role: Right-hand bat, right-arm medium bowler
Born: 29 September 1969
Height: 5ft 10in **Weight:** 12st 6lbs
Nickname: Splash
County debut: 1991
1st-Class 50s: 2
1st-Class catches: 5
Place in batting averages: 148th av. 26.18
Parents: Nicholas and Dorothy
Marital status: Single
Family links with cricket: Father played club cricket and manages Worcester U14 side
Education: Gigmill Junior School; High Park Comprehensive; King Edward V College, Stourbridge

Qualifications: 5 O-levels, 1 A-level, senior cricket coaching award
Overseas teams played for: Sunrise Sports Club, Zimbabwe 1989-90
Cricketers particularly admired: Ian Botham, Graeme Hick, Graham Gooch, Malcolm Marshall
Other sports followed: Football (Aston Villa)
Relaxations: Playing golf or squash, watching videos
Extras: Represented England Schools U15
Best batting: 66 Worcestershire v Glamorgan, Worcester 1992

1992 Season

	M	Inns	NO	Runs	HS	Avge	100s	50s	Ct	St	O	M	Runs	Wkts	Avge	Best	5wI	10wM
Test																		
All First	9	13	2	288	66	26.18	-	2	3	-	45.2	13	128	0	-		-	-	-
1-day Int																		
NatWest	1	1	0	5	5	5.00	-	-	-	-	10	0	80	0	-		-	-
B & H	3	3	2	36	19 *	36.00	-	-	2	-	30	4	93	3	31.00	2-22	-
Sunday	9	5	0	56	26	11.20	-	-	1	-	54	2	209	1	209.00	1-18	-

Career Performances

	M	Inns	NO	Runs	HS	Avge	100s	50s	Ct	St	Balls	Runs	Wkts	Avge	Best	5wI	10wM
Test																	
All First	13	17	3	339	66	24.21	-	2	5	-	388	210	0	-		-	-	-
1-day Int																	
NatWest	1	1	0	5	5	5.00	-	-	-	-	60	80	0	-		-	-
B & H	3	3	2	36	19 *	36.00	-	-	2	-	180	93	3	31.00	2-22	-
Sunday	9	5	0	56	26	11.20	-	-	1	-	324	209	1	209.00	1-18	-

90. Which school had which two former pupils playing together for England last season?

91. What is the cricketing claim to fame of R. De Smidt, ex-Western Province?

HEADLEY, D. W. Kent

Name: Dean Warren Headley
Role: Right-hand bat, right-arm fast-medium
bowler
Born: 27 January 1970, Stourbridge
Height: 6ft 4in **Weight:** 13st 7lbs
Nickname: Besty, Decos
County debut: 1991 (Middlesex)
1st-Class 50s scored: 2
1st-Class 5 w. in innings: 2
1st-Class catches: 10
Place in batting averages: 164th av. 24.54
(1991 238th av. 13.42)
Place in bowling averages: 113th av. 40.58
(1991 124th av. 43.37)
Strike rate: 74.51 (career 71.45)
Parents: Ronald George Alphonso and Gail
Marital status: Single
Family links with cricket: Father Ron
played for Worcestershire, Jamaica and

West Indies and grandfather George played
for Jamaica and West Indies
Education: Gigmill Junior School; Oldswinford Hospital School; Royal Grammar
School, Worcester
Qualifications: 7 O-levels
Career outside cricket: 'Not yet established.'
Off-season: Playing club cricket in Jamaica or Trinidad
Overseas tours: RGS Worcester to Zimbabwe 1988; Christians in Sport to India 1990
Overseas teams played for: Melbourne, Jamaica 1991-92
Cricketers particularly admired: Clive Lloyd, Michael Holding, Ian Botham, Robin
Smith, Malcolm Marshall, Angus Fraser – 'learned most from my father Ron'
Other sports followed: Rugby, football, basketball, golf
Injuries: Stress fracture in left foot, out for four weeks
Relaxations: Music, socialising with friends and colleagues
Extras: Took 5 wickets on debut including a wicket with his first ball in Championship
cricket. Played for Worcestershire 2nd XI 1988-89. Left Middlesex at the end of the 1992
season and signed for Kent
Opinions on cricket: 'One bouncer per over must go. Wickets should be prepared in
whatever way the club wants as long as it isn't dangerous. The game should be marketed
better. Helmets should only be used by batsmen not fielders.'
Best batting: 91 Middlesex v Leicestershire, Leicester 1992
Best bowling: 5-46 Middlesex v Yorkshire, Lord's 1991

1992 Season

	M	Inns	NO	Runs	HS	Avge	100s	50s	Ct	St	O	M	Runs	Wkts	Avge	Best	5wI	10wM
Test																		
All First	17	14	3	270	91	24.54	-	1	5	-	385	74	1258	31	40.58	3-31	-	-
1-day Int																		
NatWest	1	1	1	7	7 *	-	-	-	-	-	8.1	4	20	5	4.00	5-20	1	
B & H	4	1	0	11	11	11.00	-	-	1	-	31	5	123	4	30.75	4-19	-	
Sunday	15	1	1	4	4 *	-	-	-	4	-	90.1	2	457	19	24.05	4-23	-	

Career Performances

	M	Inns	NO	Runs	HS	Avge	100s	50s	Ct	St	Balls	Runs	Wkts	Avge	Best	5wI	10wM
Test																	
All First	29	29	4	472	91	18.88	-	2	10	-	4287	2516	60	41.93	5-46	2	-
1-day Int																	
NatWest	2	2	2	18	11 *	-	-	-	-	-	121	71	5	14.20	5-20	1	
B & H	8	4	0	41	26	10.25	-	-	2	-	439	303	7	43.28	4-19	-	
Sunday	23	3	2	14	6 *	14.00	-	-	4	-	877	753	20	37.65	4-23	-	

HEGG, W. K.   Lancashire

Name: Warren Kevin Hegg
Role: Right-hand bat, wicket-keeper
Born: 23 February 1968, Radcliffe, Lancashire
Height: 5ft 10in **Weight:** 12st 7lbs
Nickname: Chucky
County debut: 1986
1st-Class 50s scored: 16
1st-Class 100s scored: 2
1st-Class catches: 284
1st-Class stumpings: 35
Place in batting averages: 90th av. 36.35 (1991 97th av. 32.66)
Parents: Kevin and Glenda
Marital status: Single
Family links with cricket: Father and brother Martin play in local leagues
Education: Unsworth High School; Stand College, Whitefield
Qualifications: 5 O-levels, 7 CSEs; qualified coach
Career outside cricket: Groundsman – worked in textile warehouse
Off-season: Playing in Australia

Overseas tours: NCA North U19 to Bermuda 1985; England U19 to Sri Lanka 1986-87, to Youth World Cup in Australia 1988; England A to Pakistan and Sri Lanka 1990-91
Overseas teams played for: Sheffield, Tasmania 1988-90, 1992-93
Cricketers particularly admired: Ian Botham, Alan Knott, Bob Taylor, Gehan Mendis (for perseverance)
Other sports followed: Football, golf, fishing, Aussie rules
Injuries: Slipped disc in back, out for three weeks
Relaxations: Listening to music, walking on my own
Extras: First player to make county debut from Lytham CC. Youngest player to score a 100 for Lancashire for thirty years, 130 v Northamptonshire in fourth first-class game. Eleven victims in match v Derbyshire – to equal world record
Opinions on cricket: 'Players should be given more time to prepare for games. There should always be a travelling day for long journeys.'
Best batting: 130 Lancashire v Northamptonshire, Northampton 1987

1992 Season

	M	Inns	NO	Runs	HS	Avge	100s	50s	Ct	St	O	M	Runs	Wkts	Avge	Best	5wI	10wM
Test																		
All First	18	24	7	618	80	36.35	-	4	33	6								
1-day Int																		
NatWest	2	1	0	7	7	7.00	-	-	6	-								
B & H	5	3	1	29	19	14.50	-	-	7	-								
Sunday	13	8	5	109	34	36.33	-	-	10	2								

Career Performances

	M	Inns	NO	Runs	HS	Avge	100s	50s	Ct	St	Balls	Runs	Wkts	Avge	Best	5wI	10wM
Test																	
All First	127	179	34	3698	130	25.50	2	16	284	35	6	7	0	-	-	-	-
1-day Int																	
NatWest	14	8	1	118	29	16.85	-	-	20	-							
B & H	28	12	5	123	31 *	17.57	-	-	40	1							
Sunday	78	37	20	356	47 *	20.94	-	-	79	10							

92. Who has scored the most ever runs in Sheffield Shield cricket?

HEMMINGS, E. E.   Sussex

Name: Edward Ernest Hemmings
Role: Right-hand bat, off-spin bowler
Born: 20 February 1949, Leamington Spa, Warwickshire
Height: 5ft 10in **Weight:** 13st
Nickname: Eddie, Whale, Fossil 'with many thanks to Angus Fraser for the last of my nicknames'
County debut: 1966 (Warwicks), 1979 (Nottinghamshire)
County cap: 1974 (Warwicks), 1980 (Notts)
Benefit: 1987
Test debut: 1982
Tests: 16
One-Day Internationals: 33
50 wickets in a season: 14
1st-Class 50s scored: 27
1st-Class 100s scored: 1
1st-Class 5 w. in innings: 66
1st-Class 10 w. in match: 14
1st-Class catches: 196
One-Day 50s: 1
Place in batting averages: 173rd av. 22.00 (1991 248th av. 11.91)
Place in bowling averages: 70th av. 33.44 (1991 103rd av. 37.41)
Strike rate: 86.61 (career 66.94)
Parents: Edward and Dorothy Phyliss
Wife and date of marriage: Christine Mary, 23 October 1971
Children: Thomas Edward, 26 July 1977; James Oliver, 9 September 1979
Family links with cricket: Father and father's father played Minor Counties and League cricket
Education: Campion School, Leamington Spa
Overseas tours: England to Australia and New Zealand 1982-83, to Pakistan (World Cup), Australia and New Zealand 1987-88, to India and West Indies 1989-90, to Australia 1990-91
Cricketers particularly admired: Tim Robinson, Clive Rice, John Jameson
Other sports followed: Golf, football
Relaxations: 'Watching football at any level – especially junior. Dining out with my wife. Golf, real ale – and sleeping it off!'
Extras: Took a hat-trick for Warwickshire in 1977; hit first century – 127* for Nottinghamshire v Yorkshire at Worksop, July 1982 – after sixteen years in first-class game. Released by Notts end of the 1992 season and signed by Sussex
Best batting: 127* Nottinghamshire v Yorkshire, Worksop 1982
Best bowling: 10-175 International XI v West Indies XI, Kingston 1982-83

	M	Inns	NO	Runs	HS	Avge	100s	50s	Ct	St	O	M	Runs	Wkts	Avge	Best	5wI	10wM
Test																		
All First	7	11	5	132	52 *	22.00	-	1	2	-	259.5	95	602	18	33.44	4-30	-	-
1-day Int																		
NatWest																			
B & H	4	2	1	9	5 *	9.00	-	-	1	-	42	5	137	6	22.83	3-32	-	
Sunday	4	1	0	3	3	3.00	-	-	1	-	28	0	135	2	67.50	1-27	-	

Career Performances

	M	Inns	NO	Runs	HS	Avge	100s	50s	Ct	St	Balls	Runs	Wkts	Avge	Best	5wI	10wM
Test	16	21	4	383	95	22.52	-	2	5	-	4437	1825	43	42.44	6-58	1	-
All First	482	627	146	9297	127 *	19.32	1	27	196	-	93989	41461	1404	29.53	10-175	66	14
1-day Int	33	12	6	30	8 *	5.00	-	-	5	-	1752	1293	37	34.94	4-52	-	
NatWest	42	30	11	255	31 *	13.42	-	-	8	-	2794	1591	46	34.58	3-27	-	
B & H	89	53	17	505	61 *	14.02	-	1	20	-	5335	2853	82	34.79	4-47	-	
Sunday	268	166	50	1593	44 *	13.73	-	-	82	-	10459	8034	274	29.32	5-22	4	

HEMP, D. L.   Glamorgan

Name: David Lloyd Hemp
Role: Left-hand bat, right-arm medium bowler
Born: 15 November 1970, Bermuda
Height: 6ft **Weight:** 12st
Nickname: Hempy
County debut: 1991
1st-Class 50s scored: 2
1st-Class catches: 7
Place in batting averages: 176th av. 21.73
Parents: Clive and Elisabeth
Marital status: Single
Family links with cricket: Father plays for Ffynone and brother plays for Swansea
Education: Olchfa Comprehensive School; Millfield School
Qualifications: 5 O-levels, 2 A-levels
Career outside cricket: Working in an accountancy office
Off-season: Playing and coaching in Durban, South Africa
Overseas tours: Welsh Schools U19 to Australia 1986-87; Welsh Cricket Association

U18 to Barbados 1987; Glamorgan to Trinidad 1990; South Wales Cricket Association to New Zealand and Australia 1991-92

Cricketers particularly admired: David Gower, Viv Richards, Keith Arthurton

Other sports followed: Football

Relaxations: Watching football and TV, listening to music

Extras: Scored 258* for Wales v MCC 1991. In 1990 scored 104* & 101* for Welsh Schools U19 v Scottish Schools U19 and 120 & 102* v Irish Schools U19

Opinions on cricket: 'All 2nd XI games should be played on county grounds rather than club grounds at the quality of wickets is usually poorer at clubs, also they do not have such good facilities for covering wickets.'

Best batting: 84* Glamorgan v Hampshire, Portsmouth 1992

1992 Season

	M	Inns	NO	Runs	HS	Avge	100s	50s	Ct	St	O	M	Runs	Wkts	Avge	Best	5wl	10wM
Test																		
All First	12	17	2	326	84 *	21.73	-	2	7	-								
1-day Int																		
NatWest																		
B & H																		
Sunday	4	3	1	15	10	7.50	-	-	1	-								

Career Performances

	M	Inns	NO	Runs	HS	Avge	100s	50s	Ct	St	Balls	Runs	Wkts	Avge	Best	5wl	10wM
Test																	
All First	13	19	3	338	84 *	21.12	-	2	7	-							
1-day Int																	
NatWest																	
B & H																	
Sunday	5	4	1	22	10	7.33	-	-	1	-							

93. At which cricket ground do you find the Diglis end?

94. At which cricket ground do you find the Trafalgar Square end?

HENDERSON, J. A. L.   Lancashire

Name: Jonathan Andrew Lloyd Henderson
Role: Right-hand bat, right-arm fast bowler
Born: 16 January 1975, Cardiff
Height: 6ft 3in **Weight:** 12st
Nickname: Hendo
County debut: No first team appearance
Parents: Andrew and Carole
Marital status: Single
Family links with cricket: Father played county 2nd XI cricket with Sussex and Glamorgan
Education: Hulme Grammar School, Oldham
Qualifications: 9 GCSEs
Off-season: Still at school studying for A-levels, playing basketball, light training, running, spending time with family and friends
Overseas tours: England U18 to South Africa 1992-93
Cricketers particularly admired: Richard Hadlee, Wasim Akram
Other sports followed: Football, basketball, American football
Relaxations: Watching television, reading the newspapers, shopping, listening to music
Extras: Played for Rochdale in Central Lancashire League in 1992. Has represented Lancashire Schools U19, Lancashire Federation, England U17, U18 and U19, Central Lancashire League, League Cricket Conference

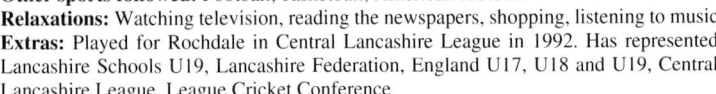

95. At which ground do you find the Vulture Street end?

96. At which ground do you find the Top Rank end?

HENDERSON, P. W.   Durham

Name: Paul William Henderson
Role: Right-hand bat, right-arm fast-medium bowler
Born: 22 October 1974, Stockton-on-Tees
Height: 6ft
County debut: 1992
1st-Class catches: 1
Place in batting averages: 212th av. 17.00
Place in bowling averages: 112th av. 40.50
Strike rate: 57.60 (career 57.60)
Marital status: Single
Education: Billingham Campus School
Off-season: Touring with Durham
Overseas tours:
Durham to Zimbabwe 1991-92
Extras: Made his debut for Durham in 1991 aged 16 against Durham University.
Best batting: 46 Durham v Glamorgan, Cardiff 1992
Best bowling: 3-59 Durham v Somerset, Darlington 1992

1992 Season

	M	Inns	NO	Runs	HS	Avge	100s	50s	Ct	St	O	M	Runs	Wkts	Avge	Best	5wI	10wM
Test																		
All First	5	7	0	119	46	17.00	-	-	1	-	96	14	405	10	40.50	3-59	-	-
1-day Int																		
NatWest																		
B & H																		
Sunday	3	2	2	13	10*	-	-	-	1	-	21	0	137	3	45.66	3-47	-	

Career Performances

	M	Inns	NO	Runs	HS	Avge	100s	50s	Ct	St	Balls	Runs	Wkts	Avge	Best	5wI	10wM
Test																	
All First	5	7	0	119	46	17.00	-	-	1	-	576	405	10	40.50	3-59	-	-
1-day Int																	
NatWest																	
B & H																	
Sunday	3	2	2	13	10*	-	-	-	1	-	126	137	3	45.66	3-47	-	

HEPWORTH, P. N. Leicestershire

Name: Peter Nash Hepworth
Role: Right-hand bat, off-spin bowler
Born: 4 May 1967, Ackworth, West Yorkshire
Height: 6ft 1in **Weight:** 12st 7lbs
Nickname: Nash
County debut: 1988
1st-Class 50s scored: 6
1st-Class 50s scored: 2
1st-Class catches: 28
Place in batting averages: 238th av. 12.35 (1991 95th av. 32.91)
Place in bowling averages: (1991 74th av. 33.07)
Strike rate: (career 70.10)
Parents: George and Zena
Marital status: Single
Family links with cricket: Father and uncle played cricket for Ackworth
Education: Bell Lane School, Ackworth; Ackworth Middle School; Hemsworth High School
Qualifications: 8 CSEs, NCA senior coaching certificate
Career outside cricket: Builder (with family firm), cricket coach
Off-season: Coaching, playing football and 'some sort of building work'
Overseas tours: Hull CC to Barbados
Overseas teams played for: Played a season in Bloemfontein 1991-92
Cricketers particularly admired: David Gower, Geoff Boycott
Other sports followed: Football (Leeds United), rugby and most other sports
Relaxations: Music and movies
Extras: Started playing for Ackworth Cricket Club following the likes of Neil Lloyd ('the best young cricketer I've ever seen'), Graham Stevenson, Tim Boon, Geoff Boycott
Best batting: 115 Leicestershire v Essex, Leicester 1991
              115 Leicestershire v Cambridge University, Fenner's 1991
Best bowling: 3-51 Leicestershire v Kent, Canterbury 1991

---

97.   Who captained Sri Lanka in the last World Cup?

1992 Season

	M	Inns	NO	Runs	HS	Avge	100s	50s	Ct	St	O	M	Runs	Wkts	Avge	Best	5wI	10wM
Test																		
All First	10	15	1	173	38	12.35	-	-	5	-	102.4	16	439	5	87.80	2-29	-	-
1-day Int																		
NatWest																		
B & H	1	1	1	11	11 *	-	-	-	1	-	11	2	44	2	22.00	2-44	-	
Sunday	4	4	1	13	8 *	4.33	-	-	-	-	21	0	115	2	57.50	1-24	-	

Career Performances

	M	Inns	NO	Runs	HS	Avge	100s	50s	Ct	St	Balls	Runs	Wkts	Avge	Best	5wI	10wM
Test																	
All First	46	75	7	1672	115	24.58	2	6	28	-	1332	902	19	47.47	3-51	-	-
1-day Int																	
NatWest																	
B & H	4	3	1	53	33	26.50	-	-	2	-	186	127	7	18.14	4-39	-	
Sunday	18	14	3	158	38	14.36	-	-	1	-	288	255	8	31.87	2-33	-	

HICK, G. A.   Worcestershire

Name: Graeme Ashley Hick
Role: Right-hand bat, off-spin bowler
Born: 23 May 1966, Harare, Zimbabwe
Height: 6ft 3in **Weight:** 14st 7lbs
Nickname: Hicky, Ash
County debut: 1984
County cap: 1986
Test debut: 1991
Tests: 11
One-Day Internationals: 21
1000 runs in a season: 8
1st-Class 50s scored: 72
1st-Class 100s scored: 67
1st-Class 200s scored: 8
1st-Class 5 w. in innings: 4
1st-Class 10 w. in match: 1
1st-Class catches: 271
One-Day 50s: 52
One-Day 100s: 9
Place in batting averages: 15th av. 53.48 (1991 96th av. 32.91)
Place in bowling averages: (1991 132nd av. 49.20)
Strike rate: (career 79.67)

Parents: John and Eve
Wife and date of marriage: Jackie, 5 October 1991
Children: Lauren Amy, 12 September 1992
Family links with cricket: Father served on Zimbabwe Cricket Union Board of Control since 1984; also played representative cricket in Zimbabwe
Education: Banket Primary; Prince Edward Boys' High School, Zimbabwe
Qualifications: 4 O-levels, NCA coaching award
Off-season: Touring with England
Overseas tours: Zimbabwe to England for 1983 World Cup, to Sri Lanka 1983-84, to England 1985; England to New Zealand and Australia (World Cup) 1991-92, to India and Sri Lanka 1992-93
Overseas teams played for: Old Hararians in Zimbabwe 1982-90; Northern Districts 1987-89; Queensland 1990-91
Cricketers particularly admired: Duncan Fletcher (Zimbabwe captain) for approach and understanding of the game, David Houghton, Basil D'Oliveira
Other sports followed: Follows Liverpool FC, golf, tennis, squash, hockey
Relaxations: 'Leaning against Steve Rhodes at first-slip.'
Extras: Made first 100 aged 6 for school team; youngest player participating in 1983 Prudential World Cup (aged 17); youngest player to represent Zimbabwe. Scored 1234 runs in Birmingham League and played for Worcestershire 2nd XI in 1984 – hitting six successive 100s. In 1986, at age 20, he became the youngest player to score 2000 runs in an English season. One of *Wisden's* Five Cricketers of the Year, 1986. In 1988 he made 405* v Somerset, the highest individual score in England since 1895, and scored 1000 first-class runs by end of May 1988, hitting a record 410 runs in April. In 1990 became youngest batsman ever to make 50 first-class 100s and scored 645 runs without being dismissed – a record for English cricket. Qualified as an English player in 1991. Scored first Test century v India in Bombay 1992-93 and was England's leading batsman, bowler and fielder. Published *Hick 'n' Dilley Circus* and *A Champion's Diary*. Also played hockey for Zimbabwe
Opinions on cricket: 'What a great game.'
Best batting: 405* Worcestershire v Somerset, Taunton 1988
Best bowling: 5-37 Worcestershire v Gloucestershire, Worcester 1990

1992 Season

	M	Inns	NO	Runs	HS	Avge	100s	50s	Ct	St	O	M	Runs	Wkts	Avge	Best	5wI	10wM
Test	4	5	0	98	51	19.60	-	1	10	-	18	3	63	0	-	-	-	-
All First	17	27	2	1337	213 *	53.48	4	5	32	-	142.3	40	415	8	51.87	3-32	-	-
1-day Int	5	5	2	187	71 *	62.33	-	2	3	-	4.2	0	15	2	7.50	2-7	-	
NatWest	1	1	0	14	14	14.00	-	-	-	-	4	0	22	0	-	-	-	
B & H	5	5	0	144	44	28.80	-	-	1	-	6	0	25	0	-	-	-	
Sunday	12	12	2	449	83 *	44.90	-	5	7	-	26.3	0	142	3	47.33	1-13	-	

Career Performances

	M	Inns	NO	Runs	HS	Avge	100s	50s	Ct	St	Balls	Runs	Wkts	Avge	Best	5wI	10wM
Test	11	17	0	307	51	18.05	-	1	22	-	774	306	6	51.00	4-126	-	-
All First	226	364	41	19083	405 *	59.08	67	72	271	-	11314	5575	142	39.26	5-37	4	1
1-day Int	21	20	4	628	86 *	39.25	-	6	11	-	148	114	4	28.50	2-7	-	
NatWest	21	21	5	941	172 *	58.81	3	4	9	-	645	376	9	41.77	4-54	-	
B & H	37	37	6	1473	109	47.51	3	11	24	-	414	285	7	40.71	3-36	-	
Sunday	105	102	17	3821	114 *	44.95	3	31	26	-	1373	1266	40	31.65	4-42	-	

HINDSON, J. E.   Nottinghamshire

Name: James Edward Hindson
Role: Right-hand bat, slow left-arm bowler
Born: 13 September 1973, Huddersfield,
Yorks
Height: 6ft 1in **Weight:** 11st 8lbs
Nickname: Jim, Muppet
County debut: 1992
1st-Class 5 w. in innings: 1
Strike rate: (career 25.25)
Parents: Robert and Gloria
Marital status: Single
Education: Robert Sherborne Infants School,
Rolleston, Staffs; Ernhale Junior School,
Arnold, Notts; St Peter's Primary School,
East Bridgford, Notts; Toot Hill
Comprehensive School, Bingham, Notts
Qualifications: 10 GCSEs, 3 A-levels
Off-season: Casual labourer in a factory
and training for England U19 tour to India
Overseas tours: England U19 to India 1992-93
Cricketers particularly admired: Richard Hadlee, Derek Randall, Robin Smith
Other sports followed: Ice hockey, football
Injuries: Rib cartilage – three weeks, on-going tendonitis in left knee
Relaxations: Anything to do with ice hockey, reading, socialising
Extras: Took five wickets on first-class debut (eight in the match). Converted from right-arm to left-arm bowler at age 6, still throws right-handed, bowled left-arm medium until 15 years old
Opinions on cricket: 'I am all for coloured clothing and names on the back of shirts in Sunday League cricket as this will give the playing public, especially the young, a chance to identify more closely with individual players, and the team they support i.e. through wearing team colours. However I cannot see the point of extending the Sunday League to

50 overs a side – the Sunday League is entertainment, and the so-called quality cricket is available in four-day matches for those wishing to see it.'

Best bowling: 5-42 Nottinghamshire v Cambridge University, Trent Bridge 1992

1992 Season

	M	Inns	NO	Runs	HS	Avge	100s	50s	Ct	St	O	M	Runs	Wkts	Avge	Best	5wI	10wM
Test																		
All First	1	0	0	0	0	-	-	-	-	-	33.4	11	74	8	9.25	5-42	1	-
1-day Int																		
NatWest																		
B & H																		
Sunday																		

Career Performances

	M	Inns	NO	Runs	HS	Avge	100s	50s	Ct	St	Balls	Runs	Wkts	Avge	Best	5wI	10wM
Test																	
All First	1	0	0	0	0	-	-	-	-	-	202	74	8	9.25	5-42	1	-
1-day Int																	
NatWest																	
B & H																	
Sunday																	

HINKS, S. G.   Gloucestershire

Name: Simon Graham Hinks
Role: Left-hand opening bat
Born: 12 October 1960, Northfleet, Kent
Height: 6ft 2in **Weight:** 13$^{1}/_{2}$-14st
Nickname: Shaba, Shinks, Hinksy
County debut: 1982 (Kent),
1992 (Gloucestershire)
County cap: 1985 (Kent)
1000 runs in a season: 3
1st-Class 50s scored: 38
1st-Class 100s scored: 11
1st-Class 200s scored: 1
One-Day 50s: 22
Place in batting averages: 122nd av. 30.07
(1991 175th av. 22.91)
Parents: Mary and Graham
Wife and date of marriage:
Vicki, September 1990
Children: Megan Rose, 15 June 1991

Family links with cricket: Father captained Gravesend CC and is now chairman. Brother Jonathan captains Gravesend and has played for Kent U19

Education: Dover Road Infant and Junior Schools, Northfleet; St George's C of E School, Gravesend; Sheffield University

Qualifications: 5 O-levels, 1 A-level, senior cricket coach, Diploma in Leisure Management

Career outside cricket: Sales rep for Reed Corrugated Cases

Off-season: Playing in South Africa

Overseas teams played for: Durbanville, South Africa 1992-93

Cricketers particularly admired: Courtney Walsh

Other sports followed: All sports

Injuries: Torn cartilage, blood clot on left knee, out for eight weeks

Relaxations: Sport, TV, DIY, gardening

Extras: Left Kent at the end of 1991 season and signed three-year contract with Gloucestershire

Opinions on cricket: 'Learn from your mistakes before it is too late. Wear the right tie.'

Best batting: 234 Kent v Middlesex, Canterbury 1990

Best bowling: 2-18 Kent v Nottinghamshire, Trent Bridge 1989

1992 Season

	M	Inns	NO	Runs	HS	Avge	100s	50s	Ct	St	O	M	Runs	Wkts	Avge	Best	5wI	10wM
Test																		
All First	10	16	3	402	88 *	30.92	-	3	3	-	2.5	1	14	0	-	-	-	-
1-day Int																		
NatWest	1	1	0	67	67	67.00	-	1	-	-								
B & H	5	5	0	127	42	25.40	-	-	-	-								
Sunday	8	8	0	90	39	11.25	-	-	2	-								

Career Performances

	M	Inns	NO	Runs	HS	Avge	100s	50s	Ct	St	Balls	Runs	Wkts	Avge	Best	5wI	10wM
Test																	
All First	164	283	18	7971	234	30.07	11	38	99	-	597	381	8	47.62	2-18	-	-
1-day Int																	
NatWest	12	12	2	481	95	48.10	-	4	3	-	18	23	0	-	-	-	-
B & H	37	36	1	835	85	23.85	-	4	7	-	246	198	5	39.60	1-15	-	
Sunday	99	99	6	2174	99	23.37	-	14	28	-	150	139	4	34.75	1-3	-	

98.   Who captained India in the last World Cup?

HODGSON, G. D. — Gloucestershire

Name: Geoffrey Dean Hodgson
Role: Right-hand opening bat
Born: 22 October 1966, Carlisle
Height: 6ft 1in **Weight:** 13st
Nickname: Deano, Harrable
County debut: 1987 (Warwicks),
1989 (Gloucestershire)
County cap: 1992
1000 runs in a season: 3
1st-Class 50s scored: 25
1st-Class 100s scored: 5
1st-Class catches: 30
One-Day 50s: 5
One-Day 100s: 1
Place in batting averages: 98th av. 34.97
(1991 118th av. 29.75)
Parents: John Geoffrey and Dorothy
Elizabeth
Marital status: Single
Education: Nelson Thomlinson
Comprehensive, Wigton; Loughborough University
Qualifications: 11 O-levels, 4 A-levels, BSc (Hons) Human Biological Sciences, NCA qualified cricket coach, PFA qualified football coach, LTA qualified tennis coach
Off-season: Playing and coaching in Argentina
Overseas tours: NCA North U19 to Bermuda 1985; Geoff Humpage Benefit Tour to Barbados 1987; Gloucestershire to Namibia 1990, to Kenya 1991
Overseas teams played for: Southern Districts, Queensland 1988-89; Wests, Brisbane 1990-91; Belgrano, Buenos Aires, Argentina 1991-92
Cricketers particularly admired: Dennis Amiss, Graham Gooch, Sunil Gavaskar, Ian Botham, Malcolm Marshall, Courtney Walsh and other players who make the most of their abilities
Other sports followed: Football, international rugby (league & union), golf, tennis, skiing
Injuries: Missed one game with 'flu
Relaxations: Listening to music ('all types depending on mood'), reading thrillers and autobiographies, watching comedies and thrillers, going to wine bars
Extras: Played Minor County Cricket for Cumberland 1982-88; also played for Lancashire (1985-87) and Worcestershire (1989) 2nd XIs, also with Warwickshire (1987-88); first-class debut for Gloucestershire in 1989. Rapid Cricketline Player of the Month August/ September 1989 while on trial with Gloucestershire. Gloucestershire Supporters Player of the Year 1990
Opinions on cricket: 'Leave Sunday League at 40 overs, 50 overs is too long coming as it does before the last day of a four-day game. Over rates are still too high, 17 per hour would

be acceptable. There should be increased awareness of players' needs in the winter. Would like to see an alternative to the benefit system, especially for those who are released before they have accumulated 8, 9 or 10 years as a capped player.'

Best batting: 147 Gloucestershire v Essex, Southend 1992

1992 Season

	M	Inns	NO	Runs	HS	Avge	100s	50s	Ct	St	O	M	Runs	Wkts	Avge	Best	5wI	10wM
Test																		
All First	21	36	1	1224	147	34.97	2	8	10	-	4	0	65	0	-	-	-	-
1-day Int																		
NatWest	3	3	0	54	29	18.00	-	-	-	-								
B & H	4	4	1	263	103 *	87.66	1	2	-	-								
Sunday	16	16	1	450	84 *	30.00	-	2	5	-								

Career Performances

	M	Inns	NO	Runs	HS	Avge	100s	50s	Ct	St	Balls	Runs	Wkts	Avge	Best	5wI	10wM
Test																	
All First	71	119	7	3705	147	33.08	5	25	30	-	24	65	0	-	-	-	-
1-day Int																	
NatWest	8	8	0	229	52	28.62	-	1	1	-							
B & H	8	8	1	283	103 *	40.42	1	2	1	-							
Sunday	29	28	3	638	84 *	25.52	-	2	12	-							

HOLLAND, E. P. M.   Glamorgan

Name: Ewan Phillip Murray Holland
Role: Right-hand bat, right-arm medium-fast bowler
Born: 1 June 1972, Hereford
Height: 6ft 4in **Weight:** 13st 7lbs
County debut: No first team appearance
Parents: Richard and Alison
Marital status: Single
Family links with cricket: Father played club cricket
Education: Christ College, Brecon; The University of the West of England, Bristol
Qualifications: 9 GCSEs, 2 A-levels
Off-season: Studying Valuation and Estate Management at University
Cricketers particularly admired: Sir Richard Hadlee,

Bob Willis, Robin Smith
Other sports followed: Rugby, squash, golf
Relaxations: Playing most sports, listening to music, watching films

HOLLIOAKE, A. J. Surrey

Name: Adam John Hollioake
Role: Right-hand bat, right-arm fast-medium bowler
Born: 5 September 1971, Melbourne, Australia
Height: 5ft 11½in **Weight:** 13st
Nickname: Smokey, Smokin' Joe, Mental, Hokey Cokey, Abo, Bong
County debut: 1992 (one-day)
Parents: John and Daria
Marital status: Single
Family links with cricket: Brother plays for England U14
Education: St Joseph's College, Sydney; Surrey Tutorial College, Guildford
Qualifications: 'Some GCSEs and A-levels'
Off-season: Playing in Australia
Overseas tours: School trip to Zimbabwe, Surrey YCs to Australia, England U19 to New Zealand
Overseas teams played for: Freemantle, Western Australia 1990-91; North Shore, Sydney 1992-93
Cricketers particularly admired: Peter Oakes, David Ligertwood, Andy Smith, Matt Church, Geoff Arnold, Waqar Younis, Keith Medlycott and 'Dad'
Other sports followed: Rugby, boxing
Injuries: 'Just a few niggles'
Relaxations: 'Phasing the coaches with Nick Peters'
Extras: Played rugby for London Counties, Middlesex and South of England as well as having a trial for England U18
Opinions on cricket: 'Too boring for spectators. If you hit the ball out of the ground you should get 12.'

---

99.   Who captained Zimbabwe in the last World Cup?

1992 Season

	M	Inns	NO	Runs	HS	Avge	100s	50s	Ct	St	O	M	Runs	Wkts	Avge	Best	5wl	10wM
Test																		
All First																		
1-day Int																		
NatWest																		
B & H																		
Sunday	2	1	0	22	22	22.00	-	-	-	-	15	0	94	1	94.00	1-37	-	

Career Performances

	M	Inns	NO	Runs	HS	Avge	100s	50s	Ct	St	Balls		Runs	Wkts	Avge	Best	5wl	10wM
Test																		
All First																		
1-day Int																		
NatWest																		
B & H																		
Sunday	2	1	0	22	22	22.00	-	-	-	-	90		94	1	94.00	1-37	-	

HOLLOWAY, P. C. L. — Warwickshire

Name: Piran Christopher Laity Holloway
Role: Left-hand bat, wicket-keeper
Born: 1 October 1970, Helston, Cornwall
Height: 5ft 8in **Weight:** 11st
Nickname: Pils, Piras, Villager, Vill
County debut: 1988
1st-Class 50s scored: 2
1st-Class 100s scored: 1
1st-Class catches: 25
1st-Class stumpings: 1
One-Day 50s: 1
Parents: Chris and Mary
Marital status: Single
Family links with cricket: 'Mum and Dad are keen supporters of Helston CC'
Education: Nansloe CP School, Helston; Millfield School; Taunton School; Loughborough University
Qualifications: 6 O-levels, 2 A-levels
Off-season: In 3rd year of degree course in sports science
Overseas tours: Millfield School to Barbados 1986; England U19 to Australia 1990
Cricketers particularly admired: Alan Knott, Roger Twose, Dermot Reeve, Bob

Woolmer

Other sports followed: Rugby (union and league), fishing, squash
Injuries: Broken finger
Relaxations: Keeping fit, training at the gym, having a few beers with the Loughborough rugby league team on a Wednesday night, reading
Best batting: 102* Warwickshire v Worcestershire, Edgbaston 1992

1992 Season

	M	Inns	NO	Runs	HS	Avge	100s	50s	Ct	St	O	M	Runs	Wkts	Avge	Best	5wI	10wM
Test																		
All First	2	3	1	133	102 *	66.50	1	-	8	-								
1-day Int																		
NatWest	1	0	0	0	0	-	-	-	-	-								
B & H	2	2	1	8	8	8.00	-	-	3	-								
Sunday	16	11	2	175	51	19.44	-	1	18	6								

Career Performances

	M	Inns	NO	Runs	HS	Avge	100s	50s	Ct	St	Balls	Runs	Wkts	Avge	Best	5wI	10wM
Test																	
All First	11	17	6	436	102 *	39.63	1	2	25	1							
1-day Int																	
NatWest	2	1	0	2	2	2.00	-	-	2	1							
B & H	6	6	1	67	27	13.40	-	-	7	-							
Sunday	23	16	5	262	51	23.81	-	1	21	6							

100. What has Dipak Patel in common with W.G. Grace, J.W.H.T. Douglas, George Giffen, and Ted Arnold?

101. Who was England's first Test captain?

HOOPER, C. L.   Kent

Name: Carl Llewellyn Hooper
Role: Right-hand bat, off-spin bowler
Born: 15 December 1966, Guyana
Height: 6ft **Weight:** 13st
County debut: 1992
County cap: 1992
Test debut: 1987-88
Tests: 32
One-Day Internationals: 80
1000 runs in a season: 2
1st-Class 50s scored: 35
1st-Class 100s scored: 15
1st-Class 5 w. in innings: 5
1st-Class catches: 120
One-Day 50s: 8
One-Day 100s: 1
Place in batting averages: 34th av. 47.46
(1991 1st av. 93.81)
Place in bowling averages: 97th av. 37.34
(1991 32nd av. 27.00)
Strike rate: 85.85 (career 74.88)
Off-season: Touring with West Indies to Australia and South Africa
Overseas tours: West Indies to India and Pakistan 1987-88, to Australia 1988-89, to Pakistan 1990-91, to England 1991, to Pakistan and Australia (World Cup) 1991-92, to Australia and South Africa 1992-93
Overseas teams played for: Guyana 1984-93
Extras: Signed a two-year contract to play for Kent from 1992
Best batting: 196 West Indies v Hampshire, Southampton 1991
Best bowling: 5-33 West Indies v Queensland, Brisbane 1988-89

1992 Season

	M	Inns	NO	Runs	HS	Avge	100s	50s	Ct	St	O	M	Runs	Wkts	Avge	Best	5wI	10wM
Test																		
All First	21	32	4	1329	131	47.46	5	7	25	-	500.5	114	1307	35	37.34	4-57	-	-
1-day Int																		
NatWest	3	3	0	67	40	22.33	-	-	1	-	35	7	110	2	55.00	1-19	-	
B & H	5	5	0	173	50	34.60	-	1	1	-	55	7	157	8	19.62	3-28	-	
Sunday	14	13	1	276	90	23.00	-	1	8	-	91	1	365	8	45.62	2-23	-	

Career Performances

	M	Inns	NO	Runs	HS	Avge	100s	50s	Ct	St	Balls	Runs	Wkts	Avge	Best	5wI	10wM
Test	32	54	4	1409	134	28.18	3	7	29	-	2920	1247	15	83.13	2-28	-	-
All First	118	178	21	6528	196	41.58	15	35	120	-	13555	6039	181	33.36	5-33	5	-
1-day Int	80	70	17	1511	113 *	28.50	1	6	33	-	3077	2254	69	32.66	4-34	-	
NatWest	3	3	0	67	40	22.33	-	-	1	-	210	110	2	55.00	1-19	-	
B & H	5	5	0	173	50	34.60	-	1	1	-	330	157	8	19.62	3-28	-	
Sunday	14	13	1	276	90	23.00	-	1	8	-	546	365	8	45.62	2-23	-	

HORRELL, R. Gloucestershire

Name: Ryan Horrell
Role: Left-hand bat, slow left-arm bowler
Born: 7 April 1973
Height: 5ft 10in **Weight:** 12st
Nickname: Creamy, Plank
County debut: No first team appearance
Parents: Robert George and Penelope Jane
Marital status: Single
Family links with cricket: Father plays local league cricket, brother plays in Devon League
Education: Picton Community College
Qualifications: 7 GCSEs, City & Guilds in Brickwork
Career outside cricket: Bricklayer
Off-season: Finishing bricklaying apprenticeship
Cricketers particularly admired: David Gower, Mark Taylor, Wasim Akram, Steve Moore (Braunton CC captain)
Other sports followed: Interested in most sports, plays football and squash
Relaxations: Playing for local side in indoor cricket league, listening to music and going out with friends
Extras: Played for Devon U16, U19 and Minor Counties before being signed for Gloucestershire

---

102. Who made two double centuries in successive Test Matches for England, twice?

HUGHES, S. P.   Durham

Name: Simon Peter Hughes
Role: Right-hand bat, right-arm fast-medium bowler
Born: 20 December 1959, Kingston, Surrey
Height: 5ft 10in **Weight:** 11st 7lbs
Nickname: Yozzer, Pluto
County debut: 1980 (Middlesex), 1992 (Durham)
County cap: 1981 (Middlesex)
Benefit: 1991 (£110,000)
50 wickets in a season: 2
1st-Class 50s scored: 1
1st-Class 5 w. in innings: 10
1st-Class catches: 49
Place in batting averages: 249th av. 11.45
Place in bowling averages: 137th av. 49.17
Strike rate: 96.79 (career 60.51)
Parents: Peter and Erica

Family links with cricket: Father very keen coach and player who owned indoor cricket school. 'Uncle once hit a ball over the school pavilion!'
Education: Latymer Upper School, Hammersmith; Durham University
Qualifications: 10 O-levels, 4 A-levels, BA General Studies
Off-season: Sundry journalism
Overseas tours: Middlesex to Zimbabwe 1980; International XI to India 1980; Bristol University to Sri Lanka 1987; International Ambassadors to India 1985-90
Overseas teams played for: Colts CC, Colombo 1979; Northern Transvaal 1982-83; Grosvenor Fynnland, Natal 1983-84; Auckland University 1984-85; Freemantle, Western Australia 1985-86; Sydney University 1986-87; Grafton, New Zealand 1988-89
Cricketers particularly admired: Clive Radley, Richard Hadlee, David Gower
Other sports followed: Soccer, rugby, tennis, golf
Relaxations: Comedy, travel, Asian food, R&B, current affairs, the environment
Extras: Took 4-82 v Kent on Championship debut, and played in County Championship and Gillette Cup winning sides in first season in 1980. Awarded cap after only 20 matches. Middlesex/Austin Reed Player of the Year 1986. First book *From Minor to Major*, on Durham's first year, published in 1992
Opinions on cricket: 'Views of players and spectators are too often ignored.'
Best batting: 53 Middlesex v Cambridge University, Fenner's 1988
Best bowling: 7-35 Middlesex v Surrey, The Oval 1986

1992 Season

	M	Inns	NO	Runs	HS	Avge	100s	50s	Ct	St	O	M	Runs	Wkts	Avge	Best	5wI	10wM
Test																		
All First	20	25	5	229	42	11.45	-	-	6	-	548.3	98	1672	34	49.17	5-25	1	-
1-day Int																		
NatWest	3	1	0	2	2	2.00	-	-	-	-	30	6	84	8	10.50	4-41	-	
B & H	4	2	0	3	3	1.50	-	-	2	-	39	3	145	7	20.71	2-31	-	
Sunday	16	4	3	16	10 *	16.00	-	-	5	-	108.2	2	545	21	25.95	3-26	-	

Career Performances

	M	Inns	NO	Runs	HS	Avge	100s	50s	Ct	St	Balls	Runs	Wkts	Avge	Best	5wI	10wM
Test																	
All First	199	218	68	1738	53	11.58	-	1	49	-	27715	14587	458	31.84	7-35	10	-
1-day Int																	
NatWest	27	14	8	47	11	7.83	-	-	1	-	1652	988	49	20.16	4-20	-	
B & H	28	17	7	74	22	7.40	-	-	5	-	1428	952	42	22.66	4-34	-	
Sunday	112	41	21	274	22 *	13.70	-	-	16	-	4612	3794	140	27.10	5-23	1	

HUMPHRIES, S.   Sussex

Name: Shaun Humphries
Role: Right-hand bat, wicket-keeper
Born: 11 January 1973, Horsham,
West Sussex
Height: 5ft 11in **Weight:** 10st
Nickname: Stanley, Moon Man
County debut: No first team appearance
Parents: Peter and Marilyn
Marital status: Single
Education: The Weald School, Billingshurst;
Kingston College of Further Education
Qualifications: 5 GCSEs, BTEC National
Diploma in Leisure Studies
Off-season: Overseas
Overseas tours: Sussex U13 to Barbados
1987; Sussex U18 to India 1990-91
Cricketers particularly admired:
Alan Knott, Peter Moores, Dean Jones,
John Berry
Other sports followed: Football (Arsenal)
Relaxations: Music, videos, football

Opinions on cricket: 'More attention should be given to the quality of pitches used by youngsters – improve safety.'

HUSSAIN, N.   Essex

Name: Nasser Hussain
Role: Right-hand bat, leg-spin bowler
Born: 28 March 1968, Madras, India
Height: 6ft 1in
Nickname: Bunny
County debut: 1987
Test debut: 1989-90
Tests: 3
One-Day Internationals: 2
1000 runs in a season: 1
1st-Class 50s scored: 24
1st-Class 100s scored: 10
1st-Class catches: 121
One-Day 50s: 7
One-Day 100s: 2
Place in batting averages:
80th av. 37.65 (1991 18th av. 54.16)
Parents: Jawad and Shireen
Marital status: Single
Family links with cricket: Father played for
Madras in Ranji Trophy 1966-67. Uncle played for Combined Indian Universities. Brother
Mel was on Hampshire staff in 1983 and 1984, and has played for England Amateur XI.
Brother Abbas played for Essex 2nd XI
Education: Forest School; Durham University
Qualifications: 9 O-levels, 3 A-levels; BSc (Hons) in Geology; NCA cricket coaching
award
Off-season: Playing in Australia
Overseas tours: England YC to Sri Lanka 1987, to Australia for Youth World Cup 1988;
England to India and West Indies 1990; England A to Pakistan and Sri Lanka 1990-91, to
Bermuda and West Indies 1991-92
Overseas teams played for: Madras 1986-87; Petersham, Sydney 1992-93
Cricketers particularly admired: Father, Keith Fletcher, Ray East, Graham Saville plus
Graham Gooch and David Gower
Other sports followed: Golf, football
Injuries: Two injuries to fingers, missed almost $1/3$ of the season
Relaxations: Golf, music, TV
Extras: Played for England Schools U15 for two years (one as captain). Youngest player
to play for Essex Schools U11 at the age of 8 and U15 at the age of 12. At 15, was considered
the best young leg-spin bowler in the country. Cricket Writers' Club Young Cricketer of
the Year, 1989. Holds record for 3rd, 4th and 5th wicket partnerships for Essex (with Salim
Malik, Mark Waugh and Mike Garnham)
Opinions on cricket: 'Better pitches please – four-day cricket welcome.'

Best batting: 197 Essex v Surrey, The Oval 1990
Best bowling: 1-38 Essex v Worcestershire, Kidderminster 1992

1992 Season

	M	Inns	NO	Runs	HS	Avge	100s	50s	Ct	St	O	M	Runs	Wkts	Avge	Best	5wI	10wM
Test																		
All First	20	26	3	866	172 *	37.65	1	5	24	-	4	0	38	1	38.00	1-38	-	-
1-day Int																		
NatWest	3	3	0	178	108	59.33	1	-	2	-								
B & H	4	4	0	92	55	23.00	-	1	2	-								
Sunday	14	11	2	130	30	14.44	-	-	4	-								

Career Performances

	M	Inns	NO	Runs	HS	Avge	100s	50s	Ct	St	Balls	Runs	Wkts	Avge	Best	5wI	10wM
Test	3	5	0	100	35	20.00	-	-	1	-							
All First	99	142	22	5163	197	43.02	10	24	121	-	207	198	1	198.00	1-38	-	-
1-day Int	2	2	1	17	15 *	17.00	-	-	1	-							
NatWest	8	7	1	318	108	53.00	1	1	6	-							
B & H	23	21	3	588	118	32.66	1	4	9	-							
Sunday	57	47	11	910	66 *	25.27	-	2	26	-							

HUTTON, S.   Durham

Name: Stewart Hutton
Role: Left-hand bat,
cover fielder
Born: 30 November 1969,
Stockton-on-Tees
Height: 6ft **Weight:** 12st
Nickname: Len
County debut: 1992
1st-Class 50s: 2
1st-Class catches: 3
One-Day 50s: 1
Place in batting averages:
140th av. 27.06
Parents: Leonard and Mavis
Marital status: Single
Education: De Brus Comprehensive;
Cleveland Technical College
Qualifications: 6 O-levels (equivalent),
A-level Economics

Overseas tours: Durham to Zimbabwe 1991-92
Cricketers particularly admired: Mike Gatting
Other sports followed: Golf, football
Injuries: Broken left thumb
Relaxations: Playing golf
Extras: Scored century for Durham on pre-season tour to Zimbabwe in 1992
Best batting: 78 Durham v Sussex, Horsham 1992

1992 Season

	M	Inns	NO	Runs	HS	Avge	100s	50s	Ct	St	O	M	Runs	Wkts	Avge	Best	5wl	10wM
Test																		
All First	8	15	0	406	78	27.06	-	2	3	-	0.1	0	4	0	-	-	-	-
1-day Int																		
NatWest																		
B & H																		
Sunday	3	3	2	107	70	107.00	-	1	2	-								

Career Performances

	M	Inns	NO	Runs	HS	Avge	100s	50s	Ct	St	Balls	Runs	Wkts	Avge	Best	5wl	10wM
Test																	
All First	8	15	0	406	78	27.06	-	2	3	-	1	4	0	-	-	-	-
1-day Int																	
NatWest																	
B & H																	
Sunday	3	3	2	107	70	107.00	-	1	2	-							

103. Who has made the highest score on a Test debut for England, and what was it?

IGGLESDEN, A. P.   Kent

Name: Alan Paul Igglesden
Role: Right-hand bat, right-arm fast bowler, outfielder
Born: 8 October 1964, Farnborough, Kent
Height: 6ft 6in **Weight:** 14st 13lbs
Nickname: Iggy, Norman, Ivor
County debut: 1986
Test debut: 1989
Tests: 1
50 wickets in a season: 3
1st-Class 5 w. in innings: 14
1st-Class 10 w. in match: 2
1st-Class catches: 29
Place in bowling averages: 51st av. 30.71
(1991 33rd av. 27.02)
Strike rate: 62.69 (career 53.66)
Parents: Alan Trevor and Gillian Catharine
Wife and date of marriage: Hilary Moira, 20 January 1990

Family links with cricket: Brother Kevin plays for Holmesdale in the Kent League
Education: St Mary's Primary School; Hosey School; Churchill Secondary School, Westerham
Qualifications: 9 CSEs, coaching certificate
Off-season: Playing and coaching in Cape Town
Overseas tours: With England A to Zimbabwe and Kenya 1989-90; Fred Rumsey's XI to Barbados 1990
Overseas teams played for: Avendale, Cape Town 1985-89; Western Province 1987-91; Green Point, Cape Town 1991-92; Boland Cricket Union 1992-93
Cricketers particularly admired: Terry Alderman, Dennis Lillee, Carl Hooper, Bed Cartwright, Alan Lewis
Other sports followed: 'Very keen Crystal Palace supporter'
Injuries: Rib cartilage and sore shins, out for five weeks
Relaxations: 'Golf, spending time with good friends, watching films with my wife.'
Opinions on cricket: 'The Sunday League should have stayed 40 overs a side, but I'm looking forward to putting the pyjamas on!'
Best batting: 41 Kent v Surrey, Canterbury 1988
Best bowling: 6-34 Kent v Surrey, Canterbury 1988

	M	Inns	NO	Runs	HS	Avge	100s	50s	Ct	St	O	M	Runs	Wkts	Avge	Best	5wI	10wM
Test																		
All First	16	13	5	67	16	8.37	-	-	5	-	480.4	95	1413	46	30.71	5-41	3	-
1-day Int																		
NatWest	2	1	1	7	7 *	-	-	-	-	-	24	3	63	1	63.00	1-33	-	
B & H	7	3	3	5	4 *	-	-	-	-	-	69	13	200	9	22.22	3-24	-	
Sunday	8	4	4	18	12 *	-	-	-	3	-	59	2	256	8	32.00	2-30	-	

Career Performances

	M	Inns	NO	Runs	HS	Avge	100s	50s	Ct	St	Balls	Runs	Wkts	Avge	Best	5wI	10wM
Test	1	1	1	2	2 *	-	-	-	1	-	222	146	3	48.66	2-91	-	-
All First	103	106	37	670	41	9.71	-	-	29	-	17601	9275	328	28.27	6-34	14	2
1-day Int																	
NatWest	9	4	3	23	12 *	23.00	-	-	3	-	500	266	13	20.46	4-29	-	
B & H	22	9	7	42	26 *	21.00	-	-	4	-	1259	790	30	26.33	3-24	-	
Sunday	50	21	13	67	13 *	8.37	-	-	13	-	2230	1517	69	21.98	5-13	1	

ILLINGWORTH, R. K. Worcestershire

Name: Richard Keith Illingworth
Role: Right-hand bat, slow left-arm bowler
Born: 23 August 1963, Bradford
Height: 6ft **Weight:** 13st
Nickname: Lucy, Harry
County debut: 1982
County cap: 1986
Test debut: 1991
Tests: 2
One-Day Internationals: 16
50 wickets in a season: 3
1st-Class 50s scored: 10
1st-Class 100s scored: 3
1st-Class 5 w. in innings: 19
1st-Class 10 w. in match: 4
1st-Class catches: 105
Place in batting averages: 179th av. 21.00
(1991 166th av. 23.81)
Place in bowling averages: 98th av. 37.61
(1991 90th av. 35.31)
Strike rate: 90.78 (career 78.36)
Parents: Keith and Margaret

Wife and date of marriage: Anne, 20 September 1985
Children: Miles, 28 August 1987; Thomas, 20 April 1989
Family links with cricket: Father played Bradford League cricket
Education: Wrose Brow Middle; Salts Grammar School ('same school as the late Jim Laker')
Qualifications: 6 O-levels, senior coaching award holder
Career outside cricket: Buyer for Golding Pipework
Off-season: Recovering from knee surgery and touring in Kenya with MCC
Overseas tours: England A to Zimbabwe and Kenya 1989-90; Pakistan and Sri Lanka 1990-91; England to New Zealand and Australia (World Cup) 1991-92; MCC to Kenya 1992-93
Overseas teams played for: Natal 1988-89
Cricketers particularly admired: Ian Botham
Other sports followed: Most sports, avid follower of Leeds United and golf
Injuries: Tendonitis in left knee
Relaxations: 'Golf, gardening, playing with my two children, cycling.'
Extras: Took 11 for 108 on South African first-class debut for Natal B v Boland 1988. Scored 120 not out as a nightwatchman for Worcestershire v Warwickshire 1988 and 106 for England A v Zimbabwe 1989-90. 11th person in history to take a wicket with their first ball in Test cricket
Best batting: 120* Worcestershire v Warwickshire, Worcester 1987
Best bowling: 7-50 Worcestershire v Oxford University, The Parks 1985

1992 Season

	M	Inns	NO	Runs	HS	Avge	100s	50s	Ct	St	O	M	Runs	Wkts	Avge	Best	5wl	10wM
Test																		
All First	20	20	6	294	43	21.00	-	-	8	-	635.3	185	1580	42	37.61	4-43	-	-
1-day Int	5	1	0	4	4	4.00	-	-	1	-	54	1	230	7	32.85	3-34	-	
NatWest	1	1	1	12	12 *	-	-	-	-	-	12	2	25	1	25.00	1-25		
B & H	5	3	2	20	14 *	20.00	-	-	2	-	55	12	146	8	18.25	2-22	-	
Sunday	14	5	3	19	8 *	9.50	-	-	1	-	100	4	397	16	24.81	3-30	-	

Career Performances

	M	Inns	NO	Runs	HS	Avge	100s	50s	Ct	St	Balls	Runs	Wkts	Avge	Best	5wl	10wM
Test	2	4	2	31	13	15.50	-	-	1	-	340	213	4	53.25	3-110	-	-
All First	243	264	70	4094	120 *	21.10	3	10	105	-	41141	16749	525	31.90	7-50	19	4
1-day Int	16	5	2	40	14	13.33	-	-	8	-	967	666	20	33.30	3-33	-	
NatWest	22	10	3	77	22	11.00	-	-	6	-	1285	636	20	31.80	4-20	-	
B & H	38	20	12	179	36 *	22.37	-	-	9	-	1890	1115	32	34.84	4-36	-	
Sunday	123	52	27	300	25 *	12.00	-	-	29	-	4432	3295	144	22.88	5-24	2	

ILOTT, M. C. Essex

Name: Mark Christopher Ilott
Role: Left-hand bat (tail end), left-arm
fast-medium bowler
Born: 27 August 1970, Watford
Height: 6ft 2in **Weight:** 13st
Nickname: Ramble, Touché, Headless
County debut: 1988
1st-Class 5 w. in innings: 5
1st-Class catches: 7
Place in bowling averages: 86th av. 35.37
Strike rate: 63.32 (career 63.65)
Parents: John and Glenys
Marital status: Single
Family links with cricket: Brother plays
Minor Counties for Hertfordshire, father is
qualified umpire and grandfather
played for Ruislip Manor for many years
Education: Francis Combe School
Qualifications: 8 O-levels, 2 A-levels,
coaching qualification, Diploma in Fitness
and Nutrition
Career outside cricket: Odd job man
Off-season: 'Hopefully working at a leisure centre until Christmas, then touring with
England A.'
Overseas tours: England A to Sri Lanka 1990-91, to Australia 1992-93
Overseas teams played for: East Torrens District, Adelaide 1989-91
Cricketers particularly admired: John Lever, Malcolm Marshall, Neil Foster, Graham
Gooch
Other sports followed: Most sports
Injuries: Groin strain, missed ten days cricket in 1992
Relaxations: Listening to music, reading, saunas and jacuzzis at the Livingwell Health
Club
Extras: Youngest player ever to play for Hertfordshire. Missed almost all 1991 season
with stress fracture of the back
Best batting: 42* Essex v Kent, Chelmsford 1990
Best bowling: 6-87 Essex v Derbyshire, Derby 1992

104. Who scored the first ever Test century for England?

1992 Season

	M	Inns	NO	Runs	HS	Avge	100s	50s	Ct	St	O	M	Runs	Wkts	Avge	Best	5wI	10wM
Test																		
All First	23	22	4	164	28	9.11	-	-	7	-	675.3	145	2264	64	35.37	6-87	3	-
1-day Int																		
NatWest	3	2	2	19	10 *	-	-	-	1	-	35	4	126	6	21.00	2-23	-	
B & H	3	2	1	5	5 *	5.00	-	-	-	-	26.5	2	71	7	10.14	4-31	-	
Sunday	11	2	1	9	7	9.00	-	-	1	-	73.1	5	361	19	19.00	4-15	-	

Career Performances

	M	Inns	NO	Runs	HS	Avge	100s	50s	Ct	St	Balls	Runs	Wkts	Avge	Best	5wI	10wM
Test																	
All First	42	39	11	331	42 *	11.82	-	-	10	-	7448	3980	117	34.01	6-87	5	-
1-day Int																	
NatWest	4	2	2	19	10 *	-	-	-	1	-	264	171	7	24.42	2-23	-	
B & H	8	2	1	5	5 *	5.00	-	-	-	-	443	233	12	19.41	4-31	-	
Sunday	23	7	2	23	7	4.60	-	-	3	-	991	746	31	24.06	4-15	-	

INNES, K. J.   Northamptonshire

Name: Kevin John Innes
Role: Right-hand bat, right-arm medium bowler
Born: 24 September 1975, Wellingborough
Height: 5ft 10in **Weight:** 11st 7lbs
Nickname: Ernie, Milkman
County debut: No first team appearance
Parents: Peter and Jane
Marital status: Single
Education: Boothville Middle School; Weston Favell Upper School, Northampton
Qualifications: 6 GCSEs, 4 O-levels
Off-season: Working, cricket tours and training
Overseas tours: England U18 to South Africa 1992-93
Cricketers particularly admired: Richard Hadlee, Viv Richards
Other sports followed: Snooker, football, tennis
Relaxations: Watching and playing most sport, music
Opinions on cricket: 'It is a shame that employment is not found at the end of the season for a lot more cricketers.'

IRANI, R.   Lancashire

Name: Ronnie Irani
Role: Right-hand bat, right-arm medium-fast bowler
Born: 26 October 1971, Leigh, Lancashire
Height: 6ft 4in **Weight:** 13st 8lbs
Nickname: Imre, Moon, Van-Damme
County debut: 1990
1st-Class catches: 4
Place in batting averages: 251st av. 11.33
Parents: Jimmy and Anne
Marital status: Single
Family links with cricket: 'Father played local league cricket in Bolton for 30 years, mother did teas for many years! '
Education: Church Road Primary School; Smithills Comprehensive School
Qualifications: 9 GCSEs
Career outside cricket: 'Working for Tesco stores, catching thieves.'
Off-season: Abroad playing cricket in Durban
Overseas tours: England U19 to Australia 1990-91
Cricketers particularly admired: Graham Gooch, Robin Smith, Wasim Akram
Other sports followed: Football
Relaxations: Music, Chinese restaurants
Extras: Played for England U19 in home series against Australia 1991, scoring a century and three 50s in six innings
Opinions on cricket: 'Cricket should be played on more sporting (maybe uncovered) wickets, as the sport is becoming more and more dominated by batsmen. This may bring more results and bowlers will take more wickets, so getting more people interested in the game and bringing the crowds back. The paying public want to be entertained, and they do contribute to our wages.'
Best batting: 31* Lancashire v Oxford University, The Parks 1991
Best bowling: 2-21 Lancashire v Nottinghamshire, Trent Bridge 1992

105. Who was coach for Sussex last season?

1992 Season

	M	Inns	NO	Runs	HS	Avge	100s	50s	Ct	St	O	M	Runs	Wkts	Avge	Best	5wI	10wM
Test																		
All First	5	6	0	68	22	11.33	-	-	4	-	33	5	137	3	45.66	2-21	-	-
1-day Int																		
NatWest																		
B & H																		
Sunday	5	1	0	3	3	3.00	-	-	1	-	5	0	36	1	36.00	1-21	-	

Career Performances

	M	Inns	NO	Runs	HS	Avge	100s	50s	Ct	St	Balls	Runs	Wkts	Avge	Best	5wI	10wM
Test																	
All First	7	7	1	99	31 *	16.50	-	-	4	-	524	292	5	58.40	2-21	-	-
1-day Int																	
NatWest																	
B & H																	
Sunday	5	1	0	3	3	3.00	-	-	1	-	30	36	1	36.00	1-21	-	

JAMES, K. D.   Hampshire

Name: Kevan David James
Role: Left-hand bat, left-arm medium bowler
Born: 18 March 1961, Lambeth,
South London
Height: 6ft 1/2in **Weight:** 13st 8lbs
Nickname: Jambo, Jaimo
County debut: 1980 (Middlesex),
1985 (Hampshire)
County cap: 1989
1000 runs in a season: 2
1st-Class 50s scored: 24
1st-Class 100s scored: 8
1st-Class 5 w. in innings: 7
1st-Class catches: 47
One-Day 50s: 3
Place in batting averages: 109th av. 32.82
(1991 31st av. 47.18)
Place in bowling averages: 147th av. 55.78
(1991 73rd av. 33.02)
Strike rate: 113.35 (career 66.25)
Parents: David (deceased) and Helen
Wife and date of marriage: Debbie, October 1987

Family links with cricket: Late father played club cricket in North London, brother Martin plays for Hertfordshire
Education: Edmonton County High School
Qualifications: 5 O-levels; qualified coach
Off-season: 'Watching the birth of our first baby in October (1992).'
Overseas tours: England YC tour of Australia 1978-79, to West Indies 1979-80
Overseas teams played for: Wellington, New Zealand 1982-83
Cricketers particularly admired: Chris Smith
Other sports followed: Football (Spurs)
Injuries: Dislocated finger, out for 10 days
Extras: Released by Middlesex at end of 1984 season and joined Hampshire
Opinions on cricket: 'Glad to see the introduction of coloured clothing.'
Best batting: 162 Hampshire v Glamorgan, Cardiff 1989
Best bowling: 6-22 Hampshire v Australia, Southampton 1985

1992 Season

	M	Inns	NO	Runs	HS	Avge	100s	50s	Ct	St	O	M	Runs	Wkts	Avge	Best	5wl	10wM
Test																		
All First	23	37	2	1149	116	32.82	1	8	10	-	264.3	65	781	14	55.78	2-23	-	-
1-day Int																		
NatWest	1	1	0	4	4	4.00	-	-	1	-	12	3	56	0	-		-	-
B & H	5	4	2	58	30	29.00	-	-	4	-	36	2	156	3	52.00	2-25	-	
Sunday	15	10	1	131	38	14.55	-	-	2	-	75	3	282	9	31.33	3-25	-	

Career Performances

	M	Inns	NO	Runs	HS	Avge	100s	50s	Ct	St	Balls	Runs	Wkts	Avge	Best	5wl	10wM
Test																	
All First	140	197	36	5379	162	33.41	8	24	47	-	14509	7228	219	33.00	6-22	7	-
1-day Int																	
NatWest	15	10	2	136	42	17.00	-	-	2	-	886	625	17	36.76	3-22	-	
B & H	31	22	4	316	45	17.55	-	-	6	-	1639	1078	28	38.50	3-31	-	
Sunday	101	67	21	1019	66	22.15	-	3	31	-	3913	2728	84	32.47	4-23	-	

106. Who was coach for Surrey last season?

JAMES, S. P.   Glamorgan

Name: Stephen Peter James
Role: Right-hand opening bat, utility fielder
Born: 7 September 1967, Lydney
Height: 6ft **Weight:** 12st 8lbs
Nickname: Jamo, Pedro, Sid
County debut: 1985
County cap: 1992
1000 runs in a season: 2
1st-Class 50s scored: 17
1st-Class 100s scored: 10
1st-Class catches: 53
One-Day 50s: 6
One-Day 100s: 1
Place in batting averages: 67th av. 39.31
(1991 125th av. 28.81)
Parents: Peter and Margaret
Marital status: Single
Family links with cricket: Father played
for Gloucestershire 2nd XI
Education: Monmouth School; University
College, Swansea; Cambridge University
Qualifications: BA (Hons) Wales – Classics; BA (Hons) Cantab –Land Economy
Off-season: Playing in Zimbabwe
Overseas tours: Welsh Schools to Barbados 1984; Monmouth Schools to Sri Lanka 1985;
Combined Universities to Barbados 1989; Glamorgan to Trinidad 1990, to Zimbabwe
1991
Overseas teams played for: Bionics, Zimbabwe 1990-92; Universals Sports Club, Zim-
babwe 1992-93
Cricketers particularly admired: Michael Atherton, Graham Gooch, Graham Burgess
Other sports followed: Most sports, especially Rugby Union
Injuries: Footballers ankle and achilles tendonitis
Relaxations: Reading, crosswords, videos, weight training
Extras: Scored maiden century in only second first-class game. Played rugby for Lydney,
Gloucestershire and Cambridge University and was on the substitutes bench for 1988 and
1989 Varsity matches
Opinions on cricket: 'Four-day cricket is long overdue.'
Best batting: 152* Glamorgan v Lancashire, Colwyn Bay 1992

1992 Season

	M	Inns	NO	Runs	HS	Avge	100s	50s	Ct	St	O	M	Runs	Wkts	Avge	Best	5wI	10wM
Test																		
All First	24	39	4	1376	152 *	39.31	3	6	20	-								
1-day Int																		
NatWest	2	2	0	30	19	15.00	-	-	-	-								
B & H	3	3	0	136	135	45.33	1	-	1	-								
Sunday	14	13	0	422	74	32.46	-	3	2	-								

Career Performances

	M	Inns	NO	Runs	HS	Avge	100s	50s	Ct	St	Balls	Runs	Wkts	Avge	Best	5wI	10wM
Test																	
All First	77	131	11	4067	152 *	33.89	10	17	53	-							
1-day Int																	
NatWest	4	4	0	62	26	15.50	-	-	-	-							
B & H	11	11	0	409	135	37.18	1	3	4	-							
Sunday	19	18	0	486	74	27.00	-	3	4	-							

JARVIS, P. W.   Yorkshire

Name: Paul William Jarvis
Role: Right-hand bat, right-arm fast-medium bowler
Born: 29 June 1965, Redcar, North Yorkshire
Height: 5ft 11in **Weight:** 12st 5lbs
Nickname: Jarv, Beaver, Gnasher
County debut: 1981
County cap: 1986
Test debut: 1987-88
Tests: 6
One-Day Internationals: 5
50 wickets in a season: 3
1st-Class 50s scored: 4
1st-Class 5 w. in innings: 18
1st-Class 10 w. in match: 3
1st-Class catches: 36
Place in batting averages: 83rd av. 37.40
Place in bowling averages: 42nd av. 29.10 (1991 3rd av. 19.58)
Strike rate: 59.05 (career 52.07)
Parents: Malcolm and Marjorie

Wife and date of marriage: Wendy Jayne, 3 December 1988
Children: Alexander Michael, 13 July 1989
Family links with cricket: Father still plays league cricket for Sudbrooke in Gwent; brother Andrew plays for Methley CC, finalists in 1992 Village Cup competition at Lord's
Education: Bydales Comprehensive School, Marske, Cleveland
Qualifications: 4 O-levels; basic and senior coaching awards
Career outside cricket: Works for Southern Africa Travel in York
Off-season: Working as above and touring in India with England
Overseas tours: Yorkshire to St Lucia and Barbados 1987; England to India/Pakistan (World Cup) and Pakistan 1986-87, to Australia and New Zealand 1987-88, to India and Sri Lanka 1992-93; unofficial English team to South Africa 1989-90
Overseas teams played for: Mossman Middle Harbour, Sydney 1984-85; Avendale, Cape Town 1985-86; Manly Warringah, Sydney 1987
Cricketers particularly admired: Dennis Lillee, Richard Hadlee, Malcolm Marshall
Other sports followed: Football and most other sports
Injuries: Slight hamstring strains (both legs), out for seven weeks
Relaxations: Fishing, golf, DIY, cooking
Extras: Youngest player ever to play for Yorkshire in County Championship (16 years, 2 months, 13 days) and youngest player to take hat-trick in JPL and Championship. Played for England YC v West Indies 1982 and Australia 1983. Banned from Test cricket for joining 1990 tour of South Africa, suspension remitted in 1992
Opinions on cricket: 'It still seems strange playing a one-day game in the middle of a four-day game!'
Best batting: 80 Yorkshire v Northamptonshire, Scarborough 1992
Best bowling: 7-55 Yorkshire v Surrey, Headingley 1986

1992 Season

	M	Inns	NO	Runs	HS	Avge	100s	50s	Ct	St	O	M	Runs	Wkts	Avge	Best	5wI	10wM
Test																		
All First	15	14	4	374	80	37.40	-	3	2	-	393.4	89	1164	40	29.10	4-27	-	-
1-day Int																		
NatWest	1	1	0	11	11	11.00	-	-	-	-	12	0	53	2	26.50	2-53	-	
B & H	2	1	0	3	3	3.00	-	-	-	-	22	4	48	7	6.85	4-34	-	
Sunday	8	6	2	48	17	12.00	-	-	3	-	58.3	4	285	11	25.90	5-29	1	

Career Performances

	M	Inns	NO	Runs	HS	Avge	100s	50s	Ct	St	Balls	Runs	Wkts	Avge	Best	5wI	10wM
Test	6	9	2	109	29 *	15.57	-	-	-	-	1347	708	14	50.57	4-107	-	-
All First	143	162	51	1896	80	17.08	-	4	36	-	23798	12571	457	27.50	7-55	18	3
1-day Int	5	2	1	5	5 *	5.00	-	-	-	-	287	187	6	31.16	4-33	-	
NatWest	14	8	2	73	16	12.16	-	-	3	-	919	573	18	31.83	4-41	-	
B & H	31	13	4	106	42	11.77	-	-	4	-	1772	966	52	18.57	4-34	-	
Sunday	89	45	19	265	29 *	10.19	-	-	23	-	3825	2784	130	21.41	6-27	3	

JEAN-JACQUES, M.   Hampshire

Name: Martin Jean-Jacques
Role: Right-hand bat, right-arm fast-medium
pace bowler
Born: 2 August 1960, Soufriere, Dominica
Height: 5ft 11in **Weight:** 12st 7lbs
Nickname: JJ
County debut: 1986
1st-Class 50s scored: 1
1st-Class 5 w. in innings: 2
1st-Class 10 w. in match: 1
1st-Class catches: 13
Place in bowling averages:
(1991 165th av. 41.33)
Strike rate: (career 60.13)
Education: Scotts Head Primary, Dominica;
Aylestone High, London
Career outside cricket: Electrician
Cricketers particularly admired:
Michael Holding
Other sports followed: Football

Relaxations: Listening to music – reggae and soul
Extras: Played Minor Counties cricket for Buckinghamshire. On debut for Derbyshire (v Yorkshire) put on a record 132 with Alan Hill for the 10th wicket. Released by Derbyshire at the end of the 1992 season
Best batting: 73 Derbyshire v Yorkshire, Sheffield 1986
Best bowling: 8-77 Derbyshire v Kent, Derby 1986

1992 Season

	M	Inns	NO	Runs	HS	Avge	100s	50s	Ct	St	O	M	Runs	Wkts	Avge	Best	5wI	10wM
Test																		
All First	2	2	0	6	6	3.00	-	-	2	-	35.4	5	135	5	27.00	4-46	-	-
1-day Int																		
NatWest																			
B & H																			
Sunday	1	0	0	0	0	-	-	-	-	-	4	0	20	0	-		-	-

107. Who was coach for Middlesex last season?

Career Performances

	M	Inns	NO	Runs	HS	Avge	100s	50s	Ct	St	Balls	Runs	Wkts	Avge	Best	5wI	10wM
Test																	
All First	53	66	14	587	73	11.28	-	1	13	-	6916	4091	115	35.57	8-77	2	1
1-day Int																	
NatWest	8	5	3	28	16	14.00	-	-	1	-	444	310	12	25.83	3-23	-	
B & H	4	2	1	4	2 *	4.00	-	-	2	-	180	164	5	32.80	3-22	-	
Sunday	30	14	1	92	23	7.07	-	-	5	-	1098	1040	27	38.51	3-36	-	

JOHNSON, P. Nottinghamshire

Name: Paul Johnson
Role: Right-hand bat, right-arm occasional bowler
Born: 24 April 1965, Newark
Height: 5ft 7in **Weight:** 11st 11lbs
Nickname: Gus, Johno, Midge
County debut: 1982
County cap: 1986
1000 runs in a season: 5
1st-Class 50s scored: 67
1st-Class 100s scored: 22
1st-Class catches: 143
1st-Class stumpings: 1
One-Day 50s: 21
One-Day 100s: 6
Place in batting averages: 41st av. 45.88 (1991 26th av. 48.46)
Parents: Donald Edward and Joyce
Marital status: Divorced

Family links with cricket: Father played local cricket and is a qualified coach
Education: Grove Comprehensive School, Newark
Qualifications: 9 CSEs, NCA advanced coach
Off-season: Coaching
Overseas tours: England A to Bermuda and West Indies 1991-92
Overseas teams played for: RAU, Johannesburg, 1985-86; Hutt District, Wellington, NZ 1988-89
Cricketers particularly admired: 'Clive Rice and Jimmy Cook – both great players who always have time to talk to players and the public.'
Other sports followed: Watches ice-hockey (Nottingham Panthers), football (Forest and County)
Injuries: Displaced knuckle and broken 5th metacarple, left little finger, missed the last

month of the season

Relaxations: 'Listening to music, crosswords and reading autobiographies.'

Extras: Played for English Schools in 1980-81 and England YC 1982 and 1983. Youngest player ever to join the Nottinghamshire CCC staff. Made 235 for Nottinghamshire 2nd XI, July 1982, aged 17. Won Man of Match award in first NatWest game (101* v Staffordshire); missed 1985 final due to appendicitis. Sunday morning soccer referee in Nottingham

Opinions on cricket: 'Who would take any notice?'

Best batting: 165* Nottinghamshire v Northamptonshire, Trent Bridge 1990

Best bowling: 1-9 Nottinghamshire v Oxford University, Trent Bridge 1984

1992 Season

	M	Inns	NO	Runs	HS	Avge	100s	50s	Ct	St	O	M	Runs	Wkts	Avge	Best	5wI	10wM
Test																		
All First	19	29	4	1147	107 *	45.88	2	10	9	-	5	0	30	0	-	-	-	-
1-day Int																		
NatWest	2	2	0	84	78	42.00	-	1	-	-								
B & H	4	4	1	214	79 *	71.33	-	2	2	-								
Sunday	12	12	2	253	90	25.30	-	1	1	-								

Career Performances

	M	Inns	NO	Runs	HS	Avge	100s	50s	Ct	St	Balls	Runs	Wkts	Avge	Best	5wI	10wM
Test																	
All First	215	353	37	11467	165 *	36.28	22	67	143	1	478	510	5	102.00	1-9	-	-
1-day Int																	
NatWest	22	22	2	545	101 *	27.25	1	1	5	-	12	16	0	-	-	-	
B & H	37	35	5	926	104 *	30.86	2	5	14	-							
Sunday	129	120	14	2789	114	26.31	3	15	44	-							

108. Who was coach for Derbyshire last season?

109. Who was coach for Hampshire last season?

JOHNSON, R. L. Middlesex

Name: Richard Leonard Johnson
Role: Right-hand bat, right-arm fast-medium
bowler, outfielder
Born: 29 December 1974, Chertsey, Surrey
Height: 6ft 2in **Weight:** 13st 6lbs
Nickname: Jono, Lenny
County debut: 1992
1st-Class catches: 1
Strike rate: 84.00 (career 84.00)
Parents: Roger and Mary Anne
Marital status: Single
Family links with cricket: Father and
grandfather played club cricket
Education: Sunbury Manor School;
Spelthorne College
Qualifications: 13 GCSEs, studying for
A-levels
Off-season: At college
Overseas tours: England U18 to South
Africa 1992-93
Cricketers particularly admired: Ian Botham, Richard Hadlee
Other sports followed: Basketball, soccer, snooker and most other sports
Injuries: Strained muscle in left side, out for five weeks
Relaxations: Sport and music
Extras: Plays for Sunbury CC, has represented Middlesex at all levels since U11
Best batting: 1 Middlesex v Surrey, The Oval 1992
Best bowling: 1-25 Middlesex v Surrey, The Oval 1992

1992 Season

	M	Inns	NO	Runs	HS	Avge	100s	50s	Ct	St	O	M	Runs	Wkts	Avge	Best	5wl	10wM
Test																		
All First	1	1	0	1	1	1.00	-	-	1	-	14	2	71	1	71.00	1-25	-	-
1-day Int																		
NatWest																		
B & H																		
Sunday																		

Career Performances

	M	Inns	NO	Runs	HS	Avge	100s	50s	Ct	St	Balls	Runs	Wkts	Avge	Best	5wI	10wM
Test																	
All First	1	1	0	1	1	1.00	-	-	1	-	84	71	1	71.00	1-25	-	-
1-day Int																	
NatWest																	
B & H																	
Sunday																	

JONES, A. J. Glamorgan

Name: Andrew James Jones
Role: Right-hand bat
Born: 5 August 1972, Swansea
Height: 5ft 8¹/₂in **Weight:** 11st
County debut: No first team appearance
Parents: Alan and Meg
Marital status: Single
Family links with cricket: Father is
Glamorgan coach and formerly opening bat
for Glamorgan and England
Education: Ysgol Gwyr School,
West Glamorgan; Monmouth School for
Boys; Exeter University
Qualifications: 8 GCSEs, 3 A-levels
Off-season: At university
Overseas teams played for:
Crusaders, Durban, South Africa
Cricketers particularly admired:
Martin Crowe, Viv Richards
Other sports followed: Rugby
Relaxations: Listening to music
Extras: Captain of Welsh Schools U19 since 1990-92. Scored a century at Lord's for MCC
Schools U19 in 1990

110. Who was coach for Warwickshire last season?

JONES, A. N. Sussex

Name: Adrian Nicholas Jones
Role: Left-hand bat, right-arm fast bowler, outfielder
Born: 22 July 1961, Woking
Height: 6ft 2in **Weight:** 14st
Nickname: Quincy, Jonah, Billy
County debut: 1981 (Sussex), 1987 (Somerset)
County cap: 1986 (Sussex), 1987 (Somerset)
50 wickets in a season: 5
1st-Class 5 w. in innings: 12
1st-Class 10 w. in match: 1
1st-Class catches: 42
Place in batting averages:
(1991 253rd av. 10.66)
Place in bowling averages: 151st av. 67.62
(1991 83rd av. 33.64)
Strike rate: 88.27 (career 54.92)

Parents: William Albert and Emily Doris
Wife and date of marriage:
Elizabeth Antoinette, 1 October 1988
Children: Amy Elizabeth, 2 May 1990; Samuel William, 27 September 1992
Family links with cricket: 'Father and brother, Glynne, both fine club cricketers'
Education: Forest Grange Preparatory School; Seaford College
Qualifications: 8 O-levels, 2 A-levels, NCA coaching qualification, financial planning and advising qualifications
Off-season: Working for QSS Office Solutions Ltd, Horsham
Overseas teams played for: Border 1981-82; Orange Free State 1986
Cricketers particularly admired: Imran Khan, Geoff Arnold, Garth le Roux, Jimmy Cook, Tony Pigott, Waqar Younis, Sylvester Clarke
Other sports followed: 'Play golf badly; hockey slightly better; rugby like an animal.'
Injuries: Slipped disc in neck and fractured left ankle, out for two months
Relaxations: 'UB40, watching Laurel and Hardy films, walking, eating, good wine and port.'
Extras: Played for England YC in 1981. Left Sussex to join Somerset at end of 1986 season, but returned for start of 1991 season
Opinions on cricket: 'There should be an alternative system for the awarding of a benefit rather than the present haphazard method. Perhaps an endowment scheme taken out when the player is capped. Too much notice is taken of averages.'
Best batting: 43* Somerset v Leicestershire, Taunton 1989
Best bowling: 7-30 Somerset v Hampshire, Southampton 1988

1992 Season

	M	Inns	NO	Runs	HS	Avge	100s	50s	Ct	St	O	M	Runs	Wkts	Avge	Best	5wI	10wM
Test																		
All First	10	9	4	56	17	11.20	-	-	1	-	161.5	17	745	11	67.72	3-76	-	-
1-day Int																		
NatWest	1	1	0	5	5	5.00	-	-	-	-	9	0	31	0	-		-	-
B & H	3	1	0	24	24	24.00	-	-	1	-	21	1	102	1	102.00	1-43	-	
Sunday																		

Career Performances

	M	Inns	NO	Runs	HS	Avge	100s	50s	Ct	St	Balls	Runs	Wkts	Avge	Best	5wI	10wM
Test																	
All First	170	147	61	998	43 *	11.60	-	-	42	-	22408	13143	408	32.21	7-30	12	1
1-day Int																	
NatWest	15	6	3	18	7	6.00	-	-	2	-	761	549	16	34.31	4-26	-	
B & H	32	15	6	102	25	11.33	-	-	3	-	1654	1185	58	20.43	5-53	1	
Sunday	94	32	22	168	37	16.80	-	-	17	-	3477	2946	139	21.19	7-41	4	

JONES, D. M. Durham

Name: Dean Mervyn Jones
Role: Right-hand bat, off-spin bowler
Born: 24 March 1963, Coburg, Melbourne, Australia
Height: 6ft 1¹/₂in **Weight:** 13st
Nickname: Deano
Test debut: 1983-84
Tests: 49
One-Day Internationals: 132
1st-Class 50s scored: 52
1st-Class 100s scored: 34
1st-Class 200s scored: 3
1st-Class catches: 119
One-Day 50s: 42
One-Day 100s: 9
Place in batting averages: 3rd av. 73.68
Wife and date of marriage:
Jane, 24 April 1986
Children: Phoebe, 26 June 1991
Family links with cricket: Father was captain/coach of Carlton, Victoria for 18 years
Education: Mt Waverley High School, Victoria

Qualifications: Higher School Certificate
Career outside cricket: Public Servant - Correctional Services
Off-season: Playing in Australia
Overseas tours: Young Australians to Zimbabwe 1983 and 1985; Australia to West Indies 1984 and 1991, to England 1985 and 1989, to India 1986 and 1987 (World Cup), to Sharjah 1986 and 1990, to Pakistan 1988, to New Zealand 1989; USA 1990
Overseas teams played for: Victoria, Australia
Cricketers particularly admired: Allan Border, Geoff Boycott, Sunil Gavaskar; Viv Richards, Javed Miandad
Other sports followed: Golf, baseball
Injuries: Broken finger
Relaxations: 'Golf and looking after my two Rottweilers, Jessica and Stanley'
Extras: Played for Victoria on their tour to England in 1991, culminating in the Britannic Assurance Challenge against Essex
Opinions on cricket: 'For slow over rates I think the penalty should be a number of runs. We should wear coloured clothing in Test matches. Test cricket should also be marketed better.'
Best batting: 248 Australian XI v Warwickshire, Edgbaston 1989

1992 Season

	M	Inns	NO	Runs	HS	Avge	100s	50s	Ct	St	O	M	Runs	Wkts	Avge	Best	5wI	10wM
Test																		
All First	14	23	7	1179	157	73.68	4	5	12	-	18.1	1	71	1	71.00	1-4	-	-
1-day Int																		
NatWest	2	2	0	71	46	35.50	-	-	1	-	2	0	16	0	-		-	-
B & H	4	4	0	25	13	6.25	-	-	2	-	7	0	34	2	17.00	2-34	-	
Sunday	11	10	2	656	114	82.00	2	5	4	-	6.1	0	41	1	41.00	1-37	-	

Career Performances

	M	Inns	NO	Runs	HS	Avge	100s	50s	Ct	St	Balls	Runs	Wkts	Avge	Best	5wI	10wM
Test	49	83	10	3355	216	45.95	10	12	32	-	198	64	1	64.00	1-5	-	-
All First	157	255	28	11780	248	51.89	34	52	119	-	1886	966	15	64.40	1-0	-	-
1-day Int	132	129	23	5048	145	47.62	7	37	47	-	106	81	3	27.00	2-34	-	
NatWest	2	2	0	71	46	35.50	-	-	1	-	12	16	0	-		-	-
B & H	4	4	0	25	13	6.25	-	-	2	-	42	34	2	17.00	2-34	-	
Sunday	11	10	2	656	114	82.00	2	5	4	-	37	41	1	41.00	1-37	-	

111. What was unusual about the first over of England's innings in the fourth Texaco Trophy match at Lord's last season?

JONES, R. O.   Glamorgan

Name: Robin Owen Jones
Role: Right-hand bat, off-spin bowler
Born: 4 October 1973, Crewe, Cheshire
Height: 5ft 10in **Weight:** 11st 7lbs
County debut: No first team appearance
Parents: G.P. and E.M.G. Jones
Marital status: Single
Family links with cricket: Brother Garri
Wyn Jones played for Cambridge University
in the 1992 Varsity match
Education: Malbank School, Nantwich,
Cheshire; Millfield School, Somerset;
Durham University
Qualifications: 10 GCSEs, 3 A-levels
Off-season: Studying economics at university
Overseas tours: Millfield School to Jamaica
1990; England U19 to India 1992-93
Cricketers particularly admired:
Viv Richards, Chris Tavare
Other sports followed: Soccer, rugby
Injuries: Slipped disc in neck and fractured left ankle, out for two months
Relaxations: Reading, modern music
Extras: Previously registered with Lancashire, played three 2nd XI matches in 1991.
Played for Welsh Schools U19 1991 and 1992, and for Bull Development XI v Australia
1991, and v Sri Lanka 1992
Opinions on cricket: 'A marvellous sport which has already taken me to many superb
places, and introduced me to some extremely pleasant people.'

112. Who captained Pakistan v England when Javed Miandad and
Salim Malik were injured?

Name: Matthew Keech
Role: Right-hand bat, Right-arm medium bowler
Born: 21 October 1970, Hampstead
Height: 6ft **Weight:** 13st 6lbs
County debut: 1991
1st-Class 50s scored: 2
1st-Class catches: 4
Parents: Ron and Brenda
Marital status: Single
Education: Northumberland Park School, Tottenham
Qualifications: 5 O-levels, NCA coaching certificate
Overseas tours: England U19 to Australia 1989-90
Overseas teams played for: Mossman, Sydney 1988-89; Lancaster Park, Christchurch NZ 1990-91

Cricketers particularly admired:
Mike Gatting, Richard Hadlee, Paul Downton
Other sports followed: Most other sports except horse racing
Relaxations: Listening to music, watching videos
Best batting: 58* Middlesex v Nottinghamshire, Lord's 1991

1992 Season (did not make any first-class or one-day appearance)

Career Performances

	M	Inns	NO	Runs	HS	Avge	100s	50s	Ct	St	Balls	Runs	Wkts	Avge	Best	5wI	10wM
Test																	
All First	15	24	3	420	58 *	20.00	-	2	4	-	84	36	0	-	-	-	-
1-day Int																	
NatWest																		
B & H	2	2	0	84	47	42.00	-	-	1	-							
Sunday	12	12	3	195	49 *	21.66	-	-	2	-							

KELLETT, S. A. Yorkshire

Name: Simon Andrew Kellett
Role: Opening bat, occasional right-arm medium bowler
Born: 16 October 1967, Mirfield
Height: 6ft 1in **Weight:** 12st 7lbs
Nickname: Kel, Ginner
County debut: 1989
County cap: 1992
1000 runs in a season: 2
1st-Class 50s scored: 23
1st-Class 100s scored: 2
1st-Class catches: 58
Place in batting averages: 79th av. 37.88
(1991 77th av. 36.17)
Parents: Brian and Valerie
Marital status: Girlfriend, Sarah
Family links with cricket: Father played local league cricket
Education: Whitcliffe Mount High School; Huddersfield Technical College
Qualifications: 5 CSEs, Sports Management course
Off-season: Playing cricket in New Zealand
Overseas tours: Yorkshire U17 to West Indies
Overseas teams played for: Upper Hutt, New Zealand 1991-92; Wellington State 1992
Cricketers particularly admired: Martyn Moxon, Graham Gooch, Tony Greig
Other sports followed: Rugby league (Bradford Northern)
Relaxations: Watching Bradford Northern
Extras: Captained NAYC against MCC; captained Yorkshire U19 to Cambridge Festival win; was out to first ball in first-class cricket
Opinions on cricket: 'Four-day cricket is good for the development of Test cricketers.'
Best batting: 125* Yorkshire v Derbyshire, Chesterfield 1991

1992 Season

	M	Inns	NO	Runs	HS	Avge	100s	50s	Ct	St	O	M	Runs	Wkts	Avge	Best	5wI	10wM
Test																		
All First	22	36	1	1326	96	37.88	-	9	23	-								
1-day Int																		
NatWest	2	2	0	38	38	19.00	-	-	3	-								
B & H	4	4	0	84	40	21.00	-	-	-	-								
Sunday	14	14	1	440	118 *	33.84	1	2	1	-								

Career Performances

	M	Inns	NO	Runs	HS	Avge	100s	50s	Ct	St	Balls	Runs	Wkts	Avge	Best	5wI	10wM
Test																	
All First	66	111	9	3422	125 *	33.54	2	23	58	-	30	19	0	-	-	-	-
1-day Int																	
NatWest	5	3	0	38	38	12.66	-	-	3	-							
B & H	12	10	1	226	45	25.11	-	-	-	-							
Sunday	24	24	2	576	118 *	26.18	1	2	4	-	18	16	0	-	-	-	

KENDRICK, N. M. *Surrey*

Name: Neil Michael Kendrick
Role: Right-hand bat, slow left-arm bowler, gully fielder
Born: 11 November 1967, Bromley
Height: 5ft 11in **Weight:** 12st 2lbs
Nickname: Kendo, Rat, Merson
County debut: 1988
50 wickets in a season: 1
1st-Class 50s scored: 3
1st-Class 5 w. in innings: 5
1st-Class 10 w. in match: 1
1st-Class catches: 35
Place in batting averages: 199th av. 19.12
Place in bowling averages: 52nd av. 30.72
(1991 8th av. 21.83)
Strike rate: 70.01 (career 71.93)
Parents: Michael Hall and Anne Patricia
Marital status: Single
Family links with cricket: Father plays club cricket for Old Wilsonians, and sister has represented Kent Ladies
Education: Hayes Primary; Wilson's Grammar School and 'the Surrey dressing room'
Qualifications: 7 O-levels, 1 A-level; senior coaching certificate
Off-season: Coaching cricket in many of Surrey's state schools
Overseas tours: Surrey U19 to Australia 1985-86
Cricketers particularly admired: Ian Botham, Graham Gooch, Bob 'The Cat' Bevin
Other sports followed: Football and most ball sports
Injuries: Fractured thumb, out for one week
Relaxations: Black music, listening to Kiss FM, going to clubs that play 'proper' music (e.g. Soul Survivors)
Opinions on cricket: 'At last – four-day cricket and coloured clothing.'

Best batting: 55 Surrey v Middlesex, Lord's 1992
Best bowling: 6-61 Surrey v Leicestershire, The Oval 1992

1992 Season

	M	Inns	NO	Runs	HS	Avge	100s	50s	Ct	St	O	M	Runs	Wkts	Avge	Best	5wl	10wM
Test																		
All First	17	21	5	306	55	19.12	-	2	16	-	595.1	171	1567	51	30.72	6-61	3	-
1-day Int																		
NatWest	1	0	0	0	0	-	-	-	-	-	12	1	51	1	51.00	1-51	-	
B & H	2	2	1	25	24	25.00	-	-	1	-	22	0	98	3	32.66	2-47	-	
Sunday	3	1	0	1	1	1.00	-	-	2	-	24	0	109	1	109.00	1-45	-	

Career Performances

	M	Inns	NO	Runs	HS	Avge	100s	50s	Ct	St	Balls	Runs	Wkts	Avge	Best	5wl	10wM
Test																	
All First	36	41	12	513	55	17.69	-	3	35	-	6834	3259	95	34.30	6-61	5	1
1-day Int																	
NatWest	1	0	0	0	0	-	-	-	-	-	72	51	1	51.00	1-51	-	
B & H	2	2	1	25	24	25.00	-	-	1	-	132	98	3	32.66	2-47	-	
Sunday	4	2	1	3	2 *	3.00	-	-	2	-	162	129	1	129.00	1-45	-	

KERR, J. I. D.   Somerset

Name: Jason Ian Douglas Kerr
Role: Right-hand bat, right-arm fast-medium
bowler
Born: 7 April 1974, Bolton, Lancashire
Height: 6ft 3in **Weight:** 13st
Nickname: Norman, Normski, Stretchy
County debut: No first team appearance
Parents: Len and Janet
Marital status: Single
Family links with cricket: 'Father manages
my league club, Tonge'
Education: Withins High School;
Bolton Met College
Qualifications: 5 GCSEs, BTEC National
Diploma in Business Studies, cricket coach
Off-season: On tour with England U19
Overseas tours: England U19 to India
1992-93
Cricketers particularly admired:
David Gower, Viv Richards, Ian Botham

Other sports followed: Golf, football (all sports)
Injuries: Ripped rib cartilage, out for two weeks
Relaxations: Playing golf, socialising, squash, TV, swimming, sleeping, listening to music
Opinions on cricket: 'Too much cricket is played. Teams can be playing for weeks on the run. This is too much for any player. 2nd XI cricket should be played on county wickets as 2nd XI is preparation for first-class.'

KERSEY, G. J. Kent

Name: Graham James Kersey
Role: Right-hand bat, wicket-keeper
Born: 19 May 1971, Greenwich
Height: 5ft 8in **Weight:** 10st
Nickname: Scuz
County debut: 1991
1st-Class catches: 14
1st-Class stumpings: 1
Parents: Don and Beryl
Marital status: Single
Family links with cricket: Brother Ian played for Kent U19 and UAU 2nd XI
Education: Bexley-Erith Technical High School
Qualifications: 6 O-levels, 1 A-level
Career outside cricket: Groundsman, installing air-conditioning
Off-season: Playing and coaching in Namibia
Overseas tours: Kent Schools U17 to Singapore and New Zealand 1987-88
Overseas teams played for: Eastern Suburbs District, Brisbane 1989-91; Windhoek College of Education, Namibia 1992-93
Cricketers particularly admired: Alan Knott, Jack Russell, David Gower, Peter Anderson (Queensland)
Other sports followed: Football
Relaxations: Keeping fit, watching films, listening to music
Opinions on cricket: 'Rules about qualifying for England are not nearly strict enough. 2nd XI cricket should be played on same standard wickets as first-class.'
Best batting: 27* Kent v Surrey, The Oval 1991

1992 Season

	M	Inns	NO	Runs	HS	Avge	100s	50s	Ct	St	O	M	Runs	Wkts	Avge	Best	5wI	10wM
Test																		
All First	2	2	1	42	22	42.00	-	-	7	1								
1-day Int																		
NatWest																		
B & H																		
Sunday	1	1	1	0	0 *	-	-	-	-	1								

Career Performances

	M	Inns	NO	Runs	HS	Avge	100s	50s	Ct	St	Balls	Runs	Wkts	Avge	Best	5wI	10wM
Test																	
All First	4	3	2	69	27 *	69.00	-	-	14	1							
1-day Int																	
NatWest																	
B & H																	
Sunday	1	1	1	0	0 *	-	-	-	-	1							

KETTLEBOROUGH, R. A.   Yorkshire

Name: Richard Allan Kettleborough
Role: Left-hand bat, right-arm medium bowler
Born: 15 March 1973, Sheffield
Height: 5ft 10in **Weight:** 11st 7lbs
Nickname: Ketts
County debut: No first team appearance
Parents: Allan and Pat
Marital status: Single
Family links with cricket: Father played for Yorkshire and is now coach at Worksop College
Education: Laughton All Saints Junior School; Worksop College; Airedale and Wharfedale College
Qualifications: 5 GCSEs, City & Guilds in Recreational Management
Career outside cricket: 'I would love to run my own pub and nightclub.'
Off-season: ' Doing some work for my Dad, playing football on Sunday mornings, doing weights and cross-country running in order to keep fit for next cricket season.'
Overseas tours: Worksop College to Australia 1988-89; England U18 to Canada 1991

Cricketers particularly admired: David Gower 'was and still is a childhood hero', Ian Botham, Viv Richards, Richard Hadlee, Malcolm Marshall
Other sports followed: Football, 'I follow Sheffield Wednesday at home and away'
Relaxations: All sports apart from horse racing. 'I like to relax with my girlfriend or with other friends in and around Sheffield.'
Extras: Won the Lord's Taverners Under 15 Award for the Most Promising Young Cricketer in 1988
Opinions on cricket: 'I'm all for four-day cricket but I think the Sunday League should be kept the same because a full day's cricket on a Sunday in the middle of a four-day county match is too much for anybody. In league cricket there should be more bonus points for wickets taken and less for runs scored to encourage people to try to bowl teams out instead of being defensive.'

KHAN, W. G. Warwickshire

Name: Wasim Gulzar Khan
Role: Left-hand bat, right-arm leg-spin bowler
Born: 26 February 1971, Birmingham
Height: 6ft 1in **Weight:** 11st 2lbs
Nickname: Mowgli, Wasby
County debut: 1992 (one-day)
Parents: Raja Gulzar (deceased) and Zarina Begum
Marital status: Single
Education: Small Heath Secondary School; Josiah Mason Sixth Form College, Birmingham
Qualifications: 6 O-levels, 1 A-level
Off-season: Playing in Australia
Overseas teams played for:
Western Suburbs, Sydney 1990-91;
North Perth, Western Australia 1991-93
Cricketers particularly admired:
Wasim Akram, Dermot Reeve, Ian Botham, Asif Din, Roger Twose, Jon Wright (Old Hill CC)
Other sports followed: Any other than horse racing
Relaxations: Listening to music, spending time with family and friends
Opinions on cricket: 'The introduction of four-day cricket this season will only improve the standard of first-class cricket. 2nd XI wickets should be similar to first-class wickets in their preparation and covering.'

1992 Season

	M	Inns	NO	Runs	HS	Avge	100s	50s	Ct	St	O	M	Runs	Wkts	Avge	Best	5wI	10wM
Test																		
All First																		
1-day Int																		
NatWest																		
B & H																		
Sunday	1	1	0	7	7	7.00	-	-	-	-								

Career Performances

	M	Inns	NO	Runs	HS	Avge	100s	50s	Ct	St	Balls	Runs	Wkts	Avge	Best	5wI	10wM
Test																	
All First																	
1-day Int																	
NatWest																	
B & H																	
Sunday	1	1	0	7	7	7.00	-	-	-	-							

KIRNON, S. Glamorgan

Name: Samuel Kirnon
Role: Right-hand bat, right-arm fast-medium bowler
Born: 25 December 1963
Height: 5ft 9¹/₂in **Weight:** 12st 7lbs
Nickname: Sammy
County debut: 1991 (one-day), 1992 (first-class)
Parents: William and Ethel
Wife and date of marriage: Shirley Anne, 20 April 1990
Family links with cricket: Father played for Montserrat, West Indies. Cousin L.O'Brien still plays for Montserrat
Education: Montserrat Secondary School, West Indies
Career outside cricket: PT Instructor with the British Army
Off-season: Playing cricket in Montserrat
Overseas tours: BAOR to Barbados 1986 and 1988; Royal Artillery to Barbados 1990
Overseas teams played for: Nijmegen, Holland 1984-90

Cricketers particularly admired: Richie Richardson, David Hemp, Steve Bastien
Other sports followed: Boxing, athletics
Relaxations: Playing squash, listening to music
Extras: Released by Glamorgan at the end of the 1992 season
Best bowling: 1-14 Glamorgan v Oxford University, The Parks 1992

1992 Season

	M	Inns	NO	Runs	HS	Avge	100s	50s	Ct	St	O	M	Runs	Wkts	Avge	Best	5wI	10wM
Test																		
All First	1	0	0	0	0	-	-	-	-	-	14	5	21	1	21.00	1-14	-	-
1-day Int																		
NatWest																		
B & H																		
Sunday	1	1	0	1	1	1.00	-	-	-	-	2	0	20	0	-	-	-	-

Career Performances

	M	Inns	NO	Runs	HS	Avge	100s	50s	Ct	St	Balls	Runs	Wkts	Avge	Best	5wI	10wM
Test																	
All First	1	0	0	0	0	-	-	-	-	-	84	21	1	21.00	1-14	-	-
1-day Int																	
NatWest																	
B & H																	
Sunday	2	2	0	1	1	0.50	-	-	-	-	60	68	2	34.00	2-48	-	

KNIGHT, N. V.   Essex

Name: Nicholas Verity Knight
Role: Left-hand bat, right-arm medium bowler, close fielder
Born: 28 November 1969, Watford
Height: 6ft **Weight:** 12st 7lbs
Nickname: Knighty, Stitch
County debut: 1991
1st-Class 50s scored: 6
1st-Class 100s scored: 3
1st-Class catches: 21
One-Day 50s: 1
Place in batting averages: 112th av. 32.25 (1991 25th av. 49.00)
Parents: John and Rosemary
Marital status: Single
Family links with cricket: Father played for Cambridgeshire, brother plays club cricket for St Giles in Cambridge
Education: Felsted Prep; Felsted School; Loughborough University

Qualifications: 9 O-levels, 3 A-level;
BSc (Hons) Sociology
Off-season: Playing cricket in Australia
Overseas tours: Felsted School to
Australia 1986-87
Overseas teams played for: Northern
Districts, Sydney 1991-92
Cricketers particularly admired:
Graham Gooch, Keith Fletcher, Malcolm
Marshall, Salim Malik and Gordon Barker
– 'my coach at Felsted'
Other sports followed: Hockey, golf,
rugby league
Injuries: Split the webbing on right hand
and broken finger on left hand
Relaxations: 'Going out for meals, eating
lots of food, putting cream on my feet,
listening to Kylie Minogue's music'
Extras: Captain of England Schools 1987
and 1988, captain of Young England v
New Zealand 1989, captain of Combined Universities 1991. Played hockey for Essex and
Young England. Played rugby for Eastern Counties.
Opinions on cricket: 'Longer tea break. Sunday League should still be 40 overs.'
Best batting: 109 Essex v Middlesex, Ilford 1992

1992 Season

	M	Inns	NO	Runs	HS	Avge	100s	50s	Ct	St	O	M	Runs	Wkts	Avge	Best	5wI	10wM
Test																		
All First	20	30	6	774	109	32.25	2	3	16	-								
1-day Int																		
NatWest	3	3	1	90	81 *	45.00	-	1	-	-								
B & H	3	3	1	22	18 *	11.00	-	-	2	-								
Sunday	16	12	2	227	35	22.70	-	-	8	-								

Career Performances

	M	Inns	NO	Runs	HS	Avge	100s	50s	Ct	St	Balls	Runs	Wkts	Avge	Best	5wI	10wM
Test																	
All First	27	40	7	1215	109	36.81	3	6	21	-	30	32	0	-	-	-	-
1-day Int																	
NatWest	3	3	1	90	81 *	45.00	-	1	-	-							
B & H	9	9	1	109	36	13.62	-	-	7	-	6	4	0	-	-	-	
Sunday	18	14	3	258	35	23.45	-	-	10	-							

KRIKKEN, K. M. G.　　　　　　　Derbyshire

Name: Karl Matthew Giles Krikken
Role: Right-hand bat, wicket-keeper
Born: 9 April 1969, Bolton
Height: 5ft 10in **Weight:** 12st
Nickname: Krikk,
County debut: 1987 (one-day),
1989 (first-class)
County cap: 1992
1st-Class 50s scored: 6
1st-Class catches: 175
1st-Class stumpings: 12
Place in batting averages: 220th av. 19.04
(1991 171st av. 23.23)
Parents: Brian and Irene
Marital status: Engaged to Liz
Family links with cricket: Father kept
wicket for Lancashire and Worcestershire
Education: Horwich Parish Church School;
Rivington and Blackrod High School
Qualifications: 6 O-levels, 3 A-levels,
Cricket coaching certificates

Off-season: Playing and coaching in Cape Town
Overseas teams played for: Griqualand West, South Africa; CBC Old Boys, Kimberley,
South Africa; Green Island, Dunedin, New Zealand
Cricketers particularly admired: Bob Taylor and Alan Knott
Other sports followed: All sports especially football
Relaxations: Music, videos, laser quest
Extras: Played first first-class game in South Africa for Griqualand West as an overseas
professional. Wicket-keeper with most dismissals in 1990
Opinions on cricket: 'No one-day cricket. 34 Championship games.'
Best batting: 77* Derbyshire v Somerset, Taunton 1990

1992 Season

	M	Inns	NO	Runs	HS	Avge	100s	50s	Ct	St	O	M	Runs	Wkts	Avge	Best	5wI	10wM
Test																		
All First	23	27	3	383	57 *	15.95	-	2	52	5								
1-day Int																		
NatWest	2	1	0	18	18	18.00	-	-	2	-								
B & H	5	4	1	52	37 *	17.33	-	-	11	-								
Sunday	17	10	2	124	28 *	15.50	-	-	16	-								

Career Performances

	M	Inns	NO	Runs	HS	Avge	100s	50s	Ct	St	Balls	Runs	Wkts	Avge	Best	5wI	10wM
Test																	
All First	74	104	16	1676	77 *	19.04	-	6	175	12	36	40	0	-	-	-	-
1-day Int																	
NatWest	2	1	0	18	18	18.00	-	-	2	-							
B & H	5	4	1	52	37 *	17.33	-	-	11	-							
Sunday	29	17	3	221	44 *	15.78	-	-	28	3							

LAMB, A. J. Northamptonshire

Name: Allan Joseph Lamb
Role: Right-hand bat, right-arm medium
bowler, county captain
Born: 20 June 1954, Langebaanweg, Cape
Province, South Africa
Height: 5ft 8in **Weight:** 12st
Nickname: Lambie, Legger, Joe
County debut: 1978
County cap: 1978
Benefit: 1988 (£134,000)
Test debut: 1982
Tests: 79
One-Day Internationals: 122
1000 runs in a season: 12
1st-Class 50s scored: 146
1st-Class 100s scored: 79
1st-Class 200s scored: 3
1st-Class catches: 320
One-Day 50s: 77
One-Day 100s: 16
Place in batting averages: 8th av. 60.83 (1991 63rd av. 38.60)
Parents: Michael and Joan
Wife and date of marriage: Lindsay, 8 December 1979
Children: Katie-Ann and Richard Edward Thomas
Family links with cricket: Father and brother played in the B section of the Currie Cup
Education: Wynberg Boys' High School; Abbotts College
Qualifications: Matriculation
Career outside cricket: Promotions company
Off-season: Playing for Western Province in South Africa
Overseas tours: With England to Australia and New Zealand 1982-83, to New Zealand
and Pakistan 1983-84, to India and Australia 1984-85, to West Indies 1985-86, to Australia

1986-87, to the World Cup in India and Pakistan 1987-88, to India and West Indies 1989-90, to Australia 1990-91, to New Zealand 1991-92

Overseas teams played for: Western Province 1972-81 and 1992-93; Orange Free State 1987-88

Cricketers particularly admired: Dennis Lillee, Viv Richards

Other sports followed: Tennis, golf, rugby and horse racing

Relaxations: Fly fishing (trout and salmon)

Extras: Was primarily a bowler when he first played school cricket in South Africa. Made first-class debut for Western Province in 1972-73. Top of first-class batting averages in 1980. One of *Wisden's* Five Cricketers of the Year, 1980. Qualified to play for England in 1982. Appointed Northamptonshire captain 1989. Captained England in Tests v West Indies in 1989-90 and v Australia in 1990-91 after injuries to Graham Gooch. Made a century in his first Test as captain v West Indies at Bridgetown. Hit three 100s in consecutive Tests v West Indies 1984. Northants Player of the Year 1992

Opinions on cricket: 'Get our one-day domestic game in line with overseas, i.e. we should play 50 overs as they do abroad, our longer competition could be 55 not 60.'

Best batting: 294 Orange Free State v Eastern Province, Bloemfontein 1987-88

Best bowling: 2-29 Northamptonshire v Lancashire, Lytham 1991

1992 Season

	M	Inns	NO	Runs	HS	Avge	100s	50s	Ct	St	O	M	Runs	Wkts	Avge	Best	5wI	10wM
Test	2	3	0	54	30	18.00	-	-	-	-								
All First	18	28	4	1460	209	60.83	6	5	12	-								
1-day Int	5	5	0	144	60	28.80	-	2	-	-								
NatWest	5	5	1	153	69	38.25	-	1	1	-								
B & H	4	4	1	214	108 *	71.33	1	1	2	-								
Sunday	13	12	2	347	120	34.70	1	-	4	-								

Career Performances

	M	Inns	NO	Runs	HS	Avge	100s	50s	Ct	St	Balls	Runs	Wkts	Avge	Best	5wI	10wM
Test	79	139	10	4656	142	36.09	14	18	75	-	30	23	1	23.00	1-6	-	-
All First	412	684	101	28495	294	48.87	79	146	320	-	305	199	8	24.87	2-29	-	-
1-day Int	122	118	16	4010	118	39.31	4	26	31	-	6	3	0	-	-	-	-
NatWest	44	43	3	1554	103	38.85	2	11	11	-	8	12	1	12.00	1-4	-	
B & H	66	60	10	2387	126 *	47.74	5	15	25	-	6	11	1	11.00	1-11	-	
Sunday	158	152	20	4751	132 *	35.99	5	25	38	-							

113. During the fourth Texaco Trophy match at Lord's last season, Wasim Akram, on 97, was described as 'approaching his century'. What century?

LAMPITT, S. R.   Worcestershire

Name: Stuart Richard Lampitt
Role: Right-hand bat, right-arm fast-medium
bowler
Born: 29 July 1966, Wolverhampton
Height: 5ft 11in **Weight:** 13st
Nickname: Jed
County debut: 1985
County cap: 1989
50 wickets in a season: 2
1st-Class 50s scored: 8
1st-Class 5 w. in innings: 8
1st-Class catches: 35
Place in batting averages: 171st av. 23.54
(1991 111th av. 30.76)
Place in bowling averages: 91st av. 35.91
(1991 46th av. 29.33)
Strike rate: 63.34 (career 56.96)
Parents: Joseph Charles and Muriel Ann
Marital status: Single
Education: Kingswinford Secondary School;

Dudley Technical College
Qualifications: 7 O-levels; Diploma in Business Studies
Career outside cricket: 'Have had several jobs and none of them were particularly attractive.'
Off-season: Playing in Perth, Australia with University C.C.
Overseas tours: NCA U19 to Bermuda; Worcestershire to Bahamas 1990, to Zimbabwe 1991, to South Africa 1992
Overseas teams played for: Mangere, Auckland 1986-88; University C.C., Perth 1991-93
Cricketers particularly admired: 'Fred Trueman and all those brilliant players of the past.'
Other sports followed: Most ball sports, particularly football (Wolves)
Injuries: Ankle ligaments, out for 2 weeks; broken thumb, out for 2 weeks
Relaxations: 'Sleeping, playing golf and taking money off the lads at Worcester.'
Extras: Took five wickets and made 42 for Stourbridge in Final of the Cockspur Cup at Lord's in 1987. One of the Whittingdale Young Players of the Year 1990
Opinions on cricket: 'Not so sure that four-day cricket is the answer after all. With our climate and pitches, cricket may turn out to be very slow and even the most ardent follower might lose interest. Good idea with the Sunday League but not with the 50 overs.'
Best batting: 93 Worcestershire v Derbyshire, Kidderminster 1991
Best bowling: 5-32 Worcestershire v Kent, Worcester 1989

1992 Season

	M	Inns	NO	Runs	HS	Avge	100s	50s	Ct	St	O	M	Runs	Wkts	Avge	Best	5wI	10wM
Test																		
All First	19	29	5	565	71 *	23.54	-	4	6	-	369.3	44	1257	35	35.91	4-57	-	-
1-day Int																		
NatWest	1	1	0	14	14	14.00	-	-	-	-	12	0	64	2	32.00	2-64	-	
B & H	5	4	1	54	23 *	18.00	-	-	2	-	35	3	143	7	20.42	3-30	-	
Sunday	12	8	5	62	19 *	20.66	-	-	3	-	67.5	3	353	17	20.76	4-40	-	

Career Performances

	M	Inns	NO	Runs	HS	Avge	100s	50s	Ct	St	Balls	Runs	Wkts	Avge	Best	5wI	10wM
Test																	
All First	89	99	22	1665	93	21.62	-	8	35	-	10595	5673	186	30.50	5-32	8	-
1-day Int																	
NatWest	10	5	2	33	14	11.00	-	-	2	-	530	371	16	23.18	5-22	1	
B & H	16	8	2	106	41	17.66	-	-	7	-	829	604	24	25.16	4-46	-	
Sunday	59	25	11	190	25 *	13.57	-	-	17	-	1835	1674	59	28.37	5-67	1	

LARKINS, W.   Durham

Name: Wayne Larkins
Role: Right-hand bat, right-arm medium bowler
Born: 22 November 1953
Height: 5ft 11in **Weight:** 12st
Nickname: Ned
County debut: 1972 (Northamptonshire) 1992 (Durham)
County cap: 1976
Benefit: 1986
Test debut: 1979-80
Tests: 13
One-Day Internationals: 25
1000 runs in a season: 12
1st-Class 50s scored: 104
1st-Class 100s scored: 53
1st-Class 200s scored: 3
1st-Class 5 w. in innings: 1
1st-Class catches: 260
One-Day 50s: 55
One-Day 100s: 18
Place in batting averages: 82nd av. 37.46 (1991 74th av. 36.50)

Parents: Mavis (father deceased)

Wife and date of marriage: Jane Elaine, 22 March 1975

Children: Philippa Jane, 30 May 1981

Family links with cricket: Father was umpire. Brother, Melvin, played for Bedford Town for many years

Education: Bushmead, Eaton Socon, Huntingdon

Overseas tours: England to Australia and India 1979-80; India and Sri Lanka 1981-82; India and West Indies 1989-90; Australia 1990-91; unofficial English team to South Africa 1981-82

Other sports followed: Golf, football (was on Notts County's books), squash

Relaxations: Gardening

Extras: Banned from Test cricket for three years for joining rebel tour of South Africa in 1982. Recalled to Test team in 1986 but withdrew due to thumb injury and missed another Test recall in 1987 because of a football injury. Eventually returned to Test cricket in the West Indies in 1989-90, nine years after his last appearance. Moved to Durham at the beginning of the 1992 season

Best batting : 252 Northamptonshire v Glamorgan, Cardiff 1983

Best bowling : 5-59 Northamptonshire v Worcestershire, Worcester 1984

1992 Season

	M	Inns	NO	Runs	HS	Avge	100s	50s	Ct	St	O	M	Runs	Wkts	Avge	Best	5wI	10wM
Test																		
All First	22	41	0	1536	143	37.46	4	8	16	-	2	1	4	0	-	-	-	-
1-day Int																		
NatWest	3	3	0	154	113	51.33	1	-	-	-								
B & H	4	4	0	150	73	37.50	-	2	4	-								
Sunday	16	15	0	357	86	23.80	-	3	6	-								

Career Performances

	M	Inns	NO	Runs	HS	Avge	100s	50s	Ct	St	Balls	Runs	Wkts	Avge	Best	5wI	10wM
Test	13	25	1	493	64	20.54	-	3	8	-							
All First	436	762	48	24384	252	34.15	53	104	260	-	3463	1858	42	44.23	5-59	1	-
1-day Int	25	24	0	591	124	24.62	1	-	9	-	15	22	0	-	-	-	-
NatWest	47	46	3	1590	121 *	36.97	2	11	19	-	455	274	4	68.50	2-38	-	
B & H	74	70	3	2238	132	33.40	5	10	18	-	675	444	16	27.75	4-37	-	
Sunday	254	244	13	6425	172 *	27.81	10	34	76	-	2033	1679	57	29.45	5-32	1	

114. Which legendary cricketer said: 'I never was superstitious. All I ever did was put my left sock, my left trouser leg, my left pad, and my left batting glove, on first'?

LATHWELL, M. N.   Somerset

Name: Mark Nicholas Lathwell
Role: Right-hand bat, right-arm medium
and off-break bowler
Born: 26 December 1971, Bletchley, Bucks
Height: 5ft 8in **Weight:** 11st 6lbs
Nickname: Lathers, Rowdy
County debut: 1991
County cap: 1992
1st-Class 50s: 11
1st-Class 100s: 1
1st-Class catches: 14
One-Day 50s: 4
Place in batting averages: 8th av. 36.75
Parents: Derek Peter and Valerie
Marital status: Single
Family links with cricket: Brother plays
local club cricket, father is a 'retired' club
cricketer and is now senior coach

Education: Overstone Primary, Wing,
Bucks; Southmead Primary, Braunton,
N Devon; Braunton Comprehensive
Qualifications: 5 GCSEs
Career outside cricket: 'Worked in Barclays bank and other office work.'
Off-season: Touring Australia with England A and 'playing darts and pool for "sticky
stumps and sticky balls".'
Overseas tours: England A to Australia 1992-93
Cricketers particularly admired: Ian Botham, Graham Gooch, Malcolm Marshall
Other sports followed: 'I prefer to play rather than watch.'
Injuries: Pulled hamstring, out for 3 weeks
Relaxations: 'Fishing, playing a range of sports, juggling, drinking, eating, sleeping.'
Extras: Spent one season on Lord's groundstaff. Played for England U19 v Australia 1991.
Young Player of the Year and Somerset Player of the Year 1992
Opinions on cricket: 'Sunday League should have stayed a 40-over game.'
Best batting: 114 Somerset v Surrey, Bath 1992
Best bowling: 1-9 Somerset v Gloucestershire, Gloucester 1992

---

115. Who won the Test series, England v Pakistan last season, and by
what margin?

1992 Season

	M	Inns	NO	Runs	HS	Avge	100s	50s	Ct	St	O	M	Runs	Wkts	Avge	Best	5wl	10wM
Test																		
All First	19	33	1	1176	114	36.75	1	11	14	-	64	14	224	4	56.00	1-9	-	-
1-day Int																		
NatWest	2	2	0	97	85	48.50	-	1	1	-								
B & H	3	3	0	98	93	32.66	-	1	-	-								
Sunday	13	13	1	396	96	33.00	-	2	6	-								

Career Performances

	M	Inns	NO	Runs	HS	Avge	100s	50s	Ct	St	Balls	Runs	Wkts	Avge	Best	5wl	10wM
Test																	
All First	21	36	1	1239	114	35.40	1	11	14	-	552	323	5	64.60	1-9	-	-
1-day Int																	
NatWest	3	3	0	113	85	37.66	-	1	1	-							
B & H	3	3	0	98	93	32.66	-	1	-	-							
Sunday	15	15	1	431	96	30.78	-	2	7	-	24	19	0	-		-	-

LAW, D. R. C. Sussex

Name: Danny Richard Charles Law
Role: Right-hand bat, right-arm fast bowler
Born: 15 July 1975, London
Height: 6ft 5in **Weight:** 13st 7lbs
County debut: No first team appearance
Parents: Richard (deceased) and Claudette
Marital status: Engaged
Education: Wolverton Hall
Off-season: Preparing for the new season
Overseas tours: England U18 to South
Africa 1992
Cricketers particularly admired:
Michael Holding, Allan Donald, Viv
Richards
Other sports followed: Football, basketball,
rugby league, rugby union and most other
sports
Relaxations: Listening to music
Opinions on cricket: 'I feel that 2nd XIs
should play four-day cricket as a proper
preparation for first-class cricket – and that they should use the same balls and the same
pitches.'

LAWRENCE, D. V.   Gloucestershire

Name: David Valentine Lawrence
Role: Right-hand bat, right-arm fast bowler
Born: 28 January 1964, Gloucester
Height: 6ft 2in **Weight:** 16st 5lbs
Nickname: Syd
County debut: 1981
County cap: 1985
Benefit: 1993
Test debut: 1988
Tests: 5
One-Day Internationals: 1
50 wickets in a season: 5
1st-Class 50s scored: 2
1st-Class 5 w. in innings: 21
1st-Class 10 w. in match: 1
1st-Class catches: 40
Place in bowling averages:
(1991 17th av. 24.18)
Strike rate: (career 52.12)
Parents: Joseph and Hilda Joyce
Children: Buster, November 1991
Family links with cricket: Father played club cricket in Jamaica
Education: Linden School, Gloucester
Qualifications: 3 CSEs
Career outside cricket: 'Ducking and diving, wheeling and dealing.'
Off-season: Touring with England
Overseas tours: England B to Sri Lanka 1986; England A to Zimbabwe 1989-90; England to New Zealand 1991-92
Overseas teams played for: Tasmania 1984; Scarborough, Perth, Western Australia 1984-85; Manly, Sydney 1987; Freemantle, Western Australia 1989
Cricketers particularly admired: Dennis Lillee, Richard Hadlee, Michael Holding
Other sports followed: Rugby union and league, American football, golf
Injuries: Missed all of the 1992 season due to shattered kneecap
Relaxations: Clothes, music, aerobics, eating out ('preferably Mexican'), looking after doberman dog called Arnold
Extras: Called up to join the England A tour in 1989-90 when Chris Lewis joined the senior squad in the West Indies. Took a hat-trick v Nottinghamshire in 1990
Best batting: 66 Gloucestershire v Glamorgan, Abergavenny 1991
Best bowling: 7-47 Gloucestershire v Surrey, Cheltenham 1988

1992 Season (did not make any first-class or one-day appearance)

Career Performances

	M	Inns	NO	Runs	HS	Avge	100s	50s	Ct	St	Balls	Runs	Wkts	Avge	Best	5wI	10wM
Test	5	6	0	60	34	10.00	-	-	-	-	1089	676	18	37.55	5-106	1	-
All First	181	205	35	1819	66	10.70	-	2	44	-	26426	16162	507	31.87	7-47	21	1
1-day Int	1	0	0	0	0	-	-	-	-	-	66	67	4	16.75	4-67	-	
NatWest	20	10	5	11	5 *	2.20	-	-	2	-	1108	763	28	27.25	5-17	1	
B&H	29	12	6	94	23	15.66	-	-	6	-	1614	1050	44	23.86	6-20	2	
Refuge	59	23	8	179	38 *	11.93	-	-	15	-	2430	2115	75	28.20	5-18	1	

LEATHERDALE, D. A. Worcestershire

Name: David Anthony Leatherdale
Role: Right-hand bat, right-arm medium bowler, cover fielder
Born: 26 November 1967, Bradford
Height: 5ft 10in **Weight:** 11st
Nickname: Lugsy, Spock
County debut: 1988
1st-Class 50s scored: 9
1st-Class 100s scored: 2
1st-Class catches: 38
One-Day 50s: 2
Place in batting averages: 134th av. 27.30
(1991 8th av. 63.16)
Parents: Paul and Rosalyn
Wife's name: Vanessa
Children: Callum Edward, 6 July 1990
Family links with cricket: Brother plays for
East Bierley in Bradford League.
Brother-in-law played for Young England
in 1979. Father played local cricket
Education: Bolton Royd Primary School; Pudsey Grangefield Secondary School
Qualifications: 8 O-levels, 2 A-levels; NCA coaching award (stage 1)
Off-season: Working for Golding Pipework Services (Birmingham)
Overseas teams played for: Pretoria Police, South Africa 1987-88
Cricketers particularly admired: Mark Scott, George Batty, Peter Kippax
Other sports followed: Football, American football
Relaxations: Golf
Opinions on cricket: 'A full circuit of 2nd XI cricket will make it easier for 2nd XI players
to move up into first-class cricket.'
Best batting: 157 Worcestershire v Somerset, Worcester 1991
Best bowling: 1-12 Worcestershire v Northamptonshire, Worcester 1988

1992 Season

	M	Inns	NO	Runs	HS	Avge	100s	50s	Ct	St	O	M	Runs	Wkts	Avge	Best	5wl	10wM
Test																		
All First	23	40	4	983	112	27.30	1	5	16	-	10	2	33	0	-	-	-	-
1-day Int																		
NatWest	1	1	0	32	32	32.00	-	-	-	-								
B & H	5	5	0	47	14	9.40	-	-	1	-								
Sunday	15	14	1	200	46	15.38	-	-	9	-	1	0	3	0	-	-	-	

Career Performances

	M	Inns	NO	Runs	HS	Avge	100s	50s	Ct	St	Balls	Runs	Wkts	Avge	Best	5wl	10wM
Test																	
All First	49	75	6	1864	157	27.01	2	9	38	-	114	59	1	59.00	1-12	-	-
1-day Int																	
NatWest	8	7	1	126	43	21.00	-	-	-	-							
B & H	7	5	0	47	14	9.40	-	-	1	-							
Sunday	39	34	6	443	62 *	15.82	-	2	17	-	60	61	0	-	-	-	

LEFEBVRE, R. P.   Glamorgan

Name: Roland Phillippe Lefebvre
Role: Right-hand bat, right-arm medium bowler
Born: 7 February 1963, Rotterdam
Height: 6ft 1in **Weight:** 12st
Nickname: Tulip, Clogsy, Dopie, Dutchie
County debut: 1990 (Somerset)
County cap: 1991 (Somerset)
1st-Class 50s scored: 2
1st-Class 100s scored: 1
1st-Class 5 w. in innings: 2
1st-Class catches: 20
Place in batting averages:
(1991 150 av. 26.14)
Place in bowling averages:
(1991 140th av. 59.72)
Strike rate: (career 95.47)
Parents: Pierre Joseph Ernest
Marital status: Single
Family links with cricket: Father and two brothers play club cricket in Holland
Education: Montessori Lyceum, Rotterdam; Hague Academy of Physiotherapy

Qualifications: Qualified physiotherapist

Career outside cricket: Physiotherapy

Off-season: Working in my private practice and touring South Africa with the Dutch team

Overseas tours: Holland tours to England, Canada, Denmark, New Zealand, Barbados, Zimbabwe, Dubai and South Africa; MCC tour of Leeward Islands 1992

Overseas teams played for: VOC Rotterdam, Flamingos; East Coast Bays Cricket Club, Auckland 1987-89; Woolston Working Men's Club, Christchurch 1990-91; Canterbury 1990-91

Cricketers particularly admired: John Prins, Ton Eldering, Renee Schoonheim

Other sports followed: Most other sports

Injuries: 'Sustained a broken arm when I was kicked by B. Donelan on the MCC tour to the Leeward Islands, missed the first 2 months of the season.'

Relaxations: Playing the piano, music of various kinds, golf, travelling

Extras: More than 80 caps for Holland. Played in 1986 and 1990 ICC Trophy competitions – voted player of tournament 1990; was a member of the Dutch team that beat England (captained by Peter Roebuck) in 1989 and West Indies in 1991. First Dutch player to score a first-class hundred. Moved to Glamorgan for the 1993 season

Opinions on cricket: 'Sunday League cricket should be 40 overs. The increase to 12 Nations for the World Cup is a great move. It enables the stronger countries out of the 2nd group to compete at the highest level and the generation of funds and publicity are of great importance to strengthen their local cricket. The stronger European countries should be allowed to play in the Benson and Hedges competition.'

Best batting: 100 Somerset v Worcestershire, Weston-super-Mare 1991

Best bowling: 6-53 Canterbury v Auckland, Auckland 1990-91

1992 Season

	M	Inns	NO	Runs	HS	Avge	100s	50s	Ct	St	O	M	Runs	Wkts	Avge	Best	5wI	10wM
Test																		
All First	3	4	0	70	36	17.50	-	-	3	-	41	11	96	5	19.20	2-33	-	-
1-day Int																		
NatWest																		
B & H																		
Sunday	8	4	2	3	2 *	1.50	-	-	3	-	50.4	0	262	8	32.75	2-18	-	

Career Performances

	M	Inns	NO	Runs	HS	Avge	100s	50s	Ct	St	Balls	Runs	Wkts	Avge	Best	5wI	10wM
Test																	
All First	43	44	10	715	100	21.02	1	2	20	-	7065	2945	74	39.79	6-53	2	-
1-day Int																	
NatWest	5	2	1	34	21 *	34.00	-	-	1	-	345	150	15	10.00	7-15	1	
B & H	10	7	3	121	37	30.25	-	-	1	-	578	380	9	42.22	3-44	-	
Sunday	33	22	5	196	28	11.52	-	-	11	-	1323	1097	34	32.26	4-35	-	

LENHAM, N. J.   Sussex

Name: Neil John Lenham
Role: Right-hand bat, right-arm medium
bowler
Born: 17 December 1965, Worthing
Height: 5ft 11in **Weight:** 11st
Nickname: Pin
County debut: 1984
County cap: 1990
1000 runs in a season: 3
1st-Class 50s scored: 28
1st-Class 100s scored: 13
1st-Class 200s scored: 1
1st-Class catches: 53
One-Day 50s: 11
Place in batting averages: 88th av. 36.65
(1991 75th av. 36.36)
Parents: Leslie John and Valerie Anne
Marital status: Single
Family links with cricket: Father played
for Sussex

Education: Broadwater Manor Prep School; Brighton College
Qualifications: 5 O-levels, 2 A-levels, N.C.A staff coach
Off-season: Cricket development officer for Eastbourne
Overseas tours: England U19 to West Indies (as captain) in 1985
Overseas teams played for: Port Elizabeth, South Africa 1987-88; Brighton, Tasmania
1989-90
Cricketers particularly admired: Ken McEwan, Ralph Dellor, Barry Richards
Other sports followed: Golf, horse racing, rugby
Relaxations: 'Keeping tropical fish, fly fishing, drinking wine, eating gherkins and golf.'
Extras: Made debut for England YC in 1983. Broke record for number of runs scored in
season at a public school in 1984 (1534 av. 80.74). Youngest player to appear for County
2nd XI at 14 years old. Appointed as Eastbourne's first Cricket Development Officer for
1992
Opinions on cricket: 'Sunday League should be 40 overs. The one bouncer an over law
should be abolished and intimidation of batsmen left to the umpire's discretion.'
Best batting: 222* Sussex v Kent, Hove 1992
Best bowling: 4-85 Sussex v Leicestershire, Leicester 1986

1992 Season

	M	Inns	NO	Runs	HS		Avge	100s	50s	Ct	St	O	M	Runs	Wkts	Avge	Best	5wI	10wM
Test																			
All First	20	34	2	1173	222	*	36.65	4	3	9	-	120.1	28	362	6	60.33	2-61	-	-
1-day Int																			
NatWest	2	1	0	14	14		14.00	-	-	-	-	11.3	3	24	1	24.00	1-24	-	
B & H	3	3	1	26	15	*	13.00	-	-	1	-	3	0	6	0	-		-	-
Sunday	13	10	3	236	81	*	33.71	-	1	1	-	26	0	171	4	42.75	2-41	-	

Career Performances

	M	Inns	NO	Runs	HS		Avge	100s	50s	Ct	St	Balls	Runs	Wkts	Avge	Best	5wI	10wM
Test																		
All First	128	218	21	6467	222	*	32.82	13	28	53	-	2652	1395	29	48.10	4-85	-	-
1-day Int																		
NatWest	8	7	1	210	66		35.00	-	1	-	-	285	157	8	19.62	2-12	-	
B & H	15	15	3	313	82		26.08	-	2	2	-	126	103	3	34.33	1-3	-	
Sunday	61	50	12	1168	86		30.73	-	8	10	-	570	599	20	29.95	2-19	-	

LEWIS, C. C.   Nottinghamshire

Name: Christopher Clairmonte Lewis
Role: Right-hand bat, right-arm fast-medium
bowler
Born: 14 February 1968, Georgetown,
Guyana
Height: 6ft 2^1/$_2$in **Weight:** 13st
Nickname: Carl
County debut: 1987 (Leicestershire)
1992 (Nottinghamshire)
County cap: 1990 (Leicestershire)
1992 (Nottinghamshire)
Test debut: 1990
Tests: 14
One-Day Internationals: 30
50 wickets in a season: 2
1st-Class 50s scored: 15
1st-Class 100s scored: 3
1st-Class 5 w. in innings: 13
1st-Class 10 w. in match: 3
1st-Class catches: 65
One-Day 50s scored: 4
Place in batting averages: 77th av. 38.00 (1991 86th av. 34.50)
Place in bowling averages: 53rd av. 30.81 (1991 24th av. 25.27)

329

Strike rate: 67.30 (career 58.48)
Parents: Philip and Patricia
Marital status: Single
Education: Willesden High School
Qualifications: 2 O-levels
Off-season: Touring India with England
Overseas tours: England YC to Australia for Youth World Cup 1987; England A to Kenya and Zimbabwe 1989-90; England to West Indies 1989-90, to Australia and New Zealand 1990-91, to New Zealand 1991-92
Cricketers particularly admired: Graham Gooch, Robin Smith
Other sports followed: Snooker, football, darts, American football, basketball
Injuries: Suffers from Raynaud's Disease, a problem of blood circulation. Has to spend one night in hospital every two months to have the disease treated.
Relaxations: Music, sleeping
Extras: Joined England's tour of West Indies in 1989-90 as a replacement for Ricky Ellcock. Suffers from Raynaud's Disease which affects his blood circulation. Left Leicestershire at the end of 1991 season and signed for Nottinghamshire. Hit first Test century v India at Madras in 1992-93 tour to India and Sri Lanka
Best batting: 189* Leicestershire v Essex, Chelmsford 1990
Best bowling: 6-22 Leicestershire v Oxford University, The Parks 1988

1992 Season

	M	Inns	NO	Runs	HS	Avge	100s	50s	Ct	St	O	M	Runs	Wkts	Avge	Best	5wI	10wM
Test	5	7	0	114	55	16.28	-	1	4	-	188	40	544	12	45.33	3-43	-	-
All First	17	26	4	836	134 *	38.00	2	5	13	-	594.3	119	1633	53	30.81	6-90	2	1
1-day Int	4	3	2	8	6 *	8.00	-	-	2	-	34	3	155	3	51.66	2-47	-	
NatWest	2	2	0	36	32	18.00	-	-	4	-	22	0	97	2	48.50	1-44	-	
B & H	4	2	0	31	26	15.50	-	-	-	-	41	4	169	9	18.77	5-46	1	
Sunday	9	7	0	172	39	24.57	-	-	1	-	68.2	2	314	5	62.80	3-34	-	

Career Performances

	M	Inns	NO	Runs	HS	Avge	100s	50s	Ct	St	Balls	Runs	Wkts	Avge	Best	5wI	10wM
Test	14	19	1	446	70	24.77	-	3	13	-	3096	1520	42	36.19	6-111	2	-
All First	91	132	17	3282	189 *	28.53	3	15	65	-	15849	7757	271	28.62	6-22	13	3
1-day Int	30	19	4	135	33	9.00	-	-	12	-	1366	1007	33	30.51	4-30	-	
NatWest	11	9	0	175	53	19.44	-	1	8	-	636	381	12	31.75	3-28	-	
B & H	17	14	5	191	28	21.22	-	-	6	-	975	674	24	28.08	5-46	1	
Sunday	61	52	12	1042	93 *	26.05	-	3	16	-	2279	1656	57	29.05	4-13	-	

116. Who won the Texaco Trophy last season between England and Pakistan, and by what margin?

LEWIS, J. J. B. Essex

Name: Jonathan James Benjamin Lewis
Role: Right-hand bat, slow medium net bowler
Born: 21 May 1970, Middlesex
Height: 5ft 9in **Weight:** 11st
Nickname: Scrubby, 'JJ which has become Judgey'
County debut: 1990
1st-Class 50s scored: 7
1st-Class 100s scored: 2
1st-Class catches: 6
Place in batting averages: 38th av. 46.62
Parents: Edward and Regina
Marital status: Single
Education: King Edward VI School, Chelmsford; Roehampton Institute of Higher Education
Qualifications: 5 O-levels, 3 A-levels, BSc (Hons) Sport Science
Off-season: Playing and coaching in Wellington
Overseas teams played for: Old Hararians, Zimbabwe 1991-92
Cricketers particularly admired: Graham Gooch, Greg Matthews, Keith Fletcher, John Childs, Keith Butler
Injuries: Double fracture of finger, out all May
Other sports followed: Football, basketball and women's tennis
Relaxations: 'Many other sports, pubs with real ale.'
Extras: Hit century on first-class debut in Essex's final Championship match of the 1990 season
Opinions on cricket: 'I do not believe close fielders should be prevented from wearing shin pads or helmet for protection, as has been suggested.'
Best batting: 133 Essex v Sussex, Hove 1992

1992 Season

	M	Inns	NO	Runs	HS	Avge	100s	50s	Ct	St	O	M	Runs	Wkts	Avge	Best	5wI	10wM
Test																		
All First	13	20	4	746	133	46.62	1	7	4	-								
1-day Int																		
NatWest	1	1	0	21	21	21.00	-	-	-	-								
B & H																			
Sunday	5	2	0	10	7	5.00	-	-	2	-								

Career Performances

	M	Inns	NO	Runs	HS	Avge	100s	50s	Ct	St	Balls	Runs	Wkts	Avge	Best	5wl	10wM
Test																	
All First	16	23	5	935	133	51.94	2	7	6	-							
1-day Int																	
NatWest	1	1	0	21	21	21.00	-	-	-	-							
B & H																	
Sunday	6	3	0	29	19	9.66	-	-	2	-							

LIGERTWOOD, D. G. C.   Surrey

Name: David George Coutts Ligertwood
Role: Right-hand bat, right arm off spin,
wicket keeper
Born: 16th May 1969, Oxford
Height: 6ft 1in **Weight:** 12st
Nickname: Hippy, Woody, Syph
County debut: 1992
Parents: Andrew and Virginia
Marital status: Single
Children: Charlene, 3rd September 1990
Family links with cricket: Brother plays
for South Australian U17 and Grandmother
is a 'fanatic'
Education: Rose Park Primary School;
Bob Burton's Finishing School; Wootton
School; Magdalen College School, Oxford;
University of Adelaide
Qualifications: Bachelor of Arts, Adelaide
University; road safety certificate
Career outside cricket: Cricket coach,
student, 'punching bag'
Off-season: 'Coming to terms with being released, Playing golf with Ricey, Barry, Nuge
& co, watching Dean Plumb.'
Overseas tours: SPSC tour of England 1986; Adelaide University IV tour of Amsterdam
1990; SACA tour of Granite Island
Overseas teams played for: Adelaide University 1987-92; South Africa 2nd XI 1990-91
Cricketers particularly admired: Ian Rice, Tony Hinton, Greg Chapple, Darren Webber,
Bob Neal, Keith Medlycott, Geoff Tolchard, Tim Pellen
Other sports followed: 'Aussie rules football, golf, picinko, cock fighting'
Injuries: Eye injury
Relaxations: 'Watching Dean Plumb, chilling out, golf, going to Rio's and Lennie's

Tavern, arguing with Charles Mayo, playing with Jules and Joanna.'
Extras: Played for Hertfordshire in the NatWest Trophy in 1991. Released by Surrey at the end of the 1992 season
Best batting: 28 Surrey v Sussex, The Oval 1992

1992 Season

	M	Inns	NO	Runs	HS	Avge	100s	50s	Ct	St	O	M	Runs	Wkts	Avge	Best	5wI	10wM
Test																		
All First	4	7	0	63	28	9.00	-	-	7	1								
1-day Int																		
NatWest																		
B & H																		
Sunday	1	0	0	0	0	-	-	-	-	1								

Career Performances

	M	Inns	NO	Runs	HS	Avge	100s	50s	Ct	St	Balls	Runs	Wkts	Avge	Best	5wI	10wM
Test																	
All First	4	7	0	63	28	9.00	-	-	7	1							
1-day Int																	
NatWest	1	1	1	37	37 *	-	-	-	-	-							
B & H																	
Sunday	1	0	0	0	0	-	-	-	-	1							

LLONG, N. J.   Kent

Name: Nigel James Llong
Role: Left-hand bat, off-spin bowler
Born: 11 February 1969, Ashford, Kent
Height: 6ft **Weight:** 11st 7lbs
Nickname: Nidge, Legend, Rigsby,
County debut: 1991
1st-Class 50s scored: 1
1st-Class catches: 9
Parents: Richard and Peggy (deceased)
Marital status: Single
Family links with cricket: Father and brother played local club cricket
Education: Ashford North Secondary School
Qualifications: 6 CSEs, NCA coaching award
Career outside cricket: Assistant groundsman, barman

Off-season: Player/coach in Cape Town, South Africa
Overseas teams played for: Ashburton, Melbourne 1988-90; Green Point, Cape Town 1990-93
Cricketers particularly admired: John Emburey, David Gower
Other sports followed: Football, tennis, golf
Relaxations: 'Socialising with friends outside cricket, fishing, playing with my two nephews.'
Opinions on cricket: 'The restriction on the size of advertising on players clothing should be lifted to let sponsors get value for money. This would hopefully bring more and bigger sponsors into the game. The money then could be used for projects for the development of young players. I also think the standard of cricket from school to second XI is getting worse due to lack of adequate coaching and playing areas (pitches especially). Also more should be done to help players winter jobs.'
Best batting: 92 Kent v Durham, Gateshead Fell 1992
Best bowling: 3-50 Kent v Cambridge University, Fenner's 1992

1992 Season

	M	Inns	NO	Runs	HS	Avge	100s	50s	Ct	St	O	M	Runs	Wkts	Avge	Best	5wI	10wM
Test																		
All First	4	5	0	137	92	27.40	-	1	4	-	55	7	212	7	30.28	3-50	-	-
1-day Int																		
NatWest	1	1	1	13	13*	-	-	-	-	-	4	0	11	1	11.00	1-11	-	
B & H																		
Sunday	6	5	2	108	44*	36.00	-	-	-	-								

Career Performances

	M	Inns	NO	Runs	HS	Avge	100s	50s	Ct	St	Balls	Runs	Wkts	Avge	Best	5wI	10wM
Test																	
All First	9	12	2	200	92	20.00	-	1	9	-	402	264	7	37.71	3-50	-	-
1-day Int																	
NatWest	1	1	1	13	13*	-	-	-	-	-	24	11	1	11.00	1-11	-	
B & H																	
Sunday	10	9	3	144	44*	24.00	-	-	-	-	36	37	1	37.00	1-20	-	

117. Who is the only player to score a century on his debut for two counties?

LLOYD, G. D.   Lancashire

Name: Graham David Lloyd
Role: Right-hand bat, right-arm medium
bowler
Born: 1 July 1969, Accrington
Height: 5ft 7in **Weight:** 13st
Nickname: Bumble, Geoff, Spamhead,
Nudenut, Slap
County debut: 1988
County cap: 1992
1000 runs in a season: 1
1st-Class 50s scored: 24
1st-Class 100s scored: 7
1st-Class catches: 44
One-Day 50s: 8
One-Day 100s: 1
Place in batting averages: 22nd av. 51.44
(1991 143rd av. 27.63)
Parents: David and Susan
Marital status: Single
Family links with cricket: Father played for Lancashire and England
Education: Hollins County High School, Accrington
Qualifications: 3 O-levels; NCA coaching certificate
Off season: Touring Australia with England A team
Overseas tours: England A to Australia 1992-93
Overseas teams played for: Marochydore C.C., Queensland 1988-89 & 1991-92
Cricketers particularly admired: Gordon Parsons, Nick Speak, David Gower, Grahame
Clinton, Justin Benson, Nigel Briers
Other sports followed: Football (Man Utd), horse racing
Relaxations: 'racing, eating, drinking'
Extras: His school did not play cricket, so he learnt at Accrington CC, playing in the same
team as his father
Best batting: 132 Lancashire v Kent, Old Trafford 1992
Best bowling: 1-57 Lancashire v Yorkshire, Old Trafford 1991

1992 Season

	M	Inns	NO	Runs	HS	Avge	100s	50s	Ct	St	O	M	Runs	Wkts	Avge	Best	5wI	10wM
Test																		
All First	23	37	10	1389	132	51.44	4	10	21	-	7	0	45	0	-	-	-	-
1-day Int																		
NatWest	2	2	0	31	24	15.50	-	-	-	-								
B & H	5	4	1	54	26	18.00	-	-	1	-								
Sunday	15	15	1	266	42 *	19.00	-	-	-	-								

	M	Inns	NO	Runs	HS	Avge	100s	50s	Ct	St	Balls	Runs	Wkts	Avge	Best	5wI	10wM
Test																	
All First	63	101	13	3478	132	39.52	7	24	44	-	151	186	1	186.00	1-57	-	-
1-day Int																	
NatWest	4	4	0	106	39	26.50	-	-	-	-							
B & H	8	7	3	71	26	17.75	-	-	1	-							
Sunday	46	44	7	1255	100 *	33.91	1	8	8	-							

LLOYD, T. A. Warwickshire

Name: Timothy Andrew Lloyd
Role: Left-hand bat, off-spin bowler,
Born: 5 November 1956, Oswestry
Height: 5ft 11in **Weight:** 12st
Nickname: Towser
County debut: 1977
County cap: 1980
Benefit: 1990 (£120,000)
Test debut: 1984
Tests: 1
One-Day Internationals: 3
1000 runs in a season: 9
1st-Class 50s scored: 87
1st-Class 100s scored: 29
1st-Class 200s scored: 1
1st-Class catches: 147
One-Day 50s: 56
One-Day 100s: 2
Place in batting averages: 161st av. 24.83
(1991 98th av. 32.60)
Strike rate: (career 101.43)
Parents: John Romer and Gwen
Wife: Gilly
Children: Georgia, Sophie
Education: Oswestry Boys' High School; Dorset College of Higher Education
Qualifications: O-levels, 2 A-levels, HND Tourism, NCA advanced coach
Career outside cricket: Business entertainment/corporate hospitality executive
Overseas tours: English Counties XI to Zimbabwe 1984-85
Overseas teams played for: Orange Free State 1978-80
Cricketers particularly admired: Allan Border, Dennis Amiss
Other sports followed: 'Most sports, but particularly racing.'

Relaxations: 'Enjoying my home, drinking good wine and beer, eating various cuisines. Also greyhounds, playing golf and walking.'
Extras: Played for Shropshire and Warwickshire 2nd XI in 1975. Captain of Warwickshire between 1988 and 1992. Was Gladstone Small's best man
Opinions on cricket: 'After-match arrangements at some grounds must be looked into more closely. Hygiene and refreshment seem low on some counties' list of priorities.'
Best batting: 208* Warwickshire v Gloucestershire, Edgbaston 1983
Best bowling: 3-7 Warwickshire v Middlesex, Lord's 1992

1992 Season

	M	Inns	NO	Runs	HS	Avge	100s	50s	Ct	St	O	M	Runs	Wkts	Avge	Best	5wI	10wM
Test																		
All First	23	39	2	919	84 *	24.83	-	5	5	-	68.5	8	295	6	49.16	3-7	-	-
1-day Int																		
NatWest	4	4	0	99	40	24.75	-	-	4	-								
B & H	4	4	0	144	61	36.00	-	2	-	-								
Sunday	15	14	1	387	71	29.76	-	4	1	-	5	0	37	2	18.50	2-37	-	

Career Performances

	M	Inns	NO	Runs	HS	Avge	100s	50s	Ct	St	Balls	Runs	Wkts	Avge	Best	5wI	10wM
Test	1	1	1	10	10 *	-	-	-	-	-							
All First	312	547	45	17211	208 *	34.28	29	87	147	-	2333	1682	23	73.13	3-7	-	-
1-day Int	3	3	0	101	49	33.66	-	-	-	-							
NatWest	37	35	3	1276	121	39.87	1	11	13	-	54	47	2	23.50	1-4	-	
B & H	56	53	3	1602	137 *	32.04	1	10	14	-	90	76	0	-	-	-	-
Sunday	183	173	19	4508	90	29.27	-	35	35	-	169	186	3	62.00	2-37	-	

118. Who did Zimbabwe play in their first ever official Test in 1992?

LONGLEY, J. I. Kent

Name: Jonathan Ian Longley
Role: Right-hand bat
Born: 12 April 1969, New Brunswick, USA
Height: 5ft 8in **Weight:** 11st 10lbs
County debut: 1989
1st-Class 100s: 1
1st-Class catches: 4
One-Day 50s: 3
Parents: Dick and Helen
Marital status: Single
Education: Tonbridge School; Durham
University
Qualifications: 9 O-levels, 3 A-levels,
BA Sociology
Off season: 'Relaxing on a beach in the
sun and playing a bit of cricket in Cape
Town – hopefully seeing many other parts
of Africa as well.'
Overseas teams played for:
Prospect District C.C., Adelaide 1991-92;
Green Point, Cape Town 1992-93
Cricketers particularly admired: Robin Smith, Gordon Greenidge, Allan Border
Other sports followed: Rugby, golf, squash, tennis
Relaxations: 'Love listening to music (Bob Dylan, Van Morrison and the Rolling Stones).
Also love old English pubs, Australian beaches and socialising with friends and family.'
Extras: Member of the Combined Universities team which reached the quarter-finals of
the B&H Cup in 1989
Opinions on cricket: 'Cannot understand why no Kent player was selected for a tour with
an England tour 1992-93 or why the ban on the rebels was lifted.'
Best batting: 110 Kent v Cambridge University, Fenner's 1992

1992 Season

	M	Inns	NO	Runs	HS	Avge	100s	50s	Ct	St	O	M	Runs	Wkts	Avge	Best	5wl	10wM
Test																		
All First	3	4	0	169	110	42.25	1	-	4	-								
1-day Int																		
NatWest																			
B & H	3	3	0	76	57	25.33	-	1	-	-								
Sunday	3	3	1	73	71	36.50	-	1	-	-								

	M	Inns	NO	Runs	HS	Avge	100s	50s	Ct	St	Balls	Runs	Wkts	Avge	Best	5wl	10wM
Test																	
All First	7	12	0	211	110	17.58	1	-	4	-							
1-day Int																	
NatWest																	
B & H	16	16	1	286	57	19.06	-	1	1	-							
Sunday	8	8	1	170	71	24.28	-	2	2	-							

LOYE, M. B. Northamptonshire

Name: Malachy Bernard Loye
Role: Right-hand bat, right-arm off-spin bowler
Born: 27 September 1972, Northampton
Height: 6ft 2in **Weight:** 12st 6lbs
Nickname: Mal, Space Man
County debut: 1991
1st-Class catches: 8
Place in batting averages: 223rd av. 15.00
Parents: Patrick and Anne
Marital status: Single
Family links with cricket: Father and brother both play for Cogenhoe
Education: Moulton Comprehensive School
Qualifications: GCSEs and coaching certificate
Off season: Playing cricket in Christchurch New Zealand
Overseas tours:
England U18 to international tournament in Canada 1991; U19 tour to Pakistan 1992
Cricketers particularly admired: Gordon Greenidge, Wayne Larkins
Other sports followed: Football, golf and basketball
Relaxations: Listening to music, reading thrillers and comical novels
Extras: Played for England U19 in the home series against Australia 1991 and against Sri Lanka 1992
Opinions on cricket: 'I disagree with the introduction of 50 overs per side in the Sunday League because the 40 over game attracts a different kind of spectator and was a success from a financial point of view. A 50 over game may risk alienating a certain kind of supporter from watching Sunday League. Tea should be extended by 10 minutes.'
Best batting: 46 Northamptonshire v Durham, Stockton 1992

1992 Season

	M	Inns	NO	Runs	HS	Avge	100s	50s	Ct	St	O	M	Runs	Wkts	Avge	Best	5wI	10wM
Test																		
All First	10	14	1	195	46	15.00	-	-	7	-								
1-day Int																		
NatWest																		
B & H																		
Sunday	2	1	1	27	27 *	-	-	-	1	-								

Career Performances

	M	Inns	NO	Runs	HS	Avge	100s	50s	Ct	St	Balls	Runs	Wkts	Avge	Best	5wI	10wM
Test																	
All First	11	15	2	198	46	15.23	-	-	8	-							
1-day Int																	
NatWest																	
B & H																	
Sunday	2	1	1	27	27 *	-	-	-	1	-							

LYNCH, M. A.   Surrey

Name: Monte Allan Lynch
Role: Right-hand bat, right-arm medium and off-spin bowler
Born: 21 May 1958, Georgetown, Guyana
Height: 5ft 8in **Weight:** 12st
Nickname: Mont
County debut: 1977
County cap: 1982
Benefit: 1991 (£107,000)
One-Day Internationals: 3
1000 runs in a season: 9
1st-Class 50s scored: 74
1st-Class 100s scored: 34
1st-Class catches: 289
One-Day 50s: 37
One-Day 100s: 5
Place in batting averages:
52nd av. 43.08 (1991 185th av. 21.37)
Parents: Lawrence and Doreen Austin
Marital status: Single
Family links with cricket: 'Father and most of family played at some time or another.'
Education: Ryden's School, Walton-on-Thames

Off season: Coaching and playing in Argentina
Overseas tours: West Indies XI to South Africa 1983-84
Overseas teams played for: Guyana 1982-83
Other sports followed: Football, table tennis
Extras: Hitting 141* for Surrey v Glamorgan at Guildford in August 1982, off 78 balls in 88 minutes, one six hit his captain Roger Knight's car. Joined West Indies Rebels in South Africa 1983-84, although qualified for England. Appeared in all three One-Day Internationals v West Indies 1988
Best batting: 172* Surrey v Kent, The Oval 1989
Best bowling: 3-6 Surrey v Glamorgan, Swansea 1981

1992 Season

	M	Inns	NO	Runs	HS	Avge	100s	50s	Ct	St	O	M	Runs	Wkts	Avge	Best	5wI	10wM
Test																		
All First	23	40	6	1465	107	43.08	3	8	24	-	21	4	85	1	85.00	1-16	-	-
1-day Int																		
NatWest	1	1	0	27	27	27.00	-	-	1	-	5	0	28	2	14.00	2-28	-	
B & H	7	7	0	282	105	40.28	1	2	5	-	4	1	13	0	-		-	-
Sunday	15	14	1	279	58	21.46	-	1	2	-	2	0	16	0	-		-	-

Career Performances

	M	Inns	NO	Runs	HS	Avge	100s	50s	Ct	St	Balls	Runs	Wkts	Avge	Best	5wI	10wM
Test																	
All First	300	483	58	15377	172 *	36.18	34	74	289	-	2117	1360	26	52.30	3-6	-	-
1-day Int	3	3	0	8	6	2.66	-	-	1	-							
NatWest	34	30	4	749	129	28.80	1	3	15	-	228	136	4	34.00	2-28	-	
B & H	56	51	3	1310	112 *	27.29	2	7	25	-	132	121	0	-		-	-
Sunday	191	177	25	4450	136	29.27	2	27	59	-	129	168	7	24.00	2-2	-	

119. Which current Test player's first name is Athanasios?

MACLEAY, K. H. Somerset

Name: Kenneth Harvey Macleay
Role: Right-hand bat, right-arm medium bowler
Born: 2 April 1959, Bradford-on-Avon, Wiltshire
Height: 6ft 4in **Weight:** 14st
Nickname: Rip, Freddie
County debut: 1991
One-Day Internationals: 16
1st-Class 50s scored: 19
1st-Class 100s scored: 3
1st-Class 5 w. in innings: 6
1st-Class catches: 79
Place in batting averages: 143rd av. 276.68 (1991 139th av. 27.80)
Place in bowling averages: (1991 83rd av. 34.88)
Strike rate: (career 73.74)
Parents: Donald and Felicity
Wife and date of marriage: Elizabeth, 1987
Family links with cricket: Father played for Devon and Combined Services
Education: Scotch College; University of Western Australia, Perth
Career outside cricket: Accountant
Off-season: as above
Overseas tours: Australia to England (World Cup) 1984
Overseas teams played for: Western Australia 1981-91
Cricketers particularly admired: Allan Border, Dennis Lillee, David Gower, Ian Botham
Other sports followed: Keen follower of most major sporting events, 'especially those involving England and Australia'
Injuries: Broken finger, inter-costal muscle strain
Relaxations: Water sports – particularly windsurfing, fishing, swimming, travelling
Extras: Released by Somerset at the end of the 1992 season
Opinions on cricket: 'County cricket should not be drastically altered solely on the basis of the national team's performance.'
Best batting: 114* Western Australia v New South Wales, Perth 1986-87
Best bowling: 6-93 Western Australia v New South Wales, Perth 1985-86

1992 Season

	M	Inns	NO	Runs	HS	Avge	100s	50s	Ct	St	O	M	Runs	Wkts	Avge	Best	5wl	10wM
Test																		
All First	12	19	3	427	74	26.68	-	3	7	-	115	28	311	9	34.55	2-33	-	-
1-day Int																		
NatWest	2	1	0	8	8	8.00	-	-	2	-	19	2	79	1	79.00	1-49	-	
B & H	6	6	0	112	43	18.66	-	-	4	-	34	1	116	0	-	-	-	-
Sunday	16	11	3	166	40 *	20.75	-	-	6	-	104.3	2	411	23	17.87	5-20	1	

Career Performances

	M	Inns	NO	Runs	HS	Avge	100s	50s	Ct	St	Balls	Runs	Wkts	Avge	Best	5wl	10wM
Test																	
All First	129	173	34	3750	114 *	26.97	3	19	79	-	22122	9080	300	30.26	6-93	6	-
1-day Int	16	13	2	139	41	12.63	-	-	2	-	857	626	15	41.73	6-39	1	
NatWest	4	2	1	33	25 *	33.00	-	-	3	-	258	146	4	36.50	2-35	-	
B & H	6	6	0	112	43	18.66	-	-	4	-	204	116	0	-	-	-	
Sunday	25	19	6	222	40 *	17.07	-	-	9	-	1005	663	32	20.71	5-20	1	

MADDY, D. L.   Leicestershire

Name: Darren Lee Maddy
Role: Right-hand bat, right-arm medium
bowler
Born: 23 May 1974, Leicester
Height: 5ft 8in
Nickname: Dazza
County debut: No first team appearance
Parents: Bill and Hilary
Marital status: Single
Family links with cricket: Father played
club cricket
Education: Herrick Junior School,
Leicester; Roundhills, Thurmaston;
Wreake Valley, Syston
Qualifications: 8 GCSEs
Off-season: Playing in South Africa
Overseas teams played for: Wanderers,
Johannesburg 1992-93
Other sports followed:
Rugby (Leicester Tigers)
Extras: Given two-year contract by Leicestershire in 1992. Had back trouble in 1991
which turned him from an all-rounder to a specialist batsman.

MAHER, B. J. M.   Derbyshire

Name: Bernard Joseph Michael Maher
Role: Right-hand bat, wicket keeper
Born: 11 February 1958, Hillingdon, Middlesex
Height: 5ft 9½in **Weight:** 13st
Nickname: B.J.
County debut: 1981
County cap: 1987
1st-Class 50s scored: 17
1st-Class 100s scored: 4
1st-Class catches: 280
1st-Class stumpings: 14
Parents: Francis Joseph and Mary Anne
Marital status: Single
Family links with cricket: Brother kept wicket for school
Education: St. Bernadette's RC Primary; Abbotsfield Comprehensive; Bishopshalt GS; Harrow College; Loughborough University
Qualifications: 3 A-Levels, 10 O-Levels,

Association of Certified Accountants Examinations, BSc (Hons) accountancy/economics
Career outside cricket: 'Accountant and also deal in promotional work and sales for a company in New Zealand.'
Off-season: 'Coaching in Dunedin for Tairi CC and Otago Cricket Association. Also Coaching Otago B side and working in sales for a financial services company.'
Overseas tours: Middlesex Cricket League to West Indies 1978; Loughborough University to Amsterdam 1981
Overseas teams played for: Zingari, Pietermaritzburg, South Africa 1982-84; Ellerslie, Aukland 198-85; Kamo and Northern Districts B 1985-88; Tairi, Dunedin, New Zealand 1989-92; Otago B, New Zealand 1992-93
Cricketers particularly admired: Allan Border, Gordon Greenidge, Richard Hadlee and Malcolm Marshall
Other sports followed: Rugby, boxing, athletics
Relaxations: 'I'm a very keen fly fisherman, fishing for trout and salmon in and around Derbyshire, Scotland and also fish all over the South Island in New Zealand. Unfortunately I'm only able to fish about three times a week. I also do a lot of hill walking in Cumbria and in North Wales.'
Opinions on cricket: 'A transfer system should operate allowing players to be bought and sold on an open market. This will allow players not receiving benefits but having been good county pro's to earn money and will make scouting and coaching of young players more wide spread and intense simply because of their possible earning potential to clubs through transfer fees. There should be a total reversal of the rules allowing players that have been

born and bred overseas to play as English Nationals. It is time Oxford and Cambridge lost their First Class status in matches they play.'
Best batting: 126 Derbyshire v New Zealand, Derby 1986
Best bowling: 2-69 Derbyshire v Glamorgan, Abergavenny 1986

1992 Season (did not make any first-class or one-day appearance)

Career Performances

	M	Inns	NO	Runs	HS	Avge	100s	50s	Ct	St	Balls	Runs	Wkts	Avge	Best	5wl	10wM
Test																	
All First	128	200	35	3667	126	22.22	4	17	280	14	270	234	4	58.50	2-69	-	-
1-day Int																	
NatWest	9	9	1	99	44	12.37	-	-	17	-							
B & H	20	13	2	256	50	23.27	-	1	25	1							
Sunday	74	63	13	776	78	15.52	-	1	58	10							

MALCOLM, D. E. Derbyshire

Name: Devon Eugene Malcolm
Role: Right-hand bat, right-arm fast bowler
Born: 22 February 1963, Kingston, Jamaica
Height: 6ft 2in **Weight:** 15st 6lbs
Nickname: Dude
County debut: 1984
County cap: 1989
Test debut: 1989
Tests: 21
One-Day Internationals: 4
50 wickets in a season: 2
1st-Class 50s scored: 1
1st-Class 5 w. in innings: 10
1st-Class 10 w. in innings: 1
1st-Class catches: 25
Place in batting averages: 261st av. 10.00
Place in bowling averages: 95th av. 36.62
(1991 84th av. 34.54)
Strike rate: 60.15 (career 55.19)
Parents: Albert and Brendalee (deceased)
Wife and date of marriage: Jennifer, October 1989
Education: St Elizabeth Technical High School; Richmond College; Derby College of Higher Education
Qualifications: College certificates, O-levels, coaching certificate

Off-season: Touring with England to India and Sri Lanka
Overseas tours: England to West Indies 1989-90, to Australia 1990-91, to India and Sri Lanka 1992-93; England A to Bermuda and West Indies 1991-92
Overseas teams played for: Ellerslie, Auckland 1985-87
Cricketers particularly admired: Michael Holding, Richard Hadlee
Other sports followed: Football, boxing
Relaxations: Music and movies
Extras: Became eligible to play for England in 1987. Played league cricket for Sheffield Works and Sheffield United. Took 10 for 137 v West Indies in Port of Spain Test, 1989-90
Best batting: 51 Derbyshire v Surrey, Derby 1989
Best bowling: 7-74 England XI v Australian XI, Hobart 1990-91

1992 Season

	M	Inns	NO	Runs	HS	Avge	100s	50s	Ct	St	O	M	Runs	Wkts	Avge	Best	5wI	10wM
Test	3	5	0	6	4	1.20	-	-	1	-	102.5	14	380	13	29.23	5-94	1	-
All First	19	19	4	150	26	10.00	-	-	6	-	451.1	64	1648	45	36.62	5-45	2	-
1-day Int																		
NatWest	2	1	1	10	10 *	-	-	-	-	-	21	1	68	4	17.00	2-29	-	
B & H	4	2	0	10	8	5.00	-	-	-	-	37	1	192	5	38.40	4-43	-	
Sunday	8	2	1	3	3 *	3.00	-	-	-	-	56.4	0	339	9	37.66	3-52	-	

Career Performances

	M	Inns	NO	Runs	HS	Avge	100s	50s	Ct	St	Balls	Runs	Wkts	Avge	Best	5wI	10wM
Test	21	29	8	105	15 *	5.00	-	-	3	-	4821	2673	74	36.12	6-77	4	1
All First	130	143	39	826	51	7.94	-	1	25	-	21746	12500	394	31.72	7-74	10	1
1-day Int	4	2	1	7	4	7.00	-	-	-	-	234	171	6	28.50	2-19	-	
NatWest	9	7	1	21	10 *	3.50	-	-	-	-	576	358	13	27.53	3-54	-	
B & H	16	9	2	52	15	7.42	-	-	-	-	918	623	22	28.31	5-27	1	
Sunday	33	14	5	66	18	7.33	-	-	4	-	1432	1281	44	29.11	4-21	-	

MALLENDER, N. A.   Somerset

Name: Neil Alan Mallender
Role: Right-hand bat, right-arm fast-medium bowler
Born: 13 August 1961, Kirk Sandall, nr Doncaster
Height: 6ft **Weight:** 13st
Nickname: Ghostie
County debut: 1980 (Northants), 1987 (Somerset)
County cap: 1984 (Northants), 1987 (Somerset)
Tests: 2
50 wickets in a season: 6

1st-Class 50s scored: 9
1st-Class 100s scored: 1
1st-Class 5 w. in innings: 33
1st-Class 10 w. in match: 5
1st-Class catches: 103
Place in batting averages: 242nd av. 11.87
(1991 236th av. 13.50)
Place in bowling averages: 11th av. 23.30
(1991 12th av. 23.07)
Strike rate: 49.97 (career 58.66)
Parents: Ron and Jean
Wife and date of marriage:
Caroline, 1 October 1984
Children: Kirstie Jane, 18 May 1988;
Dominic James 21 September 1991
Family links with cricket: Brother Graham
used to play good representative cricket
before joining the RAF
Education: Beverley Grammar School,
East Yorkshire
Qualifications: 7 O-levels, NCA Preliminary Coaching Course
Off-season: Playing and coaching in Otago in New Zealand
Overseas tours: England YC to West Indies 1980
Overseas teams played for: Otago, New Zealand 1983-92; Kalkorai, New Zealand 1983-92
Cricketers particularly admired: Richard Hadlee, Dennis Lillee, Peter Willey, Andy Hayhurst
Other sports followed: Golf, rugby league, football, American football
Injuries: Groin, abductor strain – out for July and August
Relaxations: Golf and watching TV
Extras: Joined Somerset in 1987. Equalled Somerset record for 9th wicket v Sussex at Hove in 1990 – batting with Chris Tavare. Called up to join England tour squad in New Zealand 1991-92 as cover for injured fast bowlers. On debut for England v Pakistan in 1992 at Headingley achieved a new bowling record for Test debutant at that ground by taking 8 wickets in the game. At school opened both the batting and the bowling.
Opinions on cricket: 'Still believe that new ball should be available to be taken after 85 overs in first class cricket (as in Test cricket).'
Best batting: 100 Otago v Central Districts, Palmerston North 1991-92
Best bowling: 7-27 Otago v Auckland, Auckland 1984-85

120. On what ground was Zimbabwe's first Test played?

1992 Season

	M	Inns	NO	Runs	HS	Avge	100s	50s	Ct	St	O	M	Runs	Wkts	Avge	Best	5wl	10wM
Test	2	3	0	8	4	2.66	-	-	-	-	74.5	20	215	10	21.50	5-50	1	-
All First	17	21	5	190	29 *	11.87	-	-	3	-	436.3	94	1282	55	23.30	5-29	4	-
1-day Int																		
NatWest	2	1	0	1	1	1.00	-	-	-	-	24	4	79	1	79.00	1-47	-	
B & H	6	5	2	33	14 *	11.00	-	-	1	-	63	10	259	10	25.90	4-49	-	
Sunday	14	6	4	57	19 *	28.50	-	-	3	-	90.2	4	352	11	32.00	3-16	-	

Career Performances

	M	Inns	NO	Runs	HS	Avge	100s	50s	Ct	St	Balls	Runs	Wkts	Avge	Best	5wl	10wM
Test	2	3	0	8	4	2.66	-	-	-	-	449	215	10	21.50	5-50	1	-
All First	307	343	107	3868	100 *	16.39	1	9	103	-	47929	22368	842	26.56	7-27	33	5
1-day Int																	
NatWest	24	10	3	44	11 *	6.28	-	-	5	-	1510	710	36	19.72	7-37	1	
B & H	53	25	10	91	16 *	6.06	-	-	14	-	2967	1845	64	28.82	5-53	1	
Sunday	154	68	37	419	24	13.51	-	-	28	-	6183	4532	165	27.46	5-34	1	

MARSH, S. A.   Kent

Name: Steven Andrew Marsh
Role: Right-hand bat, wicket-keeper, county vice-captain
Born: 27 January 1961, Westminster
Height: 5ft 11in **Weight:** 12st
County debut: 1982
County cap: 1986
Nickname: Marshy
1st-Class 50s scored: 30
1st-Class 100s scored: 6
1st-Class catches: 368
1st-Class stumpings: 31
One-Day 50s scored: 5
Place in batting averages: 102nd av. 34.46
(1991 89th av. 33.70)
Parents: Melvyn Graham and Valerie Ann
Wife and date of marriage:
Julie, 27 September 1986
Children: Hayley Ann, 15 May 1987;
Christian 20 November 1990
Family links with cricket: Father played local cricket for Lordswood. Father-in-law, Bob Wilson, played for Kent 1954-66

Education: Walderslade Secondary School for Boys; Mid-Kent College of Higher and Further Education
Qualifications: 6 O-levels, 2 A-levels, OND in Business Studies
Off-season: 'Working computer operator/accounts clerk for my car sponsor, Swale Motor Co., Sittingbourne.'
Cricketers particularly admired: Robin Smith, Graham Cowdrey, Matthew Fleming
Other sports followed: 'All sport except synchronised swimming.'
Injuries: Infection in right foot – out for two weeks
Extras: Appointed Kent vice-captain in 1991. Equalled world record eight catches in an innings v Middlesex 1991 and scored 113* in the same match
Best batting: 125 Kent v Yorkshire, Canterbury 1992
Best bowling: 2-20 Kent v Warwickshire, Edgbaston 1990

1992 Season

	M	Inns	NO	Runs	HS	Avge	100s	50s	Ct	St	O	M	Runs	Wkts	Avge	Best	5wl	10wM
Test																		
All First	22	30	4	896	125	34.46	1	6	44	8	8	0	126	0	-	-	-	-
1-day Int																		
NatWest	3	3	0	30	13	10.00	-	-	1	1								
B & H	7	7	1	62	26	10.33	-	-	8	-								
Sunday	14	11	1	210	36 *	21.00	-	-	14	4								

Career Performances

	M	Inns	NO	Runs	HS	Avge	100s	50s	Ct	St	Balls	Runs	Wkts	Avge	Best	5wl	10wM
Test																	
All First	172	240	45	5492	125	28.16	6	30	368	31	154	227	2	113.50	2-20	-	-
1-day Int																	
NatWest	13	8	1	76	24 *	10.85	-	-	18	2							
B & H	37	28	6	359	71	16.31	-	1	44	2							
Sunday	103	76	15	1157	59	18.96	-	4	99	14							

121. Which current Test player has played for two countries, and was born in neither?

MARSHALL, M. D.   Hampshire

Name: Malcolm Denzil Marshall
Role: Right-hand bat, right-arm fast bowler
Born: 18 April 1958, Barbados
Height: 5ft 10¹/₂in **Weight:** 12st 8lbs
Nickname: Macko
County debut: 1979
County cap: 1981
Benefit: 1987 (£61,006)
Test debut: 1978-79
Tests: 81
One-Day Internationals: 136
50 wickets in a season: 9
1st-Class 50s scored: 49
1st-Class 100s scored: 6
1st-Class 5 w. in innings: 83
1st-Class 10 w. in match: 13
1st-Class catches: 131
One-Day 50s: 4
Place in batting averages: 155th av. 25.65
(1991 182nd av. 21.77)
Place in bowling averages: 33rd av. 27.51 (1991 29th av. 26.06)
Strike rate: 64.77 (career 43.72)
Parents: Mrs Eleanor Inniss
Children: Shelly, 24 November 1984
Family links with cricket: Cousin Errol Yearwood plays for Texaco in Barbados as a fast bowler
Education: St Giles Boys' School; Parkinson Comprehensive School, Barbados
Qualifications: School passes in Maths and English
Career outside cricket: Working for Banks Brewery
Off-season: Playing for Natal, South Africa
Overseas tours: Young West Indies to Zimbabwe 1981-82; West Indies to India and Sri Lanka 1978-79, to Australia and New Zealand 1979-80, to England 1980, to Pakistan 1980-81, to Australia 1981-82, to India 1983-84, to England 1984, to Australia 1984-85, to Pakistan and New Zealand 1986-87, to England 1988, to Australia 1988-89, to Pakistan 1990-91, to England 1991, to Pakistan and Australia 1991-92
Overseas teams played for: Barbados 1977-91; Natal 1992-93
Cricketers particularly admired: Wes Hall, Gary Sobers, Viv Richards, Graham Gooch
Other sports followed: Tennis, golf
Relaxations: Soul music, reggae, golf, road tennis, lawn tennis
Extras: Took nine wickets in debut match v Glamorgan in May 1979. Scored his first first-class century (109) in Zimbabwe, October 1981. Became the leading West Indies Test wicket-taker when he overtook Lance Gibbs's total of 309. Broke record for number of

wickets taken in a 22-match English season (i.e. since 1969) with 133. Published autobiography *Marshall Arts* (1987). Nearly chose to become a wicket-keeper. 'Even now I wish sometimes I was in Jeff Dujon's place behind the stumps.' One of *Wisden's* Five Cricketers of the Year, 1982. After considering retirement, he signed a new three-year contract with Hampshire in 1990. Retired from International cricket after the 1991-92 World Cup

Opinions on cricket: 'Cricket has been my life since I could stand upright and hold a cricket bat or at least our home-made apology, built from anything that looked like one. I played morning, noon and night every day of my life. Not even school could get in the way of my obsession with the game. There was no question of playing football, or anything else, for very long. It was cricket, cricket and more cricket.'

Best batting: 117 Hampshire v Yorkshire, Headingley 1990
Best bowling: 8-71 Hampshire v Worcestershire, Southampton 1982

1992 Season

	M	Inns	NO	Runs	HS	Avge	100s	50s	Ct	St	O	M	Runs	Wkts	Avge	Best	5wI	10wM
Test																		
All First	19	25	5	513	70	25.65	-	2	11	-	529	134	1348	49	27.51	6-58	1	-
1-day Int																		
NatWest	2	1	0	7	7	7.00	-	-	1	-	24	3	69	2	34.50	2-43	-	
B & H	7	3	1	34	29 *	17.00	-	-	-	-	61	15	180	12	15.00	4-20	-	
Sunday	15	11	3	115	23 *	14.37	-	-	6	-	112	3	453	17	26.64	2-19	-	

Career Performances

	M	Inns	NO	Runs	HS	Avge	100s	50s	Ct	St	Balls	Runs	Wkts	Avge	Best	5wI	10wM
Test	81	107	11	1810	92	18.85	-	10	25	-	17585	7876	376	20.94	7-22	22	4
All First	366	464	62	9863	117	24.53	6	49	131	-	66634	28511	1524	18.70	8-71	83	13
1-day Int	136	83	19	955	66	14.92	-	2	15	-	7175	4233	157	26.96	4-18	-	
NatWest	29	20	8	317	77	26.41	-	2	3	-	1829	831	36	23.08	4-15	-	
B & H	38	28	2	374	34	14.38	-	-	6	-	2107	1042	49	21.26	4-20	-	
Sunday	133	89	22	1235	46	18.43	-	-	27	-	5889	3539	145	24.40	5-13	2	

122. Which England Test cricketer had a gap of 17 years between Tests?

MARTIN, P. J.   Lancashire

Name: Peter James Martin
Role: Right-hand bat, right-arm fast-medium bowler
Born: 15 November 1968, Accrington
Height: 6ft 5in **Weight:** 15st 7lbs
Nickname: Digger, Chinny
County debut: 1989
1st-Class 50s: 2
1st-Class 100s: 1
1st-Class catches: 15
Place in batting averages: 133rd av. 27.33
Place in bowling averages: 110th av. 40.27
(1991 99th av. 36.75)
Strike rate: 84.37 (career 80.84)
Parents: Keith and Catherine Lina
Marital status: Single
Education: Danum School, Doncaster
Qualifications: 6 O-levels, 2 A-levels
Overseas tours: England YC to Australia
for Youth World Cup, 1988 and various other
tours with Schools and NAYC
Overseas teams played for: Southern Districts, Queensland 1988-89; South Launceston, Tasmania 1989-90; South Canberra, ACT 1990-92
Cricketers particularly admired: Richard Hadlee, Ian Botham, Dennis Lillee
Other sports followed: Soccer, golf
Injuries: Back spasm, missed one First Class game
Relaxations: Music, eating, golf
Extras: Played district football and basketball for Doncaster. Played for England A v Sri Lanka 1991
Opinions on cricket: 'Alter over rate fines.'
Best batting: 133 Lancashire v Durham, Gateshead Fell 1992
Best bowling: 4-30 Lancashire v Worcestershire, Blackpool 1991

1992 Season

	M	Inns	NO	Runs	HS	Avge	100s	50s	Ct	St	O	M	Runs	Wkts	Avge	Best	5wI	10wM
Test																		
All First	22	24	6	492	133	27.33	1	2	4	-	520.2	129	1490	37	40.27	4-45	-	-
1-day Int																		
NatWest	1	0	0	0	0	-	-	-	1	-	9	1	26	2	13.00	2-26	-	
B & H																		
Sunday	8	3	2	34	18 *	34.00	-	-	2	-	52	0	243	7	34.71	2-17	-	

Career Performances

	M	Inns	NO	Runs	HS	Avge	100s	50s	Ct	St	Balls	Runs	Wkts	Avge	Best	5wI	10wM
Test																	
All First	50	46	17	641	133	22.10	1	2	15	-	7761	3814	96	39.72	4-30	-	-
1-day Int																	
NatWest	4	0	0	0	0	-	-	-	1	-	174	98	4	24.50	2-19	-	
B & H																	
Sunday	16	3	2	34	18 *	34.00	-	-	4	-	630	496	10	49.60	2-17	-	

MARU, R. J. Hampshire

Name: Rajesh Jamnadass Maru
Role: Right-hand bat, slow left-arm bowler, close fielder
Born: 28 October 1962, Nairobi
Height: 5ft 6in **Weight:** 11st
Nickname: Raj
County debut: 1980 (Middlesex), 1984 (Hampshire)
County cap: 1986 (Hampshire)
50 wickets in a season: 4
1st-Class 50s scored: 6
1st-Class 5 w. in innings: 15
1st-Class 10 w. in match: 1
1st-Class catches: 210
Place in batting averages: 225th av. 14.87 (1991 210th av. 17.04)
Place in bowling averages: 24th av. 26.11 (1991 114th av. 41.02)
Strike rate: 72.11 (career 72.67)
Parents: Jamnadass and Prabhavati
Wife and date of marriage: Amanda Jane, 21 September 1991
Family links with cricket: Father played in Kenya and in England for North London Polytechnic. Brother Pradip plays for Wembley in the Middlesex League and has played a couple of games for Middlesex 2nd XI
Education: Rooks Heath High; Pinner Sixth Form College
Qualifications: NCA advanced coach
Career outside cricket: Cricket coach
Off-season: Coaching for Hampshire CCC
Overseas tours: England YC South to Canada 1979; England YC to West Indies 1979-80; Middlesex to Zimbabwe 1980; Hampshire to Barbados 1987,1988,1990; Hampshire to Dubai 1989; Barbican International XI to Dubai 1981; MCC to Leeward Islands 1992

Overseas teams played for: Marlborough CA, Blenheim, New Zealand 1985-87
Cricketers particularly admired: David Gower, Bishen Bedi, Jimmy Cook, Richard Hadlee, Phil Edmonds, Mike Gatting, John Emburey
Other sports followed: Badminton, table tennis, squash, football, rugby – 'would watch any sport'
Injuries: Knee Injury, 'missed one or two games, but finished the season, with some pain'
Relaxations: Music, reading, DIY at home
Extras: Played for Middlesex 1980-83
Best batting: 74 Hampshire v Gloucestershire, Gloucester 1988
Best bowling: 8-41 Hampshire v Kent, Southampton 1989

1992 Season

	M	Inns	NO	Runs	HS	Avge	100s	50s	Ct	St	O	M	Runs	Wkts	Avge	Best	5wl	10wM
Test																		
All First	8	11	3	119	27	14.87	-	-	9	-	204.2	75	444	17	26.11	4-8	-	-
1-day Int																		
NatWest	2	1	0	4	4	4.00	-	-	2	-	24	1	100	0	-	-	-	
B & H	6	1	0	4	4	4.00	-	-	4	-	55.3	9	181	5	36.20	1-19	-	
Sunday	7	4	2	12	8 *	6.00	-	-	5	-	52	0	253	6	42.16	2-30	-	

Career Performances

	M	Inns	NO	Runs	HS	Avge	100s	50s	Ct	St	Balls	Runs	Wkts	Avge	Best	5wl	10wM
Test																	
All First	200	190	46	2353	74	16.34	-	6	210	-	34810	15538	479	32.43	8-41	15	1
1-day Int																	
NatWest	13	5	2	43	22	14.33	-	-	11	-	822	492	12	41.00	3-46	-	
B & H	10	2	0	13	9	6.50	-	-	5	-	495	330	9	36.66	3-46	-	
Sunday	45	19	10	122	33 *	13.55	-	-	18	-	1446	1218	32	38.06	3-30	-	

123. Who played Test cricket for 30 years?

124. Who was England's youngest Test cricketer?

MAYNARD, M. P.   Glamorgan

Name: Matthew Peter Maynard
Role: Right-hand bat, right-arm medium
'declaration' bowler, cover fielder
Born: 21 March 1966, Oldham, Lancashire
Height: 5ft 10¹/₂in **Weight:** 12st 10lbs
Nickname: Action, The Kid, Susie
County debut: 1985
County cap: 1987
Test debut: 1988
Tests: 1
1000 runs in a season: 7
1st-Class 50s scored: 65
1st-Class 100s scored: 26
1st-Class 200s scored: 2
1st-Class catches: 168
1st-Class stumpings: 2
One-Day 50s: 25
One-Day 100s: 6
Place in batting averages: 75th av. 38.09
(1991 11th av. 60.10)
Parents: Ken (deceased) and Pat
Wife and date of marriage: Susan, 27 September 1986
Children: Tom, 25 March 1989
Family links with cricket: Father played for many years for Duckinfield. Brother Charlie
plays for St Fagans
Education: Ysgol David Hughes, Anglesey
Qualifications: Cricket coach
Career outside cricket: Marketing for Glamorgan CCC
Off-season: As above and training
Overseas tours: North Wales XI to Barbados 1982; Glamorgan to Barbados, to South
Africa; Unofficial England XI to South Africa 1989-90
Overseas teams played for: St Joseph's, Whakatane, New Zealand 1986-88; Gosnells,
Perth, Western Australia 1988-89; Papakura and Northern Districts, New Zealand 1990-
92; Morrinsville College and Northern Districts 1991-92
Cricketers particularly admired: Ian Botham, Barry Richards
Other sports followed: 'Most'
Relaxations: 'Spending time with my wife, trying to control my son and playing golf.'
Extras: Scored century on debut v Yorkshire at Swansea. Youngest centurion for
Glamorgan and scored 1000 runs in first full season. Fastest ever 50 for Glamorgan (14
mins) v Yorkshire and youngest player to be awarded Glamorgan cap. Voted Young
Cricketer of the Year 1988 by the Cricket Writers Club. Banned from Test cricket for 5
years joining tour of South Africa, 1989-90, ban was remitted in 1992. Scored 987 runs in

July 1991 including a century in each innings against Gloucestershire at Cheltenham. Captained Glamorgan for most of 1992 in Alan Butcher's absence
Opinions on cricket: 'The new law concerning the number of bouncers per over is ludicrous. Four-day cricket is a must.'
Best batting: 243 Glamorgan v Hampshire, Southampton 1991
Best bowling: 3-21 Glamorgan v Oxford University, The Parks 1987

1992 Season

	M	Inns	NO	Runs	HS	Avge	100s	50s	Ct	St	O	M	Runs	Wkts	Avge	Best	5wI	10wM
Test																		
All First	23	36	4	1219	176	38.09	2	7	19	-	7	0	72	1	72.00	1-3	-	-
1-day Int																		
NatWest	3	3	0	188	87	62.66	-	2	1	-								
B & H	4	4	0	60	32	15.00	-	-	3	-								
Sunday	16	15	1	650	122 *	46.42	1	4	8	-	0.4	0	2	0	-		-	-

Career Performances

	M	Inns	NO	Runs	HS	Avge	100s	50s	Ct	St	Balls	Runs	Wkts	Avge	Best	5wI	10wM
Test	1	2	0	13	10	6.50	-	-	-	-							
All First	193	315	36	11805	243	42.31	26	65	168	2	774	566	5	113.20	3-21	-	-
1-day Int																	
NatWest	18	18	2	698	151 *	43.62	1	5	3	-							
B & H	28	28	3	900	115	36.00	2	4	7	-	24	32	0	-		-	-
Sunday	105	101	6	2749	122 *	28.93	3	16	31	-	16	27	0	-		-	-

McCAGUE, M. J. Kent

Name: Martin John McCague
Role: Right-hand bat, right-arm fast bowler
Born: 24 May 1969, Larne, Northern Ireland
Height: 6ft 6in **Weight:** 15st 10lbs
Nickname: Stinger, Oz
County debut: 1991
County cap: 1992
50 wickets in season : 1
1st-Class 5 w. in innings : 7
1st-Class 10 w. in match : 1
1st-Class catches: 4
Place in bowling averages: 29th av. 26.98 (1991 51st av. 30.06)
Strike rate: 51.77 (career 56.56)
Parents: Mal and Mary
Marital status: Single

Education: Hedland Senior High School; Carine Tafe College, Australia
Qualifications: Electrician
Career outside cricket: Electrician
Off-season: Playing in Perth, W. Australia
Overseas teams played for:
Western Australia 1990-92
Cricketers particularly admired:
Dennis Lillee, Bob Massie
Other sports followed: Australian Rules football, basketball
Injuries: Bruised heel, out for 1 week
Relaxations: Snooker, cards, TV/video
Extras: Took 5-105 on his first-class debut for Western Australia v Victoria 1990-91. 'As a British citizen and Australian resident Kent can have other overseas players as well as myself.' His 8-26 v Kent were the best bowling figures of 1992 season

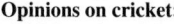

Opinions on cricket:
'With four-day cricket now, isn't an increase in overs and run ups in Sunday League asking a bit much? 40 overs was fine.'
Best batting: 29 Kent v Leicestershire, Leicester 1991
Best bowling: 8-26 Kent v Hampshire, Canterbury 1992

1992 Season

	M	Inns	NO	Runs	HS	Avge	100s	50s	Ct	St	O	M	Runs	Wkts	Avge	Best	5wI	10wM
Test																		
All First	16	18	5	120	25 *	9.23	-	-	12	-	457.2	86	1430	53	26.98	8-26	5	1
1-day Int																		
NatWest	3	3	2	21	14	21.00	-	-	-	-	26	0	104	6	17.33	2-16	-	
B & H	7	6	3	71	30	23.66	-	-	1	-	53.2	0	210	15	14.00	5-43	1	
Sunday	14	8	3	55	22 *	11.00	-	-	1	-	83.2	0	458	27	16.96	4-35	-	

Career Performances

	M	Inns	NO	Runs	HS	Avge	100s	50s	Ct	St	Balls	Runs	Wkts	Avge	Best	5wI	10wM
Test																	
All First	35	41	10	386	34	12.45	-	-	20	-	5713	2997	101	29.67	8-26	7	1
1-day Int																	
NatWest	4	4	2	30	14	15.00	-	-	-	-	198	151	6	25.16	2-16	-	
B & H	9	7	3	83	30	20.75	-	-	1	-	428	295	19	15.52	5-43	1	
Sunday	22	13	5	94	22 *	11.75	-	-	2	-	854	807	38	21.23	4-35	-	

McEWAN, S. M.   Durham

Name: Steven Michael McEwan
Role: Right-hand bat, right-arm fast-medium
bowler
Born: 5 May 1962, Worcester
Height: 6ft 1in **Weight:** 13st 7lbs
Nickname: IG, Macca
County debut: 1985 (Worcestershire),
1992 (Durham)
County cap: 1989 (Worcestershire)
50 wickets in a season: 1
1st-Class 50s scored: 1
1st-Class 5 w. in innings: 3
1st-Class catches: 24
Place in bowling averages: 128th av. 47.05
Strike rate: 80.82 (career 57.87)
Parents: Michael James and Valerie Jeanette
Wife and date of marriage:
Debbie, 30 September 1989
Family links with cricket: Father and uncle
played club cricket
Education: Worcester Royal Grammar School
Qualifications: 6 O-levels, 3 A-levels. Technician's certificate in building
Cricketers particularly admired: Richard Hadlee, Malcolm Marshall
Other sports followed: American football
Relaxations: Reading, golf, skittles, watching films
Extras: Took 10 wickets for 13 runs in an innings in 1983 for Worcester Nomads against
Moreton-in-Marsh. Also broke school bowling record, 60 wickets, at Worcester RGS,
1982. Took hat-trick for Worcestershire v Leicestershire at Leicester, 1990. Released by
Worcestershire at the end of the 1991 season and signed for Durham
Opinions on cricket: 'Second team games should be played on first-class grounds. It
seems every year a new rule is introduced which is detrimental towards the bowler. It is
probably only a matter of time before limited run-ups and the use of a tennis ball instead
of a cricket ball.'
Best batting: 54 Worcestershire v Yorkshire, Worcester 1990
Best bowling: 6-39 Worcestershire v Leicestershire, Kidderminster 1989

---

125. Who captained Zimbabwe in their first Test?

1992 Season

	M	Inns	NO	Runs	HS	Avge	100s	50s	Ct	St	O	M	Runs	Wkts	Avge	Best	5wI	10wM
Test																		
All First	10	13	1	59	22	4.91	-	-	7	-	229	44	800	17	47.05	3-52	-	-
1-day Int																		
NatWest	2	1	1	34	34 *	-	-	-	-	-	24	2	86	5	17.20	4-41	-	
B & H	4	4	3	51	29 *	51.00	-	-	-	-	36	3	154	5	30.80	3-45	-	
Sunday	14	7	4	40	18	13.33	-	-	4	-	80	4	435	11	39.54	3-27	-	

Career Performances

	M	Inns	NO	Runs	HS	Avge	100s	50s	Ct	St	Balls	Runs	Wkts	Avge	Best	5wI	10wM
Test																	
All First	65	48	17	407	54	13.12	-	1	24	-	9028	4869	156	31.21	6-39	3	-
1-day Int																	
NatWest	4	2	1	40	34 *	40.00	-	-	-	-	228	152	8	19.00	4-41	-	
B & H	5	4	3	51	29 *	51.00	-	-	-	-	282	207	7	29.57	3-45	-	
Sunday	54	18	11	86	18 *	12.28	-	-	12	-	1852	1668	50	33.36	4-35	-	

MENDIS, G. D.   Lancashire

Name: Gehan Dixon Mendis
Role: Right-hand opening bat
Born: 24 April 1955, Colombo, Ceylon
Height: 5ft 8in **Weight:** 11st
Nickname: Mendo, Dix
County debut: 1974 (Sussex), 1986 (Lancs)
County cap: 1980 (Sussex), 1986 (Lancs)
Benefit: 1993
1000 runs in a season: 12
1st-Class 50s scored: 101
1st-Class 100s scored: 40
1st-Class 200s scored: 3
1st-Class catches: 140
1st-Class stumpings: 1
One-Day 50s: 40
One-Day 100s: 8
Place in batting averages:
181st av. 20.71 (1991 73rd av. 36.68)
Parents: Sam Dixon Charles and Sonia
Marcelle (both deceased)
Wife: Gilly
Children: Hayley, 11 December 1982; Josh, 26 November 1989; Barnaby Joe, 15

February 1992

Education: St Thomas College, Mount Lavinia, Sri Lanka; Brighton, Hove & Sussex Grammar School; Bede College, Durham University

Qualifications: BEd Mathematics, Durham; NCA coaching certificate

Off-season: Organising benefit year

Cricketers particularly admired: Barry Richards, Richard Hadlee

Other sports followed: Formula One motor racing

Injuries: Multiple fracture of index finger on right hand restricted appearances to five first-class matches

Relaxations: Music, 'getting away from cricket.'

Extras: Turned down invitations to play for Sri Lanka in order to be free to be chosen for England. Left Sussex at end of 1985 to join Lancashire. Played table tennis for Sussex at junior level

Opinions on cricket: 'None, any more, as cricketers have not much say in the running of the game. Sign of old age, I guess!'

Best batting: 209* Sussex v Somerset, Hove 1984

Best bowling: 1-65 Sussex v Yorkshire, Hove 1985

1992 Season

	M	Inns	NO	Runs	HS	Avge	100s	50s	Ct	St	O	M	Runs	Wkts	Avge	Best	5wI	10wM
Test																		
All First	5	8	1	145	45	20.71	-	-	-	-								
1-day Int																		
NatWest																		
B & H	4	4	0	106	51	26.50	-	1	1	-								
Sunday																		

Career Performances

	M	Inns	NO	Runs	HS	Avge	100s	50s	Ct	St	Balls	Runs	Wkts	Avge	Best	5wI	10wM
Test																	
All First	348	609	61	20337	209 *	37.11	40	101	140	1	177	158	1	158.00	1-65	-	-
1-day Int																	
NatWest	40	40	4	1414	141 *	39.27	3	8	8	-							
B & H	72	72	3	2084	125 *	30.20	2	9	24	-							
Sunday	185	180	15	4625	125 *	28.03	3	23	48	-							

126. Who is the oldest cricketer to have played for Australia?

METCALFE, A. A. Yorkshire

Name: Ashley Anthony Metcalfe
Role: Right-hand opening bat, off-spin
bowler, county vice-captain
Born: 25 December 1963, Horsforth, Leeds
Height: 5ft 9½in **Weight:** 11st 7lbs
County debut: 1983
County cap: 1986
1000 runs in a season: 6
1st-Class 50s scored: 48
1st-Class 100s scored: 23
1st-Class 200s scored: 1
1st-Class catches: 66
One-Day 50s: 32
One-Day 100s: 4
Place in batting averages: 147th av. 26.37
(1991 119th av. 29.51)
Parents: Tony and Ann
Wife and date of marriage:
Diane, 20 April 1986

Children: Zoe, 18 July 1990
Family links with cricket: Father played in local league; father-in-law Ray Illingworth
(Yorkshire and England)
Education: Ladderbanks Middle School; Bradford Grammar School; University College,
London
Qualifications: 9 O-levels, 3 A-levels, NCA coaching certificate
Career outside cricket: 'Metcalfe & Sidebottom Associates – Sports Promotion
Company.'
Overseas teams played for: Orange Free State 1988-89
Cricketers particularly admired: Barry Richards, Doug Padgett, Don Wilson, Arnie
Sidebottom, Pete Hartley, Paul Jarvis
Other sports followed: Most, particularly golf
Relaxations: 'Relaxing at home with my family.'
Extras: Made 122 on debut v Nottinghamshire at Park Avenue in 1983, the youngest ever
Yorkshire player to do so and it was the highest ever score by a Yorkshireman on debut.
Reached 2000 runs for the season in the last match of the 1990 season with 194* and 107
v Nottinghamshire at Trent Bridge
Best batting: 216* Yorkshire v Middlesex, Headingley 1988
Best bowling: 2-18 Yorkshire v Warwickshire, Scarborough 1987

1992 Season

	M	Inns	NO	Runs	HS	Avge	100s	50s	Ct	St	O	M	Runs	Wkts	Avge	Best	5wI	10wM
Test																		
All First	11	17	1	422	73	26.37	-	1	4	-								
1-day Int																		
NatWest																		
B & H	4	4	0	79	29	19.75	-	-	1	-								
Sunday	6	6	0	123	43	20.50	-	-	1	-								

Career Performances

	M	Inns	NO	Runs	HS	Avge	100s	50s	Ct	St	Balls	Runs	Wkts	Avge	Best	5wI	10wM
Test																	
All First	177	307	18	10163	216 *	35.16	23	48	66	-	392	316	4	79.00	2-18	-	-
1-day Int																	
NatWest	16	16	3	592	127 *	45.53	1	4	3	-	42	44	2	22.00	2-44	-	
B & H	31	31	4	1277	114	47.29	1	8	8	-							
Sunday	115	114	2	3067	116	27.38	2	20	28	-							

METSON, C. P. Glamorgan

Name: Colin Peter Metson
Role: Right-hand bat, wicket-keeper
Born: 2 July 1963, Cuffley, Herts
Height: 5ft 6in **Weight:** 10st 10lbs
Nickname: Meto, Dempster
County debut: 1981 (Middlesex),
1987 (Glamorgan)
County cap: 1987 (Glamorgan)
1st-Class 50s scored: 6
1st-Class catches: 387
1st-Class stumpings: 30
Place in batting averages: 192nd av. 19.86
(1991 168th av. 23.60)
Parents: Denis Alwyn and Jean Mary
Wife and date of marriage:
Stephanie Leslie Astrid,
13 October 1991
Family links with cricket: Father captained
Winchmore Hill CC
Education: Stanborough School, Welwyn
Garden City; Enfield Grammar School;
Durham University

Qualifications: 10 O-levels, 5 A-levels, BA (Hons) Economic History, advanced cricket coach
Career outside cricket: Project co-ordinator with Allied Steel and Wire
Off-season: As above
Overseas teams played for: Payneham, Adelaide 1986-88; Rostrevor Old Boys, Adelaide 1987-88
Cricketers particularly admired: Bob Taylor, Mike Brearley, Robert Croft
Other sports followed: Football, golf, most sports except wrestling
Relaxations: Watching sport, videos, good wine, port
Extras: Young Wicket-keeper of the Year 1981. Played for England YC v India 1981. Captain Durham University 1984, losing finalists in UAU competition. Left Middlesex at end of 1986 season. Holds the Glamorgan record for most catches in an innings (7)
Opinions on cricket: 'Cricket must find ways to market itself better, and must give the sponsors value for money. Sundays should remain at 40 overs. Less one-day cricket, more emphasis on the importance of Test cricket.'
Best batting: 96 Middlesex v Gloucestershire, Uxbridge 1984

1992 Season

	M	Inns	NO	Runs	HS	Avge	100s	50s	Ct	St	O	M	Runs	Wkts	Avge	Best	5wI	10wM
Test																		
All First	23	28	6	437	46 *	19.86	-	-	49	5	1	1	0	0	-	-	-	-
1-day Int																		
NatWest	3	3	1	22	21	11.00	-	-	5	1								
B & H	4	3	1	27	14	13.50	-	-	3	-								
Sunday	15	7	4	63	15 *	21.00	-	-	12	6								

Career Performances

	M	Inns	NO	Runs	HS	Avge	100s	50s	Ct	St	Balls	Runs	Wkts	Avge	Best	5wI	10wM
Test																	
All First	166	212	46	3001	96	18.07	-	6	387	30	6	0	0	-	-	-	-
1-day Int																	
NatWest	16	9	2	50	21	7.14	-	-	16	1							
B & H	24	16	2	151	23	10.78	-	-	13	2							
Sunday	102	63	32	514	30 *	16.58	-	-	89	27							

127. Who is the oldest cricketer to have played for England?

MIDDLETON, T. C.   Hampshire

Name: Tony Charles Middleton
Role: Right-hand bat, slow left-arm bowler
Born: 1 February 1964, Winchester
Height: 5ft 10in **Weight:** 11st
Nickname: Dogun
County debut: 1984
County cap: 1990
1000 runs in a season: 2
1st-Class 50s scored: 18
1st-Class 100s scored: 12
1st-Class 200s scored: 1
1st-Class catches: 56
One-Day 50s: 12
Place in batting averages: 27th av. 49.44
(1991 117th av. 29.79)
Parents: Peter and Molly
Wife and date of marriage:
Sherralyn, 23 September 1989
Family links with cricket: Brother plays

local club cricket
Education: Weeke Infants and Junior Schools; Montgomery of Alamein Comprehensive;
Peter Symonds Sixth Form College, Winchester
Qualifications: 1 A-level, 5 O-levels
Off-season: Touring with England A
Overseas tours: Hampshire to Barbados 1989; England A to Australia 1992-93
Overseas teams played for: SA Police, Durban, South Africa 1984-86; Belmont, New-
castle, NSW, Australia 1987-89
Cricketers particularly admired: Barry Richards, Gordon Greenidge, 'I was particularly
helped by Neville Rodgers and Tim Tremlett'
Other sports followed: Football, rugby union, badminton, squash
Relaxations: Watching sport, gardening, real ale pubs, holidays
Extras: Played for England Schools 1982. Scored six consecutive 100s for Hampshire in
May 1990: 104 & 144 v Somerset II; 121 v Yorkshire II; 100 & 124 v Leics II; 104* for
1st XI v Essex. Scored 78 in NatWest final 1991, his first appearance in the competition.
Was first batsman to 1000 first-class runs in 1992
Opinions on cricket: 'Four-day cricket is a good experiment and hopefully will produce
better games of cricket.'
Best batting: 221 Hampshire v Surrey, Southampton 1992
Best bowling: 2-41 Hampshire v Kent, Canterbury 1991

1992 Season

	M	Inns	NO	Runs	HS	Avge	100s	50s	Ct	St	O	M	Runs	Wkts	Avge	Best	5wI	10wM
Test																		
All First	24	40	4	1780	221	49.44	6	7	16	-	10	0	57	0	-		-	-
1-day Int																		
NatWest	2	2	0	81	43	40.50	-	-	-	-								
B & H	6	6	0	184	65	30.66	-	1	-	-								
Sunday	12	12	2	592	98	59.20	-	6	7	-								

Career Performances

	M	Inns	NO	Runs	HS	Avge	100s	50s	Ct	St	Balls	Runs	Wkts	Avge	Best	5wI	10wM
Test																	
All First	78	130	13	4522	221	38.65	12	18	56	-	234	237	5	47.40	2-41	-	-
1-day Int																	
NatWest	3	3	0	159	78	53.00	-	1	-	-							
B & H	10	10	0	340	65	34.00	-	3	3	-							
Sunday	21	20	3	830	98	48.82	-	8	9	-							

MIKE, G. W.   Nottinghamshire

Name: Gregory Wentworth Mike
Role: Right-hand bat, right-arm medium-fast bowler
Born: 14 July 1966, Nottingham
Height: 6ft 1in **Weight:** 15st
Nickname: Wenters
County debut: 1989
1st-Class 50s scored: 2
1st-Class catches: 6
Place in bowling averages: 56th av. 31.40
Strike rate: 54.20 (career 76.57)
Parents: Clinton and Kathleen
Marital status: Single
Family links with cricket: Father played
Education: Claremont Comprehensive; Basford College
Qualifications: 5 CSEs, 2 O-levels
Career outside cricket: Youth worker
Off-season: Playing cricket in New Zealand
Overseas tours: Nottinghamshire to Barbados 1987, 1988, 1991
Overseas teams played for: Geelong City, Australia 1989-90; Lancaster Park, New Zealand 1992-93

Cricketers particularly admired: Viv Richards, Ian Botham, Richard Hadlee
Other sports followed: All sports
Injuries: Ankle, missed the whole of 1991 season and two months of 1992
Relaxations: Listening to music (swing beat, soul, reggae and dance music)
Opinions on cricket: 'I think that all captains should be more positive in their approach to winning games.'
Best batting: 61* Nottinghamshire v Warwickshire, Edgbaston 1992
Best bowling: 3-48 Nottinghamshire v Warwickshire, Edgbaston 1992

1992 Season

	M	Inns	NO	Runs	HS	Avge	100s	50s	Ct	St	O	M	Runs	Wkts	Avge	Best	5wl	10wM
Test																		
All First	5	6	2	130	61 *	32.50	-	1	2	-	90.2	17	314	10	31.40	3-48	-	-
1-day Int																		
NatWest																		
B & H																		
Sunday	7	5	1	59	26 *	14.75	-	-	-	-	44.2	1	229	5	45.80	1-18	-	

Career Performances

	M	Inns	NO	Runs	HS	Avge	100s	50s	Ct	St	Balls	Runs	Wkts	Avge	Best	5wl	10wM
Test																	
All First	10	13	4	246	61 *	27.33	-	2	6	-	1072	684	14	48.85	3-48	-	-
1-day Int																	
NatWest																	
B & H																	
Sunday	20	12	2	111	26 *	11.10	-	-	3	-	707	683	20	34.15	3-30	-	

128. Who is the oldest cricketer to have played for India?

129. Who is the oldest cricketer to have played for New Zealand?

MILBURN, S. M. Yorkshire

Name: Stuart Mark Milburn
Role: Right-hand bat, right-arm medium-fast bowler
Born: 29 September 1972, Harrogate
Height: 6ft 1in **Weight:** 12st 6lbs
Nickname: Millers
County debut: 1992
Parents: Ken and Pam
Marital status: Single
Education: Upper Nidderdale High School, Pateley Bridge, Harrogate
Qualifications: 7 GCSEs, Diploma in Catering
Off-season: Playing in South Africa
Overseas teams played for:
Somerset West, South Africa 1992-93
Cricketers particularly admired:
Ian Botham, Richard Hadlee
Other sports followed: Football and snooker
Injuries: Hip and side, missed second half of season with broken ankle
Relaxations: Playing golf and pool
Opinions on cricket: 'I would like to see pitches prepared to give batsmen and bowlers an equal chance, which should give results without having to resort to artificial declarations.'
Best batting: 5 Yorkshire v Worcestershire, Worcester 1992
Best bowling: 1-54 Yorkshire v Worcestershire, Worcester 1992

1992 Season

	M	Inns	NO	Runs	HS	Avge	100s	50s	Ct	St	O	M	Runs	Wkts	Avge	Best	5wI	10wM
Test																		
All First	1	2	1	7	5	7.00	-	-	-	-	28	2	115	1	115.00	1-54	-	-
1-day Int																		
NatWest																		
B & H																		
Sunday																		

	M	Inns	NO	Runs	HS	Avge	100s	50s	Ct	St	Balls	Runs	Wkts	Avge	Best	5wI	10wM
Test																	
All First	1	2	1	7	5	7.00	-	-	-	-	168	115	1	115.00	1-54	-	-
1-day Int																	
NatWest																	
B & H																	
Sunday																	

MILLNS, D. J. Leicestershire

Name: David James Millns
Role: Left-hand bat, right-arm fast bowler, slip fielder
Born: 27 February 1965, Mansfield
Height: 6ft 3in **Weight:** 14st 7lbs
Nickname: Rocket Man
County debut: 1988 (Notts), 1990 (Leics)
County cap: 1991
50 wickets in a season: 2
1st-Class 5 w. in innings: 11
1st-Class 10 w. in match: 2
1st-Class catches: 30
Place in batting averages: 229th av. 14.40 (1991 198th av. 19.12)
Place in bowling averages: 5th av. 20.62 (1991 56th av. 31.06)
Strike rate: 38.17 (career 46.91)
Parents: Bernard and Brenda
Marital status: Engaged to Wanda

Family links with cricket: Nottinghamshire's Andy Pick is brother-in-law. Great Uncle Richard played against the Australians for Saskatoon University, Canada in 1932 and bowled Don Bradman. Grandfather had ten brothers who all played in the same chapel team. Father played in club cricket and Notts Over 50s. Brother Paul plays for Clipstone CC
Education: Samuel Barlow Junior; Garibaldi Comprehensive
Qualifications: 9 CSEs; qualified coach
Career outside cricket: 'Yet to be decided'
Off-season: Touring with England A
Overseas tours: England A to Australia 1992-93
Overseas teams played for: Uitenhage, Port Elizabeth, South Africa 1988-89; Birkenhead, Auckland 1989-91

Cricketers particularly admired: Ian Botham, Derek Underwood, Alan Knott, Rob Sears
Other sports followed: Football, American football, Formula One motor racing, golf, rugby (Leicester Tigers)
Injuries: Displaced joint in left foot, out for five weeks
Relaxations: Music, films
Extras: Asked to be released by Nottinghamshire at the end of 1989 season and joined Leicestershire in 1990. Finished third in national bowling averages in 1990. Britannic Assurance Player of the Month in August 1991 after taking 9-37 against Derbyshire, the best Leicestershire figures since George Geary's 10-18 against Glamorgan in 1929. Players' representative on Cricketers' Association Executive for Leicestershire. Britannic Assurance Player of the Month (July)
Opinions on cricket: 'I am looking forward to the new season and hope that all the changes in the game's structure work. If only the over rate were to be reduced to 17 per hour the quality of cricket in general would be improved.'
Best batting: 44 Leicestershire v Middlesex, Uxbridge 1991
Best bowling: 9-37 Leicestershire v Derbyshire, Derby 1991

1992 Season

	M	Inns	NO	Runs	HS	Avge	100s	50s	Ct	St	O	M	Runs	Wkts	Avge	Best	5wI	10wM
Test																		
All First	19	19	9	144	33 *	14.40	-	-	12	-	470.5	107	1526	74	20.62	6-87	6	1
1-day Int																		
NatWest	3	1	1	29	29 *	-	-	-	2	-	28	3	94	6	15.66	3-22	-	
B & H	5	3	3	9	6 *	-	-	-	-	-	45	4	207	12	17.25	4-51	-	
Sunday	4	4	3	17	11 *	17.00	-	-	1	-	29	0	178	2	89.00	1-30	-	

Career Performances

	M	Inns	NO	Runs	HS	Avge	100s	50s	Ct	St	Balls	Runs	Wkts	Avge	Best	5wI	10wM
Test																	
All First	63	68	28	509	44	12.72	-	-	30	-	9148	5227	195	26.80	9-37	11	2
1-day Int																	
NatWest	5	1	1	29	29 *	-	-	-	2	-	294	181	8	22.62	3-22	-	
B & H	8	4	4	20	11 *	-	-	-	1	-	408	308	13	23.69	4-51	-	
Sunday	26	13	7	76	20 *	12.66	-	-	7	-	984	896	19	47.15	2-20	-	

130. Who is the oldest cricketer to have played for Pakistan?

MOLES, A. J.   Warwickshire

Name: Andrew James Moles
Role: Right-hand opening bat, right-arm medium bowler
Born: 12 February 1961, Solihull
Height: 5ft 10in **Weight:** 'Above average'
Nickname: Moler
County debut: 1986
County cap: 1987
1000 runs in a season: 5
1st-Class 50s scored: 62
1st-Class 100s scored: 22
1st-Class 200s scored: 3
1st-Class catches: 117
One-Day 50s: 25
One-Day 100s: 1
Place in batting averages: 92nd av. 35.76 (1991 90th av. 33.67)
Parents: Stuart Francis and Gillian Margaret
Wife and date of marriage: Jacquie, 17 December 1988
Children: Daniel
Family links with cricket: Brother plays club cricket
Education: Finham Park Comprehensive, Coventry; Henley College of Further Education; Butts College of Further Education
Qualifications: 3 O-levels, 4 CSEs, Toolmaker/Standard Room Inspector City & Guilds
Career outside cricket: Host, and sells corporate hospitality
Off-season: Coaching and playing in Argentina
Overseas teams played for: Griqualand West, South Africa 1986-88
Cricketers particularly admired: Dennis Amiss, Fred Gardner, Tom Moody
Other sports followed: Football, golf
Relaxations: Playing golf and spending time with family
Best batting: 230* Griqualand West v Northern Transvaal B, Verwoerdburg 1988-89
Best bowling: 3-21 Warwickshire v Oxford University, The Parks 1987

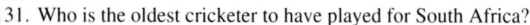

131. Who is the oldest cricketer to have played for South Africa?

1992 Season

	M	Inns	NO	Runs	HS	Avge	100s	50s	Ct	St	O	M	Runs	Wkts	Avge	Best	5wI	10wM
Test																		
All First	23	41	3	1359	122	35.76	1	12	18	-	43	8	169	2	84.50	1-16	-	-
1-day Int																		
NatWest	4	4	0	127	76	31.75	-	1	-	-								
B & H	4	4	0	37	15	9.25	-	-	2	-	15	1	54	1	54.00	1-17	-	
Sunday	17	17	1	534	96 *	33.37	-	5	4	-	7.2	0	33	0	-		-	-

Career Performances

	M	Inns	NO	Runs	HS	Avge	100s	50s	Ct	St	Balls	Runs	Wkts	Avge	Best	5wI	10wM
Test																	
All First	164	295	31	10814	230 *	40.96	22	62	117	-	3270	1763	36	48.97	3-21	-	-
1-day Int																	
NatWest	21	21	1	633	127	31.65	1	4	4	-	90	81	0	-		-	-
B & H	24	23	0	631	72	27.43	-	7	7	-	300	224	4	56.00	1-11	-	
Sunday	70	66	4	1776	96 *	28.64	-	14	19	-	446	415	7	59.28	2-24	-	

MONTGOMERIE, R. R.   Northamptonshire

Name: Richard Robert Montgomerie
Role: Right-hand opening bat, right-arm off-spin bowler
Born: 3 July 1971, Rugby
Height: 5ft 10½in **Weight:** 12st
County debut: 1991
1st-Class 50s scored: 5
1st-Class 100s scored: 1
1st-Class catches: 12
Place in batting averages: 66th av. 39.75 (1991 133rd av. 28.09)
Parents: Robert and Gillian
Marital status: Single
Family links with cricket: Father captained Oxfordshire
Education: Rugby School; Worcester College, Oxford University
Qualifications: 12 O-levels, 4 A-levels
Overseas tours: Oxford University to Namibia 1991

Cricketers particularly admired: Mick Norman, David Gower, Allan Lamb, Allan Border, Graham Gooch 'and many others'

Other sports followed: All sports, particularly hockey, rackets and real tennis
Relaxations: Playing sports – hockey, rackets, real tennis, squash, tennis etc
Extras: Scored 50s (both not out) in both innings of 1991 Varsity match. Oxford rackets blue 1990
Opinions on cricket: 'I think the introduction of the one bouncer per over per batsman rule is an odd decision. There is too much cricket during the county season. Inevitably players will not perform to the high standards that should be expected of them if they play nearly every day for 4¹/₂ months.'
Best batting: 103* Oxford University v Middlesex, The Parks 1992

1992 Season

	M	Inns	NO	Runs	HS	Avge	100s	50s	Ct	St	O	M	Runs	Wkts	Avge	Best	5wI	10wM
Test																		
All First	9	15	3	477	103 *	39.75	1	1	3	-	10	2	31	0	-	-	-	-
1-day Int																		
NatWest																		
B & H	4	4	0	157	75	39.25	-	1	-	-								
Sunday																		

Career Performances

	M	Inns	NO	Runs	HS	Avge	100s	50s	Ct	St	Balls	Runs	Wkts	Avge	Best	5wI	10wM
Test																	
All First	18	28	5	786	103 *	34.17	1	5	12	-	60	31	0	-	-	-	-
1-day Int																	
NatWest																	
B & H	4	4	0	157	75	39.25	-	1	-	-							
Sunday																	

132. Who is the oldest cricketer to have played for Sri Lanka?

MOODY, T. M.   Worcestershire

Name: Thomas Masson Moody
Role: Right-hand bat, right-arm medium bowler
Born: 2 October 1965, Adelaide
Height: 6ft 6in **Weight:** 16st
Nickname: Moods
County debut: 1990 (Warwicks)
1991 (Worcestershire)
County cap: 1990 (Warwicks)
1991 (Worcestershire)
Test debut: 1989-90
Tests: 5
One-Day Internationals: 31
1000 runs in a season: 2
1st-Class 50s scored: 39
1st-Class 100s scored: 31
1st-Class 200s scored: 2
1st-Class 5 w. in innings: 1
1st-Class 10 w. in match: 1
1st-Class catches: 102
One-Day 50s: 28

One-Day 100s: 6
Place in batting averages: 55th av. 42.58 (1991 9th av. 62.90)
Parents: John and Janet
Marital status: Single
Family links with cricket: Father played A Grade cricket
Education: Guildford Grammar School, Western Australia
Career outside cricket: Multiplex
Off-season: Playing cricket in Australia
Overseas tours: Australia to India/Pakistan (World Cup) 1987, to England 1989, to India 1989-90, to Sri Lanka 1992
Overseas teams played for: Western Australia 1985-93
Cricketers particularly admired: Dennis Lillee, Viv Richards, Allan Border
Other sports followed: Aussie Rules, football, golf, tennis
Injuries: Back and ankle
Relaxations: Golf and films
Extras: Scored 150s in both innings of 1988-89 Sheffield Shield Final for Western Australia v Queensland; hit a century against Warwickshire during Australia's 1989 tour – signed on a one-year contract for 1990. Hit centuries in first three first-class matches for Warwickshire, and seven in first eight matches – a unique achievement. Scored the fastest ever first-class century v Glamorgan in 26 minutes – taking advantage of deliberate declaration bowling. Reached 1000 first-class runs in first season of county cricket in only

12 innings – another record. Released by Warwickshire at the end of the 1990 season after they had chosen Allan Donald as their one overseas player. Signed by Worcestershire for 1991 when Graeme Hick was no longer considered an overseas player. Not resigned for 1993 season because he is expected to be touring with the Australian team

Opinions on cricket: 'Play too much of it'
Best batting: 210 Worcestershire v Warwickshire, Worcester 1991
Best bowling: 7-43 Western Australia v Victoria, Perth 1990-91

1992 Season

	M	Inns	NO	Runs	HS		Avge	100s	50s	Ct	St	O	M	Runs	Wkts	Avge	Best	5wI	10wM
Test																			
All First	11	19	2	724	178		42.58	4	1	12	-	72	13	249	8	31.12	4-50	-	-
1-day Int																			
NatWest																			
B & H	5	5	1	252	80		63.00	-	3	2	-	25	4	93	5	18.60	4-59	-	
Sunday	11	11	1	469	80	*	46.90	-	6	3	-	29	0	127	4	31.75	2-33	-	

Career Performances

	M	Inns	NO	Runs	HS		Avge	100s	50s	Ct	St	Balls	Runs	Wkts	Avge	Best	5wI	10wM
Test	5	8	0	385	106		48.12	2	2	6	-	246	68	1	68.00	1-23	-	-
All First	130	213	18	9414	210		48.27	31	39	102	-	5433	2365	73	32.39	7-43	1	1
1-day Int	31	29	3	667	89		25.65	-	6	10	-	756	542	16	33.87	3-56	-	
NatWest	4	4	1	188	58		62.66	-	2	3	-	61	41	1	41.00	1-7	-	
B & H	15	15	3	724	110	*	60.33	2	5	4	-	336	267	7	38.14	4-59	-	
Sunday	42	40	4	1768	160		49.11	4	15	10	-	537	480	11	43.63	2-33	-	

MOORES, P.   Sussex

Name: Peter Moores
Role: Right-hand bat, wicket-keeper
Born: 18 December 1962, Macclesfield, Cheshire
Height: 5ft 11³/₄in **Weight:** 13st
Nickname: Billy
County debut: 1983 (Worcs), 1985 (Sussex)
County cap: 1989
1st-Class 50s scored: 17
1st-Class 100s scored: 4
1st-Class catches: 270
1st-Class stumpings: 34
One-Day 50s: 3
Place in batting averages: 104th av. 34.04 (1991 129th av. 28.56)
Parents: Bernard and Winifred

Wife and date of marriage:
Karen, 28 September 1989
Children: Karen Jane, 28 September 1989
Family links with cricket: Three brothers,
Anthony, Stephen and Robert, all play club
cricket
Education: King Edward VI School,
Macclesfield
Qualifications: 7 O-levels, 3 A-levels.
Advanced cricket coach
Career outside cricket: 'Spent two winters
working for Britannia Building Society as an
assistant research analyst.'
Overseas tours: Christians in Sport to
India 1990; MCC to Namibia 1991;
Leeward Islands 1992
Overseas teams played for: Orange Free
State, South Africa 1988-89
Cricketers particularly admired:
Bob Taylor, Alan Knott, Clive Lloyd
Other sports followed: Football, golf
Relaxations: Photography, golf, music and real ale
Extras: On the MCC ground staff in 1982 before joining Worcestershire in latter half of
1982 season. Joined Sussex in 1985
Best batting: 116 Sussex v Somerset, Hove 1989

1992 Season

	M	Inns	NO	Runs	HS	Avge	100s	50s	Ct	St	O	M	Runs	Wkts	Avge	Best	5wI	10wM
Test																		
All First	21	30	5	851	109	34.04	1	3	32	7								
1-day Int																		
NatWest	2	2	1	14	14 *	14.00	-	-	4	-								
B & H	5	5	1	31	15	7.75	-	-	4	-								
Sunday	15	12	3	258	57	28.66	-	2	10	-								

Career Performances

	M	Inns	NO	Runs	HS	Avge	100s	50s	Ct	St	Balls	Runs	Wkts	Avge	Best	5wI	10wM
Test																	
All First	136	188	25	3933	116	24.12	4	17	270	34	12	16	0	-	-	-	-
1-day Int																	
NatWest	13	9	2	92	26	13.14	-	-	14	2							
B & H	18	14	2	196	76	16.33	-	1	17	2							
Sunday	88	61	20	655	57	15.97	-	2	75	17							

MORRIS, H.   Glamorgan

Name: Hugh Morris
Role: Left-hand bat, right-arm medium bowler, county captain
Born: 5 October 1963, Cardiff
Height: 5ft 8in **Weight:** 12st 10lbs
Nickname: Banners, Banacek, H
County debut: 1981
County cap: 1986
Test debut: 1991
Tests: 3
1000 runs in a season: 6
1st-Class 50s scored: 61
1st-Class 100s scored: 31
1st-Class catches: 126
One-Day 50s: 27
One-Day 100s: 8
Place in batting averages: 36th av. 46.97
(1991 22nd av. 53.02)
Parents: Roger and Anne
Marital status: Single
Family links with cricket: Brother played for Glamorgan U19 and currently plays local league cricket. Father played local club cricket
Education: Blundells School; South Glamorgan Institute of HE
Qualifications: 9 O-levels, 3 A-levels, 1 AO-level, BA (Hons) in Physical Education, NCA coaching award
Career outside cricket: Journalism; Sales and Marketing
Overseas tours: English Public Schoolboys to West Indies 1980-81, to Sri Lanka 1982-83; England A to Pakistan 1990-91 (called up to join England tour party in Australia), to Bermuda and West Indies 1991-92
Overseas teams played for: CBC Old Boys, Pretoria 1985-87
Cricketers particularly admired: Viv Richards, Ian Botham, Jimmy Cook
Other sports followed: Rugby, golf
Relaxations: Music, watching movies, travelling and holiday at end of the season
Extras: Highest schoolboy cricket average in 1979 (89.71), 1981 (184.6) and 1982 (149.2). Captain of England U19 Schoolboys in 1981 and 1982. Played for England YC v West Indies 1982, and captain v Australia 1983. Played first-class rugby for Aberavon 1984-85 and South Glamorgan Institute, scoring over 150 points. Appointed youngest ever Glamorgan captain 1986, but resigned in 1989 to concentrate on batting. In 1990 scored most runs in a season by a Glamorgan player (2276) and hit most 100s (10). After missing selection for the tour of Australia, appointed captain for England A's tour of Pakistan; then, after Gooch had required a hand operation and England had lost the First Test to Australia, he flew out to join the senior tour until the England captain recovered. Glamorgan Player

of the Year
Best batting: 160* Glamorgan v Derbyshire, Cardiff 1990
Best bowling: 1-6 Glamorgan v Oxford University, The Parks 1987

1992 Season

	M	Inns	NO	Runs	HS	Avge	100s	50s	Ct	St	O	M	Runs	Wkts	Avge	Best	5wI	10wM
Test																		
All First	23	37	3	1597	146	46.97	6	6	16	-	4.5	0	57	0	-	-	-	-
1-day Int																		
NatWest	3	3	0	110	55	36.66	-	1	-	-								
B & H	4	4	0	86	40	21.50	-	-	1	-	1	0	1	0	-	-	-	
Sunday	16	15	3	612	104 *	51.00	1	5	3	-								

Career Performances

	M	Inns	NO	Runs	HS	Avge	100s	50s	Ct	St	Balls	Runs	Wkts	Avge	Best	5wI	10wM
Test	3	6	0	115	44	19.16	-	-	3	-							
All First	217	367	38	12579	160 *	38.23	31	61	126	-	348	380	2	190.00	1-6	-	-
1-day Int																	
NatWest	20	20	3	997	154 *	58.64	3	4	9	-							
B & H	31	31	2	771	143 *	26.58	3	2	12	-	18	15	1	15.00	1-14	-	
Sunday	115	112	11	3194	104 *	31.62	2	21	37	-							

MORRIS, J. E. Derbyshire

Name: John Edward Morris
Role: Right-hand bat, right-arm medium
bowler, county vice-captain
Born: 1 April 1964, Crewe
Height: 5ft 10$^{1}/_{2}$in **Weight:** 13st 6lbs
Nickname: Chippendale
County debut: 1982
County cap: 1986
Test debut: 1990
Tests: 3
One-Day Internationals: 8
1000 runs in a season: 7
1st-Class 50s scored: 66
1st-Class 100s scored: 29
One-Day 50s: 21
One-Day 100s: 6
1st-Class catches: 92
Place in batting averages: 60th av. 41.15

(1991 52nd av. 41.11)
Parents: George (Eddie) and Jean
Wife and date of marriage: Sally , 30 September 1990
Children: Tom, 27 June 1991
Family links with cricket: Father played for Crewe for many years as an opening bowler
Education: Shavington Comprehensive School; Dane Bank College of Further Education
Qualifications: O-levels
Overseas tours: England to Australia 1990-91
Overseas teams played for: Griqualand West, South Africa 1988-89
Other sports followed: Athletics, motor racing, football, snooker
Relaxations: Movies, music, good food, fly-fishing
Extras: Youngest player to score a Sunday League 100
Best batting: 191 Derbyshire v Kent, Derby 1986
Best bowling: 1-13 Derbyshire v Yorkshire, Harrogate 1987
                1-13 Derbyshire v Cambridge University, Fenner's 1992

1992 Season

	M	Inns	NO	Runs	HS	Avge	100s	50s	Ct	St	O	M	Runs	Wkts	Avge	Best	5wI	10wM
Test																		
All First	23	33	0	1358	120	41.15	3	12	6	-	8	3	13	1	13.00	1-13	-	-
1-day Int																		
NatWest	2	2	0	31	31	15.50	-	-	-	-								
B & H	5	5	1	179	121	44.75	1	-	1	-								
Sunday	14	14	1	392	78	30.15	-	3	6	-								

Career Performances

	M	Inns	NO	Runs	HS	Avge	100s	50s	Ct	St	Balls	Runs	Wkts	Avge	Best	5wI	10wM
Test	3	5	2	71	32	23.66	-	-	3	-							
All First	218	359	26	12806	191	38.45	29	66	92	-	771	753	5	150.60	1-13	-	-
1-day Int	8	8	1	167	63 *	23.85	-	1	2	-							
NatWest	18	17	3	381	94 *	27.21	-	2	5	-							
B & H	40	36	4	873	123	27.28	2	3	9	-	24	14	0	-		-	-
Sunday	132	126	9	3311	134	28.29	4	15	28	-	3	7	0	-		-	-

133. Who is the oldest cricketer to have played for the West Indies?

MORRIS, R. S. M.   Hampshire

Name: Robert Sean Milner Morris
Role: Right-hand bat, right-arm slow off-spin
bowler, occasional wicket keeper
Born: 10 September 1968
Height: 6ft **Weight:** 12st
Nickname: Stowers, Mozza
County debut: 1992
1st-Class 50s scored: 2
1st-Class catches: 7
Place in batting averages: 149th av. 26.12
Parents: Stuart and Sue
Marital status: Single
Family links with cricket:
Great grandfather played for Worcestershire
Education: Swanbourne House School;
Stowe School; Durham University 'and
Yung's Bar, Bangkok'
Qualifications: 8 O-levels, 2 A-levels,
BA Dunelm sociology

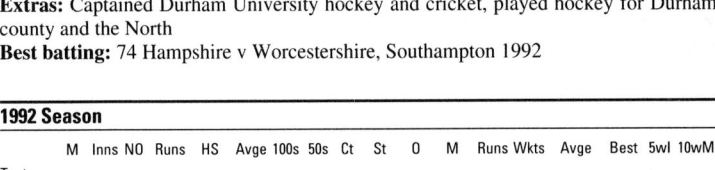

Off-season: Visiting parents in Malaysia, playing cricket in Cape Town
Overseas tours: Stowe to Australia 1982; Combined Universities to Barbados 1990
Overseas teams played for: Midland Guildford, Perth, Western Australia 1987-88; St
Albans, Buenos Aires 1991-92
Cricketers particularly admired: Malcolm Marshall, Johnny Longley 'for his hair-
raising stroke play' and Darren Flint 'for his cricketing brain'
Other sports followed: Hockey, rugby, skiing
Relaxations: 'Fast food, fast cars and fast women and pushing myself through a rigorous
fitness regime.'
Extras: Captained Durham University hockey and cricket, played hockey for Durham
county and the North
Best batting: 74 Hampshire v Worcestershire, Southampton 1992

1992 Season

	M	Inns	NO	Runs	HS	Avge	100s	50s	Ct	St	O	M	Runs	Wkts	Avge	Best	5wI	10wM
Test																		
All First	5	9	1	209	74	26.12	-	2	7	-								
1-day Int																		
NatWest																		
B & H																		
Sunday	1	1	1	4	4 *	-	-	-	-	-	-							

Career Performances

	M	Inns	NO	Runs	HS	Avge	100s	50s	Ct	St	Balls	Runs	Wkts	Avge	Best	5wI	10wM
Test																	
All First	5	9	1	209	74	26.12	-	2	7	-							
1-day Int																	
NatWest																	
B & H																	
Sunday	1	1	1	4	4*	-	-	-	-	-							

MORRISON, D. K. Lancashire

Name: Danny Kyle Morrison
Role: Right-hand bat, right-arm fast bowler
Born: 3 February 1966, Auckland,
New Zealand
County debut: 1992
Test debut: 1987-88
Tests: 25
One-Day Internationals: 46
1st-Class 5w. in innings: 9
1st-Class catches: 33
Place in batting averages: 258th av. 10.27
Place in bowling averages: 71st av. 33.58
Strike rate: 55.94 (career 58.89)
Overseas tours: New Zealand to Australia
1987-88, to India 1988-89, to Australia
1989-90, to England 1990, to Pakistan
1990-91, to Australia (World Cup) 1991-92
Overseas teams played for:
Auckland, New Zealand
Extras: Was personally coached by Dennis
Lillee. On his first appearance against England in 1988 he claimed five wickets in an
innings in Christchurch. In 1989-90 season in New Zealand was leading wicket-taker in
Tests (21), two ahead of Richard Hadlee. Signed for Lancashire on a one-year contract in
1992
Best batting: 36 Aukland v Wellington, Aukland 1986-87
Best bowling: 7-82 Aukland v Canterbury, Rangiona 1986-87

1992 Season

	M	Inns	NO	Runs	HS	Avge	100s	50s	Ct	St	O	M	Runs	Wkts	Avge	Best	5wI	10wM
Test																		
All First	14	12	1	113	30	10.27	-	-	4	-	335.4	52	1209	36	33.58	6-48	1	-
1-day Int																		
NatWest	2	0	0	0	0	-	-	-	-	-	20.1	3	89	5	17.80	3-17	-	
B & H	5	2	1	0	0 *	0.00	-	-	1	-	46	2	185	5	37.00	2-17	-	
Sunday	4	1	1	0	0 *	-	-	-	1	-	30	0	176	3	58.66	1-41	-	

Career Performances

	M	Inns	NO	Runs	HS	Avge	100s	50s	Ct	St	Balls	Runs	Wkts	Avge	Best	5wI	10wM
Test	25	35	10	146	27 *	5.84	-	-	7	-	5196	3011	78	38.60	5-69	5	-
All First	93	90	28	495	36	7.98	-	-	33	-	15665	8795	266	33.06	7-82	9	-
1-day Int	46	15	6	58	12	6.44	-	-	10	-	2240	1811	57	31.77	4-33	-	
NatWest	2	0	0	0	0	-	-	-	-	-	121	89	5	17.80	3-17	-	
B & H	5	2	1	0	0 *	0.00	-	-	1	-	276	185	5	37.00	2-17	-	
Sunday	4	1	1	0	0 *	-	-	-	1	-	180	176	3	58.66	1-41	-	

MORTENSEN, O. H — Derbyshire

Name: Ole Henrik Mortensen
Role: Right-hand bat, right-arm fast-medium bowler
Born: 29 January 1958, Vejle, Denmark
Height: 6ft 4in **Weight:** 14st 2lbs
Nickname: Stan, Blood-axe, The Great Dane
County debut: 1983
County cap: 1986
Benefit: 1994
50 wickets in a season: 3
1st-Class 50s scored: 1
1st-Class 5 w. in innings: 15
1st-Class 10 w. in match: 1
1st-Class catches: 43
Place in bowling averages: 78th av. 34.56
(1991 16th av. 23.86)
Strike rate: 88.34 (career 54.05)
Parents: Willy and Inge
Wife: Jette Jepmond
Children: Julie Jepmond, 30 August 1982 and Emilia
Family links with cricket: 'My brother, Michael, is a very talented cricketer but gave the game up to concentrate on tennis, he has played in the Davis Cup for Denmark.'

Education: Brondbyoster School; Avedore College of Higher Education, Copenhagen
Overseas tours: Denmark to East Africa, England, Scotland, Wales, Ireland and Holland
Overseas clubs played for: Ellerslie, Auckland 1983-84; Brighton, Melbourne 1984-1992
Cricketers particularly admired: 'Anyone who is successful at first-class and Test level over a number of years.'
Other sports played: Tennis, golf, football, Australian Rules football
Relaxations: Collecting stamps (only Danish) and coins, reading books about wine, sleeping in in the morning, reading newspapers
Extras: *Derbyshire's Dane* by Peter Hargreaves, published 1984. Played for Denmark in the ICC Trophy. Most economical bowler in Refuge League 1990. Played for Rest of the World XI v Australian XI in Melbourne 1990 (organised by Lord's Taverners of Australia). The only Dane at present playing first-class cricket in England. Plays as honorary Englishman under EEC regulations, i.e. not classified as overseas player
Best batting: 74* Derbyshire v Yorkshire, Chesterfield 1987
Best bowling: 6-27 Derbyshire v Yorkshire, Sheffield 1983

1992 Season

	M	Inns	NO	Runs	HS	Avge	100s	50s	Ct	St	O	M	Runs	Wkts	Avge	Best	5wl	10wM
Test																		
All First	15	13	10	47	13 *	15.66	-	-	3	-	338.4	87	795	23	34.56	2-22	-	-
1-day Int																		
NatWest	2	1	0	0	0	0.00	-	-	-	-	15	4	44	1	44.00	1-1	-	
B & H	5	2	1	9	5 *	9.00	-	-	-	-	54	11	146	8	18.25	3-39	-	
Sunday	14	3	2	5	3 *	5.00	-	-	1	-	108	9	398	8	49.75	1-9	-	

Career Performances

	M	Inns	NO	Runs	HS	Avge	100s	50s	Ct	St	Balls	Runs	Wkts	Avge	Best	5wl	10wM
Test																	
All First	145	159	89	639	74 *	9.12	-	1	43	-	22215	9673	411	23.53	6-27	15	1
1-day Int																	
NatWest	15	11	6	24	11	4.80	-	-	6	-	972	434	27	16.07	6-14	2	
B & H	36	11	6	23	5 *	4.60	-	-	2	-	2174	1058	51	20.74	3-17	-	
Sunday	125	45	33	85	11	7.08	-	-	15	-	5535	3360	119	28.23	4-10	-	

134. What is the highest innings total in first-class cricket?

MOXON, M. D.   Yorkshire

Name: Martyn Douglas Moxon
Role: Right-hand bat, right-arm medium
bowler, county captain
Born: 4 May 1960, Barnsley
Height: 6ft 1in **Weight:** 14st
Nickname: Frog
County debut: 1981
County cap: 1984
Benefit: 1993
Test debut: 1986
Tests: 10
One-Day Internationals: 8
1000 runs in a season: 9
1st-Class 50s scored: 80
1st-Class 100s scored: 33
1st-Class 200s scored: 2
1st-Class catches: 185
One-Day 50s: 35
One-Day 100s: 6
Place in batting averages: 16th av. 53.26

(1991 36th av. 46.36)
Parents: Audrey and Derek (deceased)
Wife and date of marriage: Sue, October 1985
Children: Charlotte Louise, 13 March 1990
Family links with cricket: Father and grandfather played local league cricket
Education: Holgate Grammar School, Barnsley
Qualifications: 8 O-levels, 3 A-levels, HNC in Business Studies, NCA coaching award
Off-season: Captaining England A tour to Australia
Overseas tours: England to India and Australia 1984-85, to Australia and New Zealand
1987-88; England B to Sri Lanka 1985-86; England A to Bermuda and West Indies 1991-
92, to Australia 1992-93
Overseas teams played for: Griqualand West, South Africa 1982-83 and 1983-84
Cricketers particularly admired: Viv Richards
Other sports followed: Football (supporter of Barnsley FC) and golf
Injuries: Broken and dislocated right index finger, out for six weeks
Relaxations: Listening to most types of music, having a drink with friends
Extras: Captained Yorkshire Schools U15, North of England U15 and Yorkshire Senior
Schools. Played for Wombwell Cricket Lovers' Society U18 side. First Yorkshire player
to make centuries in his first two Championship games in Yorkshire, 116 v Essex at
Headingley (on debut) and 111 v Derbyshire at Sheffield, and scored 153 in his first innings
in a Roses Match. Picked for Lord's Test of 1984 v West Indies, but had to withdraw
through injury and had to wait until 1986 to make Test debut. Appointed Yorkshire captain

in 1990. Appointed captain of England A team to tour Bermuda and West Indies 1991-92, but played no first-class cricket due to injury. Wombwell Cricket Lovers' Society Cricketer of the Year 1991
Best batting: 218* Yorkshire v Sussex, Eastbourne 1990
Best bowling: 3-24 Yorkshire v Hampshire, Southampton 1989

1992 Season

	M	Inns	NO	Runs	HS	Avge	100s	50s	Ct	St	O	M	Runs	Wkts	Avge	Best	5wI	10wM
Test																		
All First	19	28	2	1385	183	53.26	5	5	9	-	3	0	7	0	-		-	-
1-day Int																		
NatWest	2	2	0	36	34	18.00	-	-	2	-								
B & H	2	2	0	3	3	1.50	-	-	2	-	2	0	13	0	-		-	-
Sunday	12	12	0	333	57	27.75	-	3	3	-	16.1	0	75	4	18.75	2-32	-	

Career Performances

	M	Inns	NO	Runs	HS	Avge	100s	50s	Ct	St	Balls	Runs	Wkts	Avge	Best	5wI	10wM
Test	10	17	1	455	99	28.43	-	3	10	-	48	30	0	-		-	-
All First	236	401	28	15234	218 *	40.84	33	80	185	-	2626	1474	28	52.64	3-24	-	-
1-day Int	8	8	0	174	70	21.75	-	1	5	-							
NatWest	21	21	6	775	107 *	51.66	1	7	11	-	156	85	5	17.00	2-19	-	
B & H	37	37	5	1454	141 *	45.43	2	10	16	-	342	242	9	26.88	5-31	1	
Sunday	107	99	7	2982	129 *	32.41	3	17	33	-	984	868	21	41.33	3-29	-	

MULLALLY, A. D.   Leicestershire

Name: Alan David Mullally
Role: Right-hand bat, left-arm fast bowler
Born: 12 July 1969, Southend
Height: 6ft 5in **Weight:** 13st 5lb
Nickname: Aus, Spider, Long Dog
County debut: 1988 (Hampshire), 1990 (Leicestershire)
1st-Class 5 w. in innings: 1
1st-Class catches: 13
Place in bowling averages: 84th av. 35.35
Strike rate: 74.04 (career 82.42)
Parents: Michael and Ann
Marital status: Single
Education: Cannington High School, Perth, Australia; Wembley Technical College
Qualifications: 'Jack of all trades'
Off-season: House hunting
Overseas tours: Western Australia to India 1990

Overseas teams played for:
Western Australia
Cricketers particularly admired:
Robin Smith, Paul Nixon
Other sports followed: Hockey, athletics,
Australian Rules, basketball
Relaxations: Surfing, music, 'taking it easy'
Extras: English-qualified as he was born in
Southend, he made his first-class debut for
Western Australia in the 1987-88 Sheffield
Shield final, and played for Australia Youth
1988-89. Played one match for Hampshire in
1988. Joined Leicestershire for 1990 season
Opinions on cricket: 'Too much cricket is
played. Reduce the number of playing days
and the stupid over-rate fines.'
Best batting: 34 Western Australia v
Tasmania, Perth 1989-90
Best bowling: 5-119 Leicestershire v
Warwickshire, Edgbaston 1992

1992 Season

	M	Inns	NO	Runs	HS	Avge	100s	50s	Ct	St	O	M	Runs	Wkts	Avge	Best	5wI	10wM
Test																		
All First	19	23	6	118	21	6.94	-	-	4	-	518.2	125	1485	42	35.35	5-119	1	-
1-day Int																		
NatWest	5	2	1	1	1 *	1.00	-	-	2	-	50	6	167	9	18.55	2-22	-	
B & H	5	1	0	11	11	11.00	-	-	-	-	44	7	174	3	58.00	1-8	-	
Sunday	16	6	5	19	10 *	19.00	-	-	4	-	111.1	7	503	13	38.69	2-20	-	

Career Performances

	M	Inns	NO	Runs	HS	Avge	100s	50s	Ct	St	Balls	Runs	Wkts	Avge	Best	5wI	10wM
Test																	
All First	57	55	17	314	34	8.26	-	-	13	-	9809	4701	119	39.50	5-119	1	-
1-day Int																	
NatWest	6	2	1	1	1 *	1.00	-	-	2	-	372	222	11	20.18	2-22	-	
B & H	11	3	0	17	11	5.66	-	-	-	-	588	383	6	63.83	1-8	-	
Sunday	32	12	8	45	10 *	11.25	-	-	8	-	1346	984	29	33.93	2-19	-	

MUNTON, T. A. Warwickshire

Name: Timothy Alan Munton
Role: Right-hand bat, right-arm fast-medium bowler
Born: 30 July 1965, Melton Mowbray
Height: 6ft 6in **Weight:** 15st 7lbs
Nickname: Harry, Herman
County debut: 1985
County cap: 1990
Test debut: 1991
Tests: 2
50 wickets in a season: 4
1st-Class 5 w. in innings: 15
1st-Class 10 w. in match: 3
1st-Class catches: 52
Place in batting averages: 239th av. 12.33
(1991 240th av. 13.29)
Place in bowling averages: 84th av. 82.42
(1991 26th av. 25.52)
Strike rate: 75.37 (career 61.60)
Parents: Alan and Brenda
Wife and date of marriage: Helen, 20 September 1986
Children: Camilla Dallas, 13 August 1988; Harrison George Samuel, 17 February 1992
Education: Sarson High School; King Edward VII Upper School, Melton Mowbray
Qualifications: 8 O-levels, 1 A-level; NCA coaching certificate
Career outside cricket: Salesman for Bass, Mitchells and Butlers (brewery)
Off-season: As above
Overseas tours: England A to Pakistan 1990-91, to Bermuda and West Indies 1991-92
Cricketers particularly admired: Richard Hadlee
Other sports followed: Basketball, soccer
Relaxations: 'Playing basketball, spending time with my family.'
Extras: Appeared for Leicestershire 2nd XI 1982-84. Second highest wicket-taker in 1990 with 78. Called into England A squad to tour Bermuda and West Indies when Dermot Reeve replaced the injured Angus Fraser on the senior tour. Was voted Warwickshire Player of the Season 1991
Opinions on cricket: 'Full introduction of four-day cricket long overdue. I feel Sunday League cricket should have remained 40 overs with 2pm start. Concerned over the use of white balls in daylight when most cricket grounds have predominantly light coloured seats.'
Best batting: 47 Warwickshire v Kent, Edgbaston 1992
Best bowling: 8-89 Warwickshire v Middlesex, Edgbaston 1991

1992 Season

	M	Inns	NO	Runs	HS	Avge	100s	50s	Ct	St	O	M	Runs	Wkts	Avge	Best	5wI	10wM
Test	2	2	1	25	25 *	25.00	-	-	-	-	67.3	15	200	4	50.00	2-22	-	-
All First	19	19	7	148	47	12.33	-	-	7	-	640.4	176	1725	51	33.82	7-64	3	1
1-day Int																		
NatWest	4	2	0	0	0	0.00	-	-	-	-	43	7	93	3	31.00	1-17	-	
B & H	3	2	1	6	3 *	6.00	-	-	-	-	33	5	113	3	37.66	1-33	-	
Sunday	14	5	2	15	9 *	5.00	-	-	1	-	92.5	10	328	16	20.50	4-16	-	

Career Performances

	M	Inns	NO	Runs	HS	Avge	100s	50s	Ct	St	Balls	Runs	Wkts	Avge	Best	5wI	10wM
Test	2	2	1	25	25 *	25.00	-	-	-	-	405	200	4	50.00	2-22	-	-
All First	147	151	59	892	47	9.69	-	-	52	-	24148	10839	392	27.65	8-89	15	3
1-day Int																	
NatWest	18	7	3	8	5	2.00	-	-	2	-	1042	518	17	30.47	3-36	-	
B & H	23	12	7	47	13	9.40	-	-	5	-	1438	837	28	29.89	4-35	-	
Sunday	90	26	20	78	10 *	13.00	-	-	13	-	3733	2423	88	27.53	5-23	2	

MURPHY, A. J. Surrey

Name: Anthony John Murphy
Role: Right-hand bat, right-arm fast-medium bowler
Born: 6 August 1962, Manchester
Height: 5ft 11¾in **Weight:** 'Still under review'
Nickname: Headless, Murph
County debut: 1985 (Lancs), 1989 (Surrey)
50 wickets in a season: 1
1st-Class 5 w. in innings: 5
1st-Class catches: 12
Place in bowling averages: 134th av. 48.27 (1991 129th av. 47.62)
Strike rate: 97.45 (career 73.54)
Parents: John Desmond and Elizabeth Catherine
Marital status: Single
Family links with cricket: Brother captains Maori club in London; 'distant cousin's grandfather ex-captain of Southern Ireland.'
Education: Xaverian College, Manchester; Swansea University
Qualifications: 9 O-levels, 4 A-levels

Career outside cricket: 'Insider trading in the city of London'
Off-season: Coaching in Argentina and fishing in Guyana with Monte Lynch
Overseas tours: MCCA U25 to Kenya
1986; Lancashire to Jamaica 1986 and 1987; Surrey to Sharjah 1989, 1990, 1993, to Barbados 1989, 1990, to Lanzarote 1991, to Rhodes 1992
Overseas teams played for: Central Districts, New Zealand 1985-86; Hawkes Bay, New Zealand 1985-87
Cricketers particularly admired: Clive Lloyd, Michael Holding, Billy Dewsall, Bill Ellis
Other sports followed: All sports that involve action
Injuries: Groin tear and calf strain, on and off most of season
Relaxations: 'Annoying Geoff Arnold and Grahame Clinton with my outlandish views on cricket, watching old movies and listening to heavy rock.'
Extras: Surrey Bowler of the Year 1989, Man of the Match for League Cricket Conference against West Indies 1984, captain of Swansea University
Opinions on cricket: 'The ball-tampering issue has been blown out of all proportion. I think that it is just batsmen whingeing because they are unable to combat swing at pace.'
Best batting: 38 Surrey v Gloucestershire, The Oval 1989
Best bowling: 6-97 Surrey v Derbyshire, Derby 1989

1992 Season

	M	Inns	NO	Runs	HS	Avge	100s	50s	Ct	St	O	M	Runs	Wkts	Avge	Best	5wI	10wM
Test																		
All First	5	5	2	45	32	15.00	-	-	-	-	178.4	34	531	11	48.27	3-97	-	-
1-day Int																		
NatWest																		
B & H																		
Sunday	7	1	1	9	9 *	-	-	-	1	-	50.4	1	287	8	35.87	2-35	-	

Career Performances

	M	Inns	NO	Runs	HS	Avge	100s	50s	Ct	St	Balls	Runs	Wkts	Avge	Best	5wI	10wM
Test																	
All First	72	71	28	225	38	5.23	-	-	12	-	12797	6841	174	39.31	6-97	5	-
1-day Int																	
NatWest	8	2	2	1	1 *	-	-	-	-	-	524	338	8	42.25	2-34	-	
B & H	10	6	3	6	5 *	2.00	-	-	-	-	582	385	8	48.12	2-23	-	
Sunday	45	10	6	21	9 *	5.25	-	-	5	-	1936	1534	58	26.44	4-22	-	

135. Which former England captain was Best Man at David Gower's wedding in September 1992?

MUSHTAQ AHMED   Somerset

Name: Mushtaq Ahmed
Role: Right-hand bat, leg-spin and googly bowler,
Born: 28 June 1970, Sahival, Pakistan
County debut: No first team appearance
Test debut: 1991-92
Tests: 8
One-Day Internationals: 48
1st-Class 50s scored: 1
1st-Class 5w. in innings: 11
1st-Class 10w. in match: 2
1st-Class catches: 30
Place in bowling averages: 13th av. 24.54
Off-season: Touring with Pakistan
Overseas tours: Pakistan to New Zealand and Australia (World Cup) 1992, to England 1992, to New Zealand, Australia and South Africa 1992-93
Overseas teams played for:
United Bank, Pakistan
Extras: Took 6-81 against England for Punjab Chief Minister's XI 1987. Finished second to Wasim Akram as Pakistan's highest wicket-taker in the World Cup 1992 with 16 wickets. Specialist coaching from Intikhab Alam
Best batting: 75 Multan v Hyderabad, Sahival 1986-87
Best bowling: 9-93 Multan v Peshawar, Sahival 1990-91

1992 Season

	M	Inns	NO	Runs	HS	Avge	100s	50s	Ct	St	O	M	Runs	Wkts	Avge	Best	5wI	10wM
Test	5	6	0	35	11	5.83	-	-	1	-	178.4	37	475	15	31.66	3-32	-	-
All First	17	12	3	73	12	8.11	-	-	6	-	614.4	158	1620	66	24.54	5-46	4	-
1-day Int	5	3	2	29	14 *	29.00	-	-	1	-	52	2	243	2	121.50	1-34	-	
NatWest																		
B & H																		
Sunday																		

136. Who holds the record for the most first-class hundreds?

Career Performances

	M	Inns	NO	Runs	HS	Avge	100s	50s	Ct	St	Balls	Runs	Wkts	Avge	Best	5wI	10wM
Test	8	11	2	49	11	5.44	-	-	1	-	1588	716	19	37.68	3-32	-	-
All First	53	58	9	537	75	10.95	-	1	30	-	9069	4896	197	24.85	9-93	11	2
1-day Int	48	24	9	155	17 *	10.33	-	-	8	-	2403	1850	62	29.83	3-14	-	
NatWest																	
B & H																	
Sunday																	

NEALE, P. A.   Northamptonshire

Name: Phillip Anthony Neale
Role: Right-hand bat
Born: 5 June 1954, Scunthorpe
Height: 5ft 11in **Weight:** 12st 5lbs
Nickname: Phil
County debut: 1975
County cap: 1978
Benefit: 1988 (£153,005)
1000 runs in a season: 8
1st-Class 50s scored: 89
1st-Class 100s scored: 28
1st-Class catches: 134
One-Day 50s: 32
One-Day 100s: 2
Parents: Geoff and Margaret
Wife and date of marriage:
Christine, 26 September 1976
Children: Kelly Joanne, 9 November 1979;
Craig Andrew, 11 February 1982
Education: Frederick Gough Grammar School, Scunthorpe; John Leggot Sixth Form College, Scunthorpe; Leeds University
Qualifications: 10 O-levels, 2 A-levels, BA (Hons) Russian. Preliminary football and cricket coaching awards
Career outside cricket: 'Phil Neale Tours Ltd – sports tours around the world for cricket, rugby and golf, specialising in Zimbabwe.'
Cricketers particularly admired: Basil D'Oliveira, Norman Gifford, Alan Ormrod
Other sports followed: Most sports – mainly via TV
Relaxations: 'Reading, spending time with my family, trying to play golf.'
Extras: Played for Lincolnshire 1973-74. Captain of Worcestershire 1983-91. Professional footballer with Lincoln City until 1985. Celebrated his benefit season by captaining Worcestershire to a County Championship and Sunday League double in 1988. Autobiog-

raphy *A Double Life* published in 1990. Retired from Worcestershire at the end of the 1992 season to become Director of cricket at Northamptonshire
Best batting: 167 Worcestershire v Sussex, Kidderminster 1988
Best bowling: 1-15 Worcestershire v Derbyshire, Worcester 1976

1992 Season

	M	Inns	NO	Runs	HS	Avge	100s	50s	Ct	St	O	M	Runs	Wkts	Avge	Best	5wI	10wM
Test																		
All First	2	3	0	79	38	26.33	-	-	-	-								
1-day Int																		
NatWest	1	1	0	1	1	1.00	-	-	1	-								
B & H																		
Sunday																		

Career Performances

	M	Inns	NO	Runs	HS	Avge	100s	50s	Ct	St	Balls	Runs	Wkts	Avge	Best	5wI	10wM
Test																	
All First	354	571	93	17445	167	36.49	28	89	134	-	472	369	2	184.50	1-15	-	-
1-day Int																	
NatWest	37	32	3	953	98	32.86	-	6	12	-							
B & H	70	63	10	1675	128	31.60	1	10	19	-							
Sunday	225	205	50	4531	102	29.23	1	16	57	-	50	50	2	25.00	2-46	-	

NEWELL, K. Sussex

Name: Keith Newell
Role: Right-hand bat, occasional medium-pace bowler
Born: 25 March 1972, Crawley
Height: 6ft ¹/₂in **Weight:** 11st 6lbs
County debut: No first team appearance
Parents: Peter Charles and Julie Anne
Marital status: single
Family links with cricket: Father played club cricket, two brothers play for Sussex youth sides
Education: Gossops Green Junior School; Ifield Community College
Qualifications: 9 GCSEs, coaching certificate
Off-season: 'Playing cricket in either Zimbabwe or South Africa'

Overseas teams played for: Zimbabwe Universals
1989-90; Bulawayo Athletic Club 1991-92
Cricketers particularly admired: Ian Botham, 'everyone who was on the MCC young cricketers staff, 1992 season, (even Birdy).'
Other sports followed: Football, table tennis, golf and most other sports
Injuries: Strained intercostal in rib cage, out for two weeks
Relaxations: 'Listening to music, watching films, going to the pub'
Opinions on cricket: 'In the short time that I've been on the professional circuit I feel that there is too much cricket played. I think that if there was slightly less cricket played then there might be a decrease in permanent and temporary injuries

---

NEWELL, M. Nottinghamshire

Name: Michael Newell
Role: Right-hand opening bat, leg-spin bowler, occasional wicket-keeper
Born: 25 February 1965, Blackburn
Height: 5ft 9in **Weight:** 11st
Nickname: Newelly
County debut: 1984
County cap: 1987
1000 runs in a season: 1
1st-Class 50s scored: 24
1st-Class 100s scored: 6
1st-Class 200s scored: 1
1st-Class catches: 93
1st-Class stumpings: 1
One-Day 50s: 4
One-Day 100s: 1
Parents: Barry and Janet
Wife and date of marriage:
Jayne, 23 September 1989
Family links with cricket:
Father chairman of Notts Unity CC and brother, Paul, is the captain
Education: West Bridgford Comprehensive
Qualifications: 8 O-levels, 3 A-levels. NCA advanced coach
Off-season: Working for Notts CCC, coaching at all levels
Cricketers particularly admired: Chris Cairns, Richard Bates, Dave Pennett
Other sports followed: Watches rugby union, football, horse racing
Relaxations: 'Stripping wallpaper and decorating with my wife and going to the Trent Bridge Inn with Notts 2nd XI.'
Extras: Carried his bat through the Nottinghamshire innings v Warwickshire, scoring 10 out of Nottinghamshire's 44
Opinions on cricket: Apart from the fact that the Sunday League is too long a game I

believe that we have probably got the right format now for professional cricket.'
Best batting: 203* Nottinghamshire v Derbyshire, Derby 1987
Best bowling: 2-38 Nottinghamshire v Sri Lankans, Trent Bridge 1988

1992 Season

	M	Inns	NO	Runs	HS	Avge	100s	50s	Ct	St	O	M	Runs	Wkts	Avge	Best	5wI	10wM
Test																		
All First	2	3	2	75	48 *	75.00	-	-	3	-								
1-day Int																		
NatWest																		
B & H																		
Sunday																		

Career Performances

	M	Inns	NO	Runs	HS	Avge	100s	50s	Ct	St	Balls	Runs	Wkts	Avge	Best	5wI	10wM
Test																	
All First	102	178	26	4636	203 *	30.50	6	24	93	1	363	282	7	40.28	2-38	-	-
1-day Int																	
NatWest	5	5	0	136	60	27.20	-	1	3	-	6	10	0	-		-	-
B & H	10	10	1	205	39	22.77	-	-	2	-							
Sunday	24	21	4	611	109 *	35.94	1	3	8	-							

NEWPORT, P. J.   Worcestershire

Name: Philip John Newport
Role: Right-hand bat, right-arm fast-medium
bowler, outfielder
Born: 11 October 1962, High Wycombe
Height: 6ft 2in **Weight:** 13st 7lbs
Nickname: Schnozz, Newps
County debut: 1982
County cap: 1986
Test debut: 1988
Tests: 3
50 wickets in a season: 5
1st-Class 50s scored: 12
1st-Class 5 w. in innings: 27
1st-Class 10 w. in match: 3
1st-Class catches: 55
Place in batting averages: 163rd av. 24.57
(1991 191st av. 20.76)
Place in bowling averages: 23rd av. 26.02

(1991 67th av. 32.42)
Strike rate: 54.555 (career 52.19)
Parents: John and Sheila Diana
Wife and date of marriage: Christine Anne, 26 October 1985
Children: Nathan Alexander, 10 May 1989
Family links with cricket: Brother Stewart is captain of Octopus CC in North London
Education: Royal Grammar School, High Wycombe; Portsmouth University
Qualifications: 8 O-levels, 3 A-levels, BA (Hons) Geography, coaching qualification
Off-season: Playing for Northern Transvaal in South Africa
Overseas tours: NCA to Denmark 1981; selected for cancelled England tour to India 1988-89; England A to Pakistan 1990-91; England to Australia 1990-91
Overseas teams played for: Vogeltown, New Plymouth, New Zealand 1986; Boland, South Africa 1987-88; Ginnenderra and ACT, Australia 1991; Northern Transvaal, South Africa 1992-93
Other sports followed: American football, basketball, golf
Injuries: Abductor strain, out for one and a half weeks
Relaxations: 'Cinema, spending time with my son (improving his golf swing and cover drive)
Extras: Had trial as schoolboy for Southampton FC. Played cricket for NAYC England Schoolboys 1981 and for Buckinghamshire in Minor Counties Championship in 1981 and 1982. Winner of Worcestershire's Dick Lygon Award 1992. Selected as a replacement for England's tour to Australia in 1990-91. Worcestershire Player of the Year 1992
Opinions on cricket: 'County staffs will diminish in size as four-day cricket is bound to shrink each club's income,'
Best batting: 98 Worcestershire v New Zealand, Worcester 1990
Best bowling: 8-52 Worcestershire v Middlesex, Lord's 1988

1992 Season

	M	Inns	NO	Runs	HS	Avge	100s	50s	Ct	St	O	M	Runs	Wkts	Avge	Best	5wI	10wM
Test																		
All First	22	25	6	467	75 *	24.57	-	3	5	-	618.2	130	1770	68	26.02	5-22	4	-
1-day Int																		
NatWest	1	1	0	9	9	9.00	-	-	-	-	12	1	32	1	32.00	1-32	-	
B & H	5	2	0	11	9	5.50	-	-	1	-	54.5	4	189	11	17.18	5-31	1	
Sunday	13	5	2	21	7 *	7.00	-	-	1	-	92.4	6	390	16	24.37	3-27	-	

Career Performances

	M	Inns	NO	Runs	HS	Avge	100s	50s	Ct	St	Balls	Runs	Wkts	Avge	Best	5wI	10wM
Test	3	5	1	110	40 *	27.50	-	-	1	-	669	417	10	41.70	4-87	-	-
All First	194	212	66	3720	98	25.47	-	12	55	-	29646	15757	568	27.74	8-52	27	3
1-day Int																	
NatWest	18	9	2	69	25	9.85	-	-	-	-	962	532	18	29.55	4-46	-	
B & H	34	19	4	140	28	9.33	-	-	9	-	2201	1151	50	23.02	5-22	2	
Sunday	103	46	19	314	26 *	11.63	-	-	22	-	3764	2825	98	28.82	4-18	-	

NICHOLAS, M. C. J.   Hampshire

Name: Mark Charles Jefford Nicholas
Role: Right-hand bat, 'I think I bowl, but
no-one else does', county captain
Born: 29 September 1957, London
Height: 6ft **Weight:** 12st 5lbs
Nickname: Skip, Dougie, Cappy
County debut: 1978
County cap: 1982
Benefit: 1991 (£174,260)
1000 runs in a season: 8
1st-Class 50s scored: 66
1st-Class 100s scored: 29
1st-Class 200s scored: 1
1st-Class 5 w. in innings: 2
1st-Class catches: 186
One-Day 50s: 34
One-Day 100s: 1
Place in batting averages: 84th av. 37.14
(1991 113th av. 30.59)
Parents: Anne
Marital status: Single

Family links with cricket: Grandfather (F.W.H.) played for Essex as batsman and wicket-keeper and toured with MCC. Father played for Navy
Education: Fernden Prep School; Bradfield College
Qualifications: 9 O-levels, 3 A-levels
Career outside cricket: 'Not at the moment – haven't time.'
Off-season: Journalism in India and South Africa
Overseas tours: English Counties XI to Zimbabwe 1984-85; captain of England B to Sri Lanka 1985-86; captain of England A to Zimbabwe and Kenya 1989-90
Cricketers particularly admired: Barry Richards, John Snow, Mike Brearley
Other sports followed: Most – football, golf, fives, squash
Injuries: Broken knuckle and finger - missed NatWest final
Relaxations: Theatre, music, golf, going out to dinner.
Extras: Hampshire captain since 1985 but missed Hampshire's first NatWest final after having his knuckle and finger broken a few days earlier by a delivery from Waqar Younis in the Championship game between the two NatWest finalists
Opinions on cricket: 'Do anything to encourage spin-bowling - uncover pitches, change the bowler's follow through laws, i.e. 5ft and 3in either side of stumps – anything but we must have variety. Change Sunday league rules, better still abandon it.'
Best batting: 206* Hampshire v Oxford University, The Parks 1982
Best bowling: 6-37 Hampshire v Somerset, Southampton 1989

1992 Season

	M	Inns	NO	Runs	HS	Avge	100s	50s	Ct	St	O	M	Runs	Wkts	Avge	Best	5wl	10wM
Test																		
All First	21	32	5	1003	95 *	37.14	-	6	9	-	25.3	2	101	2	50.50	1-16	-	-
1-day Int																		
NatWest	2	1	0	25	25	25.00	-	-	-	-								
B & H	7	6	1	97	37 *	19.40	-	-	1	-								
Sunday	15	14	5	206	53	22.88	-	1	2	-								

Career Performances

	M	Inns	NO	Runs	HS	Avge	100s	50s	Ct	St	Balls	Runs	Wkts	Avge	Best	5wl	10wM
Test																	
All First	321	526	76	14952	206 *	33.22	29	66	195	-	5783	3208	72	44.55	6-37	2	-
1-day Int																	
NatWest	39	34	5	895	71	30.86	-	6	13	-	512	341	9	37.88	2-39	-	
B & H	58	52	7	1075	74	23.88	-	4	18	-	1020	759	24	31.62	4-34	-	
Sunday	187	170	32	3831	108	27.76	1	24	55	-	1873	1751	59	29.67	4-30	-	

NIXON, P. A. Leicestershire

Name: Paul Andrew Nixon
Role: Left-hand bat, wicket-keeper
Born: 21 October 1970, Carlisle
Height: 5ft 11in **Weight:** 12st 7lbs
Nickname: Nico, Nobby, Desert Head
County debut: 1989
1st-Class 50s: 1
1st-Class 100s: 1
1st-Class catches: 109
1st-Class stumpings: 9
One-Day 50s: 1
Place in batting averages: 128th av. 29.38
Parents: Brian and Sylvia
Marital status: Single
Family links with cricket: 'Grandfather
and father played local league cricket for
Edenhall CC where I started at home in
Penrith (Langwathby).'
Education:
Langwathby Primary; Ullswater High
Qualifications: 3 O-levels, 6 CSEs, NCA cricket coaching certificate
Career outside cricket: Working on father's farm, gardening in Australia, plasterers

labourer, cricket coaching in Cape Town

Off-season: 'Cricket development in under privileged areas in Cape Town, South Africa'

Overseas tours: Cumbria to Denmark 1985; Leicestershire to Holland 1991

Overseas teams played for: Melville and North Freemantle, Perth, Western Australia 1989-91; Cape Town, South Africa 1992

Cricketers particularly admired: John Major, Keith Piper

Other sports followed: Football (Carlisle Utd, Spurs and Leicester City FCs), rugby and 'everything really'

Injuries: Groin and cartilage

Relaxations: 'Shark fishing, bungy jumping, rally driving!'

Extras: Played for England U15, Minor Counties for Cumberland at 16, MCC Young Pro in 1988. Took eight catches in debut match v Warwickshire at Hinckley in 1989. Played for Carlisle Utd and 'once got lost in South African township at 3.30am.'

Opinions on cricket: 'There should be a change to an eight day week so we can all play even more cricket and all motorways should be closed so we must all drive on A roads between games!.'

Best batting: 107* Leicestershire v Hampshire, Leicester 1992

1992 Season

	M	Inns	NO	Runs	HS	Avge	100s	50s	Ct	St	O	M	Runs	Wkts	Avge	Best	5wI	10wM
Test																		
All First	16	25	7	529	107 *	29.38	1	1	40	5								
1-day Int																		
NatWest	5	4	2	66	32	33.00	-	-	7	1								
B & H	2	2	0	5	5	2.50	-	-	-	-								
Sunday	13	12	3	287	60	31.88	-	1	5	2								

Career Performances

	M	Inns	NO	Runs	HS	Avge	100s	50s	Ct	St	Balls	Runs	Wkts	Avge	Best	5wI	10wM
Test																	
All First	45	59	19	1081	107 *	27.02	1	1	109	9							
1-day Int																	
NatWest	6	5	2	78	32	26.00	-	-	8	1							
B & H	2	2	0	5	5	2.50	-	-	-	-							
Sunday	32	23	6	349	60	20.52	-	1	24	3							

137. Who holds the record for the fastest Test century?

NOON, W. M.

Northamptonshire

Name: Wayne Michael Noon
Role: Right-hand bat, wicket-keeper
Born: 5 February 1971, Grimsby
Height: 5ft 9^1/$_2$in **Weight:** 11st 10lbs
Nickname: Spoon Head, Noonie
County debut: 1988 (one-day),
1989 (first-class)
1st-Class catches: 23
1st-Class stumpings: 3
Parents: Trafford and Rosemary
Marital status: Single
Education: Caistor Grammar School
Qualifications: 5 O-levels
Career outside cricket: Duck farmer
Off-season: Working for Kookaburra
Overseas tours: Lincolnshire U14 to
Pakistan 1984; England YC to Australia
1989-90
Overseas teams played for: Burnside West,
Christchurch, New Zealand 1990-91
Cricketers particularly admired: Ian Botham, Alan Knott, Jack Russell
Other sports followed: Football (Lincoln City)
Injuries: Right-hand little finger – missed two weeks
Relaxations: 'Having a day's break from cricket and having a quiet beer.'
Extras: Played for England YC v New Zealand 1989; captain v Australia 1989-90 and
Pakistan 1990. Was the 1000th player to appear in the Sunday league competition
Opinions on cricket: 'I think the tea interval should be the same length as lunch and that
the cricket season should last seven months instead of six, playing the same amount of
cricket.'
Best batting: 37 Northamptonshire v Australians, Northampton 1989

1992 Season

	M	Inns	NO	Runs	HS	Avge	100s	50s	Ct	St	O	M	Runs	Wkts	Avge	Best	5wI	10wM
Test																		
All First	1	0	0	0	0	-	-	-	2	-								
1-day Int																		
NatWest																		
B & H																		
Sunday	5	2	0	13	13	6.50	-	-	3	1								

Career Performances

	M	Inns	NO	Runs	HS	Avge	100s	50s	Ct	St	Balls	Runs	Wkts	Avge	Best	5wl	10wM
Test																	
All First	12	16	2	150	37	10.71	-	-	23	3							
1-day Int																		
NatWest																		
B & H	1	0	0	0	0	-	-	-	-	-							
Sunday	14	10	2	73	21	9.12	-	-	10	2							

NORTH, J. A.   Sussex

Name: John Andrew North
Role: Right-hand bat, right-arm medium-fast
bowler, outfielder
Born: 19 November 1970, Slindon
Height: 5ft 11in **Weight:** 12st 4lbs
Nickname: Ollie
County debut: 1990
1st-Class 50s scored: 2
1st-Class catches: 2
Place in batting averages: 232nd av. 13.50
(1991 170th av. 23.28)
Place in bowling averages: 45th av. 30.09
(1991 48th av. 29.85)
Strike rate: 46.95 (career 55.30)
Parents: John Allan and Margaret Anne
Marital status: Single
Family links with cricket: Brother Mark
played county schoolboy cricket
Education: Bishop Luffa Comprehensive
School; Slindon College

Qualifications: 10 O-levels, 2 A-levels
Overseas tours: Buckingham Cavaliers to Cape Town, South Africa 1989 and 1992;
Sussex Martlets to Zimbabwe 1991
Overseas teams played for: University St Heliers, Auckland 1989-90
Cricketers particularly admired: Tony Dodemaide, Waqar Younis, Viv Richards
Other sports followed: 'Any sport without horses or rackets.'
Injuries: Chipped vertebrae of the spine after colliding with boundary boards
Relaxations: 'Films, eating out, away trips.'
Extras: Played for ESCA U15 and U17, NAYC and England YC v Pakistan 1990
Opinions on cricket: 'Politics and sport should not mix. Tea intervals should be extended.
Too much cricket crammed into a six-month season.'

Best batting: 63* Sussex v Hampshire, Hove 1991
Best bowling: 4-47 Sussex v Sri Lankans, Hove 1991

1992 Season

	M	Inns	NO	Runs	HS	Avge	100s	50s	Ct	St	O	M	Runs	Wkts	Avge	Best	5wI	10wM
Test																		
All First	5	7	1	81	53 *	13.50	-	1	-	-	96.3	14	331	11	30.09	3-51	-	-
1-day Int																		
NatWest																			
B & H	2	2	1	20	11 *	20.00	-	-	-	-	9	0	44	3	14.66	3-24	-	
Sunday	7	5	2	83	56	27.66	-	1	1	-	27	0	169	2	84.50	1-34	-	

Career Performances

	M	Inns	NO	Runs	HS	Avge	100s	50s	Ct	St	Balls	Runs	Wkts	Avge	Best	5wI	10wM
Test																	
All First	16	20	3	285	63 *	16.76	-	2	2	-	2017	1164	37	31.45	4-47	-	-
1-day Int																	
NatWest																		
B & H	7	5	1	64	22	16.00	-	-	-	-	348	300	8	37.50	3-24	-	
Sunday	15	13	4	149	56	16.55	-	1	7	-	372	376	12	31.33	3-29	-	

O'GORMAN, T. J. G. Derbyshire

Name: Timothy Joseph Gerard O'Gorman
Role: Right-hand bat
Born: 15 May 1967, Woking
Height: 6ft 2in **Weight:** 12st
County debut: 1987
County cap: 1992
1000 runs in a season: 2
1st-Class 50s scored: 17
1st-Class 100s scored: 5
1st-Class catches: 45
Place in batting averages: 93rd av. 35.55
(1991 138th av. 27.90)
Parents: Brian and Kathleen
Marital status: Single
Family links with cricket: Grandfather Joe
O'Gorman played for Surrey; father played
for Nigeria, for Sussex 2nd XI and
Middlesex 2nd XI
Education: St George's College, Weybridge;

St Chad's College, Durham University; College of Law, Guildford
Qualifications: 12 O-levels, 3 A-levels; BA (Hons) Law; Law Society finals
Career outside cricket: Solicitor
Off-season: Working at Ashurst Morris Crisp, London
Overseas tours: Troubadours to Argentina 1987, to Brazil 1989
Overseas teams played for: Alexandra, Zimbabwe; Southern Hawkes Bay, New Zealand
Cricketers particularly admired: David Gower, Greg Chappell, Richard Hadlee
Other sports followed: Tennis, golf, hockey, rugby, soccer
Relaxations: Arts, theatre, music, reading
Extras: Surrey Young Cricketer of the Year 1984. Captained Surrey Young Cricketers for three years. Trials for England schoolboys at hockey
Best batting: 148 Derbyshire v Lancashire, Old Trafford 1991
Best bowling: 1-7 Derbyshire v Cambridge University, Fenner's 1992

1992 Season

	M	Inns	NO	Runs	HS	Avge	100s	50s	Ct	St	O	M	Runs	Wkts	Avge	Best	5wI	10wM
Test																		
All First	24	37	8	1031	95	35.55	-	8	11	-	28.2	0	148	2	74.00	1-7	-	-
1-day Int																		
NatWest	2	2	0	1	1	0.50	-	-	-	-								
B & H	5	4	0	67	37	16.75	-	-	1	-								
Sunday	17	14	0	350	69	25.00	-	2	3	-								

Career Performances

	M	Inns	NO	Runs	HS	Avge	100s	50s	Ct	St	Balls	Runs	Wkts	Avge	Best	5wI	10wM
Test																	
All First	71	120	16	3228	148	31.03	5	17	45	-	260	207	3	69.00	1-7	-	-
1-day Int																	
NatWest	2	2	0	1	1	0.50	-	-	-	-							
B & H	16	14	1	270	49	20.76	-	-	4	-	6	1	0	-		-	-
Sunday	44	40	5	798	69	22.80	-	2	10	-							

138. Who holds the record for the most first-class double centuries?

OSTLER, D. P.   Warwickshire

Name: Dominic Piers Ostler
Role: Right-hand bat, right-arm medium
bowler
Born: 15 July 1970, Solihull
Height: 6ft 3in
County debut: 1990
County cap: 1991
1000 runs in a season: 2
1st-Class 50s scored: 19
1st-Class 100s scored: 4
1st-Class catches: 50
One-Day 50s: 5
Place in batting averages: 97th av. 35.00
(1991 72nd av. 36.68)
Marital status: Single
Education: Princethorpe College, Solihull
Technical College
Extras: Warwickshire 2nd XI debut in

1989; played club cricket for Moseley in the
Birmingham League; member of Warwickshire
U19 side that won ESSO National Festival in 1988 and 1989
Best batting: 192 Warwickshire v Surrey, Guildford 1992
Marital status: Single
Education: Princethorpe College, Solihull Technical College
Extras: Warwickshire 2nd XI debut in 1989; played club cricket for Moseley in the
Birmingham League; member of Warwickshire U19 side that won ESSO National Festival
in 1988 and 1989
Best batting: 192 Warwickshire v Surrey, Guildford 1992

1992 Season

	M	Inns	NO	Runs	HS	Avge	100s	50s	Ct	St	O	M	Runs	Wkts	Avge	Best	5wI	10wM
Test																		
All First	22	37	2	1225	192	35.00	3	4	20	-	13	0	83	0	-	-	-	-
1-day Int																		
NatWest	4	4	1	36	30	12.00	-	-	2	-								
B & H	4	4	1	105	65 *	35.00	-	1	2	-								
Sunday	17	17	2	365	60 *	24.33	-	2	3	-	1	0	4	0	-		-	-

Career Performances

	M	Inns	NO	Runs	HS	Avge	100s	50s	Ct	St	Balls	Runs	Wkts	Avge	Best	5wl	10wM
Test																	
All First	55	96	9	3019	192	34.70	4	19	50	-	90	90	0	-	-	-	-
1-day Int																	
NatWest	9	8	2	87	34 *	14.50	-	-	2	-							
B & H	9	9	1	205	65 *	25.62	-	1	4	-							
Sunday	38	34	6	715	62 *	25.53	-	4	8	-	6	4	0	-	-	-	

PARKER, B.   *Yorkshire*

Name: Bradley Parker
Role: Right-hand bat, cover point fielder
Born: 23 June 1970, Mirfield
Height: 5ft 11in **Weight:** 12st
Nickname: Nesty
County debut: 1992
1st-Class catches: 1
Parents: Diane and David
Marital status: Single
Family links with cricket: Father played
club cricket
Education: Bingley Grammar School
Off-season: Coaching or playing abroad
Overseas teams played for: Ellerslie,
Auckland 1990-91
Cricketers particularly admired:
Richard Hadlee, Viv Richards, Alan Border
Other sports followed: Rugby League
Relaxations: Music, watching videos
Opinions on cricket: 'We could market the game of cricket better and certainly more
should be done to speed up over rates.'
Best batting: 30 Yorkshire v Kent, Canterbury 1992

1992 Season

	M	Inns	NO	Runs	HS	Avge	100s	50s	Ct	St	O	M	Runs	Wkts	Avge	Best	5wl	10wM
Test																		
All First	1	2	0	37	30	18.50	-	-	1	-								
1-day Int																		
NatWest																		
B & H																		
Sunday																		

	M	Inns	NO	Runs	HS	Avge	100s	50s	Ct	St	Balls	Runs	Wkts	Avge	Best	5wI	10wM
Test																	
All First	1	2	0	37	30	18.50	-	-	1	-							
1-day Int																	
NatWest																	
B & H																	
Sunday																	

PARKER, P. W. G.   Durham

Name: Paul William Giles Parker
Role: Right-hand bat, leg-break bowler, cover fielder
Born: 15 January 1956, Bulawayo, Rhodesia
Height: 5ft 10¹/₂in **Weight:** 12st
Nickname: Porky, Polly
County debut: 1976 (Sussex) 1992 (Durham)
County cap: 1979 (Sussex)
Benefit: 1988 (£59,400)
Test debut: 1981
Tests: 1
1000 runs in a season: 9
1st-Class 50s scored: 86
1st-Class 100s scored: 44
1st-Class 200s scored: 1
1st-Class catches: 244
One-Day 50s: 53
One-Day 100s: 6
Place in batting averages: 64th av. 40.33 (1991 162nd av. 24.28)
Parents: Anthony John and Margaret Edna
Wife and date of marriage: Teresa, 25 January 1980
Children: James William Ralph, 6 November 1980; Jocelyn Elizabeth, 10 September 1984
Family links with cricket: Father played for Essex 2nd XI. Uncle, David Green, played for Northamptonshire and Worcestershire. Two brothers, Guy and Rupert, 'very keen and active cricketers'. Father wrote *The Village Cricket Match* and was sports editor of ITN
Education: Collyer's Grammar School; St Catharine's College, Cambridge
Qualifications: MA (Cantab.)
Career outside cricket: Teaching at Tonbridge School

Overseas teams played for: Natal, South Africa 1980-81
Cricketers particularly admired: Ken Barrington, Jimmy Cook
Other sports followed: Rugby union and to a lesser extent golf and tennis
Injuries: Hamstring tear, out for three weeks
Relaxations: Reading, crosswords, bridge, music
Extras: Cambridge Blue at cricket and was selected for Varsity rugby match in 1977 but had to withdraw through injury. Was first reserve for England on Australia tour 1979-80. Appointed captain of Sussex 1988. Left Sussex at the end of 1991 season to join Durham. Durham Player of the Year 1992
Best batting: 215 Cambridge University v Essex, Fenner's 1976
Best bowling: 2-21 Sussex v Surrey, Guildford 1984

1992 Season

	M	Inns	NO	Runs	HS	Avge	100s	50s	Ct	St	O	M	Runs	Wkts	Avge	Best	5wl	10wM
Test																		
All First	20	35	2	1331	124	40.33	3	8	16	-	3.2	0	31	0	-		-	-	-
1-day Int																		
NatWest	3	3	0	133	69	44.33	-	2	3	-								
B & H	4	4	0	75	22	18.75	-	-	3	-								
Sunday	12	11	2	242	82	26.88	-	1	6	-								

Career Performances

	M	Inns	NO	Runs	HS	Avge	100s	50s	Ct	St	Balls	Runs	Wkts	Avge	Best	5wl	10wM
Test	1	2	0	13	13	6.50	-	-	-	-							
All First	352	601	78	18495	215	35.36	44	86	244	-	985	699	11	63.54	2-21	-	-
1-day Int																	
NatWest	40	40	6	1290	109	37.94	1	11	11	-	12	17	1	17.00	1-10	-	
B & H	67	67	6	1636	87	26.82	-	11	19	-	8	6	2	3.00	2-3	-	
Sunday	205	192	26	5018	121 *	30.22	5	31	86	-	39	38	2	19.00	1-2	-	

139. Which Derbyshire and England bowler celebrated his 90th birthday on 4 September 1992?

PARKIN, O. T.   Glamorgan

Name: Owen Thomas Parkin
Role: Right-hand bat, right-arm medium-fast bowler
Born: 24 August 1972, Coventry
Height: 6ft 2in **Weight:** 11st 6lbs
Nickname: Quicky
County debut: No first team appearance
Parents: Vernon Cyrus and Sarah Patricia
Marital status: Single
Education: Bournemouth Grammar School; Bath University
Qualifications: 9 GCSEs, 4 A-levels
Career outside cricket: Student
Off-season: 'Studying?'
Cricketers particularly admired: Malcolm Marshall, Richard Hadlee
Other sports followed: Rugby, football, boxing, squash
Relaxations: Squash, badminton, cards, running, 'general socialising with friends'
Opinions on cricket: 'Best sport in the world.'

PARKS, R. J.   Hampshire

Name: Robert James Parks
Role: Right-hand bat, wicket-keeper
Born: 15 June 1959, Cuckfield, Sussex
Height: 5ft 8in **Weight:** 10st 7lbs
Nickname: Bobby
County debut: 1980
County cap: 1982
Benefit: 1992
1st-Class 50s scored: 14
1st-Class catches: 638
1st-Class stumpings: 72
Place in batting averages: 166th av. 24.14
Parents: James and Irene
Wife and date of marriage: Amanda, 30 January 1982
Family links with cricket: Father, Jim Parks, played for Sussex, Somerset and England,

grandfather, J.H. Parks, played for England and Sussex. Uncle, H.W. Parks, also played for Sussex

Education: Eastbourne Grammar School; Southampton College of Higher Education

Qualifications: 9 O-levels, 1 A-level, OND and HND in Business Studies

Career outside cricket: Training as an accountant

Off-season: 'Putting the final touches to the benefit year and playing some golf'

Overseas tours: English Counties XI to Zimbabwe 1985; MCC to Kenya

Cricketers particularly admired: Bob Taylor, Jack Russell, Alan Knott, Nick Pocock

Other sports followed: Football (Tottenham Hotspur)

Relaxations: 'Watching Spurs and playing golf'

Extras: Broke the Hampshire record for the number of dismissals in a match as a wicket-keeper, v Derbyshire, 1982 (10 catches). One of the four wicket-keepers used by England v New Zealand at Lord's, 1986 (after injury to Bruce French)

Opinions on cricket: 'Four day cricket should not be brought in. It will be detrimental to the counties who will lose revenue and consequently have to reduce the size of their staffs. Sunday cricket should be kept at 40 overs.'

Best batting: 89 Hampshire v Cambridge University, Fenner's 1984

1992 Season

	M	Inns	NO	Runs	HS	Avge	100s	50s	Ct	St	O	M	Runs	Wkts	Avge	Best	5wI	10wM
Test																		
All First	7	10	3	169	33	24.14	-	-	21	2								
1-day Int																		
NatWest	2	1	1	10	10 *	-		-	-	3	-							
B & H	1	0	0	0	0	-		-	-	2	-							
Sunday	3	2	1	19	14 *	19.00		-	-	3	-							

Career Performances

	M	Inns	NO	Runs	HS	Avge	100s	50s	Ct	St	Balls	Runs	Wkts	Avge	Best	5wI	10wM
Test																	
All First	255	284	82	3944	89	19.52	-	14	638	72	189	166	0	-		-	-	-
1-day Int																	
NatWest	33	15	7	143	27 *	17.87	-	-	41	8							
B & H	47	27	11	190	23 *	11.87	-	-	59	6							
Sunday	160	64	30	613	38 *	18.02	-	-	157	29							

---

140. Who kept wicket for MCC v Germany at Lord's in 1992?

PARSONS, G. J.   Leicestershire

Name: Gordon James Parsons
Role: Left-hand bat, right-arm medium
bowler
Born: 17 October 1959, Slough
Height: 6ft 1in **Weight:** 13st 8lbs
Nickname: Bullhead,
County debut: 1978 (Leics), 1986
(Warwicks)
County cap: 1984 (Leics), 1987 (Warwicks)
50 wickets in a season: 2
1st-Class 50s scored: 22
1st-Class 5 w. in innings: 18
1st-Class 10 w. in match: 1
1st-Class catches: 78
One-Day 50s: 1
Place in batting averages: 243rd av. 11.83
Place in bowling averages: 12th av. 24.48
Strike rate: 52.82 (career 59.36)

Parents: Dave and Evelyn
Wife and date of marriage: Hester Sophia, 8 February 1991
Children: Alexandra Suzanna, 5 June 1992
Family links with cricket: Father played club cricket , brother-in-law, Hansie Cronje,
plays for South Africa
Education: Woodside County Secondary School, Slough
Qualifications: 5 O-levels
Off-season: Managing and coaching Orange Free State B side and playing club cricket in
South Africa
Overseas tours: ESCA to India 1977-78; Derrick Robbins XI to Australasia 1980;
Leicestershire to Zimbabwe 1981
Overseas teams played for: Maharaja's, Sri Lanka 1979,1987; Boland, South Africa
1982-83; Griqualand West 1984-85; Orange Free State 1986-92
Cricketers particularly admired: 'Too many to mention'
Other sports followed: Golf
Injuries: Side strain, out for two weeks
Relaxations: 'My wife and child and I enjoy a round of golf and a few beers talking cricket'
Extras: Played for Leicester 2nd XI since 1976 and for Buckinghamshire in 1977. Left
Leicestershire after 1985 season and joined Warwickshire. Capped by Warwickshire while
in plaster and on crutches. Released at end of 1988 season and returned to his old county.
Justin Benson was best man at his wedding, 'contradiction in terms, though it is!'
Opinions on cricket: 'Looking forward to the English crowd reacting to coloured clothing
and a white ball.'
Best batting: 76 Boland v Western Province B, Cape Town 1984-85

Best bowling: 9-72 Boland v Transvaal B, Johannesburg 1984-85

1992 Season

	M	Inns	NO	Runs	HS	Avge	100s	50s	Ct	St	O	M	Runs	Wkts	Avge	Best	5wI	10wM
Test																		
All First	14	14	2	142	35	11.83	-	-	6	-	343.2	92	955	39	24.48	6-70	2	-
1-day Int																		
NatWest	4	3	1	9	5	4.50	-	-	1	-	24	4	84	2	42.00	2-29	-	
B & H	4	2	1	3	2 *	3.00	-	-	1	-	30.5	5	122	4	30.50	2-16	-	
Sunday	15	13	7	125	31 *	20.83	-	-	1	-	98	2	511	15	34.06	3-29	-	

Career Performances

	M	Inns	NO	Runs	HS	Avge	100s	50s	Ct	St	Balls	Runs	Wkts	Avge	Best	5wI	10wM
Test																	
All First	260	341	77	4929	76	18.67	-	22	78	-	35977	18436	606	30.42	9-72	18	1
1-day Int																	
NatWest	24	15	4	130	23	11.81	-	-	5	-	1315	839	18	46.61	2-11	-	
B & H	46	23	10	255	63 *	19.61	-	1	11	-	2450	1462	52	28.11	4-12	-	
Sunday	142	84	30	702	31 *	13.00	-	-	18	-	5576	4277	129	33.15	4-19	-	

PARSONS, K. A.   Somerset

Name: Keith Alan Parsons
Role: Right-hand bat, right-arm medium bowler
Born: 2 May 1973, Taunton
Height: 6ft 1in **Weight:** 13st
Nickname: Pilot, Pars
County debut: 1992
Parents: Alan and Lynne
Marital status: Single
Family links with cricket: Twin brother, Kevin, also on the Somerset staff. Father played six seasons for Somerset 2nd XI, and captained National Civil Service XI
Education: The Castle School, Taunton; Richard Huish Sixth Form College, Taunton
Qualifications: 8 GCSEs, 3 A-Levels
Off-season: Playing in New Zealand
Overseas tours: Castle School to Barbados 1989
Cricketers particularly admired: Viv Richards, Richard Hadlee, Robin Smith

Other sports followed: Rugby Union, soccer, golf

Relaxations: 'All sports.'

Extras: Captained two National Cup winning sides, Taunton St Andrews in National U15 club Championship and Richard Huish College in National U17 School Championship. Represented ESCA at U15 and U19 level

Opinions on cricket: 'Now that the First Class Championship has been changed to four-day games, in order to improve the Test team and reduce the amount of contrived finishes, shouldn't the next step be to change the 2nd XI competition to a four-day Championship also, to help the younger players, in 2nd XI, become better four-day cricketers.'

Best batting: 1 Somerset v Pakistan, Taunton 1992

1992 Season

	M	Inns	NO	Runs	HS	Avge	100s	50s	Ct	St	O	M	Runs	Wkts	Avge	Best	5wI	10wM
Test																		
All First	1	2	0	1	1	0.50	-	-	-	-								
1-day Int																		
NatWest																		
B & H																		
Sunday																		

Career Performances

	M	Inns	NO	Runs	HS	Avge	100s	50s	Ct	St	Balls	Runs	Wkts	Avge	Best	5wI	10wM
Test																	
All First	1	2	0	1	1	0.50	-	-	-	-							
1-day Int																	
NatWest																	
B & H																	
Sunday																	

141. What do the following have in common, outside cricket: W.R. Hammond, W.J. Edrich and I.T. Botham?

142. Which county cricketer played most times for England at soccer?

PARSONS, K. J. Somerset

Name: Kevin John Parsons
Role: Right-hand bat, 'very occasional wicket-keeper'
Born: 2 May 1973, Taunton
Height: 6ft 1in **Weight:** 12st 6lbs
Nickname: Barney
County debut: 1992 (one-day)
Parents: Alan and Lynne
Marital status: Single
Family links with cricket: Twin brother, Keith, also on the Somerset staff. Father played for Somerset 2nd XI
Education: The Castle School, Taunton; Richard Huish Sixth Form College, Taunton
Qualifications: 7 GCSEs, 3 A-Levels
Off-season: 'I hope to play cricket in Australia this winter'
Overseas tours: Castle School to Barbados 1989

Cricketers particularly admired:
Viv Richards, Ian Botham, David Gower
Other sports followed: Rugby Union, soccer
Relaxations: Playing golf and watching TV
Extras: Won National U15 club Championship with Taunton St Andrews and the National U17 School Championship with Richard Huish College. Played for England Schools U19 1991
Opinions on cricket: 'I think that the standard of 2nd XI wickets should be improved so that they last three days.'

1992 Season

	M	Inns	NO	Runs	HS	Avge	100s	50s	Ct	St	O	M	Runs	Wkts	Avge	Best	5wI	10wM
Test																		
All First																		
1-day Int																		
NatWest																		
B & H																		
Sunday	1	0	0	0	0	-	-	-	-	-	-							

Career Performances

	M	Inns	NO	Runs	HS	Avge	100s	50s	Ct	St	Balls	Runs	Wkts	Avge	Best	5wI	10wM
Test																	
All First																		
1-day Int																		
NatWest																		
B & H																		
Sunday	1	0	0	0	0	-	-	-	-	-	-						

PATEL, M. M. Kent

Name: Minal Mahesh Patel
Role: Right-hand bat, slow left-arm bowler
Born: 7 August 1970, Bombay, India
Height: 5ft 9in **Weight:** 9st 7lbs
Nickname: Min
County debut: 1989
1st-Class 5 w. in innings: 2
1st-Class 10 w. in match: 1
1st-Class catches: 5
Place in bowling averages:
(1991 89th av. 35.23)
Strike rate: (career 86.67)
Parents: Mahesh and Aruna
Marital status: Single
Family links with cricket: Father played good club cricket in India, Africa and England
Education: Dartford GS; Erith College of Technology; Manchester Polytechnic
Qualifications: 6 O-levels, 3 A-levels
Overseas tours: Dartford GS to Barbados 1988
Cricketers particularly admired: Bishen Bedi, Derek Underwood, Sunil Gavaskar
Other sports followed: 'All except anything to do with horses'
Relaxations: Listening to soul and dance music, playing snooker
Extras: Played for ESCA 1988,1989 and NCA England South 1989. Kent League Young Player of the Year 1987 while playing for Blackheath. First six overs in NatWest Trophy were all maidens
Best batting: 43 Kent v Leicestershire, Leicester 1991
Best bowling: 6-57 Kent v Leicestershire, Dartford 1990

1992 Season (did not make any first-class or one-day appearance)

Career Performances

	M	Inns	NO	Runs	HS	Avge	100s	50s	Ct	St	Balls	Runs	Wkts	Avge	Best	5wl	10wM
Test																	
All First	15	20	7	183	43	14.07	-	-	5	-	2947	1328	34	39.05	6-57	2	1
1-day Int																	
NatWest	1	0	0	0	0	-	-	-	-	-	72	29	2	14.50	2-29	-	
B & H																	
Sunday																	

PAYNE, A.   Somerset

Name: Andrew Payne
Role: Right-hand bat, right arm medium-fast bowler
Born: 20 October 1973, Rawtenstall, Lancashire
Height: 5ft 10in **Weight:** 12st 6lbs
Nickname: Beastie
County debut: 1992
1st-Class 50s scored: 1
Parents: Brian and Margaret
Marital status: Single
Family links with cricket: Brother represented County Junior Leagues (Lancashire), father, captain of Rawtenstall in Lancashire League
Education: Bacup and Rawtenstall Grammar School; Accrington and Rossendale College
Qualifications: 8 GCSEs, BTEC in Human Biology, BTEC in Art and Design, qualified cricket coach

Career outside cricket: In the Police Force
Off-season: Touring India with the U19 team
Overseas tours: England U19 to Pakistan 1991-92
Cricketers particularly admired: Chris Tavaré, David Gower, Robin Smith, Allan Donald
Other sports followed: 'Most sports, especially football'
Relaxations: Playing golf, watching football and socialising
Extras: Youngest ever pro in the Ribblesdale cricket league. One of the few players ever to play for all Lancashire junior teams (U11-U19)

Opinions on cricket: 'I think that the one bouncer per over rule should either be tightened up on or totally abolished because there is still uncertainty to both batsmen, bowlers and umpires as to what should be classed as a bouncer and what shouldn't. Also I would have liked the Sunday League to have stayed a forty over competition rather than fifty.'

Best batting: 51* Somerset v Gloucestershire, Taunton 1992
Best bowling: 1-71 Somerset v Gloucestershire, Taunton 1992

1992 Season

	M	Inns	NO	Runs	HS	Avge	100s	50s	Ct	St	O	M	Runs	Wkts	Avge	Best	5wI	10wM
Test																		
All First	1	1	1	51	51 *	-	-	1	-	-	27	8	71	1	71.00	1-71	-	-
1-day Int																		
NatWest																			
B & H																			
Sunday	1	1	1	6	6 *	-	-	-	-	-								

Career Performances

	M	Inns	NO	Runs	HS	Avge	100s	50s	Ct	St	Balls	Runs	Wkts	Avge	Best	5wI	10wM
Test																	
All First	1	1	1	51	51 *	-	-	1	-	-	162	71	1	71.00	1-71	-	-
1-day Int																	
NatWest																	
B & H																	
Sunday	1	1	1	6	6 *	-	-	-	-	-							

143. Who was the first woman MP to play cricket for the Lords and Commons XI?

144. Who has the highest Test batting average for England?

PEARSON, R. M.   Northamptonshire

Name: Richard Michael Pearson
Role: Right-hand bat, right arm off-break
bowler
Born: 27 January 1972, Batley, Yorkshire
Height: 6ft 4in **Weight:** 14st
Nickname: Batley, Pancho
County debut: 1992
1st-Class 5 w. in innings: 2
1st-Class catches: 4
Place in batting averages: 241st av. 12.00
Place in bowling averages: 149th av. 63.95
Strike rate: 120.75 (career 125.91)
Parents: Mike and Carol
Marital status: Single
Family links with cricket: Father played
in Yorkshire League
Education: Batley Grammar School;
St John's, Cambridge
Qualifications: 2 O-Levels, 9 GCSEs,
4 A-Levels
Career outside cricket: Student
Off-season: Studying
Overseas tours: England U19 to Pakistan 1991-92
Cricketers particularly admired: David Gower
Other sports followed: Football, rugby league
Relaxations: Playing football
Extras: Made first-class debut for Cambridge University in 1991. Has played for
Combined Universities in the Benson and Hedges Trophy since 1991
Opinions on cricket: 'Looking at the effect India's spinners had on England something
should be done to gear the pitches in England to suit the spinner more.'
Best batting: 33* Cambridge University v Surrey, Fenner's 1992
Best bowling: 5-108 Cambridge University v Warwickshire, Fenner's 1992

1992 Season

	M	Inns	NO	Runs	HS	Avge	100s	50s	Ct	St	O	M	Runs	Wkts	Avge	Best	5wI	10wM
Test																		
All First	11	13	5	96	33 *	12.00	-	-	4	-	402.3	64	1279	20	63.95	5-108	1	-
1-day Int																		
NatWest																		
B & H	4	2	1	10	8	10.00	-	-	-	-	44	4	177	4	44.25	2-31	-	
Sunday	1	0	0	0	0	-	-	-	-	-	2	0	18	0	-	-	-	

Career Performances

	M	Inns	NO	Runs	HS	Avge	100s	50s	Ct	St	Balls	Runs	Wkts	Avge	Best	5wI	10wM
Test																	
All First	21	25	6	166	33 *	8.73	-	-	6	-	4407	2377	35	67.91	5-108	1	-
1-day Int																	
NatWest																		
B & H	5	2	1	10	8	10.00	-	-	-	-	300	201	4	50.25	2-31	-	
Sunday	1	0	0	0	0	-	-	-	-	-	12	18	0	-	-	-	

PEIRCE, M. T. E.   Sussex

Name: Michael Toby Edward Peirce
Role: Left-hand bat, left arm bowler
Born: 14 June 1973, Maidenhead
Height: 5ft 10in **Weight:** 11st
Nickname: Beastie
County debut: No first team appearance
Parents: Michael Robert and Katherine Ross
Marital status: Single
Education: Ardingly College; Durham
University
Qualifications: 9 GCSEs, 3 A-Levels,
1 S-Level
Career outside cricket: Student
Off-season: At University
Overseas tours: Sussex Schools U14 to
Barbados 1987; School tour to India
1988-89; to India 1990-91
Overseas teams played for: Kilbirnie,
Wellington 1991-92; Wellington B 1991-92
Cricketers particularly admired:
David Gower, Phil Edmonds, Sangram Sawant
Other sports followed: 'Everything except swimming and the horses (rugby, football and
ice hockey especially'
Relaxations: Aviation, music and gossip
Opinions on cricket: 'Try to take each ball in turn and keep things simple.'

145. What was most unusual about the England team for the
second Test against Pakistan at Lord's, 1992?

PENBERTHY, A. L.   Northamptonshire

Name: Anthony Leonard Penberthy
Role: Left-hand bat, right-arm medium bowler
Born: 1 September 1969, Troon, Cornwall
Height: 6ft 1in **Weight:** 12st 8lbs
Nickname: Berth, Penbers, After
County debut: 1989
1st-Class 50s scored: 4
1st-Class 100s scored: 1
1st-Class catches: 25
Place in batting averages: 236th av. 12.61 (1991 220th av. 15.50)
Place in bowling averages: (1991 101st av. 37.00)
Strike rate: (career 68.04)
Parents: Gerald and Wendy
Marital status: Single
Family links with cricket: Father played in local leagues in Cornwall and is now a qualified umpire instructor
Education: Troon County Primary; Camborne Comprehensive
Qualifications: 3 O-levels, 3 CSEs, coaching certificate
Off-season: Working in Cornwall
Cricketers particularly admired: Ian Botham, David Gower, Geoff Boycott, Dennis Lillee, Viv Richards, Eldine Baptiste
Other sports followed: Football, snooker, rugby, golf
Injuries: Pulled rib cartilage, couldn't bowl for three and a half weeks; broken finger, missed two games
Relaxations: Listening to music, watching videos and comedy programmes
Extras: Had trials for Plymouth Argyle at football but came to Northampton for cricket trials instead. Took wicket with first ball in first-class cricket, Mark Taylor caught behind June 1989. Played for England YC v New Zealand 1989. Made first first-class 100 of 1990 season
Opinions on cricket: 'Don't agree with certain parts of the new Sunday League structure. For example; 50 overs per side and full run ups; lunch and tea intervals should be longer; over rate fines too strict.'
Best batting: 101* Northamptonshire v Cambridge University, Fenner's 1990
Best bowling: 4-91 Northamptonshire v Warwickshire, Northampton 1990

1992 Season

	M	Inns	NO	Runs	HS	Avge	100s	50s	Ct	St	O	M	Runs	Wkts	Avge	Best	5wI	10wM
Test																		
All First	10	14	1	164	33	12.61	-	-	6	-	108	24	313	8	39.12	3-34	-	-
1-day Int																		
NatWest	4	3	0	51	36	17.00	-	-	1	-	25.1	4	79	3	26.33	2-29	-	
B & H	1	1	1	7	7*	-	-	-	1	-	8	1	36	1	36.00	1-36	-	
Sunday	11	7	1	91	43	15.16	-	-	3	-	64	1	336	9	37.33	2-29	-	

Career Performances

	M	Inns	NO	Runs	HS	Avge	100s	50s	Ct	St	Balls	Runs	Wkts	Avge	Best	5wI	10wM
Test																	
All First	39	55	7	905	101*	18.85	1	4	25	-	3402	1909	50	38.18	4-91	-	-
1-day Int																	
NatWest	4	3	0	51	36	17.00	-	-	1	-	151	79	3	26.33	2-29	-	
B & H	4	3	1	20	10	10.00	-	-	1	-	150	101	3	33.66	2-22	-	
Sunday	26	16	4	216	43	18.00	-	-	9	-	738	675	19	35.52	3-26	-	

PENN, C.   Kent

Name: Christopher Penn
Role: Left-hand bat, right-arm fast-medium bowler
Born: 19 June 1963, Dover
Height: 6ft 1in **Weight:** 13^{1}/$_{2}$st-15st
Nickname: Penny, Gazza
County debut: 1982
County cap: 1987
50 wickets in a season: 2
1st-Class 50s scored: 6
1st-Class 100s scored: 1
1st-Class 5 w. in innings: 12
1st-Class catches: 54
Place in bowling averages:
(1991 25th av. 25.44)
Strike rate: (career 62.47)
Parents: Reg and Brenda
Wife and date of marriage: Caroline Ann, 22 March 1986
Children: Matthew Thomas, 14 October 1987; David Thomas 30 March 1990
Family links with cricket: Father played club cricket for Dover CC for 26 years; mother made the teas

Education: River Primary School; Dover Grammar School and 'Trevor Wards car'
Qualifications: 9 O-levels, 3 A-levels
Career outside cricket: Financial planning consultant. Bromley Councils sports development department. Bar manager, Granville Inn, Canterbury 'for Mr and Mrs Hilton'
Off-season: Coaching for Kent and privately. 'Participating in England's preparation for India at Lilleshall until Xmas as bowling fodder'
Overseas tours: NCA South of England U19 to Denmark 1981; Whitbread Scholarship to Australia 1982-83
Overseas teams played for: Koh-i-Noor Crescents, Johannesburg 1981-82, 1983-84 (part); West Perth, Australia 1982-83; Johannesburg Municipals 1983-84 (part); Witwatersrand University, Johannesburg 1984-85; Green Point, Cape Town 1990-91
Cricketers particularly admired: Alan Knott, Dennis Lillee, Robin Smith, 'plus those I learnt from – my father, Geoff Arnold, Colin Page, Brian Luckhurst, Graham Johnson, Barney Lock, Grahem Mart, Darryll Foster, Bob Lee and many, many more'
Other sports followed: Football (Dover FC) and all sports 'even horse racing quietly, but I will never admit to it'
Injuries: Double hernia operation; Groin strains caused by bowling, out for six weeks
Relaxations: 'Now we have a family relaxation is no longer possible but I do like music (heavy metal), art and art history (mainly impressionism), Indian food and keeping fit.'
Extras: Played for Young England and England Schools. Took hat-trick in first 2nd XI match v Middlesex when 16 years old. Coached for Transvaal Cricket Council in the Johannesburg townships during the early 80s. Kent Player of the Year 1988
Opinions on cricket: 'We are generally fortunate enough to earn a living at something we really, deep down, love doing, but we still moan. Perhaps there are more injuries now, not because we train too much but because we don't train enough to cope with the demands of the modern game.'
Best batting: 115 Kent v Lancashire, Old Trafford 1984
Best bowling: 7-70 Kent v Middlesex, Lord's 1988

1992 Season

	M	Inns	NO	Runs	HS	Avge	100s	50s	Ct	St	O	M	Runs	Wkts	Avge	Best	5wI	10wM
Test																		
All First	7	5	2	26	14 *	8.66	-	-	3	-	151	26	477	5	95.40	2-69	-	-
1-day Int																		
NatWest																			
B & H																			
Sunday																			

146. Which player has dismissed most Test opponents – in total as bowler *and* catcher – in history?

Career Performances

	M	Inns	NO	Runs	HS	Avge	100s	50s	Ct	St	Balls	Runs	Wkts	Avge	Best	5wI	10wM
Test																	
All First	123	141	36	1985	115	18.90	1	6	54	-	17681	9493	283	33.54	7-70	12	-
1-day Int																	
NatWest	8	4	1	28	20 *	9.33	-	-	1	-	480	249	10	24.90	3-30	-	
B & H	23	15	7	97	24 *	12.12	-	-	3	-	1212	780	25	31.20	4-34	-	
Sunday	61	33	9	231	40	9.62	-	-	15	-	2383	1956	62	31.54	4-15	-	

PENNETT, D. B.   Nottinghamshire

Name: David Barrington Pennett
Role: Right-hand bat, right-arm fast-medium bowler
Born: 26 October 1969, Leeds LGI
Height: 6ft **Weight:** 12st
Nickname: Yorkie, Fiery
County debut: 1992
1st-Class catches: 3
Place in bowling averages: 100th av. 37.73
Strike rate: 68.38 (career 68.38)
Parents: Barrie and Valerie
Marital status: Single
Education: Benton Park Grammar School
Qualifications: 5 O-levels, ASA teachers certificate – swimming
Career outside cricket: 'Model for numerous Northern agencies.'
Off-season: 'Either playing cricket in Australia, coaching at Trent Bridge or modelling.'
Cricketers particularly admired: Malcolm Marshall, Ian Botham, Viv Richards
Other sports followed: Football, rugby union
Relaxations: Playing football, dance music, night clubs
Extras: Joined the Yorkshire Cricket Academy in 1990 for two years. Took a hat-trick in a Bain Clarkson game for Yorkshire v Notts.
Opinions on cricket: 'There should be a better balance between bat and ball and the game should be played positively. The game should be marketed to the public more. Day/night games have got to be looked at to introduce more people to the game and to generate more money.'
Best batting: 29 Nottinghamshire v Derbyshire, Trent Bridge 1992
Best bowling: 4-58 Nottinghamshire v Warwickshire, Edgbaston 1992

1992 Season

	M	Inns	NO	Runs	HS	Avge	100s	50s	Ct	St	O	M	Runs	Wkts	Avge	Best	5wI	10wM
Test																		
All First	12	11	1	69	29	6.90	-	-	3	-	296.2	51	981	26	37.73	4-58	-	-
1-day Int																		
NatWest																		
B & H																		
Sunday	7	2	2	14	12 *	-	-	-	1	-	42	1	237	3	79.00	2-28	-	

Career Performances

	M	Inns	NO	Runs	HS	Avge	100s	50s	Ct	St	Balls	Runs	Wkts	Avge	Best	5wI	10wM
Test																	
All First	12	11	1	69	29	6.90	-	-	3	-	1778	981	26	37.73	4-58	-	-
1-day Int																	
NatWest																	
B & H																	
Sunday	7	2	2	14	12 *	-	-	-	1	-	252	237	3	79.00	2-28	-	

PENNEY, T. L.   Warwickshire

Name: Trevor Lionel Penney
Role: Right-hand bat, right-arm leg-break bowler
Born: 12 June 1968, Harare, Zimbabwe
Height: 6ft **Weight:** 11st
Nickname: T.P, Lemon Kop
County debut: 1992
1st-Class 100s scored: 3
1st-Class 50s scored: 5
1st-Class catches: 6
Place in batting averages: 17th av. 53.17
Parents: George and Bets
Marital status: Engaged
Family links with cricket: Brother Stephen played for Zimbabwe U25
Education: Blakiston Primary; Prince Edward Boys High School, Zimbabwe
Qualifications: 3 O-levels, Tobacco buyer
Career outside cricket: Tobacco buyer
Off-season: Playing and coaching cricket in Cape Town
Overseas tours: Zimbabwe to Sri Lanka 1987; ICC XI to Australia (junior World Cup)
Overseas teams played for: Old Hararians, Zimbabwe 1983-89; Scarborough, Australia

1989-90; Boland, South Africa 1991-92
Cricketers particularly admired: Colin Bland, Ian Botham, Graeme Hick
Other sports followed: Football, golf, hockey, tennis, squash
Injuries: Tore ligaments in ankle
Relaxations: Playing golf and drinking Castle on Lake Kariba
Extras: Captained the ICC team at the Junior World Cup in 1988. Played for Zimbabwe against Sri Lanka in 1987. Played hockey for Zimbabwe from 1984-87 and also made the African team who played Asia in 1987. Qualified to play for England in 1992
Opinions on cricket: 'Four-day cricket will be good for the game.'
Best batting: 151 Warwickshire v Middlesex, Lord's 1992

1992 Season

	M	Inns	NO	Runs	HS	Avge	100s	50s	Ct	St	O	M	Runs	Wkts	Avge	Best	5wI	10wM
Test																		
All First	16	24	7	904	151	53.17	3	4	5	-	5	0	35	0	-		-	-	-
1-day Int																		
NatWest	3	3	0	19	7	6.33	-	-	1	-								
B & H	2	2	0	22	17	11.00	-	-	1	1								
Sunday	13	12	6	226	53 *	37.66	-	1	7	-	1	0	2	0	-		-	-

Career Performances

	M	Inns	NO	Runs	HS	Avge	100s	50s	Ct	St	Balls	Runs	Wkts	Avge	Best	5wI	10wM
Test																	
All First	22	33	10	1146	151	49.82	3	5	6	-	36	39	0	-		-	-
1-day Int																	
NatWest	3	3	0	19	7	6.33	-	-	1	-							
B & H	2	2	0	22	17	11.00	-	-	1	1							
Sunday	13	12	6	226	53 *	37.66	-	1	7	-	6	2	0	-		-	-

PICK, R. A.   Nottinghamshire

Name: Robert Andrew Pick
Role: Left-hand bat, right-arm fast-medium bowler, gully fielder
Born: 19 November 1963, Nottingham
Height: 5ft 10in **Weight:** 13st
Nickname: Dad
County debut: 1983
County cap: 1987
50 wickets in a season: 3
1st-Class 50s scored: 3
1st-Class 5 w. in innings: 11
1st-Class 10 w. in match: 3

1st-Class catches: 32
Place in batting averages:
205th av. 18.12 (1991 243rd av. 12.90)
Place in bowling averages:
131st av. 47.88 (1991 55th av. 31.04)
Strike rate: 84.72 (career 58.25)
Parents: Bob and Lillian
Wife and date of marriage:
Jennie Ruth, 8 April 1989
Family links with cricket: Father, uncles
and cousins all play local cricket; David
Millns is brother-in-law
Education: Alderman Derbyshire
Comprehensive; High Pavement College
Qualifications: 7 O-levels, 1 A-level,
coaching qualification
Overseas tours: England A to Pakistan
1990-91; Bermuda and West Indies 1991-92
Overseas teams played for:
Wellington, New Zealand 1989-90
Cricketers particularly admired: Bob White, Mike Hendrick, Mike Harris, Franklyn
Stephenson
Other sports followed: Ice-hockey, soccer and American football
Relaxations: 'As much fishing as possible and listening to a wide range of music; eating
and drinking; going to the pictures.'
Extras: Played for England YC v Australia 1983. Played soccer for Nottingham Schoolboys
Opinions on cricket: 'Coloured clothing should be introduced for all one-day cricket.'
Best batting: 63 Nottinghamshire v Warwickshire, Nuneaton 1985
Best bowling: 7-128 Nottinghamshire v Leicestershire, Leicester 1990

1992 Season

	M	Inns	NO	Runs	HS	Avge	100s	50s	Ct	St	O	M	Runs	Wkts	Avge	Best	5wI	10wM
Test																		
All First	10	12	4	145	52	18.12	-	1	1	-	254.1	50	862	18	47.88	3-33	-	-
1-day Int																		
NatWest	2	1	1	24	24 *	-	-	-	-	-	24	1	119	2	59.50	2-66	-	
B & H	4	2	1	8	5	8.00	-	-	-	-	40	5	127	6	21.16	3-35	-	
Sunday	7	1	0	24	24	24.00	-	-	1	-	49.5	1	230	9	25.55	2-34	-	

147. What is the French for batsman?

Career Performances

	M	Inns	NO	Runs	HS	Avge	100s	50s	Ct	St	Balls	Runs	Wkts	Avge	Best	5wI	10wM
Test																	
All First	138	135	39	1430	63	14.89	-	3	32	-	20505	11521	352	32.73	7-128	11	3
1-day Int																	
NatWest	21	12	10	96	34 *	48.00	-	-	4	-	1387	888	31	28.64	5-22	1	
B & H	30	12	7	50	25 *	10.00	-	-	3	-	1821	1228	41	29.95	4-42	-	
Sunday	76	24	11	155	24	11.92	-	-	13	-	3223	2714	85	31.92	4-32	-	

PICKLES, C. S. Yorkshire

Name: Christopher Stephen Pickles
Role: Right-hand bat, right-arm medium bowler
Born: 30 January 1966, Cleckheaton
Height: 6ft 1in **Weight:** 13st 6lbs
Nickname: Pick, Oke Koke
County debut: 1985
1st-Class 50s scored: 7
1st-Class catches: 24
Place in batting averages:
216th av. 16.37 (1991 180th av. 21.84)
Place in bowling averages: 35th av. 27.64
Strike rate: 51.50 (career 77.60)
Parents: Ronnie and Christine
Wife and date of marriage: Janet,
22 October 1988
Children: Samantha, 10 October 1989
Family links with cricket: Father still plays
in the Densbury League
Education: Whitcliffe Mount Comprehensive
Qualifications: Qualified cricket coach
Overseas tours: NCA U19 to Bermuda 1985; Yorkshire to Barbados 1990
Overseas teams played for: Whangerai, New Zealand 1988-89
Cricketers particularly admired: Malcolm Marshall, Viv Richards, Graham Gooch, Robin Smith
Other sports followed: Ruby union (Cleckheaton RFC)
Relaxations: Following rugby union and 'going out for a pint'
Extras: Made debut for Northamptonshire 2nd XI as a batsman and scored 100, made debut for Yorkshire 2nd XI as a bowler and took five wickets. Released by Yorkshire at the end of the 1992 season
Opinions on cricket: 'Players should not qualify as English until they have played county

cricket for at least seven years.'
Best batting: 66 Yorkshire v Somerset, Taunton 1989
Best bowling: 4-40 Yorkshire v Northamptonshire, Northampton 1992

1992 Season

	M	Inns	NO	Runs	HS	Avge	100s	50s	Ct	St	O	M	Runs	Wkts	Avge	Best	5wI	10wM
Test																		
All First	6	9	1	131	49	16.37	-	-	2	-	120.1	27	387	14	27.64	4-40	-	-
1-day Int																		
NatWest	1	0	0	0	0	-	-	-	-	-	12	2	40	2	20.00	2-40	-	
B & H	4	4	1	74	37 *	24.66	-	-	-	-	37.1	6	129	2	64.50	1-16	-	
Sunday	10	9	4	80	26 *	16.00	-	-	2	-	59.3	2	343	5	68.60	2-62	-	

Career Performances

	M	Inns	NO	Runs	HS	Avge	100s	50s	Ct	St	Balls	Runs	Wkts	Avge	Best	5wI	10wM
Test																	
All First	58	76	21	1336	66	24.29	-	7	24	-	6441	3638	83	43.83	4-40	-	-
1-day Int																	
NatWest	3	2	0	15	12	7.50	-	-	1	-	207	111	4	27.75	2-40	-	
B & H	10	7	2	96	37 *	19.20	-	-	1	-	583	348	5	69.60	2-49	-	
Sunday	56	38	17	259	30 *	12.33	-	-	20	-	2161	1896	53	35.77	4-36	-	

PIGOTT, A. C. S. Sussex

Name: Anthony Charles Shackleton Pigott
Role: Right-hand bat, right-arm fast bowler,
slip fielder
Born: 4 June 1958, London
Height: 6ft 1in **Weight:** 13st
Nickname: Lester
County debut: 1978
County cap: 1982
Benefit: 1991 (£60,025)
Test debut: 1983-84
Tests: 1
50 wickets in a season: 5
1st-Class 50s scored: 19
1st-Class 100s scored: 1
1st-Class 5 w. in innings: 23
1st-Class 10 w. in match: 1
1st-Class catches: 115
One-Day 50s: 2

Place in batting averages: 221st av. 15.91 (1991 199th av. 18.82)
Place in bowling averages: 106th av. 39.37 (1991 109th av. 38.94)
Strike rate: 80.66 (career 55.80)
Parents: Tom and Juliet
Marital status: Divorced
Children: Elliot Sebastian, 15 March 1983
Family links with cricket: Father captained village side, mother played at school 'and claims I got my cricket ability from her'
Education: Harrow School
Qualifications: 5 O-levels, 2 A-levels; junior coaching certificate
Overseas tours: Part of England tour to New Zealand 1983-84; MCC to Leeward Islands 1992
Overseas teams played for: Wellington, New Zealand 1982-83 and 1983-84
Cricketers particularly admired: Ian Botham, Geoff Arnold, John Snow, Mike Gatting
Other sports followed: Squash, soccer, golf, rugby
Extras: Public Schools Racquets champion 1975. First three wickets in first-class cricket were a hat-trick. Had operation on back, April 1981, missing most of season, and was told by a specialist he would never play cricket again. Postponed wedding to make Test debut when called into England party on tour of New Zealand. Originally going to Somerset for 1984 season, but remained with Sussex. Was diagnosed as a diabetic after he lost 11lbs in two weeks in 1987, but recovered to take 74 wickets in 1988 season
Best batting: 104* Sussex v Warwickshire, Edgbaston 1986
Best bowling: 7-74 Sussex v Northamptonshire, Eastbourne 1982

1992 Season

	M	Inns	NO	Runs	HS	Avge	100s	50s	Ct	St	O	M	Runs	Wkts	Avge	Best	5wI	10wM
Test																		
All First	17	19	7	191	27 *	15.91	-	-	5	-	363	74	1063	27	39.37	3-34	-	-
1-day Int																		
NatWest	2	2	1	3	3 *	3.00	-	-	-	-	20	1	49	5	9.80	3-31	-	
B & H	5	4	0	41	17	10.25	-	-	1	-	50.5	2	221	6	36.83	3-39	-	
Sunday	16	8	4	55	17 *	13.75	-	-	4	-	114	2	660	19	34.73	3-49	-	

Career Performances

	M	Inns	NO	Runs	HS	Avge	100s	50s	Ct	St	Balls	Runs	Wkts	Avge	Best	5wI	10wM
Test	1	2	1	12	8 *	12.00	-	-	-	-	102	75	2	37.50	2-75	-	-
All First	234	282	63	4452	104 *	20.32	1	19	115	-	33484	18426	600	30.71	7-74	23	1
1-day Int																	
NatWest	23	13	1	163	53	13.58	-	1	6	-	1221	710	29	24.48	3-4	-	
B & H	39	27	8	263	49 *	13.84	-	-	15	-	2145	1498	49	30.57	3-29	-	
Sunday	150	87	32	993	51 *	18.05	-	1	50	-	6006	4982	224	22.24	5-24	3	

PIPER, K. J.   Warwickshire

Name: Keith John Piper
Role: Right-hand bat, wicket-keeper
Born: 18 December 1969
Height: 5ft 7in **Weight:** 10st 8lbs
Nickname: Tubbsy, Garden Boy
County debut: 1989
County cap: 1992
1st-Class 50s scored: 4
1st-Class 100s scored: 1
1st-Class catches: 158
1st-Class stumpings: 9
Place in batting averages: 185th av. 20.29
(1991 205th av. 17.50)
Parents: John and Charlotte
Marital status: Single
Family links with cricket: 'Dad plays
club cricket in Leicester.'
Education: Seven Sisters Junior;
Somerset Senior
Qualifications: Cricket senior coaching
award, basketball coaching award, volleyball coaching award
Off-season: Going to play and coach in South Africa
Overseas tours: Haringey Cricket College to Barbados 1986, to Trinidad 1987, to Jamaica 1988; Warwickshire to La Manga 1989, to St Lucia 1990
Overseas teams played for: Desmond Haynes's XI, Barbados v Haringey Cricket College
Cricketers particularly admired: Jack Russell, Alec Stewart, Dermot Reeve, Colin Metson
Other sports followed: Snooker, football, tennis
Injuries: Three broken fingers, out for eight weeks
Relaxations: Music, eating
Extras: London Young Cricketer of the Year, 1989 and in the last five, 1992. Played for Young England
Best batting: 111 Warwickshire v Somerset, Edgbaston 1990
Best bowling: 1-57 Warwickshire v Nottinghamshire, Edgbaston 1992

148. What is the French for wickets?

1992 Season

	M	Inns	NO	Runs	HS	Avge	100s	50s	Ct	St	O	M	Runs	Wkts	Avge	Best	5wI	10wM
Test																		
All First	19	25	8	345	72	20.29	-	2	41	2	4.4	0	57	1	57.00	1-57	-	-
1-day Int																		
NatWest	3	3	0	30	12	10.00	-	-	7	-								
B & H	2	2	1	1	1	1.00	-	-	1	-								
Sunday	1	0	0	0	0	-	-	-	1	-								

Career Performances

	M	Inns	NO	Runs	HS	Avge	100s	50s	Ct	St	Balls	Runs	Wkts	Avge	Best	5wI	10wM
Test																	
All First	64	85	14	1388	111	19.54	1	4	158	9	28	57	1	57.00	1-57	-	-
1-day Int																	
NatWest	7	4	0	31	12	7.75	-	-	12	-							
B & H	6	6	3	36	11 *	12.00	-	-	6	-							
Sunday	26	14	6	103	30	12.87	-	-	14	7							

POLLARD, P. R.   Nottinghamshire

Name: Paul Raymond Pollard
Role: Left-hand bat, right-arm medium bowler
Born: 24 September 1968, Carlton, Nottinghamshire
Height: 5ft 11in **Weight:** 11st 7lbs
Nickname: Polly, Sugar Ray
County debut: 1987
County cap: 1992
1000 runs in a season: 2
1st-Class 50s scored: 16
1st-Class 100s scored: 6
1st-Class catches: 76
One-Day 50s scored: 6
One-Day 100s scored: 2
Place in batting averages: 125th av. 30.00 (1991 92nd av. 33.02)
Parents: Eric (deceased) and Mary
Wife's name and date of marriage: Kate, 14 March 1992
Education: Gedling Comprehensive
Off-season: Coaching children at Trent Bridge

Overseas teams played for: Southern Districts, Brisbane 1988; North Perth 1990
Cricketers particularly admired: Derek Randall, Andy Pick, Ian Botham,
Paul Johnson, John Macmillan (Kimberley CC)
Other sports followed: 'Nottingham Forest, Nottingham Panthers and golf.'
Relaxations: Watching videos, playing golf, music and gardening
Extras: Made debut for Nottinghamshire 2nd XI in 1985. Worked in Nottinghamshire
CCC office on a Youth Training Scheme. Shared stands of 222 and 282 with Tim Robinson
v Kent 1989. Youngest player to reach 1000 runs for Nottinghamshire
Best batting: 153 Nottinghamshire v Cambridge University, Fenner's 1989
Best bowling: 1-46 Nottinghamshire v Derbyshire, Derby 1991

1992 Season

	M	Inns	NO	Runs	HS	Avge	100s	50s	Ct	St	O	M	Runs	Wkts	Avge	Best	5wI	10wM
Test																		
All First	19	33	3	900	75	30.00	-	5	21	-	4	0	33	0	-	-	-	-
1-day Int																		
NatWest	1	1	0	28	28	28.00	-	-	-	-								
B & H	4	4	1	123	76 *	41.00	-	1	-	-								
Sunday	10	9	3	269	61	44.83	-	1	2	-								

Career Performances

	M	Inns	NO	Runs	HS	Avge	100s	50s	Ct	St	Balls	Runs	Wkts	Avge	Best	5wI	10wM
Test																	
All First	81	143	7	4056	153	29.82	6	16	76	-	178	113	1	113.00	1-46	-	-
1-day Int																	
NatWest	4	4	0	61	28	15.25	-	-	-	-							
B & H	12	12	1	233	77	21.18	-	2	3	-							
Sunday	35	32	6	949	123 *	36.50	2	4	9	-							

149. In which country does the team 'Hanua' play?

POOLEY, J. C. Middlesex

Name: Jason Cavin Pooley
Role: Left-hand bat, right-arm slow bowler
Born: 8 August 1969, Hammersmith
Height: 6ft **Weight:** 13st 3lbs
County debut: 1989
1st-Class 50s scored: 4
1st-Class catches: 9
One-Day 100s: 1
Place in batting averages:
(1991 197th av. 19.38)
Parents: Dave and Kath
Marital status: Single
Family links with cricket: Father and older
brother play club cricket. Younger brother
Gregg has played for Middlesex YC and
Middlesex 2nd XI
Education: Acton High School
Career outside cricket: Working for
father's building firm
Off-season: As above
Overseas teams played for: St George's, Sydney 1988-89; Western Suburbs, Sydney
1991-92
Cricketers particularly admired: David Gower, Mike Gatting, Clive Radley, Desmond
Haynes and Mark Ramprakash
Other sports followed: Horse racing and football (Portsmouth)
Relaxations: Watching all sports
Extras: Won Rapid Cricketline 2nd XI Player of the Year in 1989, his first year on the
Middlesex staff
Opinions on cricket: 'Four-day cricket will benefit better sides.'
Best batting: 88 Middlesex v Derbyshire, Lord's 1991

1992 Season

	M	Inns	NO	Runs	HS	Avge	100s	50s	Ct	St	O	M	Runs	Wkts	Avge	Best	5wI	10wM
Test																		
All First	3	6	2	186	69	46.50	-	2	-	-								
1-day Int																		
NatWest																		
B & H																		
Sunday																		

Career Performances

	M	Inns	NO	Runs	HS	Avge	100s	50s	Ct	St	Balls	Runs	Wkts	Avge	Best	5wl	10wM
Test																	
All First	17	30	2	628	88	22.42	-	4	9	-	12	11	0	-	-	-	-
1-day Int																	
NatWest																	
B & H	3	3	0	11	8	3.66	-	-	-	-							
Sunday	4	4	0	185	109	46.25	1	-	-	-							

POTTER, L. Leicestershire

Name: Laurie Potter
Role: Right-hand bat, slow left-arm bowler, slip fielder
Born: 7 November 1962, Bexley Heath, Kent
Height: 6ft 1in **Weight:** 14st
Nickname: Potsie
County debut: 1981 (Kent), 1986 (Leics)
County cap: 1988 (Leics)
1000 runs in a season: 3
1st-Class 50s scored: 49
1st-Class 100s scored: 7
1st-Class catches: 178
One-Day 50s: 16
One-Day 100s: 2
Place in batting averages: 150th av. 26.06 (1991 107th av. 31.12)
Place in bowling averages: 108th av. 39.81 (1991 130th av. 47.78)
Strike rate: 80.03 (career 81.85)
Parents: Ronald Henry Ernest and Audrey Megan
Wife and date of marriage: Helen Louise, October 1989
Children: Michael Laurie, 14 March 1990
Family links with cricket: Father-in-law, Mike Turner, is Chief Executive of Leicestershire CCC
Education: Kelmscott Senior High School, Perth, Western Australia
Qualifications: Australian leaving exams, NCA advanced coach
Off-season: Coaching, with family
Overseas tours: Australia U19 to Pakistan 1981
Overseas teams played for: West Perth, Australia; Griqualand West, South Africa 1984-85 and 1985-86 as captain; Orange Free State 1987-88

Other sports followed: All ball games – especially hockey

Relaxations: Home and family; following sport

Extras: Captained Australia U19 team to Pakistan 1981. Captained England YC v India 1981. Parents emigrated to Australia when he was 4. His mother wrote to Kent in 1978 asking for trial for him. Decided to leave Kent after 1985 season and joined Leicestershire. Youth Development Officer for Leicestershire CCC

Best batting: 165* Griqualand West v Border, East London 1984-85

Best bowling: 4-52 Griqualand West v Boland, Stellenbosch 1985-86

1992 Season

	M	Inns	NO	Runs	HS	Avge	100s	50s	Ct	St	O	M	Runs	Wkts	Avge	Best	5wI	10wM
Test																		
All First	23	36	4	834	96	26.06	-	4	10	-	360.1	80	1075	27	39.81	4-73	-	-
1-day Int																		
NatWest	4	4	1	91	41	30.33	-	-	3	-	37	1	137	2	68.50	1-32	-	
B & H	5	4	0	14	9	3.50	-	-	1	-	23	3	92	2	46.00	1-11	-	
Sunday	14	14	2	240	52	20.00	-	1	1	-	64	1	326	8	40.75	4-33	-	

Career Performances

	M	Inns	NO	Runs	HS	Avge	100s	50s	Ct	St	Balls	Runs	Wkts	Avge	Best	5wI	10wM
Test																	
All First	211	337	40	8623	165 *	29.03	7	49	178	-	12524	6121	153	40.00	4-52	-	-
1-day Int																	
NatWest	16	16	3	379	57	29.15	-	1	6	-	444	268	5	53.60	1-28	-	
B & H	32	29	4	548	112	21.92	1	1	10	-	564	387	7	55.28	2-70	-	
Sunday	125	122	15	2630	105	24.57	1	14	44	-	1189	995	34	29.26	4-9	-	

PRESTON, N. W.   Kent

Name: Nicholas William Preston

Role: Right-hand bat, right arm medium-fast bowler

Born: 22 January 1972, Dartford

Height: 6ft 1in **Weight:** 11st 7lbs

Nickname: North end

County debut: No first team appearance

Parents: Susan and Geoffrey

Marital Status: Single

Family links with cricket: Grandfather played for Leicestershire

Education: Graves End Grammar School; Exeter University

Career outside cricket: Student

Off-season: Studying
Cricketers particularly admired:
Richard Hadlee
Other sports followed: Golf, tennis,
hockey, football, 'bit of everything'
Relaxations: Music and theatre
Opinions on cricket: 'All for coloured
clothing and more entertainment in the game.
Four-day matches will make for a better
game of cricket and provide a chance for
everyone to refine their skills to the full.'

PRICHARD, P. J. Essex

Name: Paul John Prichard
Role: Right-hand bat, cover/mid-wicket
fielder
Born: 7 January 1965, Brentwood, Essex
Height: 5ft 10in **Weight:** 12st
Nickname: Pablo, Prich
County debut: 1984
County cap: 1986
1000 runs in a season: 5
1st-Class 50s scored: 57
1st-Class 100s scored: 16
1st-Class 200s scored: 1
1st-Class catches: 125
One-Day 50s: 16
One-Day 100s: 2
Place in batting averages: 49th av. 43.67
(1991 76th av. 36.25)
Parents: John and Margaret
Wife's name and date of marriage:
Jo-Anne, 24 November 1991
Family links with cricket: Father played club cricket in Essex

Education: Brentwood County High School
Qualifications: NCA coaching certificate
Off-season: Coaching in the Essex indoor school and England A to Australia
Overseas tours: England A to Australia
Overseas teams played for: VOB Cavaliers, Cape Town 1981-82; Sutherland, Sydney 1984-87; Waverley, Sydney 1987-92
Cricketers particularly admired: Malcolm Marshall, Allan Border and all at Essex
Other sports followed: Football (West Ham)
Injuries: Achilles tendon strain, out for two games; broken toe, out for one week
Relaxations: Golf, listening to music (The Clash, Waterboys, Cold Chisel), Sydney beaches
Extras: Shared county record second wicket partnership of 403 with Graham Gooch v Leicestershire in 1990. Britannic Assurance Cricketer of the Year 1992
Opinions on cricket: 'Looking forward to playing four-day cricket but pity the bowlers having to bowl 50 overs on Sundays off their full run ups. The advent of coloured clothing, white ball etc. is a good decision especially if your club has decent looking club colours.'
Best batting: 245 Essex v Leicestershire, Chelmsford 1990
Best bowling: 1-28 Essex v Hampshire, Chelmsford 1991

1992 Season

	M	Inns	NO	Runs	HS	Avge	100s	50s	Ct	St	O	M	Runs	Wkts	Avge	Best	5wI	10wM
Test																		
All First	23	38	4	1485	136	43.67	4	9	18	-	8	0	100	0	-	-	-	-
1-day Int																		
NatWest	4	4	0	196	87	49.00	-	2	3	-								
B & H	4	4	0	54	25	13.50	-	-	1	-								
Sunday	16	13	1	447	83	37.25	-	3	5	-								

Career Performances

	M	Inns	NO	Runs	HS	Avge	100s	50s	Ct	St	Balls	Runs	Wkts	Avge	Best	5wI	10wM
Test																	
All First	194	306	38	9610	245	35.85	16	57	125	-	247	409	1	409.00	1-28	-	-
1-day Int																	
NatWest	19	18	2	559	94	34.93	-	4	9	-							
B & H	37	35	7	886	107	31.64	1	4	9	-							
Sunday	104	86	8	1915	103 *	24.55	1	8	28	-							

PRINGLE, D. R. Essex

Name: Derek Raymond Pringle
Role: Right-hand bat, right-arm fast-medium
bowler, county vice-captain
Born: 18 September 1958, Nairobi
Height: 6ft 5in **Weight:** 16st 7lbs
Nickname: Del-Boy, Ralphy, Deltoid
County debut: 1978
County cap: 1982
Benefit: 1992
Test debut: 1982
Tests: 30
One-Day Internationals: 42
50 wickets in a season: 6
1st-Class 50s scored: 42
1st-Class 100s scored: 10
1st-Class 5 w. in innings: 25
1st-Class 10 w. in match: 3
1st-Class catches: 142
One-Day 50s: 27
Place in batting averages: 58th av. 42.41
(1991 46th av. 43.35)
Place in bowling averages: 17th av. 25.04 (1991 37th av. 27.83)
Strike rate: 54.36 (career 58.54)
Parents: Donald James (deceased) and Doris May
Marital status: Single
Family links with cricket: Father represented Kenya and East Africa (played in World Cup 1975)
Education: St Mary's School, Nairobi; Felsted School, Essex; Cambridge University (Fitzwilliam College)
Qualifications: 8 O-levels, 3 A-levels, MA Cantab.
Off-season: Writing for Daily Telegraph on England's tour to India and Sri Lanka
Overseas tours: With England Schools to India 1978-79; England to Australia and New Zealand 1982-83; England B tour to Sri Lanka 1985-86; England A to Zimbabwe and Kenya 1990-91; England to New Zealand and Australia (World Cup) 1991-92
Cricketers particularly admired: Keith Fletcher ('now that he has retired'), Joel Garner
Other sports followed: Rugby union, football (Manchester United)
Relaxations: 'Getting into the wealth of largely unheard music that exists outside most playlists e.g. American Music Club, Soft Boys, The Minutemen, R.E.M., Misfits, Mid Miles Davis, X, Sunnyboys, Half Japanese. I read the Monday Telegraph every fortnight during the season for the above.'
Extras: Took all ten wickets for Nairobi Schools U13^1/$_2$ v Up Country Schools U13^1/$_2$. Captain of Cambridge University in 1982 (Blue 1979-82). Extra in 'Chariots of Fire'.

435

'Once went shark hunting with Chris Smith of Hampshire (a recklessly brave fellow) in the Maldive Islands.'

Opinions on cricket: 'Uncovered wickets don't suit our batsmen so scrap that idea. Inception of up-to-date technologies in order to reduce umpiring errors, as there is too much at stake to merely grin and accept bad decisions, i.e. anything to aid the umpires who are now in a very high-pressure situation.'

Best batting: 128 Essex v Kent, Chelmsford 1988

Best bowling: 7-18 Essex v Glamorgan, Swansea 1989

1992 Season

	M	Inns	NO	Runs	HS	Avge	100s	50s	Ct	St	O	M	Runs	Wkts	Avge	Best	5wI	10wM
Test	3	4	1	2	1	0.66	-	-	-	-	70	10	227	5	45.40	3-66	-	-
All First	16	17	5	509	112 *	42.41	2	2	4	-	425.5	98	1177	47	25.04	5-63	1	-
1-day Int	2	0	0	0	0	-	-	-	1	-	20	2	77	6	12.83	4-42	-	
NatWest	4	4	1	43	16	14.33	-	-	-	-	42	6	153	3	51.00	2-50	-	
B & H	4	4	0	39	23	9.75	-	-	2	-	35.2	10	78	4	19.50	2-40	-	
Sunday	14	8	1	127	52	18.14	-	1	2	-	88	4	414	16	25.87	3-16	-	

Career Performances

	M	Inns	NO	Runs	HS	Avge	100s	50s	Ct	St	Balls	Runs	Wkts	Avge	Best	5wI	10wM
Test	30	50	4	695	63	15.10	-	1	10	-	5287	2518	70	35.97	5-95	3	-
All First	281	383	74	8633	128	27.93	10	42	142	-	42858	19189	732	26.21	7-18	25	3
1-day Int	42	29	12	419	49 *	24.64	-	-	11	-	2253	1578	43	36.69	4-42	-	
NatWest	32	28	6	526	80 *	23.90	-	3	11	-	1901	1041	40	26.02	5-12	2	
B & H	71	60	13	1425	77 *	30.31	-	13	18	-	4058	2392	101	23.68	5-35	2	
Sunday	140	104	24	2112	81 *	26.40	-	11	39	-	5517	4406	164	26.86	5-41	1	

PURDIE, S.   Glamorgan

Name: Scott Purdie

Role: Right-hand bat, right-arm fast-medium bowler

Born: 18 April 1974, Glasgow, Scotland

Height: 6ft 3in **Weight:** 14st 4lbs

Nickname: Ravishing Rick (Rav), Julian

County debut: No first team appearance

Parents: Anne and Jim

Marital status: Single

Education: James Cook High School, Auckland; St Kentigern College, Auckland

Qualifications: Studying sports administration course

Career outside cricket: Student

Off-season: Playing club cricket in New Zealand and going for level three coaching certificate

Overseas teams played for:
Ynysygerwn 1991
Cricketers particularly admired:
Richard Hadlee, Viv Richards, Richie
Richardson, Waqar Younis
Other sports followed: Basketball, football,
rugby league, 'all sports really'
Injuries: Stress fracture in lower spine, out
for eight to ten weeks (could only bat)
Relaxations: Music, going to the beach, 'or
just lazing around'
Extras: Represented counties (minor
association) U14-U20 and First XI and
Northern Districts U14-U20
Opinions on cricket: 'We play too much
cricket! A cut down will result in better
standards all round. Have a day off for
travelling as the majority of injuries and
stiffness are caused by travelling hundreds of

miles immediately after matches. I do feel as a professional working person, one should
be entitled to accept work where one so desires.'

RADFORD, N. V. Worcestershire

Name: Neal Victor Radford
Role: Right-hand bat, right-arm fast-medium
bowler, gully fielder
Born: 7 June 1957, Luanshya, Zambia
Height: 5ft 11in **Weight:** 12st 8lbs
Nickname: Radiz, Vic
County debut: 1980 (Lancs), 1985 (Worcs)
County cap: 1985 (Worcs)
Test debut: 1986
Tests: 3
One-Day Internationals: 6
50 wickets in a season: 6
1st-Class 50s scored: 7
1st-Class 5 w. in innings: 45
1st-Class 10 w. in match: 7
1st-Class catches: 121
Place in batting averages: 175th av. 21.75
(1991 218th 15.70)
Place in bowling averages: 37th av. 27.83

(1991 48th av. 29.63)
Strike rate: 53.23 (career 49.80)
Parents: Victor Reginald and Edith Joyce
Wife: Lynne
Children: Luke Anthony, 3 June 1988; Josh Deckland 12 February 1990
Family links with cricket: Brother Wayne pro for Gowerton (SWCA) and Glamorgan 2nd XI. Also played for Orange Free State in Currie Cup
Education: Athlone Boys High School, Johannesburg
Qualifications: Matriculation and university entrance. NCA advanced coach
Off-season: 'Playing indoor cricket, spending time with my family, working on personal interests.'
Overseas teams played for: Transvaal 1979-89
Overseas tours: With England to New Zealand and Australia 1987-88
Cricketers particularly admired: Vincent van der Bijl
Other sports followed: All sports
Injuries: Had minor operation to remove burst Bursa from left knee at the end of the season
Relaxations: Music, TV, films, golf
Extras: Only bowler to take 100 first-class wickets in 1985. First player to 100 wickets in 1987. Took most first-class wickets both years. One of *Wisden's* Five Cricketers of the Year, 1985. The Cricketers' Association Cricketer of the Year 1985
Opinions on cricket: 'We play too much cricket! A cut down will result in better standards all round. Have a day off for travelling as the majority of injuries and stiffness are caused by travelling hundreds of miles immediately after matches. 50 overs on a Sunday, no thanks!'
Best batting: 76* Lancashire v Derbyshire, Blackpool 1981
Best bowling: 9-70 Worcestershire v Somerset, Worcestershire 1986

1992 Season

	M	Inns	NO	Runs	HS	Avge	100s	50s	Ct	St	O	M	Runs	Wkts	Avge	Best	5wI	10wM
Test																		
All First	22	19	7	261	73 *	21.75	-	2	4	-	532.2	99	1670	60	27.83	6-88	4	1
1-day Int																		
NatWest	1	1	0	32	32	32.00	-	-	-	-	10	1	81	2	40.50	2-81	-	
B & H	5	4	2	34	13	17.00	-	-	1	-	37.3	5	127	5	25.40	2-15	-	
Sunday	11	6	2	140	55	35.00	-	1	3	-	66.2	3	298	11	27.09	3-27	-	

Career Performances

	M	Inns	NO	Runs	HS	Avge	100s	50s	Ct	St	Balls	Runs	Wkts	Avge	Best	5wI	10wM
Test	3	4	1	21	12 *	7.00	-	-	-	-	678	351	4	87.75	2-131	-	-
All First	257	253	62	3140	76 *	16.44	-	7	121	-	44822	23469	900	26.07	9-70	45	7
1-day Int	6	3	2	0	0 *	0.00	-	-	2	-	348	230	2	115.00	1-32	-	
NatWest	27	14	4	137	37	13.70	-	-	10	-	1548	850	38	22.36	7-19	1	
B & H	43	27	14	352	40	27.07	-	-	11	-	2399	1429	66	21.65	4-25	-	
Sunday	124	70	32	825	55	21.71	-	1	31	-	4882	3706	163	22.73	5-32	1	

RADFORD, T.　　　　　　　　　　Middlesex

Name: Toby Radford
Role: Right-hand bat, 'occasional right-arm off-spin bowler'
Born: 3 December 1971, Caerphilly, Wales
Height: 5ft 10in **Weight:** 10st 4lbs
Nickname: Radders
County debut: No first team appearance
Parents: Brian and Jill
Marital status: Single
Family links with cricket: Dad is a senior coach
Education: Park House School, Newbury; St Bartholomew's School, Newbury; City University, London
Qualifications: 9 O-Levels, 3 A-Levels
Career outside cricket: Journalism
Off-season: 'Studying then playing abroad.'
Overseas tours: Young England to Australia 1990; to New Zealand 1991
Cricketers particularly admired:
Dean Jones, Desmond Haynes
Other sports followed: Football, snooker, speedway
Relaxations: Music, cinema
Opinions on cricket: 'More training facilities needed.'

150. Which cricketer, just retired, had his first Test selection greeted by the headline 'Peter Who?'?

151. Which current county cricketer has the nickname 'Map'?

RAMPRAKASH, M. R.   Middlesex

Name: Mark Ravindra Ramprakash
Role: Right-hand bat
Born: 5 September 1969, Bushey, Herts
Height: 5ft 9in **Weight:** 11st 10lbs
Nickname: Ramps, Bloodaxe
County debut: 1987
County cap: 1990
Test debut: 1991
Tests: 9
One-Day Internationals: 2
1000 runs in a season: 4
1st-Class 50s scored: 33
1st-Class 100s scored: 12
1st-Class 200s scored: 1
1st-Class catches: 48
One-Day 50s: 13
One-Day 100s scored: 4
Place in batting averages: 65th av. 39.36
(1991 58th av. 48.15)
Parents: Deonarine and Jennifer
Marital status: Single
Family links with cricket: Father played club cricket in Guyana
Education: Gayton High School; Harrow Weald Sixth Form College
Qualifications: 6 O-levels; 2 A-levels
Off-season: 'Getting away from cricket, to take a break'
Overseas tours: England YC to Sri Lanka 1987 and Australia for Youth World Cup 1988; England A to Pakistan 1990-91; to West Indies 1991-92; England to New Zealand 1991-92
Overseas teams played for: Nairobi Jafferys, Kenya 1988; North Melbourne 1989
Cricketers particularly admired: 'All the great all-rounders.'
Other sports followed: Snooker, football
Relaxations: 'Being at home with the family, going to movies, eating out.'
Extras: Won Best U15 Schoolboy of 1985 awarded by Cricket Society. Best Young Cricketer 1986. Did not begin to play cricket until he was nine years old. Made debut for Middlesex aged 17. Played for Bessborough CC at age 13. Played for ESCA U15 v Public Schools, 1984. Played in NCA Guernsey Festival Tournament and scored 204*. Played for England YC v Sri Lanka 1987 and New Zealand 1989. Played for Middlesex 2nd XI aged 16. In 1987 played for Stanmore CC and made 186* on his debut. Man of the Match in Middlesex's NatWest Trophy Final win 1988, on his debut in the competition. Cricket Society's Most Promising Player of the Year 1988.
Opinions on cricket: 'Four-day cricket must be played on reasonable wickets.'
Best batting: 233 Middlesex v Surrey, Lord's 1992

Best bowling: 1-0 Middlesex v Northamptonshire, Uxbridge 1991

1992 Season

	M	Inns	NO	Runs	HS	Avge	100s	50s	Ct	St	O	M	Runs	Wkts	Avge	Best	5wI	10wM
Test	3	5	1	31	17	7.75	-	-	1	-	1.1	0	8	0	-	-	-	-
All First	20	33	3	1199	233	39.96	3	5	8	-	11.1	1	49	0	-	-	-	-
1-day Int																		
NatWest	2	2	0	75	46	37.50	-	-	-	-	12	2	38	2	19.00	2-38	-	
B & H	6	5	2	211	108 *	70.33	1	-	2	-								
Sunday	14	12	2	363	88 *	36.30	-	3	7	-								

Career Performances

	M	Inns	NO	Runs	HS	Avge	100s	50s	Ct	St	Balls	Runs	Wkts	Avge	Best	5wI	10wM
Test	9	15	1	241	29	17.21	-	-	5	-	7	8	0	-	-	-	-
All First	117	193	32	6327	233	39.29	12	33	48	-	991	583	6	97.16	1-0	-	-
1-day Int	2	2	2	6	6 *	-	-	-	-	-							
NatWest	14	13	0	421	104	32.38	1	1	2	-	174	98	4	24.50	2-15	-	
B & H	19	18	4	457	108 *	32.64	1	1	7	-							
Sunday	59	55	13	1814	147 *	43.19	2	11	23	-	99	96	3	32.00	2-32	-	

RANDALL, D. W. Nottinghamshire

Name: Derek William Randall
Role: Right-hand bat, cover fielder
Born: 24 February 1951, Retford, Nottinghamshire
Height: 5ft 8½in **Weight:** 11st
Nickname: Arkle, Rags
County debut: 1972
County cap: 1973
Benefit: 1983 (£42,000)
Test debut: 1976-77
Tests: 47
One-Day Internationals: 49
1000 runs in a season: 13
1st-Class 50s scored: 159
1st-Class 100s scored: 52
1st-Class 200s scored: 3
1st-Class catches: 355
One-Day 50s: 74
One-Day 100s: 6
Place in batting averages: 105th av. 33.92 (1991 10th av. 62.68)

Parents: Frederick and Mavis
Wife and date of marriage: Elizabeth, September 1973
Children: Simon, June 1977
Family links with cricket: Father played local cricket – 'tried to bowl fast off a long run and off the wrong foot too!'
Education: Sir Frederick Milner Secondary Modern School, Retford
Qualifications: ONC mechanical engineering, mechanical draughtsman
Overseas tours: England to India, Sri Lanka and Australia 1976-77, to Pakistan and New Zealand 1977-78, to Australia 1978-79, to Australia and India 1979-80, to Australia and New Zealand 1982-83, to New Zealand and Pakistan 1983-84; England B to Sri Lanka 1985-86
Cricketers particularly admired: Sir Gary Sobers, Tom Graveney ('boyhood idol'), Reg Simpson
Other sports followed: Football, squash, golf
Relaxations: Listening to varied selection of tapes. Family man
Extras: Before joining Nottinghamshire staff, played for Retford CC in the Bassetlaw League, and helped in Championship wins of 1968 and 1969. Scored 174 in Centenary Test v Australia 1976-77. One of *Wisden's* Five Cricketers of the Year, 1978
Best batting: 237 Nottinghamshire v Derbyshire, Trent Bridge 1988
Best bowling: 3-15 Nottinghamshire v MCC, Lord's 1982

1992 Season

	M	Inns	NO	Runs	HS	Avge	100s	50s	Ct	St	O	M	Runs	Wkts	Avge	Best	5wl	10wM
Test																		
All First	19	29	3	882	133 *	33.92	1	5	11	-	1.2	0	8	0	-	-	-	-
1-day Int																		
NatWest	2	2	0	60	55	30.00	-	1	1	-								
B & H	4	4	2	11	7 *	5.50	-	-	3	-								
Sunday	11	10	1	406	91 *	45.11	-	4	2	-								

Career Performances

	M	Inns	NO	Runs	HS	Avge	100s	50s	Ct	St	Balls	Runs	Wkts	Avge	Best	5wl	10wM
Test	47	79	5	2470	174	33.37	7	12	31	-	16	3	0	-	-	-	-
All First	483	817	81	28176	237	38.28	52	159	355	-	489	413	13	31.76	3-15	-	-
1-day Int	49	45	5	1067	88	26.67	-	5	25	-	2	2	1	2.00	1-2	-	
NatWest	42	42	5	1169	149 *	31.59	1	8	12	-	12	23	0	-	-	-	
B & H	97	94	14	2658	103 *	33.22	2	17	45	-	17	5	0	-	-	-	
Sunday	256	239	33	6962	123	33.79	3	44	69	-	5	9	0	-	-	-	

RATCLIFFE, J. D.   Warwickshire

Name: Jason David Ratcliffe
Role: Right-hand opening bat, right-arm
medium/off-spin bowler, slip fielder
Born: 19 June 1969, Solihull
Height: 6ft 3in **Weight:** 13st 7lbs
Nickname: Ratters
County debut: 1988
1st-Class 50s scored: 14
1st-Class 100s scored: 2
1st-Class catches: 33
One-Day 50s: 2
Place in batting averages: 196th av. 19.42
(1991 102nd av. 31.76)
Parents: David and Sheila
Marital status: Single
Family links with cricket: Father
(D.P. Ratcliffe) played for Warwickshire
1956-62

Education: Meadow Green Primary School;
Sharmans Cross Secondary School; Solihull
Sixth Form College
Qualifications: 6 O-levels; NCA staff coach
Career outside cricket: Working for Birmingham City FC marketing team
Off-season: Playing cricket in Australia
Overseas tours: NCA (South) to Ireland 1988; Warwickshire to South Africa 1991-92
Overseas teams played for: West End, Kimberley, South Africa 1987-88; Belmont,
Newcastle, NSW 1990-91; Penrith, Sydney 1992-93
Cricketers particularly admired: Geoff Boycott, Dennis Amiss, Jimmy Cook, Allan
Donald, Paul Booth
Other sports followed: Football (Birmingham City) and most other sports
Relaxations: Music, reading, eating out.
Extras: Scored a century against Boland on Warwickshire tour to South Africa 1992
Opinions on cricket: 'Four-day Championship is welcomed.'
Best batting: 127* Warwickshire v Cambridge University, Fenner's 1989
Best bowling: 1-15 Warwickshire v Yorkshire, Headingley 1989

---

152. What was the real name of the team and captain that appeared
fictiously in A.G. Macdonell's *England, Their England*?

1992 Season

	M	Inns	NO	Runs	HS	Avge	100s	50s	Ct	St		O	M	Runs	Wkts	Avge	Best	5wl	10wM
Test																			
All First	7	14	0	272	50	19.42	-	1	3	-									
1-day Int																			
NatWest																			
B & H																			
Sunday																			

Career Performances

	M	Inns	NO	Runs	HS	Avge	100s	50s	Ct	St	Balls	Runs	Wkts	Avge	Best	5wl	10wM
Test																		
All First	54	102	8	2715	127 *	28.88	2	14	33	-	180	96	1	96.00	1-15	-	-
1-day Int																		
NatWest	3	3	1	153	68 *	76.50	-	2	-	-							
B & H	1	1	0	29	29	29.00	-	-	-	-							
Sunday	6	5	1	48	37	12.00	-	-	1	-	55	58	2	29.00	1-8	-	

REES, G. H. J.   Glamorgan

Name: Gareth Henry John Rees
Role: Right-hand bat, 'net' bowler
Born: 24 October 1974, Bristol
Height: 6ft 1in **Weight:** 14st 7lb
Nickname: Greeser, Sponge
County debut: No first team appearance
Parents: John and Sue
Marital status: Single
Family links with cricket: Father played for Cheltenham College
Education: Clifton College Preparatory School; Clifton College
Qualifications: 10 GCSEs
Off-season: 'Hoping to get a place at university or polytechnic'
Overseas tours: West of England U15 to Holland 1990; Clifton College to Barbados 1991

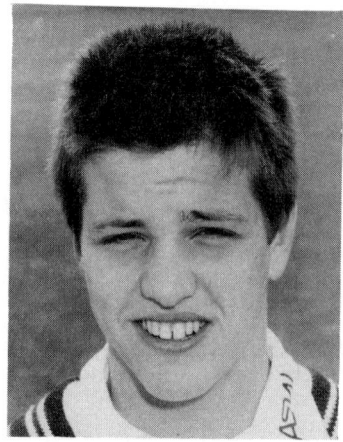

Cricketers particularly admired:
Jim Andrew, Robin Smith, Graeme Hick, Alan Jones
Other sports followed: Rugby (union nand league) and most sports
Relaxations: Playing rugby, rackets and fives. Drinking in the 'Albion', playing on fruit

machines and travelling abroad.

Extras: Record runs scorer at Clifton College, national schools fives champion, played for Clifton Flax Bourton CC in Western League and rugby for Gloucestershire Schools, Glamorgan U19 and Colts, made debut for Glamorgan 2nd XI at 16

Opinions on cricket: 'Coloured clothing is very good idea. All 2nd XI games should be played on county grounds; if not, practice facilities at other grounds should be better. Toll for the Severn Bridge should be reduced!'

REEVE, D. A.   Warwickshire

Name: Dermot Alexander Reeve
Role: Right-hand bat, right-arm fast-medium bowler, county captain
Born: 2 April 1963, Hong Kong
Height: 6ft **Weight:** 12st
Nickname: Legend, Motte
County debut: 1983 (Sussex), 1988 (Warwicks)
County cap: 1986 (Sussex), 1989 (Warwicks)
Tests: 3
One-Day Internationals: 15
1000 runs in a season: 2
50 wickets in a season: 2
1st-Class 50s scored: 42
1st-Class 100s scored: 5
1st-Class 200s scored: 1
1st-Class 5 w. in innings: 6
1st-Class catches: 128

One-Day 50s: 7
Place in batting averages: 100th av. 34.70 (1991 27th av. 48.46)
Place in bowling averages: 135th av. 48.61 (1991 7th av. 21.26)
Strike rate: 123.23 (career 64.82)
Parents: Alexander James and Monica
Wife and date of marriage: Julie, 20 December 1986
Children: Emily Kaye, 14 September 1988
Family links with cricket: Father was captain of his school XI, brother Mark is an improving club cricketer. Mother took over as scorer during the tour to India and Sri Lanka 1992-93
Education: King George V School, Kowloon, Hong Kong
Qualifications: 7 O-levels
Career outside cricket: Operations manager for Employment Agency
Off-season: Resting in Perth with daughter then touring with England

Overseas tours: England to New Zealand and Australia (World Cup) 1991-92, to India and Sri Lanka 1992-93

Cricketers particularly admired: 'Too many to mention'

Other sports followed: Football (Man Utd), most sports except motor racing and horse racing

Injuries: Stress fracture to pelvis, off for about a month

Relaxations: Swimming, golf , eating out and trying to keep in shape

Extras: Formerly on Lord's ground staff. Represented Hong Kong in the ICC Trophy competition June 1982. Hong Kong Cricketer of the Year 1980-81. Hong Kong's Cricket Sports Personality of the Year 1981. Man of the Match in 1986 NatWest Final for Sussex and 1989 Final for Warwickshire. Twice Western Australian CA Cricketer of the Year. Originally selected for England A tour to Bermuda and West Indies 1991-92 but promoted to senior tour to New Zealand when Angus Fraser was ruled out by injury. Appointed Warwickshire captain for 1993

Opinions on cricket: 'Great to see coloured clothing and white ball for Sunday cricket, but would have preferred the 40-over format to have remained and a 2 o'clock start. Would like the one bouncer per batsman per over rule to be changed and return to 1991 situation leaving the question of intimidation in the hands of the umpires.'

Best batting: 202* Warwickshire v Northamptonshire, Northampton 1990

Best bowling: 7-37 Sussex v Lancashire, Lytham 1987

1992 Season

	M	Inns	NO	Runs	HS	Avge	100s	50s	Ct	St	O	M	Runs	Wkts	Avge	Best	5wl	10wM
Test																		
All First	17	28	4	833	79	34.70	-	7	15	-	267	80	632	13	48.61	2-4	-	-
1-day Int	2	1	1	6	6 *	-	-	-	-	-	21	2	88	2	44.00	1-31	-	
NatWest	4	3	0	48	22	16.00	-	-	3	-	34	8	92	2	46.00	2-29	-	
B & H																		
Sunday	9	9	2	276	50*	39.42	-	1	2	-	51	0	229	6	38.16	2-32	-	

Career Performances

	M	Inns	NO	Runs	HS	Avge	100s	50s	Ct	St	Balls	Runs	Wkts	Avge	Best	5wl	10wM
Test	3	5	0	124	59	24.80	-	1	1	-	149	60	2	30.00	1-4	-	-
All First	189	248	63	6592	202 *	35.63	5	42	128	-	24180	10424	373	27.94	7-37	6	-
1-day Int	15	8	6	118	31 *	59.00	-	-	6	-	538	322	15	21.46	3-20	-	
NatWest	28	21	8	360	57 *	27.69	-	1	13	-	1582	743	25	29.72	4-20	-	
B & H	29	24	8	337	80	21.06	-	1	5	-	1479	1075	32	33.59	4-42	-	
Sunday	122	84	23	1568	100	25.70	1	5	34	-	4221	3318	117	28.35	5-23	1	

REMY, C. C. Sussex

Name: Carlos Charles Remy
Role: Right-hand bat, right-arm
fast-medium bowler
Born: 24 July 1968, Castries, St Lucia
Height: 5ft 10in **Weight:** 11st
Nickname: Dredd
County debut: 1989
1st-Class catches: 2
Place in batting averages: 177th av. 21.33
Parents: Mary Annette
Marital status: Single
Family links with cricket: Stepfather
played club cricket for STC in Morrant
League
Education: St William of York School,
London
Qualifications: 1 O-levels, 3 CSEs, NCA
coaching certificate
Career outside cricket: 'Doing any job'
Off-season: Playing cricket in New Zealand
Overseas tours: Haringey Cricket College to West Indies 1988, 1989
Overseas teams played for: Bionics, Harare 1989-90; Parnell, Auckland 1990-91
Cricketers particularly admired: Franklyn Stephenson, Robin Smith, Allan Border,
Malcolm Marshall
Other sports followed: Football and rugby
Injuries: Missed almost all of 1992 season with back injury, but now recovered
Relaxations: Listening to music (soul, swing, rap and ragga), dancing
Extras: 'Scored my very first hundred for Sussex in my first game for the 2nd XI'
Opinions on cricket: 'Four-day cricket is now proving to be better cricket. Sunday League
cricket should remain 40 overs and coloured clothing is good for the game.'
Best batting: 47 Sussex v Derbyshire, Eastbourne 1992
Best bowling: 3-27 Sussex v Cambridge University, Hove 1990

1992 Season

	M	Inns	NO	Runs	HS	Avge	100s	50s	Ct	St	O	M	Runs	Wkts	Avge	Best	5wl	10wM
Test																		
All First	7	9	0	192	47	21.33	-	-	1	-	96.2	12	336	6	56.00	3-27	-	-
1-day Int																		
NatWest																		
B & H																		
Sunday	6	4	0	41	15	10.25	-	-	-	-	31	0	163	10	16.30	4-31	-	

Career Performances

	M	Inns	NO	Runs	HS	Avge	100s	50s	Ct	St	Balls	Runs	Wkts	Avge	Best	5wI	10wM
Test																	
All First	10	11	1	196	47	19.60	-	-	2	-	992	593	12	49.41	4-63	-	-
1-day Int																	
NatWest	1	1	0	1	1	1.00	-	-	-	-	60	30	0	-	-	-	-
B & H																	
Sunday	12	9	1	74	15	9.25	-	-	2	-	286	265	12	22.08	4-31	-	

RHODES, S. J. Worcestershire

Name: Steven John Rhodes
Role: Right-hand bat, wicket-keeper, county vice-captain
Born: 17 June 1964, Bradford
Height: 5ft 9in **Weight:** 11st 8lbs
Nickname: Wilf, Bumpy
County debut: 1981 (Yorks), 1985 (Worcs)
County cap: 1986 (Worcs)
One-Day Internationals: 3
1st-Class 50s scored: 30
1st-Class 100s scored: 3
1st-Class catches: 503
1st-Class stumpings: 62
One-Day 50s: 3
Place in batting averages: 94th av. 35.43
(1991 82nd av. 34.88)
Parents: Bill and Norma
Marital status: Single
Family links with cricket: Father played
for Nottinghamshire 1959-64
Education: Bradford Moor Junior School; Lapage St Middle; Carlton-Bolling Comprehensive, Bradford
Qualifications: 4 O-levels, coaching certificate
Off-season: Holiday in Zimbabwe, looking for employment
Overseas tours: England B to Sri Lanka 1986-86; picked for cancelled England tour of India 1988-89; England A to Zimbabwe and Kenya 1989-90, to Pakistan 1990-91, to West Indies 1991-92
Overseas teams played for: Past Bros, Bundaberg, Queensland; Avis Vogeltown, New Plymouth, NZ
Cricketers particularly admired: Alan Knott, Bob Taylor, Graeme Hick, Richard Hadlee, Jimmy Cook

Other sports followed: Rugby league and golf

Injuries: 'Many – mainly niggles'

Relaxations: Tropical fish ('very therapeutic')

Extras: England YC v Australia in 1983. Youngest wicket-keeper to play for Yorkshire. Record for most victims in an innings for Young England. Released by Yorkshire to join Worcestershire at end of 1984 season. One of four players put on stand-by as reserves for 1992 World Cup squad. Writes a weekly cricket column.

Opinions on cricket: 'I am looking forward to finally playing in a "fair" county championship where everyone plays each other once. Thankfully the season will have a bit of continuity with one regular day off. Very pleased that coloured clothing will become a feature. I think that day/night cricket should be looked into far more seriously as matches could be played at the start and end of the season when the light fades earlier. Side view cameras should be used in big games, possibly all games, with third umpire adjudicating on stumpings and run outs. The two other umpires should interpret the judgement on all other decisions. The umpires need that extra help these days as fielding etc. is improving year after year.'

Best batting: 116* Worcestershire v Warwickshire, Worcester 1992

1992 Season

	M	Inns	NO	Runs	HS	Avge	100s	50s	Ct	St	O	M	Runs	Wkts	Avge	Best	5wI	10wM
Test																		
All First	24	34	11	815	116 *	35.43	2	2	46	5								
1-day Int																		
NatWest	1	1	0	54	54	54.00	-	1	1	-								
B & H	5	5	0	45	25	9.00	-	-	9	1								
Sunday	15	7	1	54	17	9.00	-	-	15	7								

Career Performances

	M	Inns	NO	Runs	HS	Avge	100s	50s	Ct	St	Balls	Runs	Wkts	Avge	Best	5wI	10wM
Test																	
All First	213	277	87	5939	116 *	31.25	3	30	503	62	6	30	0	-	-	-	-
1-day Int	3	2	1	9	8	9.00	-	-	3	-							
NatWest	25	18	6	259	61	21.58	-	2	26	4							
B & H	41	31	6	422	51 *	16.88	-	1	54	7							
Sunday	122	73	17	1073	48 *	19.16	-	-	119	34							

RICHARDS, I. V. A.   Glamorgan

Name: Isaac Vivian Alexander Richards
Role: Right-hand bat, off-break bowler
Born: 7 March 1952, St John's, Antigua
Height: 5ft 11in **Weight:** 13st 7lbs
Nickname: Smokey, Vivvy, Master Blaster
County debut: 1974 (Somerset),
1990 (Glamorgan)
County cap: 1974 (Somerset),
1990 (Glamorgan)
Benefit: 1982 (£56,440)
Test debut: 1974
Tests: 121
One-Day Internationals: 187
1000 runs in a season: 13
1st-Class 50s scored: 155
1st-Class 100s scored: 112
1st-Class 200s scored: 7
1st-Class 5 w. in innings: 1
1st-Class catches: 448
1st-Class stumpings: 1
One-Day 50s: 100
One-Day 100s: 24
Place in batting averages: 116th av. 36.39 (1991 14th av. 58.35)
Parents: Malcolm and Gratel
Wife and date of marriage: Miriam, 24 March 1981
Children: Matara, Mali
Family links with cricket: Father played for Antigua as an all-rounder. Half-brother Donald played for Antigua and Leeward Islands and brother Mervyn played for Antigua
Education: St John's Boys School and Antigua Grammar School
Overseas tours: West Indies to India, Sri Lanka and Pakistan 1974-75, to Australia 1975-76, to England 1976, to Australia 1979-80, to England 1980, to Pakistan 1980-81, to Australia 1981-82, to India 1983-84, to England 1984, to Australia 1984-85, to Pakistan and New Zealand 1986-87, to India 1987-88, to England 1988, to Australia 1988-89, to England 1991
Overseas teams played for: Combined Islands and Leeward Islands since 1971-72; Queensland 1976-77
Other sports followed: Football, basketball, squash. Played football for Antigua and once had a trial with Bath City FC
Injuries: Missed much of the second half of 1992 season with back problem
Relaxations: Listening to music
Extras: 'I remain a religious person to the delight of my parents. I pray every night before going to sleep; occasionally I pray for success on the field.' Helps to sponsor young

sportsmen in Antigua. 'Sounds mad but I am not a travelling man – I hate it in the air. Planes terrify me.' Captain of West Indies 1986-91. Released by Somerset at end of 1986 and played for Rishton in Lancashire League in 1987. Became first West Indian to hit 100 first-class 100s in 1988-89. Signed two-year contract with Glamorgan in 1989 but unable to play at all in his first season due to injury. Made his debut for Glamorgan in 1990 and has signed a further two-year contract for 1992 and 1993. Retired from Test cricket after The Oval Test against England in 1991. Published his autobiography *Hitting Across the Line* in 1991 and an official video biography of the same title was released in 1992. Turned down offer to play for Western Province in 1992-93 off-season on political grounds and eventually also decided not to tour South Africa with Glamorgan in Spring 1993. Toured England and Australia 1992-93 with 'King and I' (video and chat double act with Ian Botham)

Best batting: 322 Somerset v Warwickshire, Taunton 1985
Best bowling: 5-88 West Indians v Queensland, Brisbane 1981-82

1992 Season

	M	Inns	NO	Runs	HS	Avge	100s	50s	Ct	St	O	M	Runs	Wkts	Avge	Best	5wI	10wM
Test																		
All First	14	23	0	722	127	31.39	1	4	18	-	12	2	34	0	-		-	-
1-day Int																		
NatWest	3	3	0	43	25	14.33	-	-	1	-	26.3	1	98	2	49.00	2-31	-	
B & H	3	3	0	50	48	16.66	-	-	2	-	22	5	63	4	15.75	3-45	-	
Sunday	11	11	3	476	109 *	59.50	1	3	1	-	21	1	87	6	14.50	3-12	-	

Career Performances

	M	Inns	NO	Runs	HS	Avge	100s	50s	Ct	St	Balls	Runs	Wkts	Avge	Best	5wI	10wM
Test	121	182	12	8540	291	50.23	24	45	122	-	5170	1964	32	61.37	2-17	-	-
All First	490	764	56	34977	322	49.40	112	155	448	1	15107	9835	219	44.90	5-88	1	-
1-day Int	187	167	24	6721	189 *	47.00	11	45	101	-	5644	4228	118	35.83	6-41	2	
NatWest	37	37	4	1453	139 *	44.03	4	7	17	-	1126	690	22	31.36	3-15	-	
B & H	51	47	6	1549	132 *	37.78	1	10	23	-	844	488	16	30.50	3-38	-	
Sunday	169	164	20	5711	126 *	39.66	8	38	71	-	2867	2276	90	25.28	6-24	1	

153. What current cricketer played in his first Test in one black and one white sock?

RICHARDSON, A. W.   Derbyshire

Name: Alastair William Richardson
Role: Right-hand bat, right-arm fast-medium
bowler
Born: 23 October 1972, Derby
Height: 6ft 3in **Weight:** 14st 7lbs
Nickname: Big Al
County debut: 1992
Parents: William and Margaret
Marital status: Single
Family links with cricket: Grandfather
(A.W.) captained Derbyshire 1931-36;
father (G.W.) played for Derbyshire 1959-65
Education:
Oundle School; Durham University
Qualifications: 10 GCSEs, 3 A-levels
Off-season: University tour of South Africa
Overseas tours: Durham University to
South Africa 1992-93
Cricketers particularly admired:
Richard Hadlee, Ian Botham, Viv Richards
Other sports followed: Rugby union, golf, tennis, football
Relaxations: Fishing, golf, shooting, music, reading
Best batting: 5 Derbyshire v Glamorgan, Cardiff 1992
Best bowling: 2-38 Derbyshire v Glamorgan, Cardiff 1992

1992 Season

	M	Inns	NO	Runs	HS	Avge	100s	50s	Ct	St	O	M	Runs	Wkts	Avge	Best	5wI	10wM
Test																		
All First	1	1	0	5	5	5.00	-	-	-	-	13	2	38	2	19.00	2-38	-	-
1-day Int																		
NatWest																		
B & H																		
Sunday																		

Career Performances

	M	Inns	NO	Runs	HS	Avge	100s	50s	Ct	St	Balls	Runs	Wkts	Avge	Best	5wI	10wM
Test																	
All First	1	1	0	5	5	5.00	-	-	-	-	78	38	2	19.00	2-38	-	-
1-day Int																	
NatWest																	
B & H																	
Sunday																	

RICHARDSON, R. B. Yorkshire

Name: Richard Benjamin Richardson
Role: Right-hand bat, right-arm medium bowler
Born: 12 January 1962, Five Islands, Antigua
Nickname: Richie
County debut: No first team appearance
Test debut: 1983-84
Tests: 63
One-Day Internationals: 151
1st-Class 50s scored: 38
1st-Class 100s scored: 29
1st-Class 5 w. in innings: 1
1st-Class catches: 144
One-Day 50s: 37
One-Day 100s: 5
Career outside cricket: Owns duty-free shop – 'Richie Rich' – on St John's waterfront (Antigua)
Off-season: Touring Australia and South Africa with West Indies
Overseas tours: West Indies to India 1983-84, to England 1984, to Australia 1984-85, to Pakistan and New Zealand 1986-87, to India 1987-88, to England 1988, to Australia 1988-89, to England 1991, to Pakistan 1991-92, to Australia and New Zealand (World Cup) 1991-92, to Australia 1992-93, to South Africa 1992-93
Overseas teams played for: Leeward Islands 1981-1993
Relaxations: Plays guitar
Extras: Failed to make the Test team on his first visit to England in 1984 but took successive centuries off England on their 1985-86 tour, appointed captain of West Indies after the retirement of Viv Richards in 1991. Noted for his floppy red hat which will not be seen when playing for Yorkshire in 1993
Best batting: 194 West Indies v India, Georgetown 1988-89
Best bowling: 5-40 Leeward Islands v England, St John's 1985-86

1992 Season

	M	Inns	NO	Runs	HS	Avge	100s	50s	Ct	St	O	M	Runs	Wkts	Avge	Best	5wI	10wM
Test																		
All First	1	1	0	5	5	5.00	-	-	-	-								
1-day Int																		
NatWest																		
B & H																		
Sunday																		

Career Performances

	M	Inns	NO	Runs	HS	Avge	100s	50s	Ct	St	Balls	Runs	Wkts	Avge	Best	5wI	10wM
Test	63	109	10	4693	194	47.40	14	18	70	-	60	14	0	-	-	-	-
All First	151	250	22	9863	194	43.25	29	38	144	-	420	204	5	40.80	5-40	1	-
1-day Int	163	159	20	4883	122	35.12	5	37	56	-	58	46	1	46.00	1-4	-	
NatWest																	
B & H																	
Sunday																	

RIPLEY, D.   Northamptonshire

Name: David Ripley
Role: Right-hand bat, wicket-keeper
Born: 13 September 1966, Leeds
Height: 5ft 11in **Weight:** 11st 7lbs
Nickname: Rips, Spud, Oh Ah Cantona
County debut: 1984
County cap: 1987
1st-Class 50s scored: 9
1st-Class 100s scored: 6
1st-Class catches: 372
1st-Class stumpings: 55
Place in batting averages: 57th av. 42.42
(1991 122nd av. 29.18)
Parents: Arthur and Brenda
Wife and date of marriage: Jackie,
24 September 1988
Children: Joe David 11 October 1989
Education: Woodlesford Primary;
Royds High, Leeds
Qualifications: 5 O-levels, NCA senior
coaching award
Career outside cricket: Director of Gard Sports, Northampton
Off-season: Working in the shop, as above
Overseas tours: England YC to West Indies 1984-85; Northamptonshire to Durban, South Africa 1992
Overseas teams played for: Marists and Poverty Bay, New Zealand 1985-87
Cricketers particularly admired: Alan Knott, Bob Taylor 'and many other 'keepers', Clive Radley, Ian Botham, Geoff Boycott
Other sports followed: Soccer (Leeds United) and rugby league (Castleford),
Injuries: 'Nothing too serious – missed a few games with a finger injury'

Relaxations: Eating out, 'testing different beers now I'm a bitter drinker'
Extras: Finished top of wicket-keepers' dismissals list for 1988 and 1992. Played for Young England v Sri Lanka 1986. Wombwell Cricket Lovers' Best Wicket-keeper 1992
Opinions on cricket: 'I think 17 four-day games will make a better Championship. B&H and Sunday League to stay as they are with perhaps two divisions on Sundays.'
Best batting: 134* Northamptonshire v Yorkshire, Scarborough 1986
Best bowling: 2-89 Northamptonshire v Essex, Ilford 1987

1992 Season

	M	Inns	NO	Runs	HS	Avge	100s	50s	Ct	St	O	M	Runs	Wkts	Avge	Best	5wI	10wM
Test																		
All First	22	31	10	891	107 *	42.42	2	4	66	5	1	0	14	0	-	-	-	-
1-day Int																		
NatWest	5	3	2	12	6	12.00	-	-	9	-								
B & H	4	2	0	6	4	3.00	-	-	3	-								
Sunday	12	6	4	95	28	47.50	-	-	14	-								

Career Performances

	M	Inns	NO	Runs	HS	Avge	100s	50s	Ct	St	Balls	Runs	Wkts	Avge	Best	5wI	10wM
Test																	
All First	178	229	57	4268	134 *	24.81	6	9	372	55	60	103	2	51.50	2-89	-	-
1-day Int																	
NatWest	29	18	8	120	27 *	12.00	-	-	32	2							
B & H	33	22	8	280	36 *	20.00	-	-	32	4							
Sunday	98	58	27	556	36 *	17.93	-	-	65	10							

154. Who is the only England captain to have called the toss wrong on his birthday?

155. Who are the only two England captains to have called the Test toss correctly on their birthday?

ROBERTS, A. R.   Northamptonshire

Name: Andrew Richard Roberts
Role: Right-hand bat, leg-spin bowler
Born: 16 April 1971, Kettering
Height: 5ft 6in **Weight:** 10st 7lbs
Nickname: Reggie
County debut: 1989
1st-Class 50s scored: 1
1st-Class 5 w. in innings: 1
1st-Class catches: 15
Place in batting averages: 201st av. 19.00
(1991 54th av. 40.66)
Place in bowling averages: 133rd av. 48.00
(1991 94th av. 35.62)
Strike rate: 88.18 (career 78.70)
Parents: David and Shirley
Marital status: Single

Family links with cricket: Father (Dave)
played a few games for Northants 2nd XI
and brother Tim played Midlands Schools
U14 and won the Lord's Taverners Award
for U13 in 1991
Education: Bishop Stopford Comprehensive, Kettering
Qualifications: 3 O-levels, 5 CSEs, apprentice carpenter
Career outside cricket: Apprentice carpenter
Off-season: Finishing apprenticeship
Overseas tours: Northamptonshire to Durban, South Africa 1992
Overseas teams played for: Woolston Working Men's Club, Christchurch, New Zealand
1989-91
Cricketers particularly admired: Richard Williams, Wayne Larkins, Dennis Lillee, Bob
Carter
Other sports followed: Rugby and golf
Injuries: Hamstring pull on tour to South Africa
Relaxations: 'Music, sleeping, eating, a good pint!'
Extras: Played for England YC v Pakistan 1990
Opinions on cricket: 'In favour of uncovered wickets, which would produce better
technique and more exciting cricket. Don't agree with 50-over cricket on Sunday,
everyone will be knackered'
Best batting: 62 Northamptonshire v Nottinghamshire, Trent Bridge 1992
Best bowling: 6-72 Northamptonshire v Lancashire, Lytham 1991

1992 Season

	M	Inns	NO	Runs	HS	Avge	100s	50s	Ct	St	O	M	Runs	Wkts	Avge	Best	5wI	10wM
Test																		
All First	14	19	3	304	62	19.00	-	1	5	-	323.2	60	1056	22	48.00	4-101	-	-
1-day Int																		
NatWest	1	0	0	0	0	-	-	-	1	-	12	0	23	1	23.00	1-23	-	
B & H																		
Sunday	5	1	0	4	4	4.00	-	-	2	-	17	1	90	2	45.00	1-21	-	

Career Performances

	M	Inns	NO	Runs	HS	Avge	100s	50s	Ct	St	Balls	Runs	Wkts	Avge	Best	5wI	10wM
Test																	
All First	33	42	13	577	62	19.89	-	1	15	-	4801	2571	61	42.14	6-72	1	-
1-day Int																	
NatWest	1	0	0	0	0	-	-	-	1	-	72	23	1	23.00	1-23	-	
B & H																	
Sunday	8	2	0	18	14	9.00	-	-	3	-	192	167	6	27.83	3-26	-	

ROBINSON, D. D. J.   Essex

Name: Darren David John Robinson
Role: Right-hand opening bat, occasional right-arm medium bowler
Born: 2 March 1972, Braintree, Essex
Height: 5ft 10in **Weight:** 12st 8lbs
Nickname: Robbo
County debut: No first team appearance
Parents: David John and Dorothy May
Marital status: Single
Family links with cricket: Father local club cricketer for 35 years, supporter of England and Essex, 'Mother very supportive of my cricketing endeavours'
Education: Tabor High School, Braintree; Chelmsford College of Further Education
Qualifications: 5 GCSEs, BTEC National Diploma in Building and Construction
Off-season: Working holiday in Australia, playing cricket for Waverley, Sydney
Overseas tours: England U18 to Canada 1991; England U19 to Pakistan 1991-92
Overseas teams played for: Waverley, Sydney 1992-93
Cricketers particularly admired: Geoff Boycott, Graham Gooch, Keith Fletcher

457

Other sports followed: Rugby union, swimming, golf
Injuries: Groin strain, out for four weeks
Relaxations: Listening to music and socialising
Opinions on cricket: 'A very gratifying sport, which is demanding, requires dedication and considerable powers of concentration. Is frustrating at times when things are not working out. Is a good character builder providing experience of team spirit, comradeship, independence, socialising and the opportunity of international travel.'

ROBINSON, J. D. Surrey

Name: Jonathan David Robinson
Role: Left-hand bat, right-arm medium bowler
Born: 3 August 1966, Epsom, Surrey
Height: 5ft 10^1/$_2$in **Weight:** 12st 3lbs
Nickname: Robbo, Sex, Yamamoto
County debut: 1988
1st-Class 50s: 5
1st-Class catches: 12
One-Day 50s: 2
Place in batting averages: 157th av. 25.58
Place in bowling averages: 26th av. 26.23
Strike rate: 43.23 (68.67)
Parents: Peter and Wendy
Marital status: Single
Family links with cricket: Father played for Cambridge University and Esher CC; 'Mother was my coach!'
Education: Danes Hill Preparatory School; Lancing College; Bishop Otter College, Chichester
Qualifications: 6 O-levels, 3 A-levels, BA degree in Sports Studies, cricket coaching award
Career outside cricket: Marketing – training film company; gym instructor
Off-season: 'Sleeping'
Overseas tours: Lancing College to Holland, Jersey and Australia
Overseas teams played for: Manly, Sydney 1989-90
Cricketers particularly admired: David Gower, Mark Butcher, Paul Atkins, Johnny Wills, Waqar Younis, Keith Medlycott, John Glendenen, Bobby Lowe, Rehan Alikhan, 'my Dad'
Other sports followed: Rugby, squash, soccer, golf
Injuries: Broken fingers
Relaxations: 'Sun, swimming, pubs, clubs, women'
Extras: Released by Surrey at the end of the 1992 season
Opinions on cricket: 'Lunch should be one hour long and tea half an hour. A ball struck

out of the ground should be worth 10 runs thus ensuring a 10-ball hundred for Alistair Brown at least once a season.'
Best batting: 79 Surrey v Lancashire, Old Trafford 1991
Best bowling: 2-37 Surrey v Leicestershire, Leicester 1989

1992 Season

	M	Inns	NO	Runs	HS	Avge	100s	50s	Ct	St	O	M	Runs	Wkts	Avge	Best	5wI	10wM
Test																		
All First	9	17	5	307	65 *	25.58	-	2	8	-	93.4	14	341	13	26.23	3-22	-	-
1-day Int																		
NatWest	1	1	0	4	4	4.00	-	-	1	-	1	0	8	0	-		-	-
B & H																		
Sunday	10	8	1	114	27	16.28	-	-	3	-	30	0	184	4	46.00	1-14	-	

Career Performances

	M	Inns	NO	Runs	HS	Avge	100s	50s	Ct	St	Balls	Runs	Wkts	Avge	Best	5wI	10wM
Test																	
All First	31	49	10	898	79	23.02	-	5	12	-	1923	1152	28	41.14	3-22	-	-
1-day Int																	
NatWest	5	4	1	54	47	18.00	-	-	1	-	246	160	4	40.00	3-46	-	
B & H	5	5	1	79	38	19.75	-	-	3	-	182	101	5	20.20	2-31	-	
Sunday	40	34	7	478	55 *	17.70	-	2	10	-	1005	858	15	57.20	2-32	-	

ROBINSON, M. A.   Yorkshire

Name: Mark Andrew Robinson
Role: Right-hand bat, right-arm fast-medium bowler
Born: 23 November 1966, Hull
Height: 6ft 3in **Weight:** 12st 10lbs
Nickname: Smokey, Coddy, Scoop-fish, Pup
County debut: 1987 (Northamptonshire), 1991 (Yorkshire)
County cap: 1990 (Northamptonshire) 1992 (Yorkshire)
50 wickets in season: 1
1st-Class 5 w. in innings: 3
1st-Class 10 w. in match: 1
1st-Class catches: 22
Place in bowling averages: 9th av. 22.68 (1991 134th av. 49.64)

459

Strike rate: 49.66 (career 67.96)
Parents: Joan Margaret and Malcolm
Marital status: Single
Family links with cricket: Grandfather a prominent local cricketer.
Father was hostile cricketer in back garden
Education: Fifth Avenue Primary; Endike Junior High; Hull Grammar School
Qualifications: 6 O-levels, 2 A-levels, senior coach
Career outside cricket: Cricket coach
Off-season: Running my own coaching school
Overseas tours: U19 North to Bermuda; Yorkshire to Cape Town 1992
Overseas teams played for: East Shirley Christchurch, New Zealand 1988-90;
Canterbury, New Zealand 1989-90
Cricketers particularly admired: Dennis Lillee, Mike Gatting, John Emburey
Other sports followed: Hull City FC ('The Tigers')
Injuries: Fractured wrist and knee injury, out for two weeks
Relaxations: Reading, music, 'long walks with my dog Zack', watching Hull FC
Extras: Took hat-trick with first three balls of innings in Yorkshire League, playing for
Hull v Doncaster. First player to win Yorkshire U19 Bowler of the Season Award in two
successive years. Northamptonshire Uncapped Player of the Year 1989. Endured a world
record 11 innings without scoring a run during 1990 season
Opinions on cricket: 'Unless we get some better surfaces to play on there will be some
boring four-day cricket to watch next season.'
Best batting: 19* Northamptonshire v Essex, Chelmsford 1988
Best bowling: 6-57 Yorkshire v Durham, Durham University 1992

1992 Season

	M	Inns	NO	Runs	HS	Avge	100s	50s	Ct	St	O	M	Runs	Wkts	Avge	Best	5wI	10wM
Test																		
All First	17	12	5	31	12	4.42	-	-	4	-	413.5	79	1134	50	22.68	6-57	3	1
1-day Int																		
NatWest	2	1	1	1	1*	-	-	-	-	-	23.4	5	91	3	30.33	3-18	-	
B & H	1	1	0	0	0	0.00	-	-	-	-	8	1	46	1	46.00	1-46	-	
Sunday	9	2	0	4	3	2.00	-	-	3	-	62	1	286	2	143.00	2-43	-	

Career Performances

	M	Inns	NO	Runs	HS	Avge	100s	50s	Ct	St	Balls	Runs	Wkts	Avge	Best	5wI	10wM
Test																	
All First	100	95	42	126	19*	2.37	-	-	22	-	15429	7624	227	33.58	6-57	3	1
1-day Int																	
NatWest	9	4	3	4	3*	4.00	-	-	2	-	620	359	17	21.11	4-32	-	
B & H	13	5	3	2	1*	1.00	-	-	-	3	730	460	14	32.85	3-20	-	
Sunday	51	15	4	11	3	1.00	-	-	8	-	2107	1752	35	50.05	4-33	-	

ROBINSON, P. E.   Leicestershire

Name: Phillip Edward Robinson
Role: Right-hand bat, left-arm 'deccy' bowler
Born: 3 August 1963, Keighley
Height: 5ft 9in **Weight:** 13st
Nickname: Robbo
County debut: 1984 (Yorkshire),
1992 (Leicestershire)
County cap: 1988 (Yorkshire)
1000 runs in a season: 3
1st-Class 50s scored: 44
1st-Class 100s scored: 7
1st-Class catches: 96
One-Day 50s: 18
One-Day 100s: 1
Place in batting averages:
(1991 65th av. 38.02)
Parents: Keith and Lesley
Wife and date of marriage: Jane,
19 September 1986
Family links with cricket: Brother Richard
at Yorkshire Cricket Academy, mother secretary of Baldwin CC, father played and is now
umpire in Bradford League and elder brother plays in the same league and both brother-
in-laws play local league cricket
Education: Long Lee Primary; Hartington Middle; Greenhead Comprehensive
Qualifications: 2 O-levels, currently doing Open University degree
Off-season: Trying to find employment
Overseas tours: Southland CC to Tasmania 1987; Yorkshire to St Lucia and Barbados
1988
Overseas teams played for: Southland, New Zealand 1987; Eastern Southland cricket
coach 1987; Eden Roskill, Auckland 1989; Riverside, Wellington 1990
Cricketers particularly admired: Geoff Boycott, Richard Hadlee, Michael Holding
Other sports followed: 'I always watch for Meadowbank Thistle's results and watch
Keighley rugby league, golf (first hole-in-one this winter), most sports on TV'
Relaxations: Napoleonic history and watching TV
Extras: Scored the highest score by a Yorkshire 2nd XI player when he made 233 in 1983.
Scored most runs by an overseas player in the Auckland Cricket League for Eden Roskill
1989-90. Scored the fastest televised 50 in the Sunday league (19 balls) against Derbyshire
at Chesterfield 1991. Released by Yorkshire at his own request at the end of the 1991
season. Played for Cumberland in 1992 and could only play limited-overs for Leicestershire
in 1992 (apart from one match) but on full contract for 1993
Opinions on cricket: 'I think that cricket should be played over 3 days on uncovered
pitches.'

Best batting: 189 Yorkshire v Lancashire, Scarborough 1991
Best bowling: 1-10 Yorkshire v Somerset, Scarborough 1990

1992 Season

	M	Inns	NO	Runs	HS	Avge	100s	50s	Ct	St	O	M	Runs	Wkts	Avge	Best	5wI	10wM
Test																		
All First	1	2	0	19	19	9.50	-	-	-	-								
1-day Int																		
NatWest	5	5	0	221	73	44.20	-	2	-	-								
B & H																		
Sunday	10	10	0	374	104	37.40	1	2	4	-								

Career Performances

	M	Inns	NO	Runs	HS	Avge	100s	50s	Ct	St	Balls	Runs	Wkts	Avge	Best	5wI	10wM
Test																	
All First	133	219	31	6687	189	35.56	7	44	96	-	209	238	1	238.00	1-10	-	-
1-day Int																	
NatWest	13	10	0	334	73	33.40	-	3	3	-							
B & H	22	18	3	431	73 *	28.73	-	2	7	-							
Sunday	114	110	12	2568	104	26.20	1	13	41	-							

ROBINSON, R. T.   Nottinghamshire

Name: Robert Timothy Robinson
Role: Right-hand opening bat, right-arm medium bowler, county captain
Born: 21 November 1958, Sutton-in-Ashfield, Nottinghamshire
Height: 6ft **Weight:** 12st 6lbs
Nickname: Robbo
County debut: 1978
County cap: 1983
Benefit: 1992
Test debut: 1984-85
Tests: 29
One-Day Internationals: 26
1000 runs in a season: 10
1st-Class 50s scored: 100
1st-Class 100s scored: 46
1st-Class 200s scored: 2
1st-Class catches: 200
One-Day 50s: 47

One-Day 100s: 8
Place in batting averages: 13th av. 55.25 (1991 16th av. 57.69)
Parents: Eddy and Christine
Wife and date of marriage: Patricia, 2 November 1985
Children: Philip Thomas; Alex James
Family links with cricket: Father, uncle, cousin and brother all played local cricket.
Education: Dunstable Grammar School; High Pavement College, Nottingham; Sheffield University
Qualifications: BA (Hons) in Accountancy and Financial Management
Off-season: Running his own sports shop and winding up benefit year
Overseas tours: England to India and Australia 1984-85, to West Indies 1985-86, to the World Cup, India, New Zealand 1987-88; unofficial English team to South Africa 1989-90
Cricketers particularly admired: Geoffrey Boycott
Other sports followed: Golf, squash
Injuries: Broken hand, out for the first month of the season
Relaxations: Spending time with family
Extras: Played for Northamptonshire 2nd XI in 1974-75 and for Nottinghamshire 2nd XI in 1977. Had soccer trials with Portsmouth, Chelsea and QPR. One of *Wisden's* Five Cricketers of the Year, 1985. Banned from Test cricket for joining 1990 tour of South Africa, remitted in 1992
Best batting: 220* Nottinghamshire v Yorkshire, Trent Bridge 1990
Best bowling: 1-22 Nottinghamshire v Northamptonshire, Northampton 1982

1992 Season

	M	Inns	NO	Runs	HS	Avge	100s	50s	Ct	St	O	M	Runs	Wkts	Avge	Best	5wI	10wM
Test																		
All First	19	33	5	1547	189	55.25	4	8	14	-	1	0	4	0	-	-	-	-
1-day Int																		
NatWest	2	2	0	35	30	17.50	-	-	2	-								
B & H																			
Sunday	11	10	0	289	71	28.90	-	3	5	-								

Career Performances

	M	Inns	NO	Runs	HS	Avge	100s	50s	Ct	St	Balls	Runs	Wkts	Avge	Best	5wI	10wM
Test	29	49	5	1601	175	36.38	4	6	8	-	6	0	0	-	-	-	-
All First	312	544	71	20209	220 *	42.72	46	100	200	-	240	254	3	84.66	1-22	-	-
1-day Int	26	26	0	597	83	22.96	-	3	6	-							
NatWest	31	31	2	1238	139	42.69	2	5	14	-							
B & H	57	56	7	2024	120	41.30	3	14	15	-							
Sunday	164	159	20	4336	116	31.19	3	25	57	-							

ROBSON, A. G.   Sussex

Name: Andrew George Robson
Role: Right-hand bat, right-arm
fast-medium bowler
Born: 27 April 1971, Boldon,
Tyne and Wear
Height: 6ft 1in **Weight:** 13st
Nickname: George, Geordie
County debut: 1991 (Surrey), 1992 (Sussex)
1st-Class catches: 1
Parents: George William and Cynthia
Marital status: Single
Family links with cricket: Father plays for
Boldon 3rd XI and is a selector, mother is an
avid cricket watcher and scorer
Education: Whitburn Comprehensive
School, Tyne and Wear
Qualifications: 2 O-levels
Overseas tours: England U19 to Australia
1989-90
Cricketers particularly admired:
Waqar Younis, Malcolm Marshall, Ian Botham – 'also learnt a lot from Geoff Arnold'
Other sports followed: Boxing, horse racing, football
Relaxations: Watching boxing videos, eating out and socialising
Extras: Joined MCC groundstaff in 1989, signed for Surrey in June 1989. Released by
Surrey at the end of the 1991 season and joined Sussex
Best batting: 3 Surrey v Kent, The Oval 1991
Best bowling: 4-37 Sussex v Somerset, Hove 1992

1992 Season

	M	Inns	NO	Runs	HS	Avge	100s	50s	Ct	St	O	M	Runs	Wkts	Avge	Best	5wI	10wM
Test																		
All First	5	4	3	0	0*	0.00	-	-	1	-	119	24	405	8	50.62	4-37	-	-
1-day Int																		
NatWest	1	0	0	0	0	-	-	-	-	-	10	1	29	1	29.00	1-29	-	
B & H	2	1	0	0	0	0.00	-	-	-	-	22	4	61	1	61.00	1-32	-	
Sunday	11	4	3	5	3	5.00	-	-	2	-	77	5	300	8	37.50	2-14	-	

Career Performances

	M	Inns	NO	Runs	HS	Avge	100s	50s	Ct	St	Balls	Runs	Wkts	Avge	Best	5wI	10wM
Test																	
All First	7	7	3	3	3	0.75	-	-	1	-	948	508	9	56.44	4-37	-	-
1-day Int																	
NatWest	1	0	0	0	0	-	-	-	-	-	60	29	1	29.00	1-29	-	
B & H	2	1	0	0	0	0.00	-	-	-	-	132	61	1	61.00	1-32	-	
Sunday	15	4	3	5	3	5.00	-	-	2	-	648	465	16	29.06	3-42	-	

ROLLINS, R. J. Essex

Name: Robert John Rollins
Role: Right-hand bat, wicket-keeper
Born: 30 January 1974, Plaistow, London
Height: 5ft 9in **Weight:** 12st 9lbs
Nickname: Rollie
County debut: 1992
1st-Class catches: 2
Parents: Marva
Marital status: Single
Family links with cricket: Brother on
Derbyshire staff
Education: Little Ilford Comprehensive
School
Qualifications: 6 GCSEs
Off-season: Touring India with
England U19
Overseas tours: England U18 to Canada
1991; England U19 to Pakistan 1991-92, to
India 1992-93
Cricketers particularly admired:
Keith Hurst 'my uncle, who is still a very good club cricketer', John French (Clayhall CC),
Jeff Dujon, Alan Knott, Jack Russell
Other sports followed: Most sports except horse racing, golf and swimming
Relaxations: 'Spending time with my young lady and other members of my family,
especially my gran and young cousins.'
Extras: 2nd XI cap in September 1992. Essex Young Player of the Year 1992
Opinions on cricket: 'I agree with the introduction of pyjamas to the Sunday League, but
I thing 50 overs is too long.'
Best batting: 13 Essex v Pakistan, Chelmsford 1992

1992 Season

	M	Inns	NO	Runs	HS	Avge	100s	50s	Ct	St	O	M	Runs	Wkts	Avge	Best	5wI	10wM
Test																		
All First	1	2	0	19	13	9.50	-	-	2	-								
1-day Int																		
NatWest																		
B & H																		
Sunday																		

Career Performances

	M	Inns	NO	Runs	HS	Avge	100s	50s	Ct	St	Balls	Runs	Wkts	Avge	Best	5wI	10wM
Test																		
All First	1	2	0	19	13	9.50	-	-	2	-								
1-day Int																		
NatWest																		
B & H																		
Sunday																		

ROSE, G. D. Somerset

Name: Graham David Rose
Role: Right-hand bat, right-arm
fast-medium bowler, 1st slip
Born: 12 April 1964, Tottenham
Height: 6ft 4in **Weight:** 15st
Nickname: Hagar
County debut: 1985 (Middlesex),
1987 (Somerset)
County cap: 1988 (Somerset)
1000 runs in a season: 1
50 wickets in a season: 2
1st-Class 50s scored: 20
1st-Class 100s scored: 3
1st-Class 5 w. in innings: 4
1st-Class catches: 58
One-Day 50s: 9
One-Day 100s: 2
Place in batting averages: 119th av. 31.00
(1991 83rd av. 34.70)
Place in bowling averages: 125th av. 44.64
(1991 122nd av. 43.00)
Strike rate: 89.03 (career 59.85)

Parents: William and Edna
Wife and date of marriage: Teresa Julie, 19 September 1987
Children: Georgina Charlotte, 6 December 1990
Family links with cricket: Father and brothers have played club cricket
Education: Northumberland Park School, Tottenham
Qualifications: 6 O-levels, 4 A-levels. NCA coaching certificate
Career outside cricket: Trying to find a job
Off-season: Working for Stock Your Larder
Overseas teams played for: Carey Park, Bunbury, Western Australia 1984-85; Freemantle, Perth 1986-87; Paarl, Cape Town 1988-89
Cricketers particularly admired: Richard Hadlee, Malcolm Marshall, Graham Gooch, Jimmy Cook
Other sports followed: Football , rugby, golf
Injuries: Cracked bone in left hand, off for two weeks
Relaxations: Wine, music, gardening, playing golf and 'my daughter, Georgina'
Extras: Played for England YC v Australia 1983. Took 6 wickets for 41 on Middlesex debut. Joined Somerset for 1987 season and scored 95 on debut. Completed double of 1000 runs and 50 wickets in first-class cricket in 1990 and scored fastest recorded 100s in NatWest Trophy (v Devon) and Sunday League (v Glamorgan)
Opinions on cricket: 'I feel that so long as the pitches are right, then we are somewhere near the right format for county cricket. My only reservation is with the Sunday game being 50 overs long in the middle of a four-day Championship game. Will the same number of people come to watch what is virtually an all-day game on what for many people is their only day off..'
Best batting: 132 Somerset v Surrey, The Oval 1992
Best bowling: 6-41 Middlesex v Worcestershire, Worcester 1985

1992 Season

	M	Inns	NO	Runs	HS	Avge	100s	50s	Ct	St	O	M	Runs	Wkts	Avge	Best	5wI	10wM
Test																		
All First	22	34	4	930	132	31.00	1	6	12	-	392.1	84	1250	28	44.64	4-59	-	-
1-day Int																		
NatWest	2	1	0	2	2	2.00	-	-	-	-	11	2	37	1	37.00	1-24	-	
B & H	6	6	0	203	65	33.83	-	2	2	-	45.5	7	156	9	17.33	3-21	-	
Sunday	16	13	3	370	88	37.00	-	1	2	-	54	3	260	12	21.66	2-16	-	

Career Performances

	M	Inns	NO	Runs	HS	Avge	100s	50s	Ct	St	Balls	Runs	Wkts	Avge	Best	5wI	10wM
Test																	
All First	122	159	36	3726	132	30.29	3	20	58	-	15803	8340	264	31.59	6-41	4	-
1-day Int																	
NatWest	9	7	0	168	110	24.00	1	-	2	-	389	231	6	38.50	2-30	-	
B & H	32	26	3	520	65	22.60	-	3	7	-	1758	1161	40	29.02	4-37	-	
Sunday	94	78	14	1662	148	25.96	1	6	25	-	3350	2569	90	28.54	4-28	-	

ROSEBERRY, A.   Leicestershire

Name: Andrew Roseberry
Role: Right-hand bat, right-arm medium bowler
Born: 2 April 1971, Houghton-le-Spring, Sunderland
Height: 6ft **Weight:** 13st 7lbs
Nickname: Bud
County debut: 1992
Parents: Matthew and Jean
Marital status: Single
Family links with cricket: Uncle, Peter Wyness, played for Royal Navy; brother Mike plays for England A and Middlesex, father is a director of Durham CCC
Education: Tonstall Preparatory School; Durham School
Career outside cricket: Director of Roseberry Leisure
Off-season: Practising in indoor nets
Overseas teams played for:
Melville, Perth 1990-92
Other sports followed: Football, (Sunderland FC)
Relaxations: Music
Extras: Has spent three seasons with Leicestershire. Played rugby for Durham School, also represented Durham and North of England
Best batting: 14 Leicestershire v Pakistan, Leicester 1992

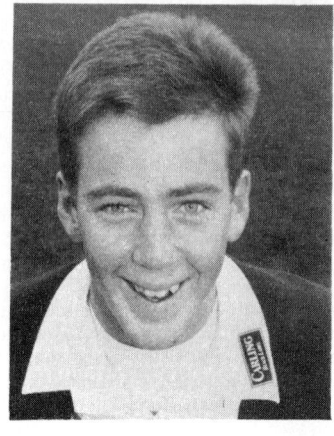

1992 Season

	M	Inns	NO	Runs	HS	Avge	100s	50s	Ct	St	O	M	Runs	Wkts	Avge	Best	5wI	10wM
Test																		
All First	1	2	0	14	14	7.00	-	-	-	-								
1-day Int																		
NatWest																		
B & H																		
Sunday																		

156. Who hit an all-run six for England v Pakistan in the fourth Test, 1992?

	M	Inns	NO	Runs	HS	Avge	100s	50s	Ct	St	Balls	Runs	Wkts	Avge	Best	5wI	10wM
Test																	
All First	1	2	0	14	14	7.00	-	-	-	-							
1-day Int																	
NatWest																	
B & H																	
Sunday																	

ROSEBERRY, M. A.   Middlesex

Name: Michael Anthony Roseberry
Role: Right-hand bat, right-arm occasional
off-break and swing bowler
Born: 28 November 1966, Houghton-le-
Spring, Sunderland
Height: 6ft 2in **Weight:** 14st
Nickname: Zorro
County debut: 1985
County cap: 1990
1000 runs in a season: 3
1st-Class 50s scored: 36
1st-Class 100s scored: 15
1st-Class catches: 83
One-Day 50s scored: 17
One-Day 100s scored: 2
Place in batting averages: 11th av. 56.77
(1991 68th av. 37.77)
Parents: Matthew and Jean
Wife and date of marriage:
Helen Louise, 22 February 1991
Children: Jordan Louise, 29 May 1992
Family links with cricket: Uncle, Peter Wyness, played for Royal Navy; brother Andrew
plays for Leicestershire, father is a director of Durham CCC
Education: Tonstall Preparatory School; Durham School
Qualifications: 5 O-levels, 1 A-level, advanced cricket coach
Career outside cricket: 'Coaching rugby and basketball at my old school'
Off-season: Training hard, watching Sunderland FC, working at McEwan's Cricket
Centre, Houghton-le-Spring, touring with England A
Overseas tours: England YC to West Indies 1985; England A to Australia 1992-93: An
England XI and Lord's Taverners to Hong Kong 'on numerous occasions'
Overseas teams played for: Freemantle, Western Australia 1986; Melville, Perth 1988

Cricketers particularly admired: Ian Botham 'for his cavalier approach', Desmond Haynes and Don Bennett 'for the great help they have given me'

Other sports followed: Football, rugby, golf and basketball

Injuries: Sore back, out from August onwards

Relaxations: 'Sport in general, going for a pint or two, eating out with my wife Helen and spending time with my daughter Jordan Louise.'

Extras: Won Lord's Taverners/MCC Cricketer of the Year 1983. Won Cricket Society's Award for Best Young Cricketer of the Year 1984 and also twice won Cricket Society award for best all-rounder in schools cricket. Played in Durham League as a professional while still at school. At age 16, playing for Durham School v St Bees, he hit 216 in 160 minutes. Scored 2044 runs in 1992 – joint highest scorer in first-class cricket, with Peter Bowler. Middlesex Player of the Year

Opinions on cricket: 'Glad to see four-day cricket. Find it a great shame for fast bowlers to only be allowed to bowl one bouncer an over.'

Best batting: 173 Middlesex v Durham, Lord's 1992

Best bowling: 1-1 Middlesex v Sussex, Hove 1988

1992 Season

	M	Inns	NO	Runs	HS	Avge	100s	50s	Ct	St	O	M	Runs	Wkts	Avge	Best	5wI	10wM
Test																		
All First	25	41	5	2044	173	56.77	9	8	14	-	13	5	71	0	-	-	-	-
1-day Int																		
NatWest	2	2	0	126	112	63.00	1	-	1	-	4	0	22	1	22.00	1-22	-	
B & H	6	6	1	287	84	57.40	-	3	1	-	1	0	2	0	-	-	-	
Sunday	17	17	2	499	76 *	33.26	-	4	4	-								

Career Performances

	M	Inns	NO	Runs	HS	Avge	100s	50s	Ct	St	Balls	Runs	Wkts	Avge	Best	5wI	10wM
Test																	
All First	120	201	25	6782	173	38.53	15	36	83	-	483	382	4	95.50	1-1	-	-
1-day Int																	
NatWest	11	11	0	355	112	32.27	1	-	4	-	36	42	1	42.00	1-22	-	
B & H	14	12	1	368	84	33.45	-	3	2	-	6	2	0	-	-	-	
Sunday	67	65	6	1833	106 *	31.06	1	14	21	-							

RUSSELL, R. C.   Gloucestershire

Name: Robert Charles Russell
Role: Left-hand bat, wicket-keeper
Born: 15 August 1963, Stroud
Height: 5ft 8¹/₂in **Weight:** 9st 8lbs
Nickname: Jack
County debut: 1981
County cap: 1985
Test debut: 1988
Tests: 31
One-Day Internationals: 26
1st-Class 50s scored: 31
1st-Class 100s scored: 4
1st-Class catches: 567
1st-Class stumpings: 84
One-Day 50s: 7
One-Day 100s: 1
Place in batting averages: 53rd av. 42.82
(1991 172nd av. 23.22)
Parents: John and Jennifer
Wife and date of marriage: Aileen Ann,
6 March 1985

Children: Stepson, Marcus Anthony; Elizabeth Ann, March 1988; Victoria, 1989; Charles David 1991
Education: Uplands County Primary School; Archway Comprehensive School
Qualifications: 7 O-levels, 2 A-levels
Career outside cricket: Professional artist – Jack Russell Art, c/o Gloucestershire CCC
Off-season: Touring with England A
Overseas tours: England to Pakistan 1987-88, to India and West Indies 1989-90, to Australia 1990-91, to New Zealand 1991-92; England A to Australia 1992-93
Cricketers particularly admired: Alan Knott, Bob Taylor
Other sports followed: Football ('a Spurs supporter, but only on television'), snooker
Relaxations: Drawing, sketching, painting (oil and watercolour). Watching comedy, Rory Bremner and Phil Cool especially
Extras: Spotted at age 9 by Gloucestershire coach, Graham Wiltshire. Record for most dismissals in a match on first-class debut: 8 (7 caught, 1 stumped) for Gloucestershire v Sri Lankans at Bristol, 1981. Youngest Gloucestershire wicket-keeper (17 years 307 days). Represented England YC v West Indies in 1982. Hat-trick of catches v Surrey at The Oval 1986. Had a three-week exhibition of his drawings in Bristol 1988 and published a book of his work entitled *A Cricketer's Art*. Co-author with Christopher Martin-Jenkins of *Sketches of a Season*, published in 1989. Was chosen as England's Man of the Test Series, England v Australia 1989. Commissioned by Dean of Gloucester to do a drawing of Gloucester Cathedral to raise funds for 900th Anniversary. Still turns out for his original

club, Stroud CC, whenever he can. Runs six miles a day to keep fit and drinks up to 20 cups of tea a day. One of *Wisden's* Five Cricketers of the Year, 1990. Appointed vice-captain to Martyn Moxon on the England A tour to Australia 1992-93
Best batting: 128* England v Australia, Old Trafford 1989
Best bowling: 1-4 Gloucestershire v West Indians, Bristol 1991

1992 Season

	M	Inns	NO	Runs	HS	Avge	100s	50s	Ct	St	O	M	Runs	Wkts	Avge	Best	5wI	10wM
Test	3	4	2	56	29 *	28.00	-	-	6	1								
All First	20	34	11	985	75	42.82	-	5	40	3								
1-day Int																		
NatWest	3	3	1	44	20	22.00	-	-	8	-								
B & H	5	5	2	78	30	26.00	-	-	4	1								
Sunday	14	11	4	226	56 *	32.28	-	1	11	1								

Career Performances

	M	Inns	NO	Runs	HS	Avge	100s	50s	Ct	St	Balls	Runs	Wkts	Avge	Best	5wI	10wM
Test	31	49	10	1060	128 *	27.17	1	3	80	8							
All First	251	351	80	7334	128 *	27.06	4	31	567	84	27	38	1	38.00	1-4	-	-
1-day Int	26	19	6	261	50	20.07	-	1	26	5							
NatWest	28	18	5	292	42 *	22.46	-	1	34	7							
B & H	43	30	10	421	51	21.05	-	1	41	8							
Sunday	128	89	24	1537	108	23.64	1	5	104	21							

SALIM MALIK   Essex

Name: Salim Malik
Role: Right-hand bat, right-arm medium bowler
Born: 16 April 1963, Lahore, Pakistan
Height: 5ft 9in
County debut: 1991
County cap: 1991
Test debut: 1981-82
Tests: 71
One-Day Internationals: 152
1000 runs in a season: 2
1st-Class 50s scored: 61
1st-Class 100s scored: 31
1st-Class 200s scored: 1
1st-Class 5 w. in innings: 2
1st-Class catches: 123
One-Day 50s: 28

One-Day 100s: 5
Place in batting averages: 1st av. 78.93 (1991 4th av. 73.03)
Strike rate: (career 53.12)
Education: Government College, Lahore
Off-season: Playing for Pakistan
Overseas tours: Pakistan U23 to Sri Lanka 1984-85; Pakistan to Australia 1981-82, to England 1982, to India 1983-84, to Australia 1983-84, to New Zealand 1984-85, to Sri Lanka 1985-86, to India 1986-87, to England 1987, to West Indies 1987-88, to New Zealand 1988-89, to Australia 1989-90, to England 1992, to New Zealand and Australia 1992-93, to South Africa and the West Indies 1992-93
Overseas teams played for: Lahore; Habib Bank
Best batting: 215 Essex v Leicestershire, Ilford 1991
Best bowling: 5-19 Habib Bank v Karachi, Karachi 1985-86

1992 Season

	M	Inns	NO	Runs	HS	Avge	100s	50s	Ct	St	O	M	Runs	Wkts	Avge	Best	5wI	10wM
Test	5	8	2	488	165	81.33	1	3	1	-	1	0	5	0	-	-	-	-
All First	15	21	6	1184	165	78.93	2	8	4	-	18.1	0	71	3	23.66	2-15	-	-
1-day Int	4	4	0	143	48	35.75	-	-	-	-								
NatWest																		
B & H																		
Sunday																		

Career Performances

	M	Inns	NO	Runs	HS	Avge	100s	50s	Ct	St	Balls	Runs	Wkts	Avge	Best	5wI	10wM
Test	71	101	18	3743	165	45.09	10	21	48	-	272	118	5	23.60	1-3	-	-
All First	189	287	46	11776	215	48.86	31	61	123	-	2975	1699	56	30.33	5-19	2	-
1-day Int	152	142	19	4038	102	32.82	5	23	45	-	586	510	14	36.42	5-35	1	
NatWest	3	3	1	55	26	27.50	-	-	4	-	36	34	0	-	-	-	
B & H	6	6	2	217	90 *	54.25	-	2	1	-	12	7	1	7.00	1-7	-	
Sunday	11	11	1	451	89	45.10	-	3	6	-	110	71	1	71.00	1-25	-	

157. Which former Test cricketer had a variety of pea named after him in 1992?

SALISBURY, I. D. K.   Sussex

Name: Ian David Kenneth Salisbury
Role: Right-hand bat, right-arm leg-spinner
Born: 2 January 1970, Northampton
Height: 5ft 11½in **Weight:** 12st
Nickname: Budgie, Sals
County debut: 1989
County cap: 1991
Test debut: 1992
Tests: 2
50 wickets in a season: 1
1st-Class 50s scored: 2
1st-Class 5 w. in innings: 9
1st-Class 10 w. in match: 2
1st-Class catches: 52
Place in batting averages: 227th av. 14.68
(1991 230th av. 14.46)
Place in bowling averages: 40th av. 28.96
(1991 118th av. 41.68)
Strike rate: 53.28 (career 72.03)
Parents: Dave and Margaret
Marital status: Engaged
Family links with cricket: 'Dad is vice-president of my first club, Brixworth.'
Education: Moulton Comprehensive, Northampton
Qualifications: 7 O-levels; NCA coaching certificate
Off-season: Touring with England in India, 'rest of the time training bloody hard at Lilleshall.'
Overseas tours: England A to Pakistan 1990-91, to Bermuda and West Indies 1991-92; England to India and Sri Lanka 1992-93
Cricketers particularly admired: 'Any that keep performing day in day out, for both country and county.'
Other sports followed: 'Most sports.'
Injuries: Pulled muscle on the back of knee, out for two weeks
Relaxations: 'Spending time with fiancée, Emma, meeting friends and relaxing with them and eating out accompanied with good wine.'
Extras: Picked to play two tests for England against Pakistan in 1992, 'proudest moments of my career.' Originally selected for England A tour to Australia 1992-93 but was asked to stay on in India and played in the first two Tests of the series. Wombwell Cricket Lovers' Young Player of the Year
Opinions on cricket: 'Hopefully people will now stop writing that they want four-day cricket and coloured clothing. Your wishes have been granted.'
Best batting: 68 Sussex v Derbyshire, Hove 1990
Best bowling: 7-54 Sussex v Yorkshire, Hove 1992

	M	Inns	NO	Runs	HS	Avge	100s	50s	Ct	St	O	M	Runs	Wkts	Avge	Best	5wI	10wM
Test	2	3	0	66	50	22.00	-	1	-	-	70.1	3	306	5	61.20	3-49	-	-
All First	20	22	3	279	50	14.68	-	1	15	-	772.4	176	2520	87	28.96	7-54	6	2
1-day Int																		
NatWest	2	1	0	4	4	4.00	-	-	2	-	21	5	49	4	12.25	3-28	-	
B & H	2	1	1	2	2*	-	-	-	1	-	16.3	2	69	2	34.50	2-43	-	
Sunday	14	5	2	50	27*	16.66	-	-	7	-	105	5	452	16	28.25	5-30	1	

Career Performances

	M	Inns	NO	Runs	HS	Avge	100s	50s	Ct	St	Balls	Runs	Wkts	Avge	Best	5wI	10wM
Test	2	3	0	66	50	22.00	-	1	-	-	421	306	5	61.20	3-49	-	-
All First	80	87	29	939	68	16.19	-	2	52	-	15128	8168	210	38.89	7-54	9	2
1-day Int																	
NatWest	6	4	2	24	14*	12.00	-	-	3	-	354	191	6	31.83	3-28	-	
B & H	8	5	2	36	17*	12.00	-	-	3	-	447	310	9	34.44	3-40	-	
Sunday	43	20	7	140	27*	10.76	-	-	13	-	1567	1237	38	32.55	5-30	1	

SARGEANT, N. F.   Surrey

Name: Neil Fredrick Sargeant
Role: Right-hand bat, wicket-keeper,
off-spin bowler
Born: 8 November 1965, Hammersmith
Height: 5ft 8in **Weight:** 11st 2lbs
Nickname: Sarge, Bilko, Grubby
County debut: 1989
1st-Class catches: 91
1st-Class stumpings: 16
Place in batting averages: 244th av. 11.73
(1991 214th av. 16.29)
Parents: Barry and Christine
Marital status: Single
Family links with cricket: Brother Lee
plays for the same club side,
Harrow Town CC
Education: Grange Primary School;
Whitmore High School
Qualifications: 2 O-levels, SAC cricket
coaching award, 'professional handy man.'
Career outside cricket: Whatever pays the most
Off-season: 'Watching QPR or Chelsea with Graham Thorpe and Alec Stewart. Working

on a building site in London with Rehan Alikhan.'
Overseas teams played for: Green Point, South Africa 1987-89; United, South Africa 1991
Cricketers particularly admired:
Alan Knott, Bob Taylor, Richie Ryall, Alec Stewart, Jack Russell, Danny Taylor
Other sports followed: Football, golf, horse racing
Injuries: Injured tendons in hand, out for one match 'but was generally rested for the last third of last season, I think'
Relaxations: Horse racing, music
Extras: Played football for Tottenham Hotspur Youth Team
Opinions on cricket: 'I think we are heading the right way with all four-day matches but I think Sunday cricket should have stayed 40 overs a side. I would also like to see 12-month contracts.'
Best batting: 49 Surrey v Lancashire, Old Trafford 1991
Best bowling: 1-88 Surrey v Gloucestershire, Guildford 1991

1992 Season

	M	Inns	NO	Runs	HS	Avge	100s	50s	Ct	St	O	M	Runs	Wkts	Avge	Best	5wI	10wM
Test																		
All First	14	19	4	176	30	11.73	-	-	35	6								
1-day Int																		
NatWest																		
B & H																		
Sunday	2	1	0	1	1	1.00	-	-	1	-								

Career Performances

	M	Inns	NO	Runs	HS	Avge	100s	50s	Ct	St	Balls	Runs	Wkts	Avge	Best	5wI	10wM
Test																	
All First	41	52	9	612	49	14.23	-	-	91	16	30	88	1	88.00	1-88	-	-
1-day Int																	
NatWest																	
B & H																	
Sunday	6	3	1	36	22	18.00	-	-	5	-							

158. The receipts for the Oval Test Match last season were over £1 million, true or false?

SAXELBY, M.   Nottinghamshire

Name: Mark Saxelby
Role: Left-hand bat, right-arm medium bowler
Born: 4 January 1969, Newark
Height: 6ft 3in **Weight:** 14st 7lbs
Nickname: Sax
County debut: 1989
1st-Class 50s scored: 7
1st-Class catches: 4
One-Day 50s: 1
Place in batting averages: 76th av. 38.50
(1991 213th av. 16.55)
Parents: George Kenneth and Hilda Margaret
Marital status: Single
Family links with cricket: Brother played for Nottinghamshire; father played local cricket

Education: Nottingham High School
Qualifications: 7 O-levels, 2 A-levels
Career outside cricket: Lab technician
Cricketers particularly admired: Richard Hadlee, Derek Randall
Other sports followed: Rugby union and league, football, American football
Relaxations: 'Good pubs, cinema, watching most sports.'
Opinions on cricket: 'Put the seam back on the ball fast. You're killing bowlers off. These flat pitches do nothing for the game.'
Best batting: 73 Nottinghamshire v Cambridge University, Fenner's 1990
                73 Nottinghamshire v Oxford University, The Parks 1992
Best bowling: 3-41 Nottinghamshire v Derbyshire, Derby 1991

1992 Season

	M	Inns	NO	Runs	HS	Avge	100s	50s	Ct	St	O	M	Runs	Wkts	Avge	Best	5wI	10wM
Test																		
All First	8	13	1	462	73	38.50	-	5	1	-	6	2	22	0	-	-	-	-
1-day Int																		
NatWest																			
B & H																			
Sunday	8	6	2	99	42 *	24.75	-	-	1	-	21	0	108	1	108.00	1-19	-	

Career Performances

	M	Inns	NO	Runs	HS	Avge	100s	50s	Ct	St	Balls	Runs	Wkts	Avge	Best	5wI	10wM
Test																	
All First	24	40	7	982	73	29.75	-	7	4	-	1086	765	9	85.00	3-41	-	-
1-day Int																	
NatWest	3	3	1	83	41	41.50	-	-	2	-	112	90	3	30.00	2-42	-	
B & H	4	3	0	37	32	12.33	-	-	-	-	156	118	1	118.00	1-36	-	
Sunday	34	26	5	485	55	23.09	-	1	8	-	936	817	22	37.13	4-29	-	

SCOTT, C. W. Durham

Name: Christopher Wilmot Scott
Role: Right-hand bat, wicket-keeper
Born: 23 January 1964, Lincoln
Height: 5ft 8in **Weight:** 11st
Nickname: George
County debut: 1981 (Nottinghamshire),
1992 (Durham)
County cap: 1988 (Nottinghamshire)
1st-Class 50s scored: 7
1st-Class catches: 162
1st-Class stumpings: 11
Parents: Kenneth and Kathleen
Wife and date of marriage:
Jacqui, 18 March 1989
Family links with cricket: Father played,
and younger brother still plays, for
Collingham, older brother plays for Newark
Rugby Club CC

Education: Robert Pattinson Comprehensive,
North Hykeham, Lincoln
Qualifications: 5 O-levels, 2 CSEs, advance cricket coach
Career outside cricket: Coaching, farming
Off-season: Working for the British Sugar
Corporation, Newark, coaching, 'improving my skiing and watching loads of Sky TV'
Overseas tours: Durham to Zimbabwe 1992
Overseas teams played for: Poverty Bay,
New Zealand 1983-84; Queensland
University 1985-86, 1987-88; Rotorua, New Zealand 1989-90
Other sports followed: Rugby union, soccer (Lincoln City)
Injuries: Broke middle finger, missed last game of the 1992 season
Relaxations: Skiing, golf (occasionally), music, films and history

Extras: One of the youngest players to make Championship debut for Nottinghamshire – 17 years 157 days. Broke the Nottinghamshire record for most catches in a match with 10 against Derbyshire in 1988. Left Nottinghamshire at the end of the 1991 season to join Durham

Opinions on cricket: 'Now that we are playing four-day cricket I think that 100 overs a day would be sufficient. If it's going to be a long game it needs to be slowed down a bit.'

Best batting: 78 Nottinghamshire v Cambridge University, Fenner's 1983

1992 Season

	M	Inns	NO	Runs	HS	Avge	100s	50s	Ct	St	O	M	Runs	Wkts	Avge	Best	5wI	10wM
Test																		
All First	18	24	5	433	57 *	22.78	-	2	27	2								
1-day Int																		
NatWest																		
B & H	1	1	0	3	3	3.00	-	-	-	-								
Sunday	1	1	1	8	8 *	-	-	-	-	-								

Career Performances

	M	Inns	NO	Runs	HS	Avge	100s	50s	Ct	St	Balls	Runs	Wkts	Avge	Best	5wI	10wM
Test																	
All First	81	96	23	1696	78	23.23	-	7	162	11	6	10	0	-	-	-	-
1-day Int																	
NatWest	3	0	0	0	0	-	-	-	4	-							
B & H	5	4	1	31	18	10.33	-	-	1	-							
Sunday	24	11	5	102	26	17.00	-	-	21	1							

159. For which Minor County did former England and Yorkshire cricketer Jim Love play last season?

SCOTT, R. J.   Gloucestershire

Name: Richard James Scott
Role: Left-hand bat, right-arm medium
bowler
Born: 2 November 1963, Bournemouth
Height: 5ft 11in **Weight:** 14st 'and a bit'
Nickname: SOS
County debut: 1986 (Hants), 1991 (Gloucs)
1st-Class 50s scored: 12
1st-Class 100s scored: 3
1st-Class catches: 33
One-Day 50s: 11
One-Day 100s: 1
Place in batting averages: 141st av. 26.82
(1991 232nd av. 18.00)
Place in bowling averages: 132nd av. 47.95
(1991 112th av. 40.93)

Strike rate: 80.30 (career 79.47)
Parents: Andy and Anne
Wife and date of marriage: Julie,
27 September 1991
Family links with cricket: Father and two brothers played for Dorset League side Colehill
Education: Queen Elizabeth School, Wimborne
Qualifications: 2 O-levels, CSEs, coaching award
Overseas teams played for: South Perth, Western Australia 1989-92
Cricketers particularly admired: Malcolm Marshall, Robin Smith, Simon O'Donnell
Other sports followed: Golf, football, rugby
Relaxations: Playing golf, pub life
Extras: Played Minor Counties cricket for Dorset since 1981. Represented Minor Counties
Cricket Association in 1985. Scored century on Gloucestershire debut
Opinions on cricket: 'Four-day game a revelation. Best side will always win Championship.'
Best batting: 127 Gloucestershire v Worcestershire, Worcester 1991
Best bowling: 3-43 Gloucestershire v Sussex, Hove 1991

1992 Season

	M	Inns	NO	Runs	HS	Avge	100s	50s	Ct	St	O	M	Runs	Wkts	Avge	Best	5wI	10wM
Test																		
All First	19	31	3	751	73	26.82	-	4	7	-	267.4	39	959	20	47.95	2-9	-	-
1-day Int																		
NatWest	3	3	0	30	25	10.00	-	-	-	-	24	3	79	4	19.75	2-32	-	
B & H																		
Sunday	15	11	5	230	50 *	38.33	-	1	1	-	97	3	428	14	30.57	3-23	-	

Career Performances

	M	Inns	NO	Runs	HS	Avge	100s	50s	Ct	St	Balls	Runs	Wkts	Avge	Best	5wI	10wM
Test																	
All First	66	111	8	2516	127	24.42	3	12	33	-	3179	1830	40	45.75	3-43	-	-
1-day Int																	
NatWest	8	7	0	63	25	9.00	-	-	-	-	278	133	10	13.30	4-22	-	
B & H	10	10	0	317	69	31.70	-	2	-	-	167	137	1	137.00	1-42	-	
Sunday	58	52	8	1330	116 *	30.22	1	9	8	-	1138	902	28	32.21	3-23	-	

SEARLE, J. P.   Durham

Name: Jason Paul Searle
Role: Right-hand bat, off-spin bowler
Born: 16 May 1976, Bath
Height: 5ft 9in **Weight:** 10st
Nickname: Jas
County debut: No first team appearance
Parents: Paul and Chris
Marital status: Single
Family links with cricket: Father played
for Chippenham and Wiltshire
Education: John Bentley School, Calne;
Wiltshire and Swindon Building College
Qualifications: Apprentice bricklayer
Career outside cricket: Bricklayer
Off-season: Bricklaying and playing for
Chippenham Town FC
Cricketers particularly admired:
Ian Botham, Robin Smith
Other sports followed: Football
Relaxations: Fishing and watching television
Opinions on cricket: 'Some of the rules should be changed: pitches should not be covered
their full length, only 4ft 6in from the wickets.'

160. For which Minor County did former England and Somerset
cricketer Peter Roebuck play last season?

SEYMOUR, A. C. H. — Worcestershire

Name: Adam Charles Hilton Seymour
Role: Left-hand bat, right-arm medium
bowler
Born: 7 December 1967, Royston,
Cambridgeshire
Height: 6ft 3in **Weight:** 13st 7lbs
Nickname: Zog, Zoggy
County debut: 1988 (Essex) 1992
(Worcestershire)
1st-Class 50s scored: 5
1st-Class 100s scored: 2
1st-Class catches: 17
Place in batting averages: 145th av. 26.47
(1991 105th av. 31.35)
Parents: Roger and Julie
Marital status: Engaged
Family links with cricket: Father captained
his school side

Education: Millfield School
Qualifications: Coaching award
Career outside cricket: 'Work for father in his pub.'
Off-season: Playing cricket in Australia
Overseas tours: Millfield School to Barbados 1987; Worcestershire to South Africa 1992
Overseas teams played for: Willetton District, Perth 1992
Cricketers particularly admired: Graham Gooch, Keith Fletcher
Other sports followed: Football, rugby, and most sports
Injuries: Foot injury
Relaxations: 'Eating out, drinking, golf, music etc.'
Extras: First played for Essex 2nd XI in 1984, aged 16. In 1989 was the county's leading
batsman in second team cricket. Left Essex at the end of the 1991 season to join Worcs
Best batting: 157 Essex v Glamorgan, Cardiff 1991

1992 Season

	M	Inns	NO	Runs	HS	Avge	100s	50s	Ct	St	O	M	Runs	Wkts	Avge	Best	5wI	10wM
Test																		
All First	11	21	0	556	133	26.47	1	1	9	-								
1-day Int																		
NatWest																		
B & H	3	3	0	49	23	16.33	-	-	-	-								
Sunday	1	1	0	9	9	9.00	-	-	-	-								

Career Performances

	M	Inns	NO	Runs	HS	Avge	100s	50s	Ct	St	Balls	Runs	Wkts	Avge	Best	5wl	10wM
Test																	
All First	25	45	4	1253	157	30.56	2	5	17	-	24	27	0	-	-	-	-
1-day Int																	
NatWest	1	1	0	0	0	0.00	-	-	1	-							
B & H	3	3	0	49	23	16.33	-	-	-	-							
Sunday	6	5	0	55	25	11.00	-	-	1	-							

SHAHID, N. Essex

Name: Nadeem Shahid
Role: Right-hand bat, leg-spin/googly bowler
Born: 23 April 1969, Karachi
Height: 6ft **Weight:** 11st 9lbs
Nickname: Prince, Biryani , Nad, Jo
County debut: 1989
1000 runs in a season: 1
1st-Class 50s scored: 11
1st-Class 100s scored: 2
1st-Class catches: 42
Place in batting averages: 131st av. 28.05
(1991 202nd av. 18.37)
Parents: Ahmed and Salma
Marital status: Single – 'but looking'
Family links with cricket: Brother plays
in the local league
Education: Stoke High; Northgate High;
Ipswich School; Plymouth Polytechnic
Qualifications: 6 O-levels, 1 A-level;
coaching certificate

Off-season: Playing for Fairfield CC, Sydney
Overseas tours: Ipswich School to Barbados (Sir Garfield Sobers Trophy) 1987; England (South) to Belfast (Youth World Tournament) 1988
Overseas teams played for: Gosnells, Perth, Western Australia 1989-91
Cricketers particularly admired: 'Abdul Qadir (for his skill), Graham Gooch (for his sheer determination), Keith Fletcher (for his shrewdness), Mark Waugh (for his timing)
Other sports followed: Rugby league and union, football (Ipswich Town)
Injuries: Broken index finger on the right hand, out for two and a half months
Relaxations: Playing golf, going to cinema, dining out, relaxing at home, listening to Kylie Minogue
Extras: Youngest Suffolk player aged 17. Played for HMC, MCC Schools, ESCA U19,

NCA Young Cricketers (Lord's and International Youth tournament in Belfast), England U25 and at every level for Suffolk. TSB Young Player of the Year 1987, winner of *The Daily Telegraph* bowling award 1987 and 1988, and Cricket Society's All-rounder of the Year, 1988

Opinions on cricket: 'Sunday League should remain 40-over competition. The rule of one bouncer per over per batsman hasn't worked very well and should therefore be abolished as it definitely favours the batsman.'

Best batting: 132 Essex v Kent, Chelmsford 1992
Best bowling: 3-91 Essex v Surrey, The Oval 1990

1992 Season

	M	Inns	NO	Runs	HS	Avge	100s	50s	Ct	St	O	M	Runs	Wkts	Avge	Best	5wI	10wM
Test																		
All First	15	21	1	561	132	28.05	1	3	8	-	40	4	167	9	18.55	2-22	-	-
1-day Int																		
NatWest	2	2	0	30	18	15.00	-	-	1	-	3	3	0	1	0.00	1-0	-	
B & H																		
Sunday	8	6	0	72	30	12.00	-	-	4	-								

Career Performances

	M	Inns	NO	Runs	HS	Avge	100s	50s	Ct	St	Balls	Runs	Wkts	Avge	Best	5wI	10wM
Test																	
All First	49	68	11	1966	132	34.49	2	11	42	-	1395	947	24	39.45	3-91	-	-
1-day Int																	
NatWest	3	2	0	30	18	15.00	-	-	2	-	18	0	1	0.00	1-0	-	
B & H	6	4	0	51	42	12.75	-	-	1	-							
Sunday	26	17	2	265	36	17.66	-	-	9	-							

SHAW, A. D.   Glamorgan

Name: Adrian David Shaw
Role: Right-hand bat, wicket-keeper, occasional off-spin bowler
Born: 17 February 1972, Neath
Height: 5ft 11in **Weight:** 12st 7lbs
Nickname: Shawsy, Doc
County debut: 1992 (one-day)
Parents: David Colin and Christina
Marital status: Single
Education: Llangatwe Comprehensive; Neath Tertiary College
Qualifications: 9 O-levels, 3 A-Levels, cricket coaching awards
Career outside cricket: Bar-man, labourer
Off-season: 'Playing rugby and visiting job centre.'
Overseas tours: Welsh Schools to Barbados 1988; Young England to

New Zealand 1991
Cricketers particularly admired:
John Crawley, Colin Metson,
Jack Russell, Jamie Bishop,
James Williams, Barry Davies
Other sports followed: Rugby union
and league
Injuries: Sciatica affected back and
groin, out for two games
Relaxations: 'Relaxing with my girlfriend,
Rebecca, watching rugby on TV or live,
enjoying mates' company especially
Jamie Bishop, Gary Butcher and James
Williams discussing politics and cricket.'
Extras: One of youngest players,
18 years, 7 days, to play first-class
rugby for Neath
Opinions on cricket: 'I would like to see
more sporting pitches to encourage spin
bowlers. In essence, a balance between bat
and ball hopefully resulting in less manufactured results. More importance should be
attached to 2nd XI issues, facilities etc. for the development of young cricketers.'

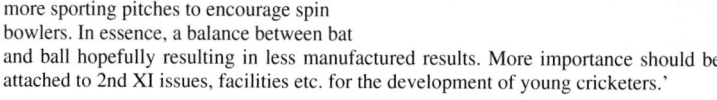

1992 Season

	M	Inns	NO	Runs	HS	Avge	100s	50s	Ct	St	O	M	Runs	Wkts	Avge	Best	5wI	10wM
Test																		
All First																		
1-day Int																		
NatWest																		
B & H																		
Sunday	1	0	0	0	0	-	-	-	-	-								

Career Performances

	M	Inns	NO	Runs	HS	Avge	100s	50s	Ct	St	Balls	Runs	Wkts	Avge	Best	5wI	10wM
Test																	
All First																	
1-day Int																	
NatWest																	
B & H																	
Sunday	1	0	0	0	0	-	-	-	-	-							

> 161. Which Minor County did former West Indies Test cricketer Alvin
> Kallicharran, play for last season?

SHINE, K. J.   Hampshire

Name: Kevin James Shine
Role: Right-hand bat, right-arm fast bowler
Born: 22 February 1969, Bracknell, Berks
Height: 6ft 3in **Weight:** 14st
Nickname: Ealham, Shoe, Eels, Slippery
County debut: 1989
1st-Class 5 w. in innings: 5
1st-Class 10 w. in match: 1
1st-Class catches: 3
Place in bowling averages: 62nd av. 32.25
(1991 106th av. 38.26)
Strike rate: 50.07 (career 54.73)
Parents: Joe and Clair
Marital status: Single
Education: Winnersh County Primary;
Maiden Erlegh Comprehensive
Qualifications: 5 O-levels, gave up
A-levels to pursue a cricket career
Off-season: Getting fitter and stronger,
working for Orico Systems Ltd a computer software and engineering company
Overseas teams played for: Merewether, Newcastle, NSW 1990
Cricketers particularly admired: Malcolm Marshall, Cardigan Connor ('the fittest first-class cricketer and personal physical training master'), Waqar Younis and Allan Donald ('the two fastest bowlers I have seen')
Other sports followed: Football, basketball, athletics
Relaxations: 'Driving and cars, relaxing with my lovely girlfriend, Wendy.'
Extras: Took a hat-trick against Lancashire at Old Trafford in May 1992. Writes (with Jason Harris) a weekly column for the Reading Chronicle
Opinions on cricket: 'The balance is still tipped far too much towards the batsmen. Please give us back the old balls or make the pitch ten yards shorter.'
Best batting: 26* Hampshire v Middlesex, Lord's 1989
Best bowling: 8-47 Hampshire v Lancashire, Old Trafford 1992

1992 Season

	M	Inns	NO	Runs	HS	Avge	100s	50s	Ct	St	O	M	Runs	Wkts	Avge	Best	5wI	10wM
Test																		
All First	16	12	6	59	22 *	9.83	-	-	-	-	333.5	49	1290	40	32.25	8-47	3	1
1-day Int																		
NatWest																		
B & H																		
Sunday																		

486

Career Performances

	M	Inns	NO	Runs	HS	Avge	100s	50s	Ct	St	Balls	Runs	Wkts	Avge	Best	5wI	10wM
Test																	
All First	41	33	16	204	26 *	12.00	-	-	3	-	5200	3384	95	35.62	8-47	5	1
1-day Int																	
NatWest																	
B & H	4	1	0	0	0	0.00	-	-	-	-	194	167	4	41.75	4-68	-	
Sunday	4	1	1	2	2 *	-	-	-	-	-	162	102	5	20.40	2-35	-	

SIMS, R. J.   Middlesex

Name: Robin Jason Sims
Role: Left-hand bat, wicket-keeper
Born: 22 November 1970, Hillingdon, Middlesex
Height: 5ft 8in **Weight:** 11st 7lbs
Nickname: Simsy, Bones, Bumper-car Billy, Inch High Private Eye, Arnie, Big Bob
County debut: 1992
Parents: Peter and Davina
Marital status: Single
Family links with cricket: Father and brother play club cricket for Ickenham
Education: Vyners Secondary School
Qualifications: 'Unfortunately have passed no exams due to circumstances beyond my control (not all that clever)'
Career outside cricket: Director of father's building company ('i.e. labourer')
Off-season: 'Directing my Dad's company'
Overseas teams played for: Stoke Nayland, Nelson, New Zealand 1987-89; Nelson representative team and Emerging Players 1987-89
Cricketers particularly admired: Phil Catchpole 'a big influence on my career', Angus Fraser, David Gower
Other sports followed: Golf, rugby, synchronised swimming, Chelsea FC follower
Relaxations: 'Going out with my girlfriend Claire, having the odd lager or two.'
Extras: MCC Young Professional, caught Allan Border as substitute fielder in the Lord's Test 1989. Scored 278* in Cockspur Cup (45 overs) 1990
Opinions on cricket: 'Should make cricket pads a bit smaller for the not so tall man.'
Best batting: 3 Middlesex v Pakistan, Lord's 1992

1992 Season

	M	Inns	NO	Runs	HS	Avge	100s	50s	Ct	St	O	M	Runs	Wkts	Avge	Best	5wI	10wM
Test																		
All First	1	1	0	3	3	3.00	-	-	-	-								
1-day Int																		
NatWest	1	1	1	13	13 *	-	-	-	-	-								
B & H	1	0	0	0	0	-	-	-	-	-								
Sunday	6	3	2	52	27 *	52.00	-	-	1	-								

Career Performances

	M	Inns	NO	Runs	HS	Avge	100s	50s	Ct	St	Balls	Runs	Wkts	Avge	Best	5wI	10wM
Test																	
All First	1	1	0	3	3	3.00	-	-	-	-							
1-day Int																	
NatWest	1	1	1	13	13 *	-	-	-	-	-							
B & H	1	0	0	0	0	-	-	-	-	-							
Sunday	6	3	2	52	27 *	52.00	-	-	1	-							

SLADDIN, R. W.   Derbyshire

Name: Richard William Sladdin
Role: Right-hand bat, slow left-arm bowler
Born: 8 January 1969, Halifax
Height: 5ft 11in **Weight:** 12st 4lbs
Nickname: Slads, Boris
County debut: 1991
1st-Class 5 w. in innings: 2
1st-Class catches: 12
Place in bowling averages: 88th av. 35.79
(1991 94th av. 35.74)
Strike rate: 76.84 (career 78.93)
Parents: Raymond and Elsie
Marital status: Single
Family links with cricket: Father watches a
lot of club cricket, eldest brother Nigel plays
club cricket
Education: Sowerby Bridge High School
Qualification: 5 O-levels, 1 A-level
Career outside cricket: Trainee accountant
Off-season: Playing and coaching in New Zealand
Cricketers particularly admired: Richard Hadlee, Derek Underwood, Abdul Qadir
Other sports followed: Football (Leeds United) and most other sports

Relaxations: Music, travelling, fishing, eating and drinking, clubs
Extras: Played for ESCA U19 in 1988 and 1989
Best batting: 39 Derbyshire v Glamorgan, Cardiff 1992
Best bowling: 6-58 Derbyshire v Cambridge University, Fenner's 1992

1992 Season

	M	Inns	NO	Runs	HS	Avge	100s	50s	Ct	St	O	M	Runs	Wkts	Avge	Best	5wI	10wM
Test																		
All First	13	16	2	131	39	9.35	-	-	6	-	499.3	138	1396	39	35.79	6-58	1	-
1-day Int																		
NatWest																		
B & H																		
Sunday	5	1	1	3	3 *	-	-	-	2	-	28	2	137	4	34.25	2-35	-	

Career Performances

	M	Inns	NO	Runs	HS	Avge	100s	50s	Ct	St	Balls	Runs	Wkts	Avge	Best	5wI	10wM
Test																	
All First	21	25	6	199	39	10.47	-	-	12	-	5210	2361	66	35.77	6-58	2	-
1-day Int																	
NatWest																	
B & H																	
Sunday	5	1	1	3	3 *	-	-	-	2	-	168	137	4	34.25	2-35	-	

SMALL, G. C.   Warwickshire

Name: Gladstone Cleophas Small
Role: Right-hand bat, right-arm
fast-medium bowler
Born: 18 October 1961, St George,
Barbados
Height: 5ft 11st **Weight:** 12st
Nickname: Gladys
County debut: 1980
County cap: 1982
Benefit: 1992
Test debut: 1986
Tests: 17
One-Day Internationals: 53
50 wickets in a season: 6
1st-Class 50s scored: 7
1st-Class 5 w. in innings: 27
1st-Class 10 w. in match: 2

1st-Class catches: 83
Place in batting averages: 215th av. 16.45 (1991 211th av. 16.81)
Place in bowling averages: 69th av. 33.43 (1991 50th av. 29.93)
Strike rate: 73.46 (career 57.86)
Parents: Chelston and Gladys
Wife: Lois
Children: Zak
Family links with cricket: Cousin, Milton Small, toured England with West Indies in 1984
Education: Moseley School; Hall Green Technical College, Birmingham
Qualifications: 2 O-levels
Overseas tours: England YC to New Zealand 1979-80; England to Australia 1986-87, to the World Cup 1987, to India and West Indies 1989-90, to Australia 1990-91, to Australia and New Zealand (World Cup) 1991-92
Overseas teams played for: South Australia 1985-86
Cricketers particularly admired: Dennis Lillee, Malcolm Marshall, Richard Hadlee, Bob Willis
Other sports followed: Athletics, golf, tennis, soccer
Relaxations: 'Playing a round of golf; listening to music and relaxing with my wife.'
Extras: Was called up for England Test squad v Pakistan at Edgbaston, July 1982, but did not play. Bowled 18-ball over v Middlesex in August 1982, with 11 no balls. Grandfather watched him take eight wickets in the Barbados Test v West Indies in 1989-90 on his return to the land of his birth. Was Andy Lloyd's best man
Opinions on cricket: 'The introduction of four-day Championship cricket will improve the first-class game: teams will have to bowl out the opposition twice instead of relying on contrived results. We should play on hard, fast and true wickets that would be beneficial to both batsmen and bowlers.'
Best batting: 70 Warwickshire v Lancashire, Old Trafford 1988
Best bowling: 7-15 Warwickshire v Nottinghamshire, Edgbaston 1988

1992 Season

	M	Inns	NO	Runs	HS	Avge	100s	50s	Ct	St	O	M	Runs	Wkts	Avge	Best	5wl	10wM
Test																		
All First	17	17	6	181	31 *	16.45	-	-	6	-	367.2	83	1003	30	33.43	3-43	-	-
1-day Int	1	0	0	0	0	-	-	-	1	-	5.1	0	28	1	28.00	1-28	-	
NatWest	4	3	1	39	23	19.50	-	-	1	-	47	10	121	4	30.25	3-28	-	
B & H	4	2	1	21	20 *	21.00	-	-	1	-	41	9	138	2	69.00	2-31	-	
Sunday	11	4	2	25	10 *	12.50	-	-	-	-	72.3	0	324	7	46.28	2-25	-	

162. Which former Australian Test player's daughter took part in the Barcelona Olympics?

Career Performances

	M	Inns	NO	Runs	HS	Avge	100s	50s	Ct	St	Balls	Runs	Wkts	Avge	Best	5wI	10wM
Test	17	24	7	263	59	15.47	-	1	9	-	3927	1871	55	34.01	5-48	2	-
All First	272	351	82	4033	70	14.99	-	7	83	-	43396	21497	750	28.66	7-15	27	2
1-day Int	53	24	9	98	18 *	6.53	-	-	7	-	2793	1942	58	33.48	4-31	-	
NatWest	34	21	7	187	33	13.35	-	-	5	-	2083	1061	38	27.92	3-22	-	
B & H	48	30	7	152	22	6.60	-	-	10	-	2738	1663	55	30.23	4-22	-	
Sunday	139	66	21	333	40 *	7.40	-	-	29	-	5904	4471	175	25.54	5-29	2	

SMITH, A. M. Gloucestershire

Name: Andrew Michael Smith
Role: Right-hand bat, left-arm medium bowler
Born: 1 October 1967, Dewsbury, West Yorks
Height: 5ft 8¹/₂in **Weight:** 11st 7lbs
Nickname: Smudge
County debut: 1991
1st-Class 50s scored: 1
1st-Class catches: 3
Place in batting averages: 203rd av. 18.77
Place in bowling averages: 80th av. 34.76 (1991 78th av. 33.89)
Strike rate: 62.33 (63.35)
Parents: Hugh and Margaret
Marital status: Engaged to Sarah
Family links with cricket: Father and uncle both played club cricket in Yorkshire, brother plays for Ossett in the Central Yorkshire League
Education: Queen Elizabeth Grammar School, Wakefield; Exeter University
Qualification: BA (Hons) French and German
Off-season: 'Decorating the house, playing golf and building myself up for next season.'
Overseas tours: Queen Elizabeth Grammar School to Holland 1985; Bradford Junior Cricket League to Barbados 1986; Exeter University to Barbados 1987; Gloucestershire to Kenya 1990
Overseas teams played for: Waimea, New Zealand 1990
Cricketers particularly admired: Richard Hadlee, Graham Gooch, Wasim Akram
Other sports followed: Football (Leeds United), golf
Relaxations: Crosswords, travel, reading
Extras: Played for ESCA U19, NAYC and represented Combined Universities in the

Benson & Hedges Cup in 1988 and 1990

Opinions on cricket: 'First-class cricket looks better organised this year but 2nd team cricket could be improved to make the step up to first-class less noticeable. 2nd XI cricket should be played at first-class venues on first-class standard pitches with more competent umpires, The 2nd team 'club' umpire should be thoroughly vetted. He can make the difference between the success and failure of a cricketer.'

Best batting: 51* Gloucestershire v Warwickshire, Bristol 1992
Best bowling: 4-41 Gloucestershire v Leicestershire, Hinckley 1991

1992 Season

	M	Inns	NO	Runs	HS	Avge	100s	50s	Ct	St	O	M	Runs	Wkts	Avge	Best	5wI	10wM
Test																		
All First	12	14	5	169	51 *	18.77	-	1	3	-	249.2	35	835	24	34.79	3-53	-	-
1-day Int																		
NatWest	3	1	0	6	6	6.00	-	-	1	-	22.1	2	90	3	30.00	3-45	-	
B & H	2	1	0	7	7	7.00	-	-	1	-	14	0	49	0	-	-	-	
Sunday	17	6	3	23	13 *	7.66	-	-	2	-	103.1	3	478	15	31.86	4-38	-	

Career Performances

	M	Inns	NO	Runs	HS	Avge	100s	50s	Ct	St	Balls	Runs	Wkts	Avge	Best	5wI	10wM
Test																	
All First	26	27	7	229	51 *	11.45	-	1	3	-	3358	1818	53	34.30	4-41	-	-
1-day Int																	
NatWest	5	1	0	6	6	6.00	-	-	1	-	229	153	5	30.60	3-45	-	
B & H	6	4	2	19	8	9.50	-	-	2	-	282	144	2	72.00	1-30	-	
Sunday	30	13	9	50	15 *	12.50	-	-	5	-	1019	856	30	28.53	4-38	-	

SMITH, A. W.   Surrey

Name: Andrew William Smith
Role: Right-hand bat, right-arm off-spin bowler
Born: 30 May 1969, Sutton, Surrey
Height: 5ft 8in
Nickname: Smudge, Smithy, Jonty, Furry
County debut: 1992 (one-day)
Parents: William and Gwendoline
Marital status: Single
Family links with cricket: Father played for Surrey 1960-70, 'mother watches, sister hates the game'
Education: Sutton Manor High School
Qualifications: 7 O-levels, NCA qualified coach
Career outside cricket: Gardener, Surrey Cricket Development staff-coaching

Off-season: Coaching around the schools in London and Surrey
Overseas teams played for: Richmond, Adelaide 1989-91
Cricketers particularly admired: Geoff Boycott, Mike Gatting, Robin Smith, Waqar Younis, John Emburey, Phil Tufnell, Jonty Rhodes 'for his fielding'
Other sports followed: All sports except wrestling
Relaxations: Cinema, go-karting, sleeping
Extras: 2nd XI Bowler of the Year 1992, took catch with first touch on first team debut in Seeboard Trophy 1992
Opinions on cricket: 'Too much cricket played, too much travelling. Four-day cricket is the best format.'

1992 Season (played only one match for Surrey in the Seeboard Trophy)

SMITH, B. F.   Leicestershire

Name: Benjamin Francis Smith
Role: Right-hand bat, right-arm medium bowler
Born: 3 April 1972, Corby
Height: 5ft 9in **Weight:** 10st 2lbs
Nickname: Smudge
County debut: 1990
1st-Class 50s scored: 6
1st-Class 100s scored: 1
1st-Class catches: 13
One-Day 50s: 5
Place in batting averages: 151st av. 25.94 (1991 69th av. 37.44)
Parents: Janet and Keith
Marital status: Single
Family links with cricket: Both uncles played for ESCA, father and grandfather played local league cricket
Education: Tugby Primary; Kibworth High;

Robert Smyth, Market Harborough
Qualifications: 5 O-levels, 3 CSEs, ESB distinction
Off-season: Playing abroad
Overseas tours: England U19 to New Zealand 1990-91; Rutland Tourists to South Africa 1992
Overseas teams played for: Alexandria, Zimbabwe 1990
Cricketers particularly admired: Paul Parker, David Gower
Other sports followed: Most sports, plays tennis and football
Injuries: Badly torn ankle tendons, out for eight weeks
Relaxations: Listening to music, cinema, eating out, Gameboy
Extras: Played tennis for Leicestershire aged 12
Best batting: 100* Leicestershire v Durham, Durham University 1992
Best bowling: 1-5 Leicestershire v Essex, Ilford 1991

1992 Season

	M	Inns	NO	Runs	HS	Avge	100s	50s	Ct	St	O	M	Runs	Wkts	Avge	Best	5wI	10wM
Test																		
All First	15	20	3	441	100*	25.94	1	3	9	-								
1-day Int																		
NatWest	2	2	0	59	49	29.50	-	-	1	-								
B & H	2	1	0	2	2	2.00	-	-	1	-								
Sunday	9	9	0	155	37	17.22	-	-	1	-								

Career Performances

	M	Inns	NO	Runs	HS	Avge	100s	50s	Ct	St	Balls	Runs	Wkts	Avge	Best	5wI	10wM
Test																	
All First	32	45	9	1134	100*	31.50	1	6	13	-	78	91	1	91.00	1-5	-	-
1-day Int																	
NatWest	4	3	0	65	49	21.66	-	-	1	-							
B & H	2	1	0	2	2	2.00	-	-	1	-							
Sunday	25	25	3	436	37	19.81	-	-	3	-	18	15	0	-		-	-

163. What have the following current county players got in common: Lance Cairns, Alec Stewart, Neil Smith?

164. Who was the first Dutchman to score a County Championship century?

SMITH, D. M.   Sussex

Name: David Mark Smith
Role: Left-hand bat, right-arm medium bowler
Born: 9 January 1956, Balham
Height: 6ft 4in **Weight:** 16st
County debut: 1973 (Surrey), 1984 (Worcs), 1989 (Sussex)
County cap: 1980 (Surrey), 1984 (Worcs), 1989 (Sussex)
Test debut: 1985-86
Tests: 2
One-Day Internationals: 2
1000 runs in a season: 7
1st-Class 50s scored: 69
1st-Class 100s scored: 27
1st-Class 200s scored: 1
1st-Class catches: 183
One-Day 50s: 34
One-Day 100s: 5
Place in batting averages: 99th av. 34.71 (1991 47th av. 42.69)

Parents: Dennis and Tina
Wife and date of marriage: Jacqui, 7 January 1977
Children: Sarah-Jane Louise, 4 April 1982
Family links with cricket: Father played cricket for the BBC
Education: Battersea Grammar School
Qualifications: 3 O-levels
Career outside cricket: Company director
Off-season: Working for my company
Overseas tours: England to West Indies 1985-86; joined tour to West Indies 1989-90 as a replacement for Graham Gooch
Overseas teams played for: Universals, Harare, Zimbabwe
Cricketers particularly admired: John Edrich, Clive Lloyd, Graham Gooch
Other sports followed: Football (Charlton Athletic), golf
Relaxations: Motor racing – 'keen to race at Le Mans and any other world series sports car event'
Extras: Played for Surrey 2nd XI in 1972. Was not retained after 1977 but was re-instated in 1978. Sacked by Surrey during 1983 season and joined Worcestershire in 1984. Rejoined Surrey in 1987, but released by Surrey at end of 1988 season. Joined Sussex for 1989. Called up as a replacement for England's tour of West Indies in 1989-90 – played in one match before breaking his thumb.
Opinions on cricket: 'There is too much cricket played. Flat wickets and seamless balls

do not make for good cricket. I dislike listening to ex-cricketers rubbishing today's players.'

Best batting: 213 Sussex v Essex, Southend 1992
Best bowling: 3-40 Surrey v Sussex, The Oval 1976

1992 Season

	M	Inns	NO	Runs	HS	Avge	100s	50s	Ct	St	O	M	Runs	Wkts	Avge	Best	5wI	10wM
Test																		
All First	19	33	2	1076	213	34.71	2	5	12	-	4	1	18	0	-	-	-	-
1-day Int																		
NatWest	2	2	0	84	62	42.00	-	1	-	-								
B & H	2	2	0	82	61	41.00	-	1	2	-								
Sunday	3	2	0	23	23	11.50	-	-	-	-								

Career Performances

	M	Inns	NO	Runs	HS	Avge	100s	50s	Ct	St	Balls	Runs	Wkts	Avge	Best	5wI	10wM
Test	2	4	0	80	47	20.00	-	-	-	-							
All First	297	476	87	14137	213	36.34	27	69	183	-	2797	1574	30	52.46	3-40	-	-
1-day Int	2	2	1	15	10 *	15.00	-	-	-	-							
NatWest	35	34	6	1388	109	49.57	2	11	10	-	186	118	4	29.50	3-39	-	
B & H	65	61	9	1899	126	36.51	3	9	37	-	336	266	8	33.25	4-29	-	
Sunday	158	144	27	3253	87 *	27.80	-	14	48	-	749	606	12	50.50	2-21	-	

SMITH, I.   Durham

Name: Ian Smith
Role: Right-hand bat, right-arm medium bowler
Born: 11 March 1967, Consett, Co Durham
Height: 6ft 3in **Weight:** 14st 5lbs
Nickname: Smudga, Cyril, Gilbert
County debut: 1985 (Glamorgan), 1992 (Durham)
1st-Class 50s scored: 7
1st-Class 100s scored: 4
1st-Class catches: 28
One-Day 50s: 2

---

165. Who is captain of Oxford University for 1993, and what county has he already played for?

Place in batting averages: 129th av. 29.00
(1991 179th av. 22.27)
Parents: Jim and Mary
Marital status: Single
Family links with cricket: Father NCA
Coach, brother played in League cricket.
'No relation to Chris, Robin, David, Neil,
Paul, Gareth, etc., etc.'
Education: Ryton Comprehensive
Qualifications: 4 O-levels, CSE; studying
for Open University degree in Social
Psychology
Overseas tours: England YC to West
Indies 1985
Cricketers particularly admired:
Ian Botham, Mike Fatkin, Viv Richards
Other sports followed: Football, table tennis
Relaxations: Music, wine, theatre, golf
Extras: Glamorgan Young Player of the
Year 1989. Offered terms by several football
clubs. Released by Glamorgan at the end of the 1991 season and signed to play for Durham
in 1992
Best batting: 116 Glamorgan v Kent, Canterbury 1989
Best bowling: 3-48 Glamorgan v Hampshire, Cardiff 1989

1992 Season

	M	Inns	NO	Runs	HS	Avge	100s	50s	Ct	St	O	M	Runs	Wkts	Avge	Best	5wI	10wM
Test																		
All First	12	16	1	435	110	29.00	1	2	4	-	90	20	242	8	30.25	3-85	-	-
1-day Int																		
NatWest	3	3	1	17	12 *	8.50	-	-	-	-	27	1	114	2	57.00	2-40	-	
B & H	1	1	1	29	29 *	-	-	-	-	-								
Sunday	10	10	2	126	26	15.75	-	-	6	-	27	1	171	4	42.75	3-32	-	

Career Performances

	M	Inns	NO	Runs	HS	Avge	100s	50s	Ct	St	Balls	Runs	Wkts	Avge	Best	5wI	10wM
Test																	
All First	74	97	14	2109	116	25.41	4	7	28	-	4252	2692	60	44.86	3-48	-	-
1-day Int																	
NatWest	8	6	1	77	33	15.40	-	-	2	-	312	237	7	33.85	3-60	-	
B & H	13	12	1	166	51	15.09	-	1	2	-	144	138	2	69.00	1-21	-	
Sunday	55	54	13	855	56 *	20.85	-	1	19	-	906	844	22	38.36	3-22	-	

SMITH, N. M. K.   Warwickshire

Name: Neil Michael Knight Smith
Role: Right-hand bat, off-spin bowler,
specialist mid-on
Born: 27 July 1967, Solihull
Height: 6ft **Weight:** 13st 7lbs
Nickname: Gurt
County debut: 1987
1st-Class 50s scored: 5
1st-Class 100s scored: 1
1st-Class 5 w. in innings: 1
1st-Class catches: 14
One-Day 50s: 1
Place in batting averages: 158th av. 25.22
(1991 116th av. 29.85)
Place in bowling averages: 136th av. 49.08
Strike rate: 83.12 (career 88.73)
Parents: Mike (M.J.K.) and Diana
Marital status: Single
Family links with cricket: Father
captained Warwickshire and England

Education: Warwick School
Qualifications: 3 O-levels (Maths, English, French); cricket coach Grade 1
Career outside cricket: 'For the last two winters I've coached sports at Oratory School,
Oxford
Off-season: As above
Overseas teams played for: Phoenix, Perth, Western Australia 1988-89
Cricketers particularly admired: David Gower, Allan Donald, Paul Smith
Other sports followed: Rugby, football, 'any really'
Relaxations: Sport and music and the occasional gamble
Best batting: 161 Warwickshire v Yorkshire, Headingley 1989
Best bowling: 5-61 Warwickshire v Middlesex, Lord's 1992

1992 Season

	M	Inns	NO	Runs	HS	Avge	100s	50s	Ct	St	O	M	Runs	Wkts	Avge	Best	5wI	10wM
Test																		
All First	12	20	2	454	67	25.22	-	1	5	-	332.3	63	1178	24	49.08	5-61	1	-
1-day Int																		
NatWest	4	3	1	41	21 *	20.50	-	-	-	-	16.5	1	56	2	28.00	1-17	-	
B & H	4	4	0	51	32	12.75	-	-	-	-	35.4	6	122	6	20.33	3-45	-	
Sunday	16	11	3	138	44	17.25	-	-	6	-	97	1	474	14	33.85	4-25	-	

Career Performances

	M	Inns	NO	Runs	HS	Avge	100s	50s	Ct	St	Balls	Runs	Wkts	Avge	Best	5wI	10wM
Test																	
All First	40	60	10	1399	161	27.98	1	5	14	-	5058	2763	57	48.47	5-61	1	-
1-day Int																	
NatWest	10	9	3	162	52	27.00	-	1	1	-	293	173	6	28.83	1-6	-	
B & H	8	7	1	115	32	19.16	-	-	1	-	328	217	7	31.00	3-45	-	
Sunday	56	38	10	462	44	16.50	-	-	17	-	1770	1539	42	36.64	4-25	-	

SMITH, P. A. Warwickshire

Name: Paul Andrew Smith
Role: Right-hand bat, right-arm
fast-medium bowler
Born: 15 April 1964, Newcastle-on-Tyne
Height: 6ft 2in **Weight:** 12st
Nickname: Smithy, Jim
County debut: 1982
County cap: 1986
1000 runs in a season: 2
1st-Class 50s scored: 44
1st-Class 100s scored: 4
1st-Class 5 w. in innings: 7
1st-Class catches: 53
One-Day 50s: 9
Place in batting averages: 202nd av. 18.90
(1991 199th av. 18.68)
Place in bowling averages: 65th av. 32.42
(1991 82nd av. 34.20)
Strike rate: 53.28 (career 55.87)
Parents: Ken and Joy
Wife and date of marriage: Caroline, 31 July 1987
Children: Oliver James, 5 February 1988
Family links with cricket: Father played for Leicestershire. Both brothers played for Warwickshire
Education: Heaton Grammar School, Newcastle
Qualifications: 5 O-levels, car restoration qualifications
Career outside cricket: 'Varies'
Off-season: Training, playing indoor cricket, going to Cape Town
Overseas teams played for: Florida, Johannesburg 1982-83, Belgrano, Buenos Aires 1983-84; Carlton, Melbourne 1984-85; St Augustine's, Cape Town 1992-93
Cricketers particularly admired: Derek Pringle, Neil Foster

Other sports followed: Most
Relaxations: Reading, gardening, working on cars
Extras: Along with Andy Moles set a new world record for most consecutive opening partnerships of over 50. In 1989, scored 140 v Worcestershire, during which scored 100 out of partnership of 123 with Dermot Reeve and took a hat-trick against Northamptonshire. In 1990 took a hat-trick against Sussex, bowling in Tim Munton's boots – two sizes too big
Opinions on cricket: 'Unlike some people I do not feel that eating bowls and bowls of muesli will make me a better player.'
Best batting: 140 Warwickshire v Worcestershire, Worcester 1989
Best bowling: 6-91 Warwickshire v Derbyshire, Edgbaston 1992

1992 Season

	M	Inns	NO	Runs	HS	Avge	100s	50s	Ct	St	O	M	Runs	Wkts	Avge	Best	5wl	10wM
Test																		
All First	19	27	5	416	45	18.90	-	-	6	-	373	57	1362	42	32.42	6-91	4	-
1-day Int																		
NatWest	1	0	0	0	0	-	-	-	1	-	2	0	15	0	-	-	-	-
B & H	4	4	0	76	37	19.00	-	-	-	-	39	3	185	6	30.83	2-41	-	
Sunday	17	10	4	123	21	20.50	-	-	1	-	95.2	2	577	17	33.94	3-25	-	

Career Performances

	M	Inns	NO	Runs	HS	Avge	100s	50s	Ct	St	Balls	Runs	Wkts	Avge	Best	5wl	10wM
Test																	
All First	193	311	38	7377	140	27.02	4	44	53	-	13578	8768	243	36.08	6-91	7	-
1-day Int																	
NatWest	22	20	3	343	79	20.17	-	2	2	-	870	563	20	28.15	3-10	-	
B & H	37	35	4	593	74	19.12	-	1	5	-	1094	789	25	31.56	3-28	-	
Sunday	129	107	23	2035	93 *	24.22	-	6	24	-	3416	3116	98	31.79	4-21	-	

166. How many times did Graham Dilley play for England, 11, 21 or 41?

167. What have the following in common: Mike Brearley, David Gower, Geoff Boycott?

SMITH, R. A.   Hampshire

Name: Robin Arnold Smith
Role: Right-hand bat, slip fielder
Born: 13 September 1963, Durban, South Africa
Height: 5ft 11in **Weight:** 14st 2lbs
Nickname: The Judge
County debut: 1982
County cap: 1985
Test debut: 1988
Tests: 36
One-Day Internationals: 47
1000 runs in a season: 6
1st-Class 50s scored: 76
1st-Class 100s scored: 33
1st-Class 200s scored: 1
1st-Class catches: 153
One-Day 50s: 45
One-Day 100s: 11
Place in batting averages:
78th av. 38.00 (1991 19th av. 53.73)
Parents: John and Joy
Wife and date of marriage: Katherine, 21 September 1988
Children: Harrison Arnold, 4 December 1991
Family links with cricket: Grandfather played for Natal in Currie Cup. Brother Chris played for Natal, Hampshire and England
Education: Northlands Boys High, Durban
Qualifications: Matriculation, '36 England caps'
Off-season: Relaxing with my family and then touring India and Sri Lanka with England
Overseas tours: England to India and West Indies 1989-90, to Australia 1990-91, to Australia and New Zealand (World Cup) 1991-92, to India and Sri Lanka 1992-93
Overseas teams played for: Natal 1980-84; Perth, Western Australia 1984-85 (grade cricket)
Cricketers particularly admired: Brother Chris, Barry Richards and Grayson Heath
Other sports followed: Soccer, athletics, rugby, golf, racing
Relaxations: 'Reading (Leslie Thomas in particular), trout fishing, assembling a good wine cellar, keeping fit and spending as much time as possible with my lovely wife, Katherine and my son, Harrison.'
Extras: Played rugby for Natal Schools and for Romsey RFC as a full-back. Held nineteen school athletics records and two South African schools records in shot put and 100-metre hurdles. One of *Wisden*'s Five Cricketers of the Year, 1990. First child was born while he was on tour in Australia last winter. Director of Holt and Haskell Ltd (sports shop)
Opinions on cricket: 'I enjoy playing cricket for Hampshire and for England and

particularly enjoy the camaraderie of the county circuit.'
Best batting: 209* Hampshire v Essex, Southampton 1987
Best bowling: 2-11 Hampshire v Surrey, Southampton 1985

1992 Season

	M	Inns	NO	Runs	HS	Avge	100s	50s	Ct	St	O	M	Runs	Wkts	Avge	Best	5wI	10wM
Test	5	8	1	314	127	44.85	1	1	7	-								
All First	17	28	3	950	127	38.00	2	5	12	-	8.1	0	41	0	-	-	-	-
1-day Int	5	5	1	258	85 *	64.50	-	3	2	-								
NatWest	2	2	1	73	59 *	73.00	-	1	-	-								
B & H	6	6	0	348	109	58.00	1	1	3	-								
Sunday	10	10	0	472	78	47.20	-	5	8	-	0.2	0	0	1	0.00	1-0	-	

Career Performances

	M	Inns	NO	Runs	HS	Avge	100s	50s	Ct	St	Balls	Runs	Wkts	Avge	Best	5wI	10wM
Test	36	66	14	2645	148 *	50.86	7	18	26	-	24	6	0	-	-	-	-
All First	230	390	68	14227	209 *	44.18	33	76	153	-	918	691	12	57.58	2-11	-	-
1-day Int	47	46	7	1547	128	39.66	2	11	18	-							
NatWest	25	25	7	1201	125 *	66.72	2	7	16	-	17	13	2	6.50	2-13	-	
B & H	32	31	7	1347	155 *	56.12	3	5	15	-	6	2	0	-	-	-	
Sunday	94	89	10	3064	131	38.78	4	22	50	-	2	0	1	0.00	1-0	-	

SNAPE, J. N. Northamptonshire

Name: Jeremy Nicholas Snape
Role: Right-hand bat, Off-spin bowler
Born: 27 April 1973, Stoke on Trent,
Staffordshire
Height: 5ft 8¹/₂in **Weight:** 11st 3lbs
Nickname: Snapey, Coot, Jez
County debut: 1992
1st-Class catches: 1
Parents: Keith and Barbara
Marital status: Single
Family links with cricket: Brother Jonathan
plays local club cricket in Staffordshire
Education: Denstone College Boarding
School, Staffordshire; Durham University
Qualifications: 8 GCSEs, 3 A-Levels,
studying BSc (Hons) in Natural Science
Off-season: Studying
Overseas tours: England U18 to Canada

1991; England U19 to Pakistan 1992; Durham University to South Africa 1992
Cricketers particularly admired: Graham Gooch, Alan Lamb, Norman Gifford
Other sports followed: Rugby, squash, 'any other big sporting event'
Injuries: 'Cut under eye after the ball hit me during fielding practice.'
Relaxations: 'Enjoy relaxing to music and good meals in restaurants.'
Extras: Gold Award winner for Combined Universities v Worcestershire 1992 (3-34) at The Parks
Opinions on cricket: 'Sunday League cricket should remain a 40-over competition. Coloured clothing is an exciting concept and it will be interesting to see it's effect on the game's following. I approve of four-day cricket as it will encourage the development of young spin bowlers.'
Best bowling: 1-20 Northamptonshire v Leicestershire, Leicester 1992

1992 Season

	M	Inns	NO	Runs	HS	Avge	100s	50s	Ct	St	O	M	Runs	Wkts	Avge	Best	5wI	10wM
Test																		
All First	1	0	0	0	0	-	-	-	1	-	26	8	62	1	62.00	1-20	-	-
1-day Int																		
NatWest	1	1	1	5	5 *	-	-	-	-	-								
B & H	4	4	1	48	26	16.00	-	-	2	-	43	3	185	7	26.42	3-35	-	
Sunday	3	1	0	6	6	6.00	-	-	1	-	24	1	116	5	23.20	3-33	-	

Career Performances

	M	Inns	NO	Runs	HS	Avge	100s	50s	Ct	St	Balls	Runs	Wkts	Avge	Best	5wI	10wM
Test																	
All First	1	0	0	0	0	-	-	-	1	-	156	62	1	62.00	1-20	-	-
1-day Int																	
NatWest	1	1	1	5	5 *	-	-	-	-	-							
B & H	4	4	1	48	26	16.00	-	-	2	-	258	185	7	26.42	3-35	-	
Sunday	3	1	0	6	6	6.00	-	-	1	-	144	116	5	23.20	3-33	-	

168. Which ex-Worcestershire player captained Auckland last season?

SNELL, R. P.   Somerset

Name: Richard Peter Snell
Role: Right-hand bat, right-arm fast bowler
Born: 12 September 1968, Durban,
South Africa
Height: 5ft 8¹/₂in **Weight:** 11st 3lbs
County debut: 1992
Tests: 1
1st-Class 50s scored: 3
1st-Class 5 w. in innings: 5
1st-Class catches: 11
One-day 50s: 1
Place in batting averages: 137th av. 27.25
Place in bowling averages: 123rd av. 44.22
Strike rate: 75.37 (career 55.29)
Off-season: Playing for South Africa v India
Overseas tours: South Africa to Australia
(World Cup) 1991-92, to West Indies
1991-92
Overseas teams played for:
Transvaal 1987-93
Extras: Joined Somerset on a one-year contract in 1992 and was replaced by Mushtaq Ahmed as Somerset's overseas player for 1993. Took eight wickets on his Test debut v West Indies at Bridgetown 1991-92
Opinions on cricket: 'Sunday League cricket should remain a 40-over competition. Coloured clothing is an exciting concept and it will be interesting to see it's effect on the game's following. I approve of four-day cricket as it will encourage the development of young spin bowlers.'
Best batting: 81 Somerset v Leicestershire, Leicester 1992
Best bowling: 6-58 Transvaal v Natal, Johannesburg 1990-91

1992 Season

	M	Inns	NO	Runs	HS	Avge	100s	50s	Ct	St	O	M	Runs	Wkts	Avge	Best	5wI	10wM
Test																		
All First	16	20	4	436	81	27.25	-	3	5	-	339.1	60	1194	27	44.22	3-29	-	-
1-day Int																		
NatWest	2	1	0	19	19	19.00	-	-	-	-	22	0	99	0	-		-	-
B & H	4	4	1	60	31	20.00	-	-	1	-	42.5	2	176	6	29.33	3-47	-	
Sunday	13	7	2	158	62	31.60	-	1	1	-	76	1	359	12	29.91	2-24	-	

Career Performances

	M	Inns	NO	Runs	HS	Avge	100s	50s	Ct	St	Balls	Runs	Wkts	Avge	Best	5wI	10wM
Test	1	2	0	6	6	3.00	-	-	-	-	204	158	8	19.75	4-74	-	-
All First	41	53	10	724	81	16.83	-	3	11	-	6856	3402	124	27.43	6-58	5	
1-day Int	15	8	2	51	16	8.50	-	-	-	-	743	575	10	57.50	3-42	-	
NatWest	2	1	0	19	19	19.00	-	-	-	-	132	99	0	-	-	-	
B & H	4	4	1	60	31	20.00	-	-	1	-	257	176	6	29.33	3-47	-	
Sunday	13	7	2	158	62	31.60	-	1	1	-	456	359	12	29.91	2-24	-	

SOLANKI, V. S. Worcestershire

Name: Vikram Singh Solanki
Role: Right-hand bat, off-spin bowler, occasional wicket-keeper
Born: 1 April 1976, Udaipur, India
Height: 6ft **Weight:** 12st
Nickname: Indian
County debut: No first team Appearance
Parents: Vijay and Florabel
Marital status: Single
Family links with cricket: Father played a high standard in India
Education: Regis School, Wolverhampton
Qualifications: 9 GCSEs
Off-season: At school
Overseas tours: England U18 to South Africa 1992-93
Cricketers particularly admired: Sachin Tendulkar, Wasim Akram, Viv Richards
Other sports followed: Many
Relaxations: 'Spending time with friends and family.'
Opinions on cricket: 'The best game in the world.'

169. What famous feat was performed on 15 September 1975 by Chris Balderstone of Leics and England?

505

SPEAK, N. J.   Lancashire

Name: Nicholas Jason Speak
Role: Right-hand opening bat, off-spin bowler
Born: 21 October 1966, Manchester
Height: 6ft **Weight:** 12st
Nickname: Twenty, Vision, Pod
County debut: 1986-87 in Jamaica
County cap: 1992
1000 runs in a season: 1
1st-Class 50s scored: 18
1st-Class 100s scored: 6
1st-Class 200s scored: 1
1st-Class catches: 35
One-Day 50s: 7
One-Day 100s: 1
Place in batting averages: 10th av. 57.33
(1991 132nd av. 28.13)
Parents: John and Irene
Wife and date of marriage:

Michelle, 11 March 1993
Family links with cricket: Father was league professional in Lancashire and Yorkshire
Education: Parrs Wood High School and Sixth Form College
Qualifications: 5 O-levels; NCA coaching certificate
Career outside cricket: Coaching in Canberra, Australia
Off-season: At North Canberra CC, Australia
Overseas tours: Lancashire to Jamaica 1987-88, to Zimbabwe 1989, to Perth 1990-91, to Johannesburg 1992
Overseas teams played for: South Canberra 1989; North Canberra 1991-93
Cricketers particularly admired: Martin Crowe, Dexter Fitton, Neil Fairbrother
Other sports followed: Most sports – Manchester City FC
Relaxations: 'Cold lager, constructive arguments with G.D. Lloyd and J.D. Fitton, Indian food and red wine.'
Extras: Scored century for Australian Capital Territories v England A at Canberra 1992-93
Opinions on cricket: 'Tea should be 10 minutes longer.'
Best batting: 232 Lancashire v Leicestershire, Leicester 1992
Best bowling: 1-0 Lancashire v Warwickshire, Old Trafford 1991

---

170. What do Bill Edrich, Robin Smith and Alan Wells have in common?

1992 Season

	M	Inns	NO	Runs	HS	Avge	100s	50s	Ct	St	O	M	Runs	Wkts	Avge	Best	5wI	10wM
Test																		
All First	22	36	3	1892	232	57.33	4	12	18	-	6	0	66	0	-		-	-	-
1-day Int																		
NatWest	2	2	0	95	60	47.50	-	1	1	-								
B & H	5	5	1	158	82	39.50	-	2	-	-								
Sunday	15	15	2	535	102 *	41.15	1	4	3	-								

Career Performances

	M	Inns	NO	Runs	HS	Avge	100s	50s	Ct	St	Balls	Runs	Wkts	Avge	Best	5wI	10wM
Test																	
All First	53	92	7	3380	232	39.76	6	18	35	-	67	92	2	46.00	1-0	-	-
1-day Int																	
NatWest	2	2	0	95	60	47.50	-	1	1	-							
B & H	6	5	1	158	82	39.50	-	2	-	-							
Sunday	21	19	3	583	102 *	36.43	1	4	6	-							

SPEIGHT, M. P. — Sussex

Name: Martin Peter Speight
Role: Right-hand bat, wicket-keeper
Born: 24 October 1967, Walsall
Height: 5ft 10in **Weight:** 12st
Nickname: Sprog, Hoover, Ginger
County debut: 1986
County cap: 1991
1000 runs in a season: 1
1st-Class 50s scored: 23
1st-Class 100s scored: 8
1st-Class catches: 58
One-Day 50s: 7
One-Day 100s: 1
Place in batting averages: 76th av. 38.06
(1991 57th av. 39.68)
Parents: Peter John and Valerie
Marital status: Single
Education: Hassocks Infants School;
The Windmills School, Hassocks;
Hurstpierpoint College Junior and Senior Schools; Durham University (St Chad's College)
Qualifications: 13 O-levels, 3 A-levels; BA (Hons) (Archaeology/Ancient History)
Career outside cricket: Artist

Off-season: 'Painting pictures for various beneficiaries and picture for a book. Possibly going to Wellington to coach/play.'

Overseas tours: NCA U19 to Bermuda 1986; England YC tour to Sri Lanka 1987

Overseas teams played for: Karori, Wellington, New Zealand 1989-90; Wellington CC, 1989-90; Victoria University of Wellington 1990-92

Cricketers particularly admired: Viv Richards, Ian Botham, David Gower

Other sports followed: Golf, rugby, hockey, horse racing

Injuries: Removal of wisdom teeth (April)

Relaxations: Most music, sports on TV painting and drawing

Extras: Member of Durham University UAU winning side 1987; played for Combined Universities in B&H Cup 1987 and 1988; Member of Durham University's men's hockey team to Barbados 1988. Sussex CCC's Most Promising Player, 1989. Painted an oil painting of the maiden first-class game at Arundel Castle between Sussex and Hampshire which was later auctioned to raise £1200 for the Sussex YC tour to India 1990-91. Limited edition has also been printed and sold. Has done paintings of Hove, Southampton and The Oval for the Benefits of Messrs. Pigott, Parks and Greig

Opinions on cricket: 'If 110 overs are bowled during a day by 6.30 there should be no over rate fines. At the moment 110 overs and ten wickets have to be taken to achieve the required over rate by 6.30. This seems unfair to me!'

Best batting: 179 Sussex v Glamorgan, Eastbourne 1992

Best bowling: 1-2 Sussex v Middlesex, Hove 1988

1992 Season

	M	Inns	NO	Runs	HS	Avge	100s	50s	Ct	St	O	M	Runs	Wkts	Avge	Best	5wI	10wM
Test																		
All First	20	33	2	1180	179	38.06	5	-	16	-	3	0	30	1	30.00	1-30	-	-
1-day Int																		
NatWest	2	2	0	29	28	14.50	-	-	-	-								
B & H	3	3	0	67	39	22.33	-	-	5	-								
Sunday	16	15	2	437	87 *	33.61	-	1	5	1								

Career Performances

	M	Inns	NO	Runs	HS	Avge	100s	50s	Ct	St	Balls	Runs	Wkts	Avge	Best	5wI	10wM
Test																	
All First	80	130	12	4164	179	35.28	8	23	58	-	21	32	2	16.00	1-2	-	-
1-day Int																	
NatWest	8	7	0	156	48	22.28	-	-	2	-							
B & H	23	21	0	530	83	25.23	-	2	16	1							
Sunday	58	50	5	1408	106 *	31.28	1	5	19	1							

171. Which was Northants bowler Paul Taylor's first county?

SPIRING, K. R.   Worcestershire

Name: Karl Reuben Spiring
Role: Right-hand opening bat
Born: 13 November 1974, Southport
Height: 5ft 11in **Weight:** 12st
County debut: No first team appearance
Parents: Peter and June
Marital status: Single
Education: Monmouth School
Qualifications: 9 GCSEs
Career outside cricket: Student
Off-season: Play and coach abroad
Cricketers particularly admired:
Graham Burgess, Tom Cartwright, Adam
Seymour and Tom Moody
Other sports followed: Rugby and golf
Relaxations: 'Watching good batsmen play
and learning from them.'
Opinions on cricket: 'Should be encouraged
and coached more at schoolboy level.'

STANLEY, N. A.   Northamptonshire

Name: Neil Alan Stanley
Role: Right-hand bat, off-spin bowler
Born: 16 May 1968, Bedford
Height: 6ft 3in **Weight:** 14st 8lbs
Nickname: Giz, Swampy, Stanners
County debut: 1988
1st-Class 50s: 7
1st-Class 100s: 1
1st-Class catches: 9
Place in batting averages:
(1991 78th av. 36.15)
Parents: Jack and Julie
Marital status: Single
Education: Bedford Modern School
Qualifications: 7 O-levels, NCA senior
coaching award
Overseas tours: Bedford Modern to
Barbados 1983; Young England to Youth

World Cup, Australia 1988
Overseas teams played for: Sydenham, Christchurch, New Zealand 1989-90
Cricketers particularly admired: Ian Botham, Wayne Larkins
Other sports followed: Snooker, golf, football
Relaxations: 'Listening to Sigue Sigue Sputnik and other loud bands. Clint Eastwood films and a good pint of bitter.'
Extras: Played for England indoor cricket team v Australia in ManuLife Test series, 1990. Missed entire 1990 season due to two cracked vertebrae, operated on in March 1990
Opinions on cricket: 'Clubs should make more effort to find winter employment in the UK for young players. 2nd team games should be played on main first-class grounds. Tea interval should be longer.'
Best batting: 132 Northamptonshire v Lancashire, Lytham 1991

1992 Season

	M	Inns	NO	Runs	HS	Avge	100s	50s	Ct	St	O	M	Runs	Wkts	Avge	Best	5wI	10wM
Test																		
All First	1	2	1	23	16	23.00	-	-	-	-								
1-day Int																		
NatWest																		
B & H																		
Sunday	2	2	0	10	9	5.00	-	-	-	-								

Career Performances

	M	Inns	NO	Runs	HS	Avge	100s	50s	Ct	St	Balls	Runs	Wkts	Avge	Best	5wI	10wM
Test																	
All First	21	35	4	1019	132	32.87	1	7	9	-	60	19	0	-	-	-	-
1-day Int																	
NatWest																	
B & H	3	2	0	13	8	6.50	-	-	1	-	6	3	1	3.00	1-3	-	
Sunday	11	10	3	88	18	12.57	-	-	2	-							

172. Who was the first foreigner to be signed by Yorkshire?

STANWORTH, J.   Lancashire

Name: John Stanworth
Role: Right-hand bat, wicket-keeper
Born: 30 September 1960
Height: 5ft 10in **Weight:** 10st 10lbs
Nickname: Stany, Ming, Stanno, Big Ears
County debut: 1983
1st-Class 50s: 1
1st-Class catches: 63
1st-Class stumpings: 10
Parents: Bob and Freda
Wife and date of marriage: Dianne,
22 March 1986
Children: Scott and Katie (twins),
6 November 1988
Family links with cricket: Father played
club cricket
Education: Chadderton Grammar School;
Padgate College
Qualifications: BEd degree
Overseas tours: British Colleges to West Indies 1981
Overseas teams played for: Norths, Queensland 1978
Cricketers particularly admired: Alan Knott and Bob Taylor ('simply the best I've
seen'), Gary Yates 'for his wholehearted approach'
Other sports followed: Rugby, football (Oldham)
Relaxations: 'Reading about Tony Murphy (ex-Lancashire, now Surrey), his interests and
relaxations in *The Cricketers' Who's Who*.'
Extras: 2nd XI captain since 1988. 'Ran pre-season training at the club until the lads
became fed up.'
Opinions on cricket: 'The *quantity* of county cricket played in this country is too high and
as a result quite often the *quality* produced isn't all that it might be. As I get older I strongly
believe that the lunch and especially the tea interval should be lengthened.'
Best batting: 50* Lancashire v Gloucestershire, Bristol 1985

1992 Season

	M	Inns	NO	Runs	HS	Avge	100s	50s	Ct	St	O	M	Runs	Wkts	Avge	Best	5wI	10wM
Test																		
All First	5	2	0	30	21	15.00	-	-	7	1								
1-day Int																		
NatWest																		
B & H																		
Sunday	1	0	0	0	0	-	-	-	-	-								

Career Performances

	M	Inns	NO	Runs	HS	Avge	100s	50s	Ct	St	Balls	Runs	Wkts	Avge	Best	5wI	10wM
Test																	
All First	44	40	11	266	50 *	9.17	-		1	63	10						
1-day Int																	
NatWest	4	1	0	0	0	0.00	-		-	6	1						
B & H	6	3	2	17	8 *	17.00	-		-	4	-						
Sunday	17	4	2	7	4 *	3.50	-		-	10	1						

STEER, I. G. Derbyshire

Name: Ian Gary Steer
Role: Right-hand opening bat, right-arm
medium bowler
Born: 17 August 1970, Birmingham
Height: 5ft 7in **Weight:** 11st 9lbs
Nickname: Steery, Steersby
County debut: 1992 (one-day)
Parents: Derrick and Vashtee
Marital status: Single
Family links with cricket: Father played
amateur cricket
Education: St Edmund Campion RC;
Sutton Coldfield College; Cheltenham
College of Higher Education
Qualifications: 7 O-levels
Career outside cricket: Currently studying
physical education degree
Off-season: At college in Cheltenham and
playing other sports
Cricketers particularly admired:
Ian Bishop, Allan Donald, Paul Smith and Simon Green
Other sports followed: Football – Aston Villa FC
Injuries: Back injury, 'no time off, I just couldn't bowl for about eight weeks'
Relaxations: 'I enjoy playing many sports and attending all of Villa's home and away
matches.'
Extras: Signed by Derbyshire from Warwickshire
Opinions on cricket: 'As many 2nd XI matches as possible should be played on County
grounds rather then at local clubs. At most club grounds there are little, or no, sufficient
covers, therefore the weather could change a game around rather than the skill of one team.'

1992 Season

	M	Inns	NO	Runs	HS	Avge	100s	50s	Ct	St	O	M	Runs	Wkts	Avge	Best	5wI	10wM
Test																		
All First																		
1-day Int																		
NatWest																		
B & H																		
Sunday	1	0	0	0	0	-	-	-	-	-								

Career Performances

	M	Inns	NO	Runs	HS	Avge	100s	50s	Ct	St	Balls	Runs	Wkts	Avge	Best	5wI	10wM
Test																	
All First																	
1-day Int																	
NatWest																	
B & H																	
Sunday	1	0	0	0	0	-	-	-	-	-							

STEMP, R. D. Yorkshire

Name: Richard David Stemp
Role: Slow left-arm bowler
Born: 11 December 1967, Erdington
Height: 6ft **Weight:** 11st 10lbs
Nickname: Stempy, Stench
County debut: 1990
1st-Class 5 w. in innings: 3
1st-Class 10 w. in match: 1
1st-Class catches: 5
Place in bowling averages: 99th av. 34.67
(1991 21st av. 25.00)
Strike rate: 72.17 (career 72.26)
Parents: Arnold and Rita Homer
Marital status: Single
Family links with cricket: Father played
Birmingham League cricket for Old Hill
Education: Britannia High School,
Rowley Regis
Qualifications: NCA coaching award
Off-season: ' Operation on shins – recuperate in South Africa.'
Overseas teams played for: Pretoria
Technikon 1988-89

Other sports followed: Indoor cricket (Australian), Australian Rules and American football

Injuries: Shin Soreness

Relaxations: Ornithology, reading, weight training

Extras: Played for England indoor cricket team v Australia in ManuLife Test series, 1990. Moved to Yorkshire at the end of the 1992 season (first English non-Yorkshireman to be signed for the county)

Opinions on cricket: 'When are players going to be able to choose the most appropriate cricket to them, for example, why change Sunday League to 50 overs when neither players, umpires or spectators agree to the format. The Cricketers Association should have far more say in the way the game is run. Get rid of age old hierarchy!'

Best batting: 16* Worcestershire v Leicestershire, Leicester 1992

Best bowling: 6-67 Worcestershire v Gloucestershire, Gloucester 1992

1992 Season

	M	Inns	NO	Runs	HS	Avge	100s	50s	Ct	St	O	M	Runs	Wkts	Avge	Best	5wI	10wM
Test																		
All First	11	6	4	70	16 *	35.00	-	-	4	-	336.5	80	1054	28	37.64	6-67	3	1
1-day Int																		
NatWest																			
B & H	1	0	0	0	0	-	-	-	-	-	11	2	29	0	-	-	-	
Sunday	3	0	0	0	0	-	-	-	-	-	9	0	58	1	58.00	1-22	-	

Career Performances

	M	Inns	NO	Runs	HS	Avge	100s	50s	Ct	St	Balls	Runs	Wkts	Avge	Best	5wI	10wM
Test																	
All First	22	16	11	103	16 *	20.60	-	-	5	-	3324	1602	46	34.82	6-67	3	1
1-day Int																	
NatWest																		
B & H	2	0	0	0	0	-	-	-	-	-	114	67	0	-	-	-	-
Sunday	9	2	1	4	3 *	4.00	-	-	3	-	258	212	6	35.33	3-18	-	

173. How many points did you get for a win in the Sunday League in 1992?

STEPHENSON, F. D.   Sussex

Name: Franklyn Dacosta Stephenson
Role: Right-hand bat, right-arm fast bowler
Born: 8 April 1959, St James, Barbados
Height: 6ft 3¹/₂in **Weight:** 13st 10lbs
Nickname: Cookie
County debut: 1982 (Gloucs), 1988 (Notts)
1992 (Sussex)
County cap: 1988 (Notts) 1992 (Sussex)
1000 runs in a season: 1
50 wickets in a season: 4
1st-Class 50s scored: 27
1st-Class 100s scored: 6
1st-Class 5 w. in innings: 32
1st-Class 10 w. in match: 8
1st-Class catches: 60
One-Day 50s: 4
Place in batting averages: 110th av. 32.38
(1991 187th av. 21.15)
Place in bowling averages: 76th av. 27.31
(1991 28th av. 25.76)
Strike rate: 70.10 (career 49.00)
Parents: Leonard Young and Violet Stevenson
Wife and date of marriage: Julia, 2 April 1981
Children: Amanda, 20 October 1981; Orissa, 6 September 1983; Tamara, 1 November 1990
Education: St John Baptist Mixed School; Samuel Jackson Prescod Polytechnic
Qualifications: School leaving certificate
Career outside cricket: Part time professional golfer
Off-season: Playing for Orange Free State, Bloemfontein, South Africa
Overseas tours: West Indies U19 to England 1978; rebel West Indies team to South Africa 1982-83 and 1983-84
Overseas teams played for: Tasmania 1981-82; Barbados 1981-82 and 1989-90; Orange Free State 1991-93
Cricketers particularly admired: Sir Garfield Sobers, Sylvester Clarke, Collis King, Richard Hadlee, Graham Gooch
Other sports followed: Golf, athletics, tennis
Injuries: Ankle, thigh, knee or 'flat-wicket-itis', out for four games
Relaxations: Playing golf, learning music and the guitar
Extras: Played League cricket for Littleborough in the Central Lancashire League in 1979, Royton in 1980 (100 wickets and 621 runs), Rawtenstall in 1981 and 1982 (100+ wickets and 500+ runs both years). Hit 165 for Barbados in 1982 having been sent in as nightwatchman. Took 10 wickets in match on debut for Tasmania. In 1988 did the double when

he scored 1018 runs and took 125 wickets in first-class cricket. Britannic Assurance Player of the Year, 1988. One of *Wisden's* Five Cricketers of the Year, 1988. Now again eligible to play for West Indies, having been banned for playing in South Africa. Left Nottinghamshire at the end of the 1991 season and signed to play for Sussex in 1992. Sussex Players' Player of the Year

Best batting: 165 Barbados v Leeward Islands, Basseterre 1981-82
Best bowling: 8-47 Nottinghamshire v Essex, Trent Bridge 1989

1992 Season

	M	Inns	NO	Runs	HS	Avge	100s	50s	Ct	St	O	M	Runs	Wkts	Avge	Best	5wI	10wM
Test																		
All First	18	25	4	680	133	32.38	1	2	10	-	467.2	93	1375	40	34.37	7-29	1	1
1-day Int																		
NatWest	2	2	0	52	40	26.00	-	-	1	-	21	6	43	5	8.60	3-8	-	
B & H	5	5	0	78	34	15.60	-	-	1	-	53	4	182	9	20.22	3-28	-	
Sunday	13	10	1	132	55 *	14.66	-	1	3	-	94.4	11	442	18	24.55	4-22	-	

Career Performances

	M	Inns	NO	Runs	HS	Avge	100s	50s	Ct	St	Balls	Runs	Wkts	Avge	Best	5wI	10wM
Test																	
All First	142	215	28	5108	165	27.31	6	27	60	-	26265	12884	536	24.03	8-47	32	8
1-day Int																	
NatWest	13	9	1	133	40	16.62	-	-	2	-	810	378	16	23.62	3-8	-	
B & H	26	23	6	395	98 *	23.23	-	2	4	-	1532	862	41	21.02	5-30	1	
Sunday	80	62	14	999	69	20.81	-	2	18	-	3581	2575	127	20.27	5-31	1	

174. Who are the only English father and son to have scored a first-class century on the same day?

STEPHENSON, J. P. Essex

Name: John Patrick Stephenson
Role: Right-hand opening bat, right-arm fast medium bowler
Born: 14 March 1965, Stebbing, Essex
Height: 6ft ¹/₂in **Weight:** 12st 7lbs
Nickname: Stan, Arnie, Svensson, Schmurdlenburglar
County debut: 1985
County cap: 1989
Test debut: 1989
Tests: 1
1000 runs in a season: 4
1st-Class 50s scored: 48
1st-Class 100s scored: 15
1st-Class 200s scored: 1
1st-Class 5 w. in innings: 2
1st-Class catches: 84
One-Day 50s: 17
One-Day 100s: 2
Place in batting averages: 48th av. 43.78
(1991 70th av. 37.39)
Place in bowling averages: 104th av. 38.81 (1991 14th av. 23.4
Strike rate: 68.68 (career 60.15)
Parents: Pat and Eve
Marital status: 'Living in sin'
Family links with cricket: Father was member of Rugby Meteors Cricketer Cup winning side in 1973. Three brothers played in Felsted 1st XI; Guy played for Essex 2nd XI and now plays for Teddington
Education: Felsted Prep School; Felsted Senior School; Durham University
Qualifications: 7 O-levels, 3 A-levels; BA General Arts (Dunelm)
Off-season: 'With Fiona, Bear and Rabbit'
Overseas tours: ESCA U19 to Zimbabwe 1982-83; England A to Kenya and Zimbabwe and Kenya 1989-90, to Bermuda and West Indies 1991-92
Overseas teams played for: Fitzroy, Melbourne 1982-83, 1987-88; Boland, South Africa 1988-89; Gold Coast Dolphins and Bond University, Australia 1990-91
Cricketers particularly admired: Brian Hardie
Injuries: Two broken fingers, 'chronic Indy 500', out for three Championship games
Relaxations: 'Collecting vinyl, e.g.. Nirvana, Slint, The Bags, Codiene, Polvo Eitzel (American music club), reading (same as music taste).'
Extras: Awarded 2nd XI cap in 1984 when leading run-scorer with Essex 2nd XI. Essex Young Player of the Year, 1985. Captained Durham University to victory in UAU Competition 1986 and captain of Combined Universities team 1987 in the first year that

it was drawn from all universities. Called up to replace the injured Michael Atherton on England A tour to Bermuda and West Indies 1991-92 and was leading wicket-taker. Two not out centuries v Somerset at Taunton and was on the field for the whole game (the first Essex player to achieve this)

Opinions on cricket: 'We should have fresh towels every day. Return to "yesterday", bring back 40 overs on Sunday. No extension of play if time is lost for rain in Championship games.'

Best batting: 202* Essex v Somerset, Bath 1990
Best bowling: 6-54 Essex v Nottinghamshire, Colchester 1992

1992 Season

	M	Inns	NO	Runs	HS	Avge	100s	50s	Ct	St	O	M	Runs	Wkts	Avge	Best	5wl	10wM
Test																		
All First	21	37	5	1401	159 *	43.78	3	8	10	-	251.5	51	854	22	38.81	6-54	1	-
1-day Int																		
NatWest	3	3	0	86	75	28.66	-	1	4	-	33.5	2	176	5	35.20	3-78	-	
B & H	4	4	0	85	66	21.25	-	1	-	-	24	0	99	4	24.75	2-47	-	
Sunday	15	14	1	396	64	30.46	-	3	4	-	93	4	444	19	23.36	5-58	1	

Career Performances

	M	Inns	NO	Runs	HS	Avge	100s	50s	Ct	St	Balls	Runs	Wkts	Avge	Best	5wl	10wM
Test	1	2	0	36	25	18.00	-	-	-	-							
All First	155	265	29	8684	202 *	36.79	15	48	84	-	5354	2903	89	32.61	6-54	2	-
1-day Int																	
NatWest	13	12	1	345	75	31.36	-	4	5	-	287	258	6	43.00	3-78	-	
B & H	26	21	2	730	142	38.42	1	5	6	-	642	437	20	21.85	3-22	-	
Sunday	79	65	8	1494	109	26.21	1	8	31	-	1442	1108	45	24.62	5-58	1	

STEWART, A. J. Surrey

Name: Alec James Stewart
Role: Right-hand bat, wicket-keeper, county captain
Born: 8 April 1963, Merton
Nickname: Stewie
Height: 5ft 11in **Weight:** 12st
County debut: 1981
County cap: 1985
Test debut: 1989-90
Tests: 22
One-Day Internationals: 41
1000 runs in a season: 7
1st-Class 50s scored: 74

1st-Class 100s scored: 23
1st-Class 200s scored: 1
1st-Class catches: 273
1st-Class stumpings: 6
One-Day 50s: 40
One-Day 100s: 8
Place in batting averages: 56th av. 42.55
(1991 42nd av. 44.65)
Parents: Michael and Sheila
Wife and date of marriage: Lynn,
28 September 1991
Family links with cricket: Father played
for England (1962-64) and Surrey
(1954 -72) and Malden Wanderers CC.
Brother Neil captains Malden Wanderers CC
Education: Tiffin Boys School
Qualifications: 4 O-levels
Off-season: Touring India and Sri Lanka
with England
Overseas tours: England to India (Nehru Cup)
1989, to West Indies 1989-90, to Australia 1990-91, to Australia and New Zealand 1991-
92 (World Cup), to India and Sri Lanka 1992-93
Overseas teams played for: Midland Guildford 1981-89
Cricketers particularly admired: Geoff Arnold, Kevin Gartrell, Tony Mann, Graham
Monkhouse, Geoff Boycott
Other sports followed: Football (Chelsea) and most other sports
Relaxations: 'Eating out, listening to Neil Kendrick talk rubbish, watching R. Alikhan
bat.'
Extras: Captained England in a Test match for the first time v India at Madras 1992-93
Opinions on cricket: 'Looking forward to four-day cricket, coloured clothing on a Sunday
(which should still be only 40 overs) and playing on good cricket wickets, which offer equal
help to both bat and ball.'
Best batting: 206* Surrey v Essex, The Oval 1989
Best bowling: 1-7 Surrey v Lancashire, Old Trafford 1989

1992 Season

	M	Inns	NO	Runs	HS	Avge	100s	50s	Ct	St	O	M	Runs	Wkts	Avge	Best	5wI	10wM
Test	5	8	1	397	190	56.71	1	2	5	-								
All First	19	33	4	1234	190	42.55	2	8	22	-	7	1	14	0	-	-	-	-
1-day Int	5	5	0	238	103	47.60	1	2	5	2								
NatWest	1	1	0	60	60	60.00	-	1	-	-								
B & H	7	7	1	267	71 *	44.50	-	2	8	1								
Sunday	11	11	2	430	105 *	47.77	2	2	18	1								

Career Performances

	M	Inns	NO	Runs	HS	Avge	100s	50s	Ct	St	Balls	Runs	Wkts	Avge	Best	5wI	10wM
Test	22	40	4	1493	190	41.47	4	6	27	-							
All First	222	366	45	12608	206 *	39.27	23	74	273	6	407	352	3	117.33	1-7	-	-
1-day Int	41	36	4	1007	103	31.46	1	6	28	3							
NatWest	22	20	3	814	107 *	47.88	1	6	14	-							
B & H	36	36	5	1189	110 *	38.35	1	9	18	3							
Sunday	120	110	11	2984	125	30.14	5	19	83	6	4	8	0	-	-	-	

SUCH, P. M. Essex

Name: Peter Mark Such
Role: Right-hand bat, off-spin bowler
Born: 12 June 1964, Helensburgh, Scotland
Height: 6ft **Weight:** 11st 7lbs
Nickname: Suchy
County debut: 1982 (Notts), 1987 (Leics),
1990 (Essex)
County cap: 1991
1st-Class 5 w. in innings: 9
1st-Class catches: 50
Place in batting averages: 252nd av. 11.30
Place in bowling averages: 19th av. 25.37
(1991 35th av. 27.44)
Strike rate: 61.77 (career 67.42)
Parents: John and Margaret
Marital status: Single
Family links with cricket: Father and
brother village cricketers

Education: Lantern Lane Primary School;
Harry Carlton Comprehensive, East Leake,
Notts
Qualifications: 9 O-levels, 3 A-levels, advanced cricket coach
Off-season: Touring Australia with England A
Overseas tours: England A to Australia 1992-93
Overseas teams played for: Kempton Park, South Africa 1982-83; Bathurst, Australia
1985-86; Matabeleland, Zimbabwe 1989-90
Cricketers particularly admired: Bob White, Eddie Hemmings, Graham Gooch, John
Childs
Other sports followed: American football
Injuries: Broken left hand, out for one week
Relaxations: Listening to music, watching movies, playing golf and hockey, gardening

Extras: Played for England YC v Australia 1983. Played for TCCB XI v New Zealand, 1985. Left Nottinghamshire at end of 1986 season. Joined Leicestershire in 1987 and released at the end of 1989. Signed by Essex for 1990. Played in one-day games for England A v Sri Lanka 1991. Is joint holder with J.H Childs of the Essex Player of the Year Award

Opinions on cricket: 'The balance has tipped too far in favour of batsmen. Wickets need pace and bounce to encourage batsmen but the bowlers have to have a chance with a small amount of sideways movement. Both green and flat wickets produce boring cricket.'

Best batting: 35* Essex v Hampshire, Chelmsford 1992

Best bowling: 6-17 Nottinghamshire v Sussex, Southend 1992

1992 Season

	M	Inns	NO	Runs	HS		Avge	100s	50s	Ct	St	O	M	Runs	Wkts	Avge	Best	5wI	10wM
Test																			
All First	15	13	3	113	35	*	11.30	-	-	6	-	411.5	126	1015	40	25.37	6-17	3	-
1-day Int																			
NatWest	3	0	0	0	0		-	-	-	-	-	24	3	74	1	74.00	1-37	-	
B & H	3	3	1	4	3		2.00	-	-	-	-	22	2	75	6	12.50	4-43	-	
Sunday	13	2	2	9	9	*	-	-	-	3	-	74.2	1	394	8	49.25	2-29	-	

Career Performances

	M	Inns	NO	Runs	HS		Avge	100s	50s	Ct	St	Balls		Runs	Wkts	Avge	Best	5wI	10wM
Test																			
All First	132	105	40	315	35	*	4.84	-	-	50	-	20296		9034	301	30.01	6-17	9	-
1-day Int																			
NatWest	6	1	1	0	0	*	-	-	-	-	-	360		176	6	29.33	2-29	-	
B & H	13	5	2	9	4		3.00	-	-	1	-	744		493	15	32.86	4-43	-	
Sunday	41	9	7	26	9	*	13.00	-	-	11	-	1484		1331	31	42.93	4-30	-	

175. Who is the only man to have made a double-century in his only first-class innings?

SYLVESTER, S. A.   Middlesex

Name: Steven Antony Sylvester
Role: Right-hand bat, left-arm fast-medium bowler
Born: 26 September 1968, Chalfont St Giles, Bucks
Height: 5ft 11in **Weight:** 12st 7lbs
Nickname: Silvers
County debut: 1991
1st-Class catches: 2
Parents: Ormond Alexander and Jennifer Irene
Marital status: Single
Family links with cricket: Father has played cricket all his life, both in St Vincent, West Indies and in England for Marlow Park and Maidenhead & Bray
Education: Wellesbourne School; The Buckinghamshire College; University of London, Goldsmith's College
Qualifications: 7 O-levels, 3 A-levels, BSc (Hons) in Psychology
Career outside cricket: 'Yet to be discovered...'
Off-season: Training hard at both fitness and technique
Overseas tours: Bucks to Zimbabwe 1992
Cricketers particularly admired: Angus Fraser, Curtly Ambrose, Gordon Greenidge
Other sports followed: Football, judo
Relaxations: Work-outs at local fitness studio, reading anything to do with sport, especiallysports psychology
Extras: Played cricket and football for Buckinghamshire. Released by Middlesex at the end of the 1992 season
Opinions on cricket: 'I believe the new ruling on one bouncer per over will give the batsman a slight advantage. While something has to be done about intimidatory bowling, I am not sure that restricting the bowler's use of the bouncer is the right way to do it. I feel batsmen will remain untested by the short-pitched delivery. '
Best batting: 0* Middlesex v Glamorgan, Lord's 1992
Best bowling: 2-34 Middlesex v Cambridge University, Fenner's 1992

---

176. Who captained South Africa on their last tour of England?

1992 Season

	M	Inns	NO	Runs	HS	Avge	100s	50s	Ct	St	O	M	Runs	Wkts	Avge	Best	5wI	10wM
Test																		
All First	4	1	1	0	0 *	-	-	-	1	-	84	22	222	4	55.50	2-34	-	-
1-day Int																		
NatWest																		
B & H	2	1	0	0	0	0.00	-	-	-	-	17	1	83	1	83.00	1-31	-	
Sunday																		

Career Performances

	M	Inns	NO	Runs	HS	Avge	100s	50s	Ct	St	Balls		Runs	Wkts	Avge	Best	5wI	10wM
Test																		
All First	5	2	1	0	0 *	0.00	-	-	2	-	624		320	4	80.00	2-34	-	-
1-day Int																		
NatWest																		
B & H	2	1	0	0	0	0.00	-	-	-	-	102		83	1	83.00	1-31	-	
Sunday																		

TAVARE, C. J.   Somerset

Name: Christopher James Tavare
Role: Right-hand bat, off-spin bowler,
slip fielder, county captain
Born: 27 October 1954, Orpington
Height: 6ft 1½in **Weight:** 12st 12lbs
Nickname: Tav, Rowdy
County debut: 1974 (Kent),
1989 (Somerset)
County cap: 1978 (Kent), 1989 (Somerset)
Benefit: 1988 (£92,318) (Kent)
Test debut: 1980
Tests: 31
One-Day Internationals: 29
1000 runs in a season: 16
1st-Class 50s scored: 136
1st-Class 100s scored: 47
1st-Class 200s scored: 1
1st-Class catches: 396
One-Day 50s: 64
One-Day 100s: 13
Place in batting averages: 69th av. 38.56 (1991 21st av. 53.86)
Parents: Andrew and June
Wife and date of marriage: Vanessa, 22 March 1980

Children: Harrison, 6 June 1992
Family links with cricket: Father, Uncle Jack Tavare, and Uncle Derrick Attwood, all played school and club cricket. Elder brother Stephen and younger brother Jeremy also both play
Education: Sevenoaks School; Oxford University
Qualifications: Zoology degree
Overseas tours: England to India and Sri Lanka 1981-82, to Australia and New Zealand 1982-83, to New Zealand and Pakistan 1983-84
Other sports followed: 'Take an interest in most sports, especially American football in winter.'
Relaxations: Music, zoology, films, gardening, woodwork, golf
Extras: Played for England Schools v India at Birmingham in 1973, scoring 124*. Oxford University cricket Blue 1975-77. Whitbread Scholarship to Perth, Australia, 1978-79. Suffers from asthma and hay-fever. Captain of Kent 1983-84. Rejected Kent's offer of a new contract for 1989 and joined Somerset as vice-captain. Appointed Somerset captain for 1990 after retirement of Vic Marks
Best batting: 219 Somerset v Sussex, Hove 1990
Best bowling: 1-3 Kent v Hampshire, Canterbury 1986

1992 Season

	M	Inns	NO	Runs	HS	Avge	100s	50s	Ct	St	O	M	Runs	Wkts	Avge	Best	5wI	10wM
Test																		
All First	21	32	2	1157	125	38.56	3	6	15	-	3.2	0	33	0	-	-	-	-
1-day Int																		
NatWest	2	2	1	62	60 *	62.00	-	1	1	-								
B & H	6	6	0	146	31	24.33	-	-	3	-								
Sunday	15	14	2	271	45	22.58	-	-	4	-								

Career Performances

	M	Inns	NO	Runs	HS	Avge	100s	50s	Ct	St	Balls	Runs	Wkts	Avge	Best	5wI	10wM
Test	31	56	2	1755	149	32.50	2	12	20	-	30	11	0	-	-	-	-
All First	418	692	74	24277	219	39.28	47	136	396	-	789	720	5	144.00	1-3	-	-
1-day Int	29	28	2	720	83 *	27.69	-	4	7	-	12	3	0	-	-	-	
NatWest	37	37	8	1556	162 *	53.65	4	9	19	-							
B & H	93	92	8	2742	143	32.64	2	16	53	-							
Sunday	219	216	29	5992	136 *	32.04	7	35	81	-							

177. When did South Africa last tour England?

TAYLOR, C. W.   Middlesex

Name: Charles William Taylor
Role: Left-hand bat, left-arm fast-medium
bowler
Born: 12 August 1966, Banbury,
Oxfordshire
Height: 6ft 5in **Weight:** 14st
Nickname: Farmer
County debut: 1990
1st-Class 5 w. in innings: 1
1st-Class catches: 5
Place in batting averages: 256th av. 10.71
Place in bowling averages: 115th av. 40.71
(1991 31st av. 26.66)
Strike rate: 70.25 (career 61.44)
Parents: Richard and Ann
Marital status: Single
Family links with cricket: Brother plays
for Banbury, father played village cricket
for Sandford St Martin

Education: Spendlove Comprehensive
School, Charlbury; North Oxon Technical College
Qualifications: City and Guilds Certificate in agriculture; 1 O-level
Career outside cricket: Farmer
Off-season: Working on the family farm
Overseas teams played for: Cricketers Club, New South Wales 1988-89
Cricketers particularly admired: Ian Bishop, Mark Waugh, Paul Tew ('my first club
captain')
Other sports followed: National Hunt racing, golf
Injuries: Broke two toes pre season, 90% fit at start of season
Relaxations: Most kinds of sports
Extras: Returned figures of 5 for 33 in second first-class match as Middlesex gained an
important win on the way to the 1990 Championship title
Best batting: 21 Middlesex v Kent, Lord's 1991
Best bowling: 5-33 Middlesex v Yorkshire, Headingley 1990

---

178. Who topped the Minor Counties batting averages last season?

1992 Season

	M	Inns	NO	Runs	HS	Avge	100s	50s	Ct	St	O	M	Runs	Wkts	Avge	Best	5wl	10wM
Test																		
All First	18	14	7	75	14	10.71	-	-	3	-	409.2	82	1425	35	40.71	4-50	-	-
1-day Int																		
NatWest	1	0	0	0	0	-	-	-	-	-	11	1	54	1	54.00	1-54	-	
B & H																			
Sunday	1	1	1	3	3*	-	-	-	-	-	7	0	46	0	-		-	-

Career Performances

	M	Inns	NO	Runs	HS	Avge	100s	50s	Ct	St	Balls	Runs	Wkts	Avge	Best	5wl	10wM
Test																	
All First	27	21	8	147	21	11.30	-	-	5	-	3625	2044	59	34.64	5-33	1	-
1-day Int																	
NatWest	1	0	0	0	0	-	-	-	-	-	66	54	1	54.00	1-54	-	
B & H																		
Sunday	6	2	1	6	3*	6.00	-	-	4	-	206	199	3	66.33	1-14	-	

TAYLOR, J. P. Northamptonshire

Name: Jonathan Paul Taylor
Role: Left-hand bat, left-arm
fast-medium bowler
Born: 8 August 1964, Ashby-de-la-Zouch,
Leicestershire
Height: 6ft 2in **Weight:** 13st 4lbs
Nickname: Roadie ('as in roadrunner'), PT
County debut: 1988 (Derbyshire),
1991 (Northamptonshire)
County cap: 1992
Test debut: 1992-93
50 wickets in a season: 1
1st-Class 50s scored: 1
1st-Class 5 w. in innings: 4
1st-Class 10 w. in match: 1
1st-Class catches: 16
Place in bowling averages: 210th av. 17.09
Place in bowling averages: 48th av. 30.47
(1991 79th av. 34.07)
Strike rate: 57.20 (career 61.71)
Parents: Derek and Janet
Marital status: Engaged to Elaine

Family links with cricket: Father and brother played local league cricket
Education: Pingle School, Swadlincote, Derbyshire
Qualifications: 6 O-levels, NCA coaching certificate
Career outside cricket: Electrical retail management, management trainee with National Coal Board
Off-season: Touring India and Sri Lanka with England
Overseas tours: Midland Club Cricket Conference to Australia 1990-91; England to India and Sri Lanka 1992-93
Overseas teams played for: Papakura, New Zealand 1984-85; Napier High School Old Boys, New Zealand 1985-86; North Kalgoorlie, Western Australia 1990-91; Great Boulder, Western Australia 1991-92
Cricketers particularly admired: Bob Taylor, John Lever, Dennis Lillee, Mike Proctor
Other sports followed: Soccer, rugby, basketball
Relaxations: 'Watching videos, eating out and spending time with my fiancee, Elaine.'
Extras: Spent four seasons on the staff at Derbyshire 1984-87. Played Minor Counties for Staffordshire 1989-90. Played first game at Lord's in NatWest Trophy final 1992
Opinions on cricket: '1. 17 four-day games will make for a much fairer County Championship. 2. The new Sunday League will be very tough, especially with it being played part way through a four-day game. I think that around August there will be some very tired bowlers around. 3. All teams should be encouraged to produce a positive result out of a game. Surely it is better to risk losing a game but giving yourself a chance to win it as well, than just playing out a boring, spectator depressing draw.'
Best batting: 74* Northamptonshire v Nottinghamshire, Northampton 1992
Best bowling: 7-23 Northamptonshire v Hampshire, Bournemouth 1992

1992 Season

	M	Inns	NO	Runs	HS	Avge	100s	50s	Ct	St	O	M	Runs	Wkts	Avge	Best	5wI	10wM
Test																		
All First	23	19	8	188	74 *	17.09	-	1	9	-	648.2	119	2072	68	30.47	7-23	3	1
1-day Int																		
NatWest	5	0	0	0	0	-	-	-	4	-	44	8	131	8	16.37	3-41	-	
B & H	4	1	0	3	3	3.00	-	-	2	-	38	3	122	4	30.50	3-38	-	
Sunday	13	3	0	17	8	5.66	-	-	3	-	98.2	7	443	15	29.53	3-38	-	

Career Performances

	M	Inns	NO	Runs	HS	Avge	100s	50s	Ct	St	Balls	Runs	Wkts	Avge	Best	5wI	10wM
Test																	
All First	43	37	14	239	74 *	10.39	-	1	16	-	6480	3479	105	33.13	7-23	4	1
1-day Int																	
NatWest	11	3	1	17	9	8.50	-	-	5	-	660	411	16	25.68	3-41	-	
B & H	8	3	2	5	3	5.00	-	-	3	-	480	228	8	28.50	3-38	-	
Sunday	29	11	2	46	16	5.11	-	-	5	-	1274	960	38	25.26	3-14	-	

Name: Neil Royston Taylor
Role: Right-hand bat, occasional off-spin bowler
Born: 21 July 1959, Farnborough, Kent
Height: 6ft 1in **Weight:** 15st
Nickname: Map
County debut: 1979
County cap: 1982
Benefit: 1992
1000 runs in a season: 9
1st-Class 50s scored: 74
1st-Class 100s scored: 38
1st-Class 200s scored: 2
1st-Class catches: 143
One-Day 50s: 30
One-Day 100s: 5
Place in batting averages: 14th av. 53.85
(1991 17th av. 56.53)
Parents: Leonard and Audrey
Wife and date of marriage: Jane Claire, 25 September 1982
Children: Amy Louise, 7 November 1985; Lauren, 21 July 1988
Family links with cricket: Brother Colin played for Kent U19 Father played club cricket
Education: Cray Valley Technical High School
Qualifications: 8 O-levels, 2 A-levels, NCA coaching certificate
Off-season: 'Finishing off my Benefit Year, resting in the New Year, playing plenty of golf and reintroducing myself to my family.'
Overseas tours: England Schools Team to India 1977-78
Cricketers particularly admired: Chris Tavare, Mark Benson and Robin Smith
Other sports followed: Rugby union, golf
Relaxations: 'Reading Wilbur Smith, Frederick Forsyth and cricket autobiographies, listening to music.'
Extras: Made 110 on debut for Kent CCC v Sri Lanka, 1979. Won four Man of the Match awards in first five matches. Scored three successive centuries in the B&H. Played for England B v Pakistan, 1982. Fielded twice as 12th man for England v India in 1982 and West Indies in 1988, both matches at The Oval. Provides a weekly contribution to Radio Kent through the summer
Opinions on cricket: 'Perhaps the groundsmen could be employed by the TCCB, so that they do not feel pressured by their county club. They can then produce their best pitches, instead of inferior ones!'
Best batting: 204 Kent v Surrey, Canterbury 1990
Best bowling: 2-20 Kent v Somerset, Canterbury 1985

1992 Season

	M	Inns	NO	Runs	HS	Avge	100s	50s	Ct	St	O	M	Runs	Wkts	Avge	Best	5wI	10wM
Test																		
All First	21	35	7	1508	144	53.85	1	11	10	-								
1-day Int																		
NatWest	3	3	0	61	43	20.33	-	-	-	-								
B & H	6	6	0	186	48	31.00	-	-	1	-								
Sunday	13	12	1	320	71	29.09	-	2	1	-								

Career Performances

	M	Inns	NO	Runs	HS	Avge	100s	50s	Ct	St	Balls	Runs	Wkts	Avge	Best	5wI	10wM
Test																	
All First	264	450	61	15623	204	40.16	38	74	143	-	1575	891	16	55.68	2-20	-	-
1-day Int																	
NatWest	23	23	1	513	85	23.31	-	2	5	-	95	48	3	16.00	3-29	-	
B & H	48	45	2	1786	137	41.53	5	7	9	-	12	5	0	-	-	-	
Sunday	123	119	10	3326	95	30.51	-	21	31	-							

TENDULKAR, S. R.   Yorkshire

Name: Sachin Ramesh Tendulkar
Role: Right-hand bat, right-arm medium/leg-spin bowler
Born: 24 April 1973
County debut: 1992
County cap: 1992
Test debut: 1989-90
Tests: 16
One-day internationals: 39
1000 runs in a season: 1
1st-Class 50s scored: 30
1st-Class 100s scored: 10
1st-Class catches: 28
One-Day 50s: 12
One-Day 100s: 1
Place in batting averages: 39th av. 46.52
Off-season: Playing for India v England
Overseas tours: India to Pakistan and New Zealand 1989-90, to England 1990, to Australia (World Cup) 1991-92, to Zimbabwe and South Africa 1992-93
Overseas teams played for: Bombay, India; West Zone

Extras: Made first-class debut in 1988-89 aged 15 and made a century. Made a stand of over 600 in school boy cricket with Vinod Kambli – both scored 300s. Test debut aged 16, and scored his first Test century aged 17 with 119* v England at Old Trafford in 1990. Signed for Yorkshire on a one-year contract in 1992 to become the county's first overseas player. Became the youngest player to score 1000 runs in Tests during India's tour to South Africa in 1992-93, aged 19

Best batting: 159 West Zone v South Zone, Rourkela 1990-91
Best bowling: 3-60 West Zone v South Zone, Rourkela 1990-91

1992 Season

	M	Inns	NO	Runs	HS	Avge	100s	50s	Ct	St	O	M	Runs	Wkts	Avge	Best	5wI	10wM
Test																		
All First	16	25	2	1070	100	46.52	1	7	10	-	62.3	10	195	4	48.75	2-35	-	-
1-day Int																		
NatWest	2	2	1	53	32 *	53.00	-	-	1									
B & H	2	2	0	23	16	11.50	-	-	1	-	20	2	65	3	21.66	2-21	-	
Sunday	13	13	1	464	107	38.66	1	1	1	-	21.2	0	102	3	34.00	2-28	-	

Career Performances

	M	Inns	NO	Runs	HS	Avge	100s	50s	Ct	St	Balls	Runs	Wkts	Avge	Best	5wI	10wM
Test	16	25	2	956	148 *	41.56	3	4	10	-	246	119	3	39.66	2-10	-	-
All First	60	97	11	4708	159	54.74	10	30	28	-	2118	1172	16	73.25	3-60	-	-
1-day Int	39	37	4	1177	84	35.66	-	11	10	-	773	570	11	51.81	4-34	-	
NatWest	2	2	1	53	32 *	53.00	-	-	1	-							
B & H	2	2	0	23	16	11.50	-	-	1	-	120	65	3	21.66	2-21	-	
Sunday	13	13	1	464	107	38.66	1	1	1	-	128	102	3	34.00	2-28	-	

TERRY, V. P.   Hampshire

Name: Vivian Paul Terry
Role: Right-hand bat, right-arm medium bowler, slip and outfielder
Born: 14 January 1959, Osnabruck, West Germany
Height: 6ft **Weight:** 13st 10lbs
County debut: 1978
County cap: 1983
Test debut: 1984
Tests: 2
1000 runs in a season: 8
1st-Class 50s scored: 67
1st-Class 100s scored: 27
1st-Class catches: 250
One-Day 50s: 39

One-Day 100s: 11
Place in batting averages: 24th av. 51.06
(1991 62nd av. 38.87)
Parents: Charles Michael and Patricia Mary
Wife and date of marriage: Bernadette
Mary, 4 June 1986
Children: Siobhan Catherine, 13 September
1987; Sean Paul, 1 August 1991
Education: Durlston Court, Hampshire;
Millfield School, Somerset
Qualifications: 8 O-levels, 1 A-level,
advanced cricket coach, squash coach
Off-season: Working for Meachers
Transport, some coaching
Overseas tours: ESCA to India 1977-78;
English Counties to Zimbabwe 1985;
Bournemouth Sports to Kenya 1986

Overseas teams played for:
Northern Districts, Sydney 1979-80;
Wakatu, Nelson 1980-81; Durban
Collegians 1982-84; Perth 1986-88, 1991-92
Cricketers particularly admired: Gordon Greenidge, Chris Smith, Viv Richards,
Malcolm Marshall
Other sports followed: Most sports – golf, rugby, football
Injuries: Dislocated thumb and back injury sciatic, out for 11 weeks
Relaxations: Sport – playing or watching, messing around with the kids
Opinions on cricket: 'Not enough done to ease pressures on cricketers during the winter.
We are expected to reach April at a level of fitness and skill but always in our own time.'
Best batting: 190 Hampshire v Sri Lanka, Southampton 1988

1992 Season

	M	Inns	NO	Runs	HS	Avge	100s	50s	Ct	St	O	M	Runs	Wkts	Avge	Best	5wl	10wM
Test																		
All First	11	17	2	766	141	51.06	3	3	7	-								
1-day Int																		
NatWest	2	2	1	217	109	217.00	2	-	-	-								
B & H	6	6	2	155	89 *	38.75	-	1	3	-								
Sunday	6	6	0	265	69	44.16	-	3	3	-								

179. Who topped the Minor Counties bowling averages last season?

Career Performances

	M	Inns	NO	Runs	HS	Avge	100s	50s	Ct	St	Balls	Runs	Wkts	Avge	Best	5wI	10wM
Test	2	3	0	16	8	5.33	-	-	2	-							
All First	227	379	38	12281	190	36.01	27	67	250	-	95	58	0	-	-	-	-
1-day Int																	
NatWest	34	32	4	1352	165 *	48.28	4	8	13	-							
B & H	46	46	5	1530	134	37.31	2	10	19	-							
Sunday	162	148	17	4130	142	31.52	5	21	83	-							

THOMAS, S. D. Glamorgan

Name: Stuart Darren Thomas
Role: Left-hand opening bat, right-arm medium-fast bowler
Born: 25 January 1975, Morriston
Height: 6ft **Weight:** 12st 7lbs
Nickname: Eric Cantona
County debut: 1992
1st-Class 5 w. in innings: 2
1st-Class catches: 1
Place in bowling averages: 8th av. 22.44
Strike rate: 37.77 (career 37.77)
Parents: Stuart and Anne
Marital status: Single
Family links with cricket: Dad played for local cricket 1st XI
Education: Craig comprehensive; Neath Tertiary College
Qualifications: 4 GCSEs
Off-season: In college
Cricketers particularly admired:
Viv Richards, Ian Botham, Imran Khan
Other sports followed: Rugby, football
Relaxations: 'Play various sports such as squash, rugby, tennis and listen to music, preferably "James".'
Extras: Youngest player to take five wickets on debut
Best batting: 10 Glamorgan v Derbyshire, Cardiff 1992
Best bowling: Glamorgan v Kent, Canterbury 1992

1992 Season

	M	Inns	NO	Runs	HS	Avge	100s	50s	Ct	St	O	M	Runs	Wkts	Avge	Best	5wI	10wM
Test																		
All First	6	7	2	25	10	5.00	-	-	1	-	113.2	18	404	18	22.44	5-79	2	-
1-day Int																		
NatWest																		
B & H																		
Sunday	3	0	0	0	0	-	-	-	1	-	11.4	1	48	1	48.00	1-34	-	

Career Performances

	M	Inns	NO	Runs	HS	Avge	100s	50s	Ct	St	Balls	Runs	Wkts	Avge	Best	5wI	10wM
Test																		
All First	6	7	2	25	10	5.00	-	-	1	-	680	404	18	22.44	5-79	2	-
1-day Int																		
NatWest																		
B & H																		
Sunday	3	0	0	0	0	-	-	-	1	-	70	48	1	48.00	1-34	-	

THORPE, G. P. Surrey

Name: Graham Paul Thorpe
Role: Left-hand bat, occasional right-arm medium bowler
Born: 1 August 1969, Farnham
Height: 5ft 10in **Weight:** 11st 7lbs
Nickname: Chalky
County debut: 1988
County cap: 1991
1000 runs in a season: 3
1st-Class 50s scored: 34
1st-Class 100s scored: 10
1st-Class 200s scored: 1
1st-Class catches: 60
One-Day 50s: 19
One-Day 100s: 1
Place in batting averages: 23rd av. 51.21
(1991 50th av. 41.48)
Parents: Geoff and Toni
Marital status: Single
Family links with cricket: Both brothers play for Farnham, father also plays cricket and mother is 'professional scorer'
Education: Weydon Comprehensive; Farnham Sixth Form College

Qualifications: 7 O-levels, PE Diploma
Off-season: Touring Australia with England A
Overseas tours: England A to Zimbabwe and Kenya 1989-90, to Pakistan 1990-91, to Bermuda and West Indies 1991-92, to Australia 1992-93
Cricketers particularly admired: Viv Richards, Grahame Clinton, David Gower
Other sports followed: Football, tennis
Extras: Played England Schools cricket U15 and U19 and England Schools football U18. Surrey Player of the Year
Best batting: 216 Surrey v Somerset, The Oval 1992
Best bowling: 2-31 Surrey v Essex, The Oval 1989

1992 Season

	M	Inns	NO	Runs	HS	Avge	100s	50s	Ct	St	O	M	Runs	Wkts	Avge	Best	5wl	10wM
Test																		
All First	24	41	4	1895	216	51.21	3	13	19	-	17.4	5	79	0	-		-	-
1-day Int																		
NatWest	1	1	0	3	3	3.00	-	-	-	-								
B & H	7	7	1	230	82	38.33	-	2	2	-								
Sunday	16	16	4	453	84	37.75	-	4	9	-	3	0	24	0	-		-	-

Career Performances

	M	Inns	NO	Runs	HS	Avge	100s	50s	Ct	St	Balls	Runs	Wkts	Avge	Best	5wl	10wM
Test																	
All First	96	157	26	5650	216	43.13	10	34	60	-	1228	738	13	56.76	2-31	-	-
1-day Int																	
NatWest	10	10	2	255	93	31.87	-	2	3	-	13	12	0	-		-	-
B & H	17	17	2	453	82	30.20	-	3	4	-	156	115	4	28.75	3-35	-	
Sunday	60	57	10	1762	115 *	37.48	1	14	19	-	216	227	5	45.40	3-21	-	

---

180. Who were overall Minor Counties champions last season?

THURSFIELD, M. J.   Hampshire

Name: Martin John Thursfield
Role: Right-hand bat, right-arm medium-fast
bowler
Born: 14 December 1971, South Shields
Height: 6ft 4in **Weight:** 13st 10lbs
Nickname: Thursy, Sticky
County debut: 1990
Parents: Anthony John and Maureen
Marital status: Single
Family links with cricket:
Great grandfather played for Yorkshire and
father is a keen club cricketer
Education: Boldon Comprehensive
Qualifications: GCSEs and NCA coaching
certificate
Off-season: 'Regaining full fitness and
coaching'
Overseas tours: England U19 to New
Zealand 1991

Cricketers particularly admired:
Robin Smith, Don Wilson, Malcolm Marshall
Other sports followed: Football, golf
Injuries: Toe operation, out for three weeks
Relaxations: 'Playing golf and following Sunderland FC.'
Extras: Bowled two balls with broken leg in first One-day international with U19 in New
Zealand
Opinions on cricket: 'If young cricketers are being nurtured to come up and play first class
cricket then the pitches must improve especially on out grounds.'
Best bowling: 1-11 Hampshire v Oxford University, The Parks 1992

1992 Season

	M	Inns	NO	Runs	HS	Avge	100s	50s	Ct	St	O	M	Runs	Wkts	Avge	Best	5wl	10wM
Test																		
All First	1	0	0	0	0	-	-	-	-	-	16	3	35	2	17.50	1-11	-	-
1-day Int																		
NatWest																		
B & H																		
Sunday																		

Career Performances

	M	Inns	NO	Runs	HS	Avge	100s	50s	Ct	St	Balls	Runs	Wkts	Avge	Best	5wI	10wM
Test																	
All First	3	0	0	0	0	-	-	-	-	-	348	165	4	41.25	1-11	-	-
1-day Int																	
NatWest																	
B & H																	
Sunday																	

TITCHARD, S. P.   Lancashire

Name: Stephen Paul Titchard
Role: Right-hand bat, right-arm medium bowler
Born: 17 December 1967, Warrington, Cheshire
Height: 6ft 3in **Weight:** 15st ('approx')
Nickname: Titch, Stainy, Tyrone
County debut: 1990
1st-Class 50s: 9
1st-Class 100s: 1
1st-Class catches: 16
One-Day 50s: 1
Place in batting averages: 114th av. 31.81
Parents: Alan and Margaret
Marital status: Single
Family links with cricket: Father, uncle and two brothers have played for Grappenhall 1st XI in the Manchester Association League
Education: Lymm County High School; Priestley College
Qualifications: 3 O-levels
Off-season: Keeping fit, playing golf
Overseas teams played for: South Canberra 1991-92
Cricketers particularly admired: Graham Gooch, Dennis Amiss, Geoff Trim ('formerly Lancs CCC, who helped me with my early development')
Other sports followed: Football (Manchester City) and rugby league (Warrington)
Injuries: Hand, out for five weeks
Relaxations: Snooker, golf, 'most sports'
Extras: Played for England U19
Opinions on cricket: 'Four-day cricket should provide a fairer way of deciding which

sides are the strongest throughout the season, as opposed to the three day games which were influenced too much by shortened games and contrived results. Tea should be extended by at least 10 minutes!'

Best batting: 135 Lancashire v Nottinghamshire, Old Trafford 1991

1992 Season

	M	Inns	NO	Runs	HS	Avge	100s	50s	Ct	St	O	M	Runs	Wkts	Avge	Best	5wI	10wM
Test																		
All First	14	24	3	668	74	31.81	-	6	8	-								
1-day Int																		
NatWest	1	1	0	20	20	20.00	-	-	-	-								
B & H	1	1	0	82	82	82.00	-	1	1	-								
Sunday	5	5	1	44	20	11.00	-	-	1	-								

Career Performances

	M	Inns	NO	Runs	HS	Avge	100s	50s	Ct	St	Balls	Runs	Wkts	Avge	Best	5wI	10wM
Test																	
All First	25	44	4	1343	135	33.57	1	9	16	-							
1-day Int																	
NatWest	1	1	0	20	20	20.00	-	-	-	-							
B & H	1	1	0	82	82	82.00	-	1	1	-							
Sunday	5	5	1	44	20	11.00	-	-	1	-							

TOLLEY, C. M.   Worcestershire

Name: Christopher Mark Tolley
Role: Right-hand bat, left-arm medium bowler
Born: 30 December 1967, Kidderminster
Height: 5ft 9in **Weight:** 11st
Nickname: Treefrog, Red dog
County debut: 1989
1st-Class catches: 14
One-Day 50s scored: 2
Place in batting averages: 226th av. 20.57 (1991 165th av. 24.00)
Place in bowling averages: 111th av. 39.07 (1991 11th av. 22.94)
Strike rate: 79.66 (career 80.71)
Parents: Ray and Liz
Marital status: Single
Family links with cricket: Father played local league; brother Richard plays in the

Birmingham League
Education: Oldswinford Primary School;
Redhill Comprehensive School;
King Edward VI College, Stourbridge; Loughborough University
Qualifications: 9 O-levels, 3 A-levels, BSc in PE Sports Science & Recreation Management
Off-season: 'Resting!'
Overseas tours: British Universities Sports Federation tour to Barbados October 1989
Cricketers particularly admired: Ian Botham, Richard Hadlee, Graeme Hick
Other sports followed: Football, athletics, hockey
Injuries: Injury to left shoulder, operation in January 1992
Relaxations: Watching TV, eating out
Extras: Played for ESCA U19 in 1986 and for the Combined Universities in the B&H Cup
Opinions on cricket: 'There is too much cricket played during the season. Players do not have time to prepare physically or mentally for each individual game.'
Best batting: 37 Worcestershire v Kent, Worcester 1989
Best bowling: 4-69 Worcestershire v Sri Lankans, Worcester 1991

1992 Season

	M	Inns	NO	Runs	HS	Avge	100s	50s	Ct	St	O	M	Runs	Wkts	Avge	Best	5wl	10wM
Test																		
All First	13	10	4	89	27	14.83	-	-	7	-	239	56	726	18	40.33	3-38	-	-
1-day Int																		
NatWest																		
B & H																		
Sunday	8	3	1	0	0 *	0.00	-	-	3	-	43	1	210	12	17.50	3-28	-	

Career Performances

	M	Inns	NO	Runs	HS	Avge	100s	50s	Ct	St	Balls	Runs	Wkts	Avge	Best	5wl	10wM
Test																	
All First	33	32	11	432	37	20.57	-	-	14	-	3390	1641	42	39.07	4-69	-	-
1-day Int																	
NatWest	1	0	0	0	0	-			-	-	36	32	0	-		-	-
B & H	9	8	1	201	77	28.71	-	2	3	-	522	336	4	84.00	1-12	-	
Sunday	15	5	2	2	1 *	0.66	-	-	5	-	468	345	15	23.00	3-28	-	

TOMLINSON, J.   Northamptonshire

Name: Jamie Tomlinson
Role: Right-hand bat, right-arm fast-medium bowler
Born: 14 August 1971, Warrington,
Height: 6ft 3in **Weight:** 13st 7lbs
Nickname: Tomo
County debut: No first team appearance

Parents: Ian And Carol Anne
Marital status: Single
Family links with cricket: Father and brother play for local teams. Father has been chairman of the Isle of Man cricket club for a number of years
Education: Murrays Road Junior school, Isle of Man; St Ninians High School, Isle of Man; Ballabermeen Junior School, Isle of Man
Qualifications: 6 CSEs
Career outside cricket: Works for Nationwide overseas Ltd, a subsidiary company of Nationwide building society
Off-season: 'Not sure yet'
Overseas tours: Isle of Man CC to Victoria, Canada (six-a-side cricket festival) 1990 and 1992
Cricketers particularly admired: Richard Hadlee, Graham Gooch
Other sports followed: Football, golf, rallying and 'anything of interest'
Relaxations: Plays for St Georges FC, Isle of Man, 'I am also a regular cinema goer and have many other interests.'

TOPLEY, T. D. Essex

Name: Thomas Donald Topley
Role: Right-hand bat, right-arm fast-medium bowler
Born: 25 February 1964, Canterbury
Height: 6ft 3in **Weight:** 15st 4lbs
Nickname: Toppers, Wimble, Jack,
County debut: 1985 (Surrey), 1985 (Essex)
County cap: 1988 (Essex)
50 wickets in a season: 3
1st-Class 50s scored: 4
1st-Class 5 w. in innings: 15
1st-Class 10 w. in match: 2
1st-Class catches: 67
Place in batting averages: 262nd av. 10.00 (1991 186th av. 21.33)
Place in bowling averages: 66th av. 32.45 (1991 66th av. 32.12)

Strike rate: 60.16 (career 52.03)

Parents: Tom (deceased) and Rhoda

Marital status: Single

Family links with cricket: Brother Peter played for Kent (1972-76), father played for Royal Navy

Education: Royal Hospital School, Holbrook, Suffolk

Qualifications: 6 O-levels, NCA advanced coach

Career outside cricket: PE teacher

Off-season: Teaching PE at Royal Hospital School

Overseas tours: Benefit tour to Barbados 1986; Zimbabwe to Australia and New Zealand (World Cup) 1992

Overseas teams played for: Noodsburg and Midlands, Natal 1985-86; Roodeburg, Transvaal 1986-87; Griqualand West, South Africa 1987-88; Harare Sports Club, Zimbabwe 1990-92

Cricketers particularly admired: Richard Hadlee, Graham Gooch, Ian Botham, Keith Fletcher 'and many bowlers'

Other sports followed: Rugby, soccer and all other ball sports

Relaxations: Photography, travel, eating out, watching Colchester FC 'and watching Peter Such facing a West Indian bowler - that is interesting!'

Extras: Spent three years prior to joining Essex on the MCC Young Professionals at Lord's. As 12th man held famous one-handed 'catch' for England v West Indies at Lord's in 1984, stepping over the boundary in taking it. Also played for Norfolk (1982-84) and Surrey (1985). Zimbabwe coach during 1991-92 World Cup

Opinions on cricket: 'The current ball being used in first-class cricket is of poor quality and that's not just because of the low seam. Was against the un-banning of the rebel tour to South Africa, however was against them being banned in the first place, hence, no confidence in the ICC. In favour of four-day cricket, but strongly oppose the new Sunday League format of 50 overs a-side.'

Best batting: 66 Essex v Yorkshire, Headingley 1987

Best bowling: 7-75 Essex v Derbyshire, Chesterfield 1988

1992 Season

	M	Inns	NO	Runs	HS	Avge	100s	50s	Ct	St	O	M	Runs	Wkts	Avge	Best	5wI	10wM
Test																		
All First	11	12	2	100	29	10.00	-	-	8	-	240.4	54	779	24	32.45	5-15	1	-
1-day Int																		
NatWest	4	3	1	35	19 *	17.50	-	-	1	-	43	2	186	8	23.25	3-47	-	
B & H	3	2	0	9	5	4.50	-	-	1	-	20	4	63	5	12.60	3-40	-	
Sunday	17	7	6	27	8	27.00	-	-	7	-	114	5	513	12	42.75	2-22	-	

181. Who topped the first-class batting averages in England last season?

Career Performances

	M	Inns	NO	Runs	HS	Avge	100s	50s	Ct	St	Balls	Runs	Wkts	Avge	Best	5wl	10wM
Test																	
All First	111	125	28	1536	66	15.83	-	4	67	-	18266	9473	351	26.98	7-75	15	2
1-day Int																	
NatWest	15	7	2	67	19 *	13.40	-	-	3	-	938	575	26	22.11	4-21	-	
B & H	24	7	4	35	10 *	11.66	-	-	7	-	1356	760	34	22.35	4-22	-	
Sunday	89	41	17	209	38 *	8.70	-	-	16	-	3706	2800	102	27.45	6-33	2	

TOWNSEND, G. T. J.   Somerset

Name: Gareth Terence John Townsend
Role: Right-hand opening batsman
Born: 28 June 1968, Tiverton, Devon
Height: 6ft **Weight:** 11st 7lbs
Nickname: Gobbler, Winscombe,
Thunder Bat
County debut: 1990
1st-Class 50s scored: 1
1st-Class catches: 10
Place in batting averages: 168th av. 22.68
Parents: Terry and Sheila
Marital status: Single
Family links with cricket: 'Father played
before giving up time to help me with my
career; older brother David played
Devon Schools cricket and club cricket,
other brother Graeme is secretary of his
club side.'
Education: Tiverton Comprehensive
School; Birmingham University
Qualifications: 7 O-levels, 4 A-levels, BA (Hons) General Studies
Career outside cricket: 'Unsure.'
Overseas teams played for: Hawks, Perth, Western Australia 1989-90; Waverley, Sydney
1991-92
Cricketers particularly admired: Gordon Greenidge, Jimmy Cook, Peter Roebuck
Other sports followed: Golf and rugby
Relaxations: 'Playing golf and socialising with mates.'
Extras: Scored 85 and 115* on 2nd XI debut v Hampshire in 1987. Released by Somerset
at the end of the 1992 season
Best batting: 53 Somerset v Sri Lankans, Taunton 1991

1992 Season

	M	Inns	NO	Runs	HS	Avge	100s	50s	Ct	St	O	M	Runs	Wkts	Avge	Best	5wl	10wM
Test																		
All First	7	13	1	272	49	22.66	-	-	4	-								
1-day Int																		
NatWest																		
B & H	1	1	0	1	1	1.00	-	-	-	-								
Sunday	1	1	0	33	33	33.00	-	-	-	-								

Career Performances

	M	Inns	NO	Runs	HS	Avge	100s	50s	Ct	St	Balls	Runs	Wkts	Avge	Best	5wl	10wM
Test																	
All First	12	22	2	414	53	20.70	-	1	10	-							
1-day Int																	
NatWest																	
B & H	1	1	0	1	1	1.00	-	-	-	-							
Sunday	3	3	0	87	33	29.00	-	-	1	-							

TRUMP, H. R. J.   Somerset

Name: Harvey Russell John Trump
Role: Right-hand bat, off-spin bowler, gully/slip fielder
Born: 11 October 1968, Taunton
Height: 6ft 2in **Weight:** 13st 7lbs
Nickname: Trumpy, Club foot
County debut: 1988
50 wickets in a season: 1
1st-Class 5 w. in innings: 6
1st-Class 10 w. in match: 1
1st-Class catches: 42
Place in batting averages: 231st av. 14.00 (1991 251st av. 10.80)
Place in bowling averages: 64th av. 32.32 (1991 117th av. 41.43)
Strike rate: 68.32 (career 77.67)
Wife and date of marriage: Nicola, 26 October 1991
Family links with cricket: Father played for Somerset 2nd XI and captained Devon
Education: Edgarley Hall (Millfield Jnr School); Millfield School; Chester College of Higher Education

Qualifications: 6 O-levels, 2 A-levels, BA (Hons) Grade 2 Level 1
Overseas tours: England YC to Sri Lanka 1987; to Australia for Junior World Cup 1988
Cricketers particularly admired: David Graveney, John Emburey, Mike Gatting, Viv Richards
Other sports followed: Hockey, rugby and most other sports
Relaxations: Reading, walking, eating out, watching sport
Extras: Played county hockey for Somerset U19. Qualified lifeguard, attaining bronze medallion life-saving award. Preliminary teacher of disabled swimming certificate. "He's the best fielder off his own bowling I've ever seen" – David Graveney, 1991
Opinions on cricket: 'Something has got to be done about the seam on the ball. Over-rates need to be looked at and adjusted appropriately. It is vitally important for youngsters to have a good grounding at junior levels in two- and three-day, cricket not just one-day.'
Best batting: 48 Somerset v Hampshire, Taunton 1988
Best bowling: 7-52 Somerset v Gloucestershire, Gloucester 1992

1992 Season

	M	Inns	NO	Runs	HS	Avge	100s	50s	Ct	St	O	M	Runs	Wkts	Avge	Best	5wI	10wM
Test																		
All First	18	18	7	154	28	14.00	-	-	14	-	558	134	1584	49	32.32	7-52	2	1
1-day Int																		
NatWest	2	1	1	1	1 *	-	-	-	1	-	13	0	47	0	-		-	-
B & H	6	3	0	3	1	1.00	-	-	1	-	47	1	168	4	42.00	2-23	-	
Sunday	12	1	1	14	14 *	-	-	-	4	-	61	1	294	8	36.75	2-8	-	

Career Performances

	M	Inns	NO	Runs	HS	Avge	100s	50s	Ct	St	Balls	Runs	Wkts	Avge	Best	5wI	10wM
Test																	
All First	66	66	18	429	48	8.93	-	-	42	-	12272	6038	158	38.21	7-52	6	1
1-day Int																	
NatWest	5	3	1	2	1 *	1.00	-	-	2	-	240	153	2	76.50	2-44	-	
B & H	6	3	0	3	1	1.00	-	-	1	-	282	168	4	42.00	2-23	-	
Sunday	32	7	2	41	19	8.20	-	-	8	-	1194	945	25	37.80	2-8	-	

182. Who topped the first-class bowling averages in England last season?

TUFNELL, P. C. R.   Middlesex

Name: Philip Clive Roderick Tufnell
Role: Right-hand bat, slow left-arm spinner
Born: 29 April 1966, Hadley Wood, Hertfordshire
Height: 6ft **Weight:** 12st 7lbs
Nickname: The Cat
County debut: 1986
County cap: 1990
Test debut: 1990-91
Tests: 10
One-Day Internationals: 15
50 wickets in a season: 3
1st-Class 5 w. in innings: 19
1st-Class 10 w. in match: 2
1st-Class catches: 49
Place in batting averages:
(1991 249th av. 11.66)
Place in bowling averages: 92nd av. 36.25
(1991 23rd av. 25.21)

Strike rate: 83.06 (career 74.21)
Parents: Sylvia and Alan
Marital status: Divorced
Education: Highgate School; Southgate School
Qualifications: O-level in Art; City & Guilds Silversmithing
Off-season: Touring India and Sri Lanka with England
Overseas tours: England U19 to West Indies 1985; England to Australia 1990-91, to New Zealand and Australia (World Cup) 1991-92, to India and Sri Lanka 1992-93
Overseas teams played for: Queensland University, Australia
Cricketers particularly admired: Jason Pooley
Other sports followed: American football
Injuries: Appendix operation (May), out for six weeks
Relaxations: Sleeping
Extras: MCC Young Cricketer of the Year 1984. Middlesex Uncapped Bowler of the Year 1987. Was originally a seam bowler and gave up cricket for three years in his mid-teens
Best batting: 37 Middlesex v Yorkshire, Headingley 1990
Best bowling: 7-47 England v New Zealand, Christchurch 1991-92

1992 Season

	M	Inns	NO	Runs	HS	Avge	100s	50s	Ct	St	O	M	Runs	Wkts	Avge	Best	5wI	10wM
Test	1	2	1	0	0*	0.00	-	-	1	-	34	9	87	1	87.00	1-87	-	-
All First	16	15	8	55	12	7.85	-	-	3	-	595.2	144	1559	43	36.25	5-83	2	-
1-day Int																		
NatWest																		
B & H	1	1	1	15	15*	-	-	-	-	-	10	0	65	0	-	-	-	-
Sunday	1	1	1	1	1*	-	-	-	-	-								

Career Performances

	M	Inns	NO	Runs	HS	Avge	100s	50s	Ct	St	Balls	Runs	Wkts	Avge	Best	5wI	10wM
Test	10	13	8	23	8	4.60	-	-	4	-	2773	1091	38	28.71	7-47	4	1
All First	114	113	45	722	37	10.61	-	-	49	-	27979	11975	377	31.76	7-47	19	2
1-day Int	15	7	6	13	5*	13.00	-	-	3	-	774	528	12	44.00	3-40	-	
NatWest	4	1	0	8	8	8.00	-	-	2	-	288	130	7	18.57	3-29	-	
B & H	7	5	3	41	18	20.50	-	-	1	-	402	330	5	66.00	3-50	-	
Sunday	8	3	3	14	13*	-	-	-	-	-	282	219	6	36.50	3-28	-	

TURNER, I. J.   Hampshire

Name: Ian John Turner
Role: Right-hand bat, slow left-arm bowler
Born: 18 July 1968, Denmead
Height: 6ft 2in **Weight:** 14st
Nickname: Turns, Bunsen, Blubs
County debut: 1989
1st-Class 5 w. in innings: 1
1st-Class catches: 5
Place in batting averages:
(1991 229th av. 14.50)
Place in bowling averages: 32nd av. 27.31
(1991 126th av. 45.50)
Strike rate: 57.68 (career 78.89)
Parents: Robert and Sheila
Marital status: Single
Family links with cricket: Father plays for Hambledon CC
Education: Cowplain Comprehensive School; South Downs College
Qualifications: 7 CSEs, pass in BTEC General Diploma in Business Studies
Career outside cricket: Bank clerk

Off-season: At home relaxing
Overseas teams played for: Waverley, Sydney 1989-90; Lomas, Argentina 1991
Cricketers particularly admired: Phil Edmonds, Rupert Cox 'for his mature behaviour'
Other sports followed: Football – 'I try to go to local games as much as I can, Portsmouth and that well-known club Waterlooville.'
Injuries: Torn muscle in thigh, out for two months
Relaxations: Listening to music, sleeping as much as possible
Opinions on cricket: 'State of pitches in 2nd XI cricket is inadequate.'
Best batting: 39* Hampshire v Glamorgan, Swansea 1991
Best bowling: 5-81 Hampshire v Essex, Chelmsford 1992

1992 Season

	M	Inns	NO	Runs	HS	Avge	100s	50s	Ct	St	O	M	Runs	Wkts	Avge	Best	5wI	10wM
Test																		
All First	6	7	1	31	16	5.16	-	-	4	-	182.4	51	519	19	27.31	5-81	1	-
1-day Int																		
NatWest																			
B & H																			
Sunday	7	0	0	0	0	-	-	-	2	-	32	3	140	4	35.00	2-31	-	

Career Performances

	M	Inns	NO	Runs	HS	Avge	100s	50s	Ct	St	Balls	Runs	Wkts	Avge	Best	5wI	10wM
Test																	
All First	20	22	7	142	39 *	9.46	-	-	9	-	3629	1628	46	35.39	5-81	1	-
1-day Int																	
NatWest																		
B & H																		
Sunday	7	0	0	0	0	-	-	-	2	-	192	140	4	35.00	2-31	-	

TURNER, R. J.   Somerset

Name: Robert Julian Turner
Role: Right-hand bat, wicket-keeper
Born: 25 November 1967, Worcestershire
Height: 6ft 2in **Weight:** 13st 8lbs
Nickname: Noddy, Doze, Teflon, Turns
County debut: 1991
1st-Class 50s scored: 4
1st-Class 100s scored: 1
1st-Class catches: 42
1st-Class stumpings: 12
Place in batting averages: (1991 142nd av. 27.66)

Parents: Derek Edward and Doris Lilian
Marital status: Single
Family links with cricket: Brother Simon
played for Somerset (1984-85) as a
wicket-keeper and is now captain of
Weston-super-Mare. Other brother Richard
also plays for Weston-super-Mare 1st team
and father is chairman of the club
Education: Uphill Primary School;
Broadoak School, Weston-super-Mare;
Millfield School; Cambridge University
Qualifications: Honours Degree in
Engineering and Diploma in Computer
Science
Career outside cricket: 'Unsure, maybe
teaching or engineering.'
Off-season: Cricket coach and maths
teacher at public school in Perth and playing
cricket for Claremont-Nedlands CC
Overseas tours: Combined Universities to
Barbados 1989

Overseas teams played for: Claremont-Nedlands, Perth, Western Australia 1991-92
Cricketers particularly admired: Andy Brassington, Stuart Turner, Peter Roebuck
Other sports followed: Nearly all sports - 'enjoy playing hockey, golf and swimming.'
Relaxations: Photography, playing the piano, reading, sleeping, eating curries, golf
Extras: Captain of Cambridge University and Combined Universities (and Cambridge
Blue) 1991
Opinions on cricket: 'The four-day game seems to be the way forward (certainly going
by Somerset's last two games of the 1992 season). Four-day cricket allows the game to take
its natural course which proves to be more pleasing and realistic to spectators.'
Best batting: 101* Somerset v Nottinghamshire, Taunton 1992

1992 Season

	M	Inns	NO	Runs	HS	Avge	100s	50s	Ct	St	O	M	Runs	Wkts	Avge	Best	5wI	10wM
Test																		
All First	7	10	5	286	101 *	57.20	1	1	6	-	2.1	0	26	0	-		-	-	-
1-day Int																		
NatWest																		
B & H																		
Sunday																		

	M	Inns	NO	Runs	HS	Avge	100s	50s	Ct	St	Balls	Runs	Wkts	Avge	Best	5wI	10wM
Test																	
All First	41	64	14	1245	101 *	24.90	1	4	42	12	13	26	0	-	-	-	-
1-day Int																	
NatWest																	
B & H	4	4	3	49	25 *	49.00	-	-	2	1							
Sunday																	

TUTT, A.   Kent

Name: Andrew Tutt
Role: Right-hand bat, right-arm medium
bowler, outfielder
Born: 21 February 1968, Bermondsey,
South London
Height: 6ft **Weight:** 14st
Nickname: Tutty, Janice
County debut: 1992
Parents: John Peter and Sylvia Helen
Marital status: Single
Family links with cricket: Father is
president and played for the same club
side. Brother played for and captained
Kent schools
Education: St Columba's RC Boys School,
Bexley Heath, Kent; Erith Technical
College, Erith, Kent

Qualifications: Honours Degree in
Engineering and Diploma in Computer
Science
Career outside cricket: Works in family floristry business and coaches youth football
teams
Off-season: 'Working hard in the family business and keeping fit in my football activities.'
Cricketers particularly admired: Andy Brassington, Stuart Turner, Peter Roebuck,
Peter Willey, John Snow
Other sports followed: Football, rugby
Injuries: Slight knee injury
Relaxations: Music, reading and 'meals and drinks with the lads'
Opinions on cricket: 'There should be more effort made to encourage cricket in schools.
2nd XI cricket should be played on better wickets to enable the younger players to
experience true First Class conditioned, and not find it a struggle to progress because of

their false performances on sub-standard grounds.'

1992 Season

	M	Inns	NO	Runs	HS	Avge	100s	50s	Ct	St	O	M	Runs	Wkts	Avge	Best	5wI	10wM
Test																		
All First	1	0	0	0	0	-	-	-	-	-	19	5	53	0	-	-	-	-
1-day Int																		
NatWest																		
B & H																		
Sunday																		

Career Performances

	M	Inns	NO	Runs	HS	Avge	100s	50s	Ct	St	Balls	Runs	Wkts	Avge	Best	5wI	10wM
Test																	
All First	1	0	0	0	0	-	-	-	-	-	114	53	0	-	-	-	-
1-day Int																	
NatWest																	
B & H																	
Sunday																	

TWEATS, T. A. Derbyshire

Name: Timothy Andrew Tweats
Role: Right-hand bat, off-spin
Born: 18 April 1974, Stoke-on-Trent
Height: 6ft 3in **Weight:** 13st
County debut: 1992
1st-Class catches: 1
Parents: Malcolm and Linda
Marital status: Single
Family links with cricket:
'Father and two brothers, Jon and Simon,
play for the local club, Leek CC, who I
played for before joining Derbyshire'
Education: Endon High School;
Stoke-on-Trent Sixth Form College;
Staffordshire University
Qualifications: 5 GCSEs, 2 A-Levels
Career outside cricket: Student
Overseas tours: Kidsgrove and District
Junior Cricket League to Australia 1991
Cricketers particularly admired: Robin Smith, Phil Tufnell

Other sports followed: Football
Best batting: 24 Derbyshire v Glamorgan, Cardiff 1992

1992 Season

	M	Inns	NO	Runs	HS	Avge	100s	50s	Ct	St	O	M	Runs	Wkts	Avge	Best	5wI	10wM
Test																		
All First	1	1	0	24	24	24.00	-	-	1	-								
1-day Int																		
NatWest																		
B & H																		
Sunday																		

Career Performances

	M	Inns	NO	Runs	HS	Avge	100s	50s	Ct	St	Balls	Runs	Wkts	Avge	Best	5wI	10wM
Test																	
All First	1	1	0	24	24	24.00	-	-	1	-							
1-day Int																	
NatWest																	
B & H																	
Sunday																	

TWOSE, R. G. Warwickshire

Name: Roger Graham Twose
Role: Left-hand bat, right-arm medium bowler
Born: 17 April 1968, Torquay ('in a car!')
Height: 6ft **Weight:** 14st 7lbs
Nickname: Twosey, Buff, Tom Cruise
County debut: 1989
County cap: 1992
1000 runs in a season: 1
1st-Class 50s scored: 18
1st-Class 100s scored: 3
1st-Class 200s scored: 1
1st-Class 5 w. in innings: 1
1st-Class catches: 36
One-Day 50s: 6
One-Day 100s: 2
Place in batting averages: 63rd av. 40.34
Place in bowling averages: 38th av. 28.35
Parents: Paul and Patricia

Marital status: Single
Family links with cricket: Father played for Devon, brother Richard plays for Devon. Uncles – Roger Tolchard (Leicestershire and England) and Jeff Tolchard (Leicestershire)
Education: Wolborough Hill, Newton Abbot, Devon; King's College, Taunton
Qualifications: 7 O-levels, 2 A-levels, NCA coaching certificate
Career outside cricket: Part-time model
Off-season: Playing first-class cricket for Central Districts in New Zealand
Overseas teams played for: Northern Districts, New Zealand 1989-90; Central Districts, New Zealand 1991-93
Cricketers particularly admired: Dermot Reeve, Mark Greatbatch
Other sports followed: Rugby, hockey etc.
Relaxations: Keeping fit, skiing (water and snow), 'all sports'
Extras: 'Once took all ten wickets in an innings whilst playing in New Zealand: a feat I plan to reproduce in first-class cricket!'. Warwickshire Player of the Year
Best batting: 233 Warwickshire v Leicestershire, Edgbaston 1992
Best bowling: 6-63 Warwickshire v Middlesex, Coventry 1992

1992 Season

	M	Inns	NO	Runs	HS	Avge	100s	50s	Ct	St	O	M	Runs	Wkts	Avge	Best	5wI	10wM
Test																		
All First	23	38	3	1412	233	40.34	1	10	17	-	249.3	48	794	28	28.35	6-63	1	-
1-day Int																		
NatWest	4	4	1	170	107 *	56.66	1	-	1	-	34	2	126	8	15.75	3-39	-	
B & H	4	4	0	140	62	35.00	-	1	1	-	13	1	49	0	-	-	-	-
Sunday	17	17	0	585	100	34.41	1	4	3	-	64.3	1	332	6	55.33	2-27	-	

Career Performances

	M	Inns	NO	Runs	HS	Avge	100s	50s	Ct	St	Balls	Runs	Wkts	Avge	Best	5wI	10wM
Test																	
All First	56	96	12	2900	233	34.52	3	18	36	-	3590	1802	55	32.76	6-63	1	-
1-day Int																	
NatWest	7	7	1	236	107 *	39.33	1	1	3	-	324	205	10	20.50	3-39	-	
B & H	8	7	0	164	62	23.42	-	1	3	-	96	65	0	-	-	-	-
Sunday	43	35	5	804	100	26.80	1	4	8	-	853	754	17	44.35	2-11	-	

183. Who scored the most runs in the Britannic Assurance Championship for Derbyshire last season?

UDAL, S. D.   Hampshire

Name: Shaun David Udal
Role: Right-hand bat, off-spin bowler,
field in the deep
Born: 18 March 1969, Farnborough
Height: 6ft 2¹/₂in **Weight:** 13st
Nickname: Uffers, Shaggy, Rodders
County debut: 1989
County cap: 1992
50 wickets in a season: 1
1st-Class 5 w. in innings: 2
1st-Class catches: 6
Place in bowling averages: 178th av. 21.05
Place in bowling averages: 79th av. 34.69
Strike rate: 71.62 (career 70.52)
Parents: Robin and Mary
Wife and date of marriage: Emma Jane,
5 October 1991
Children: Katherine Mary, 26 August 1992
Family links with cricket: Father played
for Surrey Colts and Camberley for 42 years,
brother plays for Camberley 1st XI. Grandfather played for Leicestershire and Middlesex
Education: Tower Hill Infant and Junior Schools; Cove Comprehensive School
Qualifications: 8 CSEs, qualified print finisher
Career outside cricket: Printing trade
Off-season: Salesman for printing company and getting fit for the new season
Overseas teams played for: Hamilton Wickham, Newcastle, NSW 1990
Cricketers particularly admired: Ian Botham, Malcolm Marshall, Robin Smith, David
Gower, John Emburey
Other sports followed: Football, golf
Relaxations: 'Having a couple of drinks, enjoying good company, eating out and spending
time with my daughter and wife.'
Extras: Has taken two hat-tricks in club cricket, scored a double hundred in a 40-over club
game and took 8-50 v Sussex in the first game of last season, his seventh ever Championship
match. Man of the Match on NatWest debut against Berkshire 1991
Opinions on cricket: 'Four-day cricket can only be good for the game in encouraging
spinners, but the batsmen still seem to have things their way with flat wickets and small
seams on the ball.'
Best batting: 44 Hampshire v Essex, Chelmsford 1992
Best bowling: 8-50 Hampshire v Sussex, Southampton 1992

552

1992 Season

	M	Inns	NO	Runs	HS	Avge	100s	50s	Ct	St	O	M	Runs	Wkts	Avge	Best	5wI	10wM
Test																		
All First	23	29	10	400	44	21.05	-	-	4	-	692.2	177	2012	58	34.69	8-50	2	-
1-day Int																		
NatWest	2	1	0	2	2	2.00	-	-	-	-	24	2	83	3	27.66	3-39	-	
B & H	7	1	1	3	3*	-	-	-	2	-	73	3	297	17	17.47	4-40	-	
Sunday	16	7	2	38	17	7.60	-	-	7	-	111	3	576	31	18.58	4-51	-	

Career Performances

	M	Inns	NO	Runs	HS	Avge	100s	50s	Ct	St	Balls	Runs	Wkts	Avge	Best	5wI	10wM
Test																	
All First	32	36	12	479	44	19.95	-	-	6	-	5783	3050	82	37.19	8-50	2	-
1-day Int																	
NatWest	7	1	0	2	2	2.00	-	-	2	-	444	274	9	30.44	3-39	-	
B & H	12	3	1	13	9	6.50	-	-	4	-	768	486	26	18.69	4-40	-	
Sunday	35	15	6	106	23	11.77	-	-	12	-	1502	1262	52	24.26	4-51	-	

VAN TROOST, A. P.   Somerset

Name: Adrianus Pelrus van Troost
Role: Right-hand bat, right-arm fast bowler
Born: 2 October 1972, Schiedam, Holland
Height: 6ft 7in **Weight:** 15st 2lbs
Nickname: Flappie, Rooster
County debut: 1991
1st-Class 5 w. in innings: 2
1st-Class catches: 4
Place in bowling averages: 94th av. 36.47
Strike rate: 50.19 (career 58.29)
Parents: Aad and Anneke
Marital status: Single
Family links with cricket: Father plays for Excelsior CC in Holland, brother plays for Excelsior and Holland U23. Grandfather played for Excelsior and Holland
Education: Spieringshoek College, Schiedam
Qualifications: Finished Havo schooling – specialised in languages
Career outside cricket: Works in a bank
Off-season: Touring New Zealand and South Africa with Dutch team

Overseas tours: Holland to Zimbabwe 1989, to Namibia 1990, to Dubai 1991, to Canada, New Zealand and South Africa 1992

Overseas teams played for: Excelsior, Holland 1979-91

Cricketers particularly admired: Richard Hadlee, Peter Roebuck, Roland Lefebvre, Eric Van't Zelfde, Paul Van de Bosch

Other sports followed: Football, tennis and most other sports

Relaxations: Playing football and travelling

Extras: Played for Holland at the age of 15. Third Dutch national to play professional cricket. Took 6-3 v Durham 2nd XI in 1992 season

Opinions on cricket: 'It should be made easier for Holland to play against different counties and different countries. They should also be admitted to the B & H or NatWest competition.'

Best batting: 12 Somerset v Essex, Taunton 1992

Best bowling: 6-48 Somerset v Essex, Taunton 1992

1992 Season

	M	Inns	NO	Runs	HS	Avge	100s	50s	Ct	St	O	M	Runs	Wkts	Avge	Best	5wI	10wM
Test																		
All First	11	9	5	42	12	10.50	-	-	3	-	175.4	20	766	21	36.47	6-48	2	-
1-day Int																		
NatWest																		
B & H																			
Sunday																			

Career Performances

	M	Inns	NO	Runs	HS	Avge	100s	50s	Ct	St	Balls	Runs	Wkts	Avge	Best	5wI	10wM
Test																	
All First	15	10	6	42	12	10.50	-	-	4	-	1574	1033	27	38.25	6-48	2	-
1-day Int																	
NatWest																	
B & H																		
Sunday																		

184. Who scored the most runs in the Britannic Assurance Championship for Durham last season?

VAUGHAN, J. T. C   Gloucestershire

Name: Justin Thomas Caldwell Vaughan
Role: Left-hand bat, right-arm medium bowler
Born: 30 August 1967, Hereford
Height: 6ft 1in **Weight:** 13st
Nickname: Jock, Doc, Kiwi
County debut: 1992
1st-Class 50s scored: 8
1st-Class 100s scored: 1
1st-Class 5 w. in innings: 1
1st-Class catches: 32
One-day 50s: 1
Place in batting averages: 106th av. 33.78
Place in bowling averages: 67th av. 32.66
Strike rate: 67.55 (career 71.23)
Parents: Geoff and Ailleen
Marital status: Single
Family links with cricket: Older brother Mark played for Worcestershire 2nd XI for one season in 1982
Education: Westlake Boys High School, Auckland; Auckland University
Qualifications: Qualified doctor BHB, MBchB 1990
Career outside cricket: Doctor
Off-season: Medical work and playing first-class cricket in New Zealand for Auckland
Overseas tours: New Zealand to Sri Lanka 1992-93
Overseas teams played for: Auckland 1989-92
Cricketers particularly admired: John Wright, Jeff Crowe, Courtney Walsh
Other sports followed: Most – especially rugby union, golf, tennis, Eton fives, surfing
Relaxations: Photography, playing the piano, reading, sleeping, eating curries, golf
Injuries: Knee injury, out for two weeks
Relaxations: Music, movies, photography, sunbathing, reading, travelling
Extras: Made test debut for New Zealand v Sri Lanka at Colombo, forfeiting his England qualification
Opinions on cricket: 'Abolish leg byes. Agree with new structure to county cricket. Should have a World Cup for Test cricket.'
Best batting: 106* Auckland v Wellington, Wellington 1989-90
Best bowling: 5-72 Auckland v Otago, Auckland 1991-92

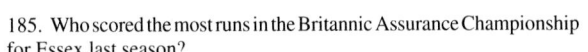

185. Who scored the most runs in the Britannic Assurance Championship for Essex last season?

1992 Season

	M	Inns	NO	Runs	HS	Avge	100s	50s	Ct	St	O	M	Runs	Wkts	Avge	Best	5wl	10wM
Test																		
All First	11	18	4	473	99	33.78	-	4	11	-	202.4	44	588	18	32.66	3-46	-	-
1-day Int																		
NatWest	2	2	1	65	54 *	65.00	-	1	-	-	16	0	57	0	-		-	-
B & H	4	3	0	24	12	8.00	-	-	-	-	38	1	177	5	35.40	3-61	-	
Sunday	6	5	1	34	20	8.50	-	-	1	-	31.3	6	110	4	27.50	3-31	-	

Career Performances

	M	Inns	NO	Runs	HS	Avge	100s	50s	Ct	St	Balls	Runs	Wkts	Avge	Best	5wl	10wM
Test																	
All First	33	53	12	1462	106 *	35.65	1	8	32	-	3063	1462	43	34.00	5-72	1	-
1-day Int																	
NatWest	2	2	1	65	54 *	65.00	-	1	-	-	96	57	0	-		-	-
B & H	4	3	0	24	12	8.00	-	-	-	-	228	177	5	35.40	3-61	-	
Sunday	6	5	1	34	20	8.50	-	-	1	-	189	110	4	27.50	3-31	-	

VAUGHAN, M. P.   Yorkshire

Name: Justin Thomas Caldwell Vaughan
Role: Right-hand bat, off-spin bowler
Born: 29 October 1974, Manchester, Lancashire
Height: 6ft 2in **Weight:** 10st 6lbs
Nickname: Virgil, Spawny
County debut: No first team appearance
Parents: Graham John and Dee
Marital status: Single
Family links with cricket: Dad played for Worsley CC and mother is related to the famous Tyldesley family (Lancashire)
Education: St Marks Junior, Manchester; Silverdale Comprehensive, Sheffield
Qualifications: 4 GCSEs
Off-season: Touring India with England U19
Overseas tours: U19 to India 1993
Cricketers particularly admired: Graham Gooch
Other sports followed: Football – Sheffield Wednesday
Relaxations: Playing golf and listening to music

Injuries: Knee injury, out for two weeks
Relaxations: Music, movies, photography, sunbathing, reading, travelling
Extras: Played club cricket for Sheffield Collegiate in the Yorkshire League

WALKER, A.   Northamptonshire

Name: Alan Walker
Role: Left-hand bat, right-arm medium-fast bowler
Born: 7 July 1962, Emley, nr Huddersfield
Height: 5ft 11in **Weight:** 12st 12lbs
Nickname: Wacky, Walks
County debut: 1983
County cap: 1987
1st-Class 5 w. in innings: 2
1st-Class catches: 37
Strike rate: (career 60.92)
Parents: Malcolm and Enid
Marital status: Engaged to Julie
Family links with cricket: Grandfather played local league
Education: Emley Junior School; Kirkburton Middle School; Shelley High School

Qualifications: 2 O-levels, 4 CSEs, qualified coal-face worker
Off-season: Building work
Overseas tours: NYCA North U19 to Denmark; Northants to Durban
Overseas teams played for: Uitenhage, South Africa 1984-85 and 1987-88
Cricketers particularly admired: Dennis Lillee, Richard Hadlee
Other sports followed: Football (Huddersfield Town and Emley), rugby league (Wakefield Trinity)
Injuries: Torn thigh and broken finger, out for six weeks
Relaxations: Cooking, drinking, gardening
Best batting: 41* Northamptonshire v Warwickshire, Edgbaston 1987
Best bowling: 6-50 Northamptonshire v Lancashire, Northampton 1986

---

186. Who scored the most runs in the Britannic Assurance Championship for Glamorgan last season?

1992 Season

	M	Inns	NO	Runs	HS	Avge	100s	50s	Ct	St	O	M	Runs	Wkts	Avge	Best	5wI	10wM
Test																		
All First	1	1	0	39	39	39.00	-	-	-	-	45	14	90	2	45.00	1-24	-	-
1-day Int																		
NatWest	1	0	0	0	0	-	-	-	-	-	10	1	46	0	-		-	-
B & H	4	2	2	3	3 *	-	-	-	-	-	38	2	180	6	30.00	2-49	-	
Sunday	11	1	0	3	3	3.00	-	-	-	-	76.2	4	382	11	34.72	3-26	-	

Career Performances

	M	Inns	NO	Runs	HS	Avge	100s	50s	Ct	St	Balls	Runs	Wkts	Avge	Best	5wI	10wM
Test																	
All First	96	91	45	664	41 *	14.43	-	-	37	-	13465	6871	221	31.09	6-50	2	-
1-day Int																	
NatWest	17	4	1	22	11	7.33	-	-	3	-	988	557	19	29.31	4-7	-	
B & H	27	10	7	38	15 *	12.66	-	-	6	-	1453	1071	30	35.70	4-46	-	
Sunday	93	19	8	76	13	6.90	-	-	22	-	3723	2734	107	25.55	4-21	-	

WALKER, D. A.   Middlesex

Name: David Anthony Walker
Role: Right-hand bat, right-arm
fast-medium bowler
Born: 18 June 1975, Hampstead
Height: 5ft 11in **Weight:** 10st 7lbs
Nickname: Dave the rave
County debut: No first team appearance
Parents: Doug and Yvonne
Marital status: single
Education: John Kelly Boys High School;
Neasden College, London
Qualifications: 5 GCSEs
Career outside cricket: Student
Cricketers particularly admired:
Mike Gatting, Malcolm Marshall
Other sports followed: Football
(Tottenham Hotspur)
Injuries: Torn thigh and broken finger, out
for six weeks
Relaxations: Listening to music
Extras: Played for England U17 against India, represented Middlesex at all levels since
U11

WALKER, M. J.   Kent

Name: Matthew Jonathan Walker
Role: Left-hand bat, right-arm slow bowler
Born: 2 January 1974, Gravesend
Height: 5ft 3in **Weight:** 12st
Nickname: Walks, Max
County debut: No first team appearance
Parents: Richard and June
Marital status: single
Family links with cricket: Grandfather
played for Kent and father was on Lord's
ground staff having played for Middlesex
and Kent 2nd XI
Education: Shorne Primary School;
King's School, Rochester
Qualifications: 9 GCSEs, 2 A-Levels
Career outside cricket: 'Yet to be decided'
Off-season: Touring India with Young
England

Overseas tours: Kent U19 to New Zealand
1991; Young England to Pakistan 1992,
to India 1993
Cricketers particularly admired: David Gower
Other sports followed: Rugby, hockey, skiing
Relaxations: Music, most other sports
Extras: Represented England U16 and U18 at hockey; represented Kent U18 at rugby.
Captained Young England tour to India 1992-93

187. Who scored the most runs in the Britannic Assurance Championship
for Gloucestershire last season?

188. Who scored the most runs in the Britannic Assurance Championship
for Hampshire last season?

WALSH, C. A.   Gloucestershire

Name: Courtney Andrew Walsh
Role: Right-hand bat, right-arm fast bowler
Born: 30 October 1962, Kingston, Jamaica
Height: 6ft 5¹/₂in **Weight:** 14st 7lbs
Nickname: Mark, Walshy, Cuddy, RP
County debut: 1984
County cap: 1985
Test debut: 1984-85
Tests: 51
One-Day Internationals: 97
50 wickets in a season: 6
1st-Class 50s scored: 6
1st-Class 5 w. in innings: 55
1st-Class 10 w. in match: 11
1st-Class catches: 68
Place in batting averages: 246th av. 11.66
Place in bowling averages: 1st av. 15.96
(1991 61st av. 31.55)
Strike rate: 38.30 (career 46.89)
Parents: Eric and Joan Wollaston
Marital status: Single
Education: Excelsior High School
Qualifications: GCE and CXL
Off-season: Playing in the West Indies

Overseas tours: West Indies YC to Zimbabwe 1983; West Indies to England 1984, to Australia 1984-85, to Pakistan, Australia and New Zealand 1986-87, to India (World Cup) 1987-88, to England 1988, to Australia 1988-89, to Pakistan 1990-91, to England 1991, to Australia and South Africa 1992-93
Overseas teams played for: Jamaica 1981-91
Other sports followed: Basketball, track and field events, football, snooker
Relaxations: Swimming, reading and listening to music
Extras: Took record 10-43 in Jamaican school cricket in 1979. On tour, he has the reputation as an insatiable collector of souvenirs. David Graveney, when captaining Gloucestershire, reckoned Walsh was the 'best old-ball bowler in the world'. One of *Wisden's* Five Cricketers of the Year, 1986. Took hat-trick for West Indies v Australia in 1988-89. Captain of Jamaica. Cricketers' Association Player of the Year. Wombwell Cricket Lovers' Cricketer of the Year
Best batting: 63* Gloucestershire v Yorkshire, Cheltenham 1990
Best bowling: 9-72 Gloucestershire v Somerset, Bristol 1986

1992 Season

	M	Inns	NO	Runs	HS	Avge	100s	50s	Ct	St	O	M	Runs	Wkts	Avge	Best	5wI	10wM
Test																		
All First	18	27	3	280	51	11.66	-	1	7	-	587.2	138	1469	92	15.96	7-27	8	2
1-day Int																		
NatWest	3	2	0	27	17	13.50	-	-	-	-	34.2	7	98	10	9.80	6-21	1	
B & H	3	2	1	13	13	13.00	-	-	-	-	32.4	2	138	4	34.50	2-46	-	
Sunday	10	7	0	39	10	5.57	-	-	4	-	66.5	8	250	15	16.66	3-23	-	

Career Performances

	M	Inns	NO	Runs	HS	Avge	100s	50s	Ct	St	Balls	Runs	Wkts	Avge	Best	5wI	10wM
Test	51	69	22	418	30 *	8.89	-	-	7	-	10114	4444	178	24.96	6-62	5	1
All First	252	306	72	2931	63 *	12.52	-	6	68	-	46379	22244	989	22.49	9-72	55	11
1-day Int	97	34	14	166	29 *	8.30	-	-	13	-	5175	3376	108	31.25	5-1	1	
NatWest	16	10	3	90	25 *	12.85	-	-	1	-	1022	549	35	15.68	6-21	2	
B & H	20	12	4	87	28	10.87	-	-	-	-	1195	712	23	30.95	2-19	-	
Sunday	74	41	7	300	35	8.82	-	-	16	-	2996	2015	99	20.35	4-19	-	

WALTON, T. C.   Northamptonshire

Name: Timothy Charles Walton
Role: Right-hand bat, right-arm medium bowler
Born: 8 November 1972, Low Lead
Height: 6ft **Weight:** 12st 10lbs
Nickname: TC, Eric Spadge
County debut: 1992 (one-day)
Parents: Alan Michael and Sally Ann
Marital status: single
Family links with cricket: Father and two brothers, Jamie and Adam, play for local village
Education: Leeds Grammar School; University of Northumbria, Newcastle
Qualifications: 7 GCSEs, 3 A-Levels, studying sports degree
Career outside cricket: Student
Off-season: 'Cocktail of beer and study'
Overseas tours: England U19 to Pakistan 1991-92
Cricketers particularly admired: Philip DeFreitas
Other sports followed: Rugby union and league

Injuries: Shoulder tendon, out for two weeks
Relaxations: Running, raving and listening to music
Opinions on cricket: 'Appearance should be irrelevant if the cricketer is good enough i.e. long hair should be of no consequence. More commerciality and one day games.'

1992 Season

	M	Inns	NO	Runs	HS	Avge	100s	50s	Ct	St	O	M	Runs	Wkts	Avge	Best	5wI	10wM
Test																		
All First																		
1-day Int																		
NatWest																		
B & H																		
Sunday	2	0	0	0	0	-	-	-	-	-	15	0	63	3	21.00	2-27	-	

Career Performances

	M	Inns	NO	Runs	HS	Avge	100s	50s	Ct	St	Balls	Runs	Wkts	Avge	Best	5wI	10wM
Test																	
All First																	
1-day Int																	
NatWest																	
B & H																	
Sunday	2	0	0	0	0	-	-	-	-	-	90	63	3	21.00	2-27	-	

WAQAR YOUNIS   Surrey

Name: Waqar Younis
Role: Right-hand bat, right-arm fast bowler
Born: 16 November 1971, Burewala, Punjab
Height: 5ft 11in **Weight:** 12st
Nickname: Wicky
County debut: 1990
County cap: 1990
Test debut: 1989-90
Tests: 19
One-Day Internationals: 47
50 wickets in a season: 2
1st-Class 50s scored: 1
1st-Class 5 w. in innings: 32
1st-Class 10 w. in match: 8
1st-Class catches: 18
Place in batting averages: (1991 227th av. 14.75)
Place in bowling averages: 14th av 24.67 (1991 1st av. 14.65)

Strike rate: 46.54 (career 34.19)
Marital status: Single
Education: Pakistani College, Sharjah;
Sadiq Public School, Burewala
Qualifications: Studying law
Off-season: Playing for Pakistan
Overseas tours: Pakistan to India, Australia
and Sharjah 1989-90, to England 1992, to
New Zealand, Australia, South Africa and
West Indies 1992-93
Overseas teams played for: United Bank,
Pakistan
Cricketers particularly admired:
Imran Khan, Wasim Akram, Geoff Arnold,
Alec Stewart
Other sports followed:
Football, badminton, squash
Relaxations: 'Sleeping and family
get-togethers.'

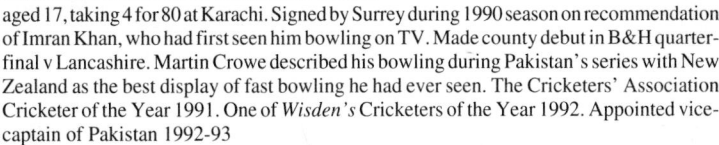

Extras: Made Test debut for Pakistan v India
aged 17, taking 4 for 80 at Karachi. Signed by Surrey during 1990 season on recommendation of Imran Khan, who had first seen him bowling on TV. Made county debut in B&H quarter-final v Lancashire. Martin Crowe described his bowling during Pakistan's series with New Zealand as the best display of fast bowling he had ever seen. The Cricketers' Association Cricketer of the Year 1991. One of *Wisden's* Cricketers of the Year 1992. Appointed vice-captain of Pakistan 1992-93
Opinions on cricket: 'There should be no over-rate fines.'
Best batting: 51 United Bank v PIA, Lahore 1989-90
Best bowling: 7-64 United Bank v ADBP, Lahore 1990-91

1992 Season

	M	Inns	NO	Runs	HS	Avge	100s	50s	Ct	St	O	M	Runs	Wkts	Avge	Best	5wl	10wM
Test	5	6	2	51	20 *	12.75	-	-	-	-	166	29	557	22	25.31	5-52	3	-
All First	10	9	4	95	23 *	19.00	-	-	1	-	287.1	50	913	37	24.67	5-22	4	-
1-day Int	3	1	0	13	13	13.00	-	-	-	-	28.2	0	167	9	18.55	4-73	-	
NatWest																		
B & H																		
Sunday																		

Career Performances

	M	Inns	NO	Runs	HS	Avge	100s	50s	Ct	St	Balls	Runs	Wkts	Avge	Best	5wI	10wM
Test	19	21	5	127	20 *	7.93	-	-	1	-	3746	1908	93	20.51	7-76	10	2
All First	80	78	31	634	51	13.48	-	1	18	-	13913	7261	355	20.45	7-64	32	8
1-day Int	47	16	8	91	20 *	11.37	-	-	4	-	2216	1581	86	18.38	6-26	5	
NatWest	6	2	0	30	26	15.00	-	-	-	-	411	233	18	12.94	5-40	1	
B & H	5	4	2	12	5 *	6.00	-	-	1	-	280	195	6	32.50	3-29	-	
Sunday	24	8	3	11	8	2.20	-	-	5	-	1026	767	52	14.75	5-26	1	

WARD, D. M.   Surrey

Name: David Mark Ward
Role: Right-hand bat, right-arm off-spin
bowler, occasional wicket-keeper
Born: 10 February 1961, Croydon, South
London
Height: 6ft 1in **Weight:** 14st
Nickname: Cocker, Wardy, Jaws,
Gnasher, Fat Boy, Piano Man
County debut: 1985
County cap: 1990
1000 runs in a season: 2
1st-Class 50s scored: 22
1st-Class 100s scored: 14
1st-Class 200s scored: 2
1st-Class catches: 100
1st-Class stumpings: 3
One-Day 50s: 17
One-Day 100s: 2
Place in batting averages: 89th av. 36.62

(1991 55th av. 40.35)
Parents: Tom and Dora
Marital status: Single
Family links with cricket: 'Uncle (John Goodey) local legend with Banstead and Temple
Bar CC.'
Education: Haling Manor High School; Croydon Technical College
Qualifications: 2 O-levels, Advanced City and Guilds in Carpentry and Joinery
Career outside cricket: Mortgage expert (Home Owners Advisory Service), carpenter
Overseas tours: Surrey to Barbados 1984, 1989, 1991; Lancashire to Mombasa 1990
Overseas teams played for: Caulfield, Melbourne 1984-87; Sunshine, Melbourne 1988-
89; Perth, Western Australia 1990-91
Cricketers particularly admired: Robert Thompson (brother of 'Candles' Thompson)

of Sturt CC, Adelaide, Geoff Howarth, Grahame Clinton
Other sports followed: Greyhound racing
Relaxations: 'Eating Chinese meal on an away trip with Keith Medlycott (when he pays)'
Extras: First Surrey batsman since John Edrich to score 2000 runs in a season in 1990 and shared county record stand of 413 for third wicket with Darren Bicknell v Kent at Canterbury. Hit century in 70 minutes for Surrey v Northants 1992
Best batting: 263 Surrey v Kent, Canterbury 1990
Best bowling: 2-66 Surrey v Gloucestershire, Guildford 1991

1992 Season

	M	Inns	NO	Runs	HS	Avge	100s	50s	Ct	St	O	M	Runs	Wkts	Avge	Best	5wI	10wM
Test																		
All First	18	30	6	879	138	36.62	3	1	3	-	4	0	16	0	-		-	-
1-day Int																		
NatWest	1	1	1	101	101 *	-	1	-	-	-								
B & H	7	6	2	77	27 *	19.25	-	-	2	-								
Sunday	15	13	4	341	63	37.88	-	2	8	-								

Career Performances

	M	Inns	NO	Runs	HS	Avge	100s	50s	Ct	St	Balls	Runs	Wkts	Avge	Best	5wI	10wM
Test																	
All First	121	192	31	6430	263	39.93	14	22	100	3	107	113	2	56.50	2-66	-	-
1-day Int																	
NatWest	14	13	1	507	101 *	42.25	1	4	7	-							
B & H	25	22	4	388	46 *	21.55	-	-	9	2							
Sunday	107	95	18	2077	102 *	26.97	1	13	53	1							

189. Who scored the most runs in the Britannic Assurance Championship for Kent last season?

Name: Alan Walker
Role: Left-hand bat, right-arm medium bowler
Born: 30 September 1972, Plymouth
Height: 5ft 8¹/₂in **Weight:** 12st
Nickname: Wardy
County debut: 1992
1st-Class catches: 1
Parents: Tony and Mary
Marital status: Single
Family links with cricket: Grandfather and father both captained Devon
Education: Millfield School
Qualifications: 8 GCSEs, 3 A-Levels
Career outside cricket: Coaching at the East Molesley Cricket School
Off-season: Training and coaching
Overseas tours: Millfield to Australia 1988-89, to Jamaica 1990; Surrey Youth to Barbados 1991

Cricketers particularly admired: David Gower, Peter Oakes, Graham Thorpe
Other sports followed: rugby, all sports
Relaxations: sleeping
Extras: Played for Surrey at all levels since U11

1992 Season

	M	Inns	NO	Runs	HS	Avge	100s	50s	Ct	St	O	M	Runs	Wkts	Avge	Best	5wI	10wM
Test																		
All First	1	1	0	0	0	0.00	-	-	1	-	8	0	35	0	-	-	-	-
1-day Int																		
NatWest																		
B & H																		
Sunday																		

190. Who scored the most runs in the Britannic Assurance Championship for Lancashire last season?

Career Performances

	M	Inns	NO	Runs	HS	Avge	100s	50s	Ct	St	Balls	Runs	Wkts	Avge	Best	5wI	10wM
Test																	
All First	1	1	0	0	0	0.00	-	-	1	-	48	35	0	-		-	-
1-day Int																	
NatWest																	
B & H																	
Sunday																	

WARD, T. R.   Kent

Name: Trevor Robert Ward
Role: Right-hand bat, occasional off-spin
bowler
Born: 18 January 1968, Farningham, Kent
Height: 5ft 11in **Weight:** 12st 11lbs
Nickname: Wardy, Chikka
County debut: 1986
County cap: 1989
1000 runs in a season: 2
1st-Class 50s scored: 32
1st-Class 100s scored: 13
1st-Class 200s scored: 1
1st-Class catches: 71
One-Day 50s: 17
Place in batting averages: 31st av. 48.47
(1991 35th av. 46.65)
Parents: Robert Henry and Hazel Ann
Wife and date of marriage: Sarah Ann,
29 September 1990
Family links with cricket: Father played
club cricket
Education: Anthony Roper County Primary; Hextable Comprehensive
Qualifications: 7 O-levels, NCA coaching award
Off-season: Playing for Gosnalls CC, Perth
Overseas tours: NCA to Bermuda 1985; England YC to Sri Lanka 1987, to Australia for
Youth World Cup 1988
Overseas teams played for: Scarborough, Perth, Western Australia 1985; Gosnalls, Perth
1993
Cricketers particularly admired: Ian Botham, Graham Gooch, Robin Smith
Other sports followed: Most sports
Relaxations: Fishing, watching, TV

Extras: A thousand runs in a season three times
Opinions on cricket: 'Four-day cricket has been proved this season to be a good thing, with matches running their course without contrived results. Sunday cricket should stay at 40 overs.'
Best batting: 235* Kent v Middlesex, Canterbury 1991
Best bowling: 2-48 Kent v Worcestershire, Canterbury 1990

1992 Season

	M	Inns	NO	Runs	HS	Avge	100s	50s	Ct	St	O	M	Runs	Wkts	Avge	Best	5wI	10wM
Test																		
All First	21	37	3	1648	153	48.47	5	9	25	-	39.5	4	109	0	-		-	-
1-day Int																		
NatWest	2	2	0	96	92	48.00	-	1	1	-								
B & H	7	7	0	83	29	11.85	-	-	1	-								
Sunday	15	14	0	507	73	36.21	-	5	4	-	1	0	11	1	11.00	1-11	-	

Career Performances

	M	Inns	NO	Runs	HS	Avge	100s	50s	Ct	St	Balls	Runs	Wkts	Avge	Best	5wI	10wM
Test																	
All First	93	160	12	5683	235 *	38.39	13	32	71	-	934	535	6	89.16	2-48	-	-
1-day Int																	
NatWest	9	9	0	354	92	39.33	-	3	1	-	72	58	1	58.00	1-58	-	
B & H	22	22	2	557	94	27.85	-	3	5	-	12	10	0	-	-	-	
Sunday	60	59	2	1522	80	26.70	-	11	11	-	228	187	6	31.16	3-20	-	

WARNER, A. E.   Derbyshire

Name: Allan Esmond Warner
Role: Right-hand bat, right-arm fast bowler, outfielder
Born: 12 May 1959, Birmingham
Height: 5ft 8in **Weight:** 10st
Nickname: Esis
County debut: 1982 (Worcs), 1985 (Derbys)
County cap: 1987 (Derbys)
1st-Class 50s scored: 14
1st-Class 5 w. in innings: 2
1st-Class catches: 39
One-Day 50s: 2
Place in batting averages: 219th av. 16.15 (1991 194th av. 19.52)
Place in bowling averages: 50th av. 30.62 (1991 71st av. 32.83)
Strike rate: 76.10 (career 64.93)
Parents: Edgar and Sarah

Children: Alvin, 6 September 1980
Education: Tabernacle School, St Kitts, West Indies
Qualifications: CSE Maths
Cricketers particularly admired: Malcolm Marshall, Michael Holding
Other sports followed: Football, boxing and athletics
Relaxations: Watching movies, music (soul, reggae and calypso)
Extras: Released by Worcestershire at end of 1984 and joined Derbyshire
Best batting: 91 Derbyshire v Leicestershire, Chesterfield 1986
Best bowling: 5-27 Worcestershire v Glamorgan, Worcester 1984

1992 Season

	M	Inns	NO	Runs	HS	Avge	100s	50s	Ct	St	O	M	Runs	Wkts	Avge	Best	5wI	10wM
Test																		
All First	17	15	2	210	55	16.15	-	1	3	-	367.5	87	888	29	30.62	4-52	-	-
1-day Int																		
NatWest	2	2	1	21	21	21.00	-	-	-	-	23	4	65	2	32.50	2-40	-	
B & H	5	3	1	39	22*	19.50	-	-	-	-	51	6	162	9	18.00	3-39	-	
Sunday	16	13	6	94	20*	13.42	-	-	2	-	112.3	5	484	23	21.04	4-23	-	

Career Performances

	M	Inns	NO	Runs	HS	Avge	100s	50s	Ct	St	Balls	Runs	Wkts	Avge	Best	5wI	10wM
Test																	
All First	163	221	40	3164	91	17.48	-	14	39	-	21170	10591	326	32.48	5-27	2	-
1-day Int																	
NatWest	13	9	2	88	32	12.57	-	-	-	-	795	503	15	33.53	4-39	-	
B & H	41	26	9	208	35*	12.23	-	-	4	-	2231	1464	59	24.81	4-36	-	
Sunday	119	87	23	922	68	14.40	-	2	19	-	4671	4004	134	29.88	5-39	1	

WARREN, R. J.   Northamptonshire

Name: Russell John Warren
Role: Right-hand bat, occasional off-spin bowler
Born: 10 September 1971, Northampton
Height: 6ft 2in **Weight:** 12st 4lbs
Nickname: Rabbit
County debut: 1992
Parents: John and Sally
Marital status: Single
Education: Whitehills Lower School; Kingsthorpe Middle and Upper Schools
Qualifications: 8 O-levels, 2 A-levels
Off-season: Recovering from foot operation in October 1992, then getting fit for next season
Overseas tours: England U19 to New Zealand 1991
Overseas teams played for: Lancaster Park, Christchurch, and Canterbury B, New Zealand 1991-92

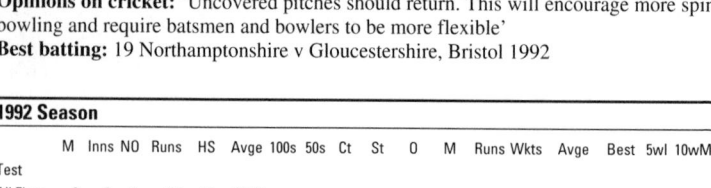

Cricketers particularly admired: Viv Richards, Wayne Larkins, Graham Gooch
Other sports followed: Most sports especially golf, football, snooker
Injuries: Sprained ankle, damaged ankle ligaments, out for two and a half weeks
Relaxations: 'Playing snooker at local club and having a relaxing nine holes of golf at Kingsthorpe GC, keen supporter of the Cobblers and Man Utd'
Opinions on cricket: 'Uncovered pitches should return. This will encourage more spin bowling and require batsmen and bowlers to be more flexible'
Best batting: 19 Northamptonshire v Gloucestershire, Bristol 1992

1992 Season

	M	Inns	NO	Runs	HS	Avge	100s	50s	Ct	St	O	M	Runs	Wkts	Avge	Best	5wI	10wM
Test																		
All First	2	3	1	27	19	13.50	-	-	-	-								
1-day Int																		
NatWest																		
B & H																		
Sunday																		

Career Performances

	M	Inns	NO	Runs	HS	Avge	100s	50s	Ct	St	Balls	Runs	Wkts	Avge	Best	5wI	10wM
Test																	
All First-	2	3	1	27	19	13.50	-	-	-	-							
1-day Int																	
NatWest																	
B & H																	
Sunday																	

WASIM AKRAM Lancashire

Name: Wasim Akram
Role: Left-hand bat, left-arm
fast-medium bowler
Born: 3 June 1966, Lahore, Pakistan
Height: 6ft 3in **Weight:** 12st 7lbs
County debut: 1988
County cap: 1989
Test debut: 1984-85
Tests: 44
One-Day Internationals: 126
50 wickets in a season: 3
1st-Class 50s scored: 10
1st-Class 100s scored: 3
1st-Class 5 w. in innings: 36
1st-Class 10 w. in match: 7
1st-Class catches: 39
One-Day 50s: 3
Place in batting averages: 191st av. 19.66
(1991 140th av. 27.70)
Place in bowling averages: 2nd av. 22.00
(1991 10th av. 22.33)
Strike rate: 36.57 (career 51.29)
Education: Islamia College
Off-season: Playing for Pakistan

Overseas tours: Pakistan U23 to Sri Lanka 1984-85, to Pakistan to New Zealand 1984-85, to Sri Lanka 1985-86, to India 1986-87, to England 1987, to West Indies 1987-88, to Australia 1989-90, to Australia and New Zealand (World Cup) 1991-92, to England 1992, to New Zealand, Australia, South Africa and West Indies 1992-93
Overseas teams played for: PACO 1984-86; Lahore Whites 1985-86
Extras: His second first-class match was playing for Pakistan on tour in New Zealand. Imran Khan wrote of him: 'I have great faith in Wasim Akram. I think he will become a

great all-rounder, as long as he realises how much hard work is required. As a bowler he is extremely gifted, and has it in him to be the best left-armer since Alan Davidson.' Hit maiden Test 100 v Australia 1989-90 during stand of 191 with Imran Khan. Signed a new 4-year contract with Lancashire in 1992. Appointed captain of Pakistan 1992-93
Best batting: 123 Pakistan v Australia, Adelaide 1989-90
Best bowling: 7-42 World XI v MCC, Scarborough 1989

1992 Season

	M	Inns	NO	Runs	HS	Avge	100s	50s	Ct	St	O	M	Runs	Wkts	Avge	Best	5wI	10wM
Test	4	7	1	118	45 *	19.66	-	-	-	-	168.5	36	462	21	22.00	6-67	2	-
All First	14	18	3	299	45 *	19.93	-	-	5	-	499.5	127	1330	82	16.22	6-32	7	2
1-day Int	4	4	1	73	34	24.33	-	-	1	-	41.4	3	180	4	45.00	2-41	-	
NatWest																		
B & H																		
Sunday																		

Career Performances

	M	Inns	NO	Runs	HS	Avge	100s	50s	Ct	St	Balls	Runs	Wkts	Avge	Best	5wI	10wM
Test	44	56	9	971	123	20.66	1	4	12	-	9631	4100	169	24.26	6-62	11	2
All First	122	158	24	2981	123	22.24	3	10	39	-	23341	10167	455	22.34	7-42	36	7
1-day Int	126	94	19	1013	86	13.50	-	1	25	-	6369	4107	171	24.01	5-21	2	
NatWest	12	10	2	129	29	16.12	-	-	3	-	736	447	20	22.35	4-27	-	
B & H	17	14	4	277	52	27.70	-	1	1	-	1066	670	33	20.30	5-27	1	
Sunday	52	40	11	683	50	23.55	-	1	9	-	2226	1703	73	23.32	4-19	-	

WATKIN, S. L.   Glamorgan

Name: Steven Llewellyn Watkin
Role: Right-hand bat, right-arm fast-medium bowler
Born: 13 September 1964, Duffryn, Rhondda, nr Port Talbot
Height: 6ft 3in **Weight:** 12st 10lbs
Nickname: Watty, Banger
County debut: 1986
County cap: 1989
Test debut: 1991
Tests: 2
50 wickets in a season: 4
1st-Class 5 w. in innings: 16
1st-Class 10 w. in match: 3
1st-Class catches: 24
Place in batting averages: (1991 245th av. 12.36)
Place in bowling averages: 54th av. 31.26 (1991 47th av. 29.39)

Strike rate: 60.83 (career 60.77)
Parents: John and Sandra
Marital status: Single
Family links with cricket: Brother plays local cricket.
Education: Cymer Afan Comprehensive; Swansea College of Further Education; South Glamorgan Institute of Higher Education
Qualifications: 8 O-levels, 2 A-levels, BA (Hons) in Human Movement Studies
Overseas tours: British Colleges to West Indies 1987; England A to Kenya and Zimbabwe 1989-90, to Pakistan and Sri Lanka 1990-91, to Bermuda and West Indies 1991-92
Overseas teams played for: Potchefstroom University, South Africa 1987-88; Aurora, Durban, South Africa 1991-92
Cricketers particularly admired:
Richard Hadlee, Dennis Lillee, Ian Botham
Other sports followed: All sports except horse racing
Relaxations: Watching TV, music, DIY, motor mechanics, 'a quiet pint'
Extras: Joint-highest wicket-taker in 1989 with 94 wickets. Sister Lynda has played for Great Britain at hockey
Opinions on cricket: 'At last four-day cricket.'
Best batting: 41 Glamorgan v Worcestershire, Worcester 1992
Best bowling: 8-59 Glamorgan v Warwickshire, Edgbaston 1988

1992 Season

	M	Inns	NO	Runs	HS	Avge	100s	50s	Ct	St	O	M	Runs	Wkts	Avge	Best	5wI	10wM
Test																		
All First	22	24	4	153	41	7.65	-	-	5	-	689.3	148	2126	68	31.26	6-97	1	-
1-day Int																		
NatWest	3	2	1	13	9	13.00	-	-	1	-	35	6	102	5	20.40	3-21	-	
B & H	2	1	0	0	0	0.00	-	-	-	-	21	10	69	5	13.80	3-49	-	
Sunday	8	2	1	9	7 *	9.00	-	-	2	-	63	2	290	5	58.00	2-25	-	

---

191. Who scored the most runs in the Britannic Assurance Championship for Leicestershire last season?

Career Performances

	M	Inns	NO	Runs	HS	Avge	100s	50s	Ct	St	Balls	Runs	Wkts	Avge	Best	5wI	10wM
Test	2	3	0	8	6	2.66	-	-	-	-	216	153	5	30.60	3-38	-	-
All First	117	122	33	738	41	8.29	-	-	24	-	22728	11532	374	30.83	8-59	16	3
1-day Int																	
NatWest	11	5	4	26	9	26.00	-	-	2	-	744	360	16	22.50	3-18	-	
B & H	15	12	6	48	15	8.00	-	-	1	-	885	568	15	37.86	3-28	-	
Sunday	54	22	7	153	31 *	10.20	-	-	10	-	2197	1775	59	30.08	5-23	1	

WATKINSON, M.   Lancashire

Name: Michael Watkinson
Role: Right-hand bat, right-arm medium or off-spin bowler
Born: 1 August 1961, Westhoughton
Height: 6ft 1½in **Weight:** 13st
Nickname: Winker
County debut: 1982
County cap: 1987
50 wickets in a season: 4
1st-Class 50s scored: 33
1st-Class 100s scored: 3
1st-Class 5 w. in innings: 21
1st-Class 10 w. in match: 1
1st-Class catches: 99
One-Day 50s: 12
Place in batting averages: 187th av. 20.08 (1991 127th av. 35.90)
Place in bowling averages: 68th av. 33.00 (1991 48th av. 33.57)
Strike rate: 60.00 (career 64.01)
Parents: Albert and Marian
Wife and date of marriage: Susan, 12 April 1986
Children: Charlotte, 24 February 1989; Liam 27 July 1991
Education: Rivington and Blackrod High School, Horwich
Qualifications: 8 O-levels, HTC Civil Engineering
Career outside cricket: Draughtsman
Off-season: Working as an estimator with William Hare Ltd, Bolton
Cricketers particularly admired: Clive Lloyd, Imran Khan
Other sports followed: Football
Relaxations: Watching Bolton Wanderers
Extras: Played for Cheshire in Minor Counties, and NatWest Trophy (v Middlesex) 1982.

Man of the Match in the first ever Refuge Cup Final 1988 and in 1990 B&H Cup Final 1990
Best batting: 138 Lancashire v Yorkshire, Old Trafford 1990
Best bowling: 7-25 Lancashire v Sussex, Lytham 1987

1992 Season

	M	Inns	NO	Runs	HS	Avge	100s	50s	Ct	St	O	M	Runs	Wkts	Avge	Best	5wI	10wM
Test																		
All First	20	25	1	482	96	20.08	-	1	10	-	660	140	2178	66	33.00	6-62	4	1
1-day Int																		
NatWest	2	2	0	122	82	61.00	-	1	-	-	19	4	56	5	11.20	3-17	-	
B & H	5	4	1	113	76	37.66	-	1	3	-	32	0	136	4	34.00	2-19	-	
Sunday	15	11	1	152	37	15.20	-	-	4	-	101.2	2	580	10	58.00	3-42	-	

Career Performances

	M	Inns	NO	Runs	HS	Avge	100s	50s	Ct	St	Balls	Runs	Wkts	Avge	Best	5wI	10wM
Test																	
All First	200	292	36	6192	138	24.18	3	33	99	-	29449	15486	460	33.66	7-25	21	1
1-day Int																	
NatWest	28	23	5	541	90	30.05	-	4	7	-	1697	1083	30	36.10	3-14	-	
B & H	49	34	8	581	76	22.34	-	3	11	-	2475	1720	57	30.17	5-49	1	
Sunday	141	109	31	1715	83	21.98	-	5	28	-	5567	4600	144	31.94	5-46	1	

WAUGH, M. E. Essex

Name: Mark Edward Waugh
Role: Right-hand bat, right-arm medium pace bowler
Born: 2 June 1965, Canterbury, New South Wales
Height: 6ft **Weight:** 13st 7lbs
County debut: 1988
County cap: 1989
Test debut: 1990-91
Tests: 11
One-Day Internationals: 34
1000 runs in a season: 3
1st-Class 50s scored: 45
1st-Class 100s scored: 35
1st-Class 200s scored: 4
1st-Class 5 w. in innings: 1
1st-Class catches: 175
One-Day 50s: 15

One-Day 100s: 5
Place in batting averages: 2nd av. 77.29
Place in bowling averages: 49th av. 30.50
Strike rate: 50.36 (career 64.41)
Parents: Rodger and Beverley
Marital status: Single
Family links with cricket: Uncle a 1st Grade cricketer in Sydney for Bankstown/ Canterbury. Twin brother Steve plays for Australia and played for Somerset in 1988. Younger brother Dean played in Bolton League with Astley Bridge in 1989 and made debut for NSW in 1990-91
Education: East Hills Boys High School
Qualifications: Higher School Certificate, cricket coach
Off-season: Playing cricket for New South Wales
Overseas tours: Young Australia to Zimbabwe 1985-86; New South Wales to Zimbabwe 1987-88; Australia to West Indies 1990-91, to Sri Lanka and New Zealand 1992-93
Overseas teams played for: New South Wales 1985-93
Cricketers particularly admired: 'Allan Border for his guts and determination, Doug Walters for his ability and sportsmanship, Greg Chappell – pure class.'
Other sports followed: 'Any – but mainly golf, football and horse racing.'
Relaxations: 'Sleeping, eating and gambling.'
Extras: Steve and Mark are only twins to score hundreds in the same innings of a first-class match and to both play international cricket. Chosen as New South Wales Cricketer of the Year, 1988 and Sheffield Shield Cricketer of the Year, jointly with D. Tazelaar of Queensland. First batsman to score a century on his Sunday League debut. Took English summer off in 1991 but returned to Essex for 1992 season. Has been replaced again by Salim Malik for the 1993 season
Opinions on cricket: 'Too much cricket is played.'
Best batting: 229 New South Wales v Western Australia, Perth 1990-91
Best bowling: 5-37 Essex v Northamptonshire, Northampton 1990

1992 Season

	M	Inns	NO	Runs	HS	Avge	100s	50s	Ct	St	O	M	Runs	Wkts	Avge	Best	5wI	10wM
Test																		
All First	16	24	7	1314	219 *	77.29	4	6	27	-	184.4	31	671	22	30.50	3-38	-	-
1-day Int																		
NatWest	3	3	0	58	25	19.33	-	-	-	-	14	1	64	1	64.00	1-51	-	
B & H	4	4	0	136	100	34.00	1	-	1	-	7.5	0	31	3	10.33	3-31	-	
Sunday	13	12	5	572	105 *	81.71	1	3	4	-	51.4	2	283	10	28.30	3-26	-	

192. Who scored the most runs in the Britannic Assurance Championship for Middlesex last season?

Career Performances

	M	Inns	NO	Runs	HS	Avge	100s	50s	Ct	St	Balls	Runs	Wkts	Avge	Best	5wI	10wM
Test	11	17	2	637	139 *	42.46	2	2	21	-	648	298	9	33.11	4-80	-	-
All First	139	217	33	10448	229 *	56.78	35	45	175	-	6764	3882	105	36.97	5-37	1	-
1-day Int	34	30	3	642	67	23.77	-	3	17	-	585	454	20	22.70	4-37	-	
NatWest	6	5	0	105	47	21.00	-	-	1	-	114	81	1	81.00	1-51	-	
B & H	16	14	1	438	100	33.69	1	2	5	-	95	76	4	19.00	3-31	-	
Sunday	47	45	11	1738	112 *	51.11	4	10	16	-	814	772	25	30.88	3-26	-	

WEEKES, P. N. Middlesex

Name: Paul Nicholas Weekes
Role: Left-hand bat, off-spin bowler
Born: 8 July 1969, Hackney
Height: 5ft 11in **Weight:** 11st 4lbs
Nickname: Weekesy, Twiddles
County debut: 1990
1st-Class 50s scored: 6
1st-Class catches: 23
Place in batting averages: 71st av. 38.50
(1991 158th av. 24.90)
Place in bowling averages: 138th av. 45.52
Strike rate: 111.00 (career 93.56)
Parents: Robert and Carol
Marital status: Single
Family links with cricket: Father played
club cricket

Education: Homerton House Secondary
School, Hackney; Hackney College
Qualifications: NCA cricket coach
Career outside cricket: Coaching cricket
in the inner city schools
Overseas teams played for: Newcastle University, NSW, Australia 1989; Sunrise,
Zimbabwe 1990
Cricketers particularly admired: David Gower, Richie Richardson
Other sports followed: Boxing – 'middle and heavyweight especially'
Relaxations: Dancing and listening to music
Extras: Scored 50 in first innings for both 2nd and 1st teams
Opinions on cricket: 'There should be more entertainment for the spectators during lunch
intervals, i.e. competitions for throwing distances and bowling speeds.'
Best batting: 95 Middlesex v Oxford University, The Parks 1992
Best bowling: 3-57 Middlesex v Worcestershire, Worcester 1991

1992 Season

	M	Inns	NO	Runs	HS	Avge	100s	50s	Ct	St	O	M	Runs	Wkts	Avge	Best	5wl	10wM
Test																		
All First	17	21	7	539	95	38.50	-	3	15	-	222	51	595	12	49.58	3-61	-	-
1-day Int																		
NatWest	2	2	0	2	2	1.00	-	-	-	-	22	6	70	1	70.00	1-47	-	
B & H	6	4	2	65	44 *	32.50	-	-	1	-	41	5	154	5	30.80	2-29	-	
Sunday	17	9	2	149	29	21.28	-	-	6	-	101	4	535	22	24.31	4-37	-	

Career Performances

	M	Inns	NO	Runs	HS	Avge	100s	50s	Ct	St	Balls	Runs	Wkts	Avge	Best	5wl	10wM
Test																	
All First	26	35	8	863	95	31.96	-	6	23	-	2152	1047	23	45.52	3-57	-	-
1-day Int																	
NatWest	3	3	0	9	7	3.00	-	-	-	-	204	100	2	50.00	1-30	-	
B & H	8	5	2	65	44 *	21.66	-	-	2	-	288	181	5	36.20	2-29	-	
Sunday	32	19	5	293	32 *	20.92	-	-	13	-	1076	965	31	31.12	4-37	-	

WELCH, G.   Warwickshire

Name: Graeme Welch
Role: Right-hand bat, right-arm medium-fast bowler
Born: 21 March 1972, Tyne and Wear
Height: 6ft **Weight:** 13st 7lbs
Nickname: Pop, Red Beard
County debut: 1992 (one-day)
Parents: Robert and Jean
Marital status: Single
Family links with cricket: Brother Barry and father
play club cricket in Durham
Education: Hetton Lyons Junior School; Hetton Comprehensive
Qualifications: 9 GCSEs, City & Guilds in Leisure Management
Off-season: Playing and coaching in Cape Town
Overseas tours: Warwickshire to Cape Town 1992
Overseas teams played for: Avendale, Cape Town 1991-93

Cricketers particularly admired: Dermot Reeve, Paul Smith, Tim Munton, Allan Donald, Carl Hooper, Mike (George) Burns
Other sports followed: Football
Injuries: Sprained ligaments in right ankle, out for three and a half weeks
Relaxations: 'Watching videos, listening to music, going out for a drink, going for meals with Lidge and playing on my Gameboy'
Extras: Played for Young England v Australia 1991
Opinions on cricket: '2nd XI cricket is supposed to be base for first-class cricket but the wickets that are played on bear no resemblance to first-class wickets. More games should be played on first-class grounds.'

1992 Season

	M	Inns	NO	Runs	HS	Avge	100s	50s	Ct	St	O	M	Runs	Wkts	Avge	Best	5wI	10wM
Test																		
All First																			
1-day Int																			
NatWest																			
B & H																			
Sunday	5	4	3	29	23	29.00	-	-	-	-	29.5	2	136	3	45.33	1-24	-	

Career Performances

	M	Inns	NO	Runs	HS	Avge	100s	50s	Ct	St	Balls	Runs	Wkts	Avge	Best	5wI	10wM
Test																	
All First																		
1-day Int																		
NatWest																		
B & H																		
Sunday	5	4	3	29	23	29.00	-	-	-	-	179	136	3	45.33	1-24	-	

193. Who scored the most runs in the Britannic Assurance Championship for Northamptonshire last season?

WELLS, A. P. Sussex

Name: Alan Peter Wells
Role: Right-hand bat, right-arm medium
bowler, county captain
Born: 2 October 1961, Newhaven
Height: 6ft **Weight:** 12st 4lbs
Nickname: Morph, Bomber
County debut: 1981
County cap: 1986
1000 runs in a season: 7
1st-Class 50s scored: 59
1st-Class 100s scored: 26
1st-Class 200s scored: 1
1st-Class catches: 131
One-Day 50s: 33
One-Day 100s: 2
Place in batting averages: 30th av. 48.83
(1991 12th 59.46)
Parents: Ernest William Charles and
Eunice Mae
Wife and date of marriage:
Melanie Elizabeth, 26 September 1987
Children: Luke William Peter 29 December 1990
Family links with cricket: Father played for many years for local club and had trial for
Sussex. Eldest brother Ray plays club cricket. Brother Colin plays for Sussex
Education: Tideway Comprehensive, Newhaven
Qualifications: 5 O-levels, NCA coaching certificate
Career outside cricket: Family packaging business
Off-season: Running the business (as above) with brother Colin
Overseas tours: Unofficial England team to South Africa 1989-90
Overseas teams played for: Border, South Africa 1981-82
Injuries: Broken toe, 'Waqar'd' – missed one game
Relaxations: Listening to music, eating out, drinking in country pubs, cooking
Extras: Played for England YC v India 1981. Banned from Test cricket for five years in
1990 for joining tour of South Africa, suspension remitted in 1992. Scored a century in each
of his first two matches as acting captain and won both matches
Best batting: 253* Sussex v Yorkshire, Middlesbrough 1991
Best bowling: 3-67 Sussex v Worcestershire, Worcester 1987

1992 Season

	M	Inns	NO	Runs	HS	Avge	100s	50s	Ct	St	O	M	Runs	Wkts	Avge	Best	5wI	10wM
Test																		
All First	22	35	5	1465	165 *	48.83	5	4	24	-	29	7	94	0	-		-	-
1-day Int																		
NatWest	2	2	1	166	119	166.00	1	-	2	-								
B & H	5	5	1	168	61	42.00	-	2	-	-								
Sunday	16	15	4	531	110 *	48.27	1	5	9	-								

Career Performances

	M	Inns	NO	Runs	HS	Avge	100s	50s	Ct	St	Balls	Runs	Wkts	Avge	Best	5wI	10wM
Test																	
All First	234	386	64	12481	253 *	38.76	26	59	131	-	961	690	9	76.66	3-67	-	-
1-day Int																	
NatWest	23	21	5	620	119	38.75	1	4	10	-	6	1	0	-		-	-
B & H	42	39	4	1052	74	30.05	-	9	9	-	60	72	3	24.00	1-17	-	
Sunday	156	141	18	3398	110 *	27.62	1	20	43	-	62	69	4	17.25	1-0	-	

WELLS, C. M. Sussex

Name: Colin Mark Wells
Role: Right-hand bat, right-arm medium bowler
Born: 3 March 1960, Newhaven
Height: 6ft **Weight:** 13st
Nickname: Bomber, Dougie
County debut: 1979
County cap: 1982
Benefit: 1993
One-Day Internationals: 2
1000 runs in a season: 6
50 wickets in a season: 2
1st-Class 50s scored: 58
1st-Class 100s scored: 20
1st-Class 200s scored: 1
1st-Class 5 w. in innings: 7
1st-Class catches: 86
One-Day 50s: 23
One-Day 100s: 4
Place in batting averages: 171st av. 22.16
(1991 91st av. 33.532)
Place in bowling averages: 63rd av. 32.30 (1991 95th av. 35.77)

Strike rate: 71.40 (career 72.68)
Parents: Ernest William Charles and Eunice Mae
Wife and date of marriage: Celia, 25 September 1982
Children: Jessica Louise, 2 October 1987
Family links with cricket: Father, Billy, had trials for Sussex and played for Sussex Cricket Association. Eldest brother Ray plays club cricket and youngest brother Alan plays for Sussex
Education: Tideway Comprehensive School, Newhaven
Qualifications: 9 O-levels, 2 CSEs, 1 A-level, intermediate coaching certificate
Off-season: Running family blister-packaging company in Newhaven
Overseas tours: England to Sharjah 1985
Overseas teams played for: Border 1980-81; Western Province 1984-85
Other sports followed: Football, rugby, hockey, basketball, tennis, table tennis
Injuries: Hamstring problems caused by lumbar spine immobility, out for approximately eight weeks
Relaxations: Sea-angling, philately, listening to music
Extras: Played in three John Player League matches in 1978. Was recommended to Sussex by former Sussex player, Ian Thomson. Vice-captain 1988-90
Opinions on cricket: 'Pleased four-day cricket has been introduced and resent clubs who have opposed it for purely financial reasons.'
Best batting: 203 Sussex v Hampshire, Hove 1984
Best bowling: 7-42 Sussex v Derbyshire, Derby 1991

1992 Season

	M	Inns	NO	Runs	HS	Avge	100s	50s	Ct	St	O	M	Runs	Wkts	Avge	Best	5wI	10wM
Test																		
All First	6	7	1	133	39	22.16	-	-	1	-	119	26	323	10	32.30	3-26	-	-
1-day Int																		
NatWest																		
B & H	3	3	0	26	16	8.66	-	-	-	-	27	4	104	2	52.00	1-32	-	
Sunday	4	1	1	4	4 *	-	-	-	-	3	-	31	2	102	5	20.40	3-16	-

Career Performances

	M	Inns	NO	Runs	HS	Avge	100s	50s	Ct	St	Balls	Runs	Wkts	Avge	Best	5wI	10wM
Test																	
All First	276	436	69	12203	203	33.25	20	58	86	-	28494	13410	392	34.20	7-42	7	-
1-day Int	2	2	0	22	17	11.00	-	-	-	-							
NatWest	29	24	3	426	76	20.28	-	1	7	-	1318	625	17	36.76	3-16	-
B & H	49	48	5	1279	117	29.74	3	4	13	-	1794	1153	35	32.94	4-21	-
Sunday	176	158	24	3553	104 *	26.51	1	18	38	-	5857	3632	118	30.78	4-15	-

WELLS, V. J.   Leicestershire

Name: Vincent John Wells
Role: Right-hand bat, right-arm medium
bowler, occasional wicket-keeper
Born: 6 August 1965, Dartford
Height: 6ft **Weight:** 13st
Nickname: Wellsy, Vinny, Both
County debut: 1987 (Kent),
1992 (Leicestershire)
1st-Class 50s scored: 6
1st-Class 5 w. in innings: 1
1st-Class catches: 13
One-Day 100s: 1
Place in batting averages: 121st av. 30.94
Place in bowling averages: 10th av. 22.75
Strike rate: 54.72 (career 51.37)
Parents: Pat and Jack
Wife and date of marriage: Deborah
Louise, 14 October 1989

Family links with cricket: Brother plays
league cricket in Kent
Education: Downs School, Dartford; Sir William Nottidge School, Whitstable
Qualifications: 1 O-level, 8 CSEs, coaching certificate
Off-season: Coaching with Leicestershire
Overseas teams played for: Parnell, Auckland 1986; Avendale, Cape Town 1987-89, 1990-91
Cricketers particularly admired: David Gower, Bob Woolmer ' for the help he gave me', Ian Botham
Other sports followed: Most sports except horse and dog racing
Injuries: Minor operation on left knee, out for three weeks
Relaxations: Eating out, keeping fit, reading.
Extras: Was a schoolboy footballer with Leyton Orient. Scored 100* on NatWest debut v Oxfordshire. Left Kent at the end of 1991 season to join Leicestershire. Missed 1992 NatWest final due to viral infection
Opinions on cricket: 'Sunday League should have been left as 40-over game starting at 2 o'clock. Coloured clothing good idea, important to give sponsors as much coverage as possible. Players should have freedom to leave clubs once they have honoured their contracts. Having List 1 and 2 players sometimes makes contracts for players pointless.'
Best batting: 58 Kent v Hampshire, Bournemouth 1990
          58 Kent v Oxford University, The Parks 1991
Best bowling: 5-43 Kent v Leicestershire, Leicester 1990

1992 Season

	M	Inns	NO	Runs	HS	Avge	100s	50s	Ct	St	O	M	Runs	Wkts	Avge	Best	5wI	10wM
Test																		
All First	17	23	6	526	56	30.94	-	3	2	-	301	93	751	33	22.75	4-26	-	
1-day Int																		
NatWest	3	3	1	27	21	13.50	-	-	-	-	22.5	2	72	5	14.40	3-38	-	
B & H	5	4	1	56	19	18.66	-	-	1	-	38	5	170	6	28.33	3-13	-	
Sunday	11	10	3	123	29 *	17.57	-	-	6	-	72.3	2	357	11	32.45	3-35	-	

Career Performances

	M	Inns	NO	Runs	HS	Avge	100s	50s	Ct	St	Balls	Runs	Wkts	Avge	Best	5wI	10wM
Test																	
All First	31	48	7	1008	58	24.58	-	6	13	-	2620	1165	51	22.84	5-43	1	-
1-day Int																	
NatWest	4	4	2	127	100 *	63.50	1	-	-	-	137	72	5	14.40	3-38	-	
B & H	9	7	2	103	25	20.60	-	-	3	-	270	203	6	33.83	3-13	-	
Sunday	21	16	5	179	29 *	16.27	-	-	11	-	573	430	18	23.88	3-17	-	

WESTON, M. J.   Worcestershire

Name: Martin John Weston
Role: Right-hand bat, right-arm medium bowler
Born: 8 April 1959, Worcester
Height: 6ft 1in **Weight:** 15st 7lbs
Nickname: Wesso
County debut: 1979
County cap: 1986
Benefit: 1993 (joint benefit with Damian D'Oliveira)
1000 runs in a season: 1
1st-Class 50s scored: 26
1st-Class 100s scored: 3
1st-Class catches: 73
One-Day 50s: 15
One-Day 100s: 1
Strike rate: (career 80.84)
Parents: John Franklyn and Sheila Margaret
Wife and date of marriage:
Angela Karen, 2 October 1992
Family links with cricket: 'Father was a pretty useful all-rounder for the British Waterways team.'

Education: St George's C of E Junior; Samuel Southall Secondary Modern, – 'and Worcester's Pavilion Bar!'

Qualifications: City & Guilds and Advanced Crafts in Bricklaying

Off-season: Working, 'hopefully'

Cricketers particularly admired: Andy Moles, Gordon Lord, Ian Botham, Peter Scudamore

Other sports followed: Horse racing, football

Relaxations: Horse racing, golf

Best batting: 145* Worcestershire v Northamptonshire, Worcester 1984

Best bowling: 4-24 Worcestershire v Warwickshire, Edgbaston 1988

1992 Season

	M	Inns	NO	Runs	HS	Avge	100s	50s	Ct	St	O	M	Runs	Wkts	Avge	Best	5wI	10wM
Test																		
All First	2	3	3	26	17*	-	-	-	1	-	19	3	58	1	58.00	1-34	-	-
1-day Int																		
NatWest																		
B & H																		
Sunday	11	4	1	19	7	6.33	-	-	2	-	79	3	291	7	41.57	2-20	-	

Career Performances

	M	Inns	NO	Runs	HS	Avge	100s	50s	Ct	St	Balls	Runs	Wkts	Avge	Best	5wI	10wM
Test																	
All First	154	245	23	5320	145*	23.96	3	26	73	-	6439	3108	80	38.85	4-24	-	-
1-day Int																	
NatWest	20	20	4	571	98	35.68	-	2	7	-	650	410	10	41.00	4-30	-	
B & H	34	34	2	744	99*	23.25	-	5	8	-	643	387	13	29.76	2-27	-	
Sunday	141	114	19	1941	109	20.43	1	8	31	-	3826	2648	77	34.39	4-11	-	

194. Who scored the most runs in the Britannic Assurance Championship for Nottinghamshire last season?

WESTON, W. P. C.   Worcestershire

Name: William Philip Christopher Weston
Role: Left-hand bat, left-arm medium bowler
Born: 16 June 1973, Durham
Height: 6ft 4in **Weight:** 13st 7lbs
Nickname: Wesso, Junior
County debut: 1991
1st-Class 50s scored: 5
1st-Class catches: 2
Place in batting averages: 81st av. 37.50
Parents: Michael Philip and Kathleen Mary
Family links with cricket: Father played
minor county
cricket for Durham and rugby for England,
brother plays for Durham CC
Education: Durham School
Qualifications: O-levels, A-Levels,
qualified NCA coach
Off-season: Playing in Australia
Overseas tours: England U19 to Canada
and New Zealand 1990-91, to Pakistan 1991-92
Cricketers particularly admired: Ian Botham, Graham Dilley, Mal Loye
Other sports followed: Most sports except golf and horse racing
Injuries: Back spasms, out for two weeks
Relaxations: Going out with friends and sleeping
Extras: Scored century for England U19 v Australia 1991. Appointed captain of England U19 for their tour to Pakistan 1991-92. Told by Keble College, Oxford that he would not be accepted if he decided to tour he chose to sacrifice his place at Oxford. Played for Northants 2nd XI and Worcestershire 2nd XI in 1989
Opinions on cricket: 'I agree with the four-day format but I am not in favour of a 50-over Sunday League.'
Best batting: 66* Worcestershire v Somerset, Weston 1992
Best bowling: 2-39 Worcestershire v Pakistan, Worcester 1992

1992 Season

	M	Inns	NO	Runs	HS	Avge	100s	50s	Ct	St	O	M	Runs	Wkts	Avge	Best	5wI	10wM
Test																		
All First	14	23	5	675	66 *	37.50	-	5	2	-	74	9	237	2	118.50	2-39	-	-
1-day Int																		
NatWest																		
B & H																		
Sunday																		

Career Performances

	M	Inns	NO	Runs	HS	Avge	100s	50s	Ct	St	Balls	Runs	Wkts	Avge	Best	5wI	10wM
Test																	
All First	16	26	5	703	66 *	33.47	-	5	2	-	444	237	2	118.50	2-39	-	-
1-day Int																	
NatWest																	
B & H																	
Sunday																	

WHITAKER, J. J.   Leicestershire

Name: John James Whitaker
Role: Right-hand bat, county vice-captain
Born: 5 May 1962, Skipton, Yorkshire
Height: 6ft **Weight:** 13st 7lbs
Nickname: Jimmy
County debut: 1983
County cap: 1986
Benefit: 1993
Test debut: 1986-87
Tests: 1
One-Day Internationals: 2
1000 runs in a season: 8
1st-Class 50s scored: 59
1st-Class 100s scored: 24
1st-Class 200s scored: 1
1st-Class catches: 142
One-Day 50s: 29
One-Day 100s: 5
Place in batting averages: 142nd av. 26.77
(1991 66th av. 37.91)
Parents: John and Ann
Family links with cricket: Father plays club cricket for Skipton
Education: Malsis Hall Prep School; Uppingham School
Qualifications: 7 O-levels
Off-season: Working on benefit; representative for Whitaker's Chocolations
Overseas tours: Uppingham to Australia 1980-81; England to Australia 1986-87; England A to Zimbabwe and Kenya 1990-91; Hong Kong Charity 6s 1991, 1992
Overseas teams played for: Glenelg, Australia 1982-83; Old Scotch, Tasmania 1983-84; Somerset West, Cape Town 1984-85
Cricketers particularly admired: Geoff Boycott, Dennis Amiss, Brian Davison
Other sports followed: Football, golf, rugby

Injuries: Fractured cheek bone, out for five weeks
Relaxations: Watching movies, reading, eating out
Extras: One of *Wisden's* Five Cricketers of the Year, 1986
Opinions on cricket: 'There is too much first-class cricket.'
Best batting: 200* Leicestershire v Nottinghamshire, Leicester 1986
Best bowling: 1-29 Leicestershire v Somerset, Leicester 1992

1992 Season

	M	Inns	NO	Runs	HS	Avge	100s	50s	Ct	St	O	M	Runs	Wkts	Avge	Best	5wl	10wM
Test																		
All First	22	34	3	830	74	26.77	-	2	13	-	8	0	86	1	86.00	1-29	-	-
1-day Int																		
NatWest	5	5	0	235	84	47.00	-	2	-	-								
B & H	5	4	0	146	73	36.50	-	1	3	-								
Sunday	15	15	2	596	118 *	45.84	1	4	3	-								

Career Performances

	M	Inns	NO	Runs	HS	Avge	100s	50s	Ct	St	Balls	Runs	Wkts	Avge	Best	5wl	10wM
Test	1	1	0	11	11	11.00	-	-	1	-							
All First	225	357	43	12003	200 *	38.22	24	59	142	-	176	268	2	134.00	1-29	-	-
1-day Int	2	2	1	48	44 *	48.00	-	-	1	-							
NatWest	21	21	1	871	155	43.55	1	4	1	-	24	9	0	-	-	-	
B & H	38	34	2	921	100	28.78	1	3	7	-							
Sunday	125	115	13	3599	132	35.28	3	22	30	-	2	4	0	-	-	-	

WHITE, C.   Yorkshire

Name: Craig White
Role: Right-hand bat, off-spin bowler, cover fielder
Born: 16 December 1969, Morley, Yorkshire
Height: 6ft 1in **Weight:** 11st 11lbs
Nickname: Chalkey, Leather
County debut: 1990
1st-Class 5 w. in innings: 1
1st-Class 50s scored: 7
1st-Class catches: 5
One-Day 50s: 2
Place in batting averages: 32nd av. 47.72
Parents: Fred Emsley and Cynthia Anne
Wife and date of marriage: Elizabeth Anne, 19 September 1992
Family links with cricket: Father played with Pudsey St Lawrence
Education: Kennington Primary; Flora Hill High School and Bendigo Senior High School

(Victoria, Australia)
Off-season: 'I'll always travel back to
Australia to play in Victoria.'
Overseas tours: Australian YC to
West Indies 1990
Overseas teams played for:
Victoria (debut 1990-91)
Cricketers particularly admired:
Allan Border, Dean Jones, David Gower,
Martyn Moxon, Sachin Tendulkar
Other sports followed: Australian Rules
football
Relaxations: Holidaying at Surfers Paradise
in Queensland, mountain bike riding
Extras: Recommended to Yorkshire CCC
by Victorian Cricket Academy. Eligible to
play for Yorkshire as he was born in the
county. 'Fred Trueman and I are the only
Yorkshire players to debut in the 1sts
before the 2nds.'

Best batting: 79* Yorkshire v Worcestershire, Worcester 1992
Best bowling: 5-74 Yorkshire v Surrey, Harrogate 1990

1992 Season

	M	Inns	NO	Runs	HS	Avge	100s	50s	Ct	St	O	M	Runs	Wkts	Avge	Best	5wI	10wM
Test																		
All First	19	26	8	859	79*	47.72	-	7	14	-	3	0	22	0	-	-	-	-
1-day Int																		
NatWest	2	1	0	41	41	41.00	-	-	-	-								
B & H	1	1	0	26	26	26.00	-	-	-	-								
Sunday	14	13	5	289	63	36.12	-	2	4	-								

Career Performances

	M	Inns	NO	Runs	HS	Avge	100s	50s	Ct	St	Balls	Runs	Wkts	Avge	Best	5wI	10wM
Test																	
All First	32	41	10	1045	79*	33.71	-	7	19	-	1140	700	15	46.66	5-74	1	-
1-day Int																	
NatWest	2	1	0	41	41	41.00	-	-	-	-							
B & H	4	3	1	44	26	22.00	-	-	1	-	54	31	1	31.00	1-31	-	
Sunday	23	19	8	414	63	37.63	-	2	7	-	145	165	5	33.00	2-49	-	

WHITTICASE, P.   Leicestershire

Name: Philip Whitticase
Role: Right-hand bat, wicket-keeper
Born: 15 March 1965, Wythall, Birmingham
Height: 5ft 8in **Weight:** 11st
Nickname: Jasper, Tracy, Boggy, Rat
County debut: 1984
County cap: 1987
1st-Class 50s scored: 15
1st-Class 100s scored: 1
1st-Class catches: 302
1st-Class stumpings: 13
Place in batting averages:
(1991 110th av. 31.00)
Parents: Larry Gordon and Ann
Marital status: Single
Family links with cricket: Grandfather and
father played local club cricket (both were
wicket-keepers)

Education: Belle Vue Junior and Middle
School; Buckpool Secondary; Crestwood
Comprehensive
Qualifications: 5 O-levels, 4 CSEs, senior coaching certificate
Overseas teams played for: South Bunbury, Western Australia 1983-85
Cricketers particularly admired: Bob Taylor, Alan Knott, Dennis Amiss
Other sports followed: Football, rugby
Relaxations: Playing soccer, watching rugby and 'a good night out'
Extras: Played schoolboy football for Birmingham City. Was Derek Underwood's last
first-class victim
Best batting: 114* Leicestershire v Hampshire, Bournemouth

1992 Season

	M	Inns	NO	Runs	HS	Avge	100s	50s	Ct	St	O	M	Runs	Wkts	Avge	Best	5wl	10wM
Test																		
All First	8	10	3	62	18*	8.85	-	-	18	1								
1-day Int																		
NatWest																		
B & H	4	2	0	29	17	14.50	-	-	4	2								
Sunday	4	4	1	35	15*	11.66	-	-	1	-								

Career Performances

	M	Inns	NO	Runs	HS	Avge	100s	50s	Ct	St	Balls	Runs	Wkts	Avge	Best	5wI	10wM
Test																	
All First	129	169	39	2963	114 *	22.79	1	15	302	13	5	7	0	-	-	-	-
1-day Int																	
NatWest	13	6	1	67	32	13.40	-	-	14	-							
B & H	26	17	6	313	45	28.45	-	-	28	4							
Sunday	68	45	9	413	38	11.47	-	-	56	4							

WHITTINGTON, J. M. S. Middlesex

Name: Jonathan Mark Smith Whittington
Role: Left-hand bat, slow left-arm bowler, specialist mid-off
Born: 17 August 1973, Marylebone
Height: 6ft 2in **Weight:** 12st 7lbs
Nickname: Basil, Elvis, Dick, Dicky Boy, Percy
County debut: 1992
Parents: Christopher and Sue
Marital status: Single
Family links with cricket: Father played club cricket
Education: Eton College; Manchester University
Qualifications: 10 GCSE/AO-levels, 3 A-levels
Off-season: At university
Cricketers particularly admired:
John Claughton, John Rice, David Gower, Robert Matheson
Other sports followed: Baseball, American football
Injuries: Split webbing, foot injury, out for six weeks
Relaxations: Poetry, music (The Grateful Dead), travelling, playing guitar
Extras: Won Daily Telegraph U19 Bowling Award 1990. Released by Middlesex at the end of the 1992 season

---

195. Who scored the most runs in the Britannic Assurance Championship for Somerset last season?

1992 Season

	M	Inns	NO	Runs	HS	Avge	100s	50s	Ct	St	O	M	Runs	Wkts	Avge	Best	5wI	10wM
Test																		
All First	1	0	0	0	0	-	-	-	-	-	19	2	44	0	-	-	-	-
1-day Int																		
NatWest																		
B & H																		
Sunday																		

Career Performances

	M	Inns	NO	Runs	HS	Avge	100s	50s	Ct	St	Balls	Runs	Wkts	Avge	Best	5wI	10wM
Test																	
All First	1	0	0	0	0	-	-	-	-	-	114	44	0	-	-	-	-
1-day Int																	
NatWest																	
B & H																	
Sunday																	

WIGHAM, G.   Durham

Name: Gary Wigham
Role: Right-hand bat, right-arm fast-medium bowler
Born: 2 March 1973, Bishop Auckland
Height: 6ft 8in **Weight:** 16st 7lbs
Nickname: Wiggy, Bill
County debut: 1992 (one-day)
Parents: Margaret and Barry
Marital status: Single
Education: Bishop Auckland Barrington Comprehensive
Qualifications: 4 GCSEs
Off-season: 'Getting a job doing anything'
Overseas tours: Durham to Zimbabwe 1992
Overseas teams played for: Riccarton, Christchurch 1991-92
Cricketers particularly admired: Ian Botham, Paul Parker, Allan Donald
Other sports followed: Golf, motor racing, football
Injuries: Groin injury, out for six weeks
Relaxations: Music, socialising, sleeping

Extras: Was on the MCC groundstaff in 1991
Opinions on cricket: 'The game is geared too much towards batsmen. I think it would be interesting if they brought back uncovered pitches.'

1992 Season

	M	Inns	NO	Runs	HS	Avge	100s	50s	Ct	St	O	M	Runs	Wkts	Avge	Best	5wI	10wM
Test																		
All First																		
1-day Int																		
NatWest																		
B & H																		
Sunday	1	0	0	0	0	-	-	-	-	-	8	1	43	1	43.00	1-43	-	

Career Performances

	M	Inns	NO	Runs	HS	Avge	100s	50s	Ct	St	Balls	Runs	Wkts	Avge	Best	5wI	10wM
Test																	
all First																	
1-day Int																	
NatWest																	
B & H																	
Sunday	1	0	0	0	0	-	-	-	-	-	48	43	1	43.00	1-43	-	

WIGHT, R. M.   Gloucestershire

Name: Robert Marcus Wight
Role: Right-hand bat, off-spin
bowler
Born: 12 September 1969, London
Height: 6ft 2in **Weight:** 13st 8lbs
Nickname: Chalky
County debut: No first team appearance
1st-Class 50s scored: 2
1st-Class catches: 3
Place in batting averages: 132nd av. 27.71
Place in bowling averages: 105th av. 39.36
Strike rate: 73.10 (career 73.10)
Parents: Philip and Penny
Marital status: Single
Family links with cricket: Cousin of
Peter Wight (ex Somerset) and Norman and
Lesley Wight (both played for the
West Indies)

Education: KCS Wimbledon; Exeter University; Cambridge University
Qualifications: 11 O-levels, 3 A-levels, BA (Hons) History, PGCE History
Career outside cricket: Financial adviser
Off-season: Working for Sun Life of Canada (UK)
Overseas tours: Surrey U21 to Australia 1989-90; MCC to Kenya 1993
Overseas teams played for: Manly, Sydney 1988
Cricketers particularly admired: Sir Garfield Sobers, Geoff Boycott
Other sports followed: Hockey, rugby, baseball, football, most sports
Relaxations: Journalism, playing hockey for Wimbledon, drinking and travelling
Extras: Was captain of Surrey U21. First-class debut for Cambridge University in the 1992 season
Opinions on cricket: 'The game has to adapt to allow as many people as possible to be able to watch and play the game. Matches could be played at night when people do not have to work. Eventually cricket supporters will be able to watch Test match cricket from around the world on television throughout the year, and so counties will have to work even harder to maintain membership levels. The dangers of wealthier clubs who can attract the best players trying to form the equivalent of football's Premier League might not be such a ridiculous notion in the future.'
Best batting: 62* Cambridge University v Oxford University, Lord's 1992
Best bowling: 3-65 Cambridge University v Kent, Fenner's 1992

1992 Season

	M	Inns	NO	Runs	HS	Avge	100s	50s	Ct	St	O	M	Runs	Wkts	Avge	Best	5wI	10wM
Test																		
All First	10	17	3	388	62 *	27.71	-	2	3	-	231.3	39	748	19	39.36	3-65	-	-
1-day Int																		
NatWest																		
B & H																		
Sunday																		

Career Performances

	M	Inns	NO	Runs	HS	Avge	100s	50s	Ct	St	Balls	Runs	Wkts	Avge	Best	5wI	10wM
Test																	
All First	10	17	3	388	62 *	27.71	-	2	3	-	1389	748	19	39.36	3-65	-	-
1-day Int																	
NatWest																	
B & H																	
Sunday																	

WILEMAN, J. R.   Nottinghamshire

Name: Jonathan Ritchie Wileman
Role: Right-hand bat
Born: 19 August 1970, Sheffield
Height: 6ft 1in **Weight:** 12st 12lbs
County debut: 1992
1st-Class 100s scored: 1
1st-Class catches: 2
Parents: Peter and Joan
Marital status: Single
Education: Malvern College; Salford
University
Qualifications: 12 O-levels, 3 A-levels
Off-season: In final year of Modern
Languages degree, playing cricket in
South Africa
Cricketers particularly admired:
Ian Botham, Geoff Boycott
Other sports followed: Football, skiing,
tennis

Relaxations: Listening to music, watching films, doing crosswords
Extras: Scored 109 on first-class debut for Notts v Cambridge University in 1992
Opinions on cricket: 'A fascinating game which is underestimated by much of the general public. It is a pity it is not played at a higher level in Europe.'
Best batting: 109 Nottinghamshire v Cambridge University, Trent Bridge 1992

1992 Season

	M	Inns	NO	Runs	HS	Avge	100s	50s	Ct	St	O	M	Runs	Wkts	Avge	Best	5wI	10wM
Test																		
All First	1	1	0	109	109	109.00	1	-	2	-								
1-day Int																		
NatWest																		
B & H																		
Sunday																		

Career Performances

	M	Inns	NO	Runs	HS	Avge	100s	50s	Ct	St	Balls	Runs	Wkts	Avge	Best	5wI	10wM
Test																	
All First	1	1	0	109	109	109.00	1	-	2	-							
1-day Int																	
NatWest																	
B & H																	
Sunday																	

WILLIAMS, J. R. A.   Glamorgan

Name: James Robert Alexander Williams
Role: Right-hand opening bat
Born: 20 July 1973, Neath
Height: 5ft 11in **Weight:** 11st 7lbs
Nickname: Vinnie
County debut: No first team appearance
Parents: John Philip and Beverly Anne
Marital status: Single
Family links with cricket: Father and
grandfather 'very competent' league
cricketers
Education: Clifton College Prep School;
Clifton College; Durham University
Qualifications: 9 GCSEs, 3 A-levels,
NCA Coaching Award
Off-season: At university
Overseas tours: Clifton College to
Barbados 1987 and 1991; Scorpions to
The Gambia 1991; Durham University
to South Africa 1992

Cricketers particularly admired: Mark Taylor, Carl Hooper
Other sports followed: Rugby, tennis
Relaxations: Most sports, music and 'perambulations'
Extras: Represented Welsh Schools and England U19
Opinions on cricket: 'I think that coloured clothing may well have a detrimental effect
on cricket at all levels.'

---

196. Who scored the most runs in the Britannic Assurance Championship
for Surrey last season?

WILLIAMS, N. F.   Middlesex

Name: Neil Fitzgerald Williams
Role: Right-hand bat, right-arm
fast-medium bowler
Born: 2 July 1962, Hopewell, St Vincent,
West Indies
Height: 5ft 10$^{1}/_{2}$in **Weight:** 11st 7lbs
Nickname: Joe
County debut: 1982
County cap: 1984
Test debut: 1990
Tests: 1
50 wickets in a season: 3
1st-Class 50s scored: 12
1st-Class 5 w. in innings: 16
1st-Class 10 w. in match: 2
1st-Class catches: 54
Place in batting averages: 234th av. 13.28
(1991 228th av. 14.62)
Place in bowling averages: 27th av. 26.72
(1991 92nd av. 35.48)

Strike rate: 54.62 (career 54.53)
Parents: Alexander and Aldreta
Marital status: Single
Family links with cricket: 'Uncle Joe was 12th man for St Vincent and played 1st Division cricket.'
Education: Cane End Primary School, St Vincent; Acland Burghley School, Tufnell Park
Qualifications: School Leaver's Certificate, 6 O-levels, 1 A-level
Off-season: May be playing in the West Indies
Overseas tours: English Counties to Zimbabwe 1985; MCC to Leeward Islands 1992
Overseas teams played for: St Vincent 1982-92; Windward Islands 1982-92; Tasmania 1983-84
Cricketers particularly admired: Viv Richards, Desmond Haynes, Mike Gatting, David Gower
Other sports followed: Athletics
Relaxations: Music (socalypso, zouk, reggae), 'cooking soul food'
Extras: Was on stand-by for England in New Zealand and Pakistan 1983-84. Test debut v India at The Oval in 1990. Took 8-75 v Gloucestershire 1992
Opinions on cricket: 'Championship cricket should not be back to back. The bouncer rule should be changed, it should be up to the umpires to intervene after the second bouncer in the over.'
Best batting: 77 Middlesex v Warwickshire, Edgbaston 1991
Best bowling: 8-75 Middlesex v Gloucestershire, Lord's 1992

1992 Season

	M	Inns	NO	Runs	HS	Avge	100s	50s	Ct	St	O	M	Runs	Wkts	Avge	Best	5wI	10wM
Test																		
All First	17	17	3	186	46 *	13.28	-	-	9	-	437	86	1283	48	26.72	8-75	2	1
1-day Int																		
NatWest	2	1	0	4	4	4.00	-	-	1	-	10	0	55	1	55.00	1-55	-	
B & H	6	3	1	32	22	16.00	-	-	2	-	57.2	8	179	9	19.88	3-25	-	
Sunday	17	4	2	10	5 *	5.00	-	-	7	-	114	7	527	18	29.27	3-34	-	

Career Performances

	M	Inns	NO	Runs	HS	Avge	100s	50s	Ct	St	Balls	Runs	Wkts	Avge	Best	5wI	10wM
Test	1	1	0	38	38	38.00	-	-	-	-	246	148	2	74.00	2-148	-	-
All First	198	232	46	3629	77	19.51	-	12	54	-	28088	15141	515	29.40	8-75	16	2
1-day Int																	
NatWest	19	10	3	49	10	7.00	-	-	4	-	913	618	15	41.20	4-36	-	
B & H	49	27	6	251	29 *	11.95	-	-	6	-	2611	1584	53	29.88	3-16	-	
Sunday	110	47	17	425	43	14.16	-	-	27	-	4509	3465	123	28.17	4-39	-	

WILLIAMS, R. C.　　　　　Gloucestershire

Name: Ricardo Cecil Williams
Role: Right-hand bat, right-arm fast-medium bowler
Born: 7 February 1968, Camberwell, London
Height: 5ft 10in **Weight:** 11st
Nickname: Raw Deal, Tricky Ricky, Gus
County debut: 1991
1st-Class catches: 0
Place in batting averages: 245th av. 11.70
Parents: Wilfred Harry Williams and Cecile Yvonne Jordan
Marital status: Single
Education: Haringey College; Ellerslie Secondary School, Barbados; Haringey Cricket College
Qualifications: 3 O-levels, NCA coaching award
Overseas tours: Haringey Cricket College to Jamaica 1988,1989,1990
Overseas teams played for:
Geelong City, Victoria, Australia 1991-92

Cricketers particularly admired: Malcolm Marshall, Viv Richards, Richie Richardson, Jimmy Cook, Gordon Greenidge, Jack Russell, David Lawrence
Other sports followed: Football, tennis, volleyball, basketball, athletics, baseball
Relaxations: Listening to music, buying clothes, relaxing with friends, watching videos
Extras: Rapid Cricketline Player of the Year
Opinions on cricket: 'Prepare faster wickets for batsmen and bowlers to compete on in both 1st and 2nd XIs.'
Best batting: 44 Gloucestershire v Nottinghamshire, Worksop 1992
Best bowling: 3-44 Gloucestershire v Pakistan, Bristol 1992

1992 Season

	M	Inns	NO	Runs	HS	Avge	100s	50s	Ct	St	O	M	Runs	Wkts	Avge	Best	5wI	10wM
Test																		
All First	7	11	1	117	44	11.70	-	-	-	-	77.3	10	300	5	60.00	3-44	-	-
1-day Int																		
NatWest																		
B & H																		
Sunday	1	0	0	0	0	-	-	-	-	-	6	0	32	0	-		-	-

Career Performances

	M	Inns	NO	Runs	HS	Avge	100s	50s	Ct	St	Balls	Runs	Wkts	Avge	Best	5wI	10wM
Test																	
All First	8	13	1	130	44	10.83	-	-	-	-	621	381	6	63.50	3-44	-	-
1-day Int																	
NatWest																	
B & H																	
Sunday	1	0	0	0	0	-	-	-	-	-	36	32	0	-		-	-

197. Who scored the most runs in the Britannic Assurance Championship for Sussex last season?

WILLIAMS, R. C. J.   Gloucestershire

Name: Richard Charles James Williams
Role: Left-hand bat, wicket-keeper
Born: 8 August 1969, Bristol
Height: 5ft 10in **Weight:** 10st 5lbs
Nickname: Reggie
County debut: 1990
1st-Class 50s scored: 2
1st-Class catches: 53
1st-Class stumpings: 12
Parents: Michael (deceased 1991)
and Angela
Marital status: Single
Family links with cricket: Father played
local club cricket
Education: Clifton College
Preparatory School, Millfield School
Qualifications: PE Diploma
Off-season: Temporary work
Overseas tours: Gloucestershire to
Namibia 1990, to Kenya 1991
Overseas teams played for: Manicaland, Zimbabwe 1990-91
Cricketers particularly admired: Andy Brassington, Jack Russell, Alan Knott, David
Gower
Other sports followed: Football, hockey, squash, windsurfing
Relaxations: Listening to music, watching and playing sport
Best batting: 55* Gloucestershire v Derbyshire, Gloucester 1991

1992 Season

	M	Inns	NO	Runs	HS	Avge	100s	50s	Ct	St	O	M	Runs	Wkts	Avge	Best	5wI	10wM
Test																		
All First	5	5	2	51	18 *	17.00	-	-	8	5								
1-day Int																		
NatWest																		
B & H																		
Sunday	3	1	0	17	17	17.00	-	-	3	-								

	M	Inns	NO	Runs	HS	Avge	100s	50s	Ct	St	Balls	Runs	Wkts	Avge	Best	5wl	10wM
Test																	
All First	23	25	8	278	55 *	16.35	-	2	53	12							
1-day Int																	
NatWest																	
B & H																	
Sunday	9	1	0	17	17	17.00	-	-	8	-							

WILLIAMS, R. G.   Northamptonshire

Name: Richard Grenville Williams
Role: Right-hand bat, off-spin bowler
Born: 10 August 1957, Bangor, Wales
Height: 5ft 6in **Weight:** 12st
Nickname: Chippy
County debut: 1974
County cap: 1979
Benefit: 1989 (£100,053)
1000 runs in a season: 6
1st-Class 50s scored: 55
1st-Class 100s scored: 18
1st-Class 5 w. in innings: 9
1st-Class catches: 99
One-Day 50s: 22
Place in batting averages:
(1991 136th av. 28.00)
Strike rate: (career 71.85)
Parents: Gordon and Rhianwen
Wife and date of marriage:
Helen Laura, 24 April 1982

Children: Bryn Reece, 3 October 1991
Family links with cricket: Father played for Caernarvonshire and North Wales
Education: Ellesmere Port Grammar School
Career outside cricket: Qualified carpenter (self-employed)
Off-season: Working – carpentry and joinery
Overseas tours: England YC to West Indies 1976; English Counties to Zimbabwe 1985
Other sports followed: Golf
Injuries: Forced to retire at end of 1992 season by a persistent knee injury
Relaxations: Fly fishing, shooting, fly tying
Extras: Debut for 2nd XI in 1972 aged 14 years 11 months. Made maiden century in 1979 and then scored four centuries in five innings. Hat-trick v Gloucestershire, at Northampton

1980. Was first player to score a century against the 1980 West Indies touring team. Was stand-by for England tour to India 1981-82.
Best batting: 175* Northamptonshire v Leicestershire, Leicester 1980
Best bowling: 7-73 Northamptonshire v Cambridge University, Fenner's 1980

1992 Season

	M	Inns	NO	Runs	HS	Avge	100s	50s	Ct	St	O	M	Runs	Wkts	Avge	Best	5wI	10wM
Test																		
All First	2	3	0	29	14	9.66	-	-	-	-	31	5	83	4	20.75	3-42	-	-
1-day Int																		
NatWest																		
B & H	4	4	2	26	18 *	13.00	-	-	-	-	16	1	64	1	64.00	1-35	-	
Sunday	3	3	1	14	9 *	7.00	-	-	-	-	11	0	78	1	78.00	1-54	-	

Career Performances

	M	Inns	NO	Runs	HS	Avge	100s	50s	Ct	St	Balls	Runs	Wkts	Avge	Best	5wI	10wM
Test																	
All First	284	447	65	11817	175 *	30.93	18	55	99	-	27016	12722	376	33.83	7-73	9	-
1-day Int																	
NatWest	36	32	6	567	94	21.80	-	2	13	-	1512	844	35	24.11	4-10	-	
B & H	55	46	13	1038	83	31.45	-	7	10	-	1656	999	30	33.30	4-41	-	
Sunday	171	141	28	2612	82	23.11	-	13	43	-	3296	2732	92	29.69	5-30	1	

WINDOWS, M. G. N.   Gloucestershire

Name: Matthew Guy Newman Windows
Role: Right-hand bat
Born: 5 April 1973, Bristol
Height: 5ft 7in
Nickname: Steamy
County debut: 1992
1st-Class 50s scored: 1
1st-Class catches: 1
Parents: Tony and Caroline
Marital status: Single
Family links with cricket: Father (A.R) played for Cambridge University and Gloucestershire
Education: Clifton College and Durham University
Career outside cricket: Student
Off-season: At university

Overseas tours: England U19 to
Pakistan 1991-92, to India 1992-93;
Durham University to South Africa 1992
Other sports followed: Rackets
Extras: Played for Lincolnshire,
England U19 home series against
Sri Lanka
Best batting:
71 Gloucestershire v Essex,
Bristol 1992

1992 Season

	M	Inns	NO	Runs	HS	Avge	100s	50s	Ct	St	O	M	Runs	Wkts	Avge	Best	5wI	10wM
Test																		
All First	1	1	0	71	71	71.00	-	1	1	-								
1-day Int																		
NatWest																		
B & H																		
Sunday																		

Career Performances

	M	Inns	NO	Runs	HS	Avge	100s	50s	Ct	St	Balls	Runs	Wkts	Avge	Best	5wI	10wM
Test																		
All First	1	1	0	71	71	71.00	-	1	1	-								
1-day Int																		
NatWest																		
B & H																		
Sunday																		

198. Who scored the most runs in the Britannic Assurance Championship
for Warwickshire last season?

WOOD, J.   Durham

Name: John Wood
Role: Right-hand bat, right-arm fast-medium bowler
Born: 22 July 1970, Wakefield
Height: 6ft 3in **Weight:** 15st
Nickname: Jugga, Angry
County debut: 1992
1st-Class 5 w. in innings: 1
1st-Class catches: 1
Place in bowling averages: 57th av. 31.41
Strike rate: 47.41 (career 47.41)
Parents: Brian and Anne
Marital status: Single
Family links with cricket: Father played village cricket for over 20 years
Education: Crofton High School; Wakefield District College; Leeds Polytechnic
Qualifications: HND in Electrical and Electronic Engineering
Off-season: 'No idea'
Overseas teams played for: Griqualand West Cricket Union, South Africa 1990-91
Cricketers particularly admired: Robin Smith, Wayne Larkins, Paul Parker
Injuries: Rib catilage, medial ligament in knee, ankle, out for two months in total
Relaxations: TV, going to the pub with friends, snooker, all sports and holidays
Extras: Has been playing in the Bradford League. Made his debut for Durham in 1991
Opinions on cricket: 'Not playing long enough to comment.'
Best batting: 28 Durham v Worcestershire, Worcester 1992
Best bowling: 5-68 Durham v Hampshire, Southampton 1992

1992 Season

	M	Inns	NO	Runs	HS	Avge	100s	50s	Ct	St	O	M	Runs	Wkts	Avge	Best	5wI	10wM
Test																		
All First	8	6	1	80	28	16.00	-	-	1	-	134.2	17	534	17	31.41	5-68	1	-
1-day Int																		
NatWest	2	0	0	0	0	-	-	-	-	-	7	1	22	2	11.00	2-22	-	
B & H																		
Sunday	4	2	1	8	4 *	8.00	-	-	-	-	19	0	117	3	39.00	2-58	-	

Career Performances

	M	Inns	NO	Runs	HS	Avge	100s	50s	Ct	St	Balls	Runs	Wkts	Avge	Best	5wI	10wM
Test																	
All First	8	6	1	80	28	16.00	-	-	1	-	806	534	17	31.41	5-68	1	-
1-day Int																	
NatWest	3	1	0	1	1	1.00	-	-	-	-	102	104	2	52.00	2-22	-	
B & H																	
Sunday	4	2	1	8	4 *	8.00	-	-	-	-	114	117	3	39.00	2-58	-	

WOOD, J. R.   Hampshire

Name: Julian Ross Wood
Role: Left-hand bat, right-arm medium
bowler
Born: 21 November 1968, Winchester,
Hampshire
Height: 5ft 7in **Weight:** 13st
Nickname: Woody, Clubber Lang
County debut: 1989
1st-Class 50s scored: 5
One-Day 50s: 3
1st-Class catches: 13
Place in batting averages: 165th av. 24.50
Parents: Ross and Susan
Marital status: Engaged to Heather
Children: Chanel Yasmin, 10 March 1992
Family links with cricket: Father
NCA coach, Minor Counties umpire, and
also played in local league
Education: St Bart's Prep School; Priors
Court School; Leighton Park School
Qualifications: 3 O-levels, NCA coach (Grade 11)
Off-season: 'Deciding where my future lies, keeping fit, coaching and trying to make ends
meet.'
Overseas tours: Berkshire U19 to Sri Lanka 1987; MCC YC to Hong Kong 1988;
Hampshire to Barbados 1990
Overseas teams played for: Newcastle City, Sydney 1989-91
Cricketers particularly admired: Ian Botham, Robin and Chris Smith, Viv Richards,
Malcolm Marshall
Other sports followed: Football (Manchester United), rugby league and most sports
Relaxations: 'Good pubs and restaurants, good beer, listening to Bryan Adams and Jimmy
Barnes, spending time with my lovely family.'

Extras: Hit first ball in first-class cricket for four as he scored 65 on debut v Sussex. England Schools U15, U19. MCC Young Professionals groundstaff. Hampshire Young Player of the Year, 1989. Won first Man of the Match award in B&H Cup against Minor Counties 1991. Hit 40 sixes in the 2nd XI Championship 1991
Opinions on cricket: '2nd team matches must be played on first-class pitches, the state of 2nd team wickets last year was a disgrace which is no help to either batsman or bowler. I think it's sad that players keep playing after their time, hanging on just to receive a benefit.'
Best batting: 96 Hampshire v Northamptonshire, Northampton 1989
Best bowling: 1-5 Hampshire v Sussex, Southampton 1989

1992 Season

	M	Inns	NO	Runs	HS	Avge	100s	50s	Ct	St	O	M	Runs	Wkts	Avge	Best	5wl	10wM
Test																		
All First	10	13	1	294	57	24.50	-	1	6	-								
1-day Int																		
NatWest																		
B & H																		
Sunday	7	7	0	96	35	13.71	-	-	2	-								

Career Performances

	M	Inns	NO	Runs	HS	Avge	100s	50s	Ct	St	Balls	Runs	Wkts	Avge	Best	5wl	10wM
Test																	
All First	26	35	3	935	96	29.21	-	5	13	-	63	38	1	38.00	1-5	-	-
1-day Int																	
NatWest	2	1	1	3	3 *	-		-	-	-							
B & H	5	5	2	133	70 *	44.33	-	1	3	-							
Sunday	24	22	0	408	66	18.54	-	2	6	-							

WOOD, N. T.   Lancashire

Name: Nathan Theodore Wood
Role: Left-hand bat, right-arm medium bowler
Born: 4 October 1974, Thornhill Edge, Yorkshire
Height: 5ft 8in **Weight:** 10st
Nickname: Bolser
County debut: No first team appearance
Parents: Barry and Janet
Marital status: Single
Family links with cricket: Father played for Lancashire and England, uncle (Ron) played for Yorkshire
Education: Altrincham Prep School;
William Holmes Grammar School

Qualifications: 8 GCSEs
Off-season: At school, touring in South Africa with England U18
Overseas tours: England U18 to South Africa 1992-93
Cricketers particularly admired: David Gower, Michael Holding
Other sports followed: Football, rugby
Relaxations: Listening to music, being with friends, socialising, reading
Extras: Represented England U14, U15, U17, U18, U19

WREN, T. N.   Kent

Name: Timothy Neil Wren
Role: Right-hand bat, left-arm medium bowler
Born: 26 March 1970, Folkestone
Height: 6ft 3in **Weight:** 14st 7lbs
Nickname: Bear
County debut: 1989 (one-day), 1990 (first-class)
1st-Class catches: 4
Parents: James and Gillian
Marital status: Single
Family links with cricket: Father played local cricket so did brother 'who is still staging a remarkable comeback'
Education: Lyminge Primary; Harvey Grammar School, Folkestone
Qualifications: 6 O-levels; NCA coaching certificate
Off-season: Working, playing rugby, staying fit
Overseas teams played for: Universals, Zimbabwe 1989-90
Cricketers particularly admired: John Lever, David Gower

Other sports followed: Rugby, golf and 'almost any other sport'
Relaxations: Real ales, good food
Extras: First played for Kent 2nd XI in 1987, aged 17
Opinions on cricket: ' The rules regarding overseas players should be revised. Sunday League should have remained 40 overs.'
Best batting: 16 Kent v Essex, Canterbury 1990
Best bowling: 3-14 Kent v Oxford University, The Parks 1991

1992 Season

	M	Inns	NO	Runs	HS	Avge	100s	50s	Ct	St	O	M	Runs	Wkts	Avge	Best	5wI	10wM
Test																		
All First	1	0	0	0	0	-	-	-	2	-	24	4	92	5	18.40	3-54	-	-
1-day Int																		
NatWest																		
B & H																		
Sunday																		

Career Performances

	M	Inns	NO	Runs	HS	Avge	100s	50s	Ct	St	Balls	Runs	Wkts	Avge	Best	5wI	10wM
Test																	
All First	7	5	2	23	16	7.66	-	-	4	-	993	629	15	41.93	3-14	-	-
1-day Int																	
NatWest																	
B & H																	
Sunday	3	1	1	0	0*	-	-	-	-	-	111	105	3	35.00	1-31	-	

199. Who scored the most runs in the Britannic Assurance Championship for Worcestershire last season?

WRIGHT, A. J.   Gloucestershire

Name: Anthony John Wright
Role: Right-hand bat, off-spin bowler,
county captain
Born: 27 July 1962, Stevenage,
Hertfordshire
Height: 6ft **Weight:** 14st
Nickname: Billy, Horace
County debut: 1982
County cap: 1987
1000 runs in a season: 4
1st-Class 50s scored: 49
1st-Class 100s scored: 12
1st-Class catches: 140
One-Day 50s: 29
One-Day 100s: 1
Place in batting averages: 153rd av. 25.73
(1991 38th av. 45.60)
Parents: Michael and Patricia
Wife and date of marriage: Rachel,
21 December 1986
Children: Hannah, 3 April 1988
Education: Alleyn's School, Stevenage
Qualifications: 6 O-levels
Cricketers particularly admired: Viv Richards, Ian Botham, Malcolm Marshall, Jack
Russell
Other sports followed: All sports except motor racing
Relaxations: Eating out, reading, playing golf
Extras: Appointed captain of Gloucestershire for 1990
Best batting: 161 Gloucestershire v Glamorgan, Bristol 1987
Best bowling: 1-16 Gloucestershire v Yorkshire, Harrogate 1989

1992 Season

	M	Inns	NO	Runs	HS	Avge	100s	50s	Ct	St	O	M	Runs	Wkts	Avge	Best	5wl	10wM
Test																		
All First	19	33	3	772	128	25.73	1	3	11	-	2	0	27	0	-	-	-	-
1-day Int																		
NatWest	3	3	1	188	107 *	94.00	1	1	-	-								
B & H	5	5	0	144	62	28.80	-	1	1	-								
Sunday	16	13	1	365	93	30.41	-	3	6	-								

Career Performances

	M	Inns	NO	Runs	HS	Avge	100s	50s	Ct	St	Balls	Runs	Wkts	Avge	Best	5wl	10wM
Test																	
All First	205	352	26	9337	161	28.64	12	49	140	-	74	68	1	68.00	1-16	-	-
1-day Int																	
NatWest	20	19	1	794	107 *	44.11	1	8	4	-							
B & H	31	28	0	787	97	28.10	-	5	5	-							
Sunday	116	105	12	2339	93	25.15	-	16	45	-	26	22	0	-		-	-

YATES, G. Lancashire

Name: Gary Yates
Role: Right-hand bat, off-spin bowler
Born: 20 September 1967,
Ashton-under-Lyne
Height: 6ft 1in **Weight:** 12st 10lbs
Nickname: Yugo, Pearly, Backyard, Zippy
County debut: 1990
1st-Class 100s scored: 2
1st-Class catches: 10
Place in batting averages:
(1991 163rd av. 24.23)
Place in bowling averages:
(1991 141st av. 61.74)
Strike rate: (career 116.61)
Parents: Alan and Patricia
Marital status: Single
Family links with cricket: Father played
in Lancashire Leagues
Education: Manchester Grammar School
Qualifications: 6 O-levels,
Australian Coaching Council coach
Off-season: Playing and coaching in South Africa
Overseas tours: Lancs to Tasmania and Western Australia 1990, to Western Australia
1991, to Johannesburg 1992, to Barbados and St Lucia 1992
Overseas teams played for: South Barwon, Geelong, Australia 1987-88; Johnsonville,
Wellington, New Zealand 1989-90; Western Suburbs, Brisbane 1991-92
Cricketers particularly admired: Michael Atherton, Ian Botham, John Emburey
Other sports followed: All sports, especially football, golf, motor rallying
Relaxations: Playing golf, watching football and good films, eating
Extras: Played for Worcestershire 2nd XI in 1987; made debut for Lancashire 2nd XI in
1988 and taken on to county staff in 1990; scored century on Championship debut v

Nottinghamshire at Trent Bridge. Rapid Cricketline Player of the Month April/May 1992
Best batting: 106 Lancashire v Nottinghamshire, Trent Bridge 1990
Best bowling: 4-94 Lancashire v Sri Lanka, Old Trafford 1990

1992 Season

	M	Inns	NO	Runs	HS	Avge	100s	50s	Ct	St	O	M	Runs	Wkts	Avge	Best	5wI	10wM
Test																		
All First																		
1-day Int																		
NatWest																		
B & H																		
Sunday	1	0	0	0	0	-	-	-	-	-								

Career Performances

	M	Inns	NO	Runs	HS	Avge	100s	50s	Ct	St	Balls	Runs	Wkts	Avge	Best	5wI	10wM
Test																	
All First	25	30	15	480	106	32.00	2	-	10	-	4548	2334	39	59.84	4-94	-	-
1-day Int																	
NatWest																	
B & H	3	0	0	0	0	-	-	-	1	-	132	85	2	42.50	2-50	-	
Sunday	5	0	0	0	0	-	-	-	-	-	120	125	2	62.50	2-45	-	

200. Who scored the most runs in the Britannic Assurance Championship for Yorkshire last season?

THE UMPIRES

BALDERSTONE, J. C.

Name: John Christopher Balderstone
Role: Right-hand opening bat, slow
left-arm bowler
Born: 16 November 1940, Huddersfield
Height: 6ft 1in **Weight:** 12st 10lbs
Nickname: Baldy
Appointed to 1st-class list: 1988
Appointed to Test panel: Stand-by
umpire in 1991
Counties: Yorkshire, Leicestershire
County debut: 1961 (Yorks); 1971 (Leics)
County cap: 1973 (Leics)
Test debut: 1976
Tests: 2
1000 runs in a season: 11
1st-Class 50s scored: 102
1st-Class 100s scored: 32
1st-Class 5 w. in innings: 5
One-Day 50s: 32
One-Day 100s: 5
1st-Class catches: 210
Parents: Frank and Jennie (deceased)
Education: Paddock County School, Huddersfield
Qualifications: Advanced cricket coach, soccer coach
Career outside cricket: Former professional footballer, sales representative for various
products, cricket and soccer coach
Off-season: Coaching cricket
Other sports followed: Played soccer for Huddersfield Town, Carlisle United, Doncaster
Rovers and Queen of the South
Cricketers particularly admired: Willie Watson and Ray Illingworth
Relaxations: Golf
Best batting: 181* Leicestershire v Gloucestershire, Leicester 1984
Best bowling: 6-25 Leicestershire v Hampshire, Southampton 1978

First-Class Career Performances

	M	Inns	NO	Runs	HS	Avge	100s	Ct	St	Runs	Wkts	Avge	Best	5wI	10wM
Test	2	4	0	39	35	9.75	-	-	1	80	1	80.00	1-80	-	-
All First	390	619	61	19034	181 *	34.11	32	210	-	8160	310	26.32	6-25	5	-

BIRD, H. D.

Name: Harold Dennis Bird, MBE
Role: Right-hand opening bat
Born: 19 April 1933, Barnsley
Height: 5ft 10in **Weight:** 12st
Nickname: Dickie
Appointed to 1st-class list: 1969
Appointed to Test panel: 1972
Tests umpired: 50
One-Day Internationals umpired: 82
Counties: Yorkshire, Leicestershire
County debut: 1956 (Yorks); 1960 (Leics)
County cap: 1960 (Leics)
1000 runs in a season: 1
1st-Class 50s scored: 14
1st-Class 100s scored: 2
1st-Class catches: 20
Parents: James Harold and Ethel
Marital status: Bachelor
Education: Raley School, Barnsley

Qualifications: MCC advanced cricket coach
Career outside cricket: 'Cricket is my life.'
Off-season: After-dinner speaking
Cricketing superstitions or habits: Twitch of the shoulders, wears distinctive white cap
Other sports followed: Football
Cricketers particularly admired: Sir Garfield Sobers, Dennis Lillee, Viv Richards
Cricketers particularly learnt from: Sir Gubby Allen, Johnny Wardle
Relaxations: Listening to recordings of Barbra Streisand and Diana Ross
Extras: Has umpired 132 international matches to date. Has umpired three World Cup finals at Lord's (1975,1979,1983). Also umpired at the World Cup in India in 1987. Umpired the Queen's Silver Jubilee Test, England v Australia 1977, the Centenary Test, England v Australia 1980 and the MCC Bi-Centenary Test, England v Rest of the World 1987. In 1982 he umpired the Women's World Cup final in Christchurch, New Zealand. During the mid-1980s he umpired several times in the various competitions staged at Sharjah, UAE. To date he has umpired 32 Cup finals all over the world, as well as the finals of other cricket events such as The Best All-rounder in the World, The Best Batsman in the World and the World Double Wicket competition. In 1977 he was voted Yorkshire Personality of the Year. He is the author of three bestselling books, Not Out, That's Out and From the Pavilion End. Despite lucrative offers to join the 'Packer circus' and to visit South Africa with rebel tours, he remained loyal to the TCCB and to the established game on which he had been brought up in Yorkshire and which had given him so much in life. In June 1986 he was made a Member of the Most Excellent Order of the British Empire (MBE) in the Queen's Birthday Honours List. With David Shepherd and Steve Bucknor

became the first ICC officially-sponsored umpires in 1992, and was appointed to stand in the Zimbabwe's first Test match (against India) in Harare. Subsequently in Zimbabwe's second Test against New Zealand (also in Harare) he became the first umpire to officiate in 50 Test matches, having passed Frank Chester's world record of 48 Tests at Bulawayo six days earlier.

Opinions on cricket: 'The greatest game in the world. A game to be enjoyed by young and old. I have consistently advocated playing through all light unless the umpires are convinced that there is genuine physical danger to the batsman

Best batting: 181* Yorkshire v Glamorgan, Bradford 1959

First-Class Career Performances

	M	Inns	NO	Runs	HS	Avge	100s	Ct	St	Runs	Wkts	Avge	Best	5wI	10wM
Test															
All First	93	170	10	3314	181 *	20.71	2	28	-	22	0	-	-	-	-

BOND, J. D.

Name: John David Bond
Role: Right-hand bat
Born: 6 May 1932, Kearsley, Lancashire
Nickname: Jackie
Appointed to 1st-class list: 1988
Counties: Lancashire, Nottinghamshire
County debut: 1955 (Lancashire); 1974 (Nottinghamshire)
County cap: 1961 (Lancashire)
1000 runs in a season: 2
1st-Class 50s scored: 54
1st-Class 100s scored: 14
1st-Class catches: 223
Education: Bolton School
Extras: Captain of Lancashire 1968-1972, during which time Lancashire won the Gillette Cup three years in succession, 1970,1971,1972, and the John Player Sunday League in 1969 and 1970. He

moved to Nottinghamshire in 1974 and was a Test selector in the same year. He was appointed Cricket Manager at Lancashire CCC in 1980 and held the position until 1986
Best batting: 157 Lancashire v Hampshire, Old Trafford 1962

First-Class Career Performances

	M	Inns	NO	Runs	HS	Avge	100s	Ct	St	Runs	Wkts	Avge	Best	5wI	10wM
Test															
All First	362	548	80	12125	157	25.90	14	222	-	69	0	-	-	-	-

BURGESS, G. I.

Name: Graham Iefvion Burgess
Role: Right-hand bat, right-arm
medium bowler
Born: 5 May 1943,
Glastonbury, Somerset
Appointed to 1st-class list: 1991
County: Somerset
County debut: 1966
County cap: 1968
Testimonial: 1977
1st-Class 100s scored: 2
1st-Class 5 w. in innings: 18
1st-Class 10 w. in match: 2
1st-Class catches: 120
Education: Millfield School
Extras: Played Minor Counties cricket
for Wiltshire 1981-82 and for
Cambridgeshire 1983-84

Best batting: 129 Somerset v Gloucestershire,
Taunton 1973
Best bowling: 7-43 Somerset v Oxford University, The Parks 1975

First-Class Career Performances

	M	Inns	NO	Runs	HS	Avge	100s	Ct	St	Runs	Wkts	Avge	Best	5wI	10wM
Test															
All First	252	414	37	7129	129	18.90	2	120	-	13543	474	28.57	7-43	18	2

CONSTANT, D. J.

Name: David John Constant
Role: Left-hand bat, slow left-arm bowler
Born: 9 November 1941,
Bradford-on-Avon, Wiltshire
Nickname: Connie
Appointed to 1st-class list: 1969
Appointed to Test panel: 1971
Tests umpired: 36
One-Day Internationals umpired: 27
Counties: Kent, Leicestershire
County debut: 1961 (Kent);
1965 (Leicestershire)
1st-Class 50s scored: 6
1st-Class catches: 33
Extras: County bowls player for
Gloucestershire 1984-86
Best batting:
80 Leicestershire v Gloucestershire,
Bristol 1966

First-Class Career Performances

	M	Inns	NO	Runs	HS	Avge	100s	Ct	St	Runs	Wkts	Avge	Best	5wl	10wM
Test															
All First	61	93	14	1517	80	19.20	-	33	-	36	1	36.00	1-28	-	-

DUDLESTON, B.

Name: Barry Dudleston
Role: Right-hand opening bat, slow
left-arm bowler, occasional wicket-keeper
Born: 16 July 1945, Bebington, Cheshire
Height: 5ft 9in **Weight:** 13st
Nickname: Danny, Dapper
Appointed to 1st-class list: 1984
Appointed to Test panel: 1991
Tests umpired: 2
One-Day Internationals umpired: 1
Counties: Leicestershire, Gloucestershire
County debut: 1966 (Leics); 1981 (Gloucs)
County cap: 1969 (Leics)
Benefit: 1980 (£25,000)
1000 runs in a season: 8
1st-Class 100s scored: 32
1st-Class 200s scored: 1
One-Day 50s: 21
One-Day 100s: 4
1st-Class catches: 234
Parents: Percy and Dorothy Vera
Marital status: Divorced
Children: Sharon Louise, 29 October 1968; Matthew Barry 12 September 1988
Education: Stockport School
Qualifications: O-levels, junior coaching certificate, Shell marketing exams
Career outside cricket: Managing Director of Sunsport Tours
Other sports followed: Most
Cricketers particularly admired: Gary Sobers, Tom Graveney
Cricketers particularly learnt from: Vinoo Mankad
Relaxations: TV, bridge, wine, golf
Extras: Played for England U25. Suffered badly from broken fingers, broke fingers on the same hand three times in 1978. Played for Rhodesia in the Currie Cup 1976-80
Opinions on cricket: 'It is still the greatest test of skill and character – beautiful to watch when played well. Am worried about the declining standards of behaviour.'
Best batting: 202 Leicestershire v Derbyshire, Leicester 1979
Best bowling: 4-6 Leicestershire v Surrey, Leicester 1972

First-Class Career Performances

	M	Inns	NO	Runs	HS	Avge	100s	Ct	St	Runs	Wkts	Avge	Best	5wl	10wM
Test															
All First	295	501	47	14747	202	32.48	32	234	7	1365	47	29.04	4-6	-	-

HAMPSHIRE, J. H.

Name: John Harry Hampshire
Role: Right-hand bat
Born: 10 February 1941,
Thurnscoe, Yorkshire
Appointed to 1st-class list: 1985
Appointed to Test panel: 1989
Tests umpired: 10
One-Day Internationals umpired: 5
Counties: Yorkshire, Derbyshire
County debut: 1961 (Yorkshire);
1982 (Derbyshire)
County cap: 1963 (Yorkshire);
1982 (Derbyshire)
Benefit: 1976
Test debut: 1969
Tests: 8
1000 runs in a season: 15
1st-Class 50s scored: 142
1st-Class 100s scored: 53
1st-Class catches: 445
1st-Class 5 w. in innings: 1
One-Day 50s: 39
One-Day 100s: 7
Parents: Jack and Vera
Wife: Judy
Children: Ian and Paul

Family links with cricket: Father (J.) and brother (A.W.) both played for Yorkshire.
Extras: Captained Yorkshire 1979-80. Played for Tasmania 1967-69 and 1977-79. Scored a century (107) in his first Test match, against West Indies at Lord's 1969. Appointed manager/coach of the Zimbabwe Test squad for their first Test matches against India and New Zealand
Best batting: 183* Yorkshire v Surrey, Hove 1971
Best bowling: 7-52 Yorkshire v Glamorgan, Cardiff 1963

First-Class Career Performances

	M	Inns	NO	Runs	HS	Avge	100s	Ct	St	Runs	Wkts	Avge	Best	5wI	10wM
Test	8	16	1	405	107	26.86	1	9	-						
All First	577	924	112	28059	183 *	34.55	43	445	-	1637	30	54.56	7-52	2	-

HARRIS, J. H.

Name: John Humphrey Harris
Role: Left-hand bat, right-arm
fast-medium bowler
Born: 13 February 1936, Taunton
Appointed to 1st-class list: 1983
County: Somerset
County debut: 1952
1st-Class catches: 6
Extras: Made his debut for Somerset
aged 16 years 99 days. Played Minor
Counties cricket for Suffolk (1960-62)
and Devon (1975)
Best batting:
41 Somerset v Worcestershire,
Taunton 1957
Best bowling:
3-29 Somerset v Worcestershire,
Bristol 1959

First-Class Career Performances

	M	Inns	NO	Runs	HS	Avge	100s	Ct	St	Runs	Wkts	Avge	Best	5wl	10wM
Test															
All First	15	18	4	154	41	11.00	-	6	-	609	19	32.05	3.29	-	-

HOLDER, J. W.

Name: John Wakefield Holder
Role: Right-hand bat, right-arm
fast-medium bowler
Born: 19 March 1945,
St George, Barbados
Height: 6ft **Weight:** 13st
Nickname: Benson
Appointed to 1st-class list: 1983
Appointed to Test panel: 1988
Tests umpired: 10
One-Day Internationals umpired: 8
County: Hampshire
County debut: 1968
50 wickets in a season: 1
1st-Class 5 w. in innings: 5
1st-Class 10 w. in match: 1
1st-Class catches: 12
Parents: Charles and Carnetta
Wife: Glenda
Children: Christopher 1968; Nigel 1970
Family links with cricket: Both sons have played for Royston in the Central Lancashire
League
Education: St Giles Boys School; Combermere High School, Barbados
Qualifications: 3 O-levels, MCC advanced cricket coach
Career outside cricket: Financial consultant
Off-season: Working as a financial consultant for Albany Life
Other sports followed: Football (Manchester United)
Cricketers particularly admired: Garfield Sobers, Richard Hadlee
Cricketers particularly learnt from: Encouraged by Everton Weekes as a schoolboy
Extras: Recorded best bowling figures in Rothmans International Cavaliers cricket
matches – 6-7 for Hampshire Cavaliers at Tichbourne Park in 1968. Played professional
league cricket in Yorkshire and Lancashire (1974-82). Took one first-class hat-trick,
Hampshire v Kent 1972, 'but finished with 3-100!'
Best batting: 33 Hampshire v Sussex, Hove 1971
Best bowling: 7-79 Hampshire v Gloucestershire, Gloucester 1972

First-Class Career Performances

	M	Inns	NO	Runs	HS	Avge	100s	Ct	St	Runs	Wkts	Avge	Best	5wI	10wM
Test															
All First	47	49	14	374	33	10.68	-	12	-	3415	139	24.56	7-79	5	1

HOLDER, V. A.

Name: Vanburn Alonza Holder
Role: Right-hand bat, right-arm
fast-medium bowler
Born: 8 October 1945,
St Michael, Barbados
Nickname: Van
Appointed to 1st-class list: 1992
County: Worcestershire
County debut: 1968
County cap: 1970
Test debut: 1969
Tests: 40
1st-Class 50s scored: 4
1st-Class 100s scored: 1
1st-Class 5 w. in innings: 38
1st-Class 10 w. in match: 3
1st-Class catches: 98
Overseas tours: West Indies to England
1969, 1973, 1976; to India Sri Lanka and

Pakistan 1974-75; Australia 1975-76; India and Sri Lanka 1978-79 (as vice-captain)
Extras: Made his debut for Barbados in the Shell Shield competition in 1966-67.
Best batting: 122 Barbados v Trinidad, Bridgetown 1973-74
Best bowling: 7-40 Worcestershire v Glamorgan, Cardiff 1974

First-Class Career Performances

	M	Inns	NO	Runs	HS	Avge	100s	Ct	St	Runs	Wkts	Avge	Best	5wI	10wM
Test	40	59	11	682	42	14.20	-	16	-	3627	109	33.27	6-28	3	-
All First	311	354	81	3559	122	13.03	1	98	-	23183	948	24.45	7-40	38	3

JONES, A. A.

Name: Alan Arthur Jones
Role: Right-hand bat, right-arm
fast-medium bowler
Born: 9 December 1947, Horley, Surrey
Height: 6ft 3in **Weight:** 14st
Nickname: Jonah
Appointed to 1st-class list: 1985
Counties: Sussex, Somerset,
Middlesex, Glamorgan
County debut: 1966 (Sussex);
1970 (Somerset); 1976 (Middlesex);
1980 (Glamorgan)
County cap: 1972 (Somerset);
1976 (Middlesex); 1980 (Glamorgan)
50 wickets in a season: 4
1st-Class 5 w. in innings: 23
1st-Class 10 w. in match: 3
1st-Class catches: 50
Parents: Leslie and Hazel
Marital status: Married
Education: St John's College, Horsham
Qualifications: 5 O-levels, MCC Advanced Coach, NCA Staff Coach
Career outside cricket: 'None at present'
Off-season: 'Generally enjoying life'
Overseas teams played for: Northern Transvaal 1972-73; Orange Free State 1976-77
Other sports followed: All sports
Cricketers particularly admired: Tom Cartwright
Cricketers particularly learnt from: Mike Brearley
Relaxations: Golf
Opinions on cricket: 'I would like to see the return of uncovered wickets in first-class cricket.'
Best batting: 33 Middlesex v Kent, Canterbury 1978
Best bowling: 9-51 Somerset v Sussex, Hove 1976

First-Class Career Performances

	M	Inns	NO	Runs	HS	Avge	100s	Ct	St	Runs	Wkts	Avge	Best	5wI	10wM
Test															
All First	214	216	68	799	33	5-39	-	50	-	15414	549	28.07	9-51	23	3

JULIAN, R.

Name: Raymond Julian
Role: Right-hand bat, wicket-keeper
Born: 23 August 1936,
Cosby, Leicestershire
Height: 5ft 11in **Weight:** 13st
Nickname: Julie
Appointed to 1st-class list: 1972
County: Leicestershire
County debut: 1953
County cap: 1961
1st-Class 50s scored: 2
1st-Class catches: 382
1st-Class stumpings: 39
Parents: George Ernest and Doris
Children:
Peter Raymond, 1 February 1958;
John Kelvin, 13 October 1960;
David Andrew, 15 October 1963;
Paul Anthony, 22 September 1967
Education: Wigston Secondary Modern
Career outside cricket: Cricket coach, painter, gardener
Cricketing superstitions or habits: Always put left shoe on first
Other sports followed: All sports. Played goalkeeper at football. First-class football referee for 15 years. Linesman on Southern League. Refereed one FA Cup fixture
Cricketers particularly admired: Gary Sobers, Keith Andrew
Cricketers particularly learnt from: Tony Lock, Willie Watson, Keith Andrew, Maurice Hallam
Relaxations: Gardening, holidays, travelling
Extras: Youngest player to make debut for Leicestershire (aged 15 years). Gave 8 lbw decisions in succession, Glamorgan v Sussex at Cardiff 1986. Played for the Army 1955-57. Has umpired three B&H semi-finals and one Gillette Cup semi-final. Took 6 catches in an innings, Leicestershire v Northants, Kettering 1965. Has been stand-by umpire for two Test matches
Opinions on cricket: 'Enjoy all cricket – believe in four-day cricket.'
Best batting: 51 Leicestershire v Worcestershire, Worcester 1962

First-Class Career Performances

	M	Inns	NO	Runs	HS	Avge	100s	Ct	St	Runs	Wkts	Avge	Best	5wI	10wM
Test															
All First	192	288	23	2581	51	9.73	-	381	40						

KITCHEN, M. J.

Name: Mervyn John Kitchen
Role: Left-hand bat, right-arm
medium bowler
Born: 1 August 1940,
Nailsea, Somerset
Appointed to 1st-class list: 1982
Appointed to Test panel: 1990
Tests umpired: 5
One-Day Internationals umpired: 5
County: Somerset
County debut: 1960
County cap: 1966
Testimonial: 1973
1000 runs in a season: 7
1st-Class 50s scored: 68
1st-Class 100s scored: 17
1st-Class catches: 157
One-Day 50s: 22
One-Day 100s: 1

Education: Blackwell Secondary Modern, Nailsea
Best batting: 189 Somerset v Pakistan, Taunton 1967

First-Class Career Performances

	M	Inns	NO	Runs	HS	Avge	100s	Ct	St	Runs	Wkts	Avge	Best	5wl	10wM
Test															
All First	354	612	32	15230	189	26.25	17	157	-	109	2	54.50	1-4	-	-

LEADBEATER, B.

Name: Barrie Leadbeater
Role: Right-hand opening bat, right-arm medium bowler, slip fielder
Born: 14 August 1943, Leeds
Height: 6ft **Weight:** 13st
Nickname: Leady
Appointed to 1st-class list: 1981
County: Yorkshire
County debut: 1966
County cap: 1969
Benefit: 1980 (joint benefit with G.A. Cope)
1st-Class 50s scored: 27
1st-Class 100s scored: 1
1st-Class catches: 82
One-Day 50s: 11
Parents: Ronnie (deceased) and Nellie
Wife and date of marriage: Jacqueline, 18 September 1971
Children: Richard Barrie, 23 November 1972; Michael Spencer, 21 March 1976; Daniel Mark Ronnie, 19 June 1981
Education: Brownhill County Primary; Harehills Secondary Modern, Leeds
Qualifications: 2 O-levels
Career outside cricket: Coach, driver
Overseas tours: Duke of Norfolk's XI to West Indies 1970
Overseas teams played for: Johannesburg Municipals 1978-79
Other sports followed: Rugby union, most other sports
Cricketers particularly admired: Colin Cowdrey, Clive Rice, Richard Hadlee, Gary Sobers, Michael Holding
Cricketers learnt from: Brian Close, Willie Watson, Arthur Mitchell, Maurice Leyland
Relaxations: Family, car maintenance, DIY, music
Opinions on cricket: 'Disappointed in players who lack self-control and professional pride and set bad examples to young players and public alike. Public should be regularly and properly informed during stoppages in play. Stoppages for bad light cause more frustration for public, players and, not least, umpires and a change in regulations may be needed soon if the game is to retain its support and credibility.'
Best batting: 140* Yorkshire v Hampshire, Portsmouth 1976

First-Class Career Performances

	M	Inns	NO	Runs	HS	Avge	100s	Ct	St	Runs	Wkts	Avge	Best	5wI	10wM
Test															
All First	147	241	29	5373	140 *	25.34	1	82	-	5	1	5.00	1-1	-	-

MEYER, B. J.

Name: Barrie John Meyer
Role: Right-hand bat, wicket-keeper
Born: 21 August 1931, Bournemouth
Height: 5ft 10$\frac{1}{2}$in **Weight:** 12st 5lbs
Nickname: BJ
Appointed to 1st-class list: 1973
Appointed to Test panel: 1978
Tests umpired: 24
One-Day Internationals umpired: 22
County: Gloucestershire
County debut: 1957
County cap: 1958
Benefit: 1971
1st-Class 50s scored: 11
1st-Class catches: 707
1st-Class stumpings: 118
Parents: Deceased
Wife and date of marriage: Gillian,
4 September 1965
Children: Stephen Barrie; Christopher John; Adrian Michael
Education: Boscombe Secondary School, Bournemouth
Career outside cricket: Salesman
Off-season: Coaching and umpiring in South Africa
Other sports followed: Golf (handicap 8), football (was a pro-footballer for Bristol Rovers, Plymouth Argyle, Newport County and Bristol City)
Cricketers particularly learnt from: Andy Wilson and Sonny Avery (coaches for Gloucestershire)
Relaxations: Golf, music, reading
Best batting: 63 (3 times) Gloucestershire v Indians, Cheltenham 1959; Gloucestershire v Oxford University, Bristol 1962; Gloucestershire v Sussex, Bristol 1964

First-Class Career Performances

	M	Inns	NO	Runs	HS	Avge	100s	Ct	St	Runs	Wkts	Avge	Best	5wI	10wM
Test															
All First	406	569	191	5367	63	14.19	-	707	118						

OSLEAR, D. O.

Name: Donald Osmund Oslear
Role: Right-hand bat, right-arm medium bowler
Born: 3 March 1929, Cleethorpes, Lincolnshire
Height: 6ft **Weight:** 14st 7lbs
Appointed to 1st-class list: 1975
Appointed to Test panel: 1980
Tests umpired: 5
One-Day Internationals umpired: 14
Parents: John Osmund and Violet Maude
Education: Elliston Street Senior School, Cleethorpes
Career outside cricket: Wholesale fish distribution, Grimsby
Off-season: 'In Sri Lanka helping their umpires and administrators to enhance their knowledge of the Laws of Cricket and standing in their four-day domestic tournament.'
Other sports followed: Professional soccer, ice hockey – 'I watch most sports.'
Cricketers particularly admired: Jimmy Cook, Garth Le Roux
Relaxations: Study of the Laws of Cricket and first-class playing regulations
Extras: Has umpired 4 one-day internationals in Zimbabwe
Opinions on cricket: 'One of the best things in recent years is the fact that South Africa will be playing again at the highest level. The worst thing will be the introduction of an independent panel of umpires.'

Did not play first-class cricket

PALMER, K. E.

Name: Kenneth Ernest Palmer
Role: Right-hand bat, right-arm
fast-medium bowler
Born: 22 April 1937, Winchester
Height: 5ft 10in **Weight:** 13st
Nickname: Pedlar
Appointed to 1st-class list: 1972
Appointed to Test panel: 1978
Tests umpired: 20
One-Day Internationals umpired: 9
County: Somerset
County debut: 1955
County cap: 1958
Testimonial: 1968
Test debut: 1965
Tests: 1
1000 runs in a season: 1
50 wickets in a season: 6
1st-Class 50s scored: 27
1st-Class 100s scored: 2
1st-Class 5 w. in innings: 46
1st-Class 10 w. in match: 5
1st-Class catches: 156
Parents: Harry and Cecilia

Wife and date of marriage: Wife deceased
Children: Gary Vincent, 6 September 1961
Education: Southbroom Secondary Modern, Devizes
Off-season: Decorating and gardening at home
Overseas tours: Commonwealth XI to Pakistan 1962; International Cavaliers to West
Indies 1963-64
Other sports followed: Football and squash
Cricketers particularly admired: Gary Sobers, Richard Hadlee, Viv Richards, David
Gower, Michael Holding, Malcolm Marshall
Cricketers particularly learnt from: Father and Maurice Tremlett
Relaxations: Car enthusiast
Extras: Called into Test side while coaching in South Africa 1964-65. Umpired two
Benson and Hedges finals and two NatWest finals. Twice on World Cup panel in England.
Won Carling Single Wicket Competition 1961. Did the 'double' in 1961 (114 wickets,
1036 runs). With Bill Alley holds the Somerset record for 6th wicket partnership.
Best batting: 125* Somerset v Northamptonshire, Northampton 1961
Best bowling: 9-57 Somerset v Nottinghamshire, Trent Bridge 1963

First-Class Career Performances

	M	Inns	NO	Runs	HS	Avge	100s	Ct	St	Runs	Wkts	Avge	Best	5wI	10wM
Test	1	1	0	10	10	10.00	-	-	-	189	1	189.00	1-113	-	-
All First	314	481	105	7771	125 *	20.66	2	156	-	18485	866	21.34	9-57	46	5

PALMER, R.

Name: Roy Palmer
Role: Right-hand bat, right-arm
fast-medium bowler
Born: 12 July 1942, Devizes, Wiltshire
Appointed to 1st-class list: 1980
Appointed to Test panel: 1992
Tests umpired: 1
One-Day Internationals umpired: 1
County: Somerset
County debut: 1965
50 wickets in a season: 1
1st-Class 50s scored: 1
1st-Class 5 w. in innings: 4
1st-Class catches: 25
Family links with cricket: Brother of
Ken Palmer, Test umpire and former
Somerset player, nephew Gary also
played for Somerset
Education: Southbroom Secondary
Modern, Devizes
Best batting:
84 Somerset v Leicestershire, Taunton 1967
Best bowling: 6-45 Somerset v Middlesex, Lord's 1967

First-Class Career Performances

	M	Inns	NO	Runs	HS	Avge	100s	Ct	St	Runs	Wkts	Avge	Best	5wI	10wM
Test															
All First	74	110	32	1037	84	13.29	-	25	-	5439	172	31.62	6-45	4	-

PLEWS, N. T.

Name: Nigel Trevor Plews
Role: Right-hand opening bat
Born: 5 September 1934, Nottingham
Height: 6ft 6½in **Weight:** 16st 8lbs
Appointed to 1st-class list: 1982
Appointed to Test panel: 1988
Tests umpired: 5
One-Day Internationals umpired: 4
Parents: Deceased
Wife and date of marriage:
Margaret, 1956
Children: Elaine, 1961; Douglas, 1964
Education: Mundella Grammar School,
Nottingham
Qualifications: School Certificate in
Commercial Subjects, RSA Advanced
Book-keeping
Career outside cricket: Nottingham City
Police for 25 years (Det Sgt in Fraud Squad)
Off-season: Employed by Touche Ross, Chartered Accountants, in insolvency work, as every year since 1980
Other sports played: Table tennis, swimming, soccer
Other sports followed: Rugby union
Relaxations: Hill-walking, reading, travel
Extras: Played local league and club cricket in Nottingham. Toured as umpire with MCC to Namibia 1991

Did not play first-class cricket

SHARP, G.

Name: George Sharp
Role: Right-hand bat, wicket-keeper
Born: 12 March 1950,
Hartlepool, County Durham
Height: 5ft 11in **Weight:** 15st
Nickname: Blunt, Razor, Sharpie
Appointed to 1st-class list: 1992
County: Northamptonshire
County debut: 1967
County cap: 1972
1st-Class catches: 565
1st-Class stumpings: 90
Parents: George and Grace
Wife: Audrey
Children: Gareth (aged 7)
Off-season: Working in Sales
Other sports followed: Most ball games
Cricketers particularly admired: Alan
Knott, Bob Taylor, Keith Andrew
Relaxations: Golf
Best batting: 98 Northamptonshire v Yorkshire, Northampton 1983

First-Class Career Performances

	M	Inns	NO	Runs	HS	Avge	100s	Ct	St	Runs	Wkts	Avge	Best	5wl	10wM
Test															
All First	306	396	81	6254	98	19.85	-	565	90	70	1	70.00	1-47	-	-

SHEPHERD, D. R.

Name: David Robert Shepherd
Role: Right-hand bat, right-arm
medium bowler
Born: 27 December 1940,
Bideford, Devon
Height: 5ft 10in **Weight:** 16st
Nickname: Shep
Appointed to 1st-class list: 1981
Appointed to Test panel: 1985
Tests umpired: 17
One-Day Internationals umpired: 'over 40'
County: Gloucestershire
County debut: 1965
County cap: 1969
Benefit: 1978 (joint benefit with J. Davey)
1000 runs in a season: 2
1st-Class 50s scored: 55
1st-Class 100s scored: 12
1st-Class catches: 95
One-Day 50s: 18
One-Day 100s: 2

Parents: Herbert and Doris (both deceased)
Marital status: Single
Education: Barnstable Grammar School; St Luke's College, Exeter
Career outside cricket: Teacher
Off-season: Assisting brother in local post office/newsagent. Umpiring World Cup in Australia/New Zealand
Cricketing superstitions or habits: 111 (Nelson!)
Other sports followed: Rugby, soccer, most ball sports
Cricketers particularly admired: Gary Sobers, Mike Procter
Relaxations: All sports, philately, TV
Extras: Played Minor Counties cricket for Devon 1959-64. Only Gloucestershire player to score a century on his first-class debut. Umpired the MCC Bi-Centenary Test, England v Rest of the World, at Lord's in 1987
Best batting: 153 Gloucestershire v Middlesex, Bristol 1968

First-Class Career Performances

	M	Inns	NO	Runs	HS	Avge	100s	Ct	St	Runs	Wkts	Avge	Best	5wl	10wM
Test															
All First	282	476	40	10672	153	24.47	12	95	-	106	2	53.00	1-1	-	-

STICKLEY, G. A.

Name: Gerald Albert Stickley
Role: Right-hand bat, wicket-keeper
Born: 24 September 1938, Birmingham
Height: 5ft 9$^{1}/_{2}$in **Weight:** 12st 6lbs
Appointed to 1st-class list: 1992
Parents: Albert and Dora (both deceased)
Wife: Janet
Children: Mark (aged 29), Diane (27),
Alan (21)
Education: Grammar school,
West Midlands
Career outside cricket: British Telecom
engineer; local government officer
(Social Services Dept)
Off-season: Employed by
Dorset County Council
Other sports followed: Soccer,
table tennis, golf
Cricketers particularly admired:
Jimmy Cook

Relaxations: Listening to music, especially jazz, reading
Opinions on cricket: 'Cricket should be entertaining with more thought given to the paying spectator.'

Did not play first-class cricket

WHITE, R. A.

Name: Robert Arthur White
Role: Left-hand bat, off-break bowler
Born: 6 October 1936, Fulham
Height: 5ft 9¹/₂in **Weight:** 12st 4lbs
Nickname: Knocker
Appointed to 1st-class list: 1982
Counties: Middlesex, Nottinghamshire
County debut: 1958 (Middlesex);
1966 (Nottinghamshire)
County cap: 1963 (Middlesex);
1966 (Nottinghamshire)
Benefit: 1974
1000 runs in a season: 1
50 wickets in a season: 2
1st-Class 50s scored: 50
1st-Class 100s scored: 5
1st-Class 5 w. in innings: 28
1st-Class 10 w. in match: 4
1st-Class catches: 190
Wife: Janice

Children: Robin and Vanessa
Education: Chiswick Grammar School
Qualifications: Matriculation
Career outside cricket: Self-employed salesman
Other sports followed: All sports – soccer, ice-hockey and horse racing in particular
Cricketers particularly admired: 'Garfield Sobers more than anyone else.'
Cricketers particularly learnt from: 'I tried to learn from everyone I encountered.'
Relaxations: Theatre-going
Extras: Made independent coaching trips to South Africa, 1959, 1960, 1966, 1967, 1968.
Together with M.J. Smedley broke the Nottinghamshire record for a 6th wicket partnership
with 204 v Surrey at The Oval 1966
Opinions on cricket: 'Too controversial to go into print.'
Best batting: 116* Nottinghamshire v Surrey, The Oval 1967
Best bowling: 7-41 Nottinghamshire v Derbyshire, Ilkeston 1971

First-Class Career Performances

	M	Inns	NO	Runs	HS	Avge	100s	Ct	St	Runs	Wkts	Avge	Best	5wI	10wM
Test															
All First	413	642	105	12452	116 *	23.18	5	190	-	21138	693	30.50	7-41	28	4

WHITEHEAD, A. G. T.

Name: Alan Geoffrey Thomas Whitehead
Role: Left-hand bat,
slow left-arm bowler
Born: 28 October 1940,
Butleigh, Somerset
Appointed to 1st-class list: 1970
Appointed to Test panel: 1982
Tests umpired: 5
County: Somerset
County debut: 1957
1st-Class 5 w. in innings: 3
1st-Class catches: 20
Best batting: 15 Somerset v Hampshire,
Southampton 1959
Best bowling: 6-74 Somerset v Sussex,
Eastbourne 1959

First-Class Career Performances

	M	Inns	NO	Runs	HS	Avge	100s	Ct	St	Runs	Wkts	Avge	Best	5wl	10wM
Test															
All First	38	49	25	137	15	5.70	-	20	-	2306	67	34.41	6-74	3	-

WIGHT, P. B.

Name: Peter Bernard Wight
Role: Right-hand bat, off-break bowler
Born: 25 June 1930,
Georgetown, British Guiana
Height: 5ft 10in **Weight:** 11st
Nickname: Flipper
Appointed to 1st-class list: 1966
County: Somerset
County debut: 1953
County cap: 1954
Benefit: 1963
1000 runs in a season: 10
1st-Class 50s scored: 207
1st-Class 100s scored: 26
1st-Class 200s scored: 2
1st-Class 5 w. in innings: 1
1st-Class catches: 204
Parents: Henry DeLisle and Mary Matilda
Wife and date of marriage: Joyce,
26 January 1957
Children: Paul Anthony and Anne-Marie
Family links with cricket: Three brothers played for British Guiana and one, G.L., played for the West Indies
Education: St Stanislaus College
Career outside cricket: Owns his own indoor cricket school
Off-season: Coaching and running his indoor school
Other sports followed: Football, hockey, squash, skittles, 'all ball games'
Cricketers particularly admired: Alec Bedser, Gary Sobers, Peter May, Ken Barrington, Tony Lock, Everton Weekes, Frank Worrell
Relaxations: Gardening, all kinds of sport
Extras: Has coached in East Africa and New Zealand. 'Encouraged in cricket by my father and brothers – Arnold, Norman and Leslie.'
Opinions on cricket: 'A game to be played and enjoyed by all. I am proud to be President of Somerset Wanderers Ladies Cricket Club.'
Best batting: 222 Somerset v Kent, Taunton 1959
Best bowling: 6-29 Somerset v Derbyshire, Chesterfield 1957

First-Class Career Performances

	M	Inns	NO	Runs	HS	Avge	100s	Ct	St	Runs	Wkts	Avge	Best	5wl	10wM
Test															
All First	333	590	53	17773	222 *	33.09	28	204	-	2262	68	33.26	6-29	1	-

WILLEY, P.

Name: Peter Willey
Role: Right-hand bat, off-break bowler
Born: 6 December 1949, Sedgefield,
Co Durham
Height: 6ft 1in **Weight:** 13st
Nickname: Chin, Will
Appointed to 1st-class list: 1993
Counties: Nothamptonshire,
Leicestershire
County debut: 1966 (Northants),
1984 (Leics)
County cap: 1971 (Northants),
1984 (Leics)
Benefit: 1981 (£31,400)
Test debut: 1976
Tests: 26
One-Day Internationals: 26
1000 runs in a season: 10
50 wickets in a season: 2
1st-Class 50s scored: 101
1st-Class 100s scored: 44
1st-Class 200s scored: 1
1st-Class 5 w. in innings: 26
1st-Class 10 w. in match: 3
1st-Class catches: 235
One-Day 50s: 63
One-Day 100s: 9

Parents: Oswald and Maisie
Wife and date of marriage: Charmaine, 23 September 1971
Children: Heather Jane, 11 September 1985
Family links with cricket: Father played local club cricket in County Durham
Education: Secondary School, Seaham, County Durham
Overseas tours: England to Australia and India 1979-80; West Indies 1980-81 and 1985-86; with unofficial England XI to South Africa 1981-82
Overseas teams played for: Eastern Province, South Africa 1982-85
Cricketers particularly admired: Bishen Bedi, Geoffrey Boycott
Other sports followed: Football, golf, rugby
Relaxations: Reading, taking Irish Setter for long walks and shooting, gardening
Extras: With Wayne Larkins, received 2016 pints of beer (seven barrels) from a brewery in Northampton as a reward for their efforts in Australia with England in 1979-80. Youngest player ever to play for Northamptonshire CCC at 16 years 180 days v Cambridge U in 1966. Banned from Test cricket for three years for joining England rebel tour of South

Africa in 1982. Left Northamptonshire at end of 1983 and moved to Leicestershire as vice-captain. Appointed Leicestershire captain for 1987, but resigned after only one season. Released by Leicestershire at the end of the 1991 season to play for Northumberland in 1992.

Opinions on cricket: 'Good pitches is the only way to get good cricketers. Four-day cricket won't make people better cricketers. Young players have things made too easy for them.'

Best batting: 227 Northamptonshire v Somerset, Northampton 1976

Best bowling: 7-37 Northamptonshire v Oxford University, The Parks 1975

First-Class Career Performances

	M	Inns	NO	Runs	HS	Avge	100s	Ct	St	Runs	Wkts	Avge	Best	5wl	10wM
Test	26	50	6	1184	102 *	26.90	2	3	-	456	7	65.14	2-73	-	-
All First	559	918	121	24361	227	30.56	44	235	-	23400	756	30.95	7-37	26	3

1992 ROLL OF HONOUR

BRITANNIC ASSURANCE CHAMPIONSHIP

Final Table

		P	W	L	D	T	Bt	Bl	Pts
1	Essex (1)	22	11	6	5	0	60	64	300
2	Kent (6)	22	9	3	10	0	60	55	259
3	Northants (10)	22	8	4	10	0	62	58	248
4	Notts (4)	22	7	7	8	0	54	58	224
5	Derbyshire (3)	22	7	6	9	0	47	63	222
6	Warwickshire (2)	22	6	8	8	0	55	68	219
7	Sussex (11)	22	6	7	9	0	60	61	217
8	Leicestershire (16)	22	7	7	8	0	40	59	211
9	Somerset (17)	22	5	4	13	0	64	62	206
10	Gloucestershire (13)	22	6	6	9	0	48	58	202
11	Middlesex (15)	22	5	3	14	0	62	60	202
12	Lancashire (8)	22	4	6	12	0	75	49	188
13	Surrey (5)	22	5	7	10	0	56	50	186
14	Glamorgan (12)	22	5	4	13	0	53	49	182
15	Hampshire (9)	22	4	6	12	0	61	57	182
16	Yorkshire (14)	22	4	6	12	0	56	52	172
17	Worcestershire (6)	22	3	4	14	0	54	65	167
18	Durham	22	2	10	10	0	46	53	131

1991 positions shown in brackets

BENSON & HEDGES CUP

Winners: Hampshire
Runners-up: Kent
Losing semi-finalists: Somerset and Surrey

NATWEST TROPHY

Winners: Northamptonshire
Runners-up: Leicestershire
Losing semi-finalists: Warwickshire and Essex

SUNDAY LEAGUE

Final Table

		P	W	L	T	NR	Away Wins	Pts	Run Rate	Runs	Balls
1	Middlesex (11)	17	14	2	0	1	6	58	93.91	3505	3732
2	Essex (6)	17	11	5	0	1	4	46	83.33	2836	3403
3	Hampshire (17)	17	10	6	0	1	3	42	76.71	2804	3655
4	Surrey (8)	17	10	7	0	0	7	40	90.46	3339	3691
5	Somerset (9)	17	9	6	0	2	3	40	81.23	2796	3442
6	Kent (10)	17	8	5	0	4	5	40	89.84	2857	3180
7	Worcs (4)	17	7	6	1	3	3	36	74.48	2441	3277
8	Gloucs (12)	17	8	8	0	1	3	34	76.04	2907	3823
9	Durham	17	7	7	0	3	4	34	89.11	3102	3481
10	Warwicks (5)	17	7	7	1	2	2	34	82.55	3171	3841
11	Sussex (13)	17	7	8	0	2	3	32	82.54	2781	3369
12	Lancashire (2)	17	6	7	0	4	3	32	84.05	2614	3110
13	Northants (3)	17	7	9	0	1	3	30	83.21	3024	3634
14	Derbyshire (15)	17	7	9	0	1	1	30	81.06	2950	3639
15	Yorkshire (7)	17	6	9	0	2	3	28	79.53	2852	3586
16	Glamorgan (16)	17	4	10	0	3	3	22	86.21	2995	3474
17	Notts (1)	17	3	11	0	3	1	18	81.17	2609	3214
18	Leics (14)	17	3	12	0	2	2	16	81.08	3108	3833

1991 positions shown in brackets

1992 AVERAGES (all first-class matches)

BATTING AVERAGES - Including fielding
Qualifying requirements : 6 completed innings and average of 20 or more

Name	Matches	Inns	NO	Runs	HS	Avge	100s	50s	Ct	St
Salim Malik	15	21	6	1184	165	78.93	2	8	4	-
M.E.Waugh	16	24	7	1314	219 *	77.29	4	6	27	-
D.M.Jones	14	23	7	1179	157	73.68	4	5	12	-
G.A.Gooch	18	29	3	1850	160	71.15	8	7	19	-
M.W.Gatting	24	36	6	2000	170	66.66	6	10	16	-
P.D.Bowler	24	38	7	2044	241 *	65.93	6	11	13	-
N.H.Fairbrother	12	18	7	689	166 *	62.63	1	5	8	-
A.J.Lamb	18	28	4	1460	209	60.83	6	5	12	-
Javed Miandad	12	17	3	809	153 *	57.78	2	4	8	-
N.J.Speak	22	36	3	1892	232	57.33	4	12	18	-
M.A.Roseberry	25	41	5	2044	173	56.77	9	8	14	-
Asif Mujtaba	16	25	6	1074	154 *	56.52	2	6	6	-
R.T.Robinson	19	33	5	1547	189	55.25	4	8	14	-
N.R.Taylor	21	35	7	1508	144	53.85	1	11	10	-
G.A.Hick	17	27	2	1337	213 *	53.48	4	5	32	-
M.D.Moxon	19	28	2	1385	183	53.26	5	5	9	-
T.L.Penney	16	24	7	904	151	53.17	3	4	5	-
K.J.Barnett	19	29	5	1270	160	52.91	4	4	5	-
Inzamam-ul-Haq	15	21	7	736	200 *	52.57	1	5	21	-
G.R.Cowdrey	21	31	6	1291	147	51.64	3	7	6	-
M.A.Atherton	21	37	6	1598	199	51.54	5	7	24	-
G.D.Lloyd	23	37	10	1389	132	51.44	4	10	21	-
G.P.Thorpe	24	41	4	1895	216	51.21	3	13	19	-
V.P.Terry	11	17	2	766	141	51.06	3	3	7	-
T.S.Curtis	23	41	5	1829	228 *	50.80	4	7	15	-
R.J.Harden	20	33	5	1387	187	49.53	3	6	14	-
T.C.Middleton	24	40	4	1780	221	49.44	6	7	16	-
A.D.Brown	11	16	1	740	175	49.33	3	3	6	-
R.J.Bailey	23	39	7	1572	167 *	49.12	2	8	22	-
A.P.Wells	22	35	5	1465	165 *	48.83	5	4	24	-
T.R.Ward	21	37	3	1648	153	48.47	5	9	25	-
C.White	19	26	8	859	79 *	47.72	-	7	14	-
G.F.Archer	7	13	3	475	117	47.50	1	4	6	-
C.L.Hooper	21	32	4	1329	131	47.46	5	7	25	-
D.I.Gower	20	33	7	1225	155	47.11	1	8	14	-
H.Morris	23	37	3	1597	146	46.97	6	6	16	-
P.A.Cottey	20	28	5	1076	141	46.78	2	6	10	-

Name	Matches	Inns	NO	Runs	HS	Avge	100s	50s	Ct	St
J.J.B.Lewis	13	20	4	746	133	46.62	1	7	4	-
S.R.Tendulkar	16	25	2	1070	100	46.52	1	7	10	-
R.J.Blakey	21	32	9	1065	125 *	46.30	2	5	44	5
P.Johnson	19	29	4	1147	107 *	45.88	2	10	9	-
D.L.Haynes	20	35	2	1513	177	45.84	3	10	8	-
J.P.Crawley	17	29	3	1175	172	45.19	2	7	11	-
M.R.Benson	21	35	2	1482	139	44.90	4	6	15	-
Shoaib Mohammad	12	21	4	761	105 *	44.76	1	7	2	-
P.Bainbridge	17	30	9	923	92 *	43.95	-	8	8	-
A.Fordham	23	41	2	1710	192	43.84	4	7	14	-
J.P.Stephenson	21	37	5	1401	159 *	43.78	3	8	10	-
P.J.Prichard	23	38	4	1485	136	43.67	4	9	18	-
B.C.Broad	14	27	3	1040	159 *	43.33	5	-	7	-
Ramiz Raja	16	26	2	1036	172	43.16	2	6	3	-
M.A.Lynch	23	40	6	1465	107	43.08	3	8	24	-
R.C.Russell	20	34	11	985	75	42.82	-	5	40	3
Aamer Sohail	17	28	2	1110	205	42.69	2	4	14	-
T.M.Moody	11	19	2	724	178	42.58	4	1	12	-
A.J.Stewart	19	33	4	1234	190	42.55	2	8	22	-
D.Ripley	22	31	10	891	107 *	42.42	2	4	66	5
D.R.Pringle	16	17	5	509	112 *	42.41	2	2	4	-
A.Dale	22	33	5	1159	150 *	41.39	2	7	8	-
J.E.Morris	23	33	0	1358	120	41.15	3	12	6	-
C.J.Adams	23	33	6	1109	140 *	41.07	4	4	20	-
C.L.Cairns	21	30	6	984	107 *	41.00	2	6	8	-
R.G.Twose	23	38	3	1412	233	40.34	1	10	17	-
P.W.G.Parker	20	35	2	1331	124	40.33	3	8	16	-
M.R.Ramprakash	20	33	3	1199	233	39.96	3	5	8	-
R.R.Montgomerie	9	15	3	477	103 *	39.75	1	1	3	-
S.P.James	24	39	4	1376	152 *	39.31	3	6	20	-
J.W.Hall	20	34	5	1125	140 *	38.79	1	8	7	-
C.J.Tavare	21	32	2	1157	125	38.56	3	6	15	-
M.Saxelby	8	13	1	462	73	38.50	-	5	1	-
P.N.Weekes	17	21	7	539	95	38.50	-	3	15	-
J.D.Carr	25	39	7	1228	114	38.37	2	8	41	-
N.E.Briers	24	42	6	1372	123	38.11	3	9	12	-
T.J.Boon	24	41	3	1448	139	38.10	2	10	15	-
M.P.Maynard	23	36	4	1219	176	38.09	2	7	19	-
M.P.Speight	20	33	2	1180	179	38.06	5	-	16	-
C.C.Lewis	17	26	4	836	134 *	38.00	2	5	13	-
R.A.Smith	17	28	3	950	127	38.00	2	5	12	-
S.A.Kellett	22	36	1	1326	96	37.88	-	9	23	-
N.Hussain	20	26	3	866	172 *	37.65	1	5	24	-
W.P.C.Weston	14	23	5	675	66 *	37.50	-	5	2	-

Name	Matches	Inns	NO	Runs	HS	Avge	100s	50s	Ct	St
W.Larkins	22	41	0	1536	143	37.46	4	8	16	-
P.W.Jarvis	15	14	4	374	80	37.40	-	3	2	-
M.C.J.Nicholas	21	32	5	1003	95 *	37.14	-	6	9	-
M.A.Crawley	25	44	9	1297	160 *	37.05	4	5	20	-
N.D.Burns	22	33	12	772	73 *	36.76	-	4	41	3
M.N.Lathwell	19	33	1	1176	114	36.75	1	11	14	-
N.J.Lenham	20	34	2	1173	222 *	36.65	4	3	9	-
D.M.Ward	18	30	6	879	138	36.62	3	1	3	-
W.K.Hegg	18	24	7	618	80	36.35	-	4	33	6
D.J.Bicknell	24	42	5	1340	120 *	36.21	2	7	6	-
A.J.Moles	23	41	3	1359	122	35.76	1	12	18	-
T.J.G.O'Gorman	24	37	8	1031	95	35.55	-	8	11	-
S.J.Rhodes	24	34	11	815	116 *	35.43	2	2	46	5
F.A.Griffith	7	10	3	248	81	35.42	-	1	6	-
G.B.T.Lovell	9	13	1	422	110 *	35.16	1	2	8	-
D.P.Ostler	22	37	2	1225	192	35.00	3	4	20	-
G.D.Hodgson	21	36	1	1224	147	34.97	2	8	10	-
D.M.Smith	19	33	2	1076	213	34.71	2	5	12	-
D.A.Reeve	17	28	4	833	79	34.70	-	7	15	-
G.Fowler	11	20	2	623	106	34.61	1	4	7	-
S.A.Marsh	22	30	4	896	125	34.46	1	6	44	8
S.C.Goldsmith	10	11	3	273	100 *	34.12	1	1	3	-
P.Moores	21	30	5	851	109	34.04	1	3	32	7
D.W.Randall	19	29	3	882	133 *	33.92	1	5	11	-
J.T.C.Vaughan	11	18	4	473	99	33.78	-	4	11	-
M.A.Feltham	13	19	6	437	50	33.61	-	1	3	-
A.N.Hayhurst	23	38	2	1197	102	33.25	1	9	6	-
K.D.James	23	37	2	1149	116	32.82	1	8	10	-
F.D.Stephenson	18	25	4	680	133	32.38	1	2	10	-
M.W.Alleyne	22	36	3	1065	93	32.27	-	7	23	-
N.V.Knight	20	30	6	774	109	32.25	2	3	16	-
C.W.J.Athey	20	32	0	1022	181	31.93	2	4	19	-
S.P.Titchard	14	24	3	668	74	31.81	-	6	8	-
N.A.Felton	22	37	3	1076	103	31.64	1	9	18	-
I.V.A.Richards	14	23	0	722	127	31.39	1	4	18	-
J.E.R.Gallian	9	15	0	468	112	31.20	1	3	7	-
I.T.Botham	17	25	2	713	105	31.00	1	4	9	-
G.D.Rose	22	34	4	930	132	31.00	1	6	12	-
J.P.Arscott	10	14	3	341	79	31.00	-	3	11	6
V.J.Wells	17	23	6	526	56	30.94	-	3	2	-
S.G.Hinks	10	16	3	402	88 *	30.92	-	3	3	-
D.G.Cork	19	21	2	578	72 *	30.42	-	3	12	-
D.Byas	20	30	4	784	100	30.15	1	6	30	-
P.R.Pollard	19	33	3	900	75	30.00	-	5	21	-

Name	Matches	Inns	NO	Runs	HS	Avge	100s	50s	Ct	St
D.J.Capel	23	34	4	892	103	29.73	1	5	16	-
D.B.D'Oliveira	13	19	1	535	100	29.72	1	2	14	-
P.A.Nixon	16	25	7	529	107 *	29.38	1	1	40	5
I.Smith	12	16	1	435	110	29.00	1	2	4	-
I.D.Austin	8	10	2	230	115 *	28.75	1	1	-	-
N.Shahid	15	21	1	561	132	28.05	1	3	8	-
R.M.Wight	10	17	3	388	62 *	27.71	-	2	3	-
P.J.Martin	22	24	6	492	133	27.33	1	2	4	-
D.A.Leatherdale	23	40	4	983	112	27.30	1	5	16	-
P.D.Atkins	7	14	0	382	99	27.28	-	2	2	-
T.H.C.Hancock	10	17	1	436	102	27.25	1	2	8	-
R.P.Snell	16	20	4	436	81	27.25	-	3	5	-
R.D.B.Croft	24	34	10	650	60 *	27.08	-	3	10	-
R.J.Bartlett	8	13	0	352	72	27.07	-	2	5	-
S.Hutton	8	15	0	406	78	27.06	-	2	3	-
R.J.Scott	19	31	3	751	73	26.82	-	4	7	-
J.J.Whitaker	22	34	3	830	74	26.77	-	2	13	-
K.H.Macleay	12	19	3	427	74	26.68	-	3	7	-
M.V.Fleming	21	32	2	797	100 *	26.56	1	4	13	-
A.C.Seymour	11	21	0	556	133	26.47	1	1	9	-
J.E.Emburey	23	27	6	554	102	26.38	1	3	21	-
A.A.Metcalfe	11	17	1	422	73	26.37	-	1	4	-
G.R.Haynes	9	13	2	288	66	26.18	-	2	3	-
R.S.M.Morris	5	9	1	209	74	26.12	-	2	7	-
L.Potter	23	36	4	834	96	26.06	-	4	10	-
B.F.Smith	15	20	3	441	100 *	25.94	1	3	9	-
K.R.Brown	25	37	7	776	106	25.86	1	3	39	11
A.J.Wright	19	33	3	772	128	25.73	1	3	11	-
C.Keey	8	13	1	308	64	25.66	-	3	1	-
M.D.Marshall	19	25	5	513	70	25.65	-	2	11	-
K.Greenfield	6	10	2	205	48	25.62	-	-	5	-
J.D.Robinson	9	17	5	307	65 *	25.58	-	2	8	-
N.M.K.Smith	12	20	2	454	67	25.22	-	1	5	-
K.M.Curran	21	30	1	730	82	25.17	-	5	10	-
P.A.J.DeFreitas	13	14	1	325	72	25.00	-	3	1	-
T.A.Lloyd	23	39	2	919	84 *	24.83	-	5	5	-
M.P.Bicknell	19	26	8	447	88	24.83	-	2	7	-
P.J.Newport	22	25	6	467	75 *	24.57	-	3	5	-
D.W.Headley	17	14	3	270	91	24.54	-	1	5	-
J.R.Wood	10	13	1	294	57	24.50	-	1	6	-
R.J.Parks	7	10	3	169	33	24.14	-	-	21	2
R.P.Davis	18	24	11	312	54 *	24.00	-	1	11	-
J.R.Ayling	18	26	1	593	121	23.72	1	2	4	-
M.A.Garnham	24	28	4	569	82 *	23.70	-	4	42	3

Name	Matches	Inns	NO	Runs	HS	Avge	100s	50s	Ct	St
Moin Khan	13	14	4	237	53	23.70	-	1	28	1
S.R.Lampitt	19	29	5	565	71 *	23.54	-	4	6	-
R.E.Bryson	11	13	2	257	76	23.36	-	1	-	-
N.A.Foster	11	14	0	326	54	23.28	-	2	12	-
J.D.R.Benson	18	28	1	623	122	23.07	1	1	30	-
R.M.Ellison	19	22	8	323	64	23.07	-	1	13	-
C.W.Scott	18	24	5	433	57 *	22.78	-	2	27	2
G.K.Brown	4	6	0	136	48	22.66	-	-	3	-
G.T.J.Townsend	7	13	1	272	49	22.66	-	-	4	-
Rashid Latif	8	8	2	136	50	22.66	-	1	28	1
J.D.Glendenen	17	28	1	607	117	22.48	1	3	5	-
C.M.Wells	6	7	1	133	39	22.16	-	-	1	-
B.T.P.Donelan	16	25	6	421	68 *	22.15	-	2	2	-
E.E.Hemmings	7	11	5	132	52 *	22.00	-	1	2	-
K.P.Evans	19	24	4	438	104	21.90	1	2	12	-
N.V.Radford	22	19	7	261	73 *	21.75	-	2	4	-
D.L.Hemp	12	17	2	326	84 *	21.73	-	2	7	-
C.C.Remy	7	9	0	192	47	21.33	-	-	1	-
S.D.Udal	23	29	10	400	44	21.05	-	-	4	-
R.K.Illingworth	20	20	6	294	43	21.00	-	-	8	-
G.W.Jones	6	12	0	249	44	20.75	-	-	1	-
G.D.Mendis	5	8	1	145	45	20.71	-	-	-	-
W.K.M.Benjamin	20	25	3	453	72	20.59	-	4	15	-
M.A.Ealham	17	27	5	452	67 *	20.54	-	4	4	-
I.R.Bishop	20	21	2	388	90	20.42	-	1	6	-
K.J.Piper	19	25	8	345	72	20.29	-	2	41	2
R.P.Gofton	5	8	1	142	75	20.28	-	1	2	-
M.Watkinson	20	25	1	482	96	20.08	-	1	10	-
A.R.Caddick	20	19	6	261	54 *	20.07	-	1	6	-
C.E.L.Ambrose	18	20	10	200	49 *	20.00	-	-	5	-

BOWLING AVERAGES
Qualifying requirements : 10 wickets taken

Name	Overs	Mdns	Runs	Wkts	Avge	Best	5wI	10wM
C.A.Walsh	587.2	138	1469	92	15.96	7-27	8	2
Wasim Akram	499.5	127	1330	82	16.22	6-32	7	2
I.R.Bishop	483	116	1118	64	17.46	7-34	4	-
J.R.Ayling	356.2	78	989	48	20.60	5-12	1	-
D.J.Millns	470.5	107	1526	74	20.62	6-87	6	1
R.P.Davis	582	150	1609	74	21.74	7-64	5	-
A.A.Donald	575.2	139	1647	74	22.25	7-37	6	-
S.D.Thomas	113.2	18	404	18	22.44	5-79	2	-
M.A.Robinson	413.5	79	1134	50	22.68	6-57	3	1
V.J.Wells	301	93	751	33	22.75	4-26	-	-
N.A.Mallender	436.3	94	1282	55	23.30	5-29	4	-
G.J.Parsons	343.2	92	955	39	24.48	6-70	2	-
Mushtaq Ahmed	614.4	158	1620	66	24.54	5-46	4	-
Waqar Younis	287.1	50	913	37	24.67	5-22	4	-
N.G.B.Cook	325.1	90	939	38	24.71	7-34	1	1
F.A.Griffith	113	31	373	15	24.86	4-33	-	-
D.R.Pringle	425.5	98	1177	47	25.04	5-63	1	-
D.J.Capel	446	92	1214	48	25.29	5-61	1	-
P.M.Such	411.5	126	1015	40	25.37	6-17	3	-
J.E.Emburey	854.5	249	2069	81	25.54	5-23	3	-
Tanvir Mehdi	94	21	307	12	25.58	3-24	-	-
M.P.Bicknell	628.5	116	1823	71	25.67	6-107	4	-
P.J.Newport	618.2	130	1770	68	26.02	5-22	4	-
R.J.Maru	204.2	75	444	17	26.11	4-8	-	-
C.E.L.Ambrose	543.4	151	1307	50	26.14	4-53	-	-
J.D.Robinson	93.4	14	341	13	26.23	3-22	-	-
N.F.Williams	437	86	1283	48	26.72	8-75	2	1
Aqib Javed	292	58	966	36	26.83	5-34	1	-
M.J.McCague	457.2	86	1430	53	26.98	8-26	5	1
A.R.Caddick	587.4	99	1918	71	27.01	6-52	3	1
J.H.Childs	684.2	205	1822	67	27.19	6-82	3	-
I.J.Turner	182.4	51	519	19	27.31	5-81	1	-
M.D.Marshall	529	134	1348	49	27.51	6-58	1	-
K.M.Curran	452.4	96	1376	50	27.52	6-45	1	-
C.S.Pickles	120.1	27	387	14	27.64	4-40	-	-
E.S.H.Giddins	247.5	52	857	31	27.64	5-32	2	-
N.V.Radford	532.2	99	1670	60	27.83	6-88	4	1
R.G.Twose	249.3	48	794	28	28.35	6-63	1	-
D.G.Cork	450.4	74	1366	48	28.45	5-36	2	-
I.D.K.Salisbury	772.4	176	2520	87	28.96	7-54	6	2
M.V.Fleming	245	46	696	24	29.00	4-63	-	-
P.W.Jarvis	393.4	89	1164	40	29.10	4-27	-	-

Name	Overs	Mdns	Runs	Wkts	Avge	Best	5wI	10wM
P.Carrick	630.1	202	1375	47	29.25	6-58	1	-
M.Davies	560.5	143	1661	56	29.66	4-73	-	-
J.A.North	96.3	14	331	11	30.09	3-51	-	-
N.A.Foster	256	63	724	24	30.16	4-47	-	-
P.J.Hartley	549.5	101	1690	56	30.17	8-111	3	-
J.P.Taylor	648.2	119	2072	68	30.47	7-23	3	1
M.E.Waugh	184.4	31	671	22	30.50	3-38	-	-
A.E.Warner	367.5	87	888	29	30.62	4-52	-	-
A.P.Igglesden	480.5	95	1413	46	30.71	5-41	3	-
N.M.Kendrick	595.1	171	1567	51	30.72	6-61	3	-
C.C.Lewis	594.3	119	1633	53	30.81	6-90	2	1
S.L.Watkin	689.3	148	2126	68	31.26	6-97	1	-
J.A.Afford	509.1	128	1599	51	31.35	6-68	2	1
G.W.Mike	90.2	17	314	10	31.40	3-48	-	-
J.Wood	134.2	17	534	17	31.41	5-68	1	-
R.D.B.Croft	657.1	124	2152	68	31.64	8-66	5	1
W.K.M.Benjamin	489	102	1498	47	31.87	4-34	-	-
P.A.J.DeFreitas	349.5	65	1091	34	32.08	6-94	1	-
A.Dale	234	62	644	20	32.20	3-30	-	-
K.J.Shine	333.5	49	1290	40	32.25	8-47	3	1
C.M.Wells	119	26	323	10	32.30	3-26	-	-
H.R.J.Trump	558	134	1584	49	32.32	7-52	2	1
P.A.Smith	373	57	1362	42	32.42	6-91	4	-
T.D.Topley	240.4	54	779	24	32.45	5-15	1	-
J.T.C.Vaughan	202.4	44	588	18	32.66	3-46	-	-
M.Watkinson	660	140	2178	66	33.00	6-62	4	1
G.C.Small	367.2	83	1003	30	33.43	3-43	-	-
E.E.Hemmings	259.5	95	602	18	33.44	4-30	-	-
D.K.Morrison	335.4	52	1209	36	33.58	6-48	1	-
M.A.Ealham	407.1	70	1243	37	33.59	4-67	-	-
T.A.Munton	640.4	176	1725	51	33.82	7-64	3	1
S.J.E.Brown	509.1	75	1973	58	34.01	7-105	3	-
M.A.Crawley	221.4	56	647	19	34.05	3-18	-	-
F.D.Stephenson	467.2	93	1375	40	34.37	7-29	1	1
Ata-ur-Rehman	159.1	29	621	18	34.50	3-69	-	-
O.H.Mortensen	338.4	87	795	23	34.56	2-22	-	-
S.D.Udal	692.2	177	2012	58	34.69	8-50	2	-
A.M.Smith	249.2	35	835	24	34.79	3-53	-	-
J.E.R.Gallian	208	41	628	18	34.88	4-29	-	-
J.Boiling	591.1	156	1579	45	35.08	6-84	1	1
C.L.Cairns	592.3	110	1974	56	35.25	6-70	2	-
A.D.Mullally	518.2	125	1485	42	35.35	5-119	1	-
S.J.W.Andrew	265	45	849	24	35.37	4-54	-	-
M.C.Ilott	675.3	145	2264	64	35.37	6-87	3	-

Name	Overs	Mdns	Runs	Wkts	Avge	Best	5wI	10wM
J.D.Fitton	171.1	38	465	13	35.76	4-81	-	-
R.W.Sladdin	499.3	138	1396	39	35.79	6-58	1	-
M.W.Alleyne	138.1	32	502	14	35.85	3-25	-	-
K.P.Evans	596.4	132	1723	48	35.89	5-27	1	-
S.R.Lampitt	369.3	44	1257	35	35.91	4-57	-	-
P.C.R.Tufnell	595.2	144	1559	43	36.25	5-83	2	-
D.Gough	255.1	53	910	25	36.40	4-43	-	-
A.P.van Troost	175.4	20	766	21	36.47	6-48	2	-
D.E.Malcolm	451.1	64	1648	45	36.62	5-45	2	-
D.J.Foster	191.3	27	820	22	37.27	5-87	1	-
C.L.Hooper	500.5	114	1307	35	37.34	4-57	-	-
R.K.Illingworth	635.3	185	1580	42	37.61	4-43	-	-
R.D.Stemp	336.5	80	1054	28	37.64	6-67	3	1
D.B.Pennett	296.2	51	981	26	37.73	4-58	-	-
Naved Anjum	107.1	24	379	10	37.90	3-73	-	-
P.J.Berry	178.3	27	649	17	38.17	7-113	1	1
M.C.J.Ball	322	61	1072	28	38.28	5-101	1	-
J.P.Stephenson	251.5	51	854	22	38.81	6-54	1	-
R.M.Wight	231.3	39	748	19	39.36	3-65	-	-
A.C.S.Pigott	363	74	1063	27	39.37	3-34	-	-
J.E.Benjamin	582.2	94	1780	45	39.55	6-30	2	-
L.Potter	360.1	80	1075	27	39.81	4-73	-	-
P.J.Bakker	162	48	441	11	40.09	4-38	-	-
P.J.Martin	520.2	129	1490	37	40.27	4-45	-	-
C.M.Tolley	239	56	726	18	40.33	3-38	-	-
P.W.Henderson	96	14	405	10	40.50	3-59	-	-
D.W.Headley	385	74	1258	31	40.58	3-31	-	-
P.Bainbridge	188.1	39	569	14	40.64	5-100	1	-
C.W.Taylor	409.2	82	1425	35	40.71	4-50	-	-
R.M.Ellison	401.5	80	1204	29	41.51	6-95	2	-
J.D.Batty	426	85	1408	33	42.66	4-34	-	-
P.A.Booth	279.4	74	814	19	42.84	4-29	-	-
D.A.Graveney	380.4	87	1201	28	42.89	3-22	-	-
C.A.Connor	417.2	69	1386	32	43.31	5-58	1	-
I.D.Austin	164.5	41	522	12	43.50	3-44	-	-
I.T.Botham	346	70	1144	26	44.00	4-72	-	-
R.P.Snell	339.1	60	1194	27	44.22	3-29	-	-
A.M.Babington	188	21	753	17	44.29	8-107	1	-
G.D.Rose	392.1	84	1250	28	44.64	4-59	-	-
M.A.Feltham	326.1	61	1125	25	45.00	4-75	-	-
S.R.Barwick	602	155	1627	36	45.19	4-67	-	-
S.M.McEwan	229	44	800	17	47.05	3-52	-	-
A.A.Barnett	595	84	2165	46	47.06	5-78	2	-
B.T.P.Donelan	404	85	1323	28	47.25	6-77	1	-

Name	Overs	Mdns	Runs	Wkts	Avge	Best	5wI	10wM
R.A.Pick	254.1	50	862	18	47.88	3-33	-	-
R.J.Scott	267.4	39	959	20	47.95	2-9	-	-
A.R.Roberts	323.2	60	1056	22	48.00	4-101	-	-
A.J.Murphy	178.4	34	531	11	48.27	3-97	-	-
D.A.Reeve	267	80	632	13	48.61	2-4	-	-
N.M.K.Smith	332.3	63	1178	24	49.08	5-61	1	-
S.P.Hughes	548.3	98	1672	34	49.17	5-25	1	-
P.N.Weekes	222	51	595	12	49.58	3-61	-	-
M.Jeh	233.5	38	846	17	49.76	3-44	-	-
S.Bastien	305.3	73	954	19	50.21	5-95	1	-
M.P.Briers	144.3	22	621	12	51.75	3-109	-	-
M.B.Abington	146.4	23	530	10	53.00	3-33	-	-
D.B.D'Oliveira	153.4	29	536	10	53.60	2-44	-	-
M.G.Field-Buss	169	29	590	11	53.63	4-71	-	-
S.W.Johnson	164	27	541	10	54.10	3-62	-	-
R.E.Bryson	333.4	41	1256	23	54.60	5-48	2	-
A.R.C.Fraser	426.4	90	1273	23	55.34	3-16	-	-
K.D.James	264.3	65	781	14	55.78	2-23	-	-
R.M.Pearson	402.3	64	1279	20	63.95	5-108	1	-
M.Frost	198.1	29	833	13	64.07	3-100	-	-
A.N.Jones	161.5	17	745	11	67.72	3-76	-	-

ANSWERS TO QUIZ

1. Hampshire
2. 1928
3. 1966
4. 1969
5. 1953
6. 1964
7. 1951
8. 1977
9. J.R. Reid, 15, for Wellington v Nothern Districts, 1962-63
10. Ian Botham, 80, in 1985
11. Sir Len Hutton, England v South Africa, Oval, 1951
12. Jim Laker, 19 for 90, England v Australia, Old Trafford, 1956
13. Northamptonshire
14. Leicestershire
15. Salim Malik
16. Alec Stewart
17. Six years
18. England's score of 363 for 7 was the highest-ever score in a One-Day International
19. Richard Blakey, Yorks
20. Nigel Briers
21. Alan Wells
22. Tony Wright
23. Phil Neale, ex-Worcestershire
24. All scored a century and a double century in the same match.
25. David Shepherd, ex-Gloucs
26. Valentine
27. Alan
28. Ravindra
29. Murphy Su'a
30. Ashley
31. Adolphus
32. Berry
33. Clairmonte
34. Eugene
35. Donald (Thomas Donald Topley!)

36. David Shepherd
37. Botham, 8 for 34, England v Pakistan, 1978
38. J.W.H.T. Douglas, Essex
39. David Gower
40. Lancashire won in one day, by eight wickets
41. P.G.H. Fender
42. Glamorgan in 1921
43. Cambridge
44. Bob Berry of Lancs, Worcs, Derbys, and England
45. Fred Titmus
46. Micky Stewart
47. J.H. Parks
48. F.L. Fane
49. Chris Tavare
50. Allan Border
51. Paul Johnson, Notts
52. They hold the record number of appearances for their country
53. Clarrie Grimmett
54. Frank Mitchell
55. 1990
56. Five
57. Tony Middleton, Hants
58. Mike Hendrick, ex-Derbyshire, Notts and England
59. *Someone Who Was*, published by Methuen
60. Ken Barrington
61. £46,000
62. £27,500
63. £27,500
64. £25,000
65. £8,000
66. £5,250
67. David Graveney
68. Matthew Engel
69. All made a century on their first-class debut

70. D.R.W. Silk, ex-Cambridge and Somerset
71. Sir Jack Hobbs, 1178, Melbourne
72. Herefordshire
73. Northumberland
74. Martin Crowe, at Wellington
75. Dennis Lillee, at Melbourne
76. John Wood, v Hants
77. South Africa and New Zealand
78. France
79. They all played Test cricket for two countries
80. They have all scored first-class centuries for three different counties
81. Greg Matthews of NSW
82. Martin Crowe, New Zealand, 114
83. Neil Fairbrother, 57
84. 1882
85. Kepler Wessels
86. John Arlott
87. Allan Donald, Warwickshire and South Africa
88. Arthur Milton of Gloucestershire, Arsenal and England
89. Ken Grieves, died 1992
90. Willesden High School, Lewis and De Freitas
91. Died at the greatest age of any first-class cricketer, 102 years 252 days, in 1986
92. David Hookes
93. Worcester
94. Scarborough
95. Brisbane
96. Southampton
97. Aravinda de Silva
98. Mohammed Azharuddin
99. David Houghton
100. Only players ever to take 10 wickets and score a double century in the same first-class game
101. James Lillywhite
102. Walter Hammond

103. R.E. Foster, 287
104. W.G. Grace
105. Norman Gifford
106. Geoff Arnold
107. Don Bennett
108. Phil Russell
109. Tim Tremlett
110. Bob Woolmer
111. Botham hit the first three balls from Wasim Akram for four
112. Ramiz Raja
113. A century of no-balls for Pakistan v England in Tests and One-Day Internationals last season.
114. Sir Leonard Hutton, Yorkshire and England
115. Pakistan, 2-1
116. England, 4-1
117. Peter Bowler, Leicestershire and Derbyshire
118. India
119. A.J.(John) Traicos, Zimbabwe
120. Harare Sports Club
121. John Traicos, South Africa and Zimbabwe, born in Egypt
122. George Gunn
123. Wilfred Rhodes, Yorkshire and England
124. Brian Close, Yorkshire and England, 18 years 149 days
125. David Houghton
126. H. Iremonger, 50 years 327 days
127. W. Rhodes, 52 years 165 days
128. M.H. Mankad, 41 years 29 days
129. J.C. Alabaster, 41 years 294 days
130. Miran Bux, 47 years 302 days
131. A.W. Nourse, 46 years 302 days
132. D.S. de Silva, 42 years 78 days
133. G.A. Headley, 44 years 236 days
134. 1107, Victoria v NSW, 1926-27
135. Chris Cowdrey
136. Sir Jack Hobbs, Surrey and England, 197
137. Viv Richards, 56 balls, 1986
138. Sir Donald Bradman, 37

139. Tommy Mitchell
140. Gary Lineker
141. All played professional football for, respectively, Bristol Rovers, Spurs and Scunthorpe
142. Geoff Hurst, Essex
143. Cheryl Gillan, Tory MP for Chesham and Amersham, 1992
144. Herbert Sutcliffe, Yorks
145. For only the third time in history, each player came from a different county
146. Ian Botham, 1505
147. Batteurs
148. Guichets
149. Germany
150. Peter Taylor, NSW, Queensland and Australia
151. Neil Taylor, Kent
152. The Invalids; Sir John Squire
153. Neil Mallender, Somerset
154. Graham Gooch, 4th Test v Pakistan, 23 July 1992
155. Peter May, Ray Illingworth
156. Mike Atherton
157. Sir Richard Hadlee
158. True
159. Lincolnshire
160. Devon
161. Shropshire
162. John Inverarity's daughter Alison, in the women's high jump
163. Their fathers were Test players
164. Roland Lefebvre, Somerset, 1991
165. Jason Gallian, Lancashire
166. 41
167. They have all opened for England as partners to Graham Gooch
168. Dipak Patel
169. He played county cricket for Leics and League football for Doncaster Rovers
170. They all scored a first-class century on the same day as their brother

171. Derbyshire
172. Craig McDermott of Australia - but he never played
173. 4
174. G. and G.V. Gunn, Notts v Warwicks, July 1931
175. Norman Callaway, NSW v Queensland, February 1915
176. Peter van der Merwe
177. 1965
178. Nick Folland, Devon
179. Geoff Miller, ex-England, Cheshire
180. Staffordshire
181. Salim Malik
182. Courtney Walsh
183. Peter Bowler, 1862
184. Wayne Larkins, 1417
185. Paul Pritchard, 1399
186. Hugh Morris, 1546
187. Dean Hodgson, 1214
188. Tony Middleton, 1628
189. Trevor Ward, 1648
190. Nick Speak, 1892
191. Tim Boon, 1383
192. Mike Gatting, 1980
193. Alan Fordham, 1693
194. Tim Robinson, 1510
195. Richard Harden, 1321
196. Graham Thorpe, 1749
197. Alan Wells, 1465
198. Roger Twose, 1368
199. Tim Curtis, 1622
200. Simon Kellett, 1326

INDEX OF PLAYERS BY COUNTY

DAWSON, R. I.
GERRARD, M. J.
HANCOCK, T. H. C.
HINKS, S. G.
HODGSON, G. D.
HORRELL, R.
LAWRENCE, D. V.
RUSSELL, R. C.
SCOTT, R. J.
SMITH, A. M.
VAUGHAN, J. T. C.
WALSH, C. A.
WIGHT, R. M.
WILLIAMS, R. C.
WILLIAMS, R. C. J.
WINDOWS, M. G. N.
WRIGHT, A. J.

HAMPSHIRE

AYLING, J. R.
AYMES, A. N.
BAKKER, P.-J.*
BYRNE, J. R.
CONNOR, C. A.
COX, R. M. F.
FLINT, D. P. J.
GARAWAY, M.
GOWER, D. I.
JAMES, K. D.
JEAN-JACQUES, M.
MARSHALL, M. D.
MARU, R. J.
MIDDLETON, T. C.
MORRIS, R. S. M.
NICHOLAS, M. C. J.
PARKS, R. J.*
SHINE, K. J.
SMITH, R. A.
TERRY, V. P.
THURSFIELD, M. J.
TURNER, I. J.
UDAL, S. D.
WOOD, J. R.

KENT

BENSON, M. R.
COWDREY, G. R.
DAVIS, R. P.
EALHAM, M. A.
ELLISON, R. M.
FLEMING, M. V.
FULTON, D. P.
HEADLEY, D. W.
HOOPER, C. L.
IGGLESDEN, A. P.
KERSEY, G. J.
LLONG, N. J.
LONGLEY, J. I.
MARSH, S. A.
McCAGUE, M. J.
PATEL, M. M.
PENN, C.
PRESTON, N. W.
TAYLOR, N. R.
TUTT, A.
WALKER, M. J.
WARD, T. R.
WREN, T. N.

LANCASHIRE

ALLOTT, P. J. W.*
ATHERTON, M. A.
AUSTIN, I. D.
BARNETT, A. A.
CHAPPLE, G.
CORDINGLEY, G. J.
CRAWLEY, J. P.
DEFREITAS, P. A. J.
FAIRBROTHER, N. H.
FIELDING, J. M.
FITTON, J. D.
FLETCHER, S. D.
GALLIAN, J. E. R.
HARVEY, M. E.
HEGG, W. K.
HENDERSON, J. A.
IRANI, R.

LLOYD, G. D.
MARTIN, P. J.
MENDIS, G. D.
MORRISON, D. K.*
SPEAK, N. J.
STANWORTH, J.
TITCHARD, S. P.
WASIM AKRAM
WATKINSON, M.
WOOD, N. T.
YATES, G.

LEICESTERSHIRE

AGNEW, J. P.
BENJAMIN, W. K. M.
BENSON, J. D. R.
BOON, T. J.
BRIERS, N. E.
COBB, R. A.
GIDLEY, M. I.
GOFTON, R. P.
HAWKES, C. J.
HAYE, A. F.
HEPWORTH, P. N.
MADDY, D. L.
MILLNS, D. J.
MULLALLY, A. D.
NIXON, P. A.
PARSONS, G. J.
POTTER, L.
ROBINSON, P. E.
ROSEBERRY, A.
SMITH, B. F.
WELLS, V. J.
WHITAKER, J. J.
WHITTICASE, P.

MIDDLESEX

AFTAB HABIB
BALLINGER, R. J.
BROWN, K. R.
CARR, J. D.
COWANS, N. G.

DUTCH, K. P.
EDMONDS, P. H.
EMBUREY, J. E.
FARBRACE, P.
FRASER, A. R. C.
GATTING, M. W.
HARRISON, J. C.
HAYNES, D. L.
JOHNSON, R. L.
KEECH, M.
POOLEY, J. C.
RADFORD, T.
RAMPRAKASH, M. R.
ROSEBERRY, M. A.
SIMS, R. J.
SYLVESTER, S. A.*
TAYLOR, C. W.
TUFNELL, P. C. R.
WALKER, D. A.
WEEKES, P. N.
WHITTINGTON, J. M. S.*
WILLIAMS, N. F.

NORTHAMPTONSHIRE

AMBROSE, C. E. L.
BAILEY, R. J.
BOWEN, M. N.
CAPEL, D. J.
COOK, N. G. B.
CURRAN, K. M.
FELTON, N. A.
FORDHAM, A.
INNES, K. J.
LAMB, A. J.
LOYE, M. B.
MONTGOMERIE, R. R.
NEALE, P. A.
NOON, W. M.
PEARSON, R. M.
PENBERTHY, A. L.
RIPLEY, D.
ROBERTS, A. R.
SNAPE, J. N.
STANLEY, N. A.

TAYLOR, J. P.
TOMLINSON, J.
WALKER, A.
WALTON, T. C.
WARREN, R. J.
WILLIAMS, R. G.*

NOTTINGHAMSHIRE

AFFORD, J. A.
ARCHER, G. F.
BATES, R. T.
BRAMHALL, S.
CAIRNS, C. L.
CHAPMAN, R. J.
COOPER, K. E.*
CRAWLEY, M. A.
DESSAUR, W. A.
DOWMAN, M. P.
EVANS, K. P.
FIELD-BUSS, M. G.
FRENCH, B. N.
HINDSON, J. E.
JOHNSON, P.
LEWIS, C. C.
MIKE, G. W.
NEWELL, M.
PICK, R. A.
PENNETT, D. B.
POLLARD, P. R.
RANDALL, D. W.
ROBINSON, R. T.
SAXELBY, M.
WILEMAN, J. R.

SOMERSET

BARTLETT, R. J.*
BURNS, N. D.
CADDICK, A. R.
COTTAM, A. C.
FLETCHER, I.
FOLLAND, N. A
HALLETT, J. C.
HARDEN, R. J.

HAYHURST, A. N.
KERR, J. I. D.
LATHWELL, M. N.
MACLEAY, K. H.*
MALLENDER, N. A.
MUSHTAQ AHMED
PARSONS, K. A.
PARSONS, K. J.
PAYNE, A.
ROSE, G. D.
SNELL, R. P.*
TAVARE, C. J.
TOWNSEND, G. T. J.*
TRUMP, H. R. J.
TURNER, R. J.
VAN TROOST, A. P.

SURREY

ALIKHAN, R. I.
ATKINS, P. D.
BAINBRIDGE, M. R.
BENJAMIN, J. E.
BICKNELL, D. J.
BICKNELL, M. P.
BOILING, J.
BROWN, A. D.
BRYSON, R. E.*
BUTCHER, M. A.
FELTHAM, M. A.*
GREIG, I. A.*
HOLLIOAKE, A. J.
KENDRICK, N. M.
LIGERTWOOD, D. G. C.*
LYNCH, M. A.
MURPHY, A. J.
ROBINSON, J. D.*
SARGEANT, N. F.
SMITH, A. W.
STEWART, A. J.
THORPE, G. P.
WAQAR YOUNIS
WARD, D. M.
WARD, I. J.

SUSSEX

ATHEY, C. W. J.
DEAN, J. W.
DONELAN, B. T. P.
GIDDINS, E. S. H.
GREENFIELD, K.
HALL, J. W.
HANLEY, R.
HANSFORD, A. R.
HEMMINGS, E. E.
HUMPHRIES, S.
JONES, A. N.
LAW, D. R. C.
LENHAM, N. J.
MOORES, P.
NEWELL, K.
NORTH, J. A.
PEIRCE, M. T. E.
PIGOTT, A. C. S.
REMY, C. C.
ROBSON, A. G.
SALISBURY, I. D. K.
SMITH, D. M.
SPEIGHT, M. P.
STEPHENSON, F. D.
WELLS, A. P.
WELLS, C. M.

WARWICKSHIRE

ASIF DIN, M.
BELL, M. A. V.
BOOTH, P. A.
BROWN, D. R.
BURNS, M.
DONALD, A. A.
GILES, A. F.
HOLLOWAY, P. C. L.
LLOYD, T. A.*
MOLES, A. J.
MUNTON, T. A.
OSTLER, D. P.
PENNEY, T. L.
PIPER, K. J.

RATCLIFFE, J. D.
REEVE, D. A.
SMALL, G. C.
SMITH, N. M. K.
SMITH, P. A.
TWOSE, R. G.
WELCH, G.

WORCESTERSHIRE

BENJAMIN, K. C. G.
BRINKLEY, J. E.
CURTIS, T. S.
DILLEY, G. R.*
D'OLIVEIRA, D. B.
EDWARDS, T.
EYERS, C. J.
HAYNES, G. R.
HICK, G. A.
ILLINGWORTH, R. K.
LAMPITT, S. R.
LEATHERDALE, D. A.
MOODY, T. M.*
NEWPORT, P. J.
RADFORD, N. V.
RHODES, S. J.
SEYMOUR, A. C. H.
SOLANKI, V. S.
SPIRING, K. R.
STEMP, R. D.
TOLLEY, C. M.
WESTON, M. J.
WESTON, W. P. C.

YORKSHIRE

BARTLE, S.
BATTY, J. D.
BLAKEY, R. J.
BROADHURST, M.
BYAS, D.
CARRICK, P.
CHAPMAN, C. A.
FOSTER, M.
GOUGH, D.

GRAYSON, A. P.
HARTLEY, P. J.
JARVIS, P. W.
KELLETT, S. A.
KETTLEBOROUGH, R. A.
METCALFE, A. A.
MILBURN, S. M.
MOXON, M. D.
PARKER, B.
PICKLES, C. S.*
RICHARDSON, R. B.
ROBINSON, M. A.
TENDULKAR, S. R.*
VAUGHAN, M. P.
WHITE, C.

*denotes not registered for 1993 season. Where players are known to have moved in the off-season they are listed under their new county.